The Nostradamus Reader

The Nostradamus Reader
by Michel Nostradamus, Lee McCann, Charles A. Ward

The Prophecies of Nostradamus
Nostradamus, The Man Who Saw Through Time
Oracles of Nostradamus

Start Publishing PD LLC
Copyright © 2024 by Start Publishing PD LLC

All rights reserved, including the right to reproduce this book or portions thereof in any form whatsoever.

Start Publishing PD is a registered trademark of Start Publishing PD LLC
Manufactured in the United States of America

Cover art: Shutterstock/Taisiya Kozorez

Cover design: Jennifer Do

10 9 8 7 6 5 4 3 2 1

ISBN 979-8-8809-1874-4

The Prophecies of Nostradamus

Table of Contents

Preface 5
Century I 10
Century II 23
Century III 36
Century IV 49
Century V 62
Century VI 75
Century VII 88
Epistle to Henry II 94
Century VIII 104
Century IX 117
Century X 130
Almanacs: 1555-1563 143
Almanacs: 1564-1567 149

Preface by M. Nostradamus to His Prophecies

Greetings and happiness to Cesar Nostradamus my son. Your late arrival, Cesar Nostredame, my son, has made me spend much time in constant nightly reflection so that I could communicate with you by letter and leave you this reminder, after my death, for the benefit of all men, of which the divine spirit has vouchsafed me to know by means of astronomy. And since it was the Almighty's will that you were not born here in this region and I do not want to talk of years to come but of the months during which you will struggle to grasp and understand the work I shall be compelled to leave you after my death: assuming that it will not be possible for me to leave you such writing as may be destroyed through the injustice of the age. The key to the hidden prediction which you will inherit will be locked inside my heart.

Also bear in mind that the events here described have not yet come to pass, and that all is ruled and governed by the power of Almighty God, inspiring us not by bacchic frenzy nor by enchantments but by astronomical assurances: predictions have been made through the inspiration of divine will alone and the spirit of prophecy in particular.

On numerous occasions and over a long period of time I have predicted specific events far in advance, attributing all to the workings of divine power and inspiration, together with other fortunate or unfortunate happenings, foreseen in their full unexpectedness, which have already come to pass in various regions of the earth. Yet I have wished to remain silent and abandon my work because of the injustice not only of the present time but also for most of the future. I will not commit to writing.

Since governments, sects and countries will undergo such sweeping changes, diametrically opposed to what now obtains, that were I to relate events to come, those in power now - monarchs, leaders of sects and religions - would find these so different from their own imaginings that they would be led to condemn what later centuries will learn how to see and understand. Bear in mind also Our Saviour's words: "Do not give anything holy to the dogs, nor throw pearls in front of swine lest they trample them with their feet and turn on you and tear you apart." For this reason I withdrew my pen from the paper, because I wished to amplify my statement touching the Vulgar Advent by means of ambiguous and enigmatic comments about future causes, even those closest to us and those I have perceived, so that some human change which may come to pass shall not unduly scandalize delicate sensibilities. The whole work is thus written in a nebulous rather than plainly prophetic form. So much so that, "You have hidden these things from the wise and the circumspect, that is from the mighty and the rulers, and you have purified those things for the small and the poor," and through Almighty God's will, revealed unto those prophets with the power to perceive what is distant and thereby to foretell things to come. For nothing can be accomplished without this faculty, whose power and goodness work so strongly in those to whom it is given that, while they contemplate within themselves, these powers are subject to other influences arising from the force of good. This warmth and strength of prophecy invests us with its influence as the sun's rays affect both animate and inanimate entities.

We human beings cannot through our natural consciousness and intelligence know anything of God the Creator's hidden secrets, For it is not for us to know the times or the instants, etc.

So much so that persons of future times may be seen in present ones, because God Almighty has wished to reveal them by means of images, together with various secrets of the future vouchsafed to orthodox astrology, as was the case in the past, so that a measure of power and divination passed through them, the flame of the spirit inspiring them to pronounce upon inspiration both human and divine. God may bring into being divine works, which are absolute; there is another level, that of angelic works; and a third way, that of the evildoers.

But my son, I address you here a little too obscurely. As regards the occult prophecies one is vouchsafed through the subtle spirit of fire, which the understanding sometimes stirs through contemplation of the distant stars as if in vigil, likewise by means of pronouncements, one finds oneself surprised at producing writings without fear of being stricken for such impudent loquacity. The reason is that all this proceeds from the divine power of Almighty God from whom all bounty proceeds.

And so once again, my son, if I have eschewed the word prophet, I do not wish to attribute to myself such lofty title at the present time, for whoever is called a prophet now was once called a seer; since a prophet, my son, is properly speaking one who sees distant things through a natural knowledge of all creatures. And it can happen that the prophet bringing about the perfect light of prophecy may make manifest things both human and divine, because this cannot be done otherwise, given that the effects of predicting the future extend far off into time.

God's mysteries are incomprehensible and the power to influence events is bound up with the great expanse of natural knowledge, having its nearest most immediate origin in free will and describing future events which cannot be understood simply through being revealed. Neither can they be grasped through men's interpretations nor through another mode of cognizance or occult power under the firmament, neither in the present nor in the total eternity to come But bringing about such an indivisible eternity through Herculean efforts, things are revealed by the planetary movements.

I am not saying, my son - mark me well, here - that knowledge of such things cannot be implanted in your deficient mind, or that events in the distant future may not be within the understanding of any reasoning being. Nevertheless, if these things current or distant are brought to the awareness of this reasoning and intelligent being they will be neither too obscure nor too clearly revealed.

Perfect knowledge of such things cannot be acquired without divine inspiration, given that all prophetic inspiration derives its initial origin from God Almighty, then from chance and nature. Since all these portents are produced impartially, prophecy comes to pass partly as predicted. For understanding created by the intellect cannot be acquired by means of the occult, only by the aid of the zodiac, bringing forth that small flame by whose light part of the future may be discerned.

Also, my son, I beseech you not to exercise your mind upon such reveries and vanities as drain the body and incur the soul's perdition, and which trouble our feeble frames. Above all avoid the vanity of that most execrable magic formerly reproved by the Holy Scriptures - only excepting the use of official astrology.

For by the latter, with the help of inspiration and divine revelation, and continual calculations, I have set down my prophecies in writing. Fearing lest this occult philosophy be condemned, I did not therefore wish to make known its dire import; also fearful that several books which had lain hidden for long centuries might be discovered, and of what might become of them, after reading them I presented them to Vulcan. And while he devoured them, the flame licking the air gave out such an unexpected light, clearer than that of an ordinary flame and resembling fire from some flashing cataclysm, and suddenly illumined the house as if it were caught in a furnace. Which is why I reduced them to ashes then, so that none might be tempted to use occult labours in searching for the perfect transmutation, whether lunar or solar, of incorruptible metals.

But as to that discernment which can be achieved by the aid of planetary scrutiny, I should like to tell you this. Eschewing any fantastic imaginings, you may through good judgement have insight into the future if you keep to the specific names of places that accord with planetary configurations, and with inspiration places and aspects yield up hidden properties, namely that power in whose presence the three times are understood as Eternity whose unfolding contains them all: for all things are naked and open.

That is why, my son, you can easily, despite your young brain, understand that events can be foretold naturally by the heavenly bodies and by the spirit of prophecy: I do not wish to ascribe to myself the title and role of prophet, but emphasize inspiration revealed to a mortal man whose perception is no further from heaven than the feet are from the earth. I cannot fail, err or be deceived, although I may be as great a sinner as anyone else upon this earth and subject to all human afflictions.

But after being surprised sometimes by day while in a trance, and having long fallen into the habit of agreeable nocturnal studies, I have composed books of prophecies, each containing one hundred astronomical quatrains, which I want to condense somewhat obscurely. The work comprises prophecies from today to the year 3797.

This may perturb some, when they see such a long timespan, and this will occur and be understood in all the fullness of the Republic; these things will be universally understood upon earth, my son. If you live the normal lifetime of man you will know upon your own soil, under your native sky, how future events are to turn out.

For only Eternal God knows the eternity of His light which proceeds from Him, and I speak frankly to those to whom His immeasurable, immense and incomprehensible greatness has been disposed to grant revelations through long, melancholy inspiration, that with the aid of this hidden element manifested by God, there are two principal factors which make up the prophet's intelligence.

The first is when the supernatural light fills and illuminates the person who predicts by astral science, while the second allows him to prophesy through inspired revelation, which is only a part of the divine eternity, whereby the prophet comes to assess what his divinatory power has given him through the grace of God and by a natural gift, namely, that what is foretold is true and ethereal in origin.

And such a light and small flame is of great efficacy and scope, and nothing less than the clarity of nature itself. The light of human nature makes the philosophers so sure of themselves that with the principles of the first cause they reach the loftiest doctrines and the deepest abysses.

But my son, lest I venture too far for your future perception, be aware that men of letters shall make grand and usually boastful claims about the way I interpreted the world, before the worldwide conflagration which is to bring so many catastrophes and such revolutions that scarcely any lands will not be covered by water, and this will last until all has perished save history and geography themselves. This is why, before and after these revolutions in various countries, the rains will be so diminished and such abundance of fire and fiery missiles shall fall from the heavens that nothing shall escape the holocaust. And this will occur before the last conflagration.

For before war ends the century and in its final stages it will hold the century under its sway. Some countries will be in the grip of revolution for several years, and others ruined for a still longer period. And now that we are in a republican era, with Almighty God's aid, and before completing its full cycle, the monarchy will return, then the Golden Age. For according to the celestial signs, the Golden Age shall return, and after all calculations, with the world near to an all-encompassing revolution - from the time of writing 177 years 3 months 11 days - plague, long famine and wars, and still more floods from now until the stated time. Before and after these, humanity shall several times be so severely diminished that scarcely anyone shall be found who wishes to take over the fields, which shall become free where they had previously been tied.

This will be after the visible judgement of heaven, before we reach the millennium which shall complete all. In the firmament of the eighth sphere, a dimension whereon Almighty God will complete the revolution, and where the constellations will resume their motion which will render the earth stable and firm, but only if He will remain unchanged for ever until His will be done.

This is in spite of all the ambiguous opinions surpassing all natural reason, expressed by Mahomet; which is why God the Creator, through the ministry of his fiery agents with their flames, will come to propose to our perceptions as well as our eyes the reasons for future predictions.

Signs of events to come must be manifested to whomever prophesies. For prophecy which stems from exterior illumination is part of that light and seeks to ally with it and bring it into being so that the part which seems to possess the faculty of understanding is not subject to a sickness of the mind.

Reason is only too evident. Everything is predicted by divine afflatus and thanks to an angelic spirit inspiring the one prophesying, consecrating his predictions through divine unction. It also divests him of all fantasies by means of various nocturnal apparitions, while with daily certainty he prophesies through the science of astronomy, with the aid of sacred prophecy, his only consideration being his courage in freedom.

So come, my son, strive to understand what I have found out through my calculations which accord with revealed inspiration, because now the sword of death approaches us, with pestilence and war more horrible than there has ever been - because of three men's work - and famine. And this sword shall smite the earth and return to it often, for the stars confirm this upheaval and it is also written: "I shall punish their injustices with iron rods, and shall strike them with blows."

For God's mercy will be poured forth only for a certain time, my son, until the majority of my prophecies are fulfilled and this fulfillment is complete. Then several times in the course of the doleful tempests the Lord shall say: Therefore I shall crush and destroy and show no mercy; and many other circumstances shall result from floods and continual rain of which I have written more fully in my other prophecies, composed at some length, not in a chronological sequence, in prose, limiting the places and times and exact dates so that future generations will see, while experiencing these inevitable events, how I have listed others in clearer language, so that despite their obscurities these things shall be understood: When the time comes for the removal of ignorance, the matter will be clearer still.

So in conclusion, my son, take this gift from your father M. Nostradamus, who hopes you will understand each prophecy in every quatrain herein. May Immortal God grant you a long life of good and prosperous happiness.

Salon, 1 March 1555

Century 1

1
Sitting alone at night in secret study;
it is placed on the brass tripod.
A slight flame comes out of the emptiness and
makes successful that which should not be believed in vain.

2
The wand in the hand is placed in the middle of the tripod's legs.
With water he sprinkles both the hem of his garment and his foot.
A voice, fear: he trembles in his robes.
Divine splendor; the God sits nearby.

3
When the litters are overturned by the whirlwind
and faces are covered by cloaks,
the new republic will be troubled by its people.
At this time the reds and the whites will rule wrongly.

4
In the world there will be made a king
who will have little peace and a short life.
At this time the ship of the Papacy will be lost,
governed to its greatest detriment.

5
They will be driven away for a long drawn out fight.
The countryside will be most grievously troubled.
Town and country will have greater struggle.
Carcassonne and Narbonne will have their hearts tried.

6
The eye of Ravenna will be forsaken,
when his wings will fail at his feet.
The two of Bresse will have made a constitution
for Turin and Vercelli, which the French will trample underfoot

7
Arrived too late, the act has been done.
The wind was against them, letters intercepted on their way.
The conspirators were fourteen of a party.
By Rousseau shall these enterprises be undertaken.

8
How often will you be captured, O city of the sun ?
Changing laws that are barbaric and vain.
Bad times approach you. No longer will you be enslaved.
Great Hadrie will revive your veins.

9
From the Orient will come the African heart
to trouble Hadrie and the heirs of Romulus.
Accompanied by the Libyan fleet
the temples of Malta and nearby islands shall be deserted.

10
A coffin is put into the vault of iron,
where seven children of the king are held.
The ancestors and forebears will come forth from the depths of hell,
lamenting to see thus dead the fruit of their line.

11
The motion of senses, heart, feet and hands
will be in agreement between Naples, Lyon and Sicily.
Swords fire, floods, then the noble Romans drowned,
killed or dead because of a weak brain.

12
There will soon be talk of a treacherous man, who rules a short time,
quickly raised from low to high estate.
He will suddenly turn disloyal and volatile.
This man will govern Verona.

13
Through anger and internal hatreds, the exiles
will hatch a great plot against the king.
Secretly they will place enemies as a threat,
and his own old (adherents) will find sedition against them.

14
From the enslaved populace, songs, chants and demands,
while Princes and Lords are held captive in prisons.
These will in the future by headless idiots
be received as divine prayers

15
.Mars threatens us with the force of war
and will cause blood to be spilt seventy times.
The clergy will be both exalted and reviled moreover,
by those who wish to learn nothing of them.

16
A scythe joined with a pond in Sagittarius
at its highest ascendant.
Plague, famine, death from military hands;
the century approaches its renewal.

17
For forty years the rainbow will not be seen.
For forty years it will be seen every day.
The dry earth will grow more parched,
and there will be great floods when it is seen.

18
Because of French discord and negligence
an opening shall be given to the Mohammedans.
The land and sea of Siena will be soaked in blood,
and the port of Marseilles covered with ships and sails.

19
When the snakes surround the altar,
and the Trojan blood is troubled by the Spanish.
Because of them, a great number will be lessened.
The leader flees, hidden in the swampy marshes.

20
The cities of Tours, Orleans, Blois, Angers, Reims and Nantes
are troubled by sudden change.
Tents will be pitched by (people) of foreign tongues;
rivers, darts at Rennes, shaking of land and sea.

21
The rock holds in its depths white clay
which will come out milk-white from a cleft
Needlessly troubled people will not dare touch it,
unaware that the foundation of the earth is of clay.

22
A thing existing without any senses
will cause its own end to happen through artifice.
At Autun, Chalan, Langres and the two Sens
there will be great damage from hail and ice.

23
In the third month, at sunrise,
the Boar and the Leopard meet on the battlefield.
The fatigued Leopard looks up to heaven
and sees an eagle playing around the sun.

24
At the New City he is thoughtful to condemn;
the bird of prey offers himself to the Gods.
After victory he pardons his captives.
At Cremona and Mantua great hardships will be suffered.

25
The lost thing is discovered, hidden for many centuries.
Pasteur will be celebrated almost as a God-like figure.
This is when the moon completes her great cycle,
but by other rumors he shall be dishonored.

26
The great man will be struck down in the day by a thunderbolt.
An evil deed, foretold by the bearer of a petition.
According to the prediction another falls at night time.
Conflict at Reims, London, and pestilence in Tuscany.

27
Beneath the oak tree of Gienne, struck by lightning,
the treasure is hidden not far from there.
That which for many centuries had been gathered,
when found, a man will die, his eye pierced by a spring.

28
Tobruk will fear the barbarian fleet for a time,
then much later the Western fleet.
Cattle, people, possessions, all will be quite lost.
What a deadly combat in Taurus and Libra.

29
When the fish that travels over both land and sea
is cast up on to the shore by a great wave,
its shape foreign, smooth and frightful.
From the sea the enemies soon reach the walls.

30
Because of the storm at sea the foreign ship
will approach an unknown port.
Notwithstanding the signs of the palm branches,
afterwards there is death and pillage. Good advice comes too late.

31
The wars in France will last for so many years
beyond the reign of the Castulon kings.
An uncertain victory will crown three great ones,
the Eagle, the Cock, the Moon, the Lion, the Sun in its house.

32
The great Empire will soon be exchanged
for a small place, which soon will begin to grow.
A small place of tiny area
in the middle of which he will come to lay down his scepter.

33
Near a great bridge near a spacious plain
the great lion with the Imperial forces
will cause a falling outside the austere city.
Through fear the gates will be unlocked for him.

34
The bird of prey flying to the left,
before battle is joined with the French, he makes preparations.
Some will regard him as good, others bad or uncertain.
The weaker party will regard him as a good omen.

35
The young lion will overcome the older one,
in a field of combat in single fight:
He will pierce his eyes in their golden cage;
two wounds in one, then he dies a cruel death.

36
Too late the king will repent
that he did not put his adversary to death.
But he will soon come to agree to far greater things
which will cause all his line to die.

37
Shortly before sun set, battle is engaged.
A great nation is uncertain.
Overcome, the sea port makes no answer,
the bridge and the grave both in foreign places.

38
The Sun and the Eagle will appear to the victor.
An empty answer assured to the defeated.
Neither bugle nor shouts will stop the soldiers.
Liberty and peace, if achieved in time through death.

39
At night the last one will be strangled in his bed
because he became too involved with the blond heir elect.
The Empire is enslaved and three men substituted.
He is put to death with neither letter nor packet read.

40
The false trumpet concealing madness
will cause Byzantium to change its laws.
From Egypt there will go forth a man who wants
the edict withdrawn, changing money and standards.

41
The city is besieged and assaulted by night;
few have escaped; a battle not far from the sea.
A woman faints with joy at the return of her son,
poison in the folds of the hidden letters.

42
The tenth day of the April Calends, calculated in Gothic fashion
is revived again by wicked people.
The fire is put out and the diabolic gathering
seek the bones of the demon of Psellus.

43
Before the Empire changes
a very wonderful event will take place.
The field moved, the pillar of porphyry
put in place, changed on the gnarled rock.

44
In a short time sacrifices will be resumed,
those opposed will be put (to death) like martyrs.
The will no longer be monks, abbots or novices.
Honey shall be far more expensive than wax.

45
A founder of sects, much trouble for the accuser:
A beast in the theater prepares the scene and plot.
The author ennobled by acts of older times;
the world is confused by schismatic sects.

46
Very near Auch, Lectoure and Mirande
a great fire will fall from the sky for three nights.
The cause will appear both stupefying and marvelous;
shortly afterwards there will be an earthquake.

47
The speeches of Lake Leman will become angered,
the days will drag out into weeks,
then months, then years, then all will fail.
The authorities will condemn their useless powers.

48
When twenty years of the Moon's reign have passed
another will take up his reign for seven thousand years.
When the exhausted Sun takes up his cycle
then my prophecy and threats will be accomplished.

49
Long before these happenings
the people of the East, influenced by the Moon,
in the year 1700 will cause many to be carried away,
and will almost subdue the Northern area.

50
From the three water signs will be born a man
who will celebrate Thursday as his holiday.
His renown, praise, rule and power will grow
on land and sea, bringing trouble to the East.

51
The head of Aries, Jupiter and Saturn.
Eternal God, what changes !
Then the bad times will return again after a long century;
what turmoil in France and Italy.

52
Two evil influences in conjunction in Scorpio.
The great lord is murdered in his room.
A newly appointed king persecutes the Church,
the lower (parts of) Europe and in the North.

53
Alas, how we will see a great nation sorely troubled
and the holy law in utter ruin.
Christianity (governed) throughout by other laws,
when a new source of gold and silver is discovered.

54
Two revolutions will be caused by the evil scythe bearer
making a change of reign and centuries.
The mobile sign thus moves into its house:
Equal in favor to both sides.

55
In the land with a climate opposite to Babylon
there will be great shedding of blood.
Heaven will seem unjust both on land and sea and in the air.
Sects, famine, kingdoms, plagues, confusion.

56
Sooner and later you will see great changes made,
dreadful horrors and vengeances.
For as the moon is thus led by its angel
the heavens draw near to the Balance.

57
The trumpet shakes with great discord.
An agreement broken: lifting the face to heaven:
the bloody mouth will swim with blood;
the face anointed with milk and honey lies on the ground.

58
Through a slit in the belly a creature will be born with two heads
and four arms: it will survive for some few years.
The day that Alquiloie celebrates his festivals
Fossana, Turin and the ruler of Ferrara will follow.

59
The exiles deported to the islands
at the advent of an even more cruel king
will be murdered. Two will be burnt
who were not sparing in their speech.

60
An Emperor will be born near Italy,
who will cost the Empire very dearly.
They will say, when they see his allies,
that he is less a prince than a butcher.

61
The wretched, unfortunate republic
will again be ruined by a new authority.
The great amount of ill will accumulated in exile
will make the Swiss break their important agreement.

62
Alas! what a great loss there will be to learning
before the cycle of the Moon is completed.
Fire, great floods, by more ignorant rulers;
how long the centuries until it is seen to be restored.

63
Pestilences extinguished, the world becomes smaller,
for a long time the lands will be inhabited peacefully.
People will travel safely through the sky (over) land and seas:
then wars will start up again.

64
At night they will think they have seen the sun,
when the see the half pig man:
Noise, screams, battles seen fought in the skies.
The brute beasts will be heard to speak.

65
A child without hands, never so great a thunderbolt seen,
the royal child wounded at a game of tennis.
At the well lightning strikes, joining together
three trussed up in the middle under the oaks.

66
He who then carries the news,
after a short while will (stop) to breathe:
Viviers, Tournon, Montferrand and Praddelles;
hail and storms will make them grieve.

67
The great famine which I sense approaching
will often turn (in various areas) then become worldwide.
It will be so vast and long lasting that (they) will grab
roots from the trees and children from the breast.

68
O to what a dreadful and wretched torment
are three innocent people going to be delivered.
Poison suggested, badly guarded, betrayal.
Delivered up to horror by drunken executioners.

69
The great mountain, seven stadia round,
after peace, war, famine, flooding.
It will spread far, drowning great countries,
even antiquities and their mighty foundations.

70
Rain, famine and war will not cease in Persia;
too great a faith will betray the monarch.
Those (actions) started in France will end there,
a secret sign for on to be sparing.

71
The marine tower will be captured and retaken three times
by Spaniards, Barbarians and Ligurians.
Marseilles and Aix, Ales by men of Pisa,
devastation, fire, sword, pillage at Avignon by the Turinese.

72
The inhabitants of Marseilles completely changed,
fleeing and pursued as far as Lyons.
Narbonne, Toulouse angered by Bordeaux;
the killed and captive are almost one million.

73
France shall be accused of neglect by her five partners.
Tunis, Algiers stirred up by the Persians.
Leon, Seville and Barcelona having failed,
they will not have the fleet because of the Venetians.

74
After a rest they will travel to Epirus,
great help coming from around Antioch.
The curly haired king will strive greatly for the Empire,
the brazen beard will be roasted on a spit.

75
The tyrant of Siena will occupy Savona,
having won the fort he will restrain the marine fleet.
Two armies under the standard of Ancona:
the leader will examine them in fear.

76
The man will be called by a barbaric name
that three sisters will receive from destiny.
He will speak then to a great people in words and deeds,
more than any other man will have fame and renown.

77
A promontory stands between two seas:
A man who will die later by the bit of a horse;
Neptune unfurls a black sail for his man;
the fleet near Gibraltar and Rocheval.

78
To an old leader will be born an idiot heir,
weak both in knowledge and in war.
The leader of France is feared by his sister,
battlefields divided, conceded to the soldiers.

79
Bazas, Lectoure, Condom, Auch and Agen
are troubled by laws, disputes and monopolies.
Carcassone, Bordeaux, Toulouse and Bayonne will be ruined
when they wish to renew the massacre.

80
From the sixth bright celestial light
it will come to thunder very strongly in Burgundy.
Then a monster will be born of a very hideous beast:
In March, April, May and June great wounding and worrying.

81
Nine will be set apart from the human flock,
separated from judgment and advise.
Their fate is to be divided as they depart.
K. Th. L. dead, banished and scattered.

82
When the great wooden columns tremble
in the south wind, covered with blood.
Such a great assembly then pours forth
that Vienna and the land of Austria will tremble.

83
The alien nation will divide the spoils.
Saturn in dreadful aspect in Mars.
Dreadful and foreign to the Tuscans and Latins,
Greeks who will wish to strike.

84
The moon is obscured in deep gloom,
his brother becomes bright red in color.
The great one hidden for a long time in the shadows
will hold the blade in the bloody wound.

85
The king is troubled by the queen's reply.
Ambassadors will fear for their lives.
The greater of his brothers will doubly disguise his action,
two of them will die through anger, hatred and envy.

86
When the great queen sees herself conquered,
she will show an excess of masculine courage.
Naked, on horseback, she will pass over the river
pursued by the sword: she will have outraged her faith

87
Earthshaking fire from the center of the earth
will cause tremors around the New City.
Two great rocks will war for a long time,
then Arethusa will redden a new river.

88
The divine wrath overtakes the great Prince,
a short while before he will marry.
Both supporters and credit will suddenly diminish.
Counsel, he will die because of the shaven heads.

89
Those of Lerida will be in the Moselle,
kill all those from the Loire and Seine.
The seaside track will come near the high valley,
when the Spanish open every route.

90
Bordeaux and Poitiers at the sound of the bell
will go with a great fleet as fast as Langon.
A great rage will surge up against the French,
when a hideous monster is born near Orgon.

91
The Gods will make it appear to mankind
that they are the authors of a great war.
Before the sky was seen to bee free of weapons and rockets:
the greatest damage will be inflicted on the left.

92
Under one man peace will be proclaimed everywhere,
but not long after will be looting and rebellion.
Because of a refusal, town, land and see will be broached.
About a third of a million dead or captured.

93
The Italian lands near the mountains will tremble.
The Cock and the Lion not strongly united.
In place of fear they will help each other.
Freedom alone moderates the French.

94
The tyrant Selim will be put to death at the harbor
but Liberty will not be regained, however.
A new war arises from vengeance and remorse.
A lady is honored through force of terror.

95
In front of a monastery will be found a twin infant
from the illustrious and ancient line of a monk.
His fame, renown and power through sects and speech
is such that they will say the living twin is deservedly chosen.

96
A man will be charged with the destruction
of temples and sects, altered by fantasy.
He will harm the rocks rather than the living,
ears filled with ornate speeches.

97
That which neither weapon nor flame could accomplish
will be achieved by a sweet speaking tongue in council.
Sleeping, in a dream, the king will see
the enemy not in war or of military blood.

98
The leader who will conduct great numbers of people
far from their skies, to foreign customs and language.
Five thousand will die in Crete and Thessaly,
the leader fleeing in a sea going supply ship.

99
The great king will join
with two kings, united in friendship.
How the great household will sigh:
around Narbon what pity for the children.

100
For a long time a gray bird will be seen in the sky
near Dôle and the lands of Tuscany.
He holds a flowering branch in his beak,
but he dies too soon and the war ends.

Century II

1
Towards Aquitaine by the British Isles
By these themselves great incursions.
Rains, frosts will make the soil uneven,
Port Selyn will make mighty invasions

2
The blue head will inflict upon the white head
As much evil as France has done them good:
Dead at the sail-yard the great one hung on the branch.
When seized by his own the King will say how much.

3
Because of the solar heat on the sea
From Negrepont the fishes half cooked:
The inhabitants will come to cut them,
When food will fail in Rhodes and Genoa.

4
From Monaco to near Sicily
The entire coast will remain desolated:
There will remain there no suburb, city or town
Not pillaged and robbed by the Barbarians.

5
That which is enclosed in iron and letter in a fish,
Out will go one who will then make war,
He will have his fleet well rowed by sea,
Appearing near Latin land.

6
Near the gates and within two cities
There will be two scourges the like of which was never seen,
Famine within plague, people put out by steel,
Crying to the great immortal God for relief.

7
Amongst several transported to the isles,
One to be born with two teeth in his mouth
They will die of famine the trees stripped,
For them a new King issues a new edict.

8
Temples consecrated in the original Roman manner,
They will reject the excess foundations,
Taking their first and humane laws,
Chasing, though not entirely, the cult of saints.

9
Nine years the lean one will hold the realm in peace,
Then he will fall into a very bloody thirst:
Because of him a great people will die without faith and law
Killed by one far more good-natured.

10
Before long all will be set in order,
We will expect a very sinister century,
The state of the masked and solitary ones much changed,
Few will be found who want to be in their place.

11
The nearest son of the elder will attain
Very great height as far as the realm of the privileged:
Everyone will fear his fierce glory,
But his children will be thrown out of the realm.

12
Eyes closed, opened by antique fantasy,
The garb of the monks they will be put to naught:
The great monarch will chastise their frenzy,
Ravishing the treasure in front of the temples.

13
The body without soul no longer to be sacrificed:
Day of death put for birthday:
The divine spirit will make the soul happy,
Seeing the word in its eternity.

14
At Tours, Gien, guarded, eyes will be searching,
Discovering from afar her serene Highness:
She and her suite will enter the port,
Combat, thrust, sovereign power.

15
Shortly before the monarch is assassinated,
Castor and Pollux in the ship, bearded star:
The public treasure emptied by land and sea,
Pisa, Asti, Ferrara, Turin land under interdict.

16
Naples, Palermo, Sicily, Syracuse,
New tyrants, celestial lightning fires:
Force from London, Ghent, Brussels and Susa,
Great slaughter, triumph leads to festivities.

17
The field of the temple of the vestal virgin,
Not far from Elne and the Pyrenees mountains:
The great tube is hidden in the trunk.
To the north rivers overflown and vines battered.

18
New, impetuous and sudden rain
Will suddenly halt two armies.
Celestial stone, fires make the sea stony,
The death of seven by land and sea sudden.

19
Newcomers, place built without defense,
Place occupied then uninhabitable:
Meadows, houses, fields, towns to take at pleasure,
Famine, plague, war, extensive land arable.

20
Brothers and sisters captive in diverse places
Will find themselves passing near the monarch:
Contemplating them his branches attentive,
Displeasing to see the marks on chin, forehead and nose.

21
The ambassador sent by biremes,
Halfway repelled by unknown ones:
Reinforced with salt four triremes will come,
In Euboea bound with ropes and chains.

22
The imprudent army of Europe will depart,
Collecting itself near the submerged isle:
The weak fleet will bend the phalanx,
At the navel of the world a greater voice substituted.

23
Palace birds, chased out by a bird,
Very soon after the prince has arrived:
Although the enemy is repelled beyond the river,
Outside seized the trick upheld by the bird.

24
Beasts ferocious from hunger will swim across rivers:
The greater part of the region will be against the Hister,
The great one will cause it to be dragged in an iron cage,
When the German child will observe nothing.

25
The foreign guard will betray the fortress,
Hope and shadow of a higher marriage:
Guard deceived, fort seized in the press,
Loire, Saone, Rhone, Garonne, mortal outrage.

26
Because of the favor that the city will show
To the great one who will soon lose the field of battle,
Fleeing the Po position, the Ticino will overflow
With blood, fires, deaths, drowned by the long-edged blow.

27
The divine word will be struck from the sky,
One who cannot proceed any further:
The secret closed up with the revelation,
Such that they will march over and ahead.

28
The penultimate of the surname of the Prophet
Will take Diana [Thursday] for his day and rest:
He will wander far because of a frantic head,
And delivering a great people from subjection.

29
The Easterner will leave his seat,
To pass the Apennine mountains to see Gaul:
He will transpire the sky, the waters and the snow,
And everyone will be struck with his rod.

30
One who the infernal gods of Hannibal
Will cause to be reborn, terror of mankind
Never more horror nor worse of days
In the past than will come to the Romans through Babel.

31
In Campania the Capuan [river] will do so much
That one will see only fields covered by waters:
Before and after the long rain
One will see nothing green except the trees.

32
Milk, frog's blood prepared in Dalmatia.
Conflict given, plague near Treglia:
A great cry will sound through all Slavonia,
Then a monster will be born near and within Ravenna.

33
Through the torrent which descends from Verona
Its entry will then be guided to the Po,
A great wreck, and no less in the Garonne,
When those of Genoa march against their country.

34
The senseless ire of the furious combat
Will cause steel to be flashed at the table by brothers:
To part them death, wound, and curiously,
The proud duel will come to harm France.

35
The fire by night will take hold in two lodgings,
Several within suffocated and roasted.
It will happen near two rivers as one:
Sun, Sagittarius and Capricorn all will be reduced.

36
The letters of the great Prophet will be seized,
They will come to fall into the hands of the tyrant:
His enterprise will be to deceive his King,
But his extortions will very soon trouble him.

37
Of that great number that one will send
To relieve those besieged in the fort,
Plague and famine will devour them all,
Except seventy who will be destroyed.

38
A great number will be condemned
When the monarchs will be reconciled:
But for one of them such a bad impediment will arise
That they will be joined together but loosely.

39.
One year before the Italian conflict,
Germans, Gauls, Spaniards for the fort:
The republican schoolhouse will fall,
There, except for a few, they will be choked dead.

40
Shortly afterwards, without a very long interval,
By sea and land a great uproar will be raised:
Naval battle will be very much greater,
Fires, animals, those who will cause greater insult.

41
The great star will burn for seven days,
The cloud will cause two suns to appear:
The big mastiff will howl all night
When the great pontiff will change country.

42
Cock, dogs and cats will be satiated with blood
And from the wound of the tyrant found dead,
At the bed of another legs and arms broken,
He who was not afraid to die a cruel death.

43
During the appearance of the bearded star.
The three great princes will be made enemies:
Struck from the sky, peace earth quaking,
Po, Tiber overflowing, serpent placed upon the shore.

44
The Eagle driven back around the tents
Will be chased from there by other birds:
When the noise of cymbals, trumpets and bells
Will restore the senses of the senseless lady.

45.
Too much the heavens weep for the Androgyne begotten,
Near the heavens human blood shed:
Because of death too late a great people re-created,
Late and soon the awaited relief comes.

46
After great trouble for humanity, a greater one is prepared
The Great Mover renews the ages:
Rain, blood, milk, famine, steel and plague,
Is the heavens fire seen, a long spark running.

47
The great old enemy mourning dies of poison,
The sovereigns subjugated in infinite numbers:
Stones raining, hidden under the fleece,
Through death articles are cited in vain.

48
The great force which will pass the mountains.
Saturn in Sagittarius Mars turning from the fish:
Poison hidden under the heads of salmon,
Their war-chief hung with cord.

49
The advisers of the first monopoly,
The conquerors seduced for Malta:
Rhodes, Byzantium for them exposing their pole:
Land will fail the pursuers in flight.

50
When those of Hainault, of Ghent and of Brussels
Will see the siege laid before Langres:
Behind their flanks there will be cruel wars,
The ancient wound will do worse than enemies.

52
The blood of the just will commit a fault at London,
Burnt through lightning of twenty threes the six:
The ancient lady will fall from her high place,
Several of the same sect will be killed.

52
For several nights the earth will tremble:
In the spring two efforts in succession:
Corinth, Ephesus will swim in the two seas:
War stirred up by two valiant in combat.

53
The great plague of the maritime city
Will not cease until there be avenged the death
Of the just blood, condemned for a price without crime,
Of the great lady outraged by pretense.

54.
Because of people strange, and distant from the Romans
Their great city much troubled after water:
Daughter handless, domain too different,
Chief taken, lock not having been picked.

55
In the conflict the great one who was worth little
At his end will perform a marvelous deed:
While Adria will see what he was lacking,
During the banquet the proud one stabbed.

56
One whom neither plague nor steel knew how to finish,
Death on the summit of the hills struck from the sky:
The abbot will die when he will see ruined
Those of the wreck wishing to seize the rock.

57
Before the conflict the great wall will fall,
The great one to death, death too sudden and lamented,
Born imperfect: the greater part will swim:
Near the river the land stained with blood.

58
With neither foot nor hand because of sharp and strong tooth
Through the crowd to the fort of the pork and the elder born:
Near the portal treacherous proceeds,
Moon shining, little great one led off.

59
Gallic fleet through support of the great guard
Of the great Neptune, and his trident soldiers,
Provence reddened to sustain a great band:
More at Narbonne, because of javelins and darts.

60
The Punic faith broken in the East,
Ganges, Jordan, and Rhone, Loire, and Tagus will change:
When the hunger of the mule will be satiated,
Fleet sprinkles, blood and bodies will swim.

61
Bravo, ye of Tamins, Gironde and La Rochelle:
O Trojan blood! Mars at the port of the arrow
Behind the river the ladder put to the fort,
Points to fire great murder on the breach.

62
Mabus then will soon die, there will come
Of people and beasts a horrible rout:
Then suddenly one will see vengeance,
Hundred, hand, thirst, hunger when the comet will run.

64
The Gauls Ausonia will subjugate very little,
Po, Marne and Seine Parma will make drunk:
He who will prepare the great wall against them,
He will lose his life from the least at the wall.

64
The people of Geneva drying up with hunger, with thirst,
Hope at hand will come to fail:
On the point of trembling will be the law of him of the Cevennes,
Fleet at the great port cannot be received.

65
The sloping park great calamity
To be done through Hesperia and Insubria:
The fire in the ship, plague and captivity,
Mercury in Sagittarius Saturn will fade.

66
Through great dangers the captive escaped:
In a short time great his fortune changed.
In the palace the people are trapped,
Through good omen the city besieged.

67
The blond one will come to compromise the fork-nosed one
Through the duel and will chase him out:
The exiles within he will have restored,
Committing the strongest to the marine places.

68
The efforts of Aquilon will be great:
The gate on the Ocean will be opened,
The kingdom on the Isle will be restored:
London will tremble discovered by sail.

69
The Gallic King through his Celtic right arm
Seeing the discord of the great Monarchy:
He will cause his scepter to flourish over the three parts,
Against the cope of the great Hierarchy.

70
The dart from the sky will make its extension,
Deaths speaking: great execution.
The stone in the tree, the proud nation restored,
Noise, human monster, purge expiation.

71
The exiles will come into Sicily
To deliver form hunger the strange nation:
At daybreak the Celts will fail them:
Life remains by reason: the King joins.

72
Celtic army vexed in Italy
On all sides conflict and great loss:
Romans fled, O Gaul repelled!
Near the Ticino, Rubicon uncertain battle.

73
The shore of Lake Garda to Lake Fucino,
Taken from the Lake of Geneva to the port of L'Orguion:
Born with three arms the predicted warlike image,
Through three crowns to the great Endymion.

74
From Sens, from Autun they will come as far as the Rhone
To pass beyond towards the Pyrenees mountains:
The nation to leave the March of Ancona:
By land and sea it will be followed by great suites.

75
The voice of the rare bird heard,
On the pipe of the air-vent floor:
So high will the bushel of wheat rise,
That man will be eating his fellow man.

76.
Lightning in Burgundy will perform a portentous deed,
One which could never have been done by skill,
Sexton made lame by their senate
Will make the affair known to the enemies.

77
Hurled back through bows, fires, pitch and by fires:
Cries, howls heard at midnight:
Within they are place on the broken ramparts,
The traitors fled by the underground passages.

78.
The great Neptune of the deep of the sea
With Punic race and Gallic blood mixed.
The Isles bled, because of the tardy rowing:
More harm will it do him than the ill-concealed secret.

79
The beard frizzled and black through skill
Will subjugate the cruel and proud people:
The great Chyren will remove from far away
All those captured by the banner of Selin

80
After the conflict by the eloquence of the wounded one
For a short time a soft rest is contrived:
The great ones are not to be allowed deliverance at all:
They are restored by the enemies at the proper time.

81
Through fire from the sky the city almost burned:
The Urn threatens Deucalion again:
Sardinia vexed by the Punic foist,
After Libra will leave her Phaethon.

82
Through hunger the prey will make the wolf prisoner,
The aggressor then in extreme distress.
The heir having the last one before him,
The great one does not escape in the middle of the crowd.

83
The large trade of a great Lyons changed,
The greater part turns to pristine ruin
Prey to the soldiers swept away by pillage:
Through the Jura mountain and Suevia drizzle.

84
Between Campania, Siena, Florence, Tuscany,
Six months nine days without a drop of rain:
The strange tongue in the Dalmatian land,
It will overrun, devastating the entire land.

85
The old full beard under the severe statute
Made at Lyon over the Celtic Eagle:
The little great one perseveres too far:
Noise of arms in the sky: Ligurian sea red.

86
Wreck for the fleet near the Adriatic Sea:
The land trembles stirred up upon the air placed on land:
Egypt trembles Mahometan increase,
The Herald surrendering himself is appointed to cry out.

87
After there will come from the outermost countries
A German Prince, upon the golden throne:
The servitude and waters met,
The lady serves, her time no longer adored.

88
The circuit of the great ruinous deed,
The seventh name of the fifth will be:
Of a third greater the stranger warlike:
Sheep, Paris, Aix will not guarantee.

89
One day the two great masters will be friends,
Their great power will be seen increased:
The new land will be at its high peak,
To the bloody one the number recounted.

90
Though life and death the realm of Hungary changed:
The law will be more harsh than service:
Their great city cries out with howls and laments,
Castor and Pollux enemies in the arena.

91.
At sunrise one will see a great fire,
Noise and light extending towards Aquilon:
Within the circle death and one will hear cries,
Through steel, fire, famine, death awaiting them.

92
Fire color of gold from the sky seen on earth:
Heir struck from on high, marvelous deed done:
Great human murder: the nephew of the great one taken,
Deaths spectacular the proud one escaped.

93
Very near the Tiber presses Death:
Shortly before great inundation:
The chief of the ship taken, thrown into the bilge:
Castle, palace in conflagration.

94
Great Po, great evil will be received through Gauls,
Vain terror to the maritime Lion:
People will pass by the sea in infinite numbers,
Without a quarter of a million escaping.

95
The populous places will be uninhabitable:
Great discord to obtain fields:
Realms delivered to prudent incapable ones:
Then for the great brothers dissension and death.

96
Burning torch will be seen in the sky at night
Near the end and beginning of the Rhone:
Famine, steel: the relief provided late,
Persia turns to invade Macedonia.

97
Roman Pontiff beware of approaching
The city that two rivers flow through,
Near there your blood will come to spurt,
You and yours when the rose will flourish.

98
The one whose face is splattered with the blood
Of the victim nearly sacrificed:
Jupiter in Leon, omen through presage:
To be put to death then for the bride.

99
Roman land as the omen interpreted
Will be vexed too much by the Gallic people:
But the Celtic nation will fear the hour,
The fleet has been pushed too far by the north wind.

100
Within the isles a very horrible uproar,
One will hear only a party of war,
So great will be the insult of the plunderers
That they will come to be joined in the great league.

Century III

1
After combat and naval battle,
The great Neptune in his highest belfry:
Red adversary will become pale with fear,
Putting the great Ocean in dread.

2
The divine word will give to the sustenance,
Including heaven, earth, gold hidden in the mystic milk:
Body, soul, spirit having all power,
As much under its feet as the Heavenly see.

3
Mars and Mercury, and the silver joined together,
Towards the south extreme drought:
In the depths of Asia one will say the earth trembles,
Corinth, Ephesus then in perplexity.

4
When they will be close the lunar ones will fail,
From one another not greatly distant,
Cold, dryness, danger towards the frontiers,
Even where the oracle has had its beginning.

5
Near, far the failure of the two great luminaries
Which will occur between April and March.
Oh, what a loss! but two great good-natured ones
By land and sea will relieve all parts.

6
Within the closed temple the lightning will enter,
The citizens within their fort injured:
Horses, cattle, men, the wave will touch the wall,
Through famine, drought, under the weakest armed.

7
The fugitives, fire from the sky on the pikes:
Conflict near the ravens frolicking,
From land they cry for aid and heavenly relief,
When the combatants will be near the walls.

8
The Cimbri joined with their neighbors
Will come to ravage almost Spain:
Peoples gathered in Guienne and Limousin
Will be in league, and will bear them company.

9
Bordeaux, Rouen and La Rochelle joined
Will hold around the great Ocean sea,
English, Bretons and the Flemings allied
Will chase them as far as Roanne.

10
Greater calamity of blood and famine,
Seven times it approaches the marine shore:
Monaco from hunger, place captured, captivity,
The great one led crunching in a metaled cage.

11
The arms to fight in the sky a long time,
The tree in the middle of the city fallen:
Sacred bough clipped, steel, in the face of the firebrand,
Then the monarch of Adria fallen.

12
Because of the swelling of the Ebro, Po, Tagus, Tiber and Rhône
And because of the pond of Geneva and Arezzo,
The two great chiefs and cities of the Garonne,
Taken, dead, drowned: human booty divided.

13.
Through lightning in the arch gold and silver melted,
Of two captives one will eat the other:
The greatest one of the city stretched out,
When submerged the fleet will swim.

14
Through the branch of the valiant personage
Of lowest France: because of the unhappy father
Honors, riches, travail in his old age,
For having believed the advice of a simple man.

15
The realm, will change in heart, vigor and glory,
In all points having its adversary opposed:
Then through death France an infancy will subjugate,
A great Regent will then be more contrary.

16
An English prince Marc in his heavenly heart
Will want to pursue his prosperous fortune,
Of the two duels one will pierce his gall:
Hated by him well loved by his mother.

17
Mount Aventine will be seen to burn at night:
The sky very suddenly dark in Flanders:
When the monarch will chase his nephew,
Then Church people will commit scandals.

18
After the rather long rain milk,
In several places in Reims the sky touched:
Alas, what a bloody murder is prepared near them,
Fathers and sons Kings will not dare approach.

19
In Lucca it will come to rain blood and milk,
Shortly before a change of praetor:
Great plague and war, famine and drought will be made visible
Far away where their prince and rector will die.

20
Through the regions of the great river Guadalquivir
Deep in Iberia to the Kingdom of Grenada
Crosses beaten back by the Mahometan peoples
One of Cordova will betray his country

21
In the Conca by the Adriatic Sea
There will appear a horrible fish,
With face human and its end aquatic,
Which will be taken without the hook.

22
Six days the attack made before the city:
Battle will be given strong and harsh:
Three will surrender it, and to them pardon:
The rest to fire and to bloody slicing and cutting.

23
If, France, you pass beyond the Ligurian Sea,
You will see yourself shut up in islands and seas:
Mahomet contrary, more so the Adriatic Sea:
You will gnaw the bones of horses and asses.

24
Great confusion in the enterprise,
Loss of people, countless treasure:
You ought not to extend further there.
France, let what I say be remembered.

25
He who will attain to the kingdom of Navarre
When Sicily and Naples will be joined:
He will hold Bigorre and Landes through Foix and Oloron
From one who will be too closely allied with Spain.

26
They will prepare idols of Kings and Princes,
Soothsayers and empty prophets elevated:
Horn, victim of gold, and azure, dazzling,
The soothsayers will be interpreted.

27
Libyan Prince powerful in the West
Will come to inflame very much French with Arabian.
Learned in letters condescending he will
Translate the Arabian language into French.

28
Of land weak and parentage poor,
Through piece and peace he will attain to the empire.
For a long time a young female to reign,
Never has one so bad come upon the kingdom.

29
The two nephews brought up in diverse places:
Naval battle, land, fathers fallen:
They will come to be elevated very high in making war
To avenge the injury, enemies succumbed.

30
He who during the struggle with steel in the deed of war
Will have carried off the prize from on greater than he:
By night six will carry the grudge to his bed,
Without armor he will surprised suddenly.

31
On the field of Media, of Arabia and of Armenia
Two great armies will assemble thrice:
The host near the bank of the Araxes,
They will fall in the land of the great Suleiman.

32
The great tomb of the people of Aquitaine
Will approach near to Tuscany,
When Mars will be in the corner of Germany
And in the land of the Mantuan people.

33
In the city where the wolf will enter,
Very near there will the enemies be:
Foreign army will spoil a great country.
The friends will pass at the wall and Alps.

34
When the eclipse of the Sun will then be,
The monster will be seen in full day:
Quite otherwise will one interpret it,
High price unguarded: none will have foreseen it.

35
From the very depths of the West of Europe,
A young child will be born of poor people,
He who by his tongue will seduce a great troop:
His fame will increase towards the realm of the East.

36
Buried apoplectic not dead,
He will be found to have his hands eaten:
When the city will condemn the heretic,
He who it seemed to them had changed their laws.

37
The speech delivered before the attack,
Milan taken by the Eagle through deceptive ambushes:
Ancient wall driven in by cannons,
Through fire and blood few given quarter.

38
The Gallic people and a foreign nation
Beyond the mountains, dead, captured and killed:
In the contrary month and near vintage time,
Through the Lords drawn up in accord.

39
The seven in three months in agreement
To subjugate the Apennine Alps:
But the tempest and cowardly Ligurian,
Destroys them in sudden ruins.

40
The great theater will come to be set up again:
The dice cast and the snares already laid.
Too much the first one will come to tire in the death knell,
Prostrated by arches already a long time split.

41
Hunchback will be elected by the council,
A more hideous monster not seen on earth,
The willing blow will put out his eye:
The traitor to the King received as faithful.

42
The child will be born with two teeth in his mouth,
Stones will fall during the rain in Tuscany:
A few years after there will be neither wheat nor barley,
To satiate those who will faint from hunger.

43
People from around the Tarn, Lot and Garonne
Beware of passing the Apennine mountains:
Your tomb near Rome and Ancona,
The black frizzled beard will have a trophy set up.

44
When the animal domesticated by man
After great pains and leaps will come to speak:
The lightning to the virgin will be very harmful,
Taken from earth and suspended in the air.

45
The five strangers entered in the temple,
Their blood will come to pollute the land:
To the Toulousans it will be a very hard example
Of one who will come to exterminate their laws.

46
The sky (of Plancus' city) forebodes to us
Through clear signs and fixed stars,
That the time of its sudden change is approaching,
Neither for its good, nor for its evils.

47
The old monarch chased out of his realm
Will go to the East asking for its help:
For fear of the crosses he will fold his banner:
To Mitylene he will go through port and by land.

48
Seven hundred captives bound roughly.
Lots drawn for the half to be murdered:
The hope at hand will come very promptly
But not as soon as the fifteenth death.

49
Gallic realm, you will be much changed:
To a foreign place is the empire transferred:
You will be set up amidst other customs and laws:
Rouen and Chartres will do much of the worst to you.

50
The republic of the great city
Will not want to consent to the great severity:
King summoned by trumpet to go out,
The ladder at the wall, the city will repent.

51
Paris conspires to commit a great murder
Blois will cause it to be fully carried out:
Those of Orléans will want to replace their chief,
Angers, Troyes, Langres will commit a misdeed against them.

52
In Campania there will be a very long rain,
In Apulia very great drought.
The Cock will see the Eagle, its wing poorly finished,
By the Lion will it be put into extremity.

53
When the greatest one will carry off the prize
Of Nuremberg, of Augsburg, and those of Bâle
Through Cologne the chief Frankfort retaken
They will cross through Flanders right into Gaul.

54
One of the greatest ones will flee to Spain
Which will thereafter come to bleed in a long wound:
Armies passing over the high mountains,
Devastating all, and then to reign in peace.

55
In the year that one eye will reign in France,
The court will be in very unpleasant trouble:
The great one of Blois will kill his friend:
The realm placed in harm and double doubt.

56
Montauban, Nîmes, Avignon and Béziers,
Plague, thunder and hail in the wake of Mars:
Of Paris bridge, Lyons wall, Montpellier,
After six hundreds and seven score three pairs.

57
Seven times will you see the British nation change,
Steeped in blood in 290 years:
Free not at all its support Germanic.
Aries doubt his Bastarnian pole.

58
Near the Rhine from the Noric mountains
Will be born a great one of people come too late,
One who will defend Sarmatia and the Pannonians,
One will not know what will have become of him.

59
Barbarian empire usurped by the third,
The greater part of his blood he will put to death:
Through senile death the fourth struck by him,
For fear that the blood through the blood be not dead.

60
Throughout all Asia (Minor) great proscription,
Even in Mysia, Lycia and Pamphilia.
Blood will be shed because of the absolution
Of a young black one filled with felony.

61
The great band and sect of crusaders
Will be arrayed in Mesopotamia:
Light company of the nearby river,
That such law will hold for an enemy.

62
Near the Douro by the closed Tyrian sea,
He will come to pierce the great Pyrenees mountains.
One hand shorter his opening glosses,
He will lead his traces to Carcassone.

63
The Roman power will be thoroughly abased,
Following in the footsteps of its great neighbor:
Hidden civil hatreds and debates
Will delay their follies for the buffoons.

64
The chief of Persia will occupy great Olchades,
The trireme fleet against the Mahometan people
From Parthia, and Media: and the Cyclades pillaged:
Long rest at the great Ionian port.

65
When the sepulcher of the great Roman is found,
The day after a Pontiff will be elected:
Scarcely will he be approved by the Senate
Poisoned, his blood in the sacred chalice.

66
The great Bailiff of Orléans put to death
Will be by one of blood revengeful:
Of death deserved he will not die, nor by chance:
He made captive poorly by his feet and hands.

67
A new sect of Philosophers
Despising death, gold, honors and riches
Will not be bordering upon the German mountains:
To follow them they will have power and crowds.

68
Leaderless people of Spain and Italy
Dead, overcome within the Peninsula:
Their dictator betrayed by irresponsible folly,
Swimming in blood everywhere in the latitude.

69
The great army led by a young man,
It will come to surrender itself into the hands of the enemies:
But the old one born to the half-pig,
He will cause Châlon and Mâcon to be friends.

70
The great Britain including England
Will come to be flooded very high by waters
The new League of Ausonia will make war,
So that they will come to strive against them.

71
Those in the isles long besieged
Will take vigor and force against their enemies:
Those outside dead overcome by hunger,
They will be put in greater hunger than ever before.

72
The good old man buried quite alive,
Near the great river through false suspicion:
The new old man ennobled by riches,
Captured on the road all his gold for ransom.

73
When the cripple will attain to the realm,
For his competitor he will have a near bastard:
He and the realm will become so very mangy
That before he recovers, it will be too late.

74
Naples, Florence, Faenza and Imola,
They will be on terms of such disagreement
As to delight in the wretches of Nola
Complaining of having mocked its chief.

75
Pau, Verona, Vicenza, Saragossa,
From distant swords lands wet with blood:
Very great plague will come with the great shell,
Relief near, and the remedies very far.

76
In Germany will be born diverse sects,
Coming very near happy paganism,
The heart captive and returns small,
They will return to paying the true tithe.

77
The third climate included under Aries
The year 1727 in October,
The King of Persia captured by those of Egypt:
Conflict, death, loss: to the cross great shame.

78
The chief of Scotland, with six of Germany,
Captive of the Eastern seamen:
They will pass Gibraltar and Spain,
Present in Persia for the fearful new King.

79
The fatal everlasting order through the chain
Will come to turn through consistent order:
The chain of Marseilles will be broken:
The city taken, the enemy at the same time.

80
The worthy one chased out of the English realm,
The adviser through anger put to the fire:
His adherents will go so low to efface themselves
That the bastard will be half received.

81
The great shameless, audacious bawler,
He will be elected governor of the army:
The boldness of his contention,
The bridge broken, the city faint from fear.

82
Fréjus, Antibes, towns around Nice,
They will be thoroughly devastated by sea and by land:
The locusts by land and by sea the wind propitious,
Captured, dead, bound, pillaged without law of war.

83
The long hairs of Celtic Gaul
Accompanied by foreign nations,
They will make captive the people of Aquitaine,
For succumbing to their designs.

84
The great city will be thoroughly desolated,
Of the inhabitants not a single one will remain there:
Wall, sex, temple and virgin violated,
Through sword, fire, plague, cannon people will die.

85
The city taken through deceit and guile,
Taken in by means of a handsome youth:
Assault given by the Robine near the Aude,
He and all dead for having thoroughly deceived.

86
A chief of Ausonia will go to Spain
By sea, he will make a stop in Marseilles:
Before his death he will linger a long time:
After his death one will see a great marvel.

87
Gallic fleet, do not approach Corsica,
Less Sardinia, you will rue it:
Every one of you will die frustrated of the help of the cape:
You will swim in blood, captive you will not believe me.

88
From Barcelona a very great army by sea,
All Marseilles will tremble with terror:
Isles seized help shut off by sea,
Your traitor will swim on land.

89
At that time Cyprus will be frustrated
Of its relief by those of the Aegean Sea:
Old ones slaughtered: but by speeches and supplications
Their King seduced, Queen outraged more.

90
The great Satyr and Tiger of Hyrcania,
Gift presented to those of the Ocean:
A fleet's chief will set out from Carmania,
One who will take land at the Tyrren Phocaean.

91
The tree which had long been dead and withered,
In one night it will come to grow green again:
The Cronian King sick, Prince with club foot,
Feared by his enemies he will make his sail bound.

92
The world near the last period,
Saturn will come back again late:
Empire transferred towards the Dusky nation,
The eye plucked out by the Goshawk at Narbonne.

93
In Avignon the chief of the whole empire
Will make a stop on the way to desolated Paris:
Tricast will hold the anger of Hannibal:
Lyons will be poorly consoled for the change.

94
For five hundred years more one will keep count of him
Who was the ornament of his time:
Then suddenly great light will he give,
He who for this century will render them very satisfied.

95
The law of More will be seen to decline:
After another much more seductive:
Dnieper first will come to give way:
Through gifts and tongue another more attractive.

96
The Chief of Fossano will have his throat cut
By the leader of the bloodhound and greyhound:
The deed executed by those of the Tarpeian Rock,
Saturn in Leo February 13.

97
New law to occupy the new land
Towards Syria, Judea and Palestine:
The great barbarian empire to decay,
Before the Moon completes it cycle.

98
Two royal brothers will wage war so fiercely
That between them the war will be so mortal
That both will occupy the strong places:
Their great quarrel will fill realm and life.

99
In the grassy fields of Alleins and Vernègues
Of the Lubéron range near the Durance,
The conflict will be very sharp for both armies,
Mesopotamia will fail in France.

100
The last one honored amongst the Gauls,
Over the enemy man will he be victorious:
Force and land in a moment explored,
When the envious one will die from an arrow shot.

Century IV

1
That of the remainder of blood unshed:
Venice demands that relief be given:
After having waited a very long time,
City delivered up at the first sound of the horn.

2
Because of death France will take to making a journey,
Fleet by sea, marching over the Pyrenees Mountains,
Spain in trouble, military people marching:
Some of the greatest Ladies carried off to France.

3
From Arras and Bourges many banners of Dusky Ones,
A greater number of Gascons to fight on foot,
Those along the Rhône will bleed the Spanish:
Near the mountain where Sagunto sits.

4
The impotent Prince angry, complaints and quarrels,
Rape and pillage, by cocks and Africans:
Great it is by land, by sea infinite sails,
Italy alone will be chasing Celts.

5
Cross, peace, under one the divine word accomplished,
Spain and Gaul will be united together:
Great disaster near, and combat very bitter:
No heart will be so hardy as not to tremble.

6
By the new clothes after the find is made,
Malicious plot and machination:
First will die he who will prove it,
Color Venetian trap.

7
The minor son of the great and hated Prince,
He will have a great touch of leprosy at the age of twenty:
Of grief his mother will die very sad and emaciated,
And he will die where the loose flesh falls.

8
The great city by prompt and sudden assault
Surprised at night, guards interrupted:
The guards and watches of Saint-Quentin
Slaughtered, guards and the portals broken.

9
The chief of the army in the middle of the crowd
Will be wounded by an arrow shot in the thighs,
When Geneva in tears and distress
Will be betrayed by Lausanne and the Swiss.

10
The young Prince falsely accused
Will plunge the army into trouble and quarrels:
The chief murdered for his support,
Scepter to pacify: then to cure scrofula.

11.
He who will have the government of the great cope
Will be prevailed upon to perform several deeds:
The twelve red one who will come to soil the cloth,
Under murder, murder will come to be perpetrated.

12
The greater army put to flight in disorder,
Scarcely further will it be pursued:
Army reassembled and the legion reduced,
Then it will be chased out completely from the Gauls.

13
News of the greater loss reported,
The report will astonish the army:
Troops united against the revolted:
The double phalanx will abandon the great one.

14
The sudden death of the first personage
Will have caused a change and put another in the sovereignty:
Soon, late come so high and of low age,
Such by land and sea that it will be necessary to fear him.

15
From where they will think to make famine come,
From there will come the surfeit:
The eye of the sea through canine greed
For the one the other will give oil and wheat.

16
The city of liberty made servile:
Made the asylum of profligates and dreamers.
The King changed to them not so violent:
From one hundred become more than a thousand.

17
To change at Beaune, Nuits, Châlon and Dijon,
The duke wishing to improve the Carmelite [nun]
Marching near the river, fish, diver's beak
Will see the tail: the gate will be locked.

18
Some of those most lettered in the celestial facts
Will be condemned by illiterate princes:
Punished by Edict, hunted, like criminals,
And put to death wherever they will be found.

19
Before Rouen the siege laid by the Insubrians,
By land and sea the passages shut up:
By Hainaut and Flanders, by Ghent and those of Liége
Through cloaked gifts they will ravage the shores.

20
Peace and plenty for a long time the place will praise:
Throughout his realm the fleur-de-lis deserted:
Bodies dead by water, land one will bring there,
Vainly awaiting the good fortune to be buried there.

21
The change will be very difficult:
City and province will gain by the change:
Heart high, prudent established, chased out one cunning,
Sea, land, people will change their state.

22
The great army will be chased out,
In one moment it will be needed by the King:
The faith promised from afar will be broken,
He will be seen naked in pitiful disorder.

23
The legion in the marine fleet
Will burn lime, lodestone sulfur and pitch:
The long rest in the secure place:
Port Selyn and Monaco, fire will consume them.

24
Beneath the holy earth of a soul the faint voice heard,
Human flame seen to shine as divine:
It will cause the earth to be stained with the blood of the monks,
And to destroy the holy temples for the impure ones.

25
Lofty bodies endlessly visible to the eye,
Through these reasons they will come to obscure:
Body, forehead included, sense and head invisible,
Diminishing the sacred prayers.

26
The great swarm of bees will arise,
Such that one will not know whence they have come;
By night the ambush, the sentinel under the vines
City delivered by five babblers not naked.

27
Salon, Tarascon, Mausol, the arch of SEX.,
Where the pyramid is still standing:
They will come to deliver the Prince of Annemark,
Redemption reviled in the temple of Artemis.

28
When Venus will be covered by the Sun,
Under the splendor will be a hidden form:
Mercury will have exposed them to the fire,
Through warlike noise it will be insulted.

29
The Sun hidden eclipsed by Mercury
Will be placed only second in the sky:
Of Vulcan Hermes will be made into food,
The Sun will be seen pure, glowing red and golden.

30
Eleven more times the Moon the Sun will not want,
All raised and lowered by degree:
And put so low that one will stitch little gold:
Such that after famine plague, the secret uncovered.

31
The Moon in the full of night over the high mountain,
The new sage with a lone brain sees it:
By his disciples invited to be immortal,
Eyes to the south. Hands in bosoms, bodies in the fire.

32
In the places and times of flesh giving way to fish,
The communal law will be made in opposition:
It will hold strongly the old ones, then removed from the midst,
Loving of Everything in Common put far behind.

33
Jupiter joined more to Venus than to the Moon
Appearing with white fullness:
Venus hidden under the whiteness of Neptune
Struck by Mars through the white stew.

34
The great one of the foreign land led captive,
Chained in gold offered to King Chyren:
He who in Ausonia, Milan will lose the war,
And all his army put to fire and sword.

35
The fire put out the virgins will betray
The greater part of the new band:
Lightning in sword and lance the lone Kings will guard
Etruria and Corsica, by night throat cut.

36
The new sports set up again in Gaul,
After victory in the Insubrian campaign:
Mountains of Hesperia, the great ones tied and trussed up:
Romania and Spain to tremble with fear.

37
The Gaul will come to penetrate the mountains by leaps:
He will occupy the great place of Insubria:
His army to enter to the greatest depth,
Genoa and Monaco will drive back the red fleet.

38
While he will engross the Duke, King and Queen
With the captive Byzantine chief in Samothrace:
Before the assault one will eat the order:
Reverse side metaled will follow the trail of the blood.

39
The Rhodians will demand relief,
Through the neglect of its heirs abandoned.
The Arab empire will reveal its course,
The cause set right again by Hesperia.

40
The fortresses of the besieged shut up,
Through gunpowder sunk into the abyss:
The traitors will all be stowed away alive,
Never did such a pitiful schism happen to the sextons.

41
Female sex captive as a hostage
Will come by night to deceive the guards:
The chief of the army deceived by her language
Will abandon her to the people, it will be pitiful to see.

42
Geneva and Langres through those of Chartres and Dôle
And through Grenoble captive at Montélimar
Seyssel, Lausanne, through fraudulent deceit,
They will betray them for sixty marks of gold.

43
Arms will be heard clashing in the sky:
That very same year the divine ones enemies:
They will want unjustly to discuss the holy laws:
Through lightning and war the complacent one put to death.

44
Two large ones of Mende, of Rodez and Milhau
Cahors, Limoges, Castres bad week
By night the entry, from Bordeaux an insult
Through Périgord at the peal of the bell.

45
Through conflict a King will abandon his realm:
The greatest chief will fail in time of need:
Dead, ruined few will escape it,
All cut up, one will be a witness to it.

46
The fact well defended by excellence,
Guard yourself Tours from your near ruin:
London and Nantes will make a defense through Reims
Not passing further in the time of the drizzle.

47
The savage black one when he will have tried
His bloody hand at fire, sword and drawn bows:
All of his people will be terribly frightened,
Seeing the greatest ones hung by neck and feet.

48
The fertile, spacious Ausonian plain
Will produce so many gadflies and locusts,
The solar brightness will become clouded,
All devoured, great plague to come from them.

49
Before the people blood will be shed,
Only from the high heavens will it come far:
But for a long time of one nothing will be heard,
The spirit of a lone one will come to bear witness against it.

50
Libra will see the Hesperias govern,
Holding the monarchy of heaven and earth:
No one will see the forces of Asia perished,
Only seven hold the hierarchy in order.

51
A Duke eager to follow his enemy
Will enter within impeding the phalanx:
Hurried on foot they will come to pursue so closely
That the day will see a conflict near Ganges.

52
In the besieged city men and woman to the walls,
Enemies outside the chief ready to surrender:
The wind will be strongly against the troops,
They will be driven away through lime, dust and ashes.

53
The fugitives and exiles recalled:
Fathers and sons great garnishing of the deep wells:
The cruel father and his people choked:
His far worse son submerged in the well.

54
Of the name which no Gallic King ever had
Never was there so fearful a thunderbolt,
Italy, Spain and the English trembling,
Very attentive to a woman and foreigners.

55
When the crow on the tower made of brick
For seven hours will continue to scream:
Death foretold, the statue stained with blood,
Tyrant murdered, people praying to their Gods.

56
After the victory of the raving tongue,
The spirit tempered in tranquillity and repose:
Throughout the conflict the bloody victor makes orations,
Roasting the tongue and the flesh and the bones.

57
Ignorant envy upheld before the great King,
He will propose forbidding the writings:
His wife not his wife tempted by another,
Twice two more neither skill nor cries.

58
To swallow the burning Sun in the throat,
The Etruscan land washed by human blood:
The chief pail of water, to lead his son away,
Captive lady conducted into Turkish land.

59
Two beset in burning fervor:
By thirst for two full cups extinguished,
The fort filed, and an old dreamer,
To the Genevans he will show the track from Nira.

60
The seven children left in hostage,
The third will come to slaughter his child:
Because of his son two will be pierced by the point,
Genoa, Florence, he will come to confuse them.

61
The old one mocked and deprived of his place,
By the foreigner who will suborn him:
Hands of his son eaten before his face,
His brother to Chartres, Orléans Rouen will betray.

62
A colonel with ambition plots,
He will seize the greatest army,
Against his Prince false invention,
And he will be discovered under his arbor.

63
The Celtic army against the mountaineers,
Those who will be learned and able in bird-calling:
Peasants will soon work fresh presses,
All hurled on the sword's edge.

64
The transgressor in bourgeois garb,
He will come to try the King with his offense:
Fifteen soldiers for the most part bandits,
Last of life and chief of his fortune.

65
Towards the deserter of the great fortress,
After he will have abandoned his place,
His adversary will exhibit very great prowess,
The Emperor soon dead will be condemned.

66
Under the feigned color of seven shaven heads
Diverse spies will be scattered:
Wells and fountains sprinkled with poisons,
At the fort of Genoa devourers of men.

67
The year that Saturn and Mars are equal fiery,
The air very dry parched long meteor:
Through secret fires a great place blazing from burning heat,
Little rain, warm wind, wars, incursions.

68
The two greatest ones of Asia and of Africa,
From the Rhine and Lower Danube they will be said to have come,
Cries, tears at Malta and the Ligurian side.

69
The exiles will hold the great city,
The citizens dead, murdered and driven out:
Those of Aquileia will promise Parma
To show them the entry through the untracked places.

70
Quite contiguous to the great Pyrenees mountains,
One to direct a great army against the Eagle:
Veins opened, forces exterminated,
As far as Pau will he come to chase the chief.

71
In place of the bride the daughters slaughtered,
Murder with great error no survivor to be:
Within the well vestals inundated,
The bride extinguished by a drink of Aconite.

72

Those of Nîmes through Agen and Lectoure
At Saint-Félix will hold their parliament:
Those of Bazas will come at the unhappy hour
To seize Condom and Marsan promptly.

73
The great nephew by force will test
The treaty made by the pusillanimous heart:
The Duke will try Ferrara and Asti,
When the pantomime will take place in the evening.

74
Those of lake Geneva and of Mâcon:
All assembled against those of Aquitaine:
Many Germans many more Swiss,
They will be routed along with those of the Humane.

75
Ready to fight one will desert,
The chief adversary will obtain the victory:
The rear guard will make a defense,
The faltering ones dead in the white territory.

76
The people of Agen by those of Périgord
Will be vexed, holding as far as the Rhône:
The union of Gascons and Bigorre
To betray the temple, the priest giving his sermon.

77
Selin monarch Italy peaceful,
Realms united by the Christian King of the World:
Dying he will want to lie in Blois soil,
After having chased the pirates from the sea.

78
The great army of the civil struggle,
By night Parma to the foreign one discovered,
Seventy-nine murdered in the town,
The foreigners all put to the sword.

79
Blood Royal flee, Monheurt, Mas, Aiguillon,
The Landes will be filled by Bordelais,
Navarre, Bigorre points and spurs,
Deep in hunger to devour acorns of the cork oak.

80
Near the great river, great ditch, earth drawn out,
In fifteen parts will the water be divided:
The city taken, fire, blood, cries, sad conflict,
And the greatest part involving the coliseum.

81
Promptly will one build a bridge of boats,
To pass the army of the great Belgian Prince:
Poured forth inside and not far from Brussels,
Passed beyond, seven cut up by pike.

82
A throng approaches coming from Slavonia,
The old Destroyer the city will ruin:
He will see his Romania quite desolated,
Then he will not know how to put out the great flame.

83
Combat by night the valiant captain
Conquered will flee few people conquered:
His people stirred up, sedition not in vain,
His own son will hold him besieged.

84
A great one of Auxerre will die very miserable,
Driven out by those who had been under him:
Put in chains, behind a strong cable,
In the year that Mars, Venus and Sun are in conjunction in summer.

85
The white coal will be chased by the black one,
Made prisoner led to the dung cart,
Moor Camel on twisted feet,
Then the younger one will blind the hobby falcon.

86
The year that Saturn will be conjoined in Aquarius
With the Sun, the very powerful King
Will be received and anointed at Reims and Aix,
After conquests he will murder the innocent.

87
A King's son learned in many languages,
Different from his senior in the realm:
His handsome father understood by the greater son,
He will cause his principal adherent to perish.

88
Anthony by name great by the filthy fact
Of Lousiness wasted to his end:
One who will want to be desirous of lead,
Passing the port he will be immersed by the elected one.

89
Thirty of London will conspire secretly
Against their King, the enterprise on the bridge:
He and his satellites will have a distaste for death,
A fair King elected, native of Frisia.

90
The two armies will be unable to unite at the walls,
In that instant Milan and Pavia to tremble:
Hunger, thirst, doubt will come to plague them very strongly
They will not have a single morsel of meat, bread or victuals.

91
For the Gallic Duke compelled to fight in the duel,
The ship of Melilla will not approach Monaco,
Wrongly accused, perpetual prison,
His son will strive to reign before his death.

92
The head of the valiant captain cut off,
It will be thrown before his adversary:
His body hung on the sail-yard of the ship,
Confused it will flee by oars against the wind.

93
A serpent seen near the royal bed,
It will be by the lady at night the dogs will not bark:
Then to be born in France a Prince so royal,
Come from heaven all the Princes will see him.

94
Two great brothers will be chased out of Spain,
The elder conquered under the Pyrenees mountains:
The sea to redden, Rhône, bloody Lake Geneva from Germany,
Narbonne, Béziers contaminated by Agde.

95
The realm left to two they will hold it very briefly,
Three years and seven months passed by they will make war:
The two Vestals will rebel in opposition,
Victor the younger in the land of Brittany.

96
The elder sister of the British Isle
Will be born fifteen years before her brother,
Because of her promise procuring verification,
She will succeed to the kingdom of the balance.

97
The year that Mercury, Mars, Venus in retrogression,
The line of the great Monarch will not fail:
Elected by the Portuguese people near Cadiz,
One who will come to grow very old in peace and reign.

98
Those of Alba will pass into Rome,
By means of Langres the multitude muffled up,
Marquis and Duke will pardon no man,
Fire, blood, smallpox no water the crops to fail.

99
The valiant elder son of the King's daughter,
He will hurl back the Celts very far,
Such that he will cast thunderbolts, so many in such an array
Few and distant, then deep into the Hesperias.

100
From the celestial fire on the Royal edifice,
When the light of Mars will go out,
Seven months great war, people dead through evil
Rouen, Evreux the King will not fail.

Century V

1
Before the coming of Celtic ruin,
In the temple two will parley
Pike and dagger to the heart of one mounted on the steed,
They will bury the great one without making any noise.

2
Seven conspirators at the banquet will cause to flash
The iron out of the ship against the three:
One will have the two fleets brought to the great one,
When through the evil the latter shoots him in the forehead.

3
The successor to the Duchy will come,
Very far beyond the Tuscan Sea:
A Gallic branch will hold Florence,
The nautical Frog in its bosom be agreement.

4
The large mastiff expelled from the city
Will be vexed by the strange alliance,
After having chased the stag to the fields
The wolf and the Bear will defy each other.

5
Under the shadowy pretense of removing servitude,
He will himself usurp the people and city:
He will do worse because of the deceit of the young prostitute,
Delivered in the field reading the false poem.

6
The Augur putting his hand upon the head of the King
Will come to pray for the peace of Italy:
He will come to move the scepter to his left hand,
From King he will become pacific Emperor.

7
The bones of the Triumvir will be found,
Looking for a deep enigmatic treasure:
Those from thereabouts will not be at rest,
Digging for this thing of marble and metallic lead.

8
There will be unleashed live fire, hidden death,
Horrible and frightful within the globes,
By night the city reduced to dust by the fleet,
The city afire, the enemy amenable.

9
The great arch demolished down to its base,
By the chief captive his friend forestalled,
He will be born of the lady with hairy forehead and face,
Then through cunning the Duke overtaken by death.

10
A Celtic chief wounded in the conflict
Seeing death overtaking his men near a cellar:
Pressed by blood and wounds and enemies,
And relief by four unknown ones.

11
The sea will not be passed over safely by those of the Sun,
Those of Venus will hold all Africa:
Saturn will no longer occupy their realm,
And the Asiatic part will change.

12
To near the Lake of Geneva will it be conducted,
By the foreign maiden wishing to betray the city:
Before its murder at Augsburg the great suite,
And those of the Rhine will come to invade it.

13
With great fury the Roman Belgian King
Will want to vex the barbarian with his phalanx:
Fury gnashing, he will chase the African people
From the Pannonias to the pillars of Hercules.

14
Saturn and Mars in Leo Spain captive,
By the African chief trapped in the conflict,
Near Malta, Herod taken alive,
And the Roman scepter will be struck down by the Cock.

15
The great Pontiff taken captive while navigating,
The great one thereafter to fail the clergy in tumult:
Second one elected absent his estate declines,
His favorite bastard to death broken on the wheel.

16
The Sabaean tear no longer at its high price,
Turning human flesh into ashes through death,
At the isle of Pharos disturbed by the Crusaders,
When at Rhodes will appear a hard phantom.

17
By night the King passing near an Alley,
He of Cyprus and the principal guard:
The King mistaken, the hand flees the length of the Rhône,
The conspirators will set out to put him to death.

18
The unhappy abandoned one will die of grief,
His conqueress will celebrate the hecatomb:
Pristine law, free edict drawn up,
The wall and the Prince falls on the seventh day.

19
The great Royal one of gold, augmented by brass,
The agreement broken, war opened by a young man:
People afflicted because of a lamented chief,
The land will be covered with barbarian blood.

20
The great army will pass beyond the Alps,
Shortly before will be born a monster scoundrel:
Prodigious and sudden he will turn
The great Tuscan to his nearest place.

21
By the death of the Latin Monarch,
Those whom he will have assisted through his reign:
The fire will light up again the booty divided,
Public death for the bold ones who incurred it.

22
Before the great one has given up the ghost at Rome,
Great terror for the foreign army:
The ambush by squadrons near Parma,
Then the two red ones will celebrate together.

23
The two contented ones will be united together,
When for the most part they will be conjoined with Mars:
The great one of Africa trembles in terror,
Duumvirate disjoined by the fleet.

24
The realm and law raised under Venus,
Saturn will have dominion over Jupiter:
The law and realm raised by the Sun,
Through those of Saturn it will suffer the worst.

25
The Arab Prince Mars, Sun, Venus, Leo,
The rule of the Church will succumb by sea:
Towards Persia very nearly a million men,
The true serpent will invade Byzantium and Egypt.

26
The slavish people through luck in war
Will become elevated to a very high degree:
They will change their Prince, one born a provincial,
An army raised in the mountains to pass over the sea.

27
Through fire and arms not far from the Black Sea,
He will come from Persia to occupy Trebizond:
Pharos, Mytilene to tremble, the Sun joyful,
The Adriatic Sea covered with Arab blood.

28
His arm hung and leg bound,
Face pale, dagger hidden in his bosom,
Three who will be sworn in the fray
Against the great one of Genoa will the steel be unleashed.

29
Liberty will not be recovered,
A proud, villainous, wicked black one will occupy it,
When the matter of the bridge will be opened,
The republic of Venice vexed by the Danube.

30
All around the great city
Soldiers will be lodged throughout the fields and towns:
To give the assault Paris, Rome incited,
Then upon the bridge great pillage will be carried out.

31
Through the Attic land fountain of wisdom,
At present the rose of the world:
The bridge ruined, and its great pre-eminence
Will be subjected, a wreck amidst the waves.

32
Where all is good, the Sun all beneficial and the Moon
Is abundant, its ruin approaches:
From the sky it advances to change your fortune.
In the same state as the seventh rock.

33
Of the principal ones of the city in rebellion
Who will strive mightily to recover their liberty:
The males cut up, unhappy fray,
Cries, groans at Nantes pitiful to see.

34
From the deepest part of the English West
Where the head of the British isle is
A fleet will enter the Gironde through Blois,
Through wine and salt, fires hidden in the casks.

35
For the free city of the great Crescent sea,
Which still carries the stone in its stomach,
The English fleet will come under the drizzle
To seize a branch, war opened by the great one.

36
The sister's brother through the quarrel and deceit
Will come to mix dew in the mineral:
On the cake given to the slow old woman,
She dies tasting it she will be simple and rustic.

37
Three hundred will be in accord with one will
To come to the execution of their blow,
Twenty months after all memory
Their king betrayed simulating feigned hate.

38
He who will succeed the great monarch on his death
Will lead an illicit and wanton life:
Through nonchalance he will give way to all,
So that in the end the Salic law will fail.

39
Issued from the true branch of the fleur-de-lis,
Placed and lodged as heir of Etruria:
His ancient blood woven by long hand,
He will cause the escutcheon of Florence to bloom.

40
The blood royal will be so very mixed,
Gauls will be constrained by Hesperia:
One will wait until his term has expired,
And until the memory of his voice has perished.

41
Born in the shadows and during a dark day,
He will be sovereign in realm and goodness:
He will cause his blood to rise again in the ancient urn,
Renewing the age of gold for that of brass.

42
Mars raised to his highest belfry
Will cause the Savoyards to withdraw from France:
The Lombard people will cause very great terror
To those of the Eagle included under the Balance.

43
The great ruin of the holy things is not far off,
Provence, Naples, Sicily, Sées and Pons:
In Germany, at the Rhine and Cologne,
Vexed to death by all those of Mainz.

44
On sea the red one will be taken by pirates,
Because of him peace will be troubled:
Anger and greed will he expose through a false act,
The army doubled by the great Pontiff.

45
The great Empire will soon be desolated
And transferred to near the Ardennes:
The two bastards beheaded by the oldest one,
And Bronzebeard the hawk-nose will reign.

46
Quarrels and new schism by the red hats
When the Sabine will have been elected:
They will produce great sophism against him,
And Rome will be injured by those of Alba.

47
The great Arab will march far forward,
He will be betrayed by the Byzantians:
Ancient Rhodes will come to meet him,
And greater harm through the Austrian Hungarians.

48
After the great affliction of the scepter,
Two enemies will be defeated by them:
A fleet from Africa will appear before the Hungarians,
By land and sea horrible deeds will take place.

49
Not from Spain but from ancient France
Will one be elected for the trembling bark,
To the enemy will a promise be made,
He who will cause a cruel plague in his realm.

50
The year that the brothers of the lily come of age,
One of them will hold the great Romania:
The mountains to tremble, Latin passage opened,
Agreement to march against the fort of Armenia.

51
The people of Dacia, England, Poland
And of Bohemia will make a new league:
To pass beyond the pillars of Hercules,
The Barcelonians and Tuscans will prepare a cruel plot.

52
There will be a King who will give opposition,
The exiles raised over the realm:
The pure poor people to swim in blood,
And for a long time will he flourish under such a device.

53
The law of the Sun and of Venus in strife,
Appropriating the spirit of prophecy:
Neither the one nor the other will be understood,
The law of the great Messiah will hold through the Sun.

54
From beyond the Black Sea and great Tartary,
There will be a King who will come to see Gaul,
He will pierce through Alania and Armenia,
And within Byzantium will he leave his bloody rod.

55
In the country of Arabia Felix
There will be born one powerful in the law of Mahomet:
To vex Spain, to conquer Grenada,
And more by sea against the Ligurian people.

56
Through the death of the very old Pontiff
A Roman of good age will be elected,
Of him it will be said that he weakens his see,
But long will he sit and in biting activity.

57
There will go from Mont and Aventin,
One who through the hole will warn the army:
Between two rocks will the booty be taken,
Of Sectus' mausoleum the renown to fail.

58
By the aqueduct of Uzès over the Gard,
Through the forest and inaccessible mountain,
In the middle of the bridge there will be cut in the fist
The chief of Nîmes who will be very terrible.

59
Too long a stay for the English chief at Nîmes,
Towards Spain Redbeard to the rescue:
Many will die by war opened that day,
When a bearded star will fall in Artois.

60
By the shaven head a very bad choice will come to be made,
Overburdened he will not pass the gate:
He will speak with such great fury and rage,
That to fire and blood he will consign the entire sex.

61
The child of the great one not by his birth,
He will subjugate the high Apennine mountains:
He will cause all those of the balance to tremble,
And from the Pyrenees to Mont Cenis.

62
One will see blood to rain on the rocks,
Sun in the East, Saturn in the West:
Near Orgon war, at Rome great evil to be seen,
Ships sunk to the bottom, taken by Trident.

63
From the vain enterprise honor and undue complaint,
Boats tossed about among the Latins, cold, hunger, waves
Not far from the Tiber the land stained with blood,
And diverse plagues will be upon mankind.

64
Those assembled by the tranquillity of the great number,
By land and sea counsel countermanded:
Near Antonne Genoa, Nice in the shadow
Through fields and towns in revolt against the chief.

65
Come suddenly the terror will be great,
Hidden by the principal ones of the affair:
And the lady on the charcoal will no longer be in sight,
Thus little by little will the great ones be angered.

66
Under the ancient vestal edifices,
Not far from the ruined aqueduct:
The glittering metals are of the Sun and Moon,
The lamp of Trajan engraved with gold burning.

67
When the chief of Perugia will not venture his tunic
Sense under cover to strip himself quite naked:
Seven will be taken Aristocratic deed,
Father and son dead through a point in the collar.

68
In the Danube and of the Rhine will come to drink
The great Camel, not repenting it:
Those of the Rhône to tremble, and much more so those of the Loire,
and near the Alps the Cock will ruin him.

69
No longer will the great one be in his false sleep,
Uneasiness will come to replace tranquillity:
A phalanx of gold, azure and vermilion arrayed
To subjugate Africa and gnaw it to the bone,

70
Of the regions subject to the Balance,
They will trouble the mountains with great war,
Captives the entire sex enthralled and all Byzantium,
So that at dawn they will spread the news from land to land.

71
By the fury of one who will wait for the water,
By his great rage the entire army moved:
Seventeen boats loaded with the noble,
The messenger come late along the Rhône.

72
For the pleasure of the voluptuous edict,
One will mix poison in the faith:
Venus will be in a course so virtuous
As to becloud the whole quality of the Sun.

73
The Church of God will be persecuted,
And the holy Temples will be plundered,
The child will put his mother out in her shift,
Arabs will be allied with the Poles.

74
Of Trojan blood will be born a Germanic heart
Who will rise to very high power:
He will drive out the foreign Arabic people,
Returning the Church to its pristine pre-eminence.

75
He will rise high over the estate more to the right,
He will remain seated on the square stone,
Towards the south facing to his left,
The crooked staff in his hand his mouth sealed.

76
In a free place will he pitch his tent,
And he will not want to lodge in the cities:
Aix, Carpentras, L'Isle, Vaucluse Mont, Cavaillon,
Throughout all these places will he abolish his trace.

77
All degrees of Ecclesiastical honor
Will be changed to that of Jupiter and Quirinus:
The priest of Quirinus to one of Mars,
Then a King of France will make him one of Vulcan.

78
The two will not be united for very long,
And in thirteen years to the Barbarian Satrap:
On both sides they will cause such loss
That one will bless the Bark and its cope.

79
The sacred pomp will come to lower its wings,
Through the coming of the great legislator:
He will raise the humble, he will vex the rebels,
His like will not appear on this earth.

80
Ogmios will approach great Byzantium,
The Barbaric League will be driven out:
Of the two laws the heathen one will give way,
Barbarian and Frank in perpetual strife.

81
The royal bird over the city of the Sun,
Seven months in advance it will deliver a nocturnal omen:
The Eastern wall will fall lightning thunder,
Seven days the enemies directly to the gates.

82
At the conclusion of the treaty outside the fortress
Will not go he who is placed in despair:
When those of Arbois, of Langres against Bresse
Will have the mountains of Dôle an enemy ambush.

83
Those who will have undertaken to subvert,
An unparalleled realm, powerful and invincible:
They will act through deceit, nights three to warn,
When the greatest one will read his Bible at the table.

84
He will be born of the gulf and unmeasured city,
Born of obscure and dark family:
He who the revered power of the great King
Will want to destroy through Rouen and Evreux.

85
Through the Suevi and neighboring places,
They will be at war over the clouds:
Swarm of marine locusts and gnats,
The faults of Geneva will be laid quite bare.

86
Divided by the two heads and three arms,
The great city will be vexed by waters:
Some great ones among them led astray in exile,
Byzantium hard pressed by the head of Persia.

87
The year that Saturn is out of bondage,
In the Frank land he will be inundated by water:
Of Trojan blood will his marriage be,
And he will be confined safely be the Spaniards.

88
Through a frightful flood upon the sand,
A marine monster from other seas found:
Near the place will be made a refuge,
Holding Savona the slave of Turin.

89
Into Hungary through Bohemia, Navarre,
and under that banner holy insurrections:
By the fleur-de-lis legion carrying the bar,
Against Orléans they will cause disturbances.

90
In the Cyclades, in Perinthus and Larissa,
In Sparta and the entire Pelopennesus:
Very great famine, plague through false dust,
Nine months will it last and throughout the entire peninsula.

91
At the market that they call that of liars,
Of the entire Torrent and field of Athens:
They will be surprised by the light horses,
By those of Alba when Mars is in Leo and Saturn in Aquarius.

92
After the see has been held seventeen years,
Five will change within the same period of time:
Then one will be elected at the same time,
One who will not be too comfortable to the Romans.

93
Under the land of the round lunar globe,
When Mercury will be dominating:
The isle of Scotland will produce a luminary,
One who will put the English into confusion.

94
He will transfer into great Germany
Brabant and Flanders, Ghent, Bruges and Boulogne:
The truce feigned, the great Duke of Armenia
Will assail Vienna and Cologne.

95
The nautical oar will tempt the shadows,
Then it will come to stir up the great Empire:
In the Aegean Sea the impediments of wood
Obstructing the diverted Tyrrhenian Sea.

96
The rose upon the middle of the great world,
For new deeds public shedding of blood:
To speak the truth, one will have a closed mouth,
Then at the time of need the awaited one will come late.

97
The one born deformed suffocated in horror,
In the habitable city of the great King:
The severe edict of the captives revoked,
Hail and thunder, Condom inestimable.

98
At the forty-eighth climacteric degree,
At the end of Cancer very great dryness:
Fish in sea, river, lake boiled hectic,
Béarn, Bigorre in distress through fire from the sky.

99
Milan, Ferrara, Turin and Aquileia,
Capua, Brindisi vexed by the Celtic nation:
By the Lion and his Eagle's phalanx,
When the old British chief Rome will have.

100
The incendiary trapped in his own fire,
Of fire from the sky at Carcassonne and the Comminges:
Foix, Auch, Mazères, the high old man escaped,
Through those of Hesse and Thuringia, and some Saxons.

Century VI

1
Around the Pyrenees mountains a great throng
Of foreign people to aid the new King:
Near the great temple of Le Mas by the Garonne,
A Roman chief will fear him in the water.

2
In the year five hundred eighty more or less,
One will await a very strange century:
In the year seven hundred and three the heavens witness thereof,
That several kingdoms one to five will make a change.

3
The river that tries the new Celtic heir
Will be in great discord with the Empire:
The young Prince through the ecclesiastical people
Will remove the scepter of the crown of concord.

4
The Celtic river will change its course,
No longer will it include the city of Agrippina:
All changed except the old language,
Saturn, Leo, Mars, Cancer in plunder.

5
Very great famine through pestiferous wave,
Through long rain the length of the arctic pole:
Samarobryn one hundred leagues from the hemisphere,
The will live without law exempt from politics.

6
There will appear towards the North
Not far from Cancer the bearded star:
Susa, Siena, Boeotia, Eretria,
The great one of Rome will die, the night over.

7
Norway and Dacia and the British Isle
Will be vexed by the united brothers:
The Roman chief sprung from Gallic blood
And his forces hurled back into the forests.

8
Those who were in the realm for knowledge
Will become impoverished at the change of King:
Some exiled without support, having no gold,
The lettered and letters will not be at a high premium.

9
In the sacred temples scandals will be perpetrated,
They will be reckoned as honors and commendations:
Of one of whom they engrave medals of silver and of gold,
The end will be in very strange torments.

10
In a short time the temples with colors
Of white and black of the two intermixed:
Red and yellow ones will carry off theirs from them,
Blood, land, plague, famine, fire extinguished by water.

11
The seven branches will be reduced to three,
The elder ones will be surprised by death,
The two will be seduced to fratricide,
The conspirators will be dead while sleeping.

12
To raise forces to ascend to the empire
In the Vatican the Royal blood will hold fast:
Flemings, English, Spain with Aspire
Against Italy and France will he contend.

13
A doubtful one will not come far from the realm,
The greater part will want to uphold him:
A Capitol will not want him to reign at all,
He will be unable to bear his great burden.

14
Far from his land a King will lose the battle,
At once escaped, pursued, then captured,
Ignorant one taken under the golden mail,
Under false garb, and the enemy surprised.

15
Under the tomb will be found a Prince
Who will be valued above Nuremberg:
The Spanish King in Capricorn thin,
Deceived and betrayed by the great Wittenberg.

16
That which will be carried off by the young Hawk,
By the Normans of France and Picardy:
The black ones of the temple of the Black Forest place
Will make an inn and fire of Lombardy.

17
After the files the ass-drivers burned,
They will be obliged to change diverse garbs:
Those of Saturn burned by the millers,
Except the greater part which will not be covered.

18
The great King abandoned by the Physicians,
By fate not the Jew's art he remains alive,
He and his kindred pushed high in the realm,
Pardon given to the race which denies Christ.

19
The true flame will devour the lady
Who will want to put the Innocent Ones to the fire:
Before the assault the army is inflamed,
When in Seville a monster in beef will be seen.

20
The feigned union will be of short duration,
Some changed most reformed:
In the vessels people will be in suffering,
Then Rome will have a new Leopard.

21
When those of the arctic pole are united together,
Great terror and fear in the East:
Newly elected, the great trembling supported,
Rhodes, Byzantium stained with Barbarian blood.

22
Within the land of the great heavenly temple,
Nephew murdered at London through feigned peace:
The bark will then become schismatic,
Sham liberty will be proclaimed everywhere.

23
Coins depreciated by the spirit of the realm,
And people will be stirred up against their King:
New peace made, holy laws become worse,
Paris was never in so severe an array.

24
Mars and the scepter will be found conjoined
Under Cancer calamitous war:
Shortly afterwards a new King will be anointed,
One who for a long time will pacify the earth.

25
Through adverse Mars will the monarchy
Of the great fisherman be in ruinous trouble:
The young red black one will seize the hierarchy,
The traitors will act on a day of drizzle.

26
For four years the see will be held with some little good,
One libidinous in life will succeed to it:
Ravenna, Pisa and Verona will give support,
Longing to elevate the Papal cross.

27
Within the Isles of five rivers to one,
Through the expansion of the great Chyren Selin:
Through the drizzles in the air the fury of one,
Six escaped, hidden bundles of flax.

28
The great Celt will enter Rome,
Leading a throng of the exiled and banished:
The great Pastor will put to death every man
Who was united at the Alps for the cock.

29
The saintly widow hearing the news,
Of her offspring placed in perplexity and trouble:
He who will be instructed to appease the quarrels,
He will pile them up by his pursuit of the shaven heads.

30
Through the appearance of the feigned sanctity,
The siege will be betrayed to the enemies:
In the night when they trusted to sleep in safety,
Near Brabant will march those of Liège.

31
The King will find that which he desired so much
When the Prelate will be blamed unjustly:
His reply to the Duke will leave him dissatisfied,
He who in Milan will put several to death.

32
Beaten to death by rods for treason,
Captured he will be overcome through his disorder:
Frivolous counsel held out to the great captive,
When Berich will come to bite his nose in fury.

33
His last hand through sanguinary,
He will be unable to protect himself by sea:
Between two rivers he will fear the military hand,
The black and irate one will make him rue it.

34
The device of flying fire
Will come to trouble the great besieged chief:
Within there will be such sedition
That the profligate ones will be in despair.

35
Near the Bear and close to the white wool,
Aries, Taurus, Cancer, Leo, Virgo,
Mars, Jupiter, the Sun will burn a great plain,
Woods and cities letters hidden in the candle.

36
Neither good nor evil through terrestrial battle
Will reach the confines of Perugia,
Pisa to rebel, Florence to see an evil existence,
King by night wounded on a mule with black housing.

37
The ancient work will be finished,
Evil ruin will fall upon the great one from the roof:
Dead they will accuse an innocent one of the deed,
The guilty one hidden in the copse in the drizzle.

38
The enemies of peace to the profligates,
After having conquered Italy:
The bloodthirsty black one, red, will be exposed,
Fire, blood shed, water colored by blood.

39
The child of the realm through the capture of his father
Will be plundered to deliver him:
Near the Lake of Perugia the azure captive,
The hostage troop to become far too drunk.

40
To quench the great thirst the great one of Mainz
Will be deprived of his great dignity:
Those of Cologne will come to complain so loudly
That the great rump will be thrown into the Rhine.

41
The second chief of the realm of Annemark,
Through those of Frisia and of the British Isle,
Will spend more than one hundred thousand marks,
Exploiting in vain the voyage to Italy.

42
To Ogmios will be left the realm
Of the great Selin, who will in fact do more:
Throughout Italy will he extend his banner,
He will be ruled by a prudent deformed one.

43
For a long time will she remain uninhabited,
Around where the Seine and the Marne she comes to water:
Tried by the Thames and warriors,
The guards deceived in trusting in the repulse.

44
By night the Rainbow will appear for Nantes,
By marine arts they will stir up rain:
In the Gulf of Arabia a great fleet will plunge to the bottom,
In Saxony a monster will be born of a bear and a sow.

45
The very learned governor of the realm,
Not wishing to consent to the royal deed:
The fleet at Melilla through contrary wind
Will deliver him to his most disloyal one.

46
A just one will be sent back again into exile,
Through pestilence to the confines of Nonseggle,
His reply to the red one will cause him to be misled,
The King withdrawing to the Frog and the Eagle.

47
The two great ones assembled between two mountains
Will abandon their secret quarrel:
Brussels and Dôle overcome by Langres,
To execute their plague at Malines.

48
The too false and seductive sanctity,
Accompanied by an eloquent tongue:
The old city, and Parma too premature,
Florence and Siena they will render more desert.

49
The great Pontiff of the party of Mars
Will subjugate the confines of the Danube:
The cross to pursue, through sword hook or crook,
Captives, gold, jewels more than one hundred thousand rubies.

50
Within the pit will be found the bones,
Incest will be committed by the stepmother:
The state changed, they will demand fame and praise,
And they will have Mars attending as their star.

51
People assembled to see a new spectacle,
Princes and Kings amongst many bystanders,
Pillars walls to fall: but as by a miracle
The King saved and thirty of the ones present.

52
In place of the great one who will be condemned,
Outside the prison, his friend in his place:
The Trojan hope in six months joined, born dead,
The Sun in the urn rivers will be frozen.

53
The great Celtic Prelate suspected by the King,
By night in flight he will leave the realm:
Through a Duke fruitful for his great British King,
Byzantium to Cyprus and Tunis unsuspected.

54
At daybreak at the second crowing of the cock,
Those of Tunis, of Fez and of Bougie,
By the Arabs the King of Morocco captured,
The year sixteen hundred and seven, of the Liturgy.

55
By the appeased Duke in drawing up the contract,
Arabesque sail seen, sudden discovery:
Tripoli, Chios, and those of Trebizond,
Duke captured, the Black Sea and the city a desert.

56
The dreaded army of the Narbonne enemy
Will frighten very greatly the Hesperians:
Perpignan empty through the blind one of Arbon,
Then Barcelona by sea will take up the quarrel.

57
He who was well forward in the realm,
Having a red chief close to the hierarchy,
Harsh and cruel, and he will make himself much feared,
He will succeed to the sacred monarchy.

58
Between the two distant monarchs,
When the clear Sun is lost through Selin:
Great enmity between two indignant ones,
So that liberty is restored to the Isles and Siena.

59
The Lady in fury through rage of adultery,
She will come to conspire not to tell her Prince:
But soon will the blame be made known,
So that seventeen will be put to martyrdom.

60
The Prince outside his Celtic land
Will be betrayed, deceived by the interpreter:
Rouen, La Rochelle through those of Brittany
At the port of Blaye deceived by monk and priest.

61
The great carpet folded will not show
But by halved the greatest part of history:
Driven far out of the realm he will appear harsh,
So that everyone will come to believe in his warlike deed.

62
Too late both the flowers will be lost,
The serpent will not want to act against the law:
The forces of the Leaguers confounded by the French,
Savona, Albenga through Monaco great martyrdom.

63
The lady left alone in the realm
By the unique one extinguished first on the bed of honor:
Seven years will she be weeping in grief,
Then with great good fortune for the realm long life.

64
No peace agreed upon will be kept,
All the subscribers will act with deceit:
In peace and truce, land and sea in protest,
By Barcelona fleet seized with ingenuity.

65
Gray and brown in half-opened war,
By night they will be assaulted and pillaged:
The brown captured will pass through the lock,
His temple opened, two slipped in the plaster.

66
At the foundation of the new sect,
The bones of the great Roman will be found,
A sepulcher covered by marble will appear,
Earth to quake in April poorly buried.

67
Quite another one will attain to the great Empire,
Kindness distant more so happiness:
Ruled by one sprung not far from the brothel,
Realms to decay great bad luck.

68
When the soldiers in a seditious fury
Will cause steel to flash by night against their chief:
The enemy Alba acts with furious hand,
Then to vex Rome and seduce the principal ones.

69
The great pity will occur before long,
Those who gave will be obliged to take:
Naked, starving, withstanding cold and thirst,
To pass over the mountains committing a great scandal.

70
Chief of the world will the great Chyren be,
Plus Ultra behind, loved, feared, dreaded:
His fame and praise will go beyond the heavens,
And with the sole title of Victor will he be quite satisfied.

71
When they will come to give the last rites to the great King
Before he has entirely given up the ghost:
He who will come to grieve over him the least,
Through Lions, Eagles, cross crown sold.

72
Through feigned fury of divine emotion
The wife of the great one will be violated:
The judges wishing to condemn such a doctrine,
She is sacrificed a victim to the ignorant people.

73
In a great city a monk and artisan,
Lodged near the gate and walls,
Secret speaking emptily against Modena,
Betrayed for acting under the guise of nuptials.

74
She chased out will return to the realm,
Her enemies found to be conspirators:
More than ever her time will triumph,
Three and seventy to death very sure.

75
The great Pilot will be commissioned by the King,
To leave the fleet to fill a higher post:
Seven years after he will be in rebellion,
Venice will come to fear the Barbarian army.

76
The ancient city the creation of Antenor,
Being no longer able to bear the tyrant:
The feigned handle in the temple to cut a throat,
The people will come to put his followers to death.

77
Through the fraudulent victory of the deceived,
Two fleets one, German revolt:
The chief murdered and his son in the tent,
Florence and Imola pursued into Romania.

78
To proclaim the victory of the great expanding Selin:
By the Romans will the Eagle be demanded,
Pavia, Milan and Genoa will not consent thereto,
Then by themselves the great Lord claimed.

79
Near the Ticino the inhabitants of the Loire,
Garonne and Saône, the Seine, the Tain and Gironde:
They will erect a promontory beyond the mountains,
Conflict given, Po enlarged, submerged in the wave.

80
From Fez the realm will reach those of Europe,
Their city ablaze and the blade will cut:
The great one of Asia by land and sea with great troop,
So that blues and Pers[ians] the cross will pursue to death.

81
Tears, cries and laments, howls, terror,
Heart inhuman, cruel, black and chilly:
Lake of Geneva the Isles, of Genoa the notables,
Blood to pour out, wheat famine to none mercy.

82
Through the deserts of the free and wild place,
The nephew of the great Pontiff will come to wander:
Felled by seven with a heavy club,
By those who afterwards will occupy the Chalice.

83
He who will have so much honor and flattery
At his entry into Belgian Gaul:
A while after he will act very rudely,
And he will act very warlike against the flower.

84
The Lame One, he who lame could not reign in Sparta,
He will do much through seductive means:
So that by the short and long, he will be accused
Of making his perspective against the King.

85
The great city of Tarsus by the Gauls
Will be destroyed, all of the Turban captives:
Help by sea from the great one of Portugal,
First day of summer Urban's consecration.

86
The great Prelate one day after his dream,
Interpreted opposite to its meaning:
From Gascony a monk will come unexpectedly,
One who will cause the great prelate of Sens to be elected.

87
The election made in Frankfort
Will be voided, Milan will be opposed:
The follower closer will seem so very strong
That he will drive him out into the marshes beyond the Rhine.

88
A great realm will be left desolated,
Near the Ebro an assembly will be formed:
The Pyrenees mountains will console him,
When in May lands will be trembling.

89
Feet and hands bound between two boats,
Face anointed with honey, and sustained with milk:
Wasps and flies, paternal love vexed,
Cup-bearer to falsify, Chalice tried.

90
The stinking abominable disgrace,
After the deed he will be congratulated:
The great excuse for not being favorable,
That Neptune will not be persuaded to peace.

91
Of the leader of the naval war,
Red one unbridled, severe, horrible whim,
Captive escaped from the elder one in the bale,
When there will be born a son to the great Agrippa.

92
Prince of beauty so comely,
Around his head a plot, the second deed betrayed:
The city to the sword in dust the face burnt,
Through too great murder the head of the King hated.

93
The greedy prelate deceived by ambition,
He will come to reckon nothing too much for him:
He and his messengers completely trapped,
He who cut the wood sees all in reverse.

94
A King will be angry with the see-breakers,
When arms of war will be prohibited:
The poison tainted in the sugar for the strawberries,
Murdered by waters, dead, saying land, land.

95
Calumny against the cadet by the detractor,
When enormous and warlike deeds will take place:
The least part doubtful for the elder one,
And soon in the realm there will be partisan deeds.

96
Great city abandoned to the soldiers,
Never was mortal tumult so close to it:
Oh, what a hideous calamity draws near,
Except one offense nothing will be spared it.

97
At forty-five degrees the sky will burn,
Fire to approach the great new city:
In an instant a great scattered flame will leap up,
When one will want to demand proof of the Normans.

98
Ruin for the Volcae so very terrible with fear,
Their great city stained, pestilential deed:
To plunder Sun and Moon and to violate their temples:
And to redden the two rivers flowing with blood.

99
The learned enemy will find himself confused,
His great army sick, and defeated by ambushes,
The Pyrenees and Pennine Alps will be denied him,
Discovering near the river ancient jugs.

100: Incantation of the law against inept critics
Let those who read this verse consider it profoundly,
Let the profane and the ignorant herd keep away:
And far away all Astrologers, Idiots and Barbarians,
May he who does otherwise be subject to the sacred rite.

Century VII

1
The arc of the treasure deceived by Achilles,
the quadrangle known to the procreators.
The invention will be known by the Royal deed;
a corpse seen hanging in the sight of the populace.

2
Opened by Mars Arles will not give war,
the soldiers will be astonished by night.
Black and white concealing indigo on land
under the false shadow you will see traitors sounded.

3
After the naval victory of France,
the people of Barcelona the Saillinons and those of Marseilles;
the robber of gold, the anvil enclosed in the ball,
the people of Ptolon will be party to the fraud.

4
The Duke of Langres besieged at Dôle
accompanied by people from Autun and Lyons.
Geneva, Augsburg allied to those of Mirandola,
to cross the mountains against the people of Ancona.

5
Some of the wine on the table will be spilt,
the third will not have that which he claimed.
Twice descended from the black one of Parma,
Perouse will do to Pisa that which he believed.

6
Naples, Palerma and all of Sicily
will be uninhabited through Barbarian hands.
Corsica, Salerno and the island of Sardinia,
hunger, plague, war the end of extended evils.

7
Upon the struggle of the great light horses,
it will be claimed that the great crescent is destroyed.
To kill by night, in the mountains,
dressed in shepherd's' clothing, red gulfs in the deep ditch.

8
Florense, flee, flee the nearest Roman,
at Fiesole will be conflict given:
blood shed, the greatest one take by the hand,
neither temple nor sex will be pardoned.

9
The lady in the absence of her great master
will be begged for love by the Viceroy.
Feigned promise and misfortune in love,
in the hands of the great Prince of Bar.

10
By the great Prince bordering Le Mans,
brave and valiant leader of the great army;
by land and sea with Bretons and Normans,
to pass Gibraltar and Barcelona to pillage the island.

11
eye, feet wounded rude disobedient;
strange and very bitter news to the lady;
more than five hundred of here people will be killed.

12
The great younger son will make an end of the war,
he assembles the pardoned before the gods;
Cahors and Moissac will go far from the prison,
a refusal at Lectoure, the people of Agen shaved.

13
From the marine tributary city,
the shaven head will take up the satrapy;
to chase the sordid man who will the be against him.
For fourteen years he will hold the tyranny.

14
He will come to expose the false topography,
the urns of the tombs will be opened.
Sect and holy philosophy to thrive,
black for white and the new for the old.

15
Before the city of the Insubrian lands,
for seven years the siege will be laid;
a very great king enters it,
the city is then free, away from its enemies.

16
The deep entry made by the great Queen
will make the place powerful and inaccessible;
the army of the three lions will be defeated
causing within a thing hideous and terrible.

17
The prince who has little pity of mercy
will come through death to change (and become) very knowledgeable.
The kingdom will be attended with great tranquillity,
when the great one will soon be fleeced.

18
The besieged will color their pacts,
but seven days later they will make a cruel exit:
thrown back inside, fire and blood, seven put to the ax
the lady who had woven the peace is a captive.

19
The fort at Nice will not engage in combat,
it will be overcome by shining metal.
This deed will be debated for a long time,
strange and fearful for the citizens.

20
Ambassadors of the Tuscan language
will cross the Alps and the sea in April and May.
The man of the calf will deliver an oration,
not coming to wipe out the French way of life.

21
By the pestilential enmity of Languedoc,
the tyrant dissimulated will be driven out.
The bargain will be made on the bridge at Sorgues
to put to death both him and his follower

22
The citizens of Mesopotamia
angry with their friends from Tarraconne;
games, rites, banquets, every person asleep,
the vicar at Rhône, the city taken and those of Ausonia.

23
The Royal scepter will be forced to take
that which his predecessors had pledged.
Because they do not understand about the ring
when they come to sack the palace.

24
He who was buried will come out of the tomb,
He will cause the fort of the bridge to be tied in chains:
Poisoned with the spawn of a pimp,
the great one from Lorraine by the Marquis du Pont.

25
Through long war all the army exhausted,
so that they do not find money for the soldiers;
instead of gold or silver, they will come to coin leather,
Gallic brass, and the crescent sign of the Moon.

26
Foists and galleys around seven ships,
a mortal war will be let loose.
The leader from Madrid will receive a wound from arrows,
two escaped and five brought to land.

27
At the wall of Vasto the great cavalry
are impeded by the baggage near Ferrara.
At Turin they will speedily commit such robbery
that in the fort they will ravish their hostage.

28
The captain will lead a great herd
on the mountain closest to the enemy.
Surrounded by fire he makes such a way,
all escape except for thirty put on the spit.

29
The great one of Alba will come to rebel,
he will betray his great forebears.
The great man of Guise will come to vanquish him,
led captive with a monument erected.

30
The sack approaches, fire and great bloodshed.
Po the great rivers, the enterprise for the clowns;
after a long wait from Genoa and Nice,
Fossano, Turin the capture at Savigliano.

31
From Languedoc and Guienne more than ten
thousand will want to cross the Alps again.
The great Savoyards march against Brindisi,
Aquino and Bresse will come to drive them back.

32
From the bank of Montereale will be born one
who bores and calculates becoming a tyrant.
To raise a force in the marches of Milan,
to drain Faenza and Florence of gold and men

33
The kingdom stripped of its forces by fraud,
the fleet blockaded, passages for the spy;
two false friends will come to rally
to awaken hatred for a long time dormant.

34
The French nation will be in great grief,
vain and lighthearted, they will believe rash things.
No bread, salt, wine nor water, venom nor ale,
the greater one captured, hunger, cold and want.

35
The great fish will come to complain and weep
for having chosen, deceived concerning his age:
he will hardly want to remain with them,
he will be deceived by those (speaking) his own tongue.

36
God, the heavens, all the divine words in the waves,
carried by seven red-shaven heads to Byzantium:
against the anointed three hundred from Trebizond,
will make two laws, first horror then trust.

37
Ten sent to put the captain of the ship to death,
are altered by one that there is open revolt in the fleet.
Confusion, the leader and another stab and bite each other
at Lerins and the Hyères, ships, prow into the darkness.

38
The elder royal one on a frisky horse
will spur so fiercely that it will bolt.
Mouth, mouthful, foot complaining in the embrace;
dragged, pulled, to die horribly.

39
The leader of the French army
will expect to lose the main phalanx.
Upon the pavement of oats and slate
the foreign nation will be undermined through Genoa.

40
Within casks anointed outside with oil and grease
twenty-one will be shut before the harbor,
at second watch; through death they will do great deeds;
to win the gates and be killed by the watch.

41
The bones of the feet and the hands locked up,
because of the noise the house is uninhabited for a long time.
Digging in dreams they will be unearthed,
the house healthy in inhabited without noise.

42
Two newly arrived have seized the poison,
to pour it in the kitchen of the great Prince.
By the scullion both are caught in the act,
taken he who thought to trouble the elder with death.

Epistle to Henry II

To the most invincible most powerful and most christian henry, king of france the second: michel nostradamus, his very humble and very obedient servant and subject, wishes victory and happiness

Ever since my long-beclouded face first presented itself before the immeasurable deity of your Majesty, O Most Christian and Most Victorious King, I have remained perpetually dazzled by that sovereign sight. I have never ceased to honor and venerate properly that date when I presented myself before a Majesty so singular and so humane. I have searched for some occasion on which to manifest high heart and stout courage, and thereby obtain even greater recognition of Your Most Serene Majesty. But I saw how obviously impossible it was for me to declare myself.

While I was seized with this singular desire to be transported suddenly from my long-beclouded obscurity to the illuminating presence of the first monarch of the universe, I was also long in doubt as to whom I would dedicate these last three Centuries of my prophecies, making up the thousand. After having meditated for a long time on an act of such rash audacity, I have ventured to address Your Majesty. I have not been daunted like those mentioned by that most grave author Plutarch, in his Life of Lycurgus, who were so astounded at the expense of the offerings and gifts brought as sacrifices to the temples of the immortal gods of that age, that they did not dare to present anything at all. Seeing your royal splendor to be accompanied by such an incomparable humanity, I have paid my address to it and not as those Kings of Persia whom one could neither stand before nor approach.

It is to a most prudent and most wise Prince that I have dedicated my nocturnal and prophetic calculations, which are composed rather out of a natural instinct, accompanied by a poetic furor, than according to the strict rules of poetry. Most of them have been integrated with astronomical calculations corresponding to the years, months and weeks of the regions, countries and most of the towns and cities of all Europe, including Africa and part of Asia, where most of all these coming events are to transpire. They are composed in a natural manner.

Indeed, someone, who would do well to blow his nose, may reply that the rhythm is as easy as the sense is difficult. That, O Most Humane king, is because most of the prophetic quatrains are so ticklish that there is no making way through them, nor is there any interpreting of them.

Nevertheless, I wanted to leave a record in writing of the years, towns, cities and regions in which most of the events will come to pass, even those of the year

1585 and of the year 1606, reckoning from the present time, which is March 14, 1557, and going far beyond to the events which will take place at the beginning of the seventh millenary, when, so far as my profound astronomical calculations and other knowledge have been able to make out, the adversaries of Jesus Christ and his Church will begin to multiply greatly.

I have calculated and composed all during choice hours of well-disposed days, and as accurately as I could, all when Minerva was free and not unfavorable. I have made computations for events over almost as long a period to come as that which has already passed, and by these they will know in all regions what is to happen in the course of time, just as it is written, with nothing superfluous added, although some may say, There can be no truth entirely determined concerning the future.

It is quite true, Sire, that my natural instinct has been inherited from my forebears, who did not believe in predicting, and that this is natural instinct has been adjusted and integrated with long calculations. At the same time, I freed my soul, mind and heart of all care, solicitude and vexation. All of these prerequisites for presaging I achieved in part by means of the brazen tripod.

There are some who would attribute to me that which is not mine at all. The eternal God alone, who is the thorough searcher of humane hearts, pious, just and merciful, is the true judge, and it is to him I pray to defend me from the calumny of evil men. These evil ones, in their slanderous way, would likewise want to inquire how all your most ancient progenitors, the Kings of France, have cured the scrofula, how those of other nations have cured the bite of snakes, how those of yet other nations have had a certain instinct for the art of divination and still others which would be too long to recite here.

Notwithstanding those who cannot contain the malignity of the evil spirit, as time elapses after my death, my writings will have more weight than during my lifetime. Should I, however, have made any errors in my calculation of dates, or prove unable to please everybody, I beg that your more than Imperial Majesty will forgive me. I protest before God and his Saints that I do not propose to insert any writings in this present Epistle that will be contrary to the true Catholic faith, whilst consulting the astronomical calculations to the best of my ability.

Such is the extent of time past, subject to correction by the most learned judgment, that the first man, Adam, came 1,242 years before Noah (not reckoning by such Gentile calculations as Varro used, but simply by the Holy Scriptures, as best my weak understanding and astronomical calculations can interpret them.) About 1,080 years after Noah and the universal flood came Abraham, who, according to some, was a first-rate astrologer and invented the Chaldean alphabet. About 515 or 516 years later came Moses, and from his time to that of David about 570 years elapsed. From the time of David to that of out Savior and Redeemer, Jesus Christ, born of the unique Virgin, 1,350 year elapsed, according to some chronographs. Some may object that this calculation cannot be true, because it differs from that of Eusebius. From the time of the human redemption to the detestable heresy of the Saracens about 621 years elapsed. From this one can easily add up the amount of time gone by.

Although my calculations may not hold good for all nations, they have, however, been determined by the celestial movements, combined with the emotion, handed down to me by my forebears, which comes over me at certain hours. But the danger of the times, O Most Serene King, requires that such secrets should not be bared except in enigmatic sentences having, however, only one sense and meaning, and nothing ambiguous or amphibological inserted. Rather they are under a cloudy obscurity, with a natural infusion not unlike the creation of the world, according to the calculation and Punic Chronicle of Joel: I will pour out my spirit upon all flesh and your sons and daughters will prophesy. But such Prophecy proceeded from the mouth of the Holy Ghost who was the sovereign and eternal power, together with the heavens, and caused some of them to predict great and marvelous events.

As for myself, I would never claim such a title, never, please God. I readily admit that all proceeds from God and render to Him thanks, honor and immortal praise. I have mixed therewith no divination coming from fate. All from God and nature, and for the most part integrated with celestial movements. It is much like seeing in a burning mirror, with clouded vision, the great events, sad, prodigious and calamitous events that in due time will fall upon the principal worshippers. First, upon the temples of God; secondly, upon those who, sustained by the earth, approach such a decadence. Also a thousand other calamitous events which will be known to happen in due time.

For God will take notice of the long barrenness of the great dame, who thereupon will conceive two principal children. But she will be in danger, and the female to whom she will have given birth will also, because of the temerity of the age, be in danger of death in her eighteenth year, and will be unable to live beyond her thirty-sixth year. She will leave three males, and one female, and of these two will not have had the same father.

There will be great differences between the three brothers, and then there will be such great cooperation and agreement between them that the three and four parts of Europe will tremble. The youngest of them will sustain and augment the Christian monarchy, and under him sects will be elevated, and suddenly cast down, Arabs will be driven back, kingdoms united and new laws promulgated.

The oldest one will rule the land whose escutcheon is that of the furious crowned lions with their paws resting upon intrepid arms.

The one second in age, accompanied by the Latins, will penetrate far, until a second furious and trembling path has been beaten to the Great St. Bernard Pass. From there he will descend to mount the Pyrenees, which will not, however, be transferred to the French crown. And this third one will cause a great inundation of human blood, and for a long time Lent will not include March.

The daughter will be given for the preservation of the Christian Church. Her lord will fall into the pagan sect of the new infidels. Of her two children, one will be faithful to the Catholic Church, the other an infidel.

The unfaithful son, who, to his great confusion and later repentance, will want to ruin her, will have three widely scattered regions, namely, the Roman, Germany and Spain, which will set up diverse sects by armed force. The 50th to the 52th degree of latitude will be left behind.

And all will render the homage of ancient religions to the region of Europe north of the 48th parallel. The latter will have trembled first in vain timidity but afterwards the regions to its west, south and east will tremble. But the nature of their power will be such that what has been brought about by concord and union will prove insuperable by warlike conquests.

In nature they will be equal, but very different in faith.

After this the barren Dame, of greater power than the second, will be received by two of the nations. First, by them made obstinate by the onetime masters of the universe. Second, by the latter themselves.

The third people will extend their forces towards the circuit of the East of Europe where, in the Pannonias, they will be overwhelmed and slaughtered. By sea they will extend their Myrmidons and Germans to Adriatic Sicily. But they will succumb wholly and the Barbarian sect will be greatly afflicted and driven out by all the Latins.

Then the great Empire of the Antichrist will begin where once was Attila's empire and the new Xerxes will descend with great and countless numbers, so that the coming of the Holy Ghost, proceeding from the 48th degree, will make a transmigration, chasing out the abomination of the Christian Church, and whose reign will be for a time and to the end of time.

This will be preceded by a solar eclipse more dark and gloomy than any since the creation of the world, except that after the death and passion of Jesus Christ. And it will be in the month of October than the great translation will be made and it will be such that one will think the gravity of the earth has lost its natural movement and that it is to be plunged into the abyss of perpetual darkness.

In the spring there will be omens, and thereafter extreme changes, reversals of realms and mighty earthquakes. These will be accompanied by the procreation of the new Babylon, miserable daughter enlarged by the abomination of the first holocaust. It will last for only seventy-three years and seven months.

Then there will issue from the stock which had remained barren for so long, proceeding from the 50th degree, one who will renew the whole Christian Church. A great place will be established, with union and concord between some of the children of opposite ideas, who have been separated by diverse realms. And such will be the peace that the instigator and promoter of military factions, born of the diversity of religions, will remain chained to the deepest pit. And the kingdom of the Furious One, who counterfeits the sage, will be united.

The countries, towns, cities, realms and provinces which will have abandoned their old customs to gain liberty, but which will in fact have enthralled themselves even more, will secretly have wearied of their liberty. Faith lost in their perfect religion, they will begin to strike to the left, only to return to the right. Holiness, for a long time overcome, will be replaced in accordance with the earliest writings.

Thereafter the great dog, the biggest of curs, will go forth and destroy all, the same old crimes being perpetrated again. Temples will be set up again as in ancient times, and the priest will be restored to his original position and he will begin his whoring and luxury, and will commit a thousand crimes.

At the eve of another desolation, when she is atop her most high and sublime dignity, some potentates and warlords will confront her, and take away her two swords, and leave her only the insignia, whose curvature attracts them. The people will make him go to the right and will not wish to submit themselves to those of the opposite extreme with the hand in acute position, who touch the ground, and want to drive spurs into them.

The people of the world from this benevolent slavery to which they had voluntary submitted. He will put himself under the protection of Mars, stripping Jupiter of all his honors and dignities, and establish himself in the free city in another scant Mesopotamia. The chief and governor will be cast out from the middle and hung up, ignorant of the conspiracy of one of the conspirators with the second Thrasibulus, who for a long time will have directed all this.

Then the impurities and abominations, with a great shame, will be brought out and manifested in the shadows of the veiled light, and will cease towards the end of the change in reign. The chiefs of the Church will be backward in the love of God, and several of them will apostatize from the true faith. Of the three sects, that which is in the middle, because of its own partisans, will be thrown a bit into decadence. The first one will be exterminated throughout all Europe and most of Africa by the third one, making use of the poor in spirit who, led by madmen to libidinous luxury, will adulterate.

The supporting common people will rise up and chase out the adherents of the legislators. From the way realms will have been weakened by the Easterners, it will seem that God the Creator has loosed Satan from the prisons of hell to give birth to the great Dog and Dogam, who will make such an abominable breach in the Churches that neither the reds nor the whites without eyes or hands will know what to make of it, and their power will be taken from them.

Then will commence a persecution of the Churches the like of which was never seen. Meanwhile, such a plague will arise that more than two thirds of the world will be removed. One will be unable to ascertain the true owners of fields and houses, and weeds growing in the streets of cities will rise higher than the knees. For the clergy there will be but utter desolation. The warlords will usurp what is returned from the City of the Sun, from Malta and the Isles of Hyhres. The great chain of the port which wakes its name from the marine ox will be opened.

And a new incursion will be made by the maritime shores, wishing to deliver the Sierra Morea from the first Mahometan recapture. Their assaults will not all be in vain, and the place which was once the abode of Abraham will be assaulted by persons who hold the Jovialists in veneration. And this city of "Achem" will be surrounded and assailed on all sides by a most powerful force of warriors. Their maritime forces will be weakened by the Westerners, and great desolation will fall upon this realm. Its greatest cities will be depopulated and those who enter will fall under the vengeance of the wrath of God.

The sepulcher, for long an object of such great veneration, will remain in the open, exposed to the sight of the heavens, the Sun and the Moon. The holy place will be converted into a stable for a herd large and small, and used for profane purposes. Oh, what a calamitous affliction will pregnant women bear at this time.

For hereupon the principal Eastern chief will be vanquished by the Northerners and Westerners, and most of his people, stirred up, will be put to death, overwhelmed or scattered. His children, offspring of many women, will be imprisoned. Then will be accomplished the prophecy of the Royal Prophet, Let him hear the groaning of the captives, that he might deliver the children of those doomed to die.

What great oppression will then fall upon the Princes and Governors of Kingdoms, especially those which will be maritime and Eastern, whose tongues will be intermingled with all others: the tongue of the Latins, and of the Arabs, via the Phoenicians. And all these Eastern Kings will be chased, overthrown and exterminated, but not altogether, by means of the forces of the Kings of the North, and because of the drawing near of our age through the three secretly united in the search for death, treacherously laying traps for one another. This renewed Triumvirate will last for seven years, and the renown of this sect will extend around the world. The sacrifice of the hole and immaculate Wafer will be sustained.

Then the Lords of "Aquilon" [the North], two in number, will be victorious over the Easterners, and so great a noise and bellicose tumult will they make amongst them that all the East will tremble in terror of these brothers, yet not brothers, of "Aquilon" [the North].

By this discourse, Sire, I present these predictions almost with confusion, especially as to when they will take place. Furthermore, the chronology of time which follows conforms very little, if at all, with that which has already been set forth. Yet it was determined by astronomy and other sources, including Holy Scriptures, and thus could not err. If I had wanted to date each quatrain, I could have done so. But this would not have been agreeable to all, least of all to those interpreting them, and was not to be done until Your Majesty granted me full power to do so, lest calumniators be furnished with an opportunity to injure me.

Anyhow, I count the years from the creation of the world to the birth of Noah as 1,506, and from the birth of Noah to the completion of the Ark, at the time of the universal deluge, as 600 (let the years be solar, or lunar, or a mixture of the ten) I hold that the Sacred Scriptures use solar years. And at the end of these 600 years, Noah entered the Ark to be saved from the deluge. This deluge was universal, and lasted one year and two months. And 295 years elapsed from the end of the flood to the birth of Abraham, and 100 from then till the birth of Isaac. And 60 years later Jacob was born. 130 years elapsed between the time he entered Egypt and the time he came out. Between the entry of Jacob into Egypt and the exodus, 430 years passed. From the exodus to the building of the Temple by Solomon in the fourth year of his reign, 480 years. According to the calculations of the Sacred Writings, it was 490 years from the building of the Temple to the time of Jesus Christ. Thus, this calculation of mine, collected from the holy writ, comes to about 4,173 years and 8 months, more or less. Because there is such a diversity of sects, I will not go beyond Jesus Christ.

I have calculated the present prophecies according to the order of the chain which contains its revolution, all by astronomical doctrine modified by my natural instinct. After a while, I found the time when Saturn turns to enter on April 7 till August 25, Jupiter on June 14 till October 7, Mars from April 17 to June 22, Venus from April 9 to May 22, Mercury from February 3 to February 24. After that, from June 1 to June 24, and from September 25 to October 16, Saturn in Capricorn, Jupiter in Aquarius, Mars in Scorpio, Venus in Pisces, Mercury for a month in Capricorn, Aquarius and Pisces, the Moon in Aquarius, the Dragon's head in Libra: its tail in opposition following a conjunction of Jupiter and Mercury with a quadrature of Mars and Mercury, and the Dragon's head coinciding with a conjunction of the Sun and Jupiter. And the year without an eclipse peaceful.

But not everywhere. It will mark the commencement of what will long endure. For beginning with this year the Christian Church will be persecuted more fiercely than it ever was in Africa, and this will last up to the year 1792, which they will believe to mark a renewal of time.

After this the Roman people will begin to re-establish themselves, chasing away some obscure shadows and recovering a bit of their ancient glory. But this will not be without great division and continual changes. Thereafter Venice will raise its wings very high in great force and power, not far short of the might of ancient Rome.

At that time the great sails of Byzantium, allied with the Ligurians and through the support and power of "Aquilon" [the Northern Realm], will impede them so greatly that the two Cretans will be unable to maintain their faith. The arks built by the Warriors of ancient times will accompany them to the waves of Neptune. In the Adriatic great discord will arise, and that which will have been united will be separated. To a house will be reduced that which was, and is, a great city, including "Pampotamia" and "Mesopotamia" of Europe at 45, and others of 41, 42 and 37 degrees.

It will be at this time and in these countries that the infernal power will set the power of its adversaries against the Church of Jesus Christ. This will constitute of the second Antichrist, who will persecute that Church and its true Vicar, by means of the power of three temporal kings who in their ignorance will be seduced by tongues which, in the hands of the madmen, will cut more than any sword.

The said reign of the Antichrist will last only to the death of him who was born at the beginning of the age and of the other one of Lyon, associated with the elected one of the House of Modena and of Ferrara, maintained by the Adriatic Ligurians and the proximity of great Sicily. Then the Great St. Bernard will be passed.

The Gallic Ogmios will be accompanied by so great a number that the Empire of his great law will extend very far. For some time thereafter the blood of the Innocent will be shed profusely by the recently elevated guilty ones. Then, because of great floods, the memory of things contained in these instruments will suffer incalculable loss, even letters. This will happen to the "Aquiloners" [the Northern People] by the will of God.

Once again Satan will be bound, universal peace will be established among men, and the Church of Jesus Christ will be delivered from all tribulations, although the Philistines would like to mix in the honey of malice and their pestilent seduction. This will be near the seventh millenary, when the sanctuary of Jesus Christ will no longer be trodden down by the infidels who come from "Aquilon" [the North]. The world will be approaching a great conflagration, although, according to my calculations in my prophecies, the course of time runs much further.

In the Epistle that some years ago I dedicated to my son, Cisar Nostradamus, I declared some points openly enough, without presage. But here, Sire, are included several great and marvelous events which those to come after will see.

During this astrological supputation, harmonized with the Holy Scriptures, the persecution of the Ecclesiastical folk will have its origin in the power of the Kings of "Aquilon" [the North], united with the Easterners. This persecution will last for eleven years, or somewhat less, for then the chief King of "Aquilon" will fall.

Thereupon the same thing will occur in the South, where for the space of three years the Church people will be persecuted even more fiercely through the Apostatic seduction of one who will hold all the absolute power in the Church militant. The hole people of God, the observer of his law, will be persecuted fiercely and such will be their affliction that the blood of the true Ecclesiastics will flow everywhere.

One of the horrible temporal Kings will be told by his adherents, as the ultimate in praise, that he has shed more of human blood of Innocent Ecclesiastics than anyone else could have spilled of wine. This King will commit incredible crimes against the Church. Human blood will flow in the public streets and temples, like water after an impetuous rain, coloring the nearby rivers red with blood. The ocean itself will be reddened by another naval battle, such that one king will say to another, Naval battles have caused the sea to blush.

Then, in this same year, and in those following, there will ensue the most horrible pestilence, made more stupendous by the famine which will have preceded it. Such great tribulations will never have occurred since the first foundation of the Christian Church. It will cover all Latin regions, and will leave traces in some countries of the Spanish.

Thereupon the third King of "Aquilon" [the North], hearing the lament of the people of his principal title, will raise a very mighty army and, defying the tradition of his predecessors, will put almost everything back in its proper place, and the great Vicar of the hood will be put back in his former state. But desolated, and then abandoned by all, he will turn to find the Holy of Holies destroyed by paganism, and the old and new Testaments thrown out and burned.

After that Antichrist will be the infernal prince again, for the last time. All the Kingdoms of Christianity will tremble, even those of the infidels, for the space of twenty-five years. Wars and battles will be more grievous and towns, cities, castles and all other edifices will be burned, desolated and destroyed, with great effusion of vestal blood, violations of married woman and widows, and sucking children dashed and broken against the walls of towns. By means of Satan, Prince Infernal, so may evils will be committed that nearly all the world will find itself undone and desolated. Before these events, some rare birds will cry in the air: Hui, Hui [Today, today] and some time later will vanish.

After this has endured for a long time, there will be almost renewed another reign of Saturn, and golden age. Hearing the affliction of his people, God the Creator will command that Satan be cast into the depths of the bottomless pit, and bound there. Then a universal peace will commence between God and man, and Satan will remain bound for around a thousand years, and then all unbound.

All these figures represent the just integration of Holy Scriptures with visible celestial bodies, namely, Saturn, Jupiter, Mars and others conjoined, as can be seen at more length in some of the quatrains. I would have calculated more profoundly and integrated them even further, Most Serene King, but for the fact that some given to censure would raise difficulties. Therefore I withdraw my pen and seek nocturnal repose.

Many events, most powerful of all Kings, of the most astounding sort are to transpire soon, but I neither could nor would fit them all into this epistle; but in order to comprehend certain horrible facts, a few must be set forth. So great is your grandeur and humanity before men, and your piety before the gods, that you alone seem worthy of the great title of the Most Christian King, and to whom the highest authority in all religion should be deferred.

But I shall only beseech you, Most Clement King, by this singular and prudent humanity of yours, to understand rather the desire of my heart, and the sovereign wish I have to obey Your Most Serene Majesty, ever since my eyes approached your solar splendor, than the grandeur of my labor can attain to or acquire. From Salon, this 27th of June, 1558.

Done by Michel Nostradamus at Salon-de-Crau in Provence.

Century VIII

1
Pau, Nay, Loron will be more of fire than blood,
to swim in praise, the great one to flee to the confluence (of rivers).
He will refuse entry to the magpies
Pampon and the Durance will keep them confined.

2
Condom and Auch and around Mirande,
I see fire from the sky which encompasses them.
Sun and Mars conjoined in Leo, then at Marmande,
lightning, great hail, a wall falls into the Garonne.

3
Within the strong castle of Vigilance and Resviers
the younger born of Nancy will be shut up.
In Turin the first ones will be burned,
when Lyons will be transported with grief.

4
The cock will be received into Monace,
the Cardinal of France will appear;
He will be deceived by the Roman legation;
weakness to the eagle, strength will be born to the cock.

5
There will appear a shining ornate temple,
the lamp and the candle at Borne and Breteuil.
For the canton of Lucerne turned aside,
when one will see the great cock in his shroud.

6
Lighting and brightness are seen at Lyons shining,
Malta is taken, suddenly it will be extinguished.
Sardon, Maurice will act deceitfully,
Geneva to London, feigning treason towards the cock.

7
Vercelli, Milan will give the news,
the wound will be given at Pavia.
To run in the Seine, water, blood and fire through Florence,
the unique one falling from high to low calling for help.

8
Near Focia enclosed in some tuns
Chivasso will plot for the eagle.
The elected one driven out, he and his people shut up,
rape with Turin, the bride led away.

9
While the eagle is united with the cock at Savonna,
the Eastern Sea and Hungary.
The army at Naples, Palermo, the marches of Ancona,
Rome and Venice a great outcry by the Barbarian.

10
A great stench will come from Lausanne,
but they will not know its origin,
they will put out all people from distant places,
fire seen in the sky, a foreign nation defeated.

11
A multitude of people will appear at Vicenza
without force, fire to burn the Basilica.
Near Lunage the great one of Valenza defeated:
at a time when Venice takes up the quarrel through custom.

12
He will appear near to Buffalora
the highly born and tall one entered into Milan.
The Abbe of Foix with those of Saint-Meur
will cause damage dressed up as serfs.

13
The crusader brother through impassioned love
will cause Bellerophon to die through Proteus;
the fleet for a thousand years, the maddened woman,
the potion drunk, both of them then die.

14
The great credit of gold and abundance of silver
will cause honor to be blinded by lust;
the offense of the adulterer will become known,
which will occur to his great dishonor.

15
Great exertions towards the North by a man-woman
to vex Europe and almost all the Universe.
The two eclipses will be put into such a rout
that they will reinforce life or death for the Hungarians.

16
At the place where HIERON has his ship built,
there will be such a great sudden flood,
that one will not have a place nor land to fall upon,
the waters mount to the Olympic Fesulan.

17
Those at ease will suddenly be cast down,
the world put into trouble by three brothers;
their enemies will seize the marine city,
hunger, fire, blood, plague, all evils doubled.

18
The cause of her death will be issued from Florence,
one time before drunk by young and old;
by the three lilies they will give her a great pause.
Save through her offspring as raw meat is dampened.

19
To support the great troubled Cappe;
the reds will march in order to clarify it;
a family will be almost overcome by death,
the red, red ones will knock down the red one.

20
The false message about the rigged election
to run through the city stopping the broken pact;
voices bought, chapel stained with blood,
the empire contracted to another one.

21
Three foists will enter the port of Agde
carrying the infection and pestilence, not the faith.
Passing the bridge they will carry off a million,
the bridge is broken by the resistance of a third.

22
Coursan, Narbonne through the salt to warn
Tuchan, the grace of Perpignan betrayed;
the red town will not wish to consent to it,
in a high flight, a copy flag and a life ended.

23
Letters are found in the queen's chests,
no signature and no name of the author.
The ruse will conceal the offers;
so that they do not know who the lover is.

24
The lieutenant at the door of the house,
will knock down the great man of Perpignan.
Thinking to save himself at Montpertuis,
the bastard of Lusignan will be deceived.

25
The heart of the lover, awakened by furtive love
will ravish the lady in the stream.
She will pretend bashfully to be half injured,
the father of each will deprive the body of its soul.

26
The bones of Cato found in Barcelona,
placed, discovered, the site found again and ruined.
The great one who holds, but does not hold,
wants Pamplona, drizzle at the abbey of Montserrat.

27
The auxiliary way, one arch upon the other,
Le Muy deserted except for the brave one and his genet.
The writing of the Phoenix Emperor,
seen by him which is (shown) to no other.

28
The copies of gold and silver inflated,
which after the theft were thrown into the lake,
at the discovery that all is exhausted and dissipated by the debt.
All scrips and bonds will be wiped out.

29
At the fourth pillar which they dedicate to Saturn
split by earthquake and by flood;
under Saturn's building an urn is found
gold carried off by Caepio and then restored.

30
In Toulouse, not far from Beluzer
making a deep pit a palace of spectacle,
the treasure found will come to vex everyone
in two places and near the Basacle.

31
The first great fruit of the prince of Perchiera,
then will come a cruel and wicked man.
In Venice he will lose his proud glory,
and is led into evil by then younger Selin.

32
French king, beware of your nephew
who will do so much that your only son
will be murdered while making his vows to Venus;
accompanied at night by three and six.

33
The great one who will be born of Verona and Vincenza
who carries a very unworthy surname;
he who at Venice will wish to take vengeance,
himself taken by a man of the watch and sign.

34
After the victory of the Lion over the Lion,
there will be great slaughter on the mountain of Jura;
floods and dark-colored people of the seventh (of a million),
Lyons, Ulm at the mausoleum death and the tomb.

35
At the entrance to Garonne and Baise
and the forest not far from Damazan,
discoveries of the frozen sea, then hail and north winds.
Frost in the Dardonnais through the mistake of the month.

36
It will be committed against the anointed brought
from Lons le Saulnier, Saint Aubin and Bell'oeuvre.
To pave with marble taken from distant towers,
not to resist Bletteram and his masterpiece.

37
The fortress near the Thames
will fall when the king is locked up inside.
He will be seen in his shirt near the bridge,
one facing death then barred inside the fortress.

38
The King of Blois will reign in Avignon,
once again the people covered in blood.
In the Rhône he will make swim
near the walls up to five, the last one near Nolle.

39
He who will have been for the Byzantine prince
will be taken away by the prince of Toulouse.
The faith of Foix through the leader of Tolentino
will fail him, not refusing the bride.

40
The blood of the Just for Taur and La Duarade
in order to avenge itself against the Saturnines.
They will immerse the band in the new lake,
then they will march against Alba.

41
a fox will be elected without speaking one word,
appearing saintly in public living on barley bread,
afterwards he will suddenly become a tyrant
putting his foot on the throats of the greatest men.

42
Through avarice, through force and violence
the chief of Orléans will come to vex his supporters.
Near St. Memire, assault and resistance.
Dead in his tent they will say he is asleep inside.

43
Through the fall of two bastard creatures
the nephew of the blood will occupy the throne.
Within Lectoure there will be blows of lances,
the nephew through fear will fold up his standard.

44
The natural offspring off Ogmios
will turn off the road from seven to nine.
To the king long friend of the half man,
Navarre must destroy the fort at Pau.

45
With his hand in a sling and his leg bandaged,
the younger brother of Calais will reach far.
At the word of the watch, the death will be delayed,
then he will bleed at Easter in the Temple.

46
Paul the celibate will die three leagues from Rome,
the two nearest flee the oppressed monster.
When Mars will take up his horrible throne,
the Cock and the Eagle, France and the three brothers.

47
Lake Trasimene will bear witness
of the conspirators locked up inside Perugia.
A fool will imitate the wise one,
killing the Teutons, destroying and cutting to pieces.

48.
Saturn in Cancer, Jupiter with Mars
in February Chaldondon'salva tierra.
Sierra Morena besieged on three sides
near Verbiesque, war and mortal conflict.

49
Saturn in Taurus, Jupiter in Aquarius. Mars in Sagittarius,
the sixth of February brings death.
Those of Tardaigne so great a breach at Bruges,
that the barbarian chief will die at Ponteroso.

50
The plague around Capellades,
another famine is near to Sagunto;
the knightly bastard of the good old man
will cause the great one of Tunis to lose his head.

51
The Byzantine makes an oblation
after having taken back Cordoba.
A long rest on his road, the vines cut down,
at sea the passing prey captured by the Pillar.

52 ---- Unfinished/Censored ----
The king of Blois to reign in Avignon,
from Amboise and Seme the length of the Indre:
claws at Poitiers holy wings ruined
before Boni. . . .

53
Within Boulogne he will want to wash away his misdeeds,
he cannot at the temple of the Sun.
He will fly away, doing very great things:
In the hierarchy he had never an equal.

54
Under the color of the marriage treaty,
a magnanimous act by the Chyren Selin:
St. Quintin and Arras recovered on the journey;
By the Spanish a second butcher's bench is made.

55
He will find himself shut in between two rivers,
casks and barrels joined to cross beyond:
eight bridges broken, their chief run through so many times,
perfect children's throats slit by the knife.

56
The weak band will occupy the land,
those of high places will make dreadful cries.
The large herd of the outer corner troubled,
near Edinburgh it falls discovered by the writings.

57
From simple soldier he will attain to Empire,
from the short robe he will grow into the long.
Brave in arms, much worse towards the Church,
he vexes the priests as water fills a sponge.

58
A kingdom divided by two quarreling brothers
to take the arms and the name of Britain.
The Anglican title will be advised to watch out,
surprised by night (the other is), led to the French air.

59
Twice put up and twice cast down,
the East will also weaken the West.
Its adversary after several battles
chased by sea will fail at time of need.

60
First in Gaul, first in Romania,
over land and sea against the English and Paris.
Marvelous deeds by that great troop,
violent, the wild beast will lose Lorraine.

61
Never by the revelation of daylight
will he attain the mark of the scepter bearer.
Until all his sieges are at rest,
bringing to the Cock the gift of the armed legion.

62
When one sees the holy temple plundered,
the greatest of the Rhône profaning their sacred things;
because of them a very great pestilence will appear,
the king, unjust, will not condemn them.

63
When the adulterer wounded without a blow
will have murdered his wife and son out of spite;
his wife knocked down, he will strangle the child;
eight captives taken, choked beyond help.

64
The infants transported into the islands,
two out of seven will be in despair.
Those of the soil will be supported by it,
the name 'shovel' taken, the hope of the leagues fails.

65
The old man disappointed in his main hope,
will attain to the leadership of his Empire.
Twenty months he will hold rule with great force,
a tyrant, cruel, giving way to one worse.

66
When the inscription D.M. is found
in the ancient cave, revealed by a lamp.
Law, the King and Prince Ulpian tried,
the Queen and Duke in the pavilion under cover.

67
Paris, Carcassone, France to ruin in great disharmony,
neither one nor the other will be elected.
France will have the love and good will of the people,
Ferara, Colonna great protection.

68
The old Cardinal is deceived by the young one,
he will find himself disarmed, out of his position:
Do not show, Arles, that the double is perceived,
both Liqueduct and the Prince embalmed.

69
Beside the young one the old angel falls,
and will come to rise above him at the end;
ten years equal to most the old one falls again,
of three two and one, the eighth seraphim.

70
He will enter, wicked, unpleasant, infamous,
tyrannizing over Mesopotamia.
All friends made by the adulterous lady,
the land dreadful and black of aspect.

71
The number of astrologers will grow so great,
that they will be driven out, banned and their books censored.
In the year 1607 by sacred assemblies
so that none will be safe from the holy ones.

72
Oh what a huge defeat on the Perugian battlefield
and the conflict very close to Ravenna.
A holy passage when they will celebrate the feast,
the conqueror banished to eat horse meat.

73
The king is struck by a barbarian soldier,
unjustly, not far from death.
The greedy will be the cause of the deed,
conspirator and realm in great remorse.

74
A king entered very far into the new land
while the subjects will come to bid him welcome;
his treachery will have such a result
that to the citizens it is a reception instead of a festival.

75
The father and son will be murdered together,
the leader within his pavilion.
The mother at Tours will have her belly swollen with a son,
a verdure chest with little pieces of paper.

76
More of a butcher than a king in England,
born of obscure rank will gain empire through force.
Coward without faith, without law he will bleed the land;
His time approaches so close that I sigh.

77
The antichrist very soon annihilates the three,
twenty-seven years his war will last.
The unbelievers are dead, captive, exiled;
with blood, human bodies, water and red hail covering the earth.

78
A soldier of fortune with twisted tongue
will come to the sanctuary of the gods.
He will open the door to heretics
and raise up the Church militant.

79
He who loses his father by the sword, born in a Nunnery,
upon this Gorgon's blood will conceive anew;
in a strange land he will do everything to be silent,
he who will burn both himself and his child.

80
The blood of innocents, widow and virgin,
so many evils committed by means of the Great Red One,
holy images placed over burning candles,
terrified by fear, none will be seen to move.

81
The new empire in desolation
will be changed from the Northern Pole.
From Sicily will come such trouble that
it will bother the enterprise tributary to Philip.

82
Thin tall and dry, playing the good valet
in the end will have nothing but his dismissal;
sharp poison and letters in his collar,
he will be seized escaping into danger.

83
The largest sail set out of the port of Zara,
near Byzantium will carry out its enterprise.
Loss of enemy and friend will not be,
a third will turn on both with great pillage and capture.

84
Paterno will hear the cry from Sicily,
all the preparations in the Gulf of Trieste;
it will be heard as far as Sicily
flee oh, flee, so may sails, the dreaded pestilence !

85
Between Bayonne and St. Jean de Luz
will be placed the promontory of Mars.
To the Hanix of the North, Nanar will remove the light,
then suffocate in bed without assistance.

86
Through Emani, Tolosa and Villefranche,
an infinite band through the mountains of Adrian.
Passes the river, Cambat over the plank for a bridge,
Bayonne will be entered all crying Bigoree.

87
A death conspired will come to its full effect,
the charge given and the voyage of death.
Elected, created, received (then) defeated by its followers,
in remorse the blood of innocence in front of him.

88
A noble king will come to Sardinia,
who will only rule for three years in the kingdom.
He will join with himself several colors;
he himself, after taunts, care spoils slumber.

89
In order not to fall into the hands of his uncle
who slaughtered his children in order to reign.
Pleasing with the people, putting his foot on Peloncle,
dead and dragged between armored horses.

90
When those of the cross are found their senses troubled,
in place of sacred things he will see a horned bull,
through the virgin the pig's place will then be filled,
order will no longer be maintained by the king.

91
Entered among the field of the Rhône
where those of the cross are almost united,
the two lands meeting in Pisces
and a great number punished by the flood.

92
Far distant from his kingdom, sent on a dangerous journey,
he will lead a great army and keep it for himself.
The king will hold his people captive and hostage,
he will plunder the whole country on his return.

93
For seven months, no longer, will he hold the office of prelate,
through his death a great schism will arise;
for seven months another acts as prelate near Venice,
peace and union are reborn.

94
In front of the lake where the dearest one was destroyed
for seven months and his army routed;
Spaniards will be devastating by means of Alba,
through delay in giving battle, loss.

95
The seducer will be placed in a ditch
and will be tied up for some time.
The scholar joins the chief with his cross.
The sharp right will draw the contented ones.

96
The sterile synagogue without any fruit,
will be received by the infidels,
the daughter of the persecuted (man) of Babylon,
miserable and sad, they will clip her wings.

97
At the end of the Var the great powers change;
near the bank three beautiful children are born.
Ruin to the people when they are of age;
in the country the kingdom is seen to grow and change more.

98
Of the church men the blood will be poured forth
as abundant as water in (amount);
for a long time it will not be restrained,
woe, woe, for the clergy ruin and grief.

99
Through the power of three temporal kings,
the sacred seat will be put in another place,
where the substance of the body and the spirit
will be restored and received as the true seat.

100
By the great number of tears shed,
from top to bottom and from the bottom to the very top,
a life is lost through a game with too much faith,
to die of thirst through a great deficiency.

Century IX

1
In the house of the translator of Bourg,
The letters will be found on the table,
One-eyed, red-haired, white, hoary-headed will hold the course,
Which will change for the new Constable.

2
From the top of the Aventine hill a voice heard,
Be gone, be gone all of you on both sides:
The anger will be appeased by the blood of the red ones,
From Rimini and Prato, the Colonna expelled.

3
The "great cow" at Racenna in great trouble,
Led by fifteen shut up at Fornase:
At Rome there will be born two double-headed monsters,
Blood, fire, flood, the greatest ones in space.

4
The following year discoveries through flood,
Two chiefs elected, the first one will not hold:
The refuge for the one of them fleeing a shadow,
The house of which will maintain the first one plundered.

5
The third toe will seem first
To a new monarch from low high,
He who will possess himself as a Tyrant of Pisa and Lucca,
To correct the fault of his predecessor.

6
An infinity of Englishmen in Guienne
Will settle under the name of Anglaquitaine:
In Languedoc, Ispalme, Bordelais,
Which they will name after Barboxitaine.

7
He who will open the tomb found,
And will come to close it promptly,
Evil will come to him, and one will be unable to prove,
If it would be better to be a Breton or Norman King.

8
The younger son made King will put his father to death,
After the conflict very dishonest death:
Inscription found, suspicion will bring remorse,
When the wolf driven out lies down ion the bedstead.

9
When the lamp burning with inextinguishable fire
Will be found in the temple of the Vestals:
Child found in fire, water passing through the sieve:
To perish in water Nîmes, Toulouse the markets to fall.

10
The child of a monk and nun exposed to death,
To die through a she-bear, and carried off by a boar,
The army will be camped by Foix and Pamiers,
Against Toulouse Carcassonne the harbinger to form.

11
Wrongly will they come to put the just one to death,
In public and in the middle extinguished:
So great a pestilence will come to arise in this place,
That the judges will be forced to flee.

12
So much silver of Diana and Mercury,
The images will be found in the lake:
The sculptor looking for new clay,
He and his followers will be steeped in gold.

13
The exiles around Sologne,
Led by night to march into Auxois,
Two of Modena for Bologna cruel,
Placed discovered by the fire of Buzanais.

14
Dyers' caldrons put on the flat surface,
Wine, honey and oil, and built over furnaces:
They will be immersed, innocent, pronounced malefactors,
Seven of Bordeaux smoke still in the cannon.

15
Near Perpignan the red ones detained,
Those of the middle completely ruined led far off:
Three cut in pieces, and five badly supported,
For the Lord and Prelate of Burgundy.

16
Out of Castelfranco will come the assembly,
The ambassador not agreeable will cause a schism:
Those of Riviera will be in the squabble,
And they will refuse entry to the great gulf.

17
The third one first does worse than Nero,
How much human blood to flow, valiant, be gone:
He will cause the furnace to be rebuilt,
Golden Age dead, new King great scandal.

18
The lily of the Dauphin will reach into Nancy,
As far as Flanders the Elector of the Empire:
New confinement for the great Montmorency,
Outside proven places delivered to celebrated punishment.

19
In the middle of the forest of Mayenne,
Lightning will fall, the Sun in Leo:
The great bastard issued from the great one Maine,
On this day a point will enter the blood of Fougères.

20
By night will come through the forest of Reines,
Two couples roundabout route Queen the white stone,
The monk king in gray in Varennes:
Elected Capet causes tempest, fire, blood, slice.

21
At the tall temple of Saint-Solenne at Blois,
Night Loire bridge, Prelate, King killing outright:
Crushing victory in the marshes of the pond,
Whence prelacy of whites miscarrying.

22
The King and his court in the place of cunning tongue,
Within the temple facing the palace:
In the garden the Duke of Mantua and Alba,
Alba and Mantua dagger tongue and palace.

23
The younger son playing outdoors under the arbor,
The top of the roof in the middle on his head,
The father King in the temple of Saint-Solonne,
Sacrificing he will consecrate festival smoke.

24
Upon the palace at the balcony of the windows,
The two little royal ones will be carried off:
To pass Orléans, Paris, abbey of Saint-Denis,
Nun, wicked ones to swallow green pits.

25
Crossing the bridges to come near the Roisiers,
Sooner than he thought, he arrived late.
The new Spaniards will come to Béziers,
So that this chase will break the enterprise.

26
Departed by the bitter letters the surname of Nice,
The great Cappe will present something, not his own;
Near Voltai at the wall of the green columns,
After Piombino the wind in good earnest.

27
The forester, the wind will be close around the bridge,
Received highly, he will strike the Dauphin.
The old craftsman will pass through the woods in a company,
Going far beyond the right borders of the Duke.

28
The Allied fleet from the port of Marseilles,
In Venice harbor to march against Hungary.
To leave from the gulf and the bay of Illyria,
Devastation in Sicily, for the Ligurians, cannon shot.

29
When the man will give way to none,
Will wish to abandon a place taken, yet not taken;
Ship afire through the swamps, bitumen at Charlieu,
St. Quintin and Calais will be recaptured.

30
At the port of Pola and of San Nicolo,
A Normand will punish in the Gulf of Quarnero:
Capet to cry alas in the streets of Byzantium,
Help from Cadiz and the great Philip.

31
The tin island of St. George half sunk;
Drowsy with peace, war will arise,
At Easter in the temple abysses opened.

32
A deep column of fine porphyry is found,
Inscriptions of the Capitol under the base;
Bones, twisted hair, the Roman strength tried,
The fleet is stirred at the harbor of Mitylene.

33
Hercules King of Rome and of "Annemark,"
With the surname of the chief of triple Gaul,
Italy and the one of St. Mark to tremble,
First monarch renowned above all.

34
The single part afflicted will be mitered,
Return conflict to pass over the tile:
For five hundred one to betray will be titled
Narbonne and Salces we have oil for knives.

35
And fair Ferdinand will be detached,
To abandon the flower, to follow the Macedonian:
In the great pinch his course will fail,
And he will march against the Myrmidons.

36
A great King taken by the hands of a young man,
Not far from Easter confusion knife thrust:
Everlasting captive times what lightning on the top,
When three brothers will wound each other and murder.

37
Bridge and mills overturned in December,
The Garonne will rise to a very high place:
Walls, edifices, Toulouse overturned,
So that none will know his place like a matron.

38
The entry at Blaye for La Rochelle and the English,
The great Macedonian will pass beyond:
Not far from Agen will wait the Gaul,
Narbonne help beguiled through conversation.

39
In Albisola to Veront and Carcara,
Led by night to seize Savona:
The quick Gascon La Turbie and L'Escarène:
Behind the wall old and new palace to seize.

40
Near Saint-Quintin in the forest deceived,
In the Abbey the Flemish will be cut up:
The two younger sons half-stunned by blows,
The rest crushed and the guard all cut to pieces.

41
The great "Chyren" will seize Avignon,
From Rome letters in honey full of bitterness:
Letter and embassy to leave from Chanignon,
Carpentras taken by a black duke with a red feather.

42
From Barcelona, from Genoa and Venice,
From Sicily pestilence Monaco joined:
They will take their aim against the Barbarian fleet,
Barbarian driven 'way back as far as Tunis.

43
On the point of landing the Crusader army
Will be ambushed by the Ishmaelites,
Struck from all sides by the ship Impetuosity,
Rapidly attacked by ten elite galleys.

44
Leave, leave Geneva every last one of you,
Saturn will be converted from gold to iron,
Raypoz will exterminate all who oppose him,
Before the coming the sky will show signs.

45
None will remain to ask,
Great Mendosus will obtain his dominion:
Far from the court he will cause to be countermanded
Piedmont, Picardy, Paris, Tuscany the worst.

46
Be gone, flee from Toulouse ye red ones,
For the sacrifice to make expiation:
The chief cause of the evil under the shade of pumpkins:
Dead to strangle carnal prognostication.

47
The undersigned to an infamous deliverance,
And having contrary advice from the multitude:
Monarch changes put in danger over thought,
Shut up in a cage they will see each other face to face.

48
The great city of the maritime Ocean,
Surrounded by a crystalline swamp:
In the winter solstice and the spring,
It will be tried by frightful wind.

49
Ghent and Brussels will march against Antwerp,
The Senate of London will put to death their King:
Salt and wine will overthrow him,
To have them the realm turned upside down.

50
Mendosus will soon come to his high realm,
Putting behind a little the Lorrainers:
The pale red one, the male in the interregnum,
The fearful youth and Barbaric terror.

51
Against the red ones sects will conspire,
Fire, water, steel, rope through peace will weaken:
On the point of dying those who will plot,
Except one who above all the world will ruin.

52
Peace is nigh on one side, and war,
Never was the pursuit of it so great:
To bemoan men, women innocent blood on the land,
And this will be throughout all France.

53
The young Nero in the three chimneys
Will cause live pages to be thrown to burn:
Happy those who will be far away from such practices,
Three of his blood will have him ambushed to death.

54
There will arrive at Porto Corsini,
Near Ravenna, he who will plunder the lady:
In the deep sea legate from Lisbon,
Hidden under a rock they will carry off seventy souls.

55
The horrible war which is being prepared in the West,
The following year will come the pestilence
So very horrible that young, old, nor beast,
Blood, fire Mercury, Mars, Jupiter in France.

56
The army near Houdan will pass Goussainville,
And at Maiotes it will leave its mark:
In an instant more than a thousand will be converted,
Looking for the two to put them back in chain and firewood.

57
In the place of Drux a King will rest,
And will look for a law changing Anathema:
While the sky will thunder so very loudly,
New entry the King will kill himself.

58
On the left side at the spot of Vitry,
The three red ones of France will be awaited:
All felled red, black one not murdered,
By the Bretons restored to safety.

59
At La Ferté-Vidame he will seize,
Nicholas held red who had produced his life:
The great Louise who will act secretly one will be born,
Giving Burgundy to the Bretons through envy.

60
Conflict Barbarian in the black Headdress,
Blood shed, Dalmatia to tremble:
Great Ishmael will set up his promontory,
Frogs to tremble Lusitania aid.

61
The plunder made upon the marine coast,
In Cittanova and relatives brought forward:
Several of Malta through the deed of Messina
Will be closely confined poorly rewarded.

62
To the great one of Ceramon-agora,
The crusaders will all be attached by rank,
The long-lasting Opium and Mandrake,
The Raugon will be released on the third of October.

63
Complaints and tears, cries and great howls,
Near Narbonne at Bayonne and in Foix:
Oh, what horrible calamities and changes,
Before Mars has made several revolutions.

64
The Macedonian to pass the Pyrenees mountains,
In March Narbonne will not offer resistance:
By land and sea he will carry on very great intrigue,
Capetian having no land safe for residence.

65
He will come to go into the corner of Luna,
Where he will be captured and put in a strange land:
The unripe fruits will be the subject of great scandal,
Great blame, to one great praise.

66
There will be peace, union and change,
Estates, offices, low high and high very low:
To prepare a trip, the first offspring torment,
War to cease, civil process, debates.

67
From the height of the mountains around the Isère,
One hundred assembled at the haven in the rock Valence:
From Châteauneuf, Pierrelatte, in Donzère,
Against Crest, Romans, faith assembled.

68
The noble of Mount Aymar will be made obscure,
The evil will come at the junction of the Saône and Rhône:
Soldiers hidden in the woods on Lucy's day,
Never was there so horrible a throne.

69
One the mountain of Saint-Bel and L'Arbresle
The proud one of Grenoble will be hidden:
Beyond Lyons and Vienne on them a very great hail,
Lobster on the land not a third thereof will remain.

70
Sharp weapons hidden in the torches.
In Lyons, the day of the Sacrament,
Those of Vienne will all be cut to pieces,
By the Latin Cantons Mâcon does not lie.

71
At the holy places animals seen with hair,
With him who will not dare the day:
At Carcassonne propitious for disgrace,
He will be set for a more ample stay.

72
Again will the holy temples be polluted,
And plundered by the Senate of Toulouse:
Saturn two three cycles completed,
In April, May, people of new leaven.

73
The Blue Turban King entered into Foix,
And he will reign less than an evolution of Saturn:
The White Turban King Byzantium heart banished,
Sun, Mars and Mercury near Aquarius.

74
In the city of Fertsod homicide,
Deed, and deed many oxen plowing no sacrifice:
Return again to the honors of Artemis,
And to Vulcan bodies dead ones to bury.

75
From Ambracia and the country of Thrace
People by sea, evil and help from the Gauls:
In Provence the perpetual trace,
With vestiges of their custom and laws.

76
With the rapacious and blood-thirsty king,
Issued from the pallet of the inhuman Nero:
Between two rivers military hand left,
He will be murdered by Young Baldy.

77
The realm taken the King will conspire,
The lady taken to death ones sworn by lot:
They will refuse life to the Queen and son,
And the mistress at the fort of the wife.

78
The Greek lady of ugly beauty,
Made happy by countless suitors:
Transferred out to the Spanish realm,
Taken captive to die a miserable death.

79
The chief of the fleet through deceit and trickery
Will make the timid ones come out of their galleys:
Come out, murdered, the chief renouncer of chrism,
Then through ambush they will pay him his wages.

80
The Duke will want to exterminate his followers,
He will send the strongest ones to strange places:
Through tyranny to ruin Pisa and Lucca,
Then the Barbarians will gather the grapes without vine.

81
The crafty King will understand his snares,
Enemies to assail from three sides:
A strange number tears from hoods,
The grandeur of the translator will come to fail.

82
By the flood and fierce pestilence,
The great city for long besieged:
The sentry and guard dead by hand,
Sudden capture but none wronged.

83
Sun twentieth of Taurus the earth will tremble very mightily,
It will ruin the great theater filled:
To darken and trouble air, sky and land,
Then the infidel will call upon God and saints.

84
The King exposed will complete the slaughter,
After having discovered his origin:
Torrent to open the tomb of marble and lead,
Of a great Roman with Medusine device.

85
To pass Guienne, Languedoc and the Rhône,
From Agen holding Marmande and La Réole:
To open through faith the wall, Marseilles will hold its throne,
Conflict near Saint-Paul-de-Mausole.

86
From Bourg-la-Reine they will come straight to Chartres,
And near Pont d'Antony they will pause:
Seven crafty as Martens for peace,
Paris closed by an army they will enter.

87
In the forest cleared of the Tuft,
By the hermitage will be placed the temple:
The Duke of Étampes through the ruse he invented
Will teach a lesson to the prelate of Montlhéry.

88
Calais, Arras, help to Thérouanne,
Peace and semblance the spy will simulate:
The soldiery of Savoy to descend by Roanne,
People who would end the rout deterred.

89
For seven years fortune will favor Philip,
He will beat down again the exertions of the Arabs:
Then at his noon perplexing contrary affair,
Young Ogmios will destroy his stronghold.

90
A captain of Great Germany
Will come to deliver through false help
To the King of Kings the support of Pannonia,
So that his revolt will cause a great flow of blood.

91
The horrible plague Perinthus and Nicopolis,
The Peninsula and Macedonia will it fall upon:
It will devastate Thessaly and Amphipolis,
An unknown evil, and from Anthony refusal.

92
The King will want to enter the new city,
Through its enemies they will come to subdue it:
Captive free falsely to speak and act,
King to be outside, he will keep far from the enemy.

93
The enemies very far from the fort,
The bastion brought by wagons:
Above the walls of Bourges crumbled,
When Hercules the Macedonian will strike.

94
Weak galleys will be joined together,
False enemies the strongest on the rampart:
Weak ones assailed Bratislava trembles,
Lübeck and Meissen will take the barbarian side.

95
The newly made one will lead the army,
Almost cut off up to near the bank:
Help from the Milanais elite straining,
The Duke deprived of his eyes in Milan in an iron cage.

96
The army denied entry to the city,
The Duke will enter through persuasion:
The army led secretly to the weak gates,
They will put it to fire and sword, effusion of blood.

97
The forces of the sea divided into three parts,
The second one will run out of supplies,
In despair looking for the Elysian Fields,
The first ones to enter the breach will obtain the victory.

98
Those afflicted through the fault of a single one stained,
The transgressor in the opposite party:
He will send word to those of Lyons that compelled
They be to deliver the great chief of Molite.

99
The "Aquilon" Wind will cause the siege to be raised,
Over the walls to throw ashes, lime and dust:
Through rain afterwards, which will do them much worse,
Last help against their frontier.

100
Naval battle night will be overcome,
Fire in the ships to the West ruin:
New trick, the great ship colored,
Anger to the vanquished, and victory in a drizzle.

Century X

1
To the enemy, the enemy faith promised
Will not be kept, the captives retained:
One near death captured, and the remainder in their shirts,
The remainder damned for being supported.

2
The ship's veil will hide the sail galley,
The great fleet will come the lesser one to go out:
Ten ships near will turn to drive it back,
The great one conquered the united ones to join to itself.

3
After that five will not put out the flock,
A fugitive for Penelon he will turn loose:
To murmur falsely then help to come,
The chief will then abandon the siege.

4
At midnight the leader of the army
Will save himself, suddenly vanished:
Seven years later his reputation unblemished,
To his return they will never say yes.

5
Albi and Castres will form a new league,
Nine Arians Lisbon and the Portuguese:
Carcassonne and Toulouse will end their intrigue,
When the chief new monster from the Lauraguais.

6
The Gardon will flood Nîmes so high
That they will believe Deucalion reborn:
Into the colossus the greater part will flee,
Vesta tomb fire to appear extinguished.

7
The great conflict that they are preparing for Nancy,
The Macedonian will say I subjugate all:
The British Isle in anxiety over wine and salt,
"Hem. mi." Philip two Metz will not hold for long.

8
With forefinger and thumb he will moisten the forehead,
The Count of Senigallia to his own son:
The Venus through several of thin forehead,
Three in seven days wounded dead.

9
In the Castle of Figueras on a misty day
A sovereign prince will be born of an infamous woman:
Surname of breeches on the ground will make him posthumous,
Never was there a King so very bad in his province.

10
Stained with murder and enormous adulteries,
Great enemy of the entire human race:
One who will be worse than his grandfathers, uncles or fathers,
In steel, fire, waters, bloody and inhuman.

11
At the dangerous passage below Junquera,
The posthumous one will have his band cross:
To pass the Pyrenees mountains without his baggage,
From Perpignan the duke will hasten to Tende.

12
Elected Pope, as elected he will be mocked,
Suddenly unexpectedly moved prompt and timid:
Through too much goodness and kindness provoked to die,
Fear extinguished guides the night of his death.

13
Beneath the food of ruminating animals,
led by them to the belly of the fodder city:
Soldiers hidden, their arms making a noise,
Tried not far from the city of Antibes.

14
Urnel Vaucile without a purpose on his own,
Bold, timid, through fear overcome and captured:
Accompanied by several pale whores,
Convinced in the Carthusian convent at Barcelona.

15
Father duke old in years and choked by thirst,
On his last day his don denying him the jug:
Into the well plunged alive he will come up dead,
Senate to the thread death long and light.

16
Happy in the realm of France, happy in life,
Ignorant of blood, death, fury and plunder:
For a flattering name he will be envied,
A concealed King, too much faith in the kitchen.

17
The convict Queen seeing her daughter pale,
Because of a sorrow locked up in her breast:
Lamentable cries will come then from Angoulême,
And the marriage of the first cousin impeded.

18
The house of Lorraine will make way for Vendôme,
The high put low, and the low put high:
The son of Mammon will be elected in Rome,
And the two great ones will be put at a loss.

29
The day that she will be hailed as Queen,
The day after the benediction the prayer:
The reckoning is right and valid,
Once humble never was one so proud.

20
All the friend who will have belonged to the party,
For the rude in letters put to death and plundered:
Property up for sale at fixed price the great one annihilated.
Never were the Roman people so wronged.

21
Through the spite of the King supporting the lesser one,
He will be murdered presenting the jewels to him:
The father wishing to impress nobility on the son
Does as the Magi did of yore in Persia.

22
For not wishing to consent to the divorce,
Which then afterwards will be recognized as unworthy:
The King of the Isles will be driven out by force,
In his place put one who will have no mark of a king.

23
The remonstrances made to the ungrateful people,
Thereupon the army will seize Antibes:
The complaints will place Monaco in the arch,
And at Fréjus the one will take the shore from the other

24
The captive prince conquered in Italy
Will pass Genoa by sea as far as Marseilles:
Through great exertion by the foreigners overcome,
Safe from gunshot, barrel of bee's liquor.

25
Through the Ebro to open the passage of Bisanne,
Very far away will the Tagus make a demonstration:
In Pelligouxe will the outrage be committed,
By the great lady seated in the orchestra.

26
The successor will avenge his brother-in-law,
To occupy the realm under the shadow of vengeance:
Obstacle slain his blood for the death blame,
For a long time will Brittany hold with France.

27
Through the fifth one and a great Hercules
They will come to open the temple by hand of war:
One Clement, Julius and Ascanius set back,
The sword, key, eagle, never was there such a great animosity.

28
Second and third which make prime music
By the King to be sublimated in honor:
Through the fat and the thin almost emaciated,
By the false report of Venus to be debased.

29
In a cave of Saint-Paul-de-Mausole a goat
Hidden and seized pulled out by the beard:
Led captive like a mastiff beast
By the Bigorre people brought to near Tarbes.

30
Nephew and blood of the new saint come,
Through the surname he will sustain arches and roof:
They will be driven out put to death chased nude,
Into red and black will they convert their green.

31
The Holy Empire will come into Germany,
The Ishmaelites will find open places:
The asses will want also Carmania,
The supporters all covered by earth.

32
The great empire, everyone would be of it,
One will come to obtain it over the others:
But his realm and state will be of short duration,
Two years will he be able to maintain himself on the sea.

33
The cruel faction in the long robe
Will come to hide under the sharp daggers:
The Duke to seize Florence and the diphthong place,
Its discovery by immature ones and sycophants.

34
The Gaul who will hold the empire through war,
He will be betrayed by his minor brother-in-law:
He will be drawn by a fierce, prancing horse,
The brother will be hated for the deed for a long time

35
The younger son of the king flagrant in burning lust
To enjoy his first cousin:
Female attire in the Temple of Artemis,
Going to be murdered by the unknown one of Maine.

36
Upon the King of the stump speaking of wars,
The United Isle will hold him in contempt:
For several good years one gnawing and pillaging,
Through tyranny in the isle esteem changing.

37
The great assembly near the Lake of Bourget,
They will meet near Montmélian:
Going beyond the thoughtful ones will draw up a plan,
Chambéry, Saint-Jean-de-Maurienne, Saint-Julien combat.

38
Sprightly love lays the siege not far,
The garrisons will be at the barbarian saint:
The Orsini and Adria will provide a guarantee for the Gauls,
For fear delivered by the army to the Grisons.

39
First son, widow, unfortunate marriage,
Without any children two Isles in discord:
Before eighteen, incompetent age,
For the other one the betrothal will take place while younger.

40
The young heir to the British realm,
Whom his dying father will have recommended:
The latter dead Lonole will dispute with him,
And from the son the realm demanded.

41
On the boundary of Caussade and Caylus,
Not at all far from the bottom of the valley:
Music from Villefranche to the sound of lutes,
Encompassed by cymbals and great stringing.

42
The humane realm of Anglican offspring,
It will cause its realm to hold to peace and union:
War half-captive in its enclosure,
For long will it cause them to maintain peace.

43
Too much good times, too much of royal goodness,
Ones made and unmade, quick, sudden, neglectful:
Lightly will he believe falsely of his loyal wife,
He put to death through his benevolence.

44
When a King will be against his people,
A native of Blois will subjugate the Ligurians,
Memel, Cordoba and the Dalmatians,
Of the seven then the shadow to the King, New Year's money and ghosts.

45
The shadow of the realm of Navarre untrue,
It will make his life one of fate unlawful:
The vow made in Cambrai wavering,
King Orléans will give a lawful wall.

46
In life, fate and death a sordid, unworthy man of gold,
He will not be a new Elector of Saxony:
From Brunswick he will send for a sign of love,
The false seducer delivering it to the people.

47
At the Garland lady of the town of Burgos,
They will impose for the treason committed:
The great prelate of Leon through Formande,
Undone by false pilgrims and ravishers.

48
Banners of the deepest part of Spain,
Coming out from the tip and ends of Europe:
Troubles passing near the bridge of Laigne,
Its great army will be routed by a band.

49
Garden of the world near the new city,
In the path of the hollow mountains:
It will be seized and plunged into the Tub,
Forced to drink waters poisoned by sulfur.

50
The Meuse by day in the land of Luxembourg,
It will find Saturn and three in the urn:
Mountain and plain, town, city and borough,
Flood in Lorraine, betrayed by the great urn.

51
Some of the lowest places of the land of Lorraine
Will be united with the Low Germans:
Through those of the see Picards, Normans, those of Main,
And they will be joined to the cantons.

52
At the place where the Lys and the Scheldt unite,
The nuptials will be arranged for a long time:
At the place in Antwerp where they carry the chaff,
Young old age wife undefiled.

53
The three concubines will fight each other for a long time,
The greatest one the least will remain to watch:
The great Selin will no longer be her patron,
She will call him fire shield white route.

54
She born in this world of a furtive concubine,
At two raised high by the sad news:
She will be taken captive by her enemies,
And brought to Malines and Brussels.

55
The unfortunate nuptials will be celebrated
In great joy but the end unhappy:
Husband and mother will slight the daughter-in-law,
The Apollo dead and the daughter-in-law more pitiful.

56
The royal prelate his bowing too low,
A great flow of blood will come out of his mouth:
The Anglican realm a realm pulled out of danger,
For long dead as a stump alive in Tunis.

57
The uplifted one will not know his scepter,
He will disgrace the young children of the greatest ones:
Never was there a more filthy and cruel being,
For their wives the king will banish them to death.

58
In the time of mourning the feline monarch
Will make war upon the young Macedonian:
Gaul to shake, the bark to be in jeopardy,
Marseilles to be tried in the West a talk.

59
Within Lyons twenty-five of one mind,
Five citizens, Germans, Bressans, Latins:
Under a noble one they will lead a long train,
And discovered by barks of mastiffs.

60
I weep for Nice, Monaco, Pisa, Genoa,
Savona, Siena, Capua, Modena, Malta:
For the above blood and sword for a New Year's gift,
Fire, the earth will tremble, water an unhappy reluctance.

61
Betta, Vienna, Emorte, Sopron,
They will want to deliver Pannonia to the Barbarians:
Enormous violence through pike and fire,
The conspirators discovered by a matron.

62
Near "Sorbia" to assail Hungary,
The herald of "Brudes" (dark ones?) will come to warn them:
Byzantine chief, Salona of Slavonia,
He will come to convert them to the law of the Arabs.

63
Cydonia, Ragusa, the city of St. Jerome,
With healing help to grow green again:
The King's son dead because of the death of two heroes,
Araby and Hungary will take the same course.

64
Weep Milan, weep Lucca and Florence,
As your great Duke climbs into the chariot:
The see to change it advances to near Venice,
When at Rome the Colonna will change.

65
O vast Rome, thy ruin approaches,
Not of thy walls, of thy blood and substance:
The one harsh in letters will make a very horrible notch,
Pointed steel driven into all up to the hilt.

66
The chief of London through the realm of America,
The Isle of Scotland will be tried by frost:
King and Reb will face an Antichrist so false,
That he will place them in the conflict all together.

67
A very mighty trembling in the month of May,
Saturn in Capricorn, Jupiter and Mercury in Taurus:
Venus also, Cancer, Mars in Virgo,
Hail will fall larger than an egg.

68
The army of the sea will stand before the city,
Then it will leave without making a long passage:
A great flock of citizens will be seized on land,
Fleet to return to seize it great robbery.

69
The shining deed of the old one exalted anew,
Through the South and Aquilon they will be very great:
Raised by his own sister great crowds,
Fleeing, murdered in the thicket of Ambellon.

70
Through an object the eye will swell very much,
Burning so much that the snow will fall:
The fields watered will come to shrink,
As the primate succumbs at Reggio.

71
The earth and air will freeze a very great sea,
When they will come to venerate Thursday:
That which will be never was it so fair,
From the four parts they will come to honor it.

72
The year 1999, seventh month,
From the sky will come a great King of Terror:
To bring back to life the great King of the Mongols,
Before and after Mars to reign by good luck.

73
The present time together with the past
Will be judged by the great Joker:
The world too late will be tired of him,
And through the clergy oath-taker disloyal.

74
The year of the great seventh number accomplished,
It will appear at the time of the games of slaughter:
Not far from the great millennial age,
When the buried will go out from their tombs.

75
Long awaited he will never return
In Europe, he will appear in Asia:
One of the league issued from the great Hermes,
And he will grow over all the Kings of the East.

76
The great Senate will ordain the triumph
For one who afterwards will be vanquished, driven out:
At the sound of the trumpet of his adherents there will be
Put up for sale their possessions, enemies expelled.

77
Thirty adherents of the order of Quirites
Banished, their possessions given their adversaries:
All their benefits will be taken as misdeeds,
Fleet dispersed, delivered to the Corsairs.

78
Sudden joy to sudden sadness,
It will occur at Rome for the graces embraced:
Grief, cries, tears, weeping, blood, excellent mirth,
Contrary bands surprised and trussed up.

79
The old roads will all be improved,
One will proceed on them to the modern Memphis:
The great Mercury of Hercules fleur-de-lis,
Causing to tremble lands, sea and country.

80
In the realm the great one of the great realm reigning,
Through force of arms the great gates of brass
He will cause to open, the King and Duke joining,
Fort demolished, ship to the bottom, day serene.

81
A treasure placed in a temple by Hesperian citizens,
Therein withdrawn to a secret place:
The hungry bonds to open the temple,
Retaken, ravished, a horrible prey in the midst.

82
Cries, weeping, tears will come with knives,
Seeming to flee, they will deliver a final attack,
Parks around to set up high platforms,
The living pushed back and murdered instantly.

83
The signal to give battle will not be given,
They will be obliged to go out of the park:
The banner around Ghent will be recognized,
Of him who will cause all his followers to be put to death.

84
The illegitimate girl so high, high, not low,
The late return will make the grieved ones contended:
The Reconciled One will not be without debates,
In employing and losing all his time.

85
The old tribune on the point of trembling,
He will be pressed not to deliver the captive:
The will, non-will, speaking the timid evil,
To deliver to his friends lawfully.

86
Like a griffin will come the King of Europe,
Accompanied by those of Aquilon:
He will lead a great troop of red ones and white ones,
And they will go against the King of Babylon.

87
A Great King will come to take port near Nice,
Thus the death of the great empire will be completed:
In Antibes will he place his heifer,
The plunder by sea all will vanish.

88
Foot and Horse at the second watch,
They will make an entry devastating all by sea:
Within the port of Marseilles he will enter,
Tears, cries, and blood, never times so bitter.

89
The walls will be converted from brick to marble,
Seven and fifty pacific years:
Joy to mortals, the aqueduct renewed,
Health, abundance of fruits, joy and mellifluous times.

90
A hundred times will the inhuman tyrant die,
In his place put one learned and mild,
The entire Senate will be under his hand,
He will be vexed by a rash scoundrel.

91
In the year 1609, Roman clergy,
At the beginning of the year you will hold an election:
Of one gray and black issued from Campania,
Never was there one so wicked as he.

92
Before his father the child will be killed,
The father afterwards between ropes of rushes:
The people of Geneva will have exerted themselves,
The chief lying in the middle like a log.

93
The new bark will take trips,
There and near by they will transfer the Empire:
Beaucaire, Arles will retain the hostages,
Near by, two columns of Porphyry found.

94
Scorn from Nîmes, from Arles and Vienne,
Not to obey the Hesperian edict:
To the tormented to condemn the great one,
Six escaped in seraphic garb.

95
To the Spains will come a very powerful King,
By land and sea subjugating the South:
This evil will cause, lowering again the crescent,
Clipping the wings of those of Friday.

96
The Religion of the name of the seas will win out
Against the sect of the son of Adaluncatif:
The stubborn, lamented sect will be afraid
Of the two wounded by A and A.

97
Triremes full of captives of every age,
Good time for bad, the sweet for the bitter:
Prey to the Barbarians hasty they will be too soon,
Anxious to see the feather wail in the wind.

98
For the merry maid the bright splendor
Will shine no longer, for long will she be without salt:
With merchants, bullies, wolves odious,
All confusion universal monster.

99
The end of wolf, lion, ox and ass,
Timid deer they will be with mastiffs:
No longer will the sweet manna fall upon them,
More vigilance and watch for the mastiffs.

100
The great empire will be for England,
The all-powerful one for more than three hundred years:
Great forces to pass by sea and land,
The Lusitanians will not be satisfied thereby.

Almanacs: 1555-1563

Almanac of 1555

The soul touched from a distance by the divine spirit presages,
Trouble, famine, plague, war to hasten:
Water, droughts, land and sea stained with blood,
Peace, truce, prelates to be born, princes to die.

The Tyrrhenian Sea, the Ocean for the defense,
The great Neptune and his trident soldiers:
Provence secure because of the hand of the great Tende,
More Mars Narbonne the heroic de Villars.

The big bronze one which regulates the time of day,
Upon the death of the Tyrant it will be dismissed:
Tears, laments and cries, waters, ice bread does not give,
V.S.C. peace, the army will pass away.

Near Geneva terror will be great,
Through the counsel, that cannot fail:
The new King has his league prepare,
The young one dies, famine, fear will cause failure.

O cruel Mars, how you should be feared,
More is the scythe with the silver conjoined:
Fleet, forces, water, wind of shadow to fear,
Sea and land in a truce. The friends has joined L.V.

For not having a guard you will be more offended,
The weak fort, Pinquiet uneasy and pacific:
They cry "famine," the people are oppressed,
The sea reddens, the Long one proud and iniquitous.

The five, six, fifteen, late and soon they remain,
The heir's bloodline ended: the cities revolted:
The herald of peace twenty and three return,
The open-hearted five locked up, news invented.

At a distance, near the Aquarius, Saturn turns back,
That year great Mars will give a fire opposition,
Towards the North to the south the great proud female,
Florida in contemplation will hold the port.

Eight, fifteen, and five what disloyalty
The evil spy will come to be permitted:
Fire in the sky, lightning, fear, Papal terror,
The west trembles, pressing too hard the Salty wine.

Six, twelve, thirteen, twenty will speak to the Lady,
The older one by a woman will be corrupted:
Dijon, Guienne hail, lightning makes the first cut into it,
The insatiable one of blood and wine satisfied.

The sky to weep for him, made to do that!
The sea is being prepared, Hannibal to plan his ruse:
Denis [drops anchor], fleet delays, does not remain silent,
Has not known the secret, and by which you are amused!

Venus Neptune will pursue the enterprise,
Pensive one imprisoned, adversaries troubled:
Fleet in the Adriatic, cities towards the Thames,
The fourth clamor, by night, the reposing ones wounded.

The great one of the sky the cape will give,
Relief, Adriatic makes an offer to the port:
He who will be able will save himself from dangers,
By night the Great One wounded pursues.

The port protests too fraudulently and false,
The maw opened, condition of peace:
Rhone in crystal, water, snow, ice stained,
The death, death, wind, through rain the burden broken.

Almanac of 1558

The young King makes a funeral wedding soon,
Holy one stirred up, feasts, of the said, Mars dormant:
Night tears they cry, they conduct the lady outside,
The arrest and peace broken on all sides.

Vain rumor within the Hierarchy,
Genoa to rebel: courses, offenses, tumults:
For the greater King will be the monarchy,
Election, conflict, covert burials.

Through discord in the absence to fail,
One suddenly will put him back on top:
Towards the North will be noises so loud,
Lesions, points to travel, above.

On the Tyrrhenian Sea, of different sail,

On the Ocean there will be diverse assaults:
Plague, poison, blood in the house of canvas,
Prefects, Legates stirred up to march high seas.

There where the faith was it will be broken,
The enemies will feed upon the enemies:
Fire rains [from the] Sky, it will burn, interrupted,
Enterprise by night. Chief will make quarrels.

War, thunder, forces fields, depopulated,
Terror and noise, assault on the frontier:
Great Great One fallen, pardon for the exiles,
Germans, Spaniards, by the sea the Barbarian banner.

The noise will be vain, the faltering ones bundled up,
The Shaven Ones captured: the all-powerful One elected:
The two Reds and four true crusaders to fail,
Rain troublesome to the powerful Monarch.

Rain, wind, forces, Barbarossa Hister, the Tyrrhenian Sea,
Vessels to pass Orkneys and beyond Gibraltar, grain and soldiers provided:
Retreats too well executed by Florence, Siena crossed,
The two will be dead, friendships joined.

Venus the beautiful will enter Florence.
The secret exiles will leave the place behind:
Many widows, they deplore the death of the Great One,
To remove from the realm, the Great Great one does not threaten.

Games, feasts, nuptials, dead Prelate of renown.
Noise, peace of truce while the enemy threatens:
Sea, land and sky noise, deed of the great Brennus,
Cries gold, silver, the enemy they ruin.

Almanac of 1560

Day's journey, diet, interim, no council,
The year peace is being prepared, plague, schismatic famine:
Put outside inside, sky to change, domicile,
End of holiday, hierarchical revolt.

Diet to break up, the ancient sacred one to recover,
Under the two, fire through pardon to result:
Consecration without arms: the tall Red will want to have,
Peace of neglect, the Elected One, the Widower, to live.

To be made to appear elected with novelty,
Place of day-labor to go beyond the boundaries:

The feigned goodness to change to cruelty,
From the suspected place quickly will they all go out.

With the place chosen, the Shaved Ones will not be contented,
Led from Lake Geneva, unproven,
They will cause the old times to be renewed:
They will expose the frighten off the plot so well hatched.

Savoy peace will be broken,
The last hand will cause a strong levy:
The great conspirator will not be corrupted,
And the new alliance approved.

A long comet to wrong the Governor,
Hunger, burning fever, fire and reek of blood:
To all estates Jovial Ones in great honor,
Sedition by the Shaven ones, ignited.

Plague, famine, fire and ardor incessant,
Lightning, great hail, temple struck from the sky:
The Edict, arrest, and grievous law broken,
The chief inventor his people and himself snatched up.

Deprived will be the Shaven Ones of their arms,
It will augment their quarrel much:
Father Liber deceived lightning Albanians,
Sects will be gnawed to the marrow.

The modest request will be received,
They will be driven out and then restored on top:
The Great Great woman will be found content,
Blind ones, deaf ones will be put uppermost.

He will not be placed, the New Ones expelled,
Black king and the Great One will hold hard:
To have recourse to arms. Exiles expelled further,
To sing of victory, not free, consolation.

The mourning left behind, supreme alliances,
Great Shaven One dead, refusal given at the entrance:
Upon return kindness to be in oblivion,
The death of the just one perpetrated at a banquet.

Almanac of 1562

Season of winter, good spring, sound, bad summer,
Pernicious autumn, dry, wheat rare:
Of wine enough, bad eyes, deeds, molested,

War, mutiny, seditious waste.

The hidden desire for the good will succeed,
Religion, peace, love and concord:
The nuptial song will not be completely in accord,
The high ones, who are low, and high, put to the rope.

For the Shaven Ones the Chief will not reach the end,
Edicts changed, the secret ones set at large:
Great One found dead, less of faith, low standing,
Dissimulated, shuddering, wounded in the boar's lair.

Moved by Lion, near Lion he will undermine,
Taken, captive, pacified by a woman:
He will not hold as well as they will waver,
Placed unpassed, to oust the soul from rage.

From Lion he will come to arouse to move,
Vain discovery against infinite people:
Known by none the evil for the duty,
In the kitchen found dead and finished.

Nothing in accord, worse and more severe trouble,
As it was, land and sea to quieten:
All arrested, it will not be worth a double,
The iniquitous one will speak, Counsel of annihilation.

Portentous deed, horrible and incredible,
Typhoon will make the wicked ones move:
Those who then afterwards supported by the cable,
And the greater part exiled on the fields.

Right put on the throne come into France from the sky,
The whole world pacified by Virtue:
Much blood to scatter, sooner change to come,
By the birds, and by fire, and not by vers.

The colored ones, the Sacred malcontents,
Then suddenly through the happy Androgynes:
Of the great part to see, the time not come,
Several amongst them will make their soups weak.

They will be returned to their full power,
Conjoined at one point of the accord, not in accord:
All defied, more promised to the Shaven Ones,
Several amongst them outflanked in a band.

For the legate of terrestrial and dawn,

The great Cape will accommodate himself to all:
Tacit LORRAINE, to be listening,
He whose advice they will not want to agree with.

The enemy wind will impede the troop,
For the greatest one advance put in difficulty:
Wine with poison will be put in the cup,
To pass the great gun without horse-power.

Through crystal the enterprise is broken,
Games and feats, in LYONS to repose more:
No longer will he take his repast with the Great Ones,
Sudden catarrh, blessed water, to bathe him.

Almanacs: 1564-1567

Almanac of 1564

The sextile year rains, wheat to abound, hatreds,
Joy to men, Princes, King divorced:
Herd to perish, human mutations,
People oppressed and poison under the surface.

Times very diverse, discord discovered,
Council of war, change taken in, changed:
The Great Woman must not be, conspirators through water lost,
Great hostility, for the great one all steady.

The bit of the enemy's tongue approaches,
The Debonair one to peace will want to reduce:
The obstinate ones will want to lose the kinswoman,
Surprised, Captives, and suspects fury to injure.

Fathers and mothers dead of infinite sorrows,
Women in mourning, the pestilent she-monster:
The Great One to be no more, all the world to end,
Under peace, repose and every single one in opposition.

Princes and Christendom stirred up in debates,
Foreign nobles, Christ's See molested:
Become very evil, much good, mortal sight.
Death in the East, plague, famine, evil treaty.

Land to tremble, killed, wasteful, monster,
Captives without number, to do, undone, done:
To go over the sea misfortune will occur,
Proud against the proud evil done in disguise.

The unjust one lowered, they will molest him fiercely,
Hail, to flood, treasure, and engraved marble:
Chief of Persuasion people will kill to death,
And attached will be the blade to the tree.

Of what not evil? inexcusable result,
The fire not double, the Legate outside confused:
Against the worse wounded the fight will not be made,
The end of June the thread cut by firing.

Fine bonds enfeebled by accords,
Mars and Prelates united will not stop:
The great ones confused by gifts of mutilated bodies,
Dignified ones, undignified ones will seize the well endowed.

From good to the evil times will change,
The peace in the South, the expectation of the Greatest Ones:
The Great Ones grieving Louis too much more will stumble,
Well-known Shaven Ones have neither power not understanding.

This is the month for evils so many as to be doubled,
Deaths, plague to drain all, famine, to quarrel:
Those of the reverse of exile will come to note,
Great Ones, secrets, deaths, not to censure.

Through death, death to bite, counsel, robbery, pestiferous,
They will not dare to attack the Marines:
Deucalion a final trouble to make,
Few young people: half-dead to give a start.

Dead through spite he will cause the others to shine,
And in an exalted place some great evils to occur:
Sad concepts will come to harm each one,
Temporal dignified, the Mass to succeed.

Almanac of 1566

For the greatest ones death, loss of honor and violence,
Professors of the faith, their estate and their sect:
For the two great Churches diverse noise, decadence,
Evil neighbors quarreling serfs of the Church without a head.

Waste, great loss, and not without violence,
All those of the faith, more for religion,
The Greatest Ones will lose their lives, their honor and fortunes
Both the two Churches, the sin in their faction.

For the two very Great Ones pernicious loss to arise,
The Greatest Ones will cause loss, goods, of honor, and of life,
As much great noises will run, the urn very odious,
Great maladies to be, meeting-house, mass in envy.

The servants of the Churches will betray their Lords,
Of other Lords also by the undivided of the fields:
Neighbors of meeting-house and mass will quarrel amongst them,
Rumors, noises to augment, to death are several lying.

Of all blessings abundance, the earth will produce for us,

No din of war in France, sedition put outside:
Man-slayers, robbers one will find on the highway,
Little faith, burning fever, people in commotion.

Between people discord, brutal enmity,
War, death of great Princes, several parts:
Universal plague, stronger in the West,
Times good and full, but very dry and exhausted.

The grains not to be plentiful, in all other fruits, plenty,
The Summer, spring humid, winter long, snow, ice:
The East in arms, France reinforces herself,
Death of beasts much honey, the place to be besieged.

Through pestilence and fire fruits of trees will perish,
Signs of oil to abound. Father Denis not scarce:
Some great ones to die, but few foreigners will sally forth in attack,
Offense, Barbarian marines, and dangers at the frontiers.

Rains very excessive, and of blessings abundance,
The cattle price to be just, women outside of danger:
Hail, rain, thunder: people depressed in France,
Through death they will work, death to reprove people.

Arms, plagues to cease, death of the seditious ones,
Great Father Liber will not much abound:
Evil ones will be seized by more malicious ones,
France more than ever victorious will triumph.

Up to this month the great drought will endure,
For Italy and Provence all fruits to half:
The Great One less of enemies prisoner of their band,
For the scroungers, Pirates, and the enemy to die.

The enemy so much to be feared to retire into Thrace,
Leaving cries, howls, and pillage desolated:
To leave noise on sea and land, religion murdered,
Jovial Ones put on the road, every sect to become angry.

Nostradamus, The Man Who Saw Through Time

Table of Contents

Foreword	154
PART ONE	157
A Prophet Is Born	157
The Education of a Genius	166
Personages and Politics	179
Garlands of Fame	191
The Plague Returns	204
A Prophet's Eyry	217
Purpose	230
On to Paris	242
The Court of the Valois	255
Towards Familiar Country	269
PART TWO	285
The Cycle of Valois-Navarre	285
Claude De Savoie	301
In the Twentieth Century	305

Foreword

THE RICH, ACTIVELY FULFILLED LIFE of the French prophet, Michel de Nostradame, is the story of genius not only in its rarest but its most modern form. His ability foreshadowed a hope, now gaining a first hearing in this our day, that science may, in some not too remote tomorrow, discover principles of mental forces which will permit every man to realize within himself a reflection of the powers of Nostradamus.

Many prophets have crossed the brightly lighted stage of history and paused to utter some astounding bit of prescience. But they are seldom remembered for more than a single episode, some ray of strange illumination that for a moment spotlighted the fate of a throne or a battle. Actually there exist but two written documents of prophecy which have pictured a grand-scale continuity of history, and unfolded a tapestry of world futures. One of these is, of course, the mighty word of Scripture. The other is that cryptic romaunt of Europe's fate, the Centuries, written by Nostradamus, Provençal troubadour of destiny.

No one knows as yet what forces shape a prophet, nor how it is that to "remembrance of things past," he adds "remembrance of the things that are to come." Perhaps the Red Queen knew more about it than most.

When Alice asked her why she cried out before, instead of after, she had pricked her finger, her majesty sagely observed that it is a poor rule which doesn't work both ways. Nostradamus would have enjoyed that bit of wit, so like his own, and pertinent to prophecy.

What is "before" and "after"? What is up or down when considered outside the limited, inaccurate criteria of the five senses? The fourth-dimensional vision of Nostradamus, like the Red Queen's cry, transcended the meanings which we give these words. The man who saw through time watched, as through a telescope, the distant stars of future events rise and set, beyond the eye of the present, over a period of four hundred years.

"Heaven from all creatures hide the book of Fate,
All but the page prescrib'd, their present state."

Pope was within his sceptical rights when he penned that couplet, because the vaticinating exceptions among heaven's creatures have always been so few that for people as a whole his words were true. Another Englishman, the modernist Dean Inge, had however a better perspective. As a churchman he accepted prophecy. As an intelligent modern he said that the phenomenon of prevision was quite possibly part of an evolutionary process which would one day become a developed faculty general to man. Considered in this light, Nostradamus, astounding as are his prophecies, is himself, the man, of even greater fascination than his work, because he attained in its completeness the faculty to which it is at least a possibility that all may eventually aspire.

It was only a few years ago that several thousand New Yorkers unhinged one of the bronze doors of the American Museum of Natural History in an effort to hear a talk that few could understand when heard. The lecture was on the mathematics of the strange, and to them, new, fourth dimension which they had visualized, confounding it with the psychic world, as opening exciting secret vistas and miraculous powers. Such an incident is indicative of a dawning intensity of popular interest in the world of unseen forces, physical and metaphysical. Vitamins and visions, telescopes and telepathy, all go together as part of the thrilling new universe expanding within the consciousness of the twentieth century.

Science works always first with physical properties and objectives. Our breakfast newspapers tell of atoms cracked and a new element found, and radio serves us up freshly discovered planets with the evening meal. In all this inrush of knowledge nothing has been of such captivating interest as the new discoveries about time which are giving rise to a new point of view as significant for layman as for scientist. Einstein has substituted new time-concepts and time-mechanics for old in the study of the universe. For half a century new inventions in communications have been telescoping time, bringing true Mother Shipton's words:

"Around the world thoughts shall fly
In the twinkling of an eye."

Now, doctors are timing and graphing the electrical thought impulses of the human brain. And universities are experimenting in psychology departments with a kind of time-sense to which may be linked the phenomena of the psyche.

We are so accustomed to thinking of time as the straight road separated by present experience into its two parts, yesterday and tomorrow. But the scientist is beginning to perceive what the mystic has always known, that time is an unknown country stretching boundlessly in all directions. Nostradamus, in whom awareness of this set him apart from his fellows, was the Marco Polo of time's uncharted land, in which he traveled the future as we travel a continent. From these transcendental voyagings, like Polo, he returned with incredible stories of strange sights. The prophet's rare okapis were a vision of events to come.

Both of these men, whose discoveries were beyond the comprehension of their age, have come late into their own. Archaeology and exploration have verified the narrative of Polo's travels. History, not only since the sixteenth century, but daily, is verifying the time-travels of that other and greater explorer, Nostradamus. He is of yesterday, today, and still a long tomorrow. By virtue of what he was, and of our own hopes, he deserves the distinguished position today which he had in the Renaissance, and serious study in the light of what science is teaching us of the power and forces of the mind.

It is an old and tenaciously held popular idea that interest in and concentration on extra-dimensional qualities of the mind tend inevitably to some form of imbalance which may run the gamut from credulity to insanity. Too often in the past superstition has added to this its dark aura of witchcraft and abnormal rites. Nostradamus was, throughout his life, a striking refutation of such beliefs. His intellectual achievements and emotional balance, his social adaptation and vigorous health show him as the pattern of the well-rounded man. Considering his unique gift, he may be said to have had, besides his genius for prophecy, a veritable genius for normality. Had he never written the

Centuries, his title to fame would still be clear. The brilliant skill and self-sacrificing devotion which made him the greatest physician in France of his day would alone keep his memory green. Physician, linguist, scholar, diplomat, writer, teacher, religieux and prophet, his life touched all phases of Renaissance thought and activity from the hovels of France, where he fought the plague, to the court of the Valois, where he was honored beyond any seer in history.

The Book of Joel, which seems to have made a strong impression upon Nostradamus, contains within its grim forecast the lovely, well-known passage:

"and your sons and your daughters shall prophesy, your old men shall dream dreams, your young men shall see visions." Nostradamus was the greatest of all who since Biblical ages have given to these words the substance of fulfillment. And perhaps his life was prelusive to the "clear seeing" which may be the glory of the coming age.

The major facts of the life of Nostradamus are known and fully attested. Much confusion, however, exists concerning a number of biographical details. Such questions as which one of the prophet's grandfathers it was who educated him, what was the year of his second marriage, and which of his sons was the eldest born are matters of conflicting opinion. Some commentators have assumed that his son, César, was born in 1555 simply because Nostradamus dedicated his prophecies to him in that year. It is impossible to find out the exact truth about these and other discrepancies because of the loss or destruction of old documents which would provide the proof. In such instances, the author has chosen from old accounts the story which has seemed in her opinion to be best supported by inference and available evidence.

The fictional treatment employed to present certain incidents is used in an attempt to give more vitality to the faded colors of time, but each has underlying facts or substantial inference. There is one exception to this, the attributed purpose in the writing of the Centuries. Other commentators besides the author believe, however, that this theory is true. It agrees with what is known of the prophet's character and type of mind, and is supported by indications from within the prophecies.

L. M.

Part One: a Prophet Is Born

IT WAS NEARLY CHRISTMAS, of the year 1503. San Rémy, ancient Provençal town, namesake of the Saint who baptized Clovis on Christmas Day, was astir with preparations for the coming activities. Everywhere in town and countryside people stopped in the sunshine to greet and talk of plans for Calèndo, the Romance word which Provençals still use for Christmas. Great ladies in silken finery, blithe young knights attended by their squires riding down from châteaux in the hills, peasant women in full skirts and bright-colored bodices, jolly monks, dark-eyed girls and sober town fathers, all were preparing for the year's greatest celebration.

In the town square men talked about yule-logs. Some who owned groves were going to cut down an olive or an almond tree that was too old to be worth keeping. But more would go to the forest to cut their logs, and drag them home behind uncoupled oxen as men had done since the days of the Druids. San Rémy housewives crowded the market-stalls, buying almonds and honey to make Christmas nougat. They chatted of New Year's gifts in the making, and gossiped about holiday masques at the Governor's palace at Aix. Troubadours tuned their harps and memorized romaunts. Through church windows drifted the voices of choir-boys practicing Christmas music, chanting their welcome to the Son of Man, singing of peace on earth which then as now seldom prevailed.

The ancient town, gay with the season, little imagined, least of all the expectant parents, that this child, born in their midst that day, would bring to his birthplace a fame enduring for centuries. Who then could foresee that a future Europe would search his words for an answer to the grim riddle of its fate? Over the Midi town the stars had taken stance to endow this infant with stranger wisdom than prophet had held since the faraway years of those who foretold the coming of the Christ.

On this the 14th day of December by the Julian calendar, "near to the twelve hours of noon," so the chronicle runs, the son of Jacques and Renée de Nostradame was born. The voice of the bronze bell speaking the hour from the town belfry was carried on breezes fragrant of meadows. In the hearts of the parents the bell-notes chimed the olden gratitude: "Unto us a child is born, unto us a son is given."

How long the family of baby Michel de Nostra-dame had been settled in Provence is not known. But long enough for them to be assimilated into the annals of the country, to have made their contribution of science and service, and to reap the rewards of prestige.

The statement that Michel was of Jewish birth has been insistently asserted by most commentators. There seems to be no warrant for this outside of unverified rumors after his lifetime. His race is not important except in relation to his prophecies. But it is of essential interest to know whether he was the last inheritor of the grand Hebrew tradition of prophecy. Or, has the Gentile race, lacking such tradition, really produced one prophet of distinction in whom they can take pride, and whose forecasts are concerned with their destiny? One who, if not comparable to the sublime poetry and exaltation of the prophets of Israel, can be compared with them in the accuracy and authority of his vision.

Nostradamus, in his letter of dedication to King Henry II, speaks of the Biblical computation of years. He says: "I hold that the Scripture takes them to be solar." To a scholar this should be proof enough that Nostradamus did not have Jewish background; if he had, he could not have escaped knowing that the Jewish calculations were always according to the lunar calendar.

Jean-Ayme de Chavigny, doctor of theology, magistrate of Beaune, presumably dependable, was the close friend and pupil of Nostradamus. His biographical sketch of the prophet is the only first-hand account, still available, that has been handed down. He makes no mention of Jewish descent. He writes:

"His grandfathers, maternal and paternal, had a reputation as great savants in mathematics and medicine, one being physician to René, King of Jerusalem and Sicily, and Count of Provence, the other, of Jean, Duke of Calabria, son of King René. This closes the mouth of the envious who, because they are misinformed, have reflected upon his birth."

The sixteenth century was a period of bitter anti-Semitism and general intolerance. Jews, it is true, were not persecuted in Provence, and many of them rose to wealth and secure standing there. Had Nostradamus been a Jew, his reputation might not have suffered from it in the place of his birth. But it would have suffered as his fame spread to larger fields, particularly Paris. During his lifetime his enemies called him charlatan and sorcerer. Had he been vulnerable to the accusation, he would certainly have been branded as a Jew by attackers overlooking no point that could be raised against him.

Doctor Theophilus Garencières, one of the early commentators, who states that all his life he had been in contact with people who either knew all about Nostradamus or thought they did, likewise makes no mention of Jewish descent. His concern was how God could reveal himself to a man of merely average social position. He says that this wonder agitated the minds of many people who admired Nostradamus as a prophet. This was not because the caste-conscious Renaissance had forgotten the birth of the Son of the Carpenter, but because they had reconciled His origin with their own social standards. Ferne's Blazen of Gentry, a sixteenth-century work on heraldry, is at pains to inform its readers that the twelve apostles were all gentlemen of blood, reduced to servile work only through misfortune.

It may have been wishful thinking that led some writers who favored Nostradamus to assert that he was of noble birth. But it must be inferred from the events of his life that he was at least gently born of people whose standing was excellent.

When Nostradamus visited the court of Henry II, as the king's guest, he was accorded almost the honor of a ranking personage, and lodged in the palace of a prince-cardinal of the blood. Henry would have known through his Provençal governor, a lifelong friend of the prophet, the history and standing of the de Nostradame family. It is to be feared that he would not have received the prophet with such public acclaim if the family position had not met with his approval.

It has been argued that the learning of Nostradamus' grandfathers was in advance of Gentile culture, and was therefore Jewish. It is true that the Jews in France had a fine record in the scholarly professions, and particularly in medicine. But there is another theory which, while it cannot be proved, would account for much.

A king of Provence went with Saint Louis to the Crusades, and shared his imprisonment in the Orient. The Saracens, marvelously advanced in medicine and mathematics, showed the Crusaders many wonders. Some of their knowledge found its way back to Europe in this manner. Ancestors of Nostradamus may have been of those who benefited by Arab learning in its own great centers; there may even have been a strain of Arab ancestry. Either or both would account for the prestige which the prophet's grandfathers enjoyed at the court of King René of Provence. It might also account for some ancient, inherited medical recepte which crusading ancestors brought back from the Orient, and which Nostradamus may have used to conquer the plague; something older than the known, standardized Arab remedies of his own times.

King René had a curious Turko-Arab complex. He preferred people of such blood and customs above all others. Consequently his court for half a century attracted every one who had a drop of the blood or any of its associations and culture. Every Levantine and Arab who had something to sell and the price of the trip came there with his wares. If a subject wanted to put anything across, he had to make the king an Eastern present. René dressed himself and the court in Oriental costume, and his Turkish and Arabian masques were famous.

One amusing incident of Rene's feeling in such matters concerns a grandfather of Nostradamus. René's queen had a laundress, Charlotte the Turk. In some way Charlotte injured her leg. Anywhere else, she would have been too far below the salt to rate attention from the royal physician. But because of Charlotte's Turkish blood, the king thought nothing too good for her. His own doctor, none other than Doctor de Nostradame, was ordered to attend her with all care, which presumably he did. It is logical to suppose that the learned grandfathers of Nostradamus contributed in some way to the king's passion for Turks and Arabs, and held his patronage to some extent through superiority in the kind of lore and training he most respected and valued.

The grandfathers had long been friends and associates at the court of Provence. When Jacques, the son of Pierre de Nostradame, married Renée, the daughter of Jean de Rémy, it had cemented more closely their existing ties of affection and mutual interest.

Jacques de Nostradame, the father of Michel, was a notary public. This occupation, dwarfed in importance today, had then a scholarly and important rating when so many of the population, even among the upper circles, could not so much as write their name. They depended on the notary, who was called on for services that ranged from writing a love-letter to arranging a transfer of property. His field was a wide one, and included nearly everything in business and property matters that did not require the actual practice of law.

Jacques' income would have provided a comfortable home in keeping with good standards of Provençal living. Through his doors passed the active flow of town affairs, personal, business and civic. Many would seek him out because, through his father and father-in-law, his contacts at the capital were somewhat influential. His house was probably near the center of the town, easy of access to his clients.

Young Michel's earliest recollections of his parents' home would center about its cheerful, fragrant kitchen which, typical of all Provençal homes in the sixteenth century, was the room where both the domestic and the social life was carried on. The center and symbol of the room's activity was the great fireplace, majestic, cavernous, holding a banked fire that had never gone out since first his father and mother came there to live. Shining pots and pans of brass hung low from the mantle shelf, convenient for his mother to bake her delicious bread, cook thick nourishing stews or roast a fowl. At either angle of the fireplace was an oak settle where the grandfathers liked to laze and talk when they came to visit. Across the room stood the buffet. Atop this was the long, flaring wooden trough in which his mother mixed and kneaded the bread. In one corner was a cupboard with shelves and drawers holding all manner of household goods. This, like the buffet, was of strong, deep-toned oak. Michel knew every line of the severe carving in geometrical design which caught the firelight on its mellow wood.

On the walls hung light cabinet shelves holding salt and spice boxes, small pieces of gay earthenware, and special treasures. Perhaps there was an enamel cup or a vase of cunning workmanship, a present from grandfather who had got it at a bargain from a Levantine merchant come to sell his wares at court.

Michel could remember the deep, embrasured windows of his home, and the narrow stoop at the door, points of vantage from which he got his earliest pictures of the life of the town as it streamed by in colorful show on fête days and market days. The charm of the procession was unending, rich merchants on ambling mules with silver bells on the harness, carts piled up with the reds and yellows of oranges and pomegranates for the market, peasants bringing in butter and cheeses from the country, shepherds with their droves, knights and ladies with feathers in their hats, riding on prancing horses.

Unforgettable, too, the first time his mother took him to Mass at the ancient church. Through the great doors, older than the Gothic spire, into the lofty vastness of dim light, he had clung affrighted to his mother's hand, staring into the rich mystery of dusk and gold and stained-glass saints. Kneeling, he had looked up to the carved Virgin and the tapers like flowers at her feet. The notes of the organ and the high clear chant of the choir-boys enfolded him, drew him with ecstasy as if to his mother's breast. It was source and beginning of his passionate, unswerving observance and devotion -to the Roman ritual from which he never deviated throughout his life. Such observance was to him never a duty, it was the sacred embroidery of his delight in God.

Another ritual that captivated young Michel was that which pertained to his father's business. He could not remember the time when he had not been fascinated by the things on his father's writing-table. The pewter ink-well with the long quills standing at attention in the small side holes, the little bowl of clean sand, and the rolls of white sheepskin neatly disposed, called to his hands to touch and try them.

He early listened to all that he could of his father's talk of the goings-on in San Rémy. With the big ears for which little pitchers are proverbial he placed together scraps which the grown-ups thought he was too young to take in. He was as curious as a cat about the news from Aix, the capital, and the rumors from Paris, that faraway city, no more than a name to him. He wondered what levies were and why his father said the people grumbled about them; he wondered if the King would go to war with Italy, and what war was like. He found out about the new elections to the town council, and who was traveling to Aix to see the Governor.

His mind observed and pigeonholed with childish literalness all that went on about him. It was his initiation, the beginning of his interest in affairs of state that were so to enchant his later years. Here was the acorn that grew into the tree of the Centuries.

It was the charm of these early recollections that kept Nostradamus, the man, always a small-town boy by inclination as he was by birth. In his day as in ours most people were the bits of steel pulled upon by the glamour-magnets of the great cities. The complex brilliance of cities and their mirage of opportunity were woven into the dreams of youth and the ambitions of manhood, and in France all roads led to Paris. Michel remained curiously immune to this lure. He learned early to prize the smaller world of the town, that can be compassed in its entirety, its figures known and studied against their background of the generations. Here in Provence were his personal interests; these were his people.

Michel was a strong boy, quick and active, full of the eager vitality of youth. His grandfathers set him early at his tasks of learning, but being physicians they wisely allowed him plenty of leisure for boyish adventure in ranging the countryside under the Midi sunshine. There was a deeply-felt bond between him and this lovely Provençal country. Boy and man he never wanted to be away from it for long. The breath of its perfume and past drew him always back to its ancient, fertile valleys watered by winding streams below the lift of Alpine hills. As a child he learned the seasons by the pink bloom of almond trees, the dun green of the olive, the gold of harvests and the blood-purple of vineyards. And always there was music accompanying the beauty of Nature's drama, harp and lute, dancing and song. For Provence is a land set to music by the Troubadours.

The genius of the Troubadours made an early and lasting impression on Michel and his brother. The famous lays which told of the honor, the chivalry, the high adventure of the heroes of Provence were captivating to the imagination of the romantic youngsters. Nor had it been long since these poets had gone their way, singing, into the past. Their patron, the minstrel-monarch René, had been the last to go. Their memory was ever green through the treasure of their songs, intimately known and sung by all of high and low degree. Michel and Jean heard them with their nursery rhymes. Le Roman de Renart seems to have made the deepest impression on Michel, perhaps because it is an allegory in which the characters are animals and the plot tells of their struggle for forest leadership. Cunning and hypocrisy are pitted against force, and weakness as usual loses out. Nostradamus, in the Centuries, uses the same animals, denoting the same qualities, as symbols of the contending powers of Europe. The Wolf, the Bear, the Lion, the Fox, the Eagle, the Stag, all play their parts again, in his minstrelsy of destiny.

Michel's brother was gifted with a great voice. The home rang with Jean's singing of the Roman de la Rose, the Chanson de Roland and other celebrated lays et fabliaux. Jean, in later life, followed the prosaic though profitable career of attorney for the parliament of Arles. But as his real contribution he left behind him a history of the Troubadours, a monumental tome entitled: "Lives of the Most Famous Ancient Provençal Poets Who Flourished in the Times of the Counts of Provence."

Some say that the songs of the Troubadours weakened the spirit and resistance of Provence. If so, it was in the sense in which today the more sensitive standards of civilization are at the mercy of aimed force. "If God would only send peace!" cries Nostradamus in the Centuries. He learned his ideals of peace and honor and gentle manners from the minstrels of old Provence.

Sir Walter Scott, in Anne of Geierstein, gives a delightful glimpse of the influence of the Troubadours on this land.

He sketches a scene which was familiar to Michel's boyhood:

"The shepherd literally marched abroad in the morning piping his flock to pasture with some love sonnet of an amorous Troubadour. His 'fleecy care' seemed actually under the influence of the music. Instead of being driven before the shepherd, they followed him, and did not disperse to feed, until facing them, he executed variations on his air. His huge wolf-dog, guardian of the flock, followed his master with ears pricked like the chief critic of the performance. At noon the shepherd's audience would be increased by comely matron or blooming maiden who joined her voice to his as they rendezvoused beside some antique fountain. In the cool of the evening there was dancing on the village green or concert before the hamlet door. Travellers were invited to share the little repast of fruits, cheese and bread. Everything gave charm to the illusion and pointed to Provence as the Arcadia of France.

"The greatest singularity was the absence of aimed men and soldiers in this peaceful country. In England, no one stirred without his long-bow, sword and buckler. In France, the hind wore armor even betwixt the stilts of the plough. In Germany you could not look along a mile of road without seeing clouds of dust from which emerged waving feathers and flashing armor. But in Provence all was quiet and peaceful, as if the music of the land had lulled to sleep all wrathful passions. Now and then a mounted cavalier would pass, harp at saddle-bow or carried by an attendant, attesting his character as Troubadour. The short sword, worn on the left thigh, was for show rather than use."

Besides its "dance and Provençal song and sunburnt mirth," there is in this country another kind of life, silent but no less vital. One that touched profoundly the spirit of young Michel, and which permeates the Centuries. It is the life of the ancient past. Provence is an old land where people and races have come and gone, yet not passed utterly away. Long-dead creeds and customs, rooted deep in antiquity, survive entranced. Celts, Romans, Phoenicians, Greeks, Goths, all have left their traces, blended now in the Christian race.

Nostradamus refers particularly to the long influence of Greece upon Provence in one of his quatrains:

IX-75
From the regions of Epirus and Thracia
People in misfortune shall come by sea seeking help of France,

The same people who have left in Provence their perpetual trace
In the survivals of their dress and laws.

Across the countryside and in the cities rises the pallor of marble ruins and monuments. Triumphal arches, crumbling amphitheaters, delicate fountains, ghost-peopled by the shades of their builders. In such memory-haunted spots, the whispering speech of the past reaches only ears that are attuned to its mysterious language. Michel, sensitive even in childhood to the enigma of past and future held in the eternal now, felt the spell of these remnants of a mighty past. He grew up in the midst of two worlds, the living present of his own day, and the majestic dead of the long ago. The first gave him its earthy warmth, its gayety, its sturdy common sense. The other opened to him its secret realm, serene, imperiously aloof, where within its twilight lay dreaming the sword of Caesar, the sails of Greece and Carthage, and the golden bracelets of the Goth.

When Michel was old enough to be curious about the history of the ruins, he liked to go on rambles of discovery with one or other of the grandfathers who could tell him the story of what he saw. It is easy to picture him at the side of the old man stately in his physician's robe and four-pointed cap, a uniform which the boy would later wear with honor. Michel was a little under height, but vigorous, with rosy-apple cheeks, color he kept so long as he lived. His hair was brown above a high, square forehead. His straight, determined features were lighted by large, extremely keen gray eyes.

On a day when the two are rambling through San Rémy they stop to admire the noble arch of triumph which Julius Caesar built to the memory of Marius and his mighty victory there. Michel is curious about the carvings on the arch. What do they mean, he asks his grandfather.

"They record how long ago the Roman general, Marius, once saved our land. You see," the old man tells him, "the barbarians had poured over the country. Nearly half a million fierce fighting men they had, besides all their families."

"Did the Romans come here to fight on our side?"

"Yes. But longer ago than that, Hannibal had crossed here with three thousand elephants on his way to conquer Rome. Our Celtic folk had fought for the Romans then, and Rome remembered. She sent us Marius, her finest general, in our time of peril."

"Did he bring a great army, grandfather?"

"No, lad, he didn't need a great army. He had great soldiers, the legions of Rome. And he had with him the prophetess Marta, a Syrian woman who had a familiar spirit and could foretell the future. She promised Marius a victory."

"What, sir, is a familiar spirit? How could the prophetess tell that Marius would win?"

"There are such people, Michel. I myself have some slight gift at mind-reading. Some day I will open your eyes a little. But prophecy is, of course, a greater faculty. The Romans called such prophets sibyls, and set great store by them. Marius did. He paid Marta high honor. Even had his wife Julia come on from Rome after the battle just to meet her. Sometime I will show you the marble stela carved with their meeting."

"Tell me more about the prophetess, please."

"There is not much to tell. Foolish folk believe she still speaks from the cavern of Lou Garagoule where a hundred of the barbarians were thrown to death at her bidding."

"Why? Surely many were killed in the battle."

"Yes. But you see, lad, she was a pagan. Before the coming of our Lord who forbade cruelty, men worshipped gods who, so they thought, must have a special sacrifice of blood to pay for their favors. Marius, no doubt, thought it cheap at the price."

"Grandfather, where is Lou Garagoule? Is it far?"

"Too far for your short legs," grandfather chuckles. "'Tis some miles beyond Aix, near to the top of Mont Saint Victoire. There is a deep cleft in the rock, with the monastery perching across it like an eagle. Under it runs a cavern so far down that it has never been plumbed. It has a secret passage leading down. 'Tis said the monks unlock it for fools who pay them enough to expiate their sin of consulting Marta, or what they think is Marta."

"But does she really speak to them?"

"Of course not. She is long dead. But they go through heathenish incantations and wait six hours in the darkness. Then all they hear is the howl of the wind in the mountain passages. Never try it, 'tis contrary to the spirit of God, and the monks do ill to allow it."

"Still, I should like to see it, grandfather."

"That you shall. When your mother thinks you are old enough to be up the night, you will go to Mont Saint Victoire on the twenty-fourth of April, the anniversary of the battle. You will see where the legions of Marius stood. You will march in the great celebration of the victory they hold there every year, for folk in these parts will never forget."

"Will there be dancing and music?"

"Drums and trumpets, tambourines and singing. They build big bonfires on the Mont, and all night long they dance the farandole, and shout 'Victory, Victory.'"

"Did you go, grandfather?"

"In my youth. Many times. At dawn there is Mass, and everyone goes to give thanks for the saving of our land."

"Tell me about the battle." Youth is never weary.

"Well, the Roman legions were posted on Mont Saint Victoire, 'tis called so after the battle. Here were the barbarians in San Rémy and stretching all the way across the plain to Aix. Between them and the Mont, Marius had dug a great line of deep ditches, the Fossa of Marius, as men still call them--"

As the story proceeded, the little boy listened enthralled until the final overthrow of the last barbarian.

"The Greek historian, Plutarch, has set down the story of the battle of Marius better than I can tell it, Michel," Grandfather finished. "You will read about it for yourself, and many other interesting happenings, when you have mastered classic language. 'Twill be an incentive to your study. Now, the hour grows late."

One wonders if the tale of ancient battle, heard in childhood, returned in age to mingle its memory of victory with the seer's bitter foresight of the ruin of France, making more desolate the vision by contrast. In the prophet's verses which tell the story of 1940 is a quatrain describing the Maginot Line. In this he uses the word fosse, French for ditch, from the Latin fossa. Perhaps his vision compared the futility of the greatest defensive ditch ever built with the primitive, victorious one of the Roman general.

IV-80

Near the great river the earth will be excavated to construct a huge Line (fosse)

Divided into fifteen parts according to the lay of the waters.

The city (Paris) will be captured, there will be the fires of battle, bloodshed and hand-to-hand fighting,

The greater part of the nation will be involved in the shock.

Alas that Marius should be so long time dead. Gone, too, the ancient Roman friendship. Left, but the sadness which cast its gloomy shadow backwards and touched the mantle of the prophet writing those words four hundred years ago.

But such foreknowledge was yet a long way off from Michel's joyous boyhood. After such adventure with his grandfather, he would go home with his head full of battle and wonder. He would dream over it by the fireside where the sleepy flames burnished the copper cooking-pots like a legionnaire's helmet. When night fell in his small, starkly furnished room, and he felt the straw of his pallet beneath him, he would pretend, like boys the world over, that he was Marius on the hillside. The moon, slanting in on the tall wardrobe in the corner, transformed its dark shape mysteriously into the outlines of the prophetess Marta.

There were a thousand such fascinating stories that the grandfathers could tell, out of which Michel and Jean wove their own picture of the ancient splendor of Provence. Tales of emperors, of lost kings and queens and popes who had built their castles there. Stories, too, of the mysteries of the Camargue where giant flame-colored birds flew high in the mists. Stories of gladiatorial games, of bullfights, of crusaders who were sovereigns in the land of Christ. Legends of all the heroes who had laughed under blue Provençal skies, and feasted at Pan's rose-wreathed board which perpetually invites in this land of classic beauty.

As for grandfather's promise to Michel to show him something of the secret marvels of the mind, it is written in the record that he kept his word. Michel would have given him scant rest until he did. "One day, by way of diversion," it is said, grandfather gave a little demonstration of the workings of hidden mental forces. What kind of demonstration is not known, but it was probably a simple experiment in mind-reading. It was, however, a perfect introduction to such mysteries for the boy who was to become an adept in their use. Given casually and naturally by grandfather, it robbed the subject of the superstitions and ideas of devil's magic which permeated the age. It gave the boy an opportunity for a normal attitude toward extra-sensory experience. The incident could take its place, without distortion or disproportion, in Michel's active gathering of assorted knowledge. Its naturalness held a protective significance toward the later development of the prophet's gift, and its influence can be traced in the honesty and fearlessness of his attitude toward his own mysterious power.

The Education of a Genius

DOCTOR DE RÉMY, Michel's maternal grandfather, took upon himself the early education of his elder grandson. Even today such an education as Michel received from him would be considered out of the ordinary. It was for that period perhaps unique in France. Doctor de Rémy's scholarly prestige and the liberal intelligence with which he guided and inspired his pupil provided an opportunity not often found in any home, ancient or modern. The response of the boy's genius and native love of learning made the relationship between them easy and delightful. How different this was from the usual instruction in the sixteenth century can be appreciated from Rabelais' account of Pantagruel's pilgrimage of learning.

"My will," said Gargantua, concerning the education of Pantagruel, "is to hand him over to some learned man to indoctrinate him according to his capacity and to spare nothing to that end."

"Indoctrination," in the early sixteenth century, meant stuffing the young mind like a Strasbourg goose. Lack of humane, intelligent methods of teaching was eked out with sadistic technique. Education was driven into the memories of tough-skulled, resistant youngsters with blows and floggings. Rabelais, writing of what boys had to endure for the rudiments of knowledge, said of one especially cruel master:

"If for flogging poor little children, unoffending schoolboys, pedagogues are damned, he, upon my word of honor, is now on Ixion's wheel, flogging the dock-tailed cur that turns it."

There was no idea of home instruction, and public education lacked range and had little that was useful. Fruitless, prolonged study of words, followed by equally fruitless study of interminable subtleties, made a drawnout, bewildering misery of the boy's path of knowledge. Doctor Garencières, telling of his own education in France a century later, says that he and the other children, as soon as they had learned the primer, were set to studying the Centuries of Nostradamus. "This book was the first after my Primer, wherein I did learn to read, it being then the custom of France about the year 1618 to initiate children by that book; first because of the crabbedness of the words; secondly that they might be acquainted with the old and obsolete French; and thirdly for the delightfulness and variety of the matter." The picture of babes learning like puzzled parrots the stanzas that have challenged the wits of how many scholars is poor immortality for the man whose own training was so different. Printing had so recently introduced the curse of schoolbooks to the young that there had not been time to create a pedagogic tradition. Before printing, children had grown up as free and untrammeled as Adam. They learned only to fish, hunt, roam, handle a bow and arrow and, if of good family, to buckle on a knight's armor. If the ways of doing these things improved, the pursuits were still those of the Stone Age. There was, of course, always a class of churchly scholars and a certain amount of mannered culture among the top social families. As a national development, however, few could read and write. But when printing brought books within popular reach, parents everywhere wanted their children to have this strange, new accessibility to knowledge which had been denied to them. So began the painful era of mental discipline for the young.

Doctor de Rémy and Rabelais, almost alone in their period, seemed to have envisioned the kind of education which today is taken for granted. Both believed that youth should be interested, and the book of knowledge unfolded in wonder and delight. Pantagruel, you will remember, spent years learning to say the alphabet backwards, and still more years and years on volumes of Latin commentaries, until Gargantua saw that he was turning out just a daft dreamer. So he chose a master of a different sort who taught Pantagruel the observation of nature and the examination of facts. Eventually Pantagruel returned to his father with a rounded development and an understanding of the relationship of knowledge to living. Rabelais knew this the hard way, Nostradamus learned it the easy way. He had an early joyousness toward study, he never needed spurring, nor had to shrink from what was for most boys a physically and emotionally painful experience that left its mark indelibly on a sensitive nature.

Doctor de Rémy grounded his grandson thoroughly in Latin, mathematics and astronomy, and gave him a general knowledge of nature facts. Ease and fluency in writing and speaking Latin were then of prime cultural importance, for it was the language employed by scholars and public orators. It was much used at court, too, through the reign of Francis I. It is said that the royal family, in hours when they gathered informally, enjoyed chatting affably together in Latin--an accomplishment that is perhaps as difficult for moderns to imagine as anything in the sixteenth century. But children then were put to this study very young to gain the required proficiency. The Provençal tongue still retained more of a Roman heritage than of northern France. This made the study of Latin easier for boys born, as Michel, in the Midi than in other sections of the country. Mathematics went hand in hand with astronomy. Patrons, amateurs and profound scholars of "the celestial science" were very numerous and they had to be able to prepare their own ephemerides, and to make elaborate, difficult mathematical calculations which today are available in published, labor-saving tables. Both of Michel's grandfathers were ranked as savants in mathematics and astronomy. Their teaching and his interest soon carried his knowledge far beyond his years.

For frosting on the educational cake, there were, from both grandfathers, endless memories of brilliant doings at King René's court, the little Athens of its day. History and geography took on romantic meanings from these stories. The boy never tired hearing of the gorgeous pageants and dramas which King René had never wearied of producing.

"The most splendid of them all," said grandfather, "was The War of The Seven Chiefs. It was a play out of Greek legend, about gods and men, and all the gods had golden faces. The king summoned one of the greatest artists in France to Aix to design the golden crown, the masque and the sceptre for the sun-god. The night the play was given, the King and Queen and all the court had dressed like the ancient Greeks. 'Twas like a country long gone, come back with all its music and soldiers and ladies and gods."

Another time grandfather would say, "When you are a man, Michel, you will travel. You will go to Italy, perhaps you will even see there such a singular man as Great Beard who came from Florence. Here, I will show you Florence on this map."

"--and Great Beard, grandfather?"

"A rich merchant who came to trade, and brought the king a Persian manuscript for a gift. To please the king Great Beard had gotten himself up in a splendid Turkish dress. He had on a robe of Eastern silk over a broidered chemise. And about his middle were girt three belts studded with little jewels. But the joke of it was the king couldn't see his splendid dress unless Great Beard turned his back, and that is never done to a king. His beard was so thick and so long that it covered up the front of him. None of us had ever seen the like before. Amazing vain he was of it too."

Nostradamus sometimes uses the word étranger in the Centuries, but more often the foreigner is le barbe, les barbares, and if a foreign tyrant, Ahenobarbus. Perhaps his memory kept a picture of the Florentine merchant seen through grandfather's eyes, and gave him a preference for the older, Latin-derived word.

Doctor de Nostradame did not live to see the young prodigy whom he had so lovingly trained grow up. He died when Michel was still in his 'teens. His passing was one of two deaths that marked the closing of Michel's young boyhood. The loss of his grandfather was a personal grief. The other passing was impersonal, remote, yet it ended a period to which he was to look back in later years with nostalgic longing. This was the death of Louis XII, which closed an epoch in the life of France, one which Michel would recall in sadder days as a never-returning patriarchal age of gold.

Michel's life-span saw the rulership of five kings of France. Under the reign of Louis XII, which ended in 1515, France had been ideally united. Never had the country a more popular king than Louis the Well Beloved, twenty-second king of the grand line of Capet. Louis had guided the government with fewer mistakes than most monarchs and no infringement of the people's liberties. But he was the last king of France whose reign expressed the national unity of a free people. The security of France had seemed at last firmly established. The powerful, one-pointed nationalism for which people and king had worked so long appeared near to realizing the French dream of continental leadership, a dream never to be fully realized, but persisting to Sedan. France never again in after periods reattained this early combination of apparently limitless possibilities combined with balance and simplicity of life, as just before the brook of Mediaevalism became the torrent of the Renaissance.

The kingdom of Provence had come under the sovereignty of France about twenty years before Michel's birth, and memories of its independent realm were still fresh in the minds of Provençals. René, their last king, had long known that with the passing of feudalism, Provence must come under a larger center. Himself a Capet, he wanted France rather than Spain to be his inheritor. But because of the love between him and the people of his little realm he put off the evil day. Louis XI was then King of France. He and René were both very old men, and Louis with an eye always on Spain grew nervous. He invited Cousin René, who always liked to go places, to visit him in Paris. In the interest of larger gain, the stingiest monarch in Christendom unloosed for once his purse-strings. His chamberlain was ordered to go all out with gay and splendid parties, and to be sure to have the prettiest girls in Paris there. The sly old fox successfully lured the gay old dog. René had the time of his ancient life, being then in his eighties, and when the party was over Louis had Provence in his pocket.

In Michel's time, Provence was administered on behalf of the French Crown by a provincial governor, the distinguished soldier Claude de Savoie, Count de Tende. He was a friend of the de Nostradame family, and his name appears with flattering mention in one of the quatrains.

With the death of Louis XII France came under the domination of a new king, and a different branch of the Capetian line--the House of Valois. Francis I, the glamour-boy from Angoulême, was the first of five Valois kings who succeeded to the throne of Saint Louis. Michel was then not quite thirteen years old. Boylike, he thrilled to the accounts of the brave and charming young prince on whom France set high hopes, and who was now his king. That was a year when the annual ceremonial pageant at Aix, which King René had begun in 1448, took on a dramatic meaning from the royal event. The most prized title of the French monarchs was that of très chrétien, and René's old festival procession pictured the triumph of Christianity over evil. Michel's parents took the boys to Aix for the occasion. The picturesque, wholly mediaeval solemnity of the procession was as naïve as an illuminated manuscript.

The long procession, which the boys watched absorbedly, winding slowly through the streets of Aix, was intended to show how the heathen gods and their worshipers were driven back into hell by Christ, but the presentation of the allegory would appear to have been as mixed and hard to unravel as one of the Centuries. The god Mercury led the procession, followed by the goddess of Night with Pluto attended by a galaxy of flame-dressed demons. Then came walking the huntress Diana and after her, singly, came Love, Venus and Mars. Followed then a gruesome group of lepers, behind whom were the commanders of the city and knights in armor riding proudly, then the dancers and a coterie of musicians with tambourines, lutes, fifes and drums. Now came the Queen of Sheba in silks and jewels on her way to visit Solomon. Next was Moses carrying the tables of the law, and trying to bring back to God a group of mocking Jews who danced around a pasteboard golden calf. Judas followed displaying his purse and counting his thirty pieces of silver while the other apostles belabored his head with sticks in punishment. Now in the distance, Michel and Jean, their heads uncovered, could see approaching the prelates bearing the Blessed Sacrament. Preceding them, strangely enough walked the Abbé of Youth, the Prince of Love, and the King of the Basoche. This last was the head of a guild of law clerks who staged many morality plays.

It should be plain to interpreters of the Centuries--though it has not been--that much in its writing which has baffled and perturbed scholars is traceable to the natural impression which such scenes as this procession made upon the imaginative, religious temperament of the boy Michel. The peculiar mixture of allegory, symbolism and historic allusion which abounds in his writings is less cryptic in intention than commentators will allow. Much of this was a normal reflection of Provençal expression in the romantic mediaevalism of the prophet's youth. It is difficult to interpret, mainly because modern scholarship has lost contact with so much in those older modes. When one reflects that with such a background Nostradamus was able to span and summarize prophetically the development of four centuries, it is not the obscurity but the clarity of most of his writing that is amazing.

After Michel's education had been interrupted by the death of his grandfather, his parents were faced with the problem of how best to continue it. They decided to send him to the famous university at Avignon. Jacques and Renée had probably to do some careful figuring of the family budget when they made their plans, for they were by no means wealthy, and a college education, then as now, was expensive for people of moderate means. But scholarship was a too distinguished family tradition for their sons to have anything but the best. Besides, they must have realized by then that Michel had whatever was the sixteenth-century equivalent of a striking I. Q. So to Avignon he went to take his Philosophia, as the course was called which approximated the modern degree of Bachelor of Arts. Avignon was a proud, powerful old town. Its active student and religious life was carried on within the protection of incredibly massive walls above which reared like guardian swords the stately height of its thirty-nine towers. Here the tradition of learning stretches far back into the past, beyond the true and the false popes, to shadowy Saracenic origins. Here the mistral blows, the cold raw wind which Petrarch bemoaned, against which even the flame of his love for Laura could not keep him warm.

Teachers, with an eye out for promising pupils, quite naturally hoped that young Michel, coming from a family of scholars, would make a good showing. But they must have been a little breathless when, according to old sources, he began at once to display his dazzling memory and amazing information. It is told that he needed to read a chapter but once in order to repeat it with exact accuracy. If, gentle reader, you are visualizing from this something like modern chapters, let it be stated that in those days twenty-five lines of print made a short sentence, punctuation was scanty, and paragraphs were met every few miles. Such ability as Michel's, in an age when all educational emphasis was upon memory, made an impression out of all proportion to its mental value, and was alone enough to give him top rating as a scholar. But he had even more fascinating rabbits-out-of-hat than his memory.

It is said that from the time Michel was able to reason "he was accustomed to decide for himself the meaning of all manner of small, curious facts which interested him." One suspects that it was his grandfather who did the deciding, and that the old gentleman wore himself to his grave answering his brilliant grandson's questions. However that may be, Michel had a vast store of assorted extra-curricular information that soon had his teachers dazed and his enthralled fellow students hanging on his words. Much of what he knew would today be in any child's book of knowledge, but only learned adults had such information then.

When Michel told the other boys how clouds were formed out of vapor, and how they dissolved into rain, he was a sensation to lads who had learned at home that clouds were pumped up out of the sea, as was commonly believed.

Shooting stars, he claimed astonishingly, were not stars that had become loosened from the sky. He talked about particles and gases and what made stars shine. And he insisted that the earth really was a round ball, for in spite of Columbus there were still plenty of people who did not believe this. And--incredible idea--he told them that the sun shone on the other side of the world too.

Michel was never a show-off, he had none of that quality. All who have written of him have, without exception, admitted his unassuming manner and quiet modesty. But he lost himself so completely in the interest of study and talked about it so constantly that such absorption had a spectacular effect. His pet interest at this time was astronomy, a subject on which he "gave out" as energetically as a living saxophone, and the college dubbed him "the young astronomer." He was nonetheless, in spite of his superior knowledge, popular with the students, because he was fun-loving and good company. After he had completed his university studies, which included advanced philosophy, astronomy, rhetoric, higher mathematics and Latin, he was put in charge of the astronomy class as student-teacher. This was a traditional honor for such a brilliant scholar.

During his sojourn in Avignon, Michel's devout young mind absorbed more impressions than merely those of academic training. The city was under the dominion of the papacy, as it had been from early days. Religion was emphasized here, as at Rome, by the Church as joint administrator of both the secular and spiritual government. The huge, ancient palace of the popes, though falling into disrepair, was still a potent symbol of this power, and dominated the activities of the town with its brooding, sightless stare. To Michel, it seemed to be forever waiting, somberly watching from dusty windows for the return of its holy tenant. Sometimes the boy watched the moon rise over the enormous pile, making it mysterious with shadows and silver. He thought of it, too, when he walked at sunset near the beautiful church of Notre Dame des Doms, and looked up to the Virgin of the Western Tower, whose famous statue was gold-sheathed like the gods in grandfather's story. At such times a strange feeling would come over him. A feeling of return. As if the popes some day really might come back to Avignon.

He knew by heart the history of the Avignon popes. How the German Emperor had bedeviled Clement V until he had removed himself to Avignon to be free of interference. How this had led eventually to the Great Schism in which three factions had claimed the papal election. How another German Emperor, Sigismund, had then called a great conference that deposed the false popes and then ratified the Emperor's choice, Martin Colonna, the Pope who healed the schism. Could such a terrible situation ever come about again, the boy wondered. Could there be rulers again in Germany who would do wicked things to religion? Would the Holy Father then return to Avignon? And if he did, might it not be that a French monarch would on this new occasion restore peace to God's Vicar? If a new schism ever arose, not Germany but France, he hoped, would name the new Martin Colonna. Half dreams and questions, these, that were to haunt him until the maturity of his mystical vision should give him the answers after many years.

The Centuries contain an impressive and detailed block of quatrains dealing with the prophesied return, under persecution, of the schismatic pattern within the Church, and he foresees rhapsodically that a great French monarch will restore a pope to his power in Rome, after Germany had been defeated by France. He foretells that Avignon will be for a time the headquarters of this king in his struggle to re-establish the monarchy and the exiled papacy.

Many verses elaborate this situation and the election of "The Great Shepherd," whom he calls "the new Colonna." These visions, though long distant from his time, held for him particular appeal and intimacy because of his Avignon boyhood.

When Michel returned to San Rémy after completing his humanities at Avignon, the next consideration in his life was the choice of a profession. He wanted to be an astronomer. To him astronomy was always the beloved science. But his father is said to have stepped on this idea. He desired naturally enough that Michel should be a doctor. In this field his distinguished family background would give him a send-off that would be almost a ready-made reputation in itself. Besides, there were always human ills to cure, and medicine offered a much more secure livelihood than did the far, bright face of the heavens. His father's arguments won the day. The opening of the new term saw Michel entered at the Faculté de Médecin in Montpellier, most famous university for scientific study in France.

When Michel passed through whichever of Montpellier's eleven gates, he no doubt carried in his light student's luggage some of the things that had been part of the professional equipment of his grandfather and may have been handed down from even older hands. Perhaps there was a surgeon's antique copper case complete with gleaming instruments. He would have no chance to use these in Montpellier's new dissection amphitheater, for dissection was done by the professors, but there was a warm feeling in just having these with him. There also would have been a copper or pewter shaving bowl, very important since it was used for bleeding and shaving the patient, and many a doctor at that time rose to fame through the simple technique of bleeding and purging. And perhaps Michel had a carved wooden box or a leather pouch that his grandfather had used to hold the gold and silver coins that were his fees, and which Michel hoped would one day receive his, too.

The clear air and bright color of Montpellier wore a welcome contrast to gray Avignon. The city, for southern France, was quite modern, too, since it dated only from the eighth century. Michel knew, of course, the legend of its founding. Two sisters, young and lovely, so the story runs, once owned all the land on which the city stands. But they cared nothing for this life, and longed instead for the eternal bliss of heaven. Believing that this could best be secured by giving up possession that bound them to earth, they had turned over to the Church their vast lands. It was a macabre coincidence that the first anatomical dissection ever made in France was performed in Montpellier upon the bodies of two women. Perpetuating the legend, the hills of Big and Little Sister, Mons Puellarum, rise about Montpellier. Over them in season, woad spreads a carpet of cloudy blue, and scarlet berries glow in the sun. In Michel's day, sheep browsed in leisurely contentment along their slopes.

Of a certainty, Michel's welcome at the university was a gracious one. Some of the professors had met his grandfathers; all had heard of them. Each teacher hoped that this promising student would enroll in his class. Professors then received no salary at Montpellier. Every student chose and paid his own masters. Naturally competition for pupils was keen among the faculty. The best-known and most popular teachers drew the largest classes, and, in consequence, made the most money. Not that money entered so much into the work of these distinguished men, but professors then as now had to live.

The Church was in active, executive control of the university. Pope Urban V had with high enthusiasm founded this college and made it his favorite project. Since his time it had grown enormously. Many buildings had been added, and the scope of instruction had broadened by taking advantage of new scientific advances. The university's latest cause for pride was its operating amphitheater, recently built and the first one in France. This was not used for operations on living persons, but only for the anatomical dissection of corpses. Yet so daring an innovation was it considered that it was the medical sensation of the moment.

This advance had been accomplished by the tireless efforts of Guillaume Rondelet, foremost anatomist in France and a devoté of the new Greek ideas which the Renaissance was rapidly introducing. He was idolized at Montpellier and the focus of its most progressive student life. In a journal which Nostradamus kept in later years he eulogized particularly the names of three physicians who were on the staff of Montpellier. These were Guillaume Rondelet, Antoine Saporta, and Honoré Castelin. Presumably these were his teachers. Of this trio, the name of Rondelet still shines with undimmed brilliance on the scientific roster of France as a great pioneer anatomist and naturalist. A man of dynamic enthusiasm and daring courage, he would have drawn Michel like steel to a magnet, and in return would have opened his heart to this unusual student.

A gentle, devout man was Doctor Rondelet, yet vivid too in his ability to dramatize his subjects. Everything he said and did was an exciting expression of the new scientific spirit, and his sacrificial devotion to science had but recently been put to proof. When the amphitheater was opened, Doctor Rondelet had found it all but impossible to procure corpses for dissection. The ban against this had been lifted, but prejudice and superstition were still a powerful handicap. Death took the doctor's son at this time, and in order that knowledge might increase for the saving of others' lives, he had given the body of his son, and had himself performed the dissection before the students in the new hall at Montpellier.

"We have come a long way," he told Michel, "from the days when Charles of Anjou granted this university permission to dissect one corpse a year--and that had to be the corpse of a criminal!"

"Who would have died of hanging, instead of some disease which needed study," Michel observed.

"Exactly. Now we have won freedom to experiment on broader lines. But much more important, science has gained a new approach. Mark you, we do not know any more yet than our ancestors, but thanks to Aristotle we are learning how to go after knowledge, how to observe and study facts--that is what will carry medicine forward."

"You have made a splendid beginning, sir." The young man praised him with formal respect.

"Ah, wait till I get my botanical garden! That is what I am after now. It is what we must have next. More study of the properties of plants, better distillation of essences, and experimentation with rare herbs. If only King Francis were less set on clouting Charles of Austria, and more interested in saving Frenchmen's lives it would be the better for France. I have beseeched him for funds for a plant-garden, but he, forsooth, needs the money for his troops and his new châteaux."

Rondelet did not live to see his dream of a botanical garden for Montpellier come true. But due directly to his efforts, it was eventually realized through the generous gift of that "son of Egypt" as Nostradamus unkindly called Henry IV.

"At least you will agree, sir, that the King has done a fine thing in opening the study of the Greek language to the public in his new Collège de France."

"Yes. And we need direct translations terribly. These second-hand Latin manuscripts are a mass of errors. But it will take time. We have to wait now for Greek scholars to be trained, then wait some more for translations to be made. And there is so much to be done!"

"But think you not, Doctor Rondelet, that it is more than a mere change of schools, more than the difference between Greek and Arab medicine? May not the fresh stirring in men's minds develop knowledge that even the Greeks did not have?"

"Of course I think so. And I can foresee trends which may take a hundred, five hundred, years to work out. Sometimes when I think of it, I feel like Moses on Mount Nebo. I shall not enter the promised land of science, but I have seen it from afar and found it glorious. Which reminds me, I shall let you read my new monograph on poisons, Michel. I have just completed it, and it contains material not heretofore presented. It is a case in point. My colleagues will say it is too radical, but the next generation will use it, surpass it, and then it will be old-fashioned. And that is as it should be."

This manuscript, like many others, its use long past, sleeps today on a library shelf. But its preservation records one among the early, patient steps on the long road which Rondelet foresaw.

The coming of the Renaissance had thrown the practice of medicine into a turmoil of transition from Arabic to Greek methods. Galen, Hippocrates and Aristotle were the new gods, but the dissemination of their ideas was at first badly handicapped by an almost total ignorance of the Greek language, and extreme prejudice in many quarters against its teaching. A fight over the latter was then raging in Paris. Francis I had just established the liberal Collège de France which offered the first public instruction in Greek and Hebrew given in France. The Sorbonne promptly let out fanatical howls of horror and threats of hell to those who studied there, claiming that he who studied Hebrew became a Jew and he who learned Greek was a heretic. In spite of such protests the new learning gained steadily under royal patronage. Montpellier was always in the forefront of liberal thought, but echoes of the bitter quarrel and the persecution of independent scholars reached its halls. Michel, the student, had his attention directed for the first time, hearing of all this, to the hazards with which liberal scholarship could be faced. Anything, he saw, might happen to it from division within the ranks of scholars or hostile authority without. Later he was to experience this in his own work, with jealousy and intolerance toward himself as a physician, and his strange kind of knowledge.

As prophet, he perceived the danger that either a too reactionary or a too revolutionary authority could and would bring to such men as himself, and to such institutions as Montpellier. He foresaw no end to these recurring perils when he later wrote:

I-62
Alas what loss shall be sustained by learning
Before Latona shall complete her cycle,
War and revolution, brought about more through stupid governments than from other causes,
Will create havoc that cannot for a long time be repaired.

IV-18
The greatest scholars of celestial science
Will be reproved by ignorant princes,
They will be punished by edict, driven like criminals,
And put to death on the spot.

Memories of the Inquisition, the French Revolution, of great men from Galileo to Einstein crowd to confirm this prophecy. Montpellier suffered in 1792 when its proud Chair of Royal Anatomist and Dissector, which Rondelet's work had established, was suppressed during the Revolution.

Student life in Montpellier was gay, delightful and cosmopolitan. Youths from all over France and from other countries were attracted to its famous universities. Besides its native southern hospitality, Montpellier was expert through long experience in the art of entertaining. Through its gates there was a constant passing to and fro of notables. Prelates, nobles, politicians and scientists who came there were greeted with civic celebrations of simplicity or elaborateness in keeping with the importance of the guest. The festivities included much Latin oratory which was probably as dull as are public speeches today. After that, there had always to be a gala procession in this pageant-conscious land. The students took prominent part in these festivals, which were colorful, and sometimes exciting when some great personage honored the city. Montpellier celebrated with a grand procession the fame of one of her most celebrated students, Rabelais. But it was five hundred years after he had died, when for a day the old town revived the full bloom of its sixteenth-century pageantry. Pictures of this occasion describe all of the bright processions in which he once kept lithe step.

It needs little imagination to visualize Michel or Rabelais in the spirited ranks of marching students which led off the procession. Behind them walked the archers, town lads who made Montpellier famous as the sporting center of military archery. Then came arquebusiers and halberdiers, weaponed and wearing the tin hats of their day. Then pretty, dark-eyed girls swung their wide skirts down the tortuous street, lifting flower-entwined arches in the Provençal trellis dance. Nobles and town-fathers rode on horseback, the feathers, jewels and velvets of the lords set off by the sober richness of the councilors' attire.

Scattered through the procession moved the heralds, musicians piping gay airs, and dark-frocked chanting monks. Last, and looking very like a calliope, was the grand car of honor drawn by six horses. Seated aloft in pomp was the guest, with the high dignitaries of Church, State and the university.

Michel had all too short a time to enjoy his student days. He was only twenty-one when a plague broke out in horrible virulence, devastating most of southern France. The Faculté de Médecin for the second time in its long history was forced to close its doors, as were all of the other schools in Montpellier.

What kind of plague it was is uncertain. Those early scourges were of many types, and medicine has little identification for many of them. It may have been, as Forman thinks, the black plague. Or it may have been the mysterious "sweating sickness" which attacked England a few years later when Henry VIII was courting Anne Boleyn. Whatever the nature of these epidemics, the dread word "plague" covered them all. This one appeared in the wake of the brief invasion by the Constable de Bourbon, and is supposed to have been carried by his troops. It swept the countryside like a devil's hurricane of agony and death. So furiously did the Horseman of the plague ride the countryside that burial could not keep pace with him. Unburied corpses lay in the houses and in the streets. So great was the frenzy of terror that gripped the people and so swift the mortality, that many, at the least touch of sickness, robed themselves in shrouds and disposed themselves for death, so that when it came they should not be bereft of this last decency.

The doctors were helpless; some of them as terrified as the victims; others, men of great-hearted courage, died like those they tended, heroic martyrs to the ignorance of the times. Literally nothing was known about these plagues, and the same treatment was given for all of them. Some of the medical men were beginning to get a glimmering of ideas that were the ancestors of modern technique, but they lacked the knowledge to develop them effectively.

They had figured out that contagion was spread by touch or carried through the air. To protect themselves, they wore extra clothing, plugged the nose with cotton and wore goggles, which were in a way the forerunner of the modern mask. They understood the need for prophylaxis, but all they had were "protective" oils with which they soaked their shirts. Garlic, long known for its purifying properties, was used extensively, but without the least intelligence or information as to its powers. There were no arrangements for isolating victims, and incense was burned to keep down the all-pervading stench of putrefaction. Conditions were exactly the same as when Thucydides wrote his description of the plague at Athens which, he said, killed as many through fear as through infection, because people knew that there was no medical help for the stricken.

Such was the awful scourge against which Michel de Nostradame, just attained to manhood, elected to wage single-handed combat. It was the first of three such battles he would fight, winning victories that are unique in the annals of medicine. But how he accomplished it is a mystery more profound than any contained in his writings.

It is strange that he, a junior medical student, ever thought in the first place that he could cure where the most famous doctors failed. But he did think so, and he had the courage to back his theories. He dared not try these out under the notice of the city doctors who would have stepped on such presumption quickly. He went out into the stricken countryside, where doctors were few or none. He took his rosy cheeks and vital, stimulating personality into the hovels and villages, dispensing remedies that were his own idea. Where he treated, Death withdrew. Devotedly, fearlessly, with the untiring strength of youth he travelled the roads of southern France; to Carcassonne, Nîmes, Toulouse, Narbonne, and west to Bordeaux he went his patient, unswerving way. News spread slowly then, and such news as this was unbelievable. Yet gradually and sensationally the word went out. A young man was curing--yes, curing the plague!

Wherever people who heard of him and could reach his services they did. He was overwhelmed with work. The plague was an exceedingly stubborn one. Its duration was four years, and its cost a multitude of lives. Through all that tragic period Michel fought it, using his skill and energies without stint or thought of self. When, in the course of time, the scourge wore itself out against the immunity of those who had survived, Michel had achieved a reputation that was already legendary. Wherever he went, flowers were strewn in his path, gifts and invitations were pressed on him in cottage and château. Everyone wanted to know this wonder-working student, and thousands had cause to bless his name in gratitude.

How did he do it? No one knows. Definitely not with use of his supernormal gift which had not developed at this time. Besides, medicine and the psychic world were to him always two separate fields, and in medicine he was all scientist. It may be that, due to the influence and opinions of his grandfathers, Michel had not then abandoned (nor ever did wholly) Arabic ideas of medicine. He may have had access to rare Arabic prescriptions, which had come down from his ancestors or via travelers at King René's court. The East was old in plagues and civilization when the West was dressing in skins. Little of what they knew medically ever reached the West, but the crusaders saw their marvels.

But if his remedies came from this source, or from whatever kind of knowledge, they must have been of exceedingly simple nature, easily procurable in quantity, and at little or no cost. There is only one place he could have sought supplies like this, the woods and meadows of Earth. The answer could only be that he found some herb or combination of herbs which suited his need and wrought his miracle.

A legend has come down that he effected his cures with a compound of lapis lazuli and gold. Where would a young student without means have procured these costly minerals, especially in quantity for four years' work, most of which was charity? Such a story is the product of an alchemistic imagination.

Michel, the student, had as yet no right to practice medicine, except under the stress of such an emergency as the plague. He had no diploma, and must now, after this four-year interval in which he had become a celebrity, return to Montpellier to stand his final examinations. The required course there was six years. It is probable that he had been there for about two when the epidemic broke out. His four years of field work with his brilliant handling of the plague would be credited to him, provided he passed the final tests, which were very rigid.

He returned a spectacular popular hero, the focus of so much attention and interest that it is said his examinations were held in public, and a crowd came to see and hear. Examinations at Montpellier were always exciting, because they were oral. The faculty and representatives of the Church gathered in one of the large churches which the university owned. All present fired questions, as searching and inclusive as possible, and woe to the student who knew not the answers. It is said that Michel defended his thesis with vigor and brilliance in this long drawn-out, important ordeal. When all the questions were answered and he was pronounced worthy, he was formally invested with "the four-cornered hat, the ermine-trimmed robe, the golden girdle and ring of the brotherhood of Hippocrates." From henceforth he is Doctor de Nostradame.

In Michel's graduating class was Jacques Dubois, or Sylvius, as he chose to be known in the fashion of the day. He soon was to become the foremost anatomist in Paris and to advance the knowledge of the human body with distinguished contributions. He was fifty-one years old when he received his degree, side by side with the prodigy of twenty-six. His fellow students no doubt pitied the plodding old boy, starting so late. Yet both he and Nostradamus were in their different ways conquerors of time. One was to look through time, the other ignored age. Both rose to greatness.

Doctor de Nostradame had planned to leave Montpellier after his graduation. But the students, wild over this new idol, demanded him for their teacher. The institution was pleased to have such a drawing-card on the faculty, though he was very young to be given such a coveted post.

Perhaps he did not realize when he assumed this responsibility how much of a strain the past four years had been, and how restless it had made him. He had made dangerous, strenuous efforts in the period when most young men are enjoying life to the full. It came over him that he too wanted freedom to enjoy himself. He did not want to teach. He wanted to travel. He informed the faculty that he was giving up his post. He had no plans, only to be footloose, to go where inclination led him. Regretfully his colleagues and students saw him go, wondering how he could bring himself to toss away so casually a position which not a scientist in all France but would have been proud to occupy. Unlike Rabelais, he never returned to Montpellier to do further work. The strangeness of his development tended to separate him more and more from its strictly hedged fields of thought. Yet Montpellier was proud of him, as she was of her errant Rabelais. She treasured the memory of both the sinner and the wizard. The worn cap and old gown of Rabelais, shabby with much trudging and trotting, hung on the wall at his alma mater, and were pointed out to visitors. And on their register they showed, up to the time of the Revolution, the prized signature of Nostradamus, with the date October 23, 1529.

Personages and Politics

THE NEW FREEDOM which had lured Doctor de Nostradame from Montpellier's halls was providing the kind of activity he liked best. His success had made him the rage throughout southern France. People were clamoring for him, requesting his attendance on their ills, inviting him to be their guest, for months if he would. Important doors were invitingly open. Everyone wanted to know the current sensation because he was charming, modest and had a great future. Besides, plagues had a way of returning, it was well to stand in with the only man who could cope with them. So Doctor de Nostradame, combining business with pleasure, travelled about from city to city, attending a patient in Avignon, stopping off for a visit in Salon, and moving on to Marseilles to answer new calls.

Everywhere he went he found men disturbed over the international unrest. His own native interest in internal and foreign affairs, dormant since the curiosity of his childhood, responded quickly to the incessant, exciting talk. Some of his new patients were men in a position to tell him inside facts and give him informed opinions. They enjoyed talking over these matters with the keen, witty young scientist, who listened so eagerly. These conversations bred in Nostradamus a dawning sense of political perspective that led eventually to his study of natural destinies on a plane of perception beyond the senses. Just now his picture of the great, warring forces of power politics was confused, incomplete. Too, he had been for so long in out-of-the-way pest-ridden districts where the only news was a tolling bell, that he was seriously behind on his history, for much had happened in those years.

The high noon of the Renaissance was now shedding its dazzling sunlight upon the most transcendent period-piece ever played by man. Chivalry, antiquity, and the beginnings of a different social order were mingling in a new civilization that was already ornamented with every splendor and blackened with every crime. Conquerors, alchemists, poets, lovers and heretics played their fiery roles in velvets and gems, plumes and armor, scholar's robe and monkish gown, against a background of deep, sensual reds, primeval greens and the blue of Mary's mantle. Chaos, war, unrest drove the scenes forward with climax topping climax. And always wine of violence and the scent of blood flavored the graces, the wit, and the etiquette of courts.

The initial impulse of the Renaissance had united an inherited physical dynamism, an ancestral hardihood, with a fresh, powerful increase in the electric potential of brain and spirit. The vigor was still earthy, and its forces, though far from the primitive, were still natural. It was this new electric urge of the Renaissance, expanding all horizons, which was responsible for the triumphs and tragedies of the grand age of the sword, the lyre, and the printing-press.

The costumes, armor and weapons, so different from ours, seem remote as we read of them. But the political set-up of the age had amazing similarities to what the world is enduring today. If a file of current newspapers could be handed back through time to a man of the sixteenth century, he would be astonished, not because our methods are so different, but because we bring them to bear on the same old situations as of his day. "Persecutions of Jews," "Fresh Axis Threats," "Books Banned," "Massacre of Religious Orders," "New Invention by Scientist," "Communism Gains Ground," "Parliament Asked for More Money"--such headlines would be quite familiar to a gentleman of the Renaissance. Nostradamus knew them all.

Martin Luther was making his bid for power with the new ideology of the Reformation. Sir Thomas More was publishing Utopia, the ancestor of Communism. Indeed, Nostradamus in writing of modern Communism calls it "the doctrine of the camel, More." Leonardo was playing with designs for aircraft and hydraulic pumps; Rabelais and other liberal scholars were fighting the ban on their books; and a new star of first magnitude, the Hitler of his day, had risen on the political horizon. It would perhaps be unfair to call Charles V, King of Spain and Holy Roman Emperor, the first totalitarian, since he was without benefit of national socialism. But he certainly thought that Europe should belong totally to him, and he got his hands on more of it than did anyone else before Hitler. In the matter of real estate, Charles, like Browning's Last Duchess, liked whate'er he looked on and his looks went everywhere.

Trouble between France and Spain had started about the time that Michel was entering Montpellier. Francis I had quickly transformed the easy-going government of Louis XII into a cast-iron autocracy. He had flouted Parliament, and lie had made the offices of the clergy into a crown benefice, a situation which continued until the Revolution. Francis hoped soon to apply these tactics to the international scene, pick up some spare parts of Italy, and eventually get the best of Spain. But the curtain went up before Francis was ready, on a drama he had not planned.

A Bourbon and a woman opened the scene. They were the Constable of France and Louise of Savoy, mother of Francis. In a short fifty years more, the duel between another Bourbon and another queen-mother, Henry of Bourbon-Navarre and Catherine de' Medici, would ring down the curtain upon the Valois dynasty. Two hundred and fifty years later, the Revolution would begin its drama with the blood of a Bourbon and "the Austrian woman." And shortly, within our own years--so the prophet has foretold--the last and greatest of the Bourbons shall arise to lead France back to power. His reign is to close the cycle of this dynasty which has alternately troubled or glorified France since the time of Nostradamus.

It was a Frenchman, Balzac, who wrote: "To the heart there are no little events. Love magnifies everything. It places in the same scale the fate of an empire and the dropping of a woman's glove. Almost always the glove outweighs the empire." This has been tragically true of France, where passion and politics have gone together from the distant yesterday of Louise and Bourbon to the recent yesterday of Daladier, Reynaud and their plotting loves.

The court drama of the queen-mother's infatuation and revenge which brought the Spaniards on French soil and opened the long conflict between the houses of Valois and Bourbon began while Michel, the student, was listening to

Doctor Rondelet lecture on bones and muscles. Except for cynical Paris, the French people had little understanding of what it was all about, nor did most of them ever find out. Palamides Tronc de Condoulet told the story to Doctor de Nostradame over a glass of ripe Provençal wine, in de Condoulet's house at Salon.

"While I was fighting the plague," Nostradamus had said, "I used to think, when I had a moment to think at all, that when it was all over, I would be an old man in a strange world. Such tricks does our time-sense play us that it seemed to me eons must have passed before I returned to the cities. I have still but little knowledge of what happened besides the plague, for at Montpellier they talk naught except science. I saw something of the passing of Spanish troops, before the plague struck. I know that our Duc de Bourbon, Constable of France, turned traitor and brought them here to seize the Crown of France for himself. But why did treachery tempt so great a man? You, my friend, who have news from everywhere, perhaps you can tell me?"

The Sieur de Condoulet, who became a lifelong friend of Nostradamus, was a good gossip. The stories he left about the prophet show that. He was a prosperous Provençal merchant who enjoyed and dealt in the good things of life. He was equipped to bring the physician up-to-date, for merchants often got news ahead of others, and in greater detail, through travelling salesmen and peddlers who went with their wares all over the country. A good salesman's best introduction to a prospective purchaser was a fresh budget of exciting, though not always reliable, news picked up at the inns along his route. Often he displayed his merchandise in châteaux and palaces, the lords and ladies making their own selections. Then the salesman had a chance to talk to the help, and many a juicy morsel was gleaned in this way.

"Bourbon's troops," said de Condoulet, "looted my warehouses and ruined my business. Then the King came rampaging down to drive him out, and his men destroyed the little I had left."

"'That which the palmerworm hath left hath the locust eaten,'" quoted the doctor, who was ever partial to the Book of Joel.

"Palmerworm or locust, whichever of the two is the hungrier, that was the Spaniards. You'd think they'd never seen food till they came to Provence."

"A conqueror's appetite is always worse than his guns. An invader brings an empty belly. But you have not answered my question," Nostradamus reminded him.

"Cherchez la femme--in this case the King's mother."

"Madame Louise!" exclaimed the doctor. "But, she must be all of--?"

"--forty-five," de Condoulet told him, "and Bourbon was but turned thirty. Some tell it that Madame Louise is arrogant, grasping, but still beautiful. Others say she is arrogant, grasping and fat. The latter insist that of her twin gods, Cupid and Cupidity, the second is so strong that even her flesh seeks gain."

"What happened?"

"She sent Milord Chancellor to Bourbon with the offer of her hand. I had that straight from the palace. Bourbon told him he would never marry an immodest i woman, to take back that word to her."

"Hé, Dieu! What insult to a royal lady."

"Insult, but understatement. The lady has looked on many a man, and one way or another usually gotten him. But not Bourbon."

"And then--?" asked Nostradamus interestedly. "Why, then, she wanted revenge. His Grace of Bourbon, besides being the handsomest man in France, had committed a more serious mistake, he was the richest. His coffers held more gold than the King's. His gentlemen wore three gold chains about the neck, and the King's but one."

"But would the King lend himself to such evil?"

"Madame Louise put the King up to it, but he was willing enough," de Condoulet said cynically. "First they took away from the Duc his command of the armies, which was cutting off France's nose to spite Francis' face. Bourbon was the best general in Europe. Then they stripped him of his last gold écu and most of his land."

"How could even the King do so?" Nostradamus asked, shocked. "There are courts of justice as well as courts of royalty."

"And the chancellor used them. He is a smart man and the queen-mother's creature. It was put over with a nice pretense of legality. And done quietly. Why, people in Bourbon's own domain didn't know what was happening."

"A tale of shame!"

"'Twas then, they say, that the Duc, with his back to the wall, wrote a letter and dispatched it by secret courier to Spanish Charles. Bourbon's friends deny this, but I had it from a peddler who heard it from a man who is cousin to the courier that carried the letter."

"I pity the Duc," Nostradamus remarked, "but I still say it was treachery to expose the country to invasion--for a personal grudge."

"It was more than a grudge, it was a man's life. Madame Louise and the King had done Bourbon too great injury to let him live. When the King got wind of that letter, he speeded up plans already made. His soldiers hunted the Duc like a wild boar through the forest. But he got away over the German border."

The physician lifted his wine-glass and quaffed deeply, as if to take away an unpleasant taste.

"King Francis and Emperor Charles had been aching for a crack at each other," de Condoulet continued. "This gave both of them an excuse. The Emperor gave Bourbon a Spanish army and backed him for a try at the French Crown. So, we had Spanish troops and their plague on French soil. And a plague on them all, I say."

"King Francis, whatever his faults, is God's anointed, and the power of Heaven protects him," said the doctor a bit sententiously.

Tronc de Condoulet eyed his friend humorously. "Heaven doesn't always protect its anointed, doctor. The same bishops would have anointed Bourbon quickly enough--if he had won."

"Why did he not, if he was such a great general?"

"The Spaniards fought badly. Their generals were jealous of him, they objected to serving under a Frenchman."

"Why, after the King had driven off Bourbon and the Spaniards, didn't he finish the job?"

"He thought he had. Why, when they fled into the Italian mountains, the Romans put up placards reading: 'Lost--an army in the mountains of Genoa. If anybody knows what became of it, let him come forward and say. He will be well rewarded.'"

"The King should have claimed the reward," the doctor murmured.

"He tried to," de Condoulet smiled. "Our King Francis, is a hero; none doubts that, but glory is too much his god. He thought the way lay open to capture Milaness and Naples, incurable madness of French kings. Hé Dieu! he almost did it. He shouted in the midst of the battle at Pavia: 'Now at last I can call myself Duke of Milan!'"

"The cup and the lip," sighed the doctor.

"True. Bourbon had a whole new army. Germans, Savoyards and Spaniards. In a few short hours our King was not Duke of Milan. He was captive of Charles V, taken by one of Bourbon's own men. He got free of Charles' dungeon about the time you left Montpellier, when you were in the very midst of the plague."

"That was one of the few pieces of news that penetrated to me," Nostradamus said, "that of the King's return to France after two years' captivity. The thought of it made even the sick feel cheerful. But to me 'twas tempered by the sadness of his two small sons having to take their father's place as hostages to Spain. Even though the Spaniards treat them not unkindly, they are too young to be taken from their home. The Spaniards are a dour, stern people, of rigid custom. Who knows what mark such enforced residence will leave upon the tender youth of the future King of France?"

One of those little boys, the younger, grew up to be Henry II, the King of France who honored the prophet Nostradamus. The sympathy and understanding with which the prophet won the friendship of the monarch had its roots in the pity he had always felt for Henry's forlorn childhood. The cold reserve, the almost shy quality of Henry's matured personality, has been attributed to the influence of those early prisoning years in Spain.

"I need not, I suppose, bring you up-to-date as to the sack of Rome by Bourbon's men," de Condoulet said. "All the world knows of that."

"Yes, horrible. I can only surmise that after enduring so much, the Duc fell into a madness."

"Not at all. He was stuck in Italy with a great army, and no gold to pay them. The Emperor promised, but he didn't send it. He, like the others, was afraid of the Duc. He wanted to use him, but keep him poor. Bourbon wouldn't have it. The Emperor had himself just held the Pope up for a mighty sum. There was more where that came from, Bourbon thought."

"He met the fate such an impious act deserved."

"Maybe. 'Tis said that from boyhood he had the prescience of an early death. Before the battle, he told his officers that he had consulted an astrologer who told him that if he went to Rome he would surely die there."

"Why is it people never take the advice of those they consult?" Nostradamus asked reflectively.

"Because they don't like the advice," his friend answered. "Almost the last words of the Duc were that he cared but little for dying there, if but his corpse be left with endless glory throughout the world."

"Ah, glory--tragic mirage."

"And he didn't die in glory. He died of a shot from the arquebus of a common brawler. But perhaps not so common, since he is a metal worker to whom I hear both the King and His Holiness give commissions. A man named Cellini."

"And now, after all that treachery, we have a Spaniard for our queen, the Emperor's sister."

"Power politics," de Condoulet shrugged. "But that too was a cruel jest on Bourbon. She was his affianced, and King Francis took her away from him while he was in jail. Ye God, but our King is ever a great one with women. Another glass of this heartening wine, mon ami."

"No more. The hour grows late."

"What of it? And speaking of women, there are pretty girls in Salon, well dowered too. Let me find a wife for you who will keep you with us always in this town."

"Your wish is dear to me, my friend. Perhaps, some day--I like this town, and the country hereabout is pleasing. Perhaps I shall come back to you. Now, the road still beckons. But my thoughts are lingering on all that you have told me. The House of Bourbon is puissant and able. The Duc is dead, but the Bourbons still remember. A Bourbon may yet one day displace a Valois."

"I never saw such a man for always thinking toward the future. Come, come, you shall take one more glass." And the friends drank a final toast.

It was some time later that Doctor de Nostradame received a call that took him travelling to the haunts of his first school-days, Avignon. The papal legate there, Cardinal de Claremont, had been ill and wished the services of the rising star of medicine. Many were the welcomes and congratulations which greeted the doctor's return to this town where he was so well remembered as a boyhood prodigy.

The prelate gave him his blessing, and brightened up at his visit, as did most of his patients.

"It seems only yesterday," Cardinal de Claremont told him, "that I was hearing tales of how you talked about the stars like an old astronomer. But alas, it is more than yesterday, and my old bones tell me so. Each year I feel the cold of the mistral more. I hope you are not going to bleed me."

"I wouldn't think of it," the doctor replied. "There is altogether too much of that, and purging too. I am going to give you a strengthening remedy in which I have great confidence."

"Good," the legate relaxed with a relieved sigh. "We hear great things of what you can do. Certainly next to the salvation of souls comes the saving of their earthly tenements. I think mine is in considerable need of repair."

"Perhaps. But surely the ivy of Christ's spirit grows ever greener on its walls."

"I would like to think so, especially in these troubled times. Draw your chair nearer to my bedside that we may talk the better. I want to hear something of your experience."

It was inevitable that in the course of the conversation the subject of the Lutheran heresy should come up. The frightening gains of "the religion," as it was called, were agitating the minds of all Catholic churchmen.

"That renegade monk, that Martin Luther, is at the bottom of every piece of trouble that afflicts the world," the legate railed, propping himself up straighter on his pillows. "Reform, Luther calls it. May the Holy Son of God preserve us from such evil kind."

"And does not Your Grace think that the disturbed state of politics and warring sovereigns play overwell into the hands of Luther?" the doctor asked.

"Of course they do. When rulers lose all godliness in pursuit of power, shall ignorant common people do less than follow them!"

"That is what I mean. Take the sack of Rome, the most grievous horror the Church has faced since the Caesars. The army of assault was made up of German Lutherans, I am told. But they were led by our French Duc de Bourbon, of the Roman faith, who commanded for the Holy Roman Emperor Charles. That is what shocks me so deeply. That men sworn to uphold the Church--"

"Kings and princes are putting lust for power before the love of God," the prelate broke in. "Power politics cares not with what bedfellow it couches, let it be Christian, heretic or Moslem infidel."

"It is that very thing which makes me question the sincerity of these Lutherans. Numbers are no doubt sincere though deluded. But most of them seem as willing to fight under a Catholic banner, if it suits their ambition, as are Catholic kings to employ them."

"Ay. You put your finger on it. Those of the religion are already making their bid for power. It is the kingdoms of earth they want, and already they are tools for leaders of unscrupulous ambition. Proof of this lies in the fact that if the Church had its faults it has gone a long way to cleanse them, but still the Protestants will have none of it."

"Has His Holiness recovered from the dreadful experience of the siege?"

"You don't recover from a shock like that," the legate said feelingly. "He is as well as may be. Know you that George Freundsberg, Bourbon's Protestant general, had got himself made a great gold chain--and I quote--'to hang and strangle the Pope with his own hand, because since the Pope called himself premier in Christendom, he must be deferred to somewhat more than others.'"

The sack of Rome by the Lutheran landesknechten of Bourbon had occurred some two years previously, during the plague. It still holds a record in military savagery unequalled except perhaps by Hitler at Warsaw. The Catholic world had not yet recovered from the horror of this crime against their holy city. The troops, while en route to the assault on Rome, had stopped briefly before Florence where, in the quiet of the Dominican Nunnery, a little nine-year-old girl had heard and trembled at the thunder of their passing. Later she had listened to the nuns tell of the massacre, the looting, rape and burning of Rome. She heard of the terror that drove her own uncle, Pope Clement VII, narrowly escaping death, to barricade himself in the old Castel San Angelo. The little girl was Catherine de' Medici. In a few short years she would be Queen of France. Another span of years would see her also queen of Saint Bartholomew's.

"And yet," marveled the doctor, "men call the Emperor, under whose banner this took place, devout."

"Devout he is," the prelate said bitterly. "Asked his confessor if it was a sin for him to take any thought to his personal life. But his very title of Holy Roman Emperor is in my opinion a trouble breeder when borne by a temporal ruler. The Church is the only Holy Empire."

"Temporal power lasts not long in any man's hands," the physician observed thoughtfully, "but the Church endures. It is the rock. The spread of heresy is a cankerous growth of another sort, far more serious. How menacing are its proportions, thinks Your Grace?"

"Look how its forest fire has swept all Germany! The sparks are falling now on France. If this fire be not extinguished and quickly, by any means, our country may be next. The intellectuals, the very men who should know better, are taking it up, spreading false doctrine with the aid of the printing-press, which I sometimes think was an invention of the Devil. The king is vacillating. He will adopt no strong policy of extermination of the heretics. Their impudence is even shielded by the King's own sister, Marguerite, a royal daughter of France."

"Strange that there should be so many converts among people strictly trained in the true faith."

"It is all this new freedom that they are demanding. Nobody is willing to submit to authority any more, not even to the discipline of God's Church. They must be free to think for themselves, whether they have any brains to think with or not. They must be free to act as they please, and free to spend their money instead of giving the Church her righteous tithes."

"It sounds as if it were the worst danger since the Great Schism."

"It is more serious." The legate sat upright in his zeal. "Then, at least, there was no argument over the right of the papacy to exist. Luther, if he dared, would deny us even that."

"The seal of Divine authority received from the hand of Saint Peter--Luther has not that."

"True, and the Church will fight to keep that authority. With fire and sword, faggot and rack, the Church will struggle with Satan's armies. 'Blow ye the trumpet in Zion, and sound an alarm in my holy mountain.'"

"But," argued the doctor gently, "is not the special glory of the Church those early martyrs who did not fight back? Was it not the blood of martyrs which made the perpetuation of the Church secure?"

The churchman regarded him frowningly. "That was different. The Christians had not then come into their power. Had a Christian sat where Nero sat, then had Nero been lion's meat as he should have been."

The Church of France drew its descent from prelates who wielded their broadswords beside Charlemagne, and from the embattled bishops who aided Hugh Capet. Sword-clanging lines of Archbishop Turpin in the Chanson de Roland flashed across the doctor's memory:

> The good archbishop could not brook
> On pagan such as he to look.
> You pagan, so it seems to me
> A grievous heretic must be.
> 'Twere best to slay him, though I died.
> Cowards I never could abide.

"This time," the cardinal continued, "the Church has the power to fight, and she will use it to the extermination of the last heretic."

"'Ha, bravely struck!' the Frenchmen yell, 'Our Bishop guards the Cross right well.'"

"You will be giving Luther the martyrs," Doctor de Nostradame told the churchman shrewdly.

"Not all of them I fear," the cardinal answered grimly. This young man was a bit too free-spoken. Cardinal de Claremont opened his mouth to rebuke him. Then he bethought himself of his rheumatic bones, and how much he hoped for from the ministrations of the doctor. Curbing his speech, he pursed his lips and sat glumly silent.

Doctor de Nostradame made his patient comfortable and left with him a tincture and directions for its use. Promising to look in again shortly, he took his leave, his mind full of the cardinal's conversation.

Power! He was beginning to get the picture. They were all playing the same game, inside the Church and outside. He could see that. Still it had to be admitted that right was on the side of King and Church who held their offices from God. Doctor de Nostradame's religion and politics were mediaeval to the marrow, and he had no more tolerance for a heretic than had Archbishop Turpin. His quatrains on the deaths of Coligny and Condé show that. But he was essentially a man of peace, and his life was dedicated to the saving of life. He saw with horror the gentle name of Christ become a trumpet call to violence. And he was too much the mystic not to realize that the true function of the Church must lie in keeping the open road to the house not built by hands. This could not be done in an enlightened age by choking that road with the slain, tortured bodies of victims, heretics though they were. Better a thousand times that the Church should suffer fresh martyrdom than confer that crown upon its enemies.

Yet he could see and sympathize with the point of view of the Church--his church. The pattern of Christianity, he reflected, had been a violent one. The forcible conversion of Europe's hordes, the Crusades with their religious orders militant, the constant persecution of Jews, all these had made it natural for the Church to turn in its new hour of peril to the violent methods which had served her so well for so long.

He could appreciate, too, how the Church felt about the uninhibited spread of the new learning. Even while he himself reached eagerly for the long-lost treasures of ancient culture, reclaimed by the printing-press, though he thrilled to the beauty and mirage of the budding knowledge which promised to every man the kingdoms of the intellect, he was alive to its dangers. The influx and spread of knowledge would bring a glory, but already he could perceive how it might also breed a slow madness and frost of disillusion in men's minds. And what would the stake and the rack breed? For the competition of these with the new freedom grew daily more claimant for fresh victims. What tragedies might not all this be setting in train for the unsullied future? Where on the time-road would it end?

Nostradamus later lamented:

X-66
Oh great Rome thy ruin approaches,
Not of thy walls but of thy blood and substance,
The printed word will work terrible havoc,
The point of the dagger will be driven home to the hilt.

Near the time of these two conversations, occurred another which interested the doctor even more because it concerned the East, of which he knew little. This came as the result of a call to attend a celebrated patient, which gave him a boyish thrill of anticipation. It would be, he told himself, like meeting a hero out of an old romaunt.

The dying flame of chivalry was fast being smothered under ideas of the new order. But there were two brilliant sparks, the last, which lighted its final ashes, two soldiers whom history recalls as the last knight and the last Crusader. The former, Chevalier Bayard, the parfait, gentil knight, was gone, struck down not by a noble lance or sword, but killed by a shot, a modern insult, while commanding Francis' troops against the Constable de Bourbon. Nostradamus had never known Bayard, except by reputation, but he had mourned with all France at the news of his passing. Only in written romances would his like be met again.

But that other valiant soldier, the Crusader, still lived and fought for the glory of God and France. He it was, the famous, colorful Villiers de L'Isle Adam, who needed the services of Doctor Nostradamus. His name had recently rung through Christendom as the hero of the siege of Rhodes, the last important outpost of all that the Crusaders had won for Europe. The sword of Villiers de L'Isle Adam, some three centuries later, was given by Napoleon to Czar Alexander. After the Emperor had returned to Paris from the session on the raft at Tilsit, he sent the ancient steel as his imperial compliment to the ruler of Russia in token that the Czar, as defender of Christianity against the Turks, was worthy of it.

William Stearns Davis, in his History of the Near East, calls Adam and his soldiers at Rhodes, "a little band of military monks clinging to a ruined cliff," and tells how that little band fought off twenty assaults by the army of Solyman the Great, and killed a hundred thousand of the flower of the Turkish Army in one of the greatest defenses recorded in history. Of course Rhodes fell to the Sultan in the end, for Solyman's resources were unlimited, and no single galley went from Christendom to help Adam.

The Grand Commander of Rhodes and his fighting monks, for all their courage, appear to have been virtually pirates. At Rhodes they had lived by forays against the Moslem coast, and done themselves so well that the Turks put up loud squawks to Solyman. The Sultan needed the island, anyway, to complete his defenses and further threaten the Western Mediterranean. Solyman, though not a Christian, was something of a parfait, gentil knight himself. When Rhodes fell to him, he permitted Adam and his remnant of men to withdraw with honor. More, he expressed his regret at dislodging such brave men from the island they had for so long called their home.

The Western world, feeling perhaps a little conscience stricken, gave to the returning hero and his order the island of Malta as a permanent home. This was, however, with the understanding that he would earn his board and keep by helping the powers resist the serious encroachments of pirates preying on their shipping.

It was on one of Commander Adam's visits to the mainland of France that he heard of the new medical celebrity and requested his services.

The doctor saw, when he made his call, a powerful man, of the old

Burgundian type, grizzled, darkened, and weathered like oaken timber exposed to many suns and seas. His eyes, cold and keen as a blade, were brushed unfathomably with a brooding quality which only long association with the East can give.

"The old wounds ache me, Doctor," the old soldier said. "Days when the wind blows damply with mist, the scars of Solyman's scimitars plague me like fresh wounds."

"That can be helped, though I fear not cured," was the reply. "You have been too hard a taskmaster to your body these many years."

"Do your best. I hear great things of you, sir. By Saint John, my patron, I never envied Solyman his soldiers. 'Twas the other way round. But many's the time I envied him his physicians. The infidels have rare skill in medicine, especially in the poulticing and healing of wounds."

"So my grandfathers held, and taught me something of Eastern methods, which, as I am about to use them in your behalf, may seem familiar. But first, an examination."

The doctor's eye, straying momentarily from his skillful, probing hands, lighted upon the lean, wicked length of an extraordinarily long sword that lay upon the near walnut table. It was the type known technically as bastard, from its unusual proportions.

"Is that, Sir Knight, the sword to which, in your hands, Christendom owes so much?"

"Right, Sir Medic, that is my trusty Durandal. Perhaps it has not drunk the blood of as many paynim as did the sword of Roland, but it has not gone thirsty."

"Well I know. I wish, sir, that you would tell me something of the Turks, if you would be so kind as to enlighten my ignorance. What of menace do you think the Turks hold for western Europe?"

"In Solyman they have an abler leader than Christian Europe can boast," the Commander said. "And he has at his beck numbers enough to overflow the continent. Numbers, that was what did for me. And mark you, though Holy Writ may say that the battle is not always to the strong, if the disproportion is enough, any fighting-man knows that numbers do win."

"But surely Europe has men enough for that." "The trouble is Europe can't, or won't, pull together. And Solyman is banking on it. Look what has just happened in these last few years. The Holy Roman Emperor, Charles, takes captive The Most Christian King Francis, and fights Christ's Vicar, the Pope, at the same time. The Most Christian Francis then writes post haste to infidel Solyman to protect him against Holy Charles. Solyman, whose ancestors were skewered by mine before the walls of Jerusalem, writes back that the petition of The Most Christian King has reached the foot of his, Solyman's, throne! And so Frenchmen put up with the humiliation of being protected by the infidel Sultan of Turkey against other Christians."

Nostradamus, as he worked with bandages, hummed to himself:

"'Blow, Roland, blow, That Charles and all his hosts may know!'"

"And don't think that the Turk hasn't a proper sense of humor," the Commander continued. "He has laughs a-plenty out of the Christians and he will have more. His pirates have almost ruined commerce in the Mediterranean, and he may defeat the navy of Venice before he is through.

What sort of madness is it that grips Europe so that it does not see what lies ahead of its peoples?"

"The common people know naught of it," the doctor told him. "They have no way to learn, and needs must trust the guidance of their leaders. But surely heads of state should know if there is really peril?"

"The Turk," said Adam emphatically, "waits until the Christian armies are weakened with slaughtering each other. Then he will attack with all his forces. Europe does not know the Camel of the East, but I have lived beside him long as friend, and fought him as foe. I do know him. Beyond him lie the elephantine hordes of Asia, and there is Africa, which sleeps now, but may some day wake to our sorrow. The one thing that can save Europe is to stop this insane strife, and unite against the common foe. You would think the Pope, as head of Christendom, would be working for this, but he is no better than the rest."

"How soon do you think the Turks will try their hand at conquering Europe?" Nostradamus asked.

"I don't know," the soldier said thoughtfully. "But I would say that there will be a showdown in the next twenty-five years or so. Solyman is still consolidating his gains in his own waters. The East has patience and endless time. They will wait for opportunity to favor them."

"But are not the Turks poor fighters? Judging from the toll you took of them, I would suppose so?"

"No, they are fierce and excellent fighters, though their military science is not yet so good as ours. As for courage, the Moslems rush to welcome death in battle, and why not with their infidel beliefs? Eighty houris, with their keep and jewels guaranteed by Allah, reward each Moslem warrior who falls in battle. 'Tis enough to tempt a Christian, if he could depend on Allah's promises."

"That is all more disturbing than I dreamed of," the doctor told him.

"You cannot shave the Turk so fine but what his beard will grow again," the warrior pronounced. "The West cannot hold the East in final check. Ay, if it takes a thousand years there will come a day--a day of victory for them."

The faultless memory of Doctor de Nostradame registered for the future every detail and impression gleaned from this dynamically interesting, completely informed patient. Later, his vision searching the hinterlands of time for Moslem ambitions, he wrote many prophecies concerning them. A number of these have been brilliantly fulfilled. Not yet has history recorded this one.

II-29
The Oriental will go out from his stronghold,
He will cross the Apennines to look on Gaul,
He will sweep through the sky, across seas and over cloudy summits,
His power will smite the countries along his way.

Garlands of Fame

DOCTOR NOSTRADAMUS--he had long since adopted the Latin style of name as did most scholars--continued to enjoy the variety of scenes and personalities that made his days a panorama of interest. He felt no inclination to settle down, and prosperity filled his velvet pouch with an agreeable number of gold pieces for his needs and plans. But the bright cornucopia of fortune was not yet emptied of its gifts to him. A letter, delightful as a laurel chaplet, again brought change into his life. Julius Caesar Scaliger, than whom France boasted no more distinguished savant and man of letters, had heard of the marvels of the young doctor, and he had been captivated by reports of the originality and power of his work. He wanted to know him. He wrote to him flatteringly and charmingly that he hoped this might come to pass. Doctor Nostradamus replied at once with such modesty and wit, it is said, that the great man felt in him already a friend. Again Scaliger wrote, this time an invitation to Nostradamus to visit him at his home in Agen. We may imagine with what unaffected eagerness the youthful doctor took his quill in hand to send his acceptance. Here was a man he truly longed to know. A great philosopher with the towering mind of the ancients, a man of medicine, too, learned in botany, and to round out perfection, a poet, an authority and writer on the arts. What inspiration, what rapture of sweet converse would not this visit mean!

Scaliger was one of the most colorful men of letters in the French Renaissance. He appears to have been a mixture of authentic, versatile genius and showmanship, with a dramatic background which his enemies claimed was the invention of his fertile imagination. Be that as it may, he had put himself over in a large way. In his late forties at the time of his writing to Nostradamus, his reputation had reached so great a height that it was unsurpassed in France.

Scaliger's story, as told by himself, was that he was born at the Castle La Rocca on Lake Garda, and that he was fairly near kin of the Emperor Maximilian. A page at the age of twelve, he had fought, so he said, as soldier and captain in the service of the Emperor for seventeen years. During that time, between wars, he had been a pupil of Albrecht Dürer. At the battle of Ravenna, in 1512, his father and brother had both been killed. He had himself performed such prodigies of valor in the mêlée that the Emperor had conferred upon him the highest honors of chivalry. But unfortunately and ungratefully the Emperor had given him no money. Injuries received in the war and the onset of gout had put an end to his military career. He had then decided to turn his talents to medicine. He had the friendship and interest of the prominent della Rovere family and became their guest during five years which were necessary to take his degree from the University of Bologna. After some years more in Italy spent in medical practice, research and writing, he had gone to France as physician to Bishop della Rovere, who had received the bishopric of Agen.

Scaliger's detractors said that he was the son of a Verona school teacher, that he had got his M.D. at the less important University of Padua, and that the rest of his story was a tissue of lies. Such stories may have sprung from jealousy of the della Rovere patronage. Competition for wealthy patrons was bitterly keen in the sixteenth century. A Maecenas was a practical necessity to a scholar without independent means. Those who were lucky in this respect were natural targets for the envy, malice and undercutting of the less fortunate. It would seem probable that the della Rovere family, knowing Scaliger for so long, would have discovered the chinks, if any, in his armor. The lies were less likely Scaliger's than his enemies. With his own abilities, and the della Rovere backing as a springboard, Scaliger had risen quickly to fame through his critical writings and scientific accomplishments, and in both of these fields he made distinguished contributions.

Doctor Nostradamus traveled in leisurely fashion to Agen. He stopped off at Toulouse where he had many friends from the plague years, when his work had covered all this territory. There were patients now who wished to consult him again, and festivities planned in his honor. While there he established headquarters in an old Romanesque house said to have had architectural ornamentation of most curious symbols. Succeeding generations pointed it out with pride to visitors as the place where the celebrated Nostradamus once lived for a time in their midst. It was standing until the time of the Revolution.

After a stay of some weeks in Toulouse, the doctor fared forth to complete his journey. The road was brisk with travel in the prosperous exchange of trade between Toulouse and Agen. Had he approached from the Bordeaux side he would have noted the same thing, for Agen, midway between these two cities, was a center for their commerce. It is in the heart of rich agricultural country, and as the doctor neared it, he admired the fine fertile fields so orderly with the produce of the sower's hand. Around the farmhouses ancient trees bent their verdure, and blossoms wove a mille-fleurs tapestry upon the earth. He could understand how the Italian-born Scaliger, now a citizen of France, could settle contentedly in this simple, radiant countryside.

Soon he saw the spire of Saint Etienne's Cathedral against the sky and the Romance Tower of the church Saint Caprasius, and knew that his destination was near. When he halted his mule at the entrance of Scaliger's residence, a servant came quickly to assist him and a moment later his host appeared, moving with slow dignity, limping a little.

"My friend, my friend!" he cried joyously. "Welcome, young Galen, how I have looked forward to your coming!"

The elaborate exchange of compliments in those days partook almost of a Chinese ritual, and each must show the other that he was versed in the art. Nostradamus bowed to the great man, as he grasped his hand.

"O Micaenus edite regibus," he smilingly addressed his host, "the honor of this meeting--"

"Talk not of that," Scaliger broke in. "We shall have more exciting topics for our discourse. You must be tired too with so long riding." He drew his guest into a delightfully furnished interior alive with a sense of art and good taste.

"First, you will want to freshen up," he continued. "So I shall forbear all conversation until I have fulfilled my duty as host. I will show you to your room, and when you return there will be wine to pledge your coming."

"Thank you," returned the doctor. "But might I have a cup of water? When one has come to the Pierian Spring, you know, such a rite is fitting. And I will admit I am thirsty too."

In a trice the servant had brought a tray with a pewter pitcher of cool spring water, and a ruby goblet of Venice glass. The doctor held it up admiringly.

"You do not woo the Muses," he laughed. "You bribe them with such beauty."

"May they grant you their favors," said Scaliger. "The glass is one of a set, a gift from the Bishop della Rovere, who by the way has been as impatient to meet you as I."

And shortly there was the promised wine, and gay pledges from each to the other. Soon there was the sight and laughter of Scaliger's romping youngsters. And there was Madame Scaliger with more greetings. Doctor Nostradamus felt quickly and joyously at home.

"We shall sup al fresco," Scaliger said. "I always like to when the weather is fine."

Over the simple, delicious food they talked, and the doctor had a leisurely opportunity to study his hosts. Scaliger was a very handsome man whose vigor and magnetism made him appear much younger than his fifty years. His head was leonine, antique Roman, with broad primitive cheekbones and ridged brows. His deep-set eyes expressed every mood. They could sparkle with enthusiasm, flash red with anger and smoulder sullenly beneath his high philosopher's forehead. His rich full beard was handsomely shaped and curled. His scholar's robe was of fine material draped in classic folds. The doctor did not wonder that the young and charming Madame Scaliger so patently adored this man, though more than thirty years his junior. It was in fact one of the happiest marriages in France. He had been forty-five and she sixteen when they married. She bore him fifteen children, and the cloudless serenity of their love for each other was unmarred and lasting until his death, which did not occur until more than a quarter of a century beyond this dinner.

Roses strewn upon the board and twining the wine-cups increased the doctor's illusion that he was the guest of some imperial Roman. He said so.

Scaliger laughed. "I have been trying to wield my pen like a sword in defense of Cicero. You shall hear what I have written and give me your opinion. I call him imperator of oratory. Would that I had the gift of Cicero for Cicero's defense. I mean to show up in all its rank pretense the ignorance of this fellow Erasmus. He is making such a loud noise with his bad translations and worse philosophy that fools are following him. But I shall expose him."

"Is there controversy about Cicero?" asked the doctor. "I had not heard."

"The controversy is a general one of literary criteria. Aristotle is, of course, the supreme criterion, perfection in every word. And I shall prove it. I intend to give to the world as my monument a canon by which men can test the worth of their own and others' writings. I, Doctor Nostradamus, shall do for letters what Guillaume Rondelet has done for anatomy."

"Dissector of Literature!" the doctor's eyes glowed. "It has never been done. I can see the need for it, too. With everyone rushing into print, and the tremendous increase of translations, some of which must be very bad. Yes, it is a wonderful idea, and you of all men are fitted by your taste and learning for the work."

"There is no question of that," Scaliger agreed. "There is, in fact, no one else at all."

The doctor winced slightly. It was his first intimation of what Frederick Morgan Paddleford has called Scaliger's necessity for maintaining the delusion of his own omniscience.

Madame Scaliger, sensitive to each slightest reaction toward her husband, spoke.

"Is not the last light lovely, Doctor Nostradamus? I think it is the most beautiful of the day." She rose. "Do you wish to linger, Jules? I am going in."

Scaliger looked at her fondly. "We shall stay a while. Until the dew begins to fall."

Her graceful walk, as she left them, the doctor thought, was like a breeze-swept flower in the pale light. He remembered Tronc de Condoulet's advice to him. Perhaps de Condoulet was right. If he could be sure of finding a happiness like this--

Scaliger was talking again, as the flowing branches of the trees darkened to black olive in the retreating light. It was the mystical hour when day is a ghost haunting the woodland.

The doctor spoke suddenly. "I have the oddest impression about what you have just said--your anatomy of letters. I cannot speak from conviction since I have not read your opinions on this subject and know only what you have told me tonight. It is instead a

kind of knowing that I feel." He paused in hesitant silence.

"But what is that you feel?"

"I feel something very distinguished about it that is partly in itself and partly in those whom it will touch. An influence. I hardly know, but my mind is making pictures of foreign countries, men with books, with writings of their own, and you are somehow there too."

The dusk hid the pleasure in the philosopher's face, but the doctor knew it was there.

"You are very flattering," Scaliger murmured.

"No. That is the odd part. It is something more."

Shakespeare, Ben Jonson, whom Paddleford considers singularly akin in mind to Scaliger, Corneille, the writers of the later Italian Renaissance, and many another writer and genius were to heir and benefit from this work of Julius Caesar Scaliger, surgeon of letters. Today its principles are as sound, its reasoning as clear and incisive as when its author wrote. Many a book on the modern market telling aspiring authors how to write but retells in the fashion of its own day the practical wisdom of this sixteenth-century analyst of letters.

This was the first of many talks, glowing with interest for the two men. The doctor must tell all about how he fought the plague, his theories and ideas. In the early mornings and at sundown they walked in Scaliger's garden, where his wife claimed her roses were crowded by her husband's plantings for his botanical study.

"This is good botanical country," Scaliger told Nostradamus. "Anything will grow here. That is why I like it." He stopped beside a small, charmingly sculptured marble of Pan perched on a pedestal, piping away. "Everything that we are or do arises out of earth. Under my trees I feel the reality of Pan come back, and I ask no more than that my thoughts play Echo to his tunes."

The doctor was unconscious that he spoke out loud, as he said, "The earth is the Lord's and the fullness thereof."

The philosopher's lips quirked. "You sound like the Archbishop."

The doctor flushed and stood his ground. "I only meant that in the discovery, revelation I call it, of fresh knowledge, or in the inspiration of poetry you cannot leave that out. It is the danger of the new classic revival that it may do so. When that happens a thread is cut. Power and the road are lost."

Scaliger, who had ever to have the last word, said dryly, "Rome and Athens seem to hold their immortality."

Nostradamus tactfully turned the conversation back to medicine. He had already learned that his distinguished host and senior ill brooked a difference of opinion.

"You do not agree with Rondelet that intensive study of the properties of plants is what is now needed most?" he asked.

"No. That is all right for the practicer of medicine who must use these properties in his laboratory. But the scientist who makes discoveries for him will never widen the field that way. A pepper is hot and stimulating. It belongs, they say to Mars. I will not argue, I have disputed with Mars on too many fields of battle and come off the worse. He can have his pepper. What I want to do is to show the likeness and difference which a plant has to its fellows. Grouping and classifying them in this way we become acquainted with the structure of plant life, we begin to see the why of things."

"A wonderful purpose. It would give a completely related field forever broadening."

"That," said Scaliger, "is to be the yield this garden makes to science. A flower of knowledge fairer than a rose."

Scaliger was the first who demonstrated the necessity for abandoning the classification of plants based on their properties. and based it on their distinctive characteristics.

The news of Doctor Nostradamus' arrival in Agen had spread quickly through the town. At once a stream of callers came to pay their respects. And very prominent among these were fathers and mothers with marriageable daughters, for it was known that this famous young man was a bachelor. Invitations to fêtes and parties poured in. Scaliger, who had the Latin's love for hospitality and gayety, was eager to show off his guest, though he protested that it was not so.

"The women," he said on the evening that he and the doctor supped with the Bishop of Agen, "are wasting our time with their picnics and dances. I protest that I begrudge so much. I had planned that the doctor and I should sit beneath my green arbutus tree and hold high converse, and I must now struggle to see him at all."

The Bishop's eyes twinkled. "If I remember my Horace," he said, "that arbute tree was planned as shade for Lalage."

His guests laughed, and Scaliger cried, "Then we must find a Lalage for Nostradamus, that we may keep him settled in our midst."

The Bishop lifted his glass. "No fairer girls than the girls of Agen, eh, Scaliger. I pledge their beauty in this wine."

This desire to possess Nostradamus, to annex him to every town where he tarried, was flatteringly illustrated next day. A formal deputation of town fathers came to Scaliger's house with a proposition which would be worthy of the imagination of a modern chamber of commerce. They desired to make some kind of financial settlement on their two valuable celebrities, in return for which they said the two should agree to make Agen their permanent home. It was a smart idea, if it had worked. Both men were supreme drawing-cards. With such a double-bill attraction, Agen would have become a Mecca for all France. The town fathers would have got back their gold many times over, with fame and increase for their town.

The two doctors listened in silence, somewhat stunned. It was the visitor who spoke first.

"Has the city of Agen no poor?" Nostradamus asked the councilors. "Are there none who are ill, old, infirm, needing your help and support, that you offer gold to us? We can support ourselves, we are strong, able men. Give this money to the unfortunate, we do not want it."

Scaliger gave his great laugh. "Don't you know scholars and artists better than that?" He scoffed at the councillors. "Why, half our travels and half our lives are spent in the country of the mind. Let the gold go to those whom it will help, the hungry, the homeless, the sick."

The councillors were overwhelmed by this unexpected reaction. Practical men of affairs, they did not know whether to be disappointed that their idea had not worked, or to glory in the idealism which seemed to them to lift their idols to new heights of splendor. When in doubt, southern France always solved a problem with a festival. The town fathers departed to tell everyone of the scholars' refusal of their offer and the generous motives prompting it. Immediately a gala procession was organized in honor of the doctors. The town was wild with enthusiasm. They wreathed the brows of Scaliger and Nostradamus with chaplets, and carried the distinguished men aloft through flower-strewn streets to the accompaniment of music, dancing and cheering. It was the high point in the friendship of these two remarkable men.

It soon became apparent to Nostradamus that Scaliger had invited him to Agen in the hope of making him a brilliant satellite to his own glory. Scaliger had no desire nor intention to share that with any man. He was annoyed at the storm of popularity which the younger man attracted, and at every manifestation of it he found it harder not to show his jealousy. Nostradamus could not but notice Scaliger's resentment. He was hurt by his host's unprovoked sarcasm and attempts to take him down. All his tact seemed powerless to change this and he grieved the more because he so genuinely reverenced the older man's gifts. He was having a splendid time in Agen, he didn't want to leave. It would be difficult to withdraw from Scaliger's home and still remain in the town without hard feelings. He was in a quandary. Then Fate, still watching over her favorite of the moment, solved the situation, with her oldest device. Doctor Nostradamus fell in love.

Mystery, which haunts so consistently the life of Nostradamus, clings, too, about this girl of Agen whom he loved and married. Even her name is not known. One writer has given it as Adriete de Loubebac, but that was the name of Scaliger's wife. Was the demoiselle fair or dark? Was she of noble birth with a goodly dowry? Was she learned? We only know, from Chavigny, that she was "très belle, très aymable," very lovely and very lovable. Garencières says of her that "she was a very honorable gentlewoman." Certainly the doctor could have had his pick of beauty and dowry wherever he went. Girls had pursued him, thrown themselves at his head, and match-making mothers had tried all of their wiles and inducements to lure this eligible parti into the matrimonial net. But he had remained singularly immune to all this, content with his work and studies.

Much as one would like to know something descriptive of the looks and qualities of this girl who captivated the doctor when his friends had consigned him to permanent bachelorhood, all that we can be sure of is that Nostradamus was too much the independent idealist to marry for less than a deep love. With so little one must be content.

When he was married and settled into a home of his own in Agen, the town fathers were delighted. What their gold had not won, a daughter of Agen had brought about; they had now their idol well and permanently anchored in their midst.

Nostradamus at some time chose for his personal motto the serene words of the prior Orvian: "Happy the first age that was contented with its flocks." One would like to know if it was at this time, amid the pastoral setting of his new-found happiness, that he adopted the idyllic expression. Or was it in later years, when, heavy with melancholy of a tragic world, he looked back upon these his cloudless days as on a painted picture?

He also assumed his family coat-of-arms, not, it is said, because he himself cared about it, but as a mark of respect to the memory of his grandfather. The arms are described as showing, in the first and fourth quarterings, gules and two silver crosses arranged to form an eight-spoked wheel. The second and third quarterings exhibited an eagle and sable on gold ground.

While Nostradamus was enjoying his peaceful life in Agen, an event of national interest took place which was to affect deeply, in time, the fate of France, and bring to the doctor honors that would crown his career.

In October of 1533 occurred the marriage of the second son of Francis I, the fourteen-year-old Henry, then Duke of Orleans, to the duchessina of Florence, Catherine de' Medici. The Bishop of Agen had gone to Marseilles, as had a number of other Agenois, to see the arrival of Catherine and her uncle, Clement VII, and the great pomp and splendor of the wedding. Nostradamus accompanied Scaliger to call upon the Bishop della Rovere after his return from the festivities, to hear his account of them.

"This age," the Bishop told them, "has never seen so grand a wedding. Splendor enough to blind Charles of Spain and some others I could mention."

"The duchessina, is she beautiful?" Scaliger wanted to know.

"We-ell, you know how it is at these public weddings. About all you can see clearly is the white robe and the lace veil of the bride."

"You had better tell us what you can about those," said Nostradamus. "We have wives, you know, and that will be the first question--'Did the Bishop tell you what the duchess wore?'"

The Bishop smiled. "'Twas a wondrous robe of gold brocade, so bright that you can both tell your ladies, the lace veil seemed like a jealous cloud above it that would, yet could not, hide the sun. Her jewels were, of course, as countless as the stars."

"Report says the duchess is somewhat plain," Scaliger persisted.

The Bishop eyed him reproachfully.

"If she is a thought less fair than some," he said, "she has a spiritual grace. They say, too, that she has inherited the wit, intelligence and tact of the Medici. Besides, it was a great day for France and the papacy. It will strengthen their bonds against Spain."

"How did His Holiness appear?" questioned Doctor Nostradamus.

"Magnificent. His entry into Marseilles was superb. He has had the best artists in Rome working on plans for it from the moment the betrothal was announced. He came in a Venice galley, gorgeously carved. His ship led all the others and as it neared the harbor I could see him plainly, sitting under a golden tent with a carpet of crimson satin."

"Were many with him?" Scaliger inquired.

"Oh, yes. All the cardinals. The Blessed Sacrament was in an ostensory that took the eye, a triumph of the goldsmith's art. It was carried ahead of His Holiness on a fine white horse when they left the ship. And I was glad to see that they had stout fellows with great bulging muscles to carry the sedia gestatoria with an even walk. It detracts from even a pope's dignity to be joggled, as so often happens, when carried on the shoulders of bearers."

"I suppose the crowds went wild," the doctor observed.

"Three hundred pieces of artillery, all the church bells and the Virgin knows how many throats made them welcome. The people all kneeled while the Sacrament and the Pope were passing, and received the benediction. The streets were strewn with flowers all the way from the ship to the two palaces the king built just for this occasion, one for himself and one for His l Holiness with a covered bridge connecting them, in case of rain, I suppose."

"I paid my taxes the other day," said Nostradamus thoughtfully. "And they had risen."

"People should not grumble about a little taxation," reproved the prelate. "Church and State must have funds for such glorious and necessary occasions." He took up the thread of his description of the wedding, adding more of the sumptuous details.

It was not to be long until the death of the dauphin made Henry and Catherine heirs prospective to the throne of France. Already history was in a train, which, unsuspected by Nostradamus, would draw him within the orbit of the royal pair.

For a time after this, the doctor's friendship with Scaliger recovered, on the surface, its first enthusiasm and cordial warmth. They resumed their long, delightful discourses with the frank enjoyment of men who have much intellectually in common. Scaliger's fame continued steadily to mount, as it did, indeed, as long as he lived. He was worshipped by the littérateurs, and revered by the scientists, even though he made many enemies by his constant and caustic attacks on other men's work. He had no cause for jealousy of the quiet doctor whose sensational reputation had been so unsought, and who never wanted the limelight. But the reputation was there, and Scaliger had only himself to thank for bringing its owner into his home territory. All accounts of

Scaliger dwell on his enormous vanity. He wanted to rule alone as uncrowned king in Agen; now another and younger man shared his throne. Doctor Nostradamus had resumed his practice of medicine, with marriage, and now patients were coming to him from Bordeaux, Carcassonne, Toulouse and the whole radius of the neighboring country. Scaliger hated this, and he also disliked the obvious pleasure which his patron, the Bishop of Agen, took in the society and conversation of the man he, Scaliger, thought of as a dangerous rival.

Intellectual differences, too, made their appearance in the progress of the friendship. The two who had said they thought as one on first acquaintance discovered later that they thought very differently on many matters. One of these was literature. Neither man was an artist, but each man thought he was. Scaliger did have a profoundly critical knowledge of the basic laws of poetry, he understood the technique by which words become the clay and bronze of the poet's sculptured emotions. Nostradamus on the other hand loved a lilting rhyme that raced with a story of derring-do and high nobility, or held a philosophic thought. He admired, and later used, to the despair of his translators, the subtleties of the rhétoriqueurs. He did not care for Scaliger's sonnets which Scaliger read to him with huge delight. Man of the world though the physician was, he found them overburdened with sensuality for which there was insufficient compensation of beauty. Few of these sonnets, says Paddleford, have been translated from the Latin in which they were written, partly for this reason, partly for lack of poetic value.

Scaliger was a devoté of Vergil whose writings he held superior to Homer's. Nostradamus, son of the troubadours, was rash enough to say that he thought Homer told a better, faster-moving story about nobler characters.

"That," said Scaliger, "is because you are ignorant of what it is that makes great poetry. When Vergil describes a shipwreck, I am there upon the deck, fighting for my life against the storm. The spray of ocean stings my eyes and salts my lips. Homer had no such art. He did not know the laborious polishing of line and phrase until words became the carving of a living immortality of experience." Doctor Nostradamus still liked Homer best.

Scaliger was a perfectionist. His ideal was the precise word, the studied gesture. His home, his clothes, his writings expressed this with a scientist's thoroughness. He had a certain contempt for the younger man's failure to comprehend the high importance of this chiselled, if cold perfection. Nostradamus, for his part, marveled that a man so learned as Scaliger could not perceive that the universe did not turn on a polished phrase. That perfection, in Scaliger's meaning, was a brittle mask concealing what it was intended to reveal. Nostradamus appears to have absorbed nothing of value from Scaliger's really great power of literary analysis. It is clear, from the writing of the Centuries, that if lines rhymed and had their complement of feet, that to Nostradamus was poetry.

What caused the eventual break between the two men is not known. But their quarrel was deep, bitter and final. Nostradamus had put up with a great deal from Scaliger for a long time. Though naturally diplomatic, Nostradamus' tongue was vitriol when he chose. There probably came a moment when, goaded beyond control by Scaliger's jealousy, he let go and told his one-time friend with daggered words just what he thought of him. Then in a cooler hour, too late, he sadly contemplated their cup of friendship, its wine turned into vinegar, its twining roses dead.

The quarrel with Scaliger was the first intimation that Fortuna, the fickle, no longer smiled upon her favorite, Nostradamus. Outwardly all was serene. The pride and devotion which the town felt for its popular and famous doctor were still at peak. The social life of Agen was delightful with the open-handed hospitality of existence under southern skies. The happy marriage of Nostradamus had brought him further joy in the birth of two sons. And on these babies the parents lavished the affection and hopes of all fathers and mothers. Then, without warning, a knife thrust in the dark, death struck. His wife and two small sons were swept from him by some mysterious stroke of fatal sickness. He, to whose skill and science thousands owed their lives, could not save even one of those most dear to him. The green grass of Agen lay above three graves. Under the skies of careless, sunny blue the doctor stood alone.

Here ended the period of his happy youth. Its doors were barred behind him. Its days could never come again. Friends were of little avail to comfort him in this time of dark despair. Nostradamus was inconsolable. Every bright prospect which Agen had held out to him was blasted. His beautiful friendship with Scaliger--the man whom he had once called "a Vergil in poetry, a Cicero in eloquence, a Galen in medicine"--had gone forever. There is no record that Scaliger sent him so much as a message of sympathy in his sorrow. His family dead, there was no longer any tie to bind Nostradamus to Agen. Sadly the townspeople saw him leave them, for what destination he himself did not know. Again he was footloose, with freedom now all unwanted. Once more he took to the open road.

Nostradamus was now just thirty years old. The next ten years of his life were spent in travel, and concerning this period less is known than of any other part of his life. Yet these were the years that saw the beginning and development of his prophetic power and as such hold a vital interest for students of his life. Though so little information about him is written in the record of these years, there are inferences to be drawn which seem rather more than speculative. And there are certain speculations which the meager facts suggest may be true, but of which we can never be sure.

In the story of most great mysteries there is a journey upon the hard road of loneliness and separation. Sometimes the journey is lifelong, sometimes, as with Nostradamus, it is for a period of years. It is during such experience that the spirit is forced in upon itself through suffering and despair until nourishment, purpose and illumination are discovered in the hidden power of the self. This is the symbolic core of all sacrificial rites, Christian or pagan. The sunny warmth of homely joys and comforts is too contenting. These are the sirens that bind the wanderer, Ulysses, with their song, while on seas of mystery the ship is waiting with taut sails and straining figurehead whose eyes look toward infinity.

Nostradamus still had as his interest and refuge his love of science, his study of medicine. Too restless and unhappy to settle down or to practice, he began to travel about southern France and to study the whole field of pharmacy, medical practice and hospitalization, the last having changed little since the days of the Crusades except in the increased size of the hospitals. He may have had some idea or plan which he thought of some day carrying out, some modern, daring innovation. He kept for a time a journal of his findings, which is no longer in existence. Early commentators tell of it and quote a few facts and names from it. They mention his sharp criticism of the greed of the medical men in Avignon. The pharmacies of Marseilles he found excessively bad in their administration. Here and there he found doctors whose work and sincerity he could praise and others whose stupidity or ethics he condemned. How much time he spent in this way is not known but enough to make himself responsible for a great deal of the bitter enmity from which he suffered later on. The doctors and pharmacies that his caustic, blunt speech branded as cheats or charlatans were furious. They missed no chance to hand it back to him when occasion gave them opportunity. They were active from this time on in accusing Nostradamus of being a spy, an associate of condemned secret societies and himself a charlatan.

For three years he settled down in Dauphiny, associating himself with a doctor of fine reputation, but whether this was for medical practice or research is not stated. But his restlessness was still acute. He gave up this work and went into Italy, where he is known to have remained for a while in Milan, Genoa and Venice.

Nostradamus' practice as a physician was always that of a man of science in the strict sense, so far as is known. He did not confuse medicine with his psychic gift. Except for having the advantage of an extraordinarily brilliant mind, he was otherwise on the same footing, scientifically, as other physicians. He had his successes and he had his failures. It was 'natural that in this period he should be interested in contacting other scientists and getting their point of view, experience, and, if they had it, superior knowledge. That is why, when he had exhausted such contacts in France he turned his steps toward Italy, which had the great tradition in this field. French inspiration in science as well as general culture still drew upon Italy, though slowly emerging to independent progress. No doubt the Italian-born Bishop of Agen and also Scaliger had told Doctor Nostradamus of Italian achievements, which had fired his imagination and given him the desire to go there and see for himself.

Whether news of his own reputation in France had not preceded him, or whether his mood in these years created in him a desire for self-effacement, there are no accounts of his experience in Italy. It would have required considerable and aggressive proof from a Frenchman, at that time, to impress the Italians, anyway. They knew themselves to be the center of progressive learning and culture, and were sceptical toward the development of these qualities elsewhere. Nostradamus would, however, have had full opportunity to study the work being done there. He had, through his own family and important patients, a scientific entrée everywhere. It is said that wherever he went in Italy he sought out and talked with the most learned scholars. The interesting question is, just where did he go besides the few cities mentioned?

Nostradamus' travels in this period covered at least ten years, probably several of these spent in Italy. If he had settled in one city for a lengthy stay, his personality and abilities were so remarkable that almost certainly he would have become spectacular, as he always did, and stories would have gathered about him and some of these would be recorded. He was not a man who could remain unobserved. He had an intensely secretive nature. The Centuries with their subtle concealments are evidence of this. He was a man who gave out little concerning himself, and guarded well the secrets of others. Even after his death, so well had he trained his son, that César was careful to tell nothing that his father would not have approved when living, and added little to what was already known. This secretiveness did not develop in Nostradamus' early life; there was nothing to bring it out. But when he reached the deeply introspective period which began after his wife's death, with it went a perhaps protective concealment which still shrouds much that one would like to know.

He was deeply religious, and if in his first grief he sought surcease in active scientific work and travel, it would not have been long until he turned to the cloistered calm of monastic walls and the deep worship and contemplation which his nature perpetually craved. It is said that near the end of this ten-year period he was to be found at an abbey where the religious observances were of particularly severe character.

He would hardly have spent much time in Italy without going to Rome, the holy city of Europe. Nor would he have been likely to forego a visit to Florence, city of the Medici. He may, however, for reasons of his own have gone incognito to cities and countries other than those the record lists. If he did so, it would have been because he had become associated with the pursuit of secret knowledge which was in danger from the Inquisition.

Italy had long been the center and hotbed of alchemic research. From the East had come a vast heritage of science and philosophy which had never received the sanction of the Church. This knowledge was bootlegged through the means of secret societies. Some of these may have provided the background and inspiration for discoveries that were the noblest fruit of the Renaissance. Some, patterning after these, were degenerate groups which courted the Devil's favor with strange rites. A few even exercised a political influence, as did the far-flung Vehmgericht in Germany, whose ritual was based on old Saxon magical ceremonies that had come down from pagan times.

The true scientists who worked within these secret groups, or alone, were for the most part men of profoundly spiritual nature. But they were unwilling to be bound by the narrow orthodoxy of the current theological dogma. They had a wider vision in which the free intellect had its place and its dignity. The search for the Philosopher's Stone was at once symbol of the chemist's research, which still goes on, and of the transmutation of man's physical nature into the gold of higher forces. Copernicus in these years was hiding his theory of the universe, not daring yet to risk its publication. And many another soaring mind was working in secret with ideas beyond his time. Such men as these would have drawn the interest of Nostradamus, naturally predisposed to knowledge of this kind. Henry James Forman states in The Story of Prophecy that Nostradamus knew and used the law of gravitation and Kepler's law of the ecliptic, though Kepler was not yet born. Whether this is more than legend cannot be said, but it may well have been true. Astronomy had been a lifelong passion with him. He may in these Italian years even have known Copernicus and shared his dream of a grander universe.

Could even Italy with its treasure of enlarging thought and its antique beauties content this man who was a dynamo of restless energy, utterly alone and free to go as he pleased? Loving travel as he did, he could have gone in his quiet way to Greece, to Egypt or anywhere. No one would miss him at departure, no one would be surprised when he appeared again among those who knew him. Who knows? Under what secret influences some of these years may have been passed is a fascinating but unanswered question.

The Plague Returns

NOSTRADAMUS HAS SAID, concerning his psychic gift, that it was inherited. Undoubtedly he had been conscious for a long time that he possessed it, and had used it to divert friends occasionally, as his grandfather had amused him when he was a child. During the period of his wanderings, under the emotional tension of sorrow and loneliness, such a faculty would tend to develop even without encouragement. Occult friends and associations, if such there were, would have given impetus to experiment with this perception, and fresh insight perhaps into the laws under which it manifests.

It is said that the first striking experience of his gift came to him while he was travelling in Lorraine. If this is so, it holds a peculiar interest, because Lorraine was the home of that other great French mystic, Jeanne d'Arc. There are two incidents from his early prophetic experiences which have been handed down and are retold by all writers on Nostradamus. These stories date from the period of his travels though the time of their occurrence is not known. One of these is amusing and bears out the idea that he often used the gift to astonish and delight close friends. Had this ability not been known to them and accepted in that way, his host would hardly have been free to tease the doctor as he tried to do.

Nostradamus was a guest of Lord Florinville at the castle of Faim, where he was attending professionally on Lord Florinville's mother. The doctor and his host were crossing the courtyard where two little pigs, a black one and a white one, were running about as was the casual custom of livestock in those days. Lord Florinville said to the doctor,

"I suppose you can even foretell the fate of those two pigs!"

"Certainly I can," replied the doctor. "We shall eat the black one, and a wolf will eat the white one."

Lord Florinville saw a chance for a good joke on his guest. He privately instructed the cook to roast the white pig for supper. That evening, while they were feasting on succulent young pork, his lordship with huge mirth told Nostradamus that he was eating white pig. This the prophet vigorously denied. The pig, he said, was the black one, as he had foretold. The cook was finally called to settle the argument. "Yes," said the cook fearfully, "the pig was the black." The white one had been killed and prepared as directed. But she had stepped out of the kitchen, before putting the pig in the oven, and a tame wolf had stepped in and was doing himself very well on the pig when the cook returned. Not supposing that it would make any difference, the black one had then been quickly killed and served, exactly as predicted. This episode occurred long before the writing of the prophecies, and certainly indicates that the doctor's uncanny faculty must have been well known to a select number of his friends and patients.

The other incident happened during his stay in Italy. In the neighborhood of Ancona, along the road, Nostradamus passed a group of Franciscan Friars. Among them was a young lad, a country boy, who had but recently left his father's farm to join the order. On seeing him, Nostradamus dismounted from his mule, went up to him and dropped on his knee before him. The astonished monks asked why he did this.

"Because I must kneel before His Holiness," he told them.

They were probably more astonished than ever, and it seems that little attention was paid to such an unlikely forecast. But it was remembered by those present, and told by them when, years after Nostradamus had died, that country boy, Felice Peretti, became Pope Sixtus V. It must be inferred from his homage that Nostradamus did not confuse principle with personality. He knelt to the symbol of his religion and the office of the Holy See, not to the man, Peretti, who became Pope. Nostradamus did not admire Sixtus V. This is what he had to say of him in one of the quatrains.

The Roman clergy in the year 1609
Will hold an election at the beginning of the year.
They will elect one who comes from the country, and wears the black and gray robe,
And never was there one more sly.

The story is that during the election Cardinal Peretti pretended to be a cripple, perhaps to create sympathy or drama. Once assured of success, he threw away his crutches and sang loudly for joy. That may have no foundation. Nostradamus disliked Sixtus for his compromising complacence in dealing with Henry of Navarre, who in the prophet's uncompromising opinion was a turn-coat and a heretic. The prophet had little sympathy with what he thought was the Pope's weakness. In another verse he speaks of Sixtus as being "afraid to take off his shirt at night for fear of its being stolen." Which was a sarcastic reference to the despoiling of the Church at the hands of the Protestants and ambitious rulers.

The year, during Nostradamus' lifetime, began in France with the Spring Equinox. Sixtus V was elevated to the papacy in 1585, and the election was held April 24. If 24 is added to the number of the year it gives 1609, just one of the prophet's little subtleties which make life difficult for his interpreters! It is at least an interesting coincidence, and to those who follow astrology something more, that these three men whose lives were strangely intertwined, Nostradamus, Henry IV, and Sixtus V, all had the same birthday, with the Sun in the second degree of Capricorn. It was to Henry of Navarre that the verses of Nostradamus called Presages and Sixains were presented after the prophet's death. Henry II, the king who summoned Nostradamus to Paris, had the same degree of Capricorn on the zenith of his horoscope.

When the new dimension of time swung wide its strange doors to Nostradamus, giving upon vistas of the future in extraordinary visions, he must have suffered for a time grave concern, even though long accustomed to slighter manifestations. Such a condition would have, even for the strongest nature, a somewhat terrifying aspect. Nostradamus, too, would have pondered its source, its rightness; his conscience as a churchman would have scrutinized it. For this was the era when there was nothing more dreaded than possession by the Devil. He is thought to have spent a long retreat within a severe monastery. Some believe that it was here that he began the writing of the Centuries. It is more likely that he went for the purpose of thoroughly examining his gift within consecrated walls, under a rigid religious routine, and also to take counsel with the Abbot concerning this gift of prophecy. The Church was ever the friend of this prophet; he stood on firm ground with its heads. Although the cry of sorcery was raised madly against him, the Inquisition took no notice of it, and his first Almanachs were dedicated to the Pope. Nostradamus, alert to the dangers of his age, would have made sure of the approval of the Church before he launched himself upon a career as prophet. All the more so because his prophecies were not the usual vague cries of woes to come, but specific information dealing with political destinies.

The Abbot was a very learned man. He would have questioned the physician closely as to whether there were any sorcerous phenomena appearing with the visions. Were there any indications that the Devil was -trying to work through him? Nostradamus thought not. It was the reason that he had come to the Abbey, where its strict ritual was well calculated to discourage any such ideas of the evil one.

"In fact," he told the Abbot, "it is my very love of God, my fasting, my praise of Him and my prayers, which seem to draw the visions closer. Surely, such white and holy light as appears to me then, could come from none but heavenly sources."

"That is so," the Abbot agreed. "The pure, ineffable white flame has ever been a sign of God's favor. 'Tis very well known that the evil one must use the red flames of hell; he has no other kind of light."

"You say," continued the Abbot, "that this peculiar foresight is inherited. To what extent did your grand-sires experience it?"

"Not to the extent that I have. Their gift was more personal, they could foresee matters affecting the family or members of the community. But they foresaw these things less frequently, and never the wide scope of the world which is opening before me."

The prelate eyed him shrewdly. "My son, I will not ask you if you have gone further in efforts to develop this gift than did your grandsires. That is a matter between yourself and the confessional. But I am not unaware that there is much dark knowledge in the world."

"And I swear before Almighty God that never have I broken his Holy law touching such matters. I have done only that which I believed to be right. But if God Himself opens a door in my understanding, shall I defeat His purpose, shall I refuse to enter that door? Is not that the meaning of prophecy?"

"Yes," the Abbot said very thoughtfully, "when it is really prophecy." He touched some closely written sheets of parchment on the table beside him. "These visions you have set down touching the near future of France are depressing. I can hope, my son, that in these matters your foresight will be proved wrong."

"It will not be," said the doctor with conviction, "though I hope it no less fervently than do you."

"Well," the Abbot told him, "you have done wisely to set down the impressions that have come to you. Now we shall keep a check on this record. My advice is that you write them down, but do not show them about. Not yet. Many devout men have prophesied for a day, some have been given the sight here within these walls. Later, they are often proved mistaken in what they saw. Again sometimes, even when they were right, the vision left them as swiftly and mysteriously as it had come. That may happen to you. But if you find that over the stretch of years this knowledge continues to come to you, and that its visions are true, then you may, I think, accept it as a signal token of inspiration. It is odd, though," the Abbot said thoughtfully, "I have served Him on my knees these many years, and never have I had a vision such as nightly comes to you. It passes understanding."

After the prophet had returned to his cell, the Abbot's mind continued to dwell on this peculiar man. A goodly soul, he thought, strange, but genuinely devout. There was a power of some kind that dwelt in him, he could himself sense it, and the doctor had wrought some wondrous cures among the monks. True, his prophecies might, in the long run, not work out. So few did. Still the Abbot believed he was an honest man. He, as a churchman, could not be too careful in dealing with what might be Satan's wiles, but as yet he could see nothing in Doctor Nostradamus meriting the condemnation of the Church.

Something besides this new increase in his power was beginning at this time to make itself felt in the breast of the prophet. He realized suddenly that he was homesick. He was tired of the road. He wanted to settle down in Provence in a place of his own once more, where he could have about him his books and scientific paraphernalia. Where he could meditate and work on the knowledge and experience garnered in these long, weary years. He was now turned forty, time to stop tramping.

The question was, where should he settle? He could not return to Agen with its sadness of memories. The thing to do was to go back to Provence, look about and then decide on a new home. This he did, and no sooner did word of his return get about than it seemed as if every town in that part of the world was begging him to settle there. Friends were active, telling him of just the right house for him, and keeping him busy with kindly advice.

The City of Marseilles thought it would be wonderful if they could get this famous man to live in their midst, and sent a deputation to invite him and offer inducements. He finally decided on the little old town of Salon, because, he told his friends, it was central to Avignon, and to the other cities of Provence, and he would have a radius which would allow him to keep in touch with a wider circle, and see more of his friends than in the other places under consideration. His real reason was probably the smallness of Salon. Just as when he had fought the plague, he had been compelled to go to places that were isolated to carry out his ideas, he knew that in a different way he still faced that necessity. The jealousy and criticism, the constant watchfulness of his colleagues in larger towns would have spelled trouble in short order. In little Salon he hoped to avoid this. Besides, it was a sweet old town, and he wanted peace. Salon was overjoyed, it did its best for him. The old commentators say that "Salon gave him a wife who was well born and wealthy." Her name was Anne Ponsart Jumelle. Whether the lady was a gift from the town's grateful chamber of commerce, or whether the doctor did his own selecting, he did marry again, not long after his return.

Settled down comfortably in a house fronting a narrow street, once more prospects for some durable happiness seemed bright. He resumed his medical practice with all of his old-time popularity. Soon, too, there was the first child, a son, to bind him even more closely to his love of home. Life once more was quiet, normal and carefree.

When their boy was born the parents named him César. One wonders if Nostradamus chose this name in memory of his happy days spent in the company of Julius Caesar Scaliger before their friendship ended. He may have thought that such a compliment might heal the breach when Scaliger heard of it. But there is no record that the haughty ego of Scaliger ever softened toward his one-time friend.

It was the month of May, 1544, when a traveler coming from Aix, passing through Salon, brought the disturbing news that plague had broken out in the capital. Wealthy people were already leaving the city, though it was not known yet whether there would be few cases or an epidemic. This time the pest was the hideous charbon scourge, so called because its victims turned completely black, so that in death they resembled charred logs.

Then new rumors reached Salon that the plague cases were increasing and conditions in Aix were becoming serious. Nostradamus' young wife spoke to her husband in apprehension.

"Michel, is there any danger that you may be called to Aix to fight this scourge?"

"Probably not," he comforted her. "It is a plague which has occurred before. I have never handled a case, but other doctors have treated it and may have found certain remedies efficacious. There are a number of good doctors in Aix who will perhaps be able to arrest the contagion."

Actually he was not so sure. There was no cure for this pestilence known. The only hopeful sign that he could see was that he had not been sent for. That should mean that the pest was lessening, getting under control so that he was not needed. On the other hand it was just possible that he was needed, and badly, but that professional jealousy was keeping him from being called. He knew too well that there were doctors who would for this reason let their patients die rather than call him in, and he was too proud to offer his services unasked.

In Salon, they were wondering about this too. Strange, people said, that if the plague was really bad Aix did not send for the one man in France who had ever been able to cope with it. True, this time it was a different pest, but still a plague was a plague, was it not? And if you could cure one, why not another? Then came the news that the plague was appalling, that people were dying like flies, and still no call came in for the services of Doctor Nostradamus.

"And for that I give thanks to the Virgin and all the Saints," said Anne Nostradamus, thinking of her baby.

"Nonsense," Nostradamus told her. "You are married to a doctor. And a doctor goes where he is needed. And they must need me." He walked restlessly about the room. He was worried. Some of his dearest associations were with Aix. He should be there, helping their distress.

Came a day, some weeks after the first news of the outbreak, when a little group of hard-riding men with despair in their faces drew rein outside the house of Doctor Nostradamus. They were men from the town council of Aix.

"We have come to beg your help, Doctor Nostradamus," their spokesman said. "The situation in Aix is completely out of hand. The doctors there are powerless. The whole city is affected, and the pest is still spreading. If it cannot be checked it will spread beyond Aix, and who knows where it will reach? Our only hope is now in you."

"Why," asked the doctor coldly, "was I not sent for before this plague had gained such headway?" Inwardly he was seething with indignation, for in Aix of all places, where his grandfathers had been great, and his family known for generations, he had the right to expect trust and understanding.

There was a moment of embarrassed silence, then the councillors all began to talk at once. They had not anticipated such a rapid, deadly progress of the disease. They had thought the physicians resident in Aix could handle it, they had not wanted to ask Doctor Nostradamus to leave his young wife and child--for these and more reasons they had waited.

Nostradamus refused to spare them. "I know why you have not come before. And if you think that I am Satan's agent, you have done ill to call me now. No--" he raised his hand against their trembling protest. "This must be straightened out now. Otherwise I shall be of no use to you."

"Michel," cried one of the councillors piteously, who had known the de Nostradame family for a long time, "do not reproach us. Help us, and we will bless your name forever."

The doctor's quick sympathy could not withstand this appeal. "Very well," he replied. "Then let us get on with it at once. My servant will bring you refreshment and look to your needs while I get together a few requirements, then we shall ride at once."

"They have come for me," he told his wife soberly.

"Oh, Michel." She held their baby in her arms, and struggled to keep back the tears. Beside these two, to whom happiness had so lately come, there stood a specter now, and each knew that the other saw it. It was the vision of three narrow graves beneath the trees of Agen. What new toll might now be exacted by the grisly visitor of pest? Yet it never occurred to the doctor to consider personal interest and safety. A few simple preparations, a brief, tender farewell to the wife and baby he might never see again, and he was riding with the others at top speed down the road to Aix.

When they stopped at an inn for a quick bite and a change of horses, Nostradamus received more information about the situation.

One of the councillors told him how the cemeteries were choked with bodies. "Even piling them together," he said, "there is no more space in consecrated ground. My wife and daughter lie buried in the open field with the corpses of peasants."

"People die so fast," another told him hopelessly, "the doctors have no time for treatment or study of the remedies. In two days the stricken are dead."

Crime, they said, was complicating the problem, too. The people thought they were abandoned by God, that they had no time left to live, and they must snatch terribly at any pleasure or indulgence that was remaining. Theft, rape and even murder were stalking hand in hand with the pestilence.

"How many doctors have you there, and who are they?" Nostradamus wanted to know.

It appeared from the shamefaced admissions that there had already been a very large corps of doctors, some of them quite famous, who had been called in from outside Aix. A number of these had fallen victims of the plague, the mortality among the doctors being but little less than among the rest of the population. Some, too, had fled the place, unable to stand the horror of the scene. The rest were carrying on as best they could, but utterly helpless to save the victims or arrest the spread. It was the same familiar, tragic situation the doctor had faced fifteen years before.

Already Nostradamus was mapping his plan of campaign. "I want a good laboratory, and some trained pharmaceutical helpers," he told them. "Once I decide on a remedy, I shall want it made up in quantity. I shall give you a list of herbs and essences, and you can check your supplies at all pharmacies against it, and make arrangements to send elsewhere as shortages develop."

"We will do these things while you are resting a little when we get to Aix," they assured him.

"I want no rest," he replied. "There is not a moment to lose."

"But won't you wish to consult with the other doctors, and hear their professional accounts and findings?" he was asked.

"No," he answered with grim positiveness. "I shall not. If they knew anything, I need not have come. I shall get my information from the victims."

"Michel," the councillor who knew him best spoke hesitantly, "what precautions are you using against taking the contagion? I mean, is there something you can suggest to us that we--?"

"Nothing. I know too little as yet to recommend precautions. Of what good to plug up the nose and deprive yourself of air when the contagion may come from food or some other carrier? A clean body, internally and externally, is a general measure at all times. But the one important thing at this time is to control your fears, for fear is a killer. Put your trust in God, have courage, and pray as never before."

Nostradamus knew that these were brave men, but they had been under a terrible strain for weeks, they were exhausted and near the breaking point. It would not do to sympathize with them. His calm, matter-of-fact attitude took hold of them. Some power seemed to go out from him and reach their spirits. They were conscious of being at the same time relaxed and strengthened by his personality. Each breathed a sigh, as if a heavy load had been shouldered by another and stronger. In this man, they felt, was help. They rose to resume the ride and finish the journey, which was a full day's ride.

Along the rutted roads, where they were making all speed possible, sweet buds were bursting into blossom, framed in the fresh green leaves of the year's loveliest season. The rustle of brook-song and the notes of birds were carried on the woodland breezes. Sheep and cattle browsed content under ancient trees. Here was Nature upsurging in all her vivid beauty, with the rose of Spring at her breast. And beyond, at Aix, the stricken children of Earth were dying like the seared boughs of lightning-struck trees. As the group approached the suburbs of Aix, the doctor noted increasingly the processions of burial carts heaped high with human clay on its way to fields already thickly pitted with newly dug graves. Soon he breathed the fever-foulness weighting the air. From the town came the mournful sound, faint at first, rising in volume as they drew nearer, of the church bells tolling unceasingly their terrifying dirges.

Doctor Nostradamus preferred to stop at an inn to becoming a guest of one of the councillors. He would have more freedom at a public hostelry. Most of these had closed, but one was found which was willing to admit him to its empty rooms.

"Everything is dead, Doctor," the innkeeper told him hysterically. "The palace is closed, all the shops and every kind of business. Of course, places of amusement shut down first of all. Now even the money-lenders have put up their shutters. When that happens," he spread his hands in a weary, cynical gesture, "then truly there is no life left."

When Nostradamus had washed and put on fresh linen, he found a member of the council waiting for him accompanied by one of the Aix doctors.

The physician greeted Nostradamus cordially and said he had come to offer his services, he would be glad to work under Doctor Nostradamus, since there had seemed little that he could accomplish working alone. Nostradamus looked at him in pity, for his appearance was enough to frighten a beholder without the plague. He looked utterly exhausted, white and sunken as death itself after his long bout. He was bundled up in so much clothing that no one could say how much was man and how much wrappings. Since it was hot weather, and he was sweating profusely, perspiration mingling with the medicinal oils had soaked through his coat. Garlic added to these made the odor which he had brought into the room nearly unbearable. Nostradamus said that he was ready to begin work, and that he would like to go first to the hospital and pest-houses. He wanted to see the arrangements for handling the cases, and then settle down to a study of the symptoms and progress of the disease. He could not say how long it would be before he could begin to improvise and experiment with remedies, since he was entirely unfamiliar with the charbon plague.

When Nostradamus stepped from the cool, shadowed interior of the inn once more into the blazing Midi sunshine of the deserted streets, it was to begin his first of two hundred and seventy days of fierce and unremitting battle against the plague, days filled with unending sights of black, twisted agony, and heavy with the stench of putrefaction which no breeze could freshen. Along the way to the hospital, he saw how many of the beautiful old houses, empty now, had suffered injury from vandals and looters. There were, the other doctors told him in answer to his comment, no magistrates sitting, no pretense of the administration of justice or the apprehension of criminals. Everything was being looted, he said, and live stock driven away. People of good repute were too disconsolate to take action, those, that is, who had remained in the city. Several times in the course of their progress the doctors were forced to dodge quickly to escape being hit by corpses tossed callously from windows to lie hideously in the streets until the burial carts picked them up. Nostradamus saw that hope was indeed an exile from this ancient and opulent city.

The churches were as empty as the rest of the buildings, Nostradamus' companion said. No one, he thought, believed any longer in prayer. As for the priests they were as confused as rabbits, they ran around in utter helplessness, accomplishing little even in the way of solace.

Nostradamus found the hospital staffed by gaunt, utterly weary men. The stamp of terror was on every face there as elsewhere in the city. There was the disorganization caused by insufficient attendants and the crowding of patients far beyond hospital capacity. Sanitation, food, attention of every kind was suffering from neglect or lacking. The woebegone staff of doctors and nurses greeted him with joy and thankfulness. Hope stirred faintly in his wake like a salt sea breeze. Fear slackened in the presence of this man for whom it did not exist. Serenely he made the round of the hospital, studying conditions deliberately, questioning, now and then making some practical suggestion. He sat for a time at the bedside of the victims in various stages of the disease, observing symptoms and conditions, leaving some blessed ray of comfort where he passed.

One disadvantage in the study of this and other plagues had been the fear of contagion, which was so great it prevented the doctors from spending enough time with the victims to study properly the course of the disease, its character, and the patients' reaction to the remedies that were tried out, though the latter were still for the most part cordials, bleeding and purging. Nostradamus began by spending hours at bedsides, observing. Forman thinks that he studied excreta and may have been the father of modern ideas of antisepsis. One of the old commentators, Astruc, says that he paid careful attention to arrangements for patients, their transportation by whatever was the sixteenth-century equivalent of ambulances, and the disposition of corpses. This undoubtedly was an effort to limit the carrying of the disease.

Only after prolonged study did Nostradamus begin to try out some remedial ideas. How much trial and failure was necessary we have no record. Evidently, from the length of time the plague persisted, a great deal. Here was no easy success such as had been his youthful conquest of the plague. This bears out the idea that he had some inherited, little known and untried recepte which, in the first experience, he used with brilliant results. In the plague of Aix, he had no such assistance, he was face to face with a contagion of which he was ignorant, without theories, and on the same footing with all of the other doctors in charge.

The peculiar remedy which he at last evolved was a kind of troche to be held in the mouth. That is all that he used. Eugene Bareste, a scholarly and highly intelligent French commentator, writing in 1840 tells of his discovery of a rare little volume by Nostradamus. He found it, lying ancient and dusty in the Library of Saint Geneviève, such a rarity that not even the Library of France possessed a copy. It is entitled A Collection of Numerous Receipts For Perfumes and Lotions For Beautifying The Face and Preserving Bodily Wholeness. Also Various Liquid Confections And Other Receipts Not Hitherto Presented. It was originally in two volumes, but one, alas, had disappeared. The remaining volume, however, contained Nostradamus' description of the plague at Aix, and his formula for the troche.

Nostradamus says in this account that neither bleeding nor medical cordials had the least efficacy. "Nor was any found but this (his own remedy). All who carried it in the mouth were preserved." Here is the receipt, as given by Nostradamus himself.

"Take of the distillation of the branch of the greenest cypress-wood, one ounce; of Iris of Florence, six ounces; of cloves, three ounces, of sweet-flag, three drams, of ligni aloes, six drams. Reduce these to a mixture not overly evaporated. Then take of blood-red roses two or three hundred, completely fresh and gathered before dawn; pound these thoroughly, then blend them with the mixture. When the whole has been well mingled, make it into small pats, like troches, and set them to dry in the shade. In addition to the excellence and fragrance which this prescription affords, when held in the mouth it sweetens the breath for an entire day and relieves gaseous stomach conditions."

How, one ponders, could such slight, fragrant, medicinal pot-pourri afford resistance to the mortality of a deadly contagion? Perhaps in several ways. All historians of plagues, from Thucydides down, stress their accompaniment of destroying terror. The rose-pats of Nostradamus, considered only as bread-pills backed by his sensational reputation, would have helped enormously to relieve the fear. Anyone who could obtain something that this celebrated doctor said would save them, had already conquered fear and acquired resistance. But there is more to this old recepte than just that. One of the first symptoms of the charbon plague was frightful bleeding at the nose. Nostradamus must have believed that the infection entered through the mouth or nasal passages. This pungent, delightful little cake was designed to both stimulate and relax the nerves and passages of nose and throat, and perhaps give a mild antisepsis. There is a close connection between these nerves and the brain, so that terror in itself tends to congest them, lessening resistance to infection. His troche would have affected both physically and psychologically the particular head-area which appeared most vulnerable to the contagion.

Nostradamus, in the infinite subtlety of his mind, may have considered, too, that the red rose has been from time immemorial the symbol of life and happiness, Its fragrance and flavor would carry that message and symbolism to patients even though they were unconscious of it. It was the substitution of the idea of life and hope replacing that of death and despair. Roses are becoming a rarity in modern life; a grouping behind the plate-glass window of a florist's shop, or a few in the vases of the fortunate. They were a more vital and plentiful treasure of the ancient world, and put to many uses. Marvelous rose cordials were made by carefully guarded family receipts sometimes centuries old. The bloom was also sacred to the making of odorous pot-pourri which gave summer fragrance to the house through the winter. And confitures of rose leaves were a frequent delicacy. It would be strange if in the ancient world these glorious blooms should not have been used in some remedial way that old scientists might believe infused something of their vivid life into the fading vitality of illness. Nostradamus was fortunate in being summoned to Aix in the season when roses were abundant. The picture of him, which history presents, calling those who stood in the midst of the whirlwind of death to go into the dew-laden dawn and gather the red roses of summer for healing, is in itself symbolic of the way in which the skill and spirit of this great man touched the lives of those who turned to him for help.

For the efficacy of Nostradamus' prescription there is testimony of the most practical kind. When the plague had been at long last conquered, the city of Aix gave him the highest and most grateful credit and praise. They paid him in full for the nine months of his service, and in addition, the parliament voted him a substantial life pension which was paid to him as long as he lived. Nostradamus writing of this, says: "And it is true that in 1544 I was chosen and received compensation from the City of Aix in Provence, where by the parliament and the people I was entrusted with the preservation of the city ... Toward the end of the plague it was clearly demonstrated that I had preserved a world of people."

Wealthy citizens, besides all this, made him rich presents of money. These he distributed with his customary generosity among families victimized in the plague.

Weary with the long pull, laden with glory, he returned to Salon and his family. He had been away almost a year. The small rural town is now almost bursting with pride in their star, and richer than their wildest dreams had ever imagined. For Nostradamus, after this triumph, more than ever means business to the little place. The nobility from all the country around are pouring in to see and consult him. The nobles from Arles, Avignon, Aix, Marseilles, choke the street leading to his home with their horses, coaches and litters. These educated, sophisticated people of the great world were enchanted with a doctor whose skill could cure them while he diverted them with his learning and witty conversation. But in the background there was always the enmity of his own profession, insanely jealous of a man who could do what other doctors could not, and accomplish it by means they despised, envied, and could not comprehend. It was openly said in regard to medical innovations generally, indeed it was the credo of the old-line physicians, that it was much better for people to die under treatment approved by the majority of doctors than to have their lives saved by unorthodox methods. The only trouble with this theory was that the man whose life was at stake wasn't likely to agree, not until he got well, anyhow.

Nostradamus was now openly accused by the doctors of using bootlegged knowledge gained through association with secret, heretical societies and outlawed alchemists. These accusations were not without effect. The times were so deeply superstitious, so rent by all sorts of hatreds, that many listened, though not enough to jeopardize his position. But the snapping at his heels continued.

Nearly a year went by in which he was peaceful and happy in his home life, popular and sought after. Then came the news, once again, of the coming of the charbon plague. This time the outbreak was at Lyons, and on this occasion Nostradamus was early called on to help. When he arrived at Lyons, however, he found Jean-Antoine Sarrazin already in the field and directing the work. Sarrazin, according to the history of both Lyons and Montpellier, was considered one of the great medical figures of his day, his reputation was of the highest. He was extremely ambitious, and eager to make a record in stamping out the plague in Lyons that would equal if not surpass the work of Nostradamus for the city of Aix. He had the devotion and the courage to do this, but lacked the science. The coming of Nostradamus immediately roused his jealousy, and he stated that he intended to work alone. Nostradamus, always a modest man, having no desire except to save those whom he might, agreed at once. He said that he would gladly share with Sarrazin what had been learned about the plague in Aix, and then he and Sarrazin would take separate routes which were not in conflict. This was done.

The situation at Lyons was somewhat different from that at Aix. Lyons was one of the largest and most important cities of France. It had a long medical tradition, for it was there that the first hospital in France had been established by Childebert in the sixth century. An interesting description of a sixteenth-century hospital which may be taken as typical of the best institutions, such as that at Lyons, exists in a document sent by the Hospital of Santa Maria Nuova, at Florence, to Henry VIII. This was written at the request of the king for information which would aid him in improving the hospitals of England. The hospital staff, according to his letter, comprised a number of internes who lived in, and a larger number of visiting surgeons who paid daily visits, just as today. The hospital maintained a dispensary for the treatment of ulcers and slight disorders. This was conducted by the foremost surgeon in the city who, with his assistants, gave their services without charge to the poor, and supplied them with free medicines from the hospital pharmacy. The modern clinic continues this tradition. The large hospitals were all independently wealthy, owning extensive vineyards and other properties and industries. Revenue from these was supplemented by taxes. But since then, as now, there was never as much money as was needed, wealthy patrons endowed beds, gave annuities, and assumed responsibilities for particular comforts and various needs of the patients. All of which sounds surprisingly modern.

The Church administered the hospitals, and appears to have done so in a skilled and highly responsible way. Even Martin Luther confessed that under the papacy generous provision had always been made for all classes of suffering, while among his own followers no one contributed to the maintenance of the sick and poor. Architecturally, the hospitals were constructed on the religious pattern of the cross as established by the Crusaders. The beds were arranged in rows in one enormous room, the long section of the cross. There was no such thing as private rooms, or separate wards. Some of the hospitals provided screens which could be used to partition off the beds. But this was in the interest of privacy when religious rites were administered, rather than any consideration for the patient at other times. In times of plague, the accommodations of even the largest institution were but a drop in the bucket of need, though they served all they could. However, the hospital was the focal agency from which all plans and effort were put forth.

In the Lyons hospital Nostradamus found a trained efficiency and order, even under plague conditions, far beyond the limited facilities he had worked with at Aix. The institution had two thousand beds and a large staff of well-known doctors. Association, as doctor or interne, with the Lyons hospital carried a certain prestige such as the great medical institutions of today confer upon their chosen staffs. It was also a hotbed of gossip, hatred and controversy over new techniques and theories, and watched over with a malicious eye by the fanatics of the Sorbonne. But a few years previous, Rabelais had been a member of the staff, when his friend, the distinguished physician, Etienne Dôle, was burned at the stake by order of the Sorbonne. No liberal scholarship which was boldly acknowledged could consider itself safe here, for there were always spies. Nostradamus braved more than the plague when he excited the enmity of Sarrazin.

In the pestilence at Lyons it soon became apparent that Doctor Sarrazin, with all of his zeal, was killing a great many more people than his methods were helping. Citizens from Sarrazin's territory began rushing pell-mell to Nostradamus, who wanted no trouble with his jealous confrère. Crowds threw themselves at his feet and implored him not to abandon them. Nostradamus finally said to these groups:

"I want to help you, but you must let me experiment in my own way. I honor Doctor Sarrazin, who is my colleague, but our remedies are different. So you must choose which one of us you want to remain as medical director of the city. You must decide at once for one of us, myself or Doctor Sarrazin."

The whole deputation cried out, "We choose Doctor Nostradamus, the deliverer of Aix." Sarrazin left, discredited and furious.

One month later the plague at Lyons was completely stamped out and over. Once again the little roseleaf cakes had done their work. Once more Nostradamus took his leave heaped with glory and gratitude. A deputation of members of the city government as an escort of honor accompanied him on his return to Salon.

The municipal histories of Aix and Lyons report in detail the work of Nostradamus in these two plagues. Whatever room for controversy there is in minor matters of the physician's life, these medical achievements are incontestable. Sarrazin immediately accused Nostradamus of magical practice and spread evil rumors far and wide. This was followed a year later by a book published in Avignon bitterly attacking him, branding him as a charlatan and worse. It was the hatred of the man of today which almost invariably pursues the man of tomorrow. It is said that in later years Nostradamus was deeply wounded when, on a visit to Lyons, he found that he was no longer popular there. This was after the misrepresentations through imitations and pirating of his writings. The doctors, too, who were his enemies had no doubt reminded the former patients of Nostradamus many a time that if they had been left to die, they would by then be enjoying the delights of Paradise. That having been cured by sorcery, they might have forever forfeited those delights. A potent argument in the sixteenth century.

A Prophet's Eyry

NOSTRADAMUS HAD FOUND, up to this time, that a settled home life was about the most unattainable of his ambitions. Yet each time that he returned from his absence it had been with more acclaim and a wider, if bitterly controversial reputation. Now, once again he settled down to live quietly in Salon, surrounded by the people and things he loved. More than ever he sought an uninterrupted family life and pursuit of the profound studies that were beckoning him to their secret fascinations.

He fitted up the top floor of his home as a study and laboratory sacred to himself, and prepared to enjoy long hours of solitary concentration in the late hours of evening when the day's professional duties were done, and his dearly loved family were abed. Here in this eyry he could arrange his books and instruments, placed to his liking with scientific nicety. His library must by this time have been considerable. From his grandfathers he would have inherited incunabula, old treatises on medicine, mathematics and astronomy. He had added to these with books and manuscripts picked up here and there in his travels. He watched the printers' lists for new scientific works that seemed worthwhile, and editions of the classics. Greek, Latin, Hebrew and French, they stood in orderly array upon his shelves. Among them was a large, square Bible, its pages softened with much handling.

Near a window of the study, where the light fell most clearly, was his long work table on which were writing materials. Against the far wall there was a bed which he occasionally used when the few hours before dawn were all that was left of a night spent in study. Nostradamus, like Edison, is said to have needed but little sleep, and to have found five hours or less always sufficient. A small, but for its time, modern and well-equipped laboratory occupied part of the space in this private haunt. Its charcoal brazier, alembic, retorts, and chemicals permitted him to compound some of his prescription needs, and if he wished, to carry out some research. Hour-glasses in several sizes stood about, including a large twelve-hour time-keeper and a small one registering the half-hour, useful in timing chemical experiments. A fine astrolabe spoke eloquently of the doctor's continued interest in astronomy. Nostradamus could afford to indulge his taste for the best in scientific equipment. His patronage had been for a long time very large and wealthy. He gave liberally to charity and to the Church, but he lived simply by preference, and had plenty of income to indulge his interests and hobbies.

Inconspicuous in a corner, though startling to a beholder, stood a tripod of solid brass which might have graced the mysterious rituals of the Pythoness of Delphi. This was the "selle d'airain" of his first quatrain, upon which, he tells us, he sat when in prophetic trance. On the wall hung a mirror of soft-toned old glass in a gilded Italian frame. Some said it was a magic mirror in which he saw his visions. Others said he saw them in the large, gleaming copper bowl which was also a part of the room's furnishings and which, the whispers told, he filled to the brim with water for his occult ceremonies.

Among all of these practical furnishings there would have been, as there always are, little personal things which he liked having near him and looking at sometimes when he worked. Such as, perhaps, a childish drawing by young César, who turned out in later years to be a very good painter and sculptor. Perhaps there were also mementos of his grandfathers. Some of the things in this room would be gifts from wealthy patients. He had received many handsome presents from the time of his young days when he first fought the plague. After he became famous as a prophet gifts multiplied ad infinitum. From Delphi to Nostradamus, all great oracles have been loaded with gifts, the general idea being the hope that the favors of destiny might be commensurate with the offerings.

About the study clung the dry, pungent odors of blended herbs, of which a few clusters were visible. The rest, powdered or distilled for use, filled a variety of decorative earthenware jars. Sometimes a fresher fragrance gave its odor to the room. This was when Anne Nostradamus would climb the steep flights of narrow stairs to bring a jar of roses in her arms from her garden.

Here in his high retreat Nostradamus began enjoyably to burn the midnight oil to the scandal of the town. Late hours have long been associated in simple minds with sin and sorcery. The country town of Salon, where all knew that the Lord made the night for sleeping, to say nothing of the high cost of candles, was early and suspiciously conscious of the strange nocturnal habits of its celebrity. Nostradamus had come to this town, in part, to escape from the enmity and envy of powerful personalities in the large cities. Here he had thought that he would be entirely free. But he found out that life had its drawbacks in this place too. Because he was the one illustrious personage in its small midst, everything he did and all that could be found out about him fascinated the townspeople. Their desire for excitement fed on his doings and, as in all little towns, they watched and pried and gossiped. Who were his grand visitors, how many litters and blooded horses stood outside his house, what did he eat, where did his wife go, what did she pay for her clothes, and WHY did he sit up all night? Why couldn't he go to bed like a Christian? Was there truth in what some people said, that he trafficked in magic? One should not, of course, say too much, for he had brought prosperity to the town.

The talk and rumors kept up, in spite of the fact that the town was both fond and proud of him. Nostradamus is said to have been not too happy over all this. He had endless patience over anything related to his work, but he was psychically thin-skinned and he had an irritable side. He was hurt over the suspicions and gossip of the townspeople who owed him so much. After the vicious accusations spread by his enemies, he became more taciturn, though he still talked brilliantly in sympathetic company. There were in Salon some charming, cultivated families, such as that of the Sieur de Condoulet, with whom he and his wife were on terms of intimacy. But he felt increasingly drawn to solitude and research.

His growing family, too, demanded more of his time and interest. Five children, two boys and three girls, were born after César. The dates of their births are not known, but Michel, Charles, Magdeleine, Diane and Anne arrived in due season to add their charms of childhood to the home. In his will Magdeleine is favored above the other girls to the extent of a hundred écus above their portions. No reason for this is given, but there must have been some ill health or handicap which required particular provision. It would not have been like Nostradamus to play favorites.

One pleasant day among the calls the doctor received was a social one from the scholarly magistrate of the town of Beaune, Doctor Jean-Ayme de Chavigny. He introduced himself and mentioned a number of mutual friends in Provence, and expressed his deep admiration for the doctor's achievements and all that he had heard of him. Nostradamus was delightfully impressed with his visitor's dignified manner and intelligent talk.

"Doctor Nostradamus," Chavigny said, "I have come for something more than the great pleasure of meeting you. I want to study with you."

"To study with me!" the doctor echoed in surprise. Not since his days at Montpellier had he taught. "To study what?" he asked.

"I should like to learn something of your wisdom which seems to me to be beyond that of other men," Chavigny told him. "I have my degrees as Doctor of Law and Doctor of Theology. I have been a student all my life, which should be some preparation. I desire to continue studying, particularly those things which will give me a deeper insight into the mysteries of existence. I have never studied astronomy, except superficially. And I think that I might also find the higher branches of mathematics interesting. But if you will become my master, then I shall leave the guidance of my studies to you."

Pleased, though hesitant at first, the doctor was gradually won over to the idea, because he already liked Chavigny. The doctor agreed to plan and supervise some studies for the magistrate who was to see him reporting progress and receiving instruction from time to time. It was the beginning of a fine and lasting friendship. How deeply Doctor Chavigny penetrated into the mysteries of Nostradamus' gifts, or if he had some psychic flair of his own, is not known. But the prophet's eyry soon became familiar territory to him, and more than any other friend he was received into his confidence. Unlike the friendship with Scaliger, no disagreements marred the even tenor of the association, unbroken to the death of Nostradamus.

It is supposedly in this period of his life that Nostradamus took up for the first time the study of astrology. Garencières says that he did so because he thought it might throw some additional light on the diagnosis of disease. This would seem to be an unlikely reason. Medicine had all too lately begun to emerge from its long bondage to superstition in which a misapplied astrology had played its part. The pathology of the humors, so recently blasted by Paracelsus, had its foundation in the elemental divisions of astrology, as did many ideas of treatment then being discarded. Nostradamus was too modern, too much the scientist alive to the trends of the times to have taken up this study for medical reasons.

From Belshazzar to Hitler, astrology has been the esoteric science of courts and kings. Its oldest traditions are linked with governments and their rulers. This was still true in the sixteenth century when there was no monarch of importance but had his court astrologer. Where royalty led, the courtiers followed. What the nobles did, the common people imitated. The sixteenth century was permeated with astrological belief and practice. No picture of the Renaissance is complete which leaves out the overwhelming desire of the age to penetrate the laws of destiny, to discover and manipulate fate through prevision.

Astrology as much as astronomy was then the science of intellectuals. It had not become "The unwise daughter of a wise mother." The two were still sisters in prestige. Scholarship in one was incomplete without knowledge of the other. Nostradamus had come to the study late because his life had been filled with other activities. But keen astronomer that he was, he would quite naturally have wished to round out his education with knowledge of the sister science. Not to know it was a reflection on his scholarship.

Nostradamus, no more than a man of today, could not be invited to dinner without having his neighbor at table complain of what Saturn was doing to him and lament that it would be another year before Jupiter helped him financially. Someone, too, would be certain to ask what did Doctor Nostradamus think of the political effects of the oncoming eclipse. Doctor Nostradamus might choose to discount astrology, but it did not do for him to be ignorant of it.

Nostradamus did not need astrology for his prophetic work. The completeness of his extra-dimensional vision gave him what no astrologer could ever find in his charts. There is no record of any horoscopes cast by Nostradamus, although he may have occasionally made such charts at the request of patrons and as a personal hobby. His patients may have asked him for decumbency charts, for much was made of these horoscopes through the seventeenth century. They were horoscopes of illness, erected for the time when the person was first taken ill. From such a chart the doctor or astrologer deduced not only the nature of the illness, but its critical period, duration and chance of survival. People liked the charts because they flattered their egos and they could talk about them. "My astrologer said he never before saw anyone live through such a frightful position of Mars." It was just the way people talk of their operations today.

Nostradamus, besides his desire to be acquainted with astrology, to test it and see for himself how much truth it contained, had another reason, a very practical one, for establishing a reputation as an astrologer. This motive was self-protective. He was already deep in the psychic experiences which were to result in his written prophecies. Perhaps he was even then toying with the idea of eventually publishing some of them. He knew he would be treading on dangerous ground, and that he might risk the accusation of sorcery by the Inquisition. Astrology was more respectable than other kinds of prophecy. It was called The Celestial Science. It was patronized by the best people and the most learned minds, many of whom were high within the Church. If Nostradamus could launch his prophecies under the protective coloration of astrology, he had a better chance to escape persecution than if he put them out as revelation only. Such would be the wise course to follow, at least until he had tested public and authoritative reaction. Which is exactly what he did.

Queen Catherine was a sincere believer in astrology and came of a family who had employed court astrologers for generations. She had brought Ruggiero, the son of her father's astrologer, to France to act as her adviser. Later, after the king's death, he had apartments in the palace connected with the queen's by a private stairway, and still later she built an observatory for him at Blois and erected a column to honor him in Paris. Canny Catherine was herself an expert astrologer. So also was Renée, daughter of Louis XII, and Duchess of Ferrara, who was considered one of the most cultivated women in Europe. Pope Julius II had been known as a fine astrologer, as was Clement VIII later on. Old Doctor John Dee, the English astrologer, planned Queen Elizabeth's coronation and advised her throughout her tenure of the throne.

Seldom has an astrologer changed the course of history. Kings did as they pleased, not as they were advised. But they kept the astrologers on the pay roll because the good ones were usually right. Monarchs, even the richest, were invariably short of cash for their needs, and a good astrologer came high. He had to have a laboratory, expensive instruments, and de luxe books. Sometimes he had more worldly tastes for which he expected the king to foot the bills, as had Angelo Catho, astrologer to Louis XI. Monarchs who employed astrologers at least believed that they had value received for their money, for not one of them was keen about giving away gold. Acceptance and use by royal and powerful personalities conferred dignity upon the old science and kept it in the limelight of fashion and practice. Everybody of importance had horoscopes cast, if they did not do them themselves. Notable collections of the birth-charts of all important personages of the times were compiled, and have been handed down to the present day. These may in some future age be considered as precious as written histories. Forman says that when Kepler cast horoscopes, a generation later, "To have a nativity cast by Kepler was like having one's portrait painted by Rembrandt."

Nostradamus reiterates in both his letters, to César and to King Henry, which preface the Centuries, that he has made use of astrology in combination with his prophetic gift. But as a matter of fact the Centuries show little use of it. A prophet who could casually identify James I of England and Cromwell by the planets rising at the time they were born, which was long after his own death, had no need of astrology. Nostradamus, however, had to use a certain amount of the terminology of the science and some of the trimmings to back his assertion of its influence. What he really did--and it is a marvel of marvels, utterly unique--was to foresee clairvoyantly the kind of horoscope under which the two rulers just cited would be born.

For the rest, he used his knowledge of the heavens as an astronomer would. Instead of giving dates, he often, in the Centuries, times events by astronomical positions. Sometimes he mentions a grouping of planets, and again only Mars or the Sun. One of the great outcries against the reputation of Nostradamus came from the ranks of the astrologers themselves, after he had published his astrological Almanachs. They well knew that his prophecies transcended their limitations, and, echoing the doctors, shrieked, "Sorcery!"

No previous analyst of Nostradamus has inquired as to the precise place astrology occupies in his writings. The attitude toward this has seemed to be that in verses so cryptic, anything which puzzles the commentator must be just part of the general oddity of expression. Whereas much light is thrown on many prophecies by an understanding of how Nostradamus used his knowledge of the stars.

Nostradamus may have been influenced to take up this study at the time that he did through having seen and heard discussed a book published by Jerome Cardan at Nuremberg in 1543. Cardan was one of the great mathematicians of the epoch, and for this reason entitled to respect. He was also a famous astrologer. His book was a collection of nearly seventy nativities of public personages and a number of predictions concerning those who were living at the time. Among his horoscopes was that of Martin Luther. Nostradamus, passionately interested in all that concerned the Church and contemporary religious conditions, would have had his attention particularly caught by what Cardan had to say from an astrologer's point of view. What Cardan did say, (as quoted in Manly Hall's Story of Astrology) was:

"Incredible is the vast number of followers which this doctrine has in a brief space achieved. Already the world is on fire with the wild struggle over this madness, which, owing to the position of Mars, must ultimately break up of itself. Countless are the heads which desire to reign in it, and if nothing else could convince us of its futility, then the number of its diverse manifestations must convince us.... Nevertheless, the Sun and Saturn in the position of their future great conjunction indicate both the strength and the long duration of this heresy."

In his book Cardan predicted the hanging of the Archbishop of Saint Andrews, one of the remarkable forecasts of the period. Nine years later, this English prelate, ill of a puzzling malady, sent to the continent for the assistance of Cardan. The astrologer, after making a diagnosis which brought about a cure, told the churchman that, though he had been able to cure him, he could not change his destiny nor prevent him from being hanged, as was eventually his fate. Cardan also correctly predicted that his own son would be beheaded.

Nostradamus, mathematician and descendant of mathematicians, would have been impressed by the authority of this book and the reputation of the author as a mathematician. He would have said to himself, "I shall look into astrology--when I have the time." It was not until after the plague of Aix that he had this leisure, in 1547.

Another stimulant to his interest in the subject was the death of Francis I, which occurred in 1547. This event brought to the throne a new king, the son of Francis, who now reigned as Henry II and whose queen was Catherine de' Medici. Whenever there was a change in the government it always was, and still is, the signal for the prophets to burst into print. Prophets have an advantage over the "now it can be told" groups, because the latter have to wait for whatever happens, and spill the secrets afterwards. But no such limitation binds the reader of the future. He "tells all" before the event occurs. His disadvantage is that usually nobody believes him. Prophets of all ages have seemed to love and specialize in gloom, the motto appearing to be the opposite in most instances to the sundial, which records only the happy hours. It must have been a little hard on Henry II, the new king, to have the astrologers working on the details of his death before he had time to put his crown on straight.

Everybody in prophetic circles knew that Henry and Catherine both had afflicted nativities. Lucas Gauricus, a learned, competent astrologer whose fine collection of charts has been handed down, had published in his Tractatus Astrologus, 1542, the horoscopes of both sovereigns. He had predicted that

Henry would be killed in a duel, and warned him against any kind of single combat in his forty-first year. This prophecy, like that of Nostradamus concerning the fate of Henry, is a famous one because it was an accurate forecast. Two stories are told about it. One is that Catherine gave the birthdate to Gauricus under a false name, and that he made the prophecy not knowing whose chart it was. This would have been impossible. Royal births are timed and witnessed, information was immediately and widely accessible to astrologers. Gauricus would have recognized the horoscope at once. The other account, which the Duchess of Cleves related in her memoirs, was that the king told her that he visited Gauricus in disguise and that the prophecy was made to him. He commented on it by saying that kings did not fight duels except with equals, and he had just made peace with Charles of Spain.

Interest in his forecast centers in the fact that Gauricus could not, by the nature of astrology, have specifically predicted a duel. The violence of Henry's chart, with its Aries planets afflicted by Mars and Saturn, might have meant illness affecting the head, or war, or any number of things. Catherine, born in the same year and just two weeks later than Henry, had a chart as dangerous as his, yet her life was different and nearly twenty years longer. So that if Gauricus really predicted death through single combat, he was using the same extradimensional sense, combined with astrology, which made Nostradamus great.

There seem to have been no dramatic public forecasts about the Queen, who was to be so much more fatal to France than the short-lived husband. The French had never expected that Catherine would be their Queen. When she married Henry, he was still the second son. Then the sudden death of the Dauphin had put Henry in line for the throne. The match was considered quite a step up for the Medici, who were, in the eyes of the French aristocracy, trades-people, no matter how glorified. Had Henry been Dauphin at the time, a more patrician alliance would have been planned for him. Perhaps, thought the seers, studying these two fatalistic horoscopes of their rulers, neither one would live very long, and maybe Catherine would go first.

From the time of Henry's accession, the forecast of Gauricus seems to have been known generally and talked around. With the works of Gauricus and Cardan published in successive years, attracting the attention and discussion of scientists, scholars and court circles, it would have been strange if Doctor Nostradamus had not felt that he wished to be conversant with this much debated branch of prophecy.

The leading astrologers, whatever their limitations, were for the most part honest, high-minded scholars, with many dramatically fulfilled predictions to their credit. They were in their way a picturesque ornament of the sixteenth century. But there was another and a darker side to the century's "lust of knowing what shall not be known." Magic, the black art of witch and sorcerer, flourished surreptitiously, offering its secret, propitiatory rites to Satan, and attracting large numbers of people in all ranks of society. Whereas astrology was acknowledged by science and tolerated by the Church, the hidden ritual of Devil-worship required of its votaries a willingness to make a compact with Satan, and a little blood drawn from the worshiper's veins wherewith to seal it.

Religion was the only form of mass production which the century knew.

From the time that Clovis had presented Christianity to the Franks, saying take it or else, to the Renaissance decree forbidding any other religion within France, belief and conversion were strictly compulsory. The Inquisition was there to see that they remained so. In those days of the tremendous certitudes when, as Heywood Broun once said of the past, "heaven had a mighty low ceiling," both heaven and hell were well-mapped countries whose inhabitants, customs, flora and fauna were a matter of exact knowledge. The Devil and his minions had for many, if anything, a more omnipresent reality than had the beings of divinity. He was always prowling. Few were the peasants who had not seen on starless nights a flash of scarlet flame against black branches, and smelled the Devil's sulphur. Nor could the rustling sounds from the heart of a dark wood always be distinguished from the sinister witches' chant, by a man plodding home on a lonely road. Sometimes, even in broad daylight, he might come upon the clear track of the print of a cloven hoof, when woe betide his flocks and herds. From Egypt and Carthage, from Greece and Rome, from the Druids and all the people of the forgotten lands, the old spells lived on, woven by Satan to affright the heart and tempt the soul to its damnation.

The blessed saints wrought miracles for the benefit of mankind, but the evil one worked his magic through man and could not accomplish his works except with the aid of human co-operation. When strange misfortunes befell Jacques Bonhomme and his pious wife Marie, they knew that Satan had found his like on earth to do his bidding. If the flocks sickened and died for no reason, if the harvest was blighted, or Marie's fresh cream soured in the pan, and a child broke an arm, then someone in their community had sold out to Satan and was working mischief.

"Thou shalt not suffer a witch to live."

Stark terror and primitive fear were the witchery that drove people of the Renaissance into a kind of madness. To this, color was given by the very real number who sought Satanic contact with pentagram and incantation, incense and sacrifice in the hope of gold and power, the ancient promise of the kingdom of the world, never fulfilled.

There was only one way to protect the righteous, that was to fight the Devil with fire. So the witch-fires of the stake were lighted and burned high over Europe for more than two hundred years. While Nostradamus was a boy preparing for Avignon, five hundred of the piteous creatures accused of witchcraft were burned in Geneva. This was typical of what went on throughout Christendom. Nor was there any more tolerance among Protestants than among Catholics. It was Martin Luther who said that the Devil caused children to disappear and placed his own minions as changelings in their place to be reared, all unsuspectingly, by honest parents. Since Luther found a great many people whom he did not like, it was easy for him to spot, as he did, such changelings. Not without reason has Doctor Victor Robinson, in his Story of Medicine, called the sixteenth century the world's darkest age. The very brilliance of its blaze of glory and enlightenment made blacker the shadows that it cast.

Among the common people, such medical practice as they had sustained the belief in witchcraft. The two went hand in hand (as with the hex doctors of present-day Pennsylvania). The herbalist and the "wise woman" were the doctors in country districts and among the city poor where there was no free clinic. Here old magical ideas of the sympathetic virtues of plants were as strong as ever. These had all to be gathered in certain phases of the moon, and their distillations made under proper magical conditions. The witches' brew was a part of such beliefs, and the charlatan's decoction of the Elixir of Life.

In the upper classes, the spread of the new learning stimulated, if anything, the interest in magical practice, because the writings of Greece and Rome are filled with the most intriguing stories about it. The seeker after occult information could get from the classics new ideas and techniques with which to experiment. One of the books accessible to the times and apparently much consulted by the "evil folk," as Nostradamus calls them, was the work of an early writer, Michael Psellus, entitled provocatively enough Concerning Demons. If there was one thing above another that was adored by the sixteenth century it was the sinister doings of demons, and also with many, how to get hold of one and put him to work. Psellus gives full details of the way to do this. He also gives descriptions of degraded orgies in connection with such rites, which were once the ceremonial of the old fertility magic. Nostradamus wrote this curious quatrain about the followers of what might be called the Psellus method:

The tenth of the Calends of April, by the pre-Gregorian calendar,
Is again revived by evil gentry,
The light extinguished, the group of evil-worshipers
Seek to rouse the ancient Demon of Psellus.

No one can say today whom the prophet was accusing. The magic rites had greatest power when used on the night of Good Friday. It is supposable that he referred to a group who were experimenting in a year when this day fell on the twenty-third of April.

"Sorcery and sanctity are the only realities," wrote that English master of mystical prose, Arthur Machen. The distinction between the two is sometimes fine drawn. If the difference is to be based upon the means employed, then Nostradamus, judged by sixteenth-century standards, was, as his enemies claimed, a sorcerer. But if the distinction is one of motivation, then in his deep religious faith, in his long record of charity and good will toward men, his life followed better than most the pattern of sanctity. It is indisputable that he came deeply under the old pagan methods of divination. That is written in the record, and by his own hand. But he truly believed that the agencies which he invoked were heavenly ones.

It must be assumed that the Church also took this view. His work and his life were known in their completeness to the Church. Only acceptance by the papacy of his inspirational claims can account for the fact that throughout his life no rebuke nor interference ever came to him from the Inquisition. Had he not been sure of it he would never have dared to publish the Centuries. The hue and cry against him from the enemies within his own profession, their constant accusations of sorcery, would, at the slightest notice from the Inquisition, have carried him to the stake. Nor could the King and all the prophet's courtly patrons have availed to save him. Nostradamus was always on terms of friendship with important prelates and he may have rendered secret and valuable services to the Church, for which it was grateful. The published prophecies are but a small part of the predictive work which he carried on after he became known as a prophet and possibly before that. It is said that Europe is strewn with his forecasts made privately to noble and royal families, and never given out.

I-1
Seated at night in secret study,
Alone, at ease upon my tripod of brass,
From out the low flame of solitude
Comes realization of that in which it is not empty to believe.

I-2
Holding the bough with my hand where the branches fork,
The Branch seeking the Ripple moistens (with a spatter) the hem of my robe and my foot,
Fear and a voice make me tremble in my sleeves,
Splendor divine, the Divine Being is seated near.

In these opening lines of the Centuries, Nostradamus gives a clear, specific picture of his lone, late evenings when all the world was quiet and sleeping. He shows himself to posterity engaged in the ancient rite of divination by water, an oracle so old and universal that its origin is one with the lost river that first ran by the feet of the first man dreaming beside its banks. Nostradamus, in his letter to César, has told something of the books which were the source of his knowledge of the water-ritual, which he considered too dangerous to keep.

"Although many volumes have come before me which have lain hidden for long ages, dreading what might happen in the future, after reading them, I made an offering of them to Vulcan. As the flame caught them, the fire, licking the air, flared in unaccustomed brightness, clearer than natural flame, more like the explosion of powder. It cast a subtle illumination over the house, as if it were filled by the reflection of the conflagration. So that you might not at some time be harmed by alchemic research for the perfect lunar or solar transformation, or the hidden, incorruptible metals of earth or sea, I reduced these books to ashes."

There has been much speculation over what these books were and how Nostradamus came by them. Some commentators have thought they might have been inherited. Those who would have Nostradamus of Jewish descent have concocted the fantastic theory that the books were part of the temple treasure salvaged at the time of the Diaspora. There is no evidence for such ideas. It is most unlikely that the books were inherited. Grandfather de Rémy, be it remembered, initiated the boy Michel into some slight exhibition of extra-sensory perception. Having done this, the old man would hardly leave within the reach of a boy whose curiosity he had aroused, works which might spell danger, and even his doom at the stake. He would have withheld them for the same reason that Nostradamus destroyed them, to protect the child he loved from possible harm. Grandfather de Rémy, too, was too wise for anything else.

Europe was full of ancient books on magic; some were spurious and some authentic. When Constantinople fell in 1540, many Greeks fled to Italy and France. They brought with them all they could rescue of their written works. It was said that invariably beneath the rags of the refugee could be seen the parchment edges of some treasured rarity of manuscript. The Greeks sold many of these; they were forced to in order to live. Nostradamus almost certainly acquired his magic books during the years of his travels, and found them in either Marseilles or Italy. Both were gateways for all the world, and many strange, lost secrets of antiquity drifted in at their ports.

The particular work on water-divining was in all likelihood a Greek manuscript and one of the priceless incunabula which the refugees brought with them. Probably the manuscript contained an accurate account of the divinatory ceremonies practiced in ancient Greece in the temple of the god Branchus. Since Nostradamus mentions "long ages" in connection with these magical books, they may have been of the time of Alexander the Great, or even as early as Xerxes. The priests of Branchus were said to have sold out to the Persian invaders and fled, to escape popular anger. They were later destroyed by Alexander. The work on water-divination must have been something very special, for there is an account of the rites of Branchus in The Mysteries of Egypt, by Iamblichus, in current circulation in Nostradamus' day. His own books must have contained knowledge far more prized and secret.

The word "Branches," which Nostradamus printed in capitals to emphasize its significance, has reference to the forked branch of laurel or hazel used in this divinatory art, and also stands for the name of the god, Branchus, from whose name are derived "branch" and "bronchial." The myth of Branchus makes him the son of Apollo and a mortal. The sun-god entered the mother's mouth in a dream, and impregnated her. Branchus means throat and branches. The ancient oracle of Branchus was very famous, and it is easy to see the association of prophecy with this god of the throat. It is not so easy to see his association with water, except that speech is difficult with a dry throat! Even so it would seem more reasonable for the priestess of Branchus to take a drink of water than spill a little, as she did, on her foot and the hem of her dress. However that may be, it is undoubtedly Branchus whose ritual Nostradamus describes.

Did Nostradamus really believe in the worship of Branchus? Of course not. Nostradamus says more than once that his prophetic faculty was inherited. This ancient method of the vision by water could have stimulated, perhaps developed his gift to greater scope, but it never could have conferred it.

This man, whose intelligence was universal and of tomorrow, understood that the laws of attunement between the world of the senses and the realm beyond their range were in themselves unrelated to creed or dogma, nor were they inconsistent with the Christian life. The same force has animated the prophets of all ages, only the methods, the technique by which the psychic accord is established are different and individual. Nostradamus had found in the old Greek ritual one that suited his faculty. Mantra, incantations, chants, all such have only the purpose of attuning the prophet. That Nostradamus was familiar with the spoken words of magical ceremonies and probably used them in just this way may be judged from the passage in which he warns the frivolous and the charlatans to keep hands off his Centuries or consider themselves "cursed according to the rites of magic." Such curses were like the chants, oral pronouncements, and evidently the prophet knew their literature.

And what happened next in this strange night-life of prophecy? Let Nostradamus describe it. Writing to César, he says:

"Through some eternal power, and epileptic Herculean excitement, celestial causation is made known to me ... But the perfect knowledge of causes cannot be acquired without divine inspiration. All authentic prophecy derives its first principle from God the Creator, next from favoring conditions, and last from natural endowment."

This passage is the answer to those who call Nostradamus pagan. In his letter to Henry II, the prophet writes concerning the Centuries:

"The entire work has been composed and calculated on days and hours of best election and disposition . . ." That is to say, he began his work and carried it on under favorable planetary conditions. The choice of a desirable time for beginning any undertaking is called, in stellar parlance, an election, meaning that a time has been elected. "Disposition" refers to aspects favorably disposed. Such elections have in all times been considered of the utmost importance by astrologers. This has been particularly true of the coronations of royalty, their marriages, wars and important affairs. There is no knowing if Nostradamus did use elections or if their mention was merely part of his insistence on the importance of astrology in his work. But perhaps he did consult his ephemeris for the positions of the Moon and Mercury, watching the import of their transits upon the clarity and expression of his vision. Perhaps, too, while studying astrology he cast his own nativity, curious to see this celestial blue-print of his own destiny.

The curtains drawn, the candles lighted in his study, on some evening when the oracle is silent, he may have drawn the twelve-rayed circle upon a sheet of parchment and placed precisely the symbols of the Sun and Moon and planets.

Interestedly he studies the chart. In the eighth mansion of the chart, in the mystical water sign of the Scorpion, a waning, secret Moon is setting. The eighth house is the house of death, and of interest in all that lies behind the veil. Nostradamus sighs as he thinks how truly that portent of the Moon's position has been fulfilled from early years. But the Moon is in trine, a benefic aspect, to the powerful conjointure of Jupiter and Saturn in the Moon's own sign, Cancer. These grave planets rule the hierarchy of the Church, of the political and economic conditions, and, placed in a water sign, are a splendid augury for success as a physician and for psychic matters. "And here is my success." His finger touches the Mid-Heaven Sun. "I should not fear to dedicate my work to king or pope." Longest his eye lingered on Mercury in the sign of the Centaur, for Mercury, planet of brain and speech, is the celestial prototype of Branchus.

"Mercury," he whispered, "27 degrees of Sagittarius, it touches the Mercury of Jeanne d'Arc in the same sign. Oh, Branchus, speed the Archer's arrows, let my words be winged--for France!"

On other nights when the prophetic spirit was upon him, the candles would flicker on the forked laurel branch as it bent from the prophet's electrically sensitive hand to the clear water filling to the brim the great, gleaming copper bowl. As the seer bent above the water undulant to the laurel bough, a listener might have heard his low chanting in an ancient tongue, words that once wove a spell amidst the splendor of a long-razed temple.

The phenomenon of illumination which has always been an accompaniment of great prophets, which is mentioned in the Bible, and which has given its name, the illuminati, to those of advanced spiritual perception is referred to by Nostradamus in the letter to César in these words:

"Though everlasting God alone knows His eternity of light, yet I speak frankly to all whose long, melancholy inspiration is informed by the revelation of His immeasurable greatness. It is through the hidden source of divine light, manifested in two principal ways, that the understanding of the prophet is inspired. One way is the intuition which clarifies vision in him who predicts by the stars. The other is prophecy by inspired revelation, which is practically a participation in divine eternity. In the latter, the prophet's judgment is according to his share of divine spirit which he has received through attunement with God the Creator, and also according to native endowment. The complete efficacy of illumination and the thin flame is to recognize that what is predicted is true and of heavenly origin. For this light of prophecy descends from above no less than the light of day."

Did Nostradamus see history flow before his sight in a bowl of water? Did the "Divine Being" dictate his writing as he sat in trance? None knows. Research can pursue no further these "nocturnal studies of sweet odor." Within the prophet's study the candle and the "thin flame" burn low in mystery.

Purpose

TIME WORE ON. The fruit of the prophet's nocturnal visions multiplied enormously as the history of events to come unfolded its vast stretches before his eyes. Nostradamus, in common with most men of genius, began to feel the urge to share his vision with the world. Yet he knew he would have to move very cautiously in presenting his work to the public. Its peculiar nature made necessary all possible safeguards against suppression or destruction not only during his own lifetime but in the future centuries with which his prophecies were concerned. His plans must be carefully made, there must be no mistakes.

He had shown some of his prophetic verses to close friends, and already some of these forecasts had been fulfilled with impressive exactitude. Those who had been privileged to read them wanted to see more of them. A whole bookful, they told Nostradamus, could not hold enough of such fascinating inside information on destiny.

"Why not publish your prophecies?" his friends pressed the question continually. This enthusiasm was a good augury for the popularity of his work, Nostradamus thought, and he wanted to present it as soon as possible. Yet there were difficulties. He talked it all over with Ayme de Chavigny, who says that Nostradamus kept his prophecies by him for a long time, reluctant to bring them out because of the risks which the times made so menacing to scholars. Chavigny, himself a lawyer, scholar and theologian, saw the difficulties clearly, but he, too, was eager for the world to know the marvelous work of his teacher and friend.

"Mon ami et maitre," he said to Nostradamus, "you believe that your foreknowledge is divinely inspired. Well, then, does not that carry its own obligation to reveal it? Had the prophets of Scripture dwelt only on their dangers, we should not have the guidance of Daniel, preserved from the lions, nor Jeremiah, who was rescued from a dungeon."

"True, Ayme," the prophet smiled ruefully, "but you can see there are my wife and children to think of. They would not like either lions or dungeons. Perhaps it would be safest to wait until after my death to have the prophecies published."

"But think of your splendid horoscope," urged Chavigny, who loved to dwell on this chart in admiration of its power. "It promises great preservation."

"Yes, but you and I both realize that though valuable in certain ways, astrology cannot be too heavily relied on. You have only to follow its public prophecies to see that."

"But the astounding accuracy of what you foretell will confound your enemies."

"Oh, no." The prophet's voice was bitter. "They will say that only the Devil could supply such knowledge. You see, Ayme, if they could ever have dismissed me as a charlatan, they could forgive me. But that they will never be able to do."

Chavigny was troubled. He did not know what advice to give. It was true that there was a constant martyrdom of great scholars. Nor was the Inquisition responsible for all of it. The Protestants, when not too busy protecting their own skins, could show the zeal of Torquemada, and their numbers were increasing in Provence. Both sides were lavish patrons of the stake. For Etienne Dôle, burnt by the Catholic Sorbonne, there was Michael Servetus, burned on the order of John Calvin, with the torch applied to an imitation crown of thorns made of straw and set upon his brow.

"But the Church, Michel, is your friend," Chavigny urged. "The fanatics at the Sorbonne, the physicians who hate you, all the rest--they cannot hurt you if the power of the Church supports you. Why not talk to some of the bishops and cardinals who know you well?"

"I have," Nostradamus told him. "They are not against my publishing. Some were encouraging. But I must feel more sure."

"I do not seek to probe unduly," Chavigny said, "but back of your hesitation I seem to sense some other, unspoken reason which is influencing you."

"You are right," Nostradamus told him gravely. "There is another reason for my caution." He rose and walked restlessly about the study, the long black velvet folds of his robe swaying in sculptural rhythm to his movements. When he spoke again, it was with passionate emphasis. "Ayme, my work must live. Must, I tell you. When I think that some agency might compass its destruction, fear lays a hand on my heart."

Chavigny looked at him in astonishment. He silently waited an explanation. Nostradamus turned to his long work-table heaped with parchments. Searching among 4 these he withdrew one and handed it to Chavigny. "Read this."

Chavigny took the screed and read it carefully, first to himself, then slowly aloud.

VI-4
The Capital of France will change from the bank of the river,
No more shall the City of Agrippina hold dominion there,
Everything will be transformed, only the ancient language shall remain unchanged,
Saturn in Leo will pillage Mars in Cancer.

VII-34
The people of France will be very decadent,
Their hearts will be filled with vanities, they will put faith in irresponsible rashness,
There will be scarcity of bread and salt, of wine and ale and all kinds of brewage.
Their leader will be captive of hunger, cold and necessity.

I-8
How many times, O Paris, City of the Sun, shalt thou be captured!
While thou art changing thy empty, barbarian laws, thy great misfortune is drawing near, bringing dire slavery.
But Great Henry will see to it that your vanities are buried.

"My friend," Chavigny said distressfully, "except as you interpret them to me, I do not understand these clouded words. Only I perceive that a disaster of mighty extent stretches an evil hand toward Paris and the nation. Will it be soon? Is it the Spaniards who will conquer in spite of all?" Spain was the ever-present menace of the sixteenth century.

"No, not Spain, mon ami. Nor is it soon. To you it would seem a great way off. To my vision, telescoping time as it does, beholding now this distant tragedy, it affects me as if it were tomorrow. As a matter of fact it is nearly four hundred years away."

Chavigny released the long sigh of a man reprieved from instant calamity. Nostradamus looked at him with a smile half sad, half amused.

"You are in no personal danger, Ayme. But you do not see now what I mean? Why my work must live?"

"But of course!" Chavigny's Gallic vivacity quickly rallied. "That you may warn the country! They will know you for a true and great prophet, they will believe you, they will be saved as Jeanne d'Arc saved France. Oh, what a destiny of grandeur!"

"No. That is not it either," Nostradamus said somberly. "No prophet can contravene the laws of destiny. Would God some word of mine could save France. It is impossible."

"But that makes no sense--"

"Destiny, a man's or a nation's," Nostradamus told him, "is according to divine plan; it is the cross upon the shoulders of humanity. The prophets of Scripture did not utter to change that plan, but through perceived truth to lead men closer to God."

"But your writings pertain to affairs of state, not religion," Chavigny objected.

"That is true. If I have really any mission, it is a humble one," Nostradamus sighed. He was silent for a little, then he took up the thread of his explanation. "There will be in the years to come many crises which France must meet. Two of these will be terrible. In the first one France will for a while seem to be without her soul, but," he added a little cynically, "she will not lose her lands. In the second disaster, which will occur about a hundred and fifty years later, to which I refer in the verses you have just read, her soil will be ravished, her spirit crushed, and her people in bondage.

For a time there will appear to be nothing left. There will be famine of bread for the body and of bread for the soul."

"Horrible, unthinkable," murmured Chavigny.

"These distant calamities," the prophet continued, "will come because the people shall have forsaken spiritual law and are like lost sheep." From memory he quoted one of his verses.

IV-25
The heavenly bodies, visible in their infinite courses,
Shall cloud eventually man's judgment,
Then shall man's forehead, which is body's throne of judgment, lacking its invisible leadership,
Little incline to bend in sacred rite of prayer.

"Ah, Chavigny, could man but realize of how little worth is pride of intellect.

And they will call this strange period The Age of Reason, not knowing that when they lose heaven they lose all."

"You paint a dreadful picture," the lawyer commented. "Yet because it is so far off, I cannot somehow feel it as I should. It has no reality for me. And if you cannot avert this disaster with your warnings, what is it, my friend, that you hope to accomplish?"

"Very little, I am afraid," Nostradamus answered mournfully. "My great desire is to write something that will reach France across the centuries. I was a physician before I was a prophet. My hope is that in her day of disaster some word of mine may administer to the people the caustic of pride, the stimulant of courage, and bind about their wounds the healing salve of hope. If I could but do that much, I would ask no greater boon of God."

Emotion choked Chavigny's voice as he said, "Jeanne d'Arc did no more. I see what you mean, my friend. In the last extremity, a people must help themselves. All that can be done is to arouse them to the effort."

"Yes," Nostradamus agreed. "And here is my message to them. He handed Chavigny another piece of writing. The lawyer read:

III-24
When impotence and violence shall have bred the great confusion
Born of loss of thy people and thy innumerable treasure,
Thou should not then permit thyself to weaken,
France, this is my word to thee, remember thou thy past.

"I have not spared the faults of France. I have reported what I think are the self-wrought causes of her downfall. Do you think," Nostradamus asked anxiously, "that she will listen and heed?"

Chavigny's curiosity had reverted to the earlier quatrains. "Who is there that can conquer France if it is not Spain?" he asked belligerently. "You speak of moving the capital--how could that be? And what is the meaning of that reference to the planets, Saturn in Leo, wasn't it?"

"Slowly, my friend! In that period of lost judgment, which will cover quite a long space of years, some of which will be rich and prosperous, there will be no king in France, the government will be a republic."

"Like Venice and Florence?"

"Well--no. It will be more extreme. You have read Utopia by that misguided camel across the Channel, Thomas More. It will be more like that--at least they will have similar ideas. They will say that all men are equal."

"What folly!" cried his friend. "Men can grow in grace, if they would. But a peasant cannot equal a king."

"All political ideas will have changed," Nostradamus replied, "except the greed for power." "But you still have not told me--"

"Germany," Nostradamus cut in with his answer, "will be the dominant power. Twice it will conquer France, and the second conquest is the time I speak of as so desperate. You know, Ayme, that I like to date and to identify events by means of the positions of the heavenly bodies, which cannot lie, nor are they subject to change as is the calendar. In the chart of this Republic of France, the position of Mars will be in the sign of Cancer. There will, in the final disaster, be no real leadership. It is the government which will be both criminal and victim. That is why I designate particularly the government. Nor do I wish to give exactly the year of this downfall, but only to indicate under what constitution of the government the event will occur. But the German, the one man who will tear down the realm of France, I have identified him by the position of Saturn at the time of his birth, for in that day he is the government of Germany. In another verse about him, I have even given the precise degree, Saturn in the thirteenth degree of Leo."

"Then the meaning of this line is," said Chavigny, consulting the verse, "that this powerful German, one who has Saturn at birth in the thirteenth degree of Leo, will ravish that government of France which will have Mars in Cancer. Is that it?"

"That is correct," said Nostradamus.

In the last tragic days of June, 1940, the current astronomical position of Mars was exactly transiting the position Mars held in Cancer at the birth of the Third Republic, September 4th, 1870. Saturn was in thirteen degrees of Leo when Adolf Hitler was born.

"Will this German be of the religion?" asked Chavigny in concern.

"No, there will be a new and far worse heresy which will then arise, resembling more the pagans of the Northland." Again he quoted from his prophecies.

III-67
A new sect of Philosophers will arise
Who scorn death, gold, honor and wealth,
The mountains of Germany will not set their limits,
A following and the printing-presses will support their movement.

II-76
Germany will give birth to diversified sects
Which will approach a prosperous paganism,
But such beliefs will collect scant profits,
Eventually they will return to the payment of the true tithe. (of religion)

"Grand Dieu!" cried Chavigny, "but this is all horrible. I begin to feel its sorrow like a black shadow. Is this to be the end of France? France without her robe of glory--it is unthinkable. Is there no hope?"

"Hope! Ah, yes, take heart, my friend! Hope and splendor such as France has never known. But this will only come after a long and cruel wounding. A crucifixion of all that she holds most dear."

"And what is the nature of this great hope?" Chavigny questioned.

Nostradamus' fine features kindled to quick enthusiasm. "A king. The greatest and most glorious of the kings of earth. A son of ancient France and of the lineage of the fleur-de-lys. A prince who will restore the monarchy of France."

"Our own Capetian monarchy! It will not then have died out?" Chavigny exclaimed in surprise.

"No, indeed. The coming of this king will carry the memories of Frenchmen back to that other ancient day of darkness when all seemed lost. I mean the times of Charles VII whom the Maid of Orleans restored to his throne. The king who drove out the English and built a greater France. His name will be on men's lips again and they will liken the conquests of the new monarch to those of Charles VII, buried half a century. I will read you some of my verses about all this." Gathering up some sheets of writing in his hand, he read:

III-94
For five hundred years no accounting will be made
Of him who was the ornament of his time, (Charles VII),
Then there will come a sudden burst of brilliant light,
And the age will be made very happy.

S-49
From the dark realm of old Charon the Phoenix will be reborn,
The last and greatest of the firebird's sons,
He will relight in France the ancient flame, he will be loved by everyone,
Long shall he reign with greater honors
Than ever had his predecessors
In whose name he will achieve a memorable glory.

V-41
Born into shadows of the times and secret effort,
He will be sovereign in his rule and kindness,
His lineage will be that of the lily flowering from its ancient vase,
He will transmute the age of bronze to gold.

III-100
He will be the last reigning king whom France shall honor,
He shall be victorious over him who is the enemy,
He will put to the test his own power and his country,
With a thunderbolt he shall destroy the man of hatred.

VI-3
The river where will be the scene of his effort
Will be in great discord with the Empire,
The youthful prince with the assistance of the Church
Will offer the crown and scepter of concord.

V-6
The Pope will place his hand on the king's head,
He will implore him to establish peace in Italy,
The king will change his scepter to his left hand (the symbol of peaceful intention)
And emerge from his kingship as the peaceful Emperor.

I-80
In the great reign of the great king reigning

He will open by armed might
The great bronze doors (Rheims Cathedral); he will unite in himself the qualities of king and leader.
When the harbor is free, its defenses demolished, he will escort the barque of the Church to its font, (Rome) and day shall be serene.

VI-28
The great Celt shall enter into Rome
Leading the masses of the exiled and banished,
The Pope, great shepherd of the flock, will give asylum to all
Who for the fighting Cock (of Orleans) united in the Alps.

I-97
That which fire and sword knew not how to achieve
His gentle speech will accomplish in council,
The king will develop his ideals through repose and meditation.
There will be no more enemy, nor sword, nor blood shed in battle.

VIII-38
The King of Blois shall reign in Avignon,
Once more he shall be the sole ruler of his people,
He will build his walls on the land that is bathed by the Rhone.
Fifth of his name, and last of his rank before the second coming of Christ.

"Will not that give them hope?" the prophet cried. "And there is more that I have seen, but it is not yet shaped into verses. There is still an immense amount of work to be done on my prophecies."

"It is magnificent," Chavigny exclaimed. "There is the glory of Charlemagne and Saint Louis both about this Prince Capet. I wish that I could see his like on the throne of France today. Tell me, have you seen him, actually looked upon him?"

"Yes, I have indeed," Nostradamus said smiling. "And searching his face I find there justice, sympathy and the wisdom to serve his people. Four centuries separate him and me." A whimsical smile touched his lips. "By such standards of time I become a very ancient man compared to him. So I hope that he would not, if he knew, take it as an unbecoming liberty that I should love him as a son."

"This message of yours should mean all the world to him, 'born under shadows,' as you say. Will he recognize it, see it as himself?"

"That is my hope," Nostradamus told him. "My purpose is that he shall read it, and feel the ancient royal, strength of Hugh Capet flow through his sword arm. My hope is to give him confidence of victory, of freedom for his people--our people."

"Now I understand your anxiety for the preservation of this work," Chavigny said. "But can you not foresee its fate?"

"Yes," Nostradamus answered, "I know that it will live, and that it will avail. But I cannot be sure how much. It is harder to foresee those matters which concern oneself. What I fear is that the work may be mutilated or changed, or that others may imitate it so that people will be hard put to tell the true from the false."

"What I would fear more," his friend told him candidly, "is that people will not understand its meanings when they read it. These verses are clear enough to me now, but many that you have shown me, I frankly could make nothing of, lacking your help. In a matter so important you should write with the utmost clarity." It was the lawyer in Chavigny speaking.

"What you are pleased to call my clouded words," smiled Nostradamus, "have a purpose. Books too often survive because time forgets them, they are safe because unread. My prophecies must be read by every generation, their flame must be fed by constant interest, so that in the day of their need they will not be on musty shelves, but in the hands of the people of France." The prophet's grave eyes twinkled at Chavigny. "Can you, my learned and legal friend, think of a better way to set the generations reading than by giving them a puzzle, of which each age solves some pieces of its truth, and none ever solves it fully until the time of its fulfillment?"

The lawyer thought it over. "I see your point," he said, "it is a good one. But even, if, as you say, people cannot change their major destinies, still they have to wait for the fulfillment of a prophecy to know if it is a true one. And each accurate forecast will make them pay closer attention to what is foretold as coming next."

"And also bring them greater suffering in anticipation," Nostradamus reminded him. "No. Life holds more of sadness than of joy. Many things are better not revealed in advance. But my prophecies are not all obscure. That would not do either. Many events are clearly described, with names of persons given, and dates of occurrences. Men will know by these that there is truth in my words, and they will never leave off searching for more of it in the difficult passages. That is how I would have it."

Chavigny's mind had gone off on a tangent. "I suppose the world will be a very different kind of place in four hundred years. I doubt that I would recognize it."

"Outwardly different," Nostradamus told him. "The nations of that day will, as Scripture says, have sought out many inventions. But man himself will be the same. Unfortunately." Chavigny got up from his chair, shook out the folds of his scholar's gown and carefully adjusted them. "If I had not studied with you so long," he observed thoughtfully, "I could not credit a vision of such immensity as yours. But because I know you, know the already fulfilled prophecies that you have made, I must believe you. Yet it staggers the imagination. Four hundred years!"

"And far beyond that," the prophet told him dreamily. "My eyes have beheld the oceans of time that swirl their mighty tides against the gates of God." He too arose. "You are leaving, Ayme?"

"Yes, I must be getting back to Beaune. Besides, my mind is incapable of digesting more wonders. You are right, there is something about prophecy, even when it does not touch one's own life, that is somehow shattering."

After Chavigny had gone, Nostradamus seated himself at his table. He spread a parchment carefully before him, selected a quill, and began to write:

III-79
The fatal order of destiny is an eternal chain
Forever looping on itself in cycles consistent with its own order.

He threw aside the quill, the verse unfinished, and began to think. His friends were right; if his work was to be published, it was time to make a beginning, to try it out. Time to conquer doubts and misgivings and to get on with it. He realized and faced the fact that what he most dreaded was the fresh cries of sorcery, the calumnies and vituperation that would be heaped upon his head by the very men who should be his friends. His nature, as unselfish and affectionate as it was deeply sensitive, shrank from this ordeal. But there would be, surely, a preservation from harm. Not as Chavigny had said because of the power of his horoscope, but because he held his prophetic gift from God. Certainly, he thought it had been given to him for a divine purpose. He had never misused it. God would look after him. He would trust in that, and act with confidence.

His decision made, he began to think of details. How many verses should he publish at first? Not too many. Better see how it went. If there were interest and demand, a new edition could be quickly run off with more of the quatrains. As soon as he could leave Salon, ill patients permitting, he would go up to Lyons and look for a publisher. Macé Bonhomme was reputed a good printer of excellent standing. He would see him and make arrangements.

There was also the matter of the dedication to be planned. Chavigny, de Condoulet, all his friends would, he knew, urge him to select a powerful patron to whom he could flatteringly address his work. This would have the double advantage of protection and publicity. Moreover, it was customary. Well, he would break the precedent. He had always stood alone. Not so many men in France among the ranks of scholars or artists could say as much. Most of them couldn't exist without the gold and prestige of a patron, and fought like wolves among themselves to attract the help and protection of great prelates and nobles. But with him, Nostradamus, he proudly thought, the shoe had been on the other foot. Patrons had supplicated him, begged him to save their lives and foretell their destinies. He owed no man for gold or favors.

The dedication he decided, should be to César, his oldest and dearly loved son. Between father and son there was a fine sympathy and understanding. César was going to make a good man and one who would do well with his gifts. He thought wistfully how much he would like to see César's young manhood, and guide it. But whenever he should be called to leave the scene of his labors, he wished to leave behind something of himself that should belong exclusively to César. It should be the letter of dedication and the first book of his prophecies. In this letter he would reveal something of his gift, how it manifested itself, how he differed from other prophets of the time. And in particular he would warn his son against the danger of alchemic research and all the forms of black magic. It should be a document which César could keep always by him, recognizing therein his father's true self. César would value it and be proud of it when he, A his father, was gone.

He had told Chavigny of his plan to complete the work in twelve divisions, each one a century containing a hundred quatrains. He liked the arrangement in centuries. It suggested such periods of time and caught the imagination. Yet it really meant nothing in this sense, because he intended that the verses should be so well scrambled that only with difficulty, and usually after the event, could the prophecies be assigned to their proper dates. He decided against publishing an even number of verses, such as five hundred. Everyone would be searching for hidden meanings, and he wanted to pique interest and curiosity as much as possible. If there were but, say, four hundred and fifty odd verses, people would wonder why. They would speculate on whether those were all he had ready, or if there was a secret reason, perhaps a hidden clue to his dates--well, that might be true too, though unlikely that anyone would find it.

He had already set aside a large number of the completed verses which he had chosen to go in the book. But these must again be carefully checked, with perhaps some changes, additions and omissions. There must be enough verses about current personalities, who were immediately identifiable or in which the events predicted were of not distant occurrence, otherwise interest would languish and die at the beginning. And there must be other verses which people would think they had identified and which would work out differently, and these would keep them puzzling their wits.

Chavigny had at times wondered why he, as a scientist, did not prophesy more about future developments in this field. It was hard to make Ayme understand how he felt about it. Man's works passed away, but man himself went on. What he was, and in particular how he governed himself, was the important thing. Under a good government and wise leaders ideas expanded, invention and discovery flowered in multiple forms. Given long wars and fools at the head of things, such works disappeared, had to be rediscovered, the work done over again. And, too, there were plenty of men besides himself then living who, if they dared, could give almost as precise a picture of what science would develop in coming centuries as those men of tomorrow themselves. Leonardo had known that some day men would fly, he had foreseen many other inventions they would use. Copernicus had understood that his discovery was but the prelude to vast knowledge of the heavens that would be unfolded. Farther back, the Englishman, Roger Bacon, had written in secret of the principles that would be commonplaces of chemistry one day, but were still too dangerous to mention openly. Plenty of men had this kind of knowledge, better than himself. But these men did not have what he, Nostradamus had, the vision of men and times, the chord within which all else must work.

But, he smiled to himself, he was telling some things about science. The men of tomorrow should see that at least he had not omitted such forecasts because he was ignorant of them. Certainly he was saying enough about "gnats" and "locusts" and "strange birds." The men of the future should recognize exactly what he meant by these terms, because their flying machines looked just like that. He had watched them, in pictures of the future, swarming against the sky, blackening it like a cloud of locusts. Like insects, too, was their weird humming. In time of war they would be an insult to heaven, fighting close to its blue vault, and worse than all the plagues of Pharaoh. Man would pay for such invention; he, Nostradamus, had nothing good to say of airplanes.

He had told, too, about the strange air-bag with a hole in it--another one of those flying-devices. He had set the time quite closely for this. It was the kind of picturesque bit that he knew appealed to readers, as was the gun-part with the amusing name which Frenchmen would give to it. And for those of his own profession, he had described the strange case of an abnormal birth. People took great interest in such things and he, as a physician, did himself. Many thought such births were Devil's changelings. As a scientist, he knew that there were unknown biological laws at work in such cases, but he had often wondered if there had been a soul inclosed in such hideous shapes as he had seen and prayed God's pity on. The child of which he had written would fortunately not be born alive. It was an extraordinary case and would make talk, not only as a wonder but because he had predicted it.

Doctor Garencières, who was, like Nostradamus, a doctor of medicine, and whose translation of the Centuries first introduced Nostradamus to England, was, a hundred years later, fascinated by the prophecy of this unique case. He investigated the circumstances and interviewed one of the medical men who had to do with the preservation of the freak and could tell him all about it. In his translation he devotes considerable space to the account. This quatrain is Nostradamus' prediction.

I-22
That which shall have life, but no intelligence,
Shall have the perfection of its form injured by the steel instrument.
Langres, Autun, Chalons and the two towns of Sens
Will suffer greatly from strife and ice.

Here is the story as told by Doctor Garencières. Speaking of the verse he says:

"This is a great riddle which was never found out till now; and had I not been born in the Country where the History did happen, it might have been unknown to this day, and buried in oblivion.

"In the year of the Lord 1613, which was that of my birth, there lived in the town of Sens a Taylor's wife, named Columba Chatry, and who presently after her marriage conceived and for the space of twenty-eight years persuaded herself to be with child. She had all the signs of it, and after having gone her compleat time, began to feel the pains of a woman in labor. Then her breath failed, the motion of the child ceased and the pains subsided. For three years the poor woman kept her bed complaining of a hard swelling and griping. She frequently spoke of bearing a child as being the cause of her death. After her death her husband engaged two prominent chirurgeons to make an autopsy. On making the incision with a razor, their knives encountered a horny substance and they had to exert their full muscular strength. Within the womb was a child, perfectly formed and partly petrified, its skull shining like a horn. The wrist was broken in removing the child ("perfection of the form injured by the steel instrument") which was so grown to the mother, nor did the doctors realize what they had (in time to prevent the injury). The little body was perfectly developed and of such hardness that to this very day that little body defieth all kind of corruption. The child was kept by a Mr. Medill, a chirurgeon of Sens who kindly showed it to all strangers who came from far and near to see it."

Doctor Garencières goes on to relate that the fame of this wonder was so great that doctors in particular travelled great distances to verify the happening and see the child. A prominent English physician urged Charles I to buy it for England, but this was not done, and Venice, instead, obtained it. Of the last two lines of the quatrain, Garencières says:

"Autun, Chalons and Langres, and Sens, the Town where this did happen, did in that year suffer much damage by Hail and Ice which did come to pass, as many persons in that country may testify that are alive to this day."

César de Nostradame says in his History of Provence, that his father predicted "astronomically" the birth of a two-headed child, and that this occurred, as foretold, in 1554, in February, and was brought to Salon for his father to see.

Comets were another source of perennial appeal in older times when as portents of doom their appearance provided gloomy excitement and much agitated speculation as to where the blow would fall. Not much was known in the sixteenth century of the erratic orbits of these wanderers which were a never-failing source of astonishment and dread. Nostradamus had enough showmanship to know that comets were always good for arousing interest. He has reported a number of them in the Centuries. While he was organizing his quatrains for the first edition of the prophecies he was pleased that one of these eerie visitors could soon be expected. There was a verse about it that must certainly be included because it would only be a year until its fulfillment.

II-43
While the star with the hairy tail is visible,
Three great princes will become enemies,
Peace will receive a blow from the heavens, there will be earthly upheavals.
The Po and the Tiber will be in flood, and there will be a serpent on the shore.

There was a verse that, from the popular viewpoint, had everything, comet, royal quarrel, disturbance of the earth, and a sea serpent! Nostradamus delighted in confounding his readers by using the same words for a political upheaval as for an earthquake. This verse, it transpired later, meant some kind of actual disturbance within the earth. In March, of the following year, and less than a year after publication of the prophecies, a great comet appeared and could be seen, terrifying in the night sky, for three months. Truly enough, the new truce between France and Spain was quickly broken when the French king went to the assistance of the Pope, who was fighting the Spaniards. To make the forecast perfect, the Tiber and the Arno for no known reason, unless it was some underground disturbance, overflowed and flooded the surrounding land. When the Tiber receded, sure enough there on its bank was a very strange, large serpent, just as promised. Nostradamus knew that a verse such as this would linger in the minds of people, making an impression where events of graver import might be overlooked or forgotten. He counted on such prophecies to increase his fame and serve its continuance.

Not long after this, his letter of dedication to César finished, his verses chosen, he journeyed to Lyons and gave them into the skilled hands of the printer, Mach Bonhomme. Thereafter in due time in this same year, 1555, a slim volume containing four hundred and fifty-four prophetic verses by Maistre Michel Nostradamus was offered to a wondering world.

On to Paris

THE SUCCESS OF THE BOOK was immediate and enormous--adjectives which seem to keynote the life of Nostradamus. People were fascinated by the cryptic novelty of the verses which became the sensation of the moment. Everybody was reading, puzzling, spotting, quoting and arguing over them. Some of the verses were daringly easy of identification. Some seemed to point to certain public personalities but were debatable. These were shuffled among quatrains that no one could pretend to understand, or even guess at the persons referred to. Since the baffling prophecies were decidedly in the majority, the detractors of Nostradamus, who said that here was no prophecy but only incomprehensible gibberish, had, it must be confessed, much on their side.

When one remembers that it has taken "seven men with seven mops" working diligently all these intervening years to decipher the meanings, some of which are still controversial, and others yet not understood, it is no wonder that the derisionists of that day refused to be shouted down by the chorus of enthusiasts. Everyone who had known the prophet personally chanted his praises. From Provence to Paris people talked of him, relating the successes, legends and accusations that had grown up about his history. More than ever the narrow lanes and crooked streets of Salon were choked with the crowd pouring in to consult the new authority on destiny. Patients needing the doctor of medicine were now jostled by patronage seeking the doctor of destiny.

Paris was in those days a long way from Provence. Nostradamus' fame had hitherto been local. With the publication of the book, reports of his astonishing history reached the capital. It is not surprising that Catherine de' Medici desired at once to meet Nostradamus. Her interest in occultism was well known. What is surprising is that the King, who had no such interest, was the one who summoned the doctor to Paris. His curiosity was on this occasion at least the equal of the Queen's.

It is probable that before he extended an invitation to Nostradamus to visit Paris, he sent a cautious inquiry to his Provençal governor, seeking reliable information about this strange subject of his. A king had to be careful not to excite ridicule and criticism in such a matter.

The King could have asked no one who was better fitted to extol the prestige and abilities of Nostradamus than was Claude de Savoie, Count de Tende et de Villars, Governor of Provence. He had known Nostradamus all his life as friend, physician and seer. He knew his background and family history. He and the prophet had both been young together. Both had fought their first great battles at the same time. When Nostradamus had left Montpellier to wrestle with the plague, the Count de Tende had been holding at bay the Spanish army under the Constable de Bourbon. He had defended Marseilles and defeated the Spaniards with a valor which had established him as one of the first soldiers in France. As Governor of Provence he had endorsed the life pension with which the city of Aix had rewarded the doctor's second battle with the plague. He knew how Nostradamus' prophetic gift had come down to him through inheritance. He had seen many illustrations of its uncanny power and authority. These were all things which he could write to the King, adding that the greatest princes and prelates in the south of France called Maître Nostradamus friend.

All this he set down in his letter to the King. Then, before he closed it with the customary salutations, he sat back in his chair and nibbled his quill thoughtfully. This writing was a chore for a soldier. He would be glad to get it done. But there was one thing more that he wanted the King to know. Again his quill took up its scratching rhythm as he wrote a concluding paragraph.

"Maître Nostradamus has also honored me with a prophecy concerning the future of my line. Inasmuch as my ancestors served those of Your Majesty, and since it has been my privilege to wield my sword for Your Majesty's late father, and holding it always in readiness to strike for his most puissant son, the Very Christian King of France, it is a comfort to my declining age to learn from the inspired vision of this true prophet that in the future of times to come the sword arm of Villars shall still not fail in its valor to defend the crown of France on behalf of Your Majesty's descendants."

He added the final compliments, his signature and the date with a satisfied flourish. That did it. Now perhaps the King would ask Nostradamus what this prophecy was, and his friend would tell the King the tale of the future about the line of Villars which in a rare mood he had unfolded to him one evening when they had supped together in Aix, and had sat late by the Governor's fireside afterward, talking of many old experiences.

A Frenchman, perhaps more than men of other nationalities, is concerned over the continuance of his line and the maintenance of the prestige established by his ancestors. The Count de Tende et Villars had spoken of this to Nostradamus. The prophet had gladdened his heart by saying that there would come another Claude de Savoie in time, who would even surpass all former military achievements of his house, that he would rescue France from desperate peril, and fight his battles on a far-flung field. The Governor had begged the prophet to tell him something of this coming soldier, his namesake. It meant so much to him that his own name would be carried on to greener laurels. He felt such an old fogy in these days of new artillery, and odd gadgets on guns, all so different from the weapons he had used to defend Marseilles. That, too, had been a great fight; it had preserved France from Charles V, and made him, Claude de Savoie, famous. But that had been thirty years ago, and the world forgot so quickly.

The prophet had smiled at him quizzically. "You have," he told him, "already read without knowing it something of the battles of the coming Claude de Savoie."

"Where?" asked the Count.

"In my new book," the prophet told him. "There are several verses about him, and I have still more to foretell, perhaps in another volume."

"Tell me, old friend, I implore you." The Governor sat forward excitedly. "When is this to be? How long before it happens?"

"That I shall not tell you," answered Nostradamus, "but it is sometime off. You and I won't be here."

"I hope Saint Peter will let me see the fight, By God, I'd snatch Lord Gabriel's trumpet and sound a blast for victory!"

Nostradamus looked shocked. He did not relish the profanity of camps.

"Which are the verses, man? I must know them," the Count cried. "Don't stand me off with your puzzles. I won't tell anyone. I can keep my counsel, as you know. I understand how everyone would be at you if they found that you had broken your precedent and explained a little from that book, though I can't see why you are so unwilling. But my word as a soldier, I will not tell of the verses to anyone. Do you mention my name?"

"Yes," the seer assured him, "both names, Tende and Villars. And since I wish the men of that day to say 'like ancestor, like descendant,' I mention also Provence, so that it shall not be forgotten from what place and what fighting stock this soldier comes."

"He will be born here in Provence, I suppose?" the Count said.

"He will come from Narbonne. Your namesake will be a Gascon."

"Pah!" the Count exclaimed disgustedly. "A Gascon is a braggart who fights with words. Why can't he be born right here?" He looked at the prophet in naïve hopefulness as if it were possibly not too late to do something about it.

"I have called him 'the heroic Villars, the man who is more like Mars than Narbonne.' He will be a boaster, but he will make good his boasts when he saves his country," Nostradamus assured him.

"More like Mars than Narbonne," quoted the Count with relish. "I like that conceit, 'tis clever. Martius Narbo was the old Roman name for the city of Narbonne. Yes, it is a pretty play on words, and means, I take it, that this young Claude de Savoie will be a better fighter than a boaster. I begin to think well of him. By Saint Denis, I do!" The Count smiled broadly.

In his many verses on the War of the Spanish Succession, Nostradamus has described its hero, Marshal Villars, and told a great deal about his long struggle. It is not on the record how much he related to the Count de Tende et Villars concerning his illustrious namesake, but the verses which he left for posterity are given in Part II of this book.

In due time the Count de Tende received the royal invitation summoning Maitre Michel Nostradamus to Paris as the King's guest. The Count was requested personally to make all arrangements for the trip and to expedite it in every way as His Majesty was impatient to meet the prophet. Here was a breath-taking compliment. Kings had always used prophets, but not since the days of ancient oracles had they paid them any particular honor. Paris was then filled with seers of one kind and another. Some of them were good, and a few were famous. But such a public invitation as this from royalty was an unheard-of thing. It was the crowning honor of a sensational life.

Salon buzzed with the excitement of the news. Quickly Avignon heard about it, and soon Marseilles. All Provence, except the enemies of Nostradamus, was thrilled and proud. Wherever Nostradamus was known, wherever he had patients from as far back as the first plague, the conversation was all of a piece in marketplace, cottage, château and council hall. The King had bidden their great man to Paris!

Preparations for the journey got under way at once. Maître de Chavigny, the Sieur de Condoulet, the town fathers and a host of friends and patients poured in to offer their congratulations, give practical advice about the long trip, and tell what they knew or had heard about the customs and personages at the court of the Valois. The housewifely instincts of Madame de Nostradamus came immediately into action to look after the details of her husband's travel needs. There was brushing, steaming and airing of the doctor's best robe of Lyons velvet. Two costumes were the limit, even for the affluent in these days, and they were expected to last, if not unto the third and fourth generations, at least unto the second. There was baking and roasting to be done, a flaky loaf and a tender young fowl for the hamper in which would also go the leathern bottle of vintage wine, which a grateful patient had contributed. Perhaps the children, being French, may not have surged around shouting, "My Papa is going to Paris!" but they and the whole household would have felt the excitement.

Only the doctor was unaffected and moved about in his usual serene and casual fashion. He prepared and labeled tinctures and essences which some of the sick might require in his absence. He packed his inkhorn, his quills and writing-tablets. He might want to do a little writing in the evenings at inns along the route, since his travel would be all done by day. He would probably be too tired when night came for much effort, however, so for company he chose his well-worn copy of Aristotle to take with him, and the latest volume of poems by Ronsard, the celebrated and fashionable poet who had just received the Toulouse award and the silver statue of Minerva. Perhaps Ronsard would be at the court, and he might have the privilege of meeting him.

Nostradamus was now fifty-three years old, and no longer in good health. He had used his splendid energies throughout his life without stint or thought to himself. Premature age was taking its toll, and he was suffering from that so common ailment of the time, gout. The long trip to Paris was a great undertaking for him, even under the best conditions which the Count de Tende could arrange. There is no account of his mode of travel. But it was probably, as he had always travelled, on the back of a sturdy mule. He may have made part of the trip by coach, but coaches were still a rarity, and their build was so cumbersome and their springs so joltingly hard that they offered, outside of their impressive appearance, little relief.

Nostradamus left Salon on the 14th of July, 1555. This date, looking forward in time, and told by another calendar, would one day be pregnant with meaning to France as Bastille Day, an event of the future which the prophet sadly chronicled. Looking backward in time, it was the date when Frenchmen, fighting valiantly for their God, had seen Jerusalem fall to the Crusaders, rescued from the infidel. Nostradamus had not forgotten that page of history, now made melancholy by loss of the Crusaders' gains which his writings mention as Christendom's disgrace.

All of his friends had gathered with his family to see him off on his trip. A waving, smiling crowd from in and out of town had assembled to wish him Godspeed. The Count de Tende had ridden over from Aix to supervise the details of departure. He found a moment to whisper in the prophet's ear, while giving him his schedule of travel.

"Tell His Majesty about young Claude de Savoie, if opportunity permits. I think the King would be well satisfied to know of him."

Nostradamus smiled indulgently. "Yes," he said, "and Claude, the elder, too. A thousand thanks for all your kindness."

Since he was on the King's errand, the prophet no doubt made top speed for the times. But the roads, though more numerous, were often no better than in the days of Clovis. They were full of deep ruts, which became small ponds when it rained, and great stretches of mud. Travel at best was appallingly slow, though never having known a swifter mode, it doubtless did not seem so to Nostradamus. Besides, he was an experienced traveller and liked the road. It was his first trip of any length in a good many years and he was prepared to enjoy it. He savored the character and charm of each locality that he passed, drawing in the perfume of its herbs and flowers as a connoisseur savors a vintage bouquet.

Travelling northward through the valley of the Rhone he watched Provence roll past him, slowly receding. Its panorama never failed to enchant him, its gardens, its cypress and olive, its thyme and lavender, rosemary and rue. Besides their beauty, these held for him, as physician, the deep meaning of the soil, the healing power of earth's plants for earth's children. Across the countryside at intervals his ears caught the joyous shrilling of a flute or the tinkle of a tambourine, and occasionally there was a flash of Moorish color, or the glimpse of a festival procession.

In two weeks he had passed Lyons, and left behind him the langue d'oc, "that beautiful Provençal language, more than three-quarters Latin, formerly spoken by queens, which shepherds alone now understand." Once across the Rhone, he had entered the land of the langue d'oïl, or modern French, which had been the official language of France for some twenty years. He was now moving through the beautiful landscapes of Lorraine, drawing closer to the country of the Maid of Orleans, and the fields and blossoms bright with summer celebrated by Ronsard's verses. The prophet's memory, "almost divine," did not need to consult the volume of Ronsard's poems. Softly to himself he quoted:

"Sky, air and winds, and naked hills and plains,
Tapestried woodland halls, and green morass,
And river-shores, and pools of sombre glass,
And viny slopes, and shivering gold champaigns,
And moss-mouthed caverns' shadowy domains,
And buds and blossoms and dew-glimmering grass." *

And about him he saw lordly châteaux topping the hills, their arrogant towers lifting in conscious elegance above the half-screening woodlands. Cottages in the deep heart of bowering trees, foot bridges over streams dancing across valleys of emerald velvet, offered their northern loveliness in substitute for the high color of Provence.

While he was traversing the long road, Nostradamus had ample time to ponder the personages and conditions he would meet in Paris. He had heard a great deal about the King and Queen. He reviewed it now as a guide for his successful approach to royalty. How different, he thought, had been the lives of these two, and yet there was a pattern of similarity, too, especially, in their early youth. Both had experienced a loveless, prisoned, dangerous childhood when each had been a helpless, political pawn in the hands of savagely warring powers.

From his seventh to his eleventh year, Henry had spent shut up in a gloomy Spanish monastery, hostage, with his older brother, for their father, King

Francis. When he had finally returned to France, it had been necessary for him to relearn his own language, forbidden him in his imprisonment. A shy, alien boy, he had come home to a Spanish stepmother and a country which, though his own, seemed a stranger. He had not been the dauphin then, only the second son. He had been lonely and ill adapted to the gay court. The prisoning walls had not been wholly left behind, something of their barriers was now within himself. Then when he was only fourteen, they had married him to the pale little Italian girl from Florence, with whom he had found nothing in common, not even a child for ten years. In all the carefree glitter of his father's court, there had been only one who had taken an interest in the diffident boy growing up within his shell. Only one who had understood him and concerned herself with his boyish life. This was the gloriously beautiful Seneschal of Normandy, now Duchess of Valentinois also, Diane of Poictiers. The adolescent heart of the boy, still yearning for the mother he could not remember, had attached itself with passionate fidelity to this woman twenty years his senior. Now, all France knew and accepted its two queens, Catherine the crowned, whose diadem but scarcely gilded the indifference of her husband, and Diane the uncrowned, whose power dispensed the patronage and spent the revenues of France with arrogant assurance.

The King at this time was enjoying the first period of peace that he had experienced in some years. Six months before, he had signed a five-year truce with his enemy, Charles V. That monarch had then betaken himself to a monastery to consider his soul's salvation, after first dividing up his empire. Austria he had bestowed upon his brother. Spain, the Netherlands and possessions in Italy he had given to his son Philip. No one expected the truce between Spain and France would last. Philip II was as bitter a foe of France as his father had been, while Henry's warlike nature and inherited glory-dreams bided only an opportunity to strike at Spain. Nostradamus well knew the kind of questions that the King would ask him about all this, and he realized how little his answers would affect the course of events. For had he not seen those events transpiring in his visions?

His thoughts turned to the Queen. An intelligent, agreeable woman, by all reports. Deeply interested in occultism, too, but desiring, like all ambitious people, to profit by it rather than to live according to its laws. It was going to require more adroitness to meet and parry her questions, and at the same time satisfy her than would the inquiries of the King. He felt a vast pity for this woman, even though he knew what tragedy she would one day bring to the country. The French had never been enthusiastic over "the banker's daughter," and they remained indifferent to her. Not the least of the reasons for this was that "the three pearls," which Clement VII had optimistically mentioned as her dowry, Genoa, Naples and Milan, had so far proved uncollectible. The money she had brought from Italy had been negligible. Her wealth, and it was large, had come to her from her French mother, Madeleine de la Tour d'Auvergne. It was through her mother, too, that she was cousin to both her rivals, the older siren, Diane de Poictiers, and the young beauty, Mary Stuart, the enchantress of her son the dauphin. Not until Catherine could rid herself of the power of these two women would she have her turn.

Nostradamus, who knew her history fully, understood how Catherine's whole life had been spent in trying to hold her own--just that. And it would always be so. From the time of her birth her ears had been assaulted by the sound of trampling. First, it was the Horseman of Death, taking both her father and mother within the month of her coming into the world. Ariosto, touched by her fate, had written then of her babyhood, "A single branch grows green again with a little foliage. Fearful and hopeful, I do not know if winter will spare it or tear it from me."

The heavy tread of armies, trampling the lives and fortunes of the family great Lorenzo built, had menaced all her childhood. "Put her in a brothel so the Pope cannot marry her to a noble." "Bind her to the ramparts and see how straight the Prince of Orange aims his bullets." These were the outcries of soldiers and demagogues at the siege of Rome, when she, a child, was hidden in a convent.

At fourteen had come marriage and the transplanting to the colder soil and grayer sunlight of Paris. Then a new kind of trampling had begun. This time it was her pride and her heart that were beaten into the dust. The men and women of Europe's haughtiest court scarcely permitted her to forget that they counted their noble lineage by centuries, while she, the Medici, counted hers by years. Nor did they disguise their careless pity for her lack of beauty. Catherine had been ill equipped to compete in this new field, but she had tried. However, she soon found out that fine clothes, the grave grace of her beautiful leg flung boldly over the saddle-bow, defying convention, and the supplicating gesture of ivory and exquisite hands, were not enough. Not in that court where every woman was hand-picked for beauty.

Catherine, like Henry, had turned to age for sympathy and companionship. She had attached herself to King Francis and won his genuine affection. "She prayed the King," wrote Brantôme, "to allow her to be always at his side." Francis liked her love of sports, the wit and maturity of her mind. Always a connoisseur of women, he was the only one of his court to appreciate that his daughter-in-law was a girl of unusual interest. Then Francis, her one friend, had died. Never did life give to Catherine de' Medici the opportunity to love or be loved. Always there was defeat and frustration for her affections. Even maternity was so long denied to her, and then so continuously thrust upon her, that love for her children was never a part of her life. Ruggiero, her astrologer, whispered to her of future power through her long years of repression, sustaining her with this dark bread, while what should have been her heart turned slowly and terribly into stone.

Such were the royal pair whom Doctor Nostradamus was so soon to greet.

A month and a day had gone by from the time he left Salon until he sighted the walls and spires of Paris, ancient Lutetia. It was the feast day of Notre Dame when he arrived, late in the afternoon. There was no one to meet him, since the time of his arrival could not be known. Travel-worn and very tired, he looked about for an inn to rest his weary bones. The sign of the first hostelry that he came upon bore the name of the Inn of Saint Michel. Here were two omens, the day and the inn, which had spelled his own name, Michel de Nostradame, in silent, pleasing welcome to the city. Already he felt the friendship of Paris, how could his visit be other than successful? After he had eaten, he dispatched a messenger to the King, announcing his arrival, and holding himself at His Majesty's disposal.

Next morning he had scarcely breakfasted before he was attended by the Constable of France, Duke Anne de Montmorency, who brought the King's greetings and word of his eagerness to see the prophet. He was also there to escort the prophet to proper accommodations.

"His Majesty has provided suitable quarters for your visit, Maître Nostradamus, in the hôtel of the Cardinal de Bourbon. You will be comfortable there and under a pious roof in keeping with what is, we hear, the divine source of your inspiration."

In lodging Nostradamus in the residence of the Cardinal de Bourbon, Archbishop of Sens, the King had rather cleverly served notice on scoffers that the man of prophecy was under the approval and protection of both royalty and the Church. It was a tacit warning to sceptics to hold their opinions in leash. On the way to the Hôtel de Sens, prophet and soldier chatted enjoyably. The constable was then about sixty-five years old. He was the last of the old guard who had fought with Francis I at Pavia, who had been the friend and companion-in-arms of such men as the Chevalier Bayard, the Count de Tende, and, before his downfall, of his predecessor in office, the Constable de Bourbon. He was at this time, next to the King, the most influential figure in France. Head of the Catholic party, high in favor with the Seneschal Diane, and commander of the army of France, he wielded enormous power.

He inquired affectionately after the Count de Tende, recalling their old comradeship when together they had fought the Provencal invasions of Charles V.

"Touching this matter of prophecy," he said, "I don't know much about that field. A soldier usually makes his own destiny, and carves it out the hard way. There have been times when I could have used your vision to know what the enemy was up to, but never have I been in doubt as to how I should speak and act."

The constable was noted for his blunt, forceful words and autocratic opinion, even in the presence of the King.

"I am an old man now," the constable continued, "the prophecy of my life has about reached its last fulfillment, when other and younger hands will carry on my work. And I can make my own prophecy about that. As long as there is a Montmorency to bear the name, he will be at the forefront to defend his king as I have been. Knowing that, I am content."

There was a grand sincerity to the soldier's words that touched the seer. He was suddenly very glad that he had not included in his book a quatrain mentioning the house of Montmorency. For Nostradamus knew how much less fortunate in his famous descendant the constable would be, than his friend the Count de Tende. A future Duke de Montmorency, whom history would call "the great," would meet his end on the block, for conspiracy against the King, Louis XIII, a tragedy some seventy-five years away. The verse describing it is one of the most celebrated of the prophet's forecasts, and a favorite with commentators because it is so specific. It appeared in the later, completed volume of his prophecies.

IX-19

The dauphin shall carry the fleur de lis to Nancy
And even into Flanders to the elector of the German Empire.
A new prison shall confine the great Montmorency
Who, far from the customary sites, will be delivered to the well-known punishment. (Clerepeyne)

There was an interval in which the use of the title of dauphin was allowed to lapse, and Louis XIII was the first to revive it after the time of Nostradamus. Louis did make a triumphal personal entry with his troops into Nancy, not then a part of France, in 1633. Two years later he marched into Flanders to aid the Elector of Trèves, who had been imprisoned by the Spaniards. It was just before this, in 1632, that Henry Montmorency was taken in rebellion and conspiracy, as were a number of important nobles during the reign of Louis. It was the old fight to retain feudal powers against Richelieu's work for national unity. Montmorency was imprisoned in a newly completed building at Toulouse, and privately beheaded in the courtyard instead of one of the customary public places of execution. The soldier who beheaded him was named Clerepeyne, a name which strangely enough comes from two Latin words, clara poena, meaning well-known punishment. Nostradamus has been criticized for his double-talk, but here it was not he, but history which did the double-talking. The ironic, amazing coincidence of the executioner's name and its actual derivative meaning was merely noted with the exactitude of Nostradamus' prevision, and set down with an accuracy which history has attested. Fortunately the constable was unaware of this distant disaster to his house, as he piloted the prophet toward his new quarters.

The fine old Gothic-Renaissance Hôtel de Sens, .at the corner of the Rue de Figuier and the Rue de l'Hôtel de Ville, the town house of the Archbishop of Sens where the constable established Nostradamus in comfort, was built about the year the prophet was born, and at the time of his visit was one of only about fifty such palaces in Paris. Because of the scarcity of such establishments, and the overcrowding and cramped quarters which even wealthy nobles coming to court from out of town had to endure, it was the occasional custom for the owner of a town house, when not in residence, to place it at the disposal of the King. One infers from this, that the archbishop was not himself in Paris at this time, and that the hospitality of his mansion was under the stewardship of the King's household.

Nostradamus was quite used to being stared at. It never bothered him. The mixture of deference and intense curiosity with which the staff at the Hôtel de Sens regarded him, the half-awed, half-mocking eyes of the street crowd which had gathered outside when the Constable de Montmorency returned to conduct him to the King, concerned him not at all. On the way to the Louvre the constable remarked that the attendance at court was unusually large.

"News of your arrival has brought them all out," he told Nostradamus. "I fear they will make your visit to us a very strenuous one. All hope to consult you," he smiled cynically. "The ladies hope that you will foretell vases of gold to hold their roses of love. The men hope to savor in prophetic anticipation the rewards of ambition. Some of them, I think, will savor it no other way," he finished grimly.

Outside the Louvre more citizens had gathered, watching for the prophet's arrival, curious to see what he looked like. Another crowd confronted him when he entered the square courtyard which the palace enclosed. A colorful throng, all jockeying for position to get a front-line view, turned their battery of eyes toward the black-clad figure beside the constable. Nostradamus, smiling in pleasant salutation to the crowd, picked out with his lightning perception its carnival variety. King's gentlemen, cardinals and lovely ladies were in the forefront with the best points of vantage. Back of them pages, lackeys, servants, priests and a nondescript assortment of persons who had made business at the palace an excuse to get in, all elbowed each other and craned their necks to the utmost. Even the narrow windows that looked down on the court were filled with faces.

The constable acknowledged the salute of the gaudily dressed Swiss guards as they entered the building and directed the prophet to the stately new staircase which bears Henry's name. Upstairs there were more people, eager to catch the constable's eye. Montmorency gave a brief nod here and there but he did not slacken his long-legged stride which Nostradamus had, with his ailing foot, some ado to keep pace with. Through unfamiliar doors and corridors they swept to halt at last outside a closed door, which a gentleman in waiting swung open to them. Inside the room a man seated beside a table was reading in a small volume. He looked up as the door opened. The Constable de Montmorency announced:

"Maître Michel Nostradamus."

The prophet was in the presence of the King.

"Ha! At last!" Henry exclaimed, rising with a smile of welcome. "We are pleased that you are safely here. It has seemed a long time." He extended his hand for the kiss of homage and graciously asked Montmorency to place a chair beside the table, near him, for the prophet.

Nostradamus murmured his thanks for the privilege, to which the King answered that his guest having come so far, he would scarcely ask him to tire his body more when there was so much to ask of his mind. The constable did not linger. He quietly withdrew, leaving seer and sovereign to their talk.

Nostradamus gave a glance of swift appraisal, and understood the man who was King. The monarch studied the prophet intently, slowly, carefully adding up in his mind the sum of his observations to give him a conclusion. Each recognized in the other authority and the quality known as presence. Nostradamus saw a tall, blond, splendidly built man of thirty-seven whose bold blue eyes and handsome features were amiable but somewhat inexpressive. Threads of gold and jewel-fires made points of brilliance in the silk-on-silk of his sumptuous dress. Below his clipped beard, an overturn of fine lace half concealed his high, built-up collar. A heavy, elaborately wrought gold chain made a double loop about his neck with a beautiful medallion of gold and jewels, pendant.

The King observed a short, ruddy-cheeked man severely robed, whose extraordinary eyes somehow held him, interested him, gave him the feeling of confidence that he had wanted to feel.

What these two may have said to each other in this confidential interview is not in the record. But we may imagine that the talk ran something like this:

The King gestured toward the book which he had laid down on the table, and which Nostradamus recognized as a volume of his prophecies. "We are interested in this matter of prediction," the King said, when the amenities had been further disposed of, "yet much that is foretold never comes to pass, so that there has seemed to us to be little of guidance in it. The Queen leans more on prophecy than do we. But it is not the Queen who makes decisions; she has not our responsibility to decide for France."

"Your Majesty's valor and wisdom--" began the prophet, but the King broke in.

"No pretty speeches, Maître Nostradamus. Our court is well versed in those. Men say that you have foresight divinely inspired and therefore true. What we desire from you is truth."

"Sire," the prophet answered, "I would not demean this honor with less."

"You have written some things," the King continued, "in this book that seem to touch our family and certain persons of the court. But we shall not speak of that yet. Our personal fate is subject to God's will. It is of France that I would have you prophesy. What of our claims, what of our enemy's ambitions, how shall the glory of France be best advanced?"

"The lilies," the prophet told him, "will bloom for a great while and fill a larger garden. But I will not hide from Your Majesty that there will be troubled times and much bloodshed. But from each time of peril France will emerge greater, more powerful."

"A brave prophecy!" said the King. "The blood will no doubt be shed by Spain. Well, we expect that, though God be our witness that we have striven for peace."

"Not for long shall Spain hold her power," the prophet told him. "Her time is drawing to a close, though she will trouble France until she has passed her zenith, but her power will be surpassed by the English."

"England!" said the King in vast surprise. "An heretical people, whose rulers do not scruple to intrigue with those of the religion in France to foment sedition. The worst troubles in the history of France have been with England. I wish we might get Calais out of their hands!"

"Ah, that you will," Nostradamus told him, "and shortly. Calais, I promise you, shall return permanently to France."

Henry's eyes sparkled. "That is a forecast which tickles my ears. Now we are getting somewhere. Spain put down, and Calais back. Give us but Italy, those portions which rightly belong to France, and we shall be well content."

The prophet was silent, as the King looked at him expectantly.

"Well, Maitre Nostradamus, shall we gather in Milan, Naples and Sicily next year?"

"No, Sire. Success will not crown the war in Italy." The King's face clouded. "What! You contradict yourself. If Spain is to weaken, nothing can stop France."

"Spanish power will not vanish in Your Majesty's lifetime, but in the lifetime of one of your sons. The Italian venture will prove costly and unprofitable."

"We shall change that forecast," said Henry aggressively, "and sooner, perhaps, than we shall take Calais. The Italian lands must come to the crown of France, and we shall lead Frenchmen to take them." The King's bold blue eyes challenged the prophet's reflective gray ones. As the prophet sat silent, the

King said imperiously, "Such a matter touches the honor of the crown, and it is one which only the crown can decide."

"The future expansion of France," said Nostradamus, "will be toward the Rhine, toward which Your Majesty has already made a strong beginning." The great fortress of Metz had fallen to the French under Francis of Guise but a few years before.

"You think we shall get still more of that territory?" asked the King.

"I do, and that too is not far off. Those who now speak the French tongue under foreign sovereignty will be returned to their motherland."

"There is already enthusiasm for that policy," Henry remarked. "It is intolerable that men having this bond of our language should be subject to another rule. We have taken the matter greatly to heart. We rejoice to hear what you have to say of it."

It was during the reign of Henry II that the idea was born that people speaking a common language should be united under one flag. France used the argument to justify her conquests toward the Rhine and Belgium. It was the same argument with which Adolf Hitler opened his campaign to seize Europe.

"How long shall England hold her power?" the King desired to know.

"More than three centuries," the prophet told him.

"Body of God!" cried the King, "and what will France be doing? Will there be no French kings to wrest the strength from England? Dare not to tell me of another Agincourt."

"There will be no Agincourt," the prophet assured him gravely. "France, too, shall be an empire of far-flung grandeur. Yet there will be one time when a great soldier will arise out of England and overflow the continent. France then will be in great danger. But there will be another Claude of Savoie to rescue France."

"The Governor of Provence so wrote me." The King rose and walked about the room, pleasurably excited. "I shall enjoy telling the Queen that. Her Majesty admires the teachings of her countryman, Machiavelli. She thinks I treat my nobles too well and will pay for it in their conspiracies for power. But I will not believe it of them. Men who not only give their lifehood to France, but unasked melt the white and the red from their tables, and take the last coin from their pouches for my needs! I prefer to rule such subjects through friendship, not severity."

"A feeling which does great honor to Your Majesty's character," said the prophet warmly. "And God will preserve his anointed kings of France who have Your Majesty's strength and goodness."

"I suppose there is no future danger to the continuance of the Capetian monarch," the King said questioningly. "Can you tell me how many more kings of France there will be?"

"There are twelve more to come of the line of the fleur de lis. The last of them shall be greater than Charlemagne. His glory shall light the firmament, and be long remembered of man."

"Only twelve!" cried the King. "And after twelve?" The King leaned forward in his chair.

"The whole world shall then greatly change, and for a long time there will not be peace between God and man."

The King was silent for a time, thoughtful. Then his mind reverted to the royal obsession.

"Tell me, Maître Nostradamus, touching this thing that men call fate, how far do you think it can be changed? You say that we shall not regain Italy. Well now, if I accepted that and made no effort, then we ourselves should be furnishing the cloth to make the cloak for your prophecy. But suppose we are unwilling to be so accommodating."

"The outcome would be the same in either case," the prophet said firmly. "Only in the former circumstance, Frenchmen's lives would be saved. As to your question about fate, it is my humble belief that prophetic visions, when true, are not subject to change. I hold that they can only be perceived by the prophet because they have already transpired within the mind of Almighty God. Touching, however, the times, events and climates of which there is no prescience, these may perhaps be changed according to the will of man. God has given volition to man, and a measure of freedom in using it. Only when man misuses it does God deprive him of it and send disaster upon him."

"And have you seen our defeat in Italy?" persisted the King.

"With sorrow, Sire, I have."

"You may be right," the King admitted. "But I still shall not accept it." The prominent royal jaw set stubbornly. "To do so would make me a coward, traitorous to the just claims of my ancestors."

The King rose, this time in token that the interview was at an end. The prophet's gaze dwelt admiringly for a moment on the beautiful tapestries which covered the walls with their pictured story of the labors of Hercules.

"Were Hercules not a tapestry," he said to Henry, "but a living hero, what could he not learn with profit from a monarch whose tasks are greater and more glorious than were his."

The King smiled. "Hercules, at least, finished his work. I often despair of that. We have many more questions to ask you, Maitre Nostradamus, and we look forward to more conversations. Just now, though I count myself a man of courage, I quail at the thought of how I shall be chidden if I keep you longer. The Queen, the Duchess of Valentinois, and Madame, my sister are all impatience to meet you. The Constable of Montmorency will continue to have you in his care. He will see that you have refreshment, and will then conduct you to other interviews. For the present, adieu." Footnotes

204:* Translation from Ronsard by Morris Bishop.

The Court of the Valois

THE ARRIVAL OF THE PROPHET in Paris had stimulated afresh the popular interest in his book. Everyone who had not seen it before was reading and talking about it now. Speculation centered particularly on a few of the quatrains that seemed to yield more promise of immediate fruition than the rest. There was one which spoke of a new king, crowned at Rheims when Saturn was in water, who would "slaughter the innocents." It would be in a water sign, Cancer, again in 1561. Was that the end of Henry II, and who were the innocents? Of course if 1561-3 went by and nothing happened, then the prophecy couldn't take place for another seven or eight years. But maybe something would happen, because there was that other verse about the old lion being killed, fighting in a golden cage. The astrologers had said Henry II would die in a duel, and only a king vv as privileged to wear gilded armor. Henry II didn't have long then, did he, they gossiped.

There was the verse, too, about the Bailiff of Orleans. Would that be Jerome Groslot, the present bailiff? Condemned to die, deserving to, but saved from death--what could bring that about?

Then there was that wicked verse about Bossu. Everybody knew who that was--young Louis de Bourbon, the hunchback Prince of Condé. Well, the gossips said, he wouldn't be the first Bourbon to turn traitor and get shot for it. Already he was of the religion, like others of his family.

Bossu was then in Paris. While the fanfare of the prophet's arrival was being noised abroad, he dropped in at Admiral Coligny's quarters fuming with anger.

"You would think that God Himself had come to town," he raged. "The entire court, I hear, are making complete fools of themselves over this charlatan."

Coligny, his brother Francis d'Andelot and some other Protestant gentlemen who were present gave Condé ready agreement. D'Andelot said,

"The old sorcerer ought to be tied to the stake and a very slow fire lighted under him."

They spoke of what they considered the outrage of the quatrain about the Prince de Condé. One of the gentlemen had not heard it, and Condé repeated it:

III-41
The Hunchback will be elected by the council,
A more hideous monster never appeared on earth,
A deliberately fired shot will pierce the eye
Of the traitor who had accepted the obligation of fealty to his king.

A shocked silence greeted the words. Coligny's stern face was dark with pity and resentment as he looked at the brilliant young prince already important in Protestant councils. Louis de Bourbon, though hump-shouldered, was a very winning, virile figure. Women felt the charm of his merry blue eyes and clever, sensitive face. He was far from being a monster in appearance or character. The verse, mentioning his deformity in such bitter words, is the most bitingly cruel that Nostradamus ever wrote. Inasmuch as the young man was living and could not fail to see and recognize himself in the lines, it seems nothing short of vicious. Yet one has always to bear in mind that Nostradamus was a mediaeval Catholic, fanatically against the new heresy. He was, besides this, a political prophet who saw in the ambition of such men as Condé and Coligny the blade that would cleave France in twain, and he foresaw that the cleavage would never be completely healed, but would lead to untold tragedy and horror through the years. Condé had become to him the symbol of all that was twisted, hideous, and, from his point of view, false in the politico-religious scene rapidly developing into a death struggle between the Protestant and Catholic creeds. Nor did he see Condé as the gay young courtier whom others in that room saw and loved. He saw the later Condé, elected general by a council of Calvinist nobles. He saw the menace of his military genius, and he was glad that he could see the shot that put an end to him at the battle of Jarnac. Nostradamus could view psychically with pitiless satisfaction this gallant fighter, his leg broken by a horse's kick, helpless on the ground, deliberately shot through the eye by Henry of Anjou's captain of the guard, just as the verse described it.

Francis d'Andelot thought Nostradamus could do a great deal of harm. Coligny took the opposite view. He said

"What can he do but feed the hopes of those who are already doing all the harm they can? Francis of Guise already thinks himself the coming Charlemagne, and is out to crush us at the first opportunity. Besides, the more the court indulges in such superstitious, ungodly nonsense as this Maître Nostradamus purveys, the more quickly the intelligent masses will rally to our side."

"Has any of you seen this man?" asked one of the other gentlemen. It seemed none had.

"My dear uncle of Montmorency is shepherding him around," said Coligny disgustedly. "And my kinsman the Cardinal of Châtillon is like to burst with curiosity. I shouldn't be surprised if he paid his respects. Faugh!"

"I wonder if he has brought a vial of the Elixir of Life to Madame Diane," sneered d'Andelot.

"Does she need it?" asked Condé mockingly.

Nostradamus did not include in this first volume his bitter verses on Coligny; they came later. Coligny was at this time in no danger. He was the brave admiral of forty, needed and valued for his services in spite of his religion. But Nostradamus had seen a vision of Coligny whitened by age, watched for three nights by the murderous thugs of Guise as he sat reading his Bible. He had seen, without a qualm, the old man murdered, his body insulted and mutilated. He believed that it was the ambition of these Protestant leaders rather than the faults of Church or Crown which would precipitate the nation's tragedy.

Naturally during Nostradamus' visit Protestants were conspicuous at court by their absence, except a few drawn by curiosity to join those who gathered at the Louvre, or called to pay their respects and ask for consultation at the Hôtel de Sens, though Nostradamus had as yet no time except for royal audiences.

Next in order, after his interview with the King, had been his reception by the Queen. Catherine was accustomed to prophets. She had been brought up with them as a family tradition of the Medici, and she usually, since her marriage, patronized those who had a reputation. With Nostradamus she was calmly gracious and, as to the matter in hand, most practical and businesslike. There were certain definite things which she wanted if possible to learn. If Maître Nostradamus knew them and could tell her, Catherine was not at all concerned with whether he got his knowledge from God or Devil.

She received the prophet in company with the dauphin and Mary Stuart, his betrothed, to whom she presented Nostradamus.

"This is our son who will in time assume the royal burdens of his father. And this is our dearly loved royal daughter of Scotland who will, as my son's wife, adorn the crown with her character and learning."

Nostradamus saw a frail boy of twelve, with a kindly, ineffectual face that showed neither mentally nor physically the making of a king. He felt his heart contract as he looked into the pure, sensitive face of the fair Scottish girl whose fate he foresaw. What awful troubles beauty could bring to nations! Mary smiled at him charmingly and greeted him with a brief salutation in Latin. She was nearly two years older than Francis and her poise and assured bearing were already that of a queen. There was little curiosity in her frank regard, and the prophet was glad to see that she was too young and too happy to be as yet mistrustful of fortune's favors. Francis looked bored with the meeting. Catherine sent them away after the introductions, explaining when they had gone that she had thought the meeting might make it easier for the prophet to frame their forecasts.

Old commentators have indulged in dramatic speculation as to what went on at the sessions between Catherine and the prophet. It was said by some that he "bodied forth the angel Anael" to predict for her, others said that he made the future pass before her eyes in a magic mirror. Such suggestions of midnight spells and mystic incantations are arrant nonsense of course. Catherine was too intelligent to expect anything of that kind.

Just as Henry's interest was in the extension of the kingdom and in winning victories over other nations, Catherine was concerned with her particular problems which were of a different sort. Catherine's questions pertained to her personal power; there lay her difficulty. Her concern was on how to acquire power, which she had never possessed, what were its instruments which she could use to best advantage, and how could she most securely hold the power once she had obtained it. Undoubtedly she had accepted and thoroughly believed the prophecies of Henry's death, and she knew it might not be far off. As a practical woman she was making her plans to be ready, plotting her moves and policies that would pave the way for her ambition. Already she foresaw the coming struggle. She dreaded the influence which Francis of Guise and his brother, the Cardinal of Lorraine, would be able to use through their niece, Mary Stuart, when Mary became queen. If on the other hand, she, Catherine, played in with the Protestants to offset this, there was the predicted threat from the house of Bourbon-Navarre which the astrologers said would supplant the line of Valois. She saw herself between the frying-pan and the fire. She wanted a prophet who could show her a way out. She wanted assurance that the power she had waited for and dreamed of for years would be hers.

There had been plenty of prophecies made, and Catherine had written records of them all. Ruggiero she trusted, because he was from her home, and her family had long employed his family. But she wanted a check-up on his predictions to see where this new man would confirm and where he would differ with Ruggiero's findings.

The Queen, without doubt, had ready for the prophet her entire collection of family birth-charts together with those of the Guise and Navarre families. In Catherine's secret archives, guarded by hidden panels, there probably reposed the most complete collection of court horoscopes to be found in Europe. A large part of Ruggiero's work would have been to keep the more important charts up-to-date in the matter of progressions, eclipses, mutations and significant transits. In this way the Queen could get a coup d'oeil of what might be expected. When the Navarre charts were in difficulties she could plan her course, either an attempt to further crush them, or win their gratitude with a helping hand. She could plot the rising curve of the Guises' power and estimate how far it might go, at what time it would show weakness, when she might dare to attack it. However handy Ruggiero may or may not have been with poison and such accessories to Catherine's power as history has credited him with, he was a very fine scholar, and his astrological work must have been well organized and adequate. Catherine was herself an expert in this line and could put up a chart and read it with the best of them. Since this was a branch in which she was qualified and proud of her knowledge she would have wanted Nostradamus' opinion on her charts, as well as in his own chosen field of prophecy.

She would have discussed with him her plan, which she later carried out, of building a private observatory at Blois and requested that he note the intended placing of it, when he went there, and tell her if he thought it good.

How Ruggiero regarded this new-risen star is not known. Like his mistress, he had been well schooled in repression over many years. He may have welcomed some new light on his heavy responsibilities to Catherine. At any rate, one may be sure that this suave, stately Italian scholar greeted his confrère in prophecy with all cordiality and placed the resources of his laboratory at Maître Nostradamus' disposal.

What Nostradamus told the Queen in their first talks cannot even be surmised, except that it is known that Catherine was interested and impressed, but obviously she did not get all that she wanted to know. Whether the prophet hedged or not cannot be said. But Catherine requested him to go to Blois, where her other children were, in order to see them personally and make a closer prediction than he had so far made of their fates.

There must have been some delightful talks between these two keen minds, when prophecy was temporarily in abeyance. Catherine had an objective, intellectual grasp of many things to which emotionally she could not measure up. She could talk and write interestingly and with an impressively high moral tone, strikingly at variance with the cynical remarks made in other moods and with her actions.

Nostradamus' travels in Italy would have interested Catherine, where he went, whom he met, what he thought of Italian alchemy and astrology. As a pope's niece she would have been particularly eager to question him about the two fine verses in which he prophesied that the Church would confirm the doctrine of transubstantiation, which was done seven years later by the Council of Trent in 1563.

The Church had for some time been at work on various reforms with which to combat the theology of Luther and Calvin. Many people today do not realize that it was not until the time of the Council of Trent that the rite of the bread and wine became accepted as miraculous reality. These are the quatrains in which Nostradamus prophesied acceptance of this doctrine:

III-2
The Divine Word shall become flesh,
Through the mystical act (of transubstantiation), and the ritual of occult manifestation, celebrated on earth, shall give attunement with heaven,
And the ground beneath man's feet shall become as the footstool of God.

II-13
No longer will man's body be a soul-less sacrifice,
The day of death will be thought of as a day of birth
When the Divine Spirit shall give the soul felicity,
Perceiving The Word in its eternity.

Nostradamus expressed his wish to visit while in the city the great shrines which were the sacred pride of Paris. The Queen approved this pious desire and assured him that the guardian prelates would be happy to show him their treasures.

The prophet's first night in Paris was destined to be a restless one. From early morning he had been in the thick of audiences and introductions, and he was still not rested from his wearing journey. With more such days ahead, his bed at the Hôtel de Sens looked very good, even to a man who required but little sleep. Late in the night he was disturbed by noise at his front door. Looking out from his window he saw one of the royal pages hammering in a youth-must-be-served fashion on the portal.

"What is it, page?" called out the prophet. "You are making a lot of noise about a lost dog. Go down the Orleans road and you will find your dog being led on a leash."

This page, who came of the aristocratic family of Beauveau, had lost one of his pedigreed hounds. Perhaps he wanted to show off to his friends that he wasn't afraid of the old prophet who, he would bet, wouldn't know where his hound was anyhow. But Nostradamus did know, and the excited boy found his dog being brought home on leash by a servant, just where Nostradamus had said, on the Orleans road. Such minor incidents caught popular fancy and spread the prophet's fame, because they could be understood better than his impressively puzzling stanzas.

Naturally the Seneschal Diane, and the King's sister, Marguerite of Valois, were not kept waiting for their turn with the oracle. Nostradamus was presented to these two ladies next in order after the royal audiences.

Diane de Poictiers was then a miracle of fifty-seven years. "The old hag," her enemies called her, attacking her in street verses of scurrilous ribaldry. But this missed its mark, for she was still beautiful, still the enchantress of the King. Some said that her secret was cold baths, some said it was sorcery--whichever it was, her "pretty and pompous dress," which was always of black and white, encased her northern fairness as the printer's art holds the time-defying lines of a love-sonnet. Perhaps the prophet paid her some such compliment. It was her daily meed, but coming from a fresh source it was always pleasant. She may have inquired if he meant to immortalize her in his prophecies, as Goujon did in his sculpture. If so, he might have told her,

"A prophecy dies when it is fulfilled. But true poetry lives forever. I, Your Grace, am a prophet telling of times and seasons. Your beauty belongs to poetry, which is timeless."

Nostradamus makes few mentions of women in his prophecies, and only in their capacity as heads of state. This seems strange in a country so politically affected by women throughout its history. Perhaps the prophet disapproved of this. Or it may have been his respect for the Salic law of France forbidding women to rule in their own right, except as regent for a child.

Studying the pictured face of Diane, cool and strong like the women of old Germanic Gaul, one does not get the feeling that she would have been much interested in prophecy. She knew her strength. She could hold Henry. But with his passing her destiny would end. She had heard all about the prophecies of the King's duel and death. Did she really want to know if and when this would occur? Probably not.

In the King's sister, Marguerite, the prophet made a genuine and delightful friend. History does not tell a great deal of this princess, but it does say that she was witty and wise and learned. She was charmed with Nostradamus' conversation and ideas. They talked together of books, personalities and public trends. Nostradamus had foreseen, and indicated in a verse not then published, the marriage, eventually, of Marguerite to Emmanuel-Philibert, Duke of Savoy. He would have taken delight in informing the lively princess of the admirable and apparently happy match in store for her, and also in sketching the illustrious future of the house of Savoy destined long after to rule a united Italy.

"My brother, the King, has wanted Piedmont for years," Marguerite said. "I shall tease him about my conquest of Savoy, where his armies have failed."

Nostradamus did not tell her that the event of her betrothal to the Duke would also be the sad occasion of her brother's death in the midst of a gay tournament staged to celebrate the marriages of Marguerite and the King's young daughter, Elizabeth.

"Maître Nostradamus," Marguerite told the prophet seriously, "I shall see you again after you leave Paris. This is not the end of the friendship which you inspire in me. But there are too many people trying to talk to you now. It is bad enough with all those of my own sex appealing to your prophetic gifts, but when I must also compete with my brother and all the gentlemen of the court to get a word with you, what chance have I to talk of the things I long to know? I am going to seek you out some day in Salon!"

Nostradamus smiled indulgently at the charming young woman.

"The royal Pearl of Paris would be a glorious jewel for Provence to honor."

"You turn a compliment," the princess said, "as neatly as any courtier, yet you have spent your years far from the court."

"It is because we Provençals live in the sun, and we know that in France the sun and the monarchy are one."

Throughout the Centuries the prophet's favorite and radiant symbol for the French monarchy is Le Sol. In astrology the sun is held to rule kings in general, but the prophet applies the meaning only to the sovereign of his own country.

"I shall pick a time to come to Salon," Marguerite continued, "when all the gentlemen have gone to war, and all the ladies are occupied with children. And I shall hope, Maître Nostradamus, that all your patients will be cured. And then we shall talk, and talk!"

It was to be some time before the democratic Marguerite made good her promise, but she meant it, and eventually she did find her way to the prophet's door in Provence.

The Queen was impatient to have Nostradamus go to Blois and see the other children.

"We have not yet asked you, Maître Nostradamus," Catherine said to him, "concerning your two verses which appear to refer to our children. But surely you understand how they disturb us. It may be that when you have seen and studied all of the children, you will be able to give us an encouraging report. The health of the dauphin gives cause for anxiety, but he is young, and our physician, Ambroise Paré, thinks that he may outgrow his delicate constitution. The other children are sturdy and promising. But since, as you know, we have already been saddened by the loss of three children, a mother's heart beats in anxious solicitude for the others."

"Indeed, Madame, I comprehend that," Nostradamus gravely assured her.

Blois is about a hundred miles southwest of Paris, which meant another not inconsiderable trip for the prophet. He probably traveled in a ponderous, much begilded royal coach, but the trip required more than two days on the road. Still, it was August, with fair, warm weather, and the country, delightful all the way, was enchanting the nearer he came to the banks of the Loire. When the plateau of the palace at last loomed before his eyes and he had his first sight of the castle, its fabulous size and the enormous dignity of its towers and broad flat roofs seemed to him, more than any other building in France, to symbolize the might of the monarchy.

The kings of France always loved the banks of the Loire for their country residences, and of all the beautiful castles they built there, Blois is the one which bears the most regal stamp of the magnificence of the Orleans and Valois princes. It was set on a triangle-plateau separated from the town by a stream. Its position was isolated and formerly a strongly defended one. But its military strength was now more apparent than real, and perhaps this, too, was a symbol of the Valois dynasty which had made the latest contributions to its architectural splendor. We would like to know to which room in this vast pile the major-domo directed the steps of the prophet. All that is certain is that it was in the most modern wing, which Francis I had built, and which housed the apartments and guest rooms of the present royal family. The private rooms all faced north to escape the heat. Their balconied, arcaded windows looked out over the country of the Vendômois and the moats of the town. It was in the midst of the carved and frescoed magnificence of one of these rooms that Nostradamus was installed.

As the prophet followed the steward to his apartment, he hardly knew where to look, so bewildered was his vision by the multiplicity and variety of fantastic beauty. The stone staircase which he mounted wound upward through a hexagonal hollow tower, "an arabesque device invented by giants and executed by dwarfs to give the effect of a dream. The delicate, ingenious marvels of workmanship are like super-wrought, deeply cut Chinese ivories." So Balzac describes the staircase which the prophet is now ascending. As he mounts he can see further and further over the Loire, its living color framed in the pale, elaborate artifice of stone.

The apartments of Catherine and Henry occupied the entire first floor. The monarchs spent, however, little time at Blois, for Henry preferred other châteaux. Not until his death would Blois resume its historic role as the setting for the royal drama. When Nostradamus had rested and had something to eat he asked to see the royal children, whose laughter had already reached him from some unseen play-nook.

Blois was well staffed while the children were in residence. Besides the major-domo and his staff, there was a confessor who looked after the spiritual welfare of the young charges and the household. Each of the children had a personal nurse. Over the nurses were Madame de Curton, the governess of the three little girls, a woman whose superior virtues and abilities were eulogized in the writings of the day; and the Abbé Amyot, the instructor of the three boys, who would one day be the source of a bitter quarrel between Charles IX and Catherine, through the young king's love and loyalty toward his childhood teacher.

The confessor and the two instructors welcomed Nostradamus cordially. They, too, were used to prophets. Their young charges had been horoscoped and studied by owlish men of purported wisdom ever since their birth. To them, Nostradamus, whatever his reputation, was just one more of the same. Each was so devoted to the royal charges and so loved in return, that to imagine fate as ever cruel to these lovely children was more than their simple faith could compass. The prophet quickly established friendly relations by encouraging them to talk about the children. Enthusiastically they told him in what this one excelled, how modest the deportment of that one, and where another needed curbing. The Princess Elizabeth was so fine a Latin scholar, Madame de Curton vowed, that soon she would rival the young Queen of Scotland. Claude, it seemed, was somewhat stubborn, like her father, but with her mother's good sense. As for baby Margot, the whole staff adored her. The Abbé Amyot allowed Madame de Curton to take the floor, and when she asked in what arrangement Maitre Nostradamus would like to see the children, Amyot said promptly,

"Ladies first. Display your charges, Madame."

Elizabeth, the eldest of the daughters of Catherine and Henry, was at this time eleven years old. Nostradamus was charmed with the singular sweetness and strength of her young face, which still glows through the stiff conventionality of her portraits. It was this quality which so captivated Philip II of Spain, three years later, that he married her, although she was intended for his son. "He cut the ground under his son's feet," writes Brantôme, "and took her for himself, beginning all charity at home."

Catherine, who had expected, after Elizabeth's marriage, to pump her advantageously about the state affairs of Spain, ran up against a sense of honor rare in the Valois family. Elizabeth refused to betray Spanish confidence. She was only twenty-three when she died, and about her passing has always hung the dark aura of suspicion. Philip may not, as was reported, have poisoned his charming young wife out of jealousy of his mad son, Carlos. But the legend that he did has persisted.

She smiled on the prophet and gave him her carefully coached greeting in faultless Latin, which he praised to Madame de Curton's content. Then he talked to Elizabeth a little of her studies and her interest in flowers.

Mademoiselle Claude, who was nine, came next. She would grow up to marry the Duke of Lorraine, and to try, weeping, to shield her newly married little sister, Margot, from the horror of blood on Saint Bartholomew's night. Her life lacked the spectacular elements of the other two daughters, for which she was doubtless grateful. She, too, made her little Latin speech, but was more reserved than the frank Elizabeth.

Baby Margot was only three years old. Nostradamus had met the two older girls in one of the formal galleries. Now Madame de Curton guided the prophet to the nursery in the Queen's apartments, which occupied the first floor. These rooms had formerly been those of Queen Claude, the wife of Francis I. They were still adorned with her delicate sculpture of double C's, with a device in pure white of swans and lilies signifying her motto Candidior Candidis, the whitest of the white. The entire apartments were gorgeously furnished, and to the heavier pieces were added a profusion of little inlaid and silver tables, ivories, enamels and other objets d'art, which were for the most part of Italian workmanship.

Baby Margot was already a siren and knew it. She stopped playing with her doll when the governess and Nostradamus entered, and came running toward them. She tossed her cloud of blue-black curls, and used devastatingly her roguish brown eyes at the visitor. She chattered with adorable fearlessness to the strange, grave man and promptly claimed another conquest.

"Is she not beautiful! Is she not an angel!" cried Madame de Curton, while the nurse stood by, beaming with the same adoration.

La Reine Margot! The dry pages of history still tingle electrically with memories of her beauty, her grand romantic glamour, her loves, and her tragedies. Yet something of all the future sadness which he perceived, too, came momentarily into the prophet's eyes, causing the governess to exclaim anxiously.

"You will see no misfortune for my little ones, Maître Nostradamus? You will foretell only happiness? Surely they are too good and sweet for anything else. Is not each one a little queen of hearts?"

"Alas, Madame," the prophet told her, "hearts are the most uncertain of all thrones. But you may be very sure that your pupils will grow up to reflect every credit upon your admirable teaching, in the exalted positions which all three shall fill."

Madame de Curton and the nurse exchanged pleased looks. They read into the prophet's words their own interpretation, the fulfilled picture of a wish, so different from the realization.

Later Nostradamus walked in the gardens with the Abbé Amyot, and saw the three boys at their play. Charles, Duke of Orleans, and Henry of Anjou, were but six and five years old, and the little Duke of Alençon was a baby of two years. Nostradamus' quick perception noted the nurse in charge of the eldest boy, Charles, a deep-bosomed northern type with a face of endless patience and brooding calm. When she looked at the little boy, the prophet saw a passionate depth of devotion such as one seldom sees except in the expression of the actual mother. He mentioned it to the Abbé.

"Yes," the Abbé replied. "It is so, and she is a superb nurse. It is unfortunate that she is a Huguenot, but she handles the child, who is high-strung, so wonderfully that the Queen will not let her go. The little prince, doctor, is going to make a splendid man," the Abbé told him, smiling. "Look at his fine, honest blue eyes, the noble set of his head."

A sick feeling swept over the prophet like a spiritual nausea. He turned away from the Abbé lest it should show in his face.

This manly little child was the monarch he had seen in his visions. "The savage king," he had called him. He was to be the one who would mount the throne when Saturn came into water. He it was who would "slaughter the innocents." Dear God, that loving, happy little boy, become the bloodstained man at the palace window holding an arquebus in his hand trained on Frenchmen! The Abbé was talking on, extolling the qualities of his charge, but Nostradamus did not hear him. A tiger-kitten that licked the hand of the man who fed him could one day tear that man to bloody bits. So it would be with this child. And those who fed the tiger his first meat, they were to blame, too.

Henry of Anjou, with two small dogs leaping about him, came shyly up and stood by his teacher's knee and fixed his big violet eyes on Nostradamus.

"Our young lord of Anjou is a fine prince too." Amyot stroked Henry's wind-ruffled hair affectionately, yet his tone told the prophet that Charles was his favorite.

"Who are you?" the child wanted to know of Nostradamus.

And who are you? The prophet's thoughts echoed in suffering, the child's words. A man stood mistily between him and the boy. A man with a weary, cynical, painted face and a dagger in his hand. He could smell the perfume of his silken clothes. This was the man that Henry of Anjou would be. Only the little dogs playing at his feet were unchanged. It was unbearable. Abruptly Nostradamus got up from the stone bench where he and the Abbé were resting and walked toward the infant Duke of Alençon, who was learning his first steps. The faltering efforts stopped at his approach, and eyes that were too solemn above a nose too long for a baby fixed themselves intently upon him.

"He is doing well with his steps," the nurse said proudly. "Soon he will walk alone."

And one day to perdition and an early death, was the prophet's bitter reflection. He recalled the words of Machiavelli: "It is probable that the atmosphere is full of intelligences which announce the future out of commiseration for mortals." What of commiseration was there in foresight such as this? Nearer was he to calling his gift cursed than ever in his life. Suddenly he wished to be away from Blois. A mist of blood seemed to wreathe the castle and tint the pallid stone. He would have ordered the coach and returned to Paris but that it was late afternoon. Not until morning could he leave. The Abbé noticed his abstraction and restless movements. Tactfully he suggested that the prophet might need a little rest and reflection before they supped. Nostradamus was glad to agree, he wanted to be alone.

I-10
When the coffin is lowered behind the iron grille
Where the seven children of the king shall be laid,
The ancient and ancestral dead shall rise from the depths of the nether world
With outcry, seeing the death of this their withered fruit.

He should have changed that line, he thought. Their ancestors should rejoice for France, to see the dropping of such rotted fruit.

That evening the prophet ate little. He summoned his self-control and talked with brilliance. But he retired to his room early. He said that he was a night-owl and asked if it would be disturbing if he should roam about the castle in the late hours. The others, having heard that such visions as his usually came by night, were a little awed by his request. He was assured that he would be free to ramble, and the guard should be so instructed. Yes, the castle was all open, he could go where he liked.

Deep in the night, while all but the guards were sleeping, the prophet left his room and by the light of a lonely candle traversed the dim length of empty corridors to the moon-haunted chapel of the ancient kings of Blois who had built their temple to God in an age of surer faith. As he went his way down endless stretches of chilly stone, the ghosts of the past and the ghosts of the future peopled the shadowed halls. Out of the blackness gleamed faintly old crowns of pointed gold above stern faces, or was it a pattern of yellow moonlight? Surely the presence of Louis XII, who had so loved this castle, was near, with that of his friend, the Cardinal d'Amboise. Near, too, was the dagger, not yet forged, which would strike down young Balafré, the Guise. And here walked Catherine, the Queen, and the pale young dauphin with reproachful eyes upon his mother. From farther in the future peered the fat face of the other Medici, Marie, with treacherous d'Epernon. Some seemed to follow the prophet within the chapel, others whose hands were red, halted outside the door.

The prophet entered and knelt before the Christ and Virgin, dim in the uncertain candlelight. His fingers touched the beads of his rosary, his lips moved in prayer. The candle burned lower, guttered into blackness, unnoticed by the man whose ceaselessly moving lips pleaded for pity on the seven children of the King.

In the morning Nostradamus said farewell to Blois and left for Paris. He was beginning to feel the strain of all he was experiencing. On the way back his mind was busy with his coming interview with the Queen. Carefully he composed the answers he would make to her questions. He knew he could satisfy her ambitions. But if she asked his guidance and advice that would be difficult. There was so little to be said that would be acceptable to her or that she would follow. He sighed heavily as he thought how futile was, after all, such a gift as his to change conditions.

Catherine, who had been impatiently awaiting his return, sent for him at once on hearing that he was back. No one knows what took place at that interview. The Venetian ambassador, Lorenzo, writing in 1560, refers to Nostradamus' forecast to Catherine as very well known in France, and as predicting that her three eldest sons would all occupy the throne. The ambassador speaks of this as a prophecy which menaced the lives of the princes, since their succession could only come about through death. Many commentators have quoted this accepted story of what Catherine heard from the prophet. It would, if true, however, have been but a small part of the amplitude of information which Catherine would have demanded. All that we really know of what Nostradamus predicted are his brilliantly accurate, published verses. That, and one thing more. He satisfied the Queen and retained her confidence and friendship. Had this not been the case she would not have sought him out again, as she did.

The interview over, Nostradamus returned to the Hôtel de Sens a sick man. His foot was paining him with what appeared to be a somewhat serious attack of his enemy the gout. The food in Paris had been very hard on him. It was heavy, with too much meat, spices and sweets. He missed his green vegetables, garlic and simple, wholesome stews that he had at home, and his wife's good housekeeping. He was sick at heart, too, in the midst of all the adulation he was receiving. Paris was filled with greed, ambition and wickedness. She was like Agrippina, the mother of Nero. And Paris would pay for her sins, and then the whole of France would be involved and would suffer. He saw it coming with dreadful clarity of vision.

His foot swelled and grew steadily worse. He had to take to his bed, hating it, and remain in it helpless for ten days. The acid condition induced by change of diet and water combined with the long traveling and emotional strain of Blois were too much for him. He could no longer stand what he used to. Everyone was wonderfully kind to him in his illness. The King and Queen sent constant inquiries for his welfare, and each sent a purse heavy with a hundred gold écus. The Princess Margaret came to see him and sent him more of the indigestible food and heating wines of which he could not partake.

Ronsard sent him a tribute of verses, which pleased him greatly, likening him to an antique oracle and rebuking the scoffers. This more than offset the Latin distych of Jodelle, another famous poet of the day, who attacked Nostradamus with this punning rhyme:

"Nostradamus cum falsa damus, nam fallere nostrum est,
  Et cum falsa damus, nil nisi nostra damus."

Which means, though it has a double interpretation with a play on the name,

"We give our own when we give lies, for cheating is our affair,
  When we give what is false, we give nothing but what is our own."

His friends countered in this merry, malicious little war with a couplet using almost the same words but changed enough to give an opposite meaning.

The Hôtel de Sens was busy receiving and answering inquiries from the stream of callers that came and went all day. Scholars, physicians, prelates mingled with the courtiers in their puffed and slashed velvet costumes, their jewels and feathers. As soon as Nostradamus felt well enough, he received some of the more important of these visitors in his room.

Of the notables who prayed the exercise of his vision, the great Duke Francis of Guise was not to be denied, nor his crafty brother, the dark Cardinal of Lorraine. Even more than the Bourbons, these two were the most ambitious men in the kingdom. As the uncles of Mary Stuart, they seemed in a fair way to realize the dreams of their house, if and when the King did pass on in a duel, and the dauphin, Mary's betrothed, came to the throne. Duke Francis, the hero of the siege of Metz, was the military idol of France. A very handsome, very haughty man, he claimed descent from Charlemagne, and had pretensions to the throne itself. He had married Anne d'Este, a granddaughter of Louis XII, and daughter of the tolerant, scholarly Renée, Duchess of Ferrara. The Duke brought his wife with him, both eager for a forecast for their son Henry, whom Henry III was one day to murder in the castle of Blois.

"My mother, the Duchess of Ferrara, has rare skill with astrology," the Duchess of Guise told the prophet. "I have known her tell marvelous things. I wish that she might return to France if only for the mutual pleasure which she and the Queen might have in. such discussion."

When Renée did return several years later, one of the few bright spots in her life was the conversations which she and Catherine had on the subject of the stars in the Queen's new observatory at Blois.

Both the Duc de Guise and the Cardinal of Lorraine plied the prophet with questions. Nostradamus predicted a considerable advance in the Guise fortunes. He would scarcely have courted trouble from these fierce, proud, determined men by revealing the ultimate tragedy of their house, but he has set it down in his verses with a full sense of its dramatic significance and its disaster to France.

If he had told them that they would lose to the Bourbons, then very weak, they would probably have scoffed at him. Their star was then too powerful for the concept of defeat to enter into their minds.

The gout wore off slowly, but at last Nostradamus was free of it for the time being, and in spite of all flattery and solicitation, he was anxious to return to Salon. Nor would he be deterred. His room at the Hôtel de Sens looked like a dream of Christmas, so loaded was it with presents of every description. Some of the King's servants packed them for him, while he, himself, packed his valued ink horn and writing materials, his treasured Aristotle and the other simple needs he had brought.

César Nostradamus, writing of these gifts, after his father's death, says of them:

"As to the honors, royal gifts, and presents of jewels which he received from their Majesties, I would rather have their list on the tip of my tongue than to give myself the exquisite pleasure of relating them, fearing lest I should say more than modesty permits."

When all was in readiness for departure, Nostradamus went to the Louvre to say his farewells to royalty.

"Your Majesty," he told the King with genuine feeling, "I never thought that I should envy any man. Yet now I find myself very much envying those who have the gift of ready and golden speech. Lacking this I am but helpless to express my opinion of Your Majesty's grandeur and generosity of nature, and of the kindness which I, your humblest servant, have received from you. The treasures of gifts which your royal goodness has bestowed on me are even surpassed by the treasure of royal memories which I take away with me to brighten all my years."

The King smiled at him with genial regard.

"We have, Maitre Nostradamus, one more, and I think well deserved, token of our favor. You are herewith appointed by us to the rank of Physician-in-Ordinary and Councilor to ourself."

The prophet, deeply moved, bowed low. "Your Majesty, I am overcome with this further honor."

"We have enjoyed your visit," the King said, "and hope to profit by those matters in which you have advised us. Now, the Queen is waiting to see you."

Catherine, like Marguerite, told the prophet, "We shall see you again, Maître Nostradamus, and meanwhile you may hear from us by letter touching some further service which you can render, or some point on which we can better act through your advice."

The last farewell was finally said, the last handshake given. Over the bridge the way led, past the soot-blackened beauty of Notre Dame and the Ile de la Cité, across to the left bank, and the road to Lyons. Nostradamus looked back at the spires and towers of Paris, scene of his proudest triumph. He lifted his hand in salute to the city.

"Vale Lutetia! Ave Salona!"

Towards Familiar Country

NEARLY THREE MONTHS had gone by from the time that Nostradamus had left Salon, to his return, laden with gifts and the honor of the King's appointment. It was a great day in the life of the little town when he came back to his people with laurels of this new adventure. Family and friends rejoiced at his success. His triumphs, though pleasing to Nostradamus, made no difference in his way of life. As soon as he had rested up he resumed the busy even tenor of his days as if Paris had never called him.

Yet there was a difference. He was no longer merely the wonderful Doctor Nostradamus of Provence. He was now the celebrated prophet of France, honored by his king, and known throughout Europe. In those days when personalities counted more than policies in the political arena--because personalities then made policies--diplomatic reports on royalty were as gossipy as a tabloid. They were expected to be. In the lives of kings and queens, everything relative to them had political significance.

> "Whatever they did was an act of state
> From taking a pill to taking a mate."

The least occurrence that an ambassador could find out was incentive to him to seize his quill and write a dispatch to his sovereign. Ink had flowed like water during the visit of Nostradamus to Paris, and copious reports had been sent home by the diplomats describing this amazing man. Some of the diplomats had made an effort to meet him in order to size up what sort of influence he might exert on the King. The Queen's patronage of prophets was well known. But Henry's interest was something else. It made Nostradamus potentially high politics.

After his return to Salon, foreign rulers began to send private emissaries there to see him. This was with the double hope that he might let drop some information of value, and, on the other hand, if he was as amazing as reported, there was not a ruler in Europe who did not yearn for a little advance knowledge on the aims of his competitors. A good prophet was worth his weight in gold to any king. So the people of Salon had one more thing to wonder and gossip over in the important looking men with a foreign air who now came and went mysteriously at the house of Nostradamus. Naturally these consultations were of the utmost secrecy, and nothing is known of them except the rumors and observations of the townspeople.

In his leisure time Nostradamus took up the work on his verses for another volume of prophecies. He also turned his attention to other kinds of writing. He had published in 1552 a little book, Traité des Fardements. In 1557 he brought out in Anvers another, Des Confitures. These two were later on combined into one work, perhaps supplemented, and formed the two little volumes to which

Bareste refers, one of which contained the recipe for the troches.

It was not strange in that day for a famous doctor to occupy himself with writing about beauty secrets and cooking. In that pre-beautician, pre-dietician age, the doctor was the only safe authority on such matters. The cult of the body, which the pagan revival raised to romantic heights, demanded to be served with formulae which contributed to the effectiveness of feminine charm and preserved its loveliness from age. Every beauty of the day had her private collection of formulae. Some of these were very old family secrets, carefully guarded and passed on from mother to daughter. Valuable additions to this tested knowledge were greatly prized. Perfumes, too, were a part of the doctor's field. The sixteenth century drenched itself in sweet-smelling essences not alone because they were fashionable and much enjoyed, but they were thought to have some prophylactic value too.

There was also the matter of cooking, which was by no means beneath a physician's notice. Culinary recipes, like those for beauty, were especially important in France, and were hoarded and prized in every household. Nothing was known about diet, but it was recognized that in illness special feeding was required, and usually this took the most unfortunate form. Scurvy, which was one of the commonest diseases, was considered, then as now, a deficiency disease. They knew that much about it. But the sufferers were denied the citrus fruits which would have cured them and were "strengthened" with rich meats and heavy wines. The doctors of the day not only recommended the foods which they considered most efficacious for various types of illness, but wrote books of recipes for cooking of every sort. Their wives must have laughed in their capacious sleeves over this, for of course it was their recipes these learned doctors brought forward with such éclat. They did the cooking, and the doctor took the cash and credit. A little compendium of what every woman should know--perfumes, cookery, beauty hints, household remedies and how to keep the silver clean was a popular, practical book and met a real need. When doctors stopped writing these books, much of this old, generalized information found its way into almanacs. Doctor Nostradamus had many highborn feminine patients. These might not have cared so much for the doctor's ideas on cooking, but they would certainly have demanded that he produce a few miracle-aids for beauty.

Now that he was so famous, the plain people of the countryside, who knew well his kindness, began to claim their need of attention. Their concern was with the land, its crops and harvests. Farmers, laborers, shepherds, estate managers and gardeners swarmed to ask the prophet to tell them when to plant, how their crops would turn out, how to destroy pests, what the weather would be, how to cure livestock, and the thousand and one things a far ruer wants to know. They took up so much of his valuable time that something had to be done about it.

So Nostradamus, in order to help them, and, so it is said, for his own diversion too, wrote and published his astrological almanacs. These gave the times and seasons for the farmers' work, and included a number of public forecasts in prose. These almanacs were dedicated to Pope Paul IV, and presumably met with his august approval. King Henry II was overlooked in the matter of dedication which, one would think, by all the laws of hospitality received, would have been made to him. Unless it was that the need for the good will and protection of the Church made the gesture desirable.

Like everything he did, the almanacks caught on at once. They sold like wildfire. Printers all over France, seeing a gold-mine in Nostradamus' name, began to pirate it. Bogus almanacs, imitating his style and using his name, were put out everywhere. The common people, greedy for the prophet's words, were unable to discriminate between the publications, but they knew false prophecy when they saw it, and blamed Nostradamus. His enemies fed the fuel of undeserved criticism, and in consequence of all the ensuing furor Nostradamus' reputation took a fall among the people at large. This was not true of the court, the people of position and culture who knew him realized the situation, and their loyalty never wavered.

There were no copyright laws. The almanacs were at once translated and republished in England. They were the ancestors of Old Moore's and other famous English prophetic almanacs which have always been popular there. Nostradamus had no protection or redress. He consulted a Lyons lawyer about the misuse of his name but there was nothing to be done. In Lyons particularly, the city for which he had done so much at the time of the plague, old acquaintances cold-shouldered hint and he found that his popularity was gone. He is said to have been deeply wounded by his treatment there.

In 1557 he published at Lyons his Paraphrase of Galen, a philosophic discourse which was well received by scholars.

All was quiet in little Salon as the prophet pursued his peaceful studies. But in the great world large events were taking place, fulfilling incredibly his prophecies. While the bourgeois and the common people who bought the paper almanacs were attacking him, kings and their courts who owned and studied the small, finely bound leather volumes of his quatrains were according him new and breathless acclaim.

In January of 1557 Henry II, unable to contain himself longer, sent Guise into Italy to join the Pope in his war against Philip II of Spain.

II-72
The French army in Italy, will be troubled
Throughout the conflict, and sustain great loss,
Flee, citizens of Rome. Oh, France, driven back
Near to the Tessin in your doubtful struggle to reach the Rubicon!

Bloody Mary of England was then the wife of Philip II of Spain. Philip persuaded Mary to help him by declaring war on France.

Presage-18
The travelling herald of the Lion seeks out the Dog
While the city is consumed by battle, pillage and fresh capture,
Princes, defenses opened up, are captured by hard blows,

The Herald returns to his country, the French who went on an expedition are captured, a great alliance is contracted with a royal virgin.

The dog (sometimes the great mastiff) is a symbol sometimes used by the prophet for the guardian qualities of the kings of France, the watch dogs. The lion is here the heraldic one of the Tudor family. Mary declared war by sending a single herald to France to give in person, in the old mediaeval fashion, her personal defiance to Henry. Henry told him to begone the kingdom and that had he not come from a woman he would have told him some worse things. Philip, with some English help, then landed fifty thousand men in Picardy and Flanders. The Duke de Guise had to rush back from the Italian failure to meet this new threat as best he could. Meanwhile "the alliance with the royal virgin" goes forward and, while Philip's army is landing, Mary Stuart is married to the dauphin of France.

10-5 5
The unfortunate nuptials will be celebrated
With great joyousness, but the end will be unhappy,
Mary and the mother of the groom will scorn each other
When Phoebus, dead, is a more than piteous spouse.

This verse is in the later quatrains, then withheld. It is interesting that he used "Mary," the English word, rather than Marie, as she was called in France. The rivalry of Mary and the Medici queen, after Henry's death, is history. Piteous Phoebus, the Sun of the French Monarchy, is Francis II.

Meanwhile the armies of Philip were before Saint-Quentin, considered one of the bulwarks of France. The Spaniards were commanded by the Duke of Savoy, who would later marry the prophet's friend, the Princess Marguerite. King Henry was ill prepared to meet this siege. His forces were tied up in Italy. The defense army hurriedly mustered was only twenty thousand men. It developed that Saint-Quentin was in a deplorable state, an impressive shell with only dated equipment, as Philip had privately found out.

IV-8
The great city, suddenly and to its repentance, will be taken by assault,
Surprised in the night, its defenses will be broken down.
The guards and lines of communication at San Quentin
Will be destroyed, and its gates battered in.

VI-96
The fine city will be abandoned to the soldiery,
Never was mortal tumult closer at hand,
O what hideous death is closing in,
Except one crime, nothing will be spared the people.

Soldiers, munitions and food were all lacking. Coligny got there first, sent away the useless mouths and began trying to strengthen the weakest points. Old Constable de Montmorency, Bossu of Condé, Francis d'Andelot, men who would soon be murdering each other in deadliest hate, were there with the flower of the nobles of France of whatever creed. They stood together then as Frenchmen and fought as Frenchmen can. But it was one of those never heeded lessons in preparedness. They were unprepared and their defeat was bloody and total, just as the prophecy had said.

Francis of Guise, arriving from Italy after Saint-Quentin had fallen, sought for some brilliant counterstroke to humble Spain. Calais, like Saint-Quentin, was poorly defended and its equipment was run down. Very secretly Guise moved before Philip could get wind of it, and:

VII-28
The great Duke of Alva will enter the war
In a manner traitorous to his grandsires,
The great Duke of Guise will put an end to the war
With a captivity that shall be his enduring monument.

IX-29
The country which has accomplished nothing will give place,
It will eventually abandon what was captured but not captured,
The Church will be on fire over the bloodshed,
Guines, Calais and Oye will be returned.

The capture of Calais did indeed confer immortality upon the name of Guise and give him an enduring monument. The Pope said it was worth more than the capture of half of England. Mary Tudor, who was dying, cried out: "If they open my heart, they will find Calais graven on it." Guizot lists in his history the vast extent of the "captivity" of the British commander, "cannon and munitions, the gold and silver, furniture, merchandise, and horses" which passed to Guise. England had held Calais for over two hundred years. From this capture it remained with France until 1940. Spain had accomplished nothing whatever by the war, for the peace terms gave back to France everything she had lost, all her "captured but not captured towns." The Duke of Alva was general-in-chief for Charles V and Philip II of Spain.

All wars come to an end and this one closed with the Peace of Cateau-Cambresis in the spring of 1559. Nostradamus saw it only as the prelude to worse and internal war.

IX-52
Peace approaches from one side, but war
Will be pursued on a greater scale than ever.
Men and women will weep, innocent blood will flow throughout the land
And it will happen throughout all France.

But not while Henry lived would the storm break. Bloody Mary had died while the war was on, which changed the political lineup, as Protestant Elizabeth inherited the English throne, and it was too early yet to foresee the character of her rule. Philip and Henry had decided for a change to be friends; besides, Philip had seen young Elizabeth's picture, the little daughter of Henry II whose sweetness had so charmed the prophet at Blois.

Nostradamus has given a pen picture of Philip. This cruel king, although Nostradamus doesn't seem to think so except when Philip is fighting France or her interests, did, as Nostradamus says, continue the policy of ridding Spain of Moors, and encouraged the Inquisition to do its worst. He is to be credited with the major effort in defeating the Turks (who as Moslems hold Friday sacred) at Lepanto. Perhaps that is what the prophet means rather than the Inquisition by "returning the Church to its pre-eminence."

V-74
Sprung from Italian blood, born in the heart of Germany,
Is the leader who shall become of such high power
That he will drive the foreign Moorish people from his realm,
Returning the Church to its original prestige.

10-95
Within Spain there shall arise a very powerful ruler,
He will conquer the Midy by land and sea,
This vigorous man will beat back the Crescent
And lower the wings of the people to whom Friday is a sacred day.

Henry II decided that his sister Marguerite had better marry a late enemy too. So her marriage was planned with the Duke of Savoy on whose hands the blood of three thousand Frenchmen slain at Saint-Quentin had hardly dried. Henry had got Saint-Quentin back in the peace settlement.

VI-8
Under the pretext of a marriage settlement,
Great Henry will, conformably to the situation, act with generosity.
Quentin and Arras being recovered through a journey,
The Spanish will at this time take a back seat at slaughter.

Henry acted with generosity by presenting Mary Stuart, now dauphiness, with Saint-Quentin as a wedding present. Kings have to make rather expensive gifts, and this would stay in the family.

VI-74
The great king will acquire new relatives,
Before he shall have rendered up his soul
The people will see him take for kindred
Eagles, Lions and Cross; in doing this he will sell out the Crown.

The heraldic imperial eagle of the Spanish Empire, the Lion of Scotland and the Cross of Savoy were represented in the three royal marriages with Spain, Scotland and Savoy. But Henry's wedding presents were too much for the French. Others besides Nostradamus said the weddings had cost too much good crown land and felt it was a sell-out for France.

The peace had been signed in April. The marriages took place at the end of June. Henry II celebrated the acquisition of his new relatives with a splendid tourney.

The three-day sports event was attended by the entire royal family--even to Baby Margot. Society turned out in the full magnificence of its jewels, its laces and its stiff brocades. Before this audience of the rank, wealth and beauty of

France was played a long-awaited tragic drama. Staged against a background of damascened silks, feathers, tassels and fluttering streamers, with the trumpets of heralds in parti-colored dress calling the final act, on the 29th June 1559 occurred the "duel" in which Henry II lost his life, as prophesied.

Henry II loved to joust, a sport at which he excelled most of his court. He had already run several tilts "like a sturdy and skillful cavalier," and he wanted one more before he stopped. He challenged his young Scottish captain of the guard, the Earl of Montgomery. The Earl, like everyone else, knew the prophecy. He excused himself, but the King wouldn't have it. It was a command. The Seneschal, radiant in her black and white, was looking on from the royal dais, at her colors flying from her lover's lance and shield. The King was mounted on a curvetting Spanish barb, caparisoned with crimson velvet. Henry's armor, as was royalty's privilege, flashed with the goldsmith's art of cunning and intricate gold inlay, which covered the steel like a golden lace. His casque was gilded and crested with plumes.

A fragment of Montgomery's lance struck the King's neck--a piece forced up the visor, and a splinter of wood entered Henry's eye and injured the brain. He lingered for eleven days in horrible agony, then died.

Probably of all the prophetic verses which Nostradamus has written, none is so widely familiar as have always been the quatrains describing this tragic affair.

I-35
The young Lion shall overcome the old
In single combat on a martial field,
His eyes, encased in gold, will be put out,
When two are in the lists, fighting as one, he will receive a mortal blow and die a cruel death.

Young Montgomery was a Scot, indicated by the heraldic Lion.

III-55
In the year when a single eye reigns in France
The court will be in grievous trouble.
His friend will kill the Great One of Blois
The Kingdom will be thrown into evil condition and double uncertainty.

The Great One of Blois is of course the King, and the young Earl of Montgomery, his friend. Almost over the King's dead body the struggle began between the Guise and Bourbon factions, with Catherine as a helpless factor in the fight for power. Francis II, the boy-king, doubled the uncertainty of the situation through his frail health.

VI-63
The Royal Lady shall dwell alone in power
After the passing of her matchless husband, first on the field of honor.
For seven years she will lament her sorrow,
Then, gifted with long life, she will rule to an advanced age.

Nostradamus must have been looking ahead to the continued protection of Catherine's favor when he mentions her seven years' lament. Seven days would have been stretching it. This line was a courtier's phrase for a practical purpose. But it is true that seven years after Henry's death Catherine made a grand tour of France with Charles IX, and it was the first time she had indulged in such a public display of social pomp since King Henry's death. She lived to be seventy years old. Few royalties in her day lived so long.

The working out of the prognostications of Maître Nostradamus had the court gasping with awe. With Henry dead, everyone set to with a will for a fresh bout with the quatrains to see if they could wrest an inkling of where the next blow would fall. The boy-king, Francis II, with lovely Mary Stuart, were now the King and Queen of France. It was the triumphal hour of Francis, Duke of Guise and the Cardinal of Lorraine. It was Catherine's hour to mourn, not for Henry gone, but for herself, alive and beset by enemies on every hand. But who knows what secret prophecies she hugged to her bosom while outwardly dutifully meek, as became a sorrowing widow? Only Nostradamus and Ruggiero could have told.

Bossu, Coligny and their crowd had no intention of letting the Guises rule France without a struggle. They had their own prophecies that some day a Bourbon would unseat a Valois. And prophecy or not, they meant to keep fighting.

IV-62
There will be an ambitious plot against the crown
By a powerful army leader who will think to seize the King.
And he will feign a situation, by a planned ruse,
But the plot will be uncovered under the boughs of the forest.

Had Condé and Coligny seen that verse when the plot was hatched, and did they only scoff at the Catholic sorcerer? Did no one whisper in their ears, saying, this man has a record for truth, Saint-Quentin, the King's death and all the other things he has foretold should give you pause?

The conspiracy of Amboise was the Protestants' opening gun in the bloody religious wars that would devastate France for more than thirty years. The French historian, Malet, says that Condé, Bossu, was the secret head of the plot to kidnap the King and break up the influence of the Guises. The forces of the plotters were stationed in the forest of Amboise. There, under the trees, they were discovered, beheaded or hanged.

Nostradamus heard of all these things in Salon; there was another of his forecasts destined to come true very shortly; one he hadn't published yet, it would be included in the last three Centuries.

X-39
The widow of the unfortunate marriage will survive the death of the eldest son,
No children will be born of the marriage. Two Isles will be put in discord.
He will die before eighteen, still of incompetent age.
The succession will be harmoniously settled upon the next of age.

Mary of Scotland had married the dauphin while he was still "the eldest son" of the seven children the King was to leave behind him. There were no children of this marriage and Mary returned to her native heath, unwanted in France by Catherine, and set two Isles in discord through feud with Elizabeth. The dauphin, King at his death, poor "Phoebus," was only sixteen years old and he was king for but sixteen months.

The story has come down that before the death of Francis II the Venetian ambassador, Lorenzo, wrote to his government that all the court was quoting verse 39 of Century X under the breath. Yet this verse was not published until 1568 and the boy-king died in 1560. So many legends have grown up about Nostradamus, inspired no doubt by the natural desire of the raconteur to top the other fellow's story, that one is constantly finding these inconsistencies in old accounts. The court would have been far more likely to discuss the ingress of Saturn into Cancer hinted at as the date for a new king. That verse was in the first edition.

The month before Francis died, the blow, also predicted in the first edition, struck the Bailiff of Orleans, Jerome Groslot.

III-66
The important Bailiff of Orleans will be in peril of his life,
Through one of vindictive nature.
But neither fate nor his deserts shall bring his death,
Because though captive, his hands and feet will be loosely bound.

The court would have been watching for developments on this verse indicating a prominent man. Perhaps Groslot had studied the verse too, and taken heart from the prophecy that he would escape. He allowed the Calvinists to seize Orleans, for which the Inquisition promptly condemned him to be beheaded. Nostradamus makes it clear that he thought he deserved the sentence as a Calvinist traitor, but foresaw that he would get away. Groslot escaped death in just the way that Nostradamus said it would happen.

During this period, since Nostradamus had paid his visit to the court, while war and turmoil had brought so many of his forecasts to fulfillment, he had published another edition of his prophecies. This had been in 1558.

This edition is spoken of by many commentators as princeps, but it was the second edition supplemented by more of the verses. It contained all that the first volume printed, with three hundred and ninety-one additional quatrains, bringing the number up to seven full Centuries of a hundred verses each, and one of forty-four verses, seven hundred and forty-four in all. Between the sixth and seventh Centuries was interpolated an unnumbered Latin verse which he titled:

Invocation of the Law Against Stupid Critics
Let those who read these verses consider them with mature mind,
Let not the profane and ignorant mob be drawn to study them,
Let all of the Astrologers, the Fools and the Barbarians keep aloof,
Let him who acts otherwise be cursed according to ritual.

Nostradamus reveals in this peculiar verse his savage resentment against the people who had insulted his work. He warns that his book is for the serious minded only. And to those who have called him sorcerer he will offer a curse, as they have so long accused him of doing. It is also revealing that though he constantly asserts, for reasons of his own, in his letters that he is himself an astrologer, he includes astrologers here among the people who are to keep hands off his work. He gives away in these lines the fact that he did not use astrology, and that he even despised the popular practice of this esoteric art. His mention of the common mob seems inconsistent with the public presentation and sale of his book, as if he both wanted and hated the acclaim it brought him. There is no doubt that he was very thin-skinned to censure, for certainly he was not alone in suffering it. Every scholar who came before the public risked it. Nostradamus was indeed among the fortunate in that he never endured worse, and that the chorus of his praises swelled at all times louder than the minority voices of those who disliked him.

It seems odd that, when Nostradamus had been so recently and highly honored by the King, he did not dedicate to him this new edition, or that he did not bring out the fresh quatrains in a small separate book devoted to the King. Nostradamus knew, none better, when the King would die. If he had ever intended a dedication to Henry II, then was his last opportunity to make it, for Henry died the following year. If, however, the dedication to Henry II which prefaced the third and last book of the Centuries was never intended for this king, but was meant for another Henry, fifth of his name, who is yet to come, then it was entirely logical that Nostradamus should have arranged matters as he did. The preface to the complete edition, though written ostensibly as a letter to Henry II, was never seen by him. It was not published until he had been dead a decade. Nostradamus himself planned it that way and made his own arrangements for the letter and final volume to be brought out only after he and the King were both gone.

Moreover, the letter begins with a salutation which does not use the word deux, as one would expect, but addresses him as Henry, King of France Second. The connotation of second is a little different from deux. It has the implication of "following," and the words seem intended to convey the idea of a king of France which is to follow, or a second France.

Had he, during the King's lifetime, dedicated a book to Henry II, no one would ever have considered it as other than it seemed. It was only by holding the letter back until the man for whom it seemed to be written had died without receiving it, that he could get his idea across to some people.

Why, one may ask, all this fuss? Why didn't he just write to Henry V in the first place? Because he foresaw the Duke de Bordeaux who, if he had reigned, would have been Henry V, and did claim the title. People would have mistaken the Duke de Bordeaux for the man for whom the letter was written, then branded Nostradamus as a false prophet because he never reigned. Nostradamus' wording was perfect for his purpose. He knew that the human mind seeks always a conclusion. He knew the world would hang on to the quatrains and preserve them as long as they hadn't solved the mystery. And four hundred years have proved him right.

This would also account for his sensitivity to criticism. One can scarcely imagine his modest, natively retiring personality going after the sensational reputation which his book brought him, unless he had a secret and definite reason for doing it. He could not explain this, he could only suffer through what he felt was its necessity, when people called him a sensation-seeker and attacked him for his pretensions as a prophet.

Everything Nostradamus did, and his personal reactions in regard to the Centuries, appear to point to an ulterior purpose in writing them.

With the passing of Francis II, another boy-king assumed the throne. This time there was no lovely, inconvenient wife to menace Catherine de' Medici. Charles IX was only ten years old, and his mother ruled as regent of France in his name. Catherine's power-dream had at last come true.

IV-86
In the year when Saturn shall be in a water sign and
Conjoined with the Sun, the strong and puissant King
Will be crowned at Rheims and received and anointed at Aix,
Thereafter he will murder the conquered innocents.

Francis II had died in December of 1560. Catherine, though de facto regent at once, did not receive parliamentary confirmation of this until sometime in the following summer, just the time when Saturn was making its ingress into Cancer, a water sign. One must bear always in mind that we are looking at astrology through the eyes of the sixteenth century, remembering too that Nostradamus gave indications of the timing of events by astronomical positions. This verse is of particular interest analyzed with that understanding. One must not forget, either, the wide familiarity which cultivated people then had with famous birth-charts. Even without this verse, people who followed their charts would have said, "Oh, Oh! When Saturn goes into Cancer that will hit the King and the Queen-mother. His Sun and her Mars are closely conjoined in that sign, which bodes ill for the country staying at peace. Saturn will touch that off. There will be trouble."

The two, mother and son, were astrologically linked together. That is just what Nostradamus means when he speaks of a strong king. He refers to the mother-son combination which he treats as one force, which it was. He was not speaking alone of the little boy he had seen at Blois, who was still unspoiled and fine. In another passage forecasting the eventual rise of Henry of Navarre he says, "he will shave the beard of Catherine." Indication enough that she was the strong king, it would be only as accessory that the boy would be responsible for "the slaughter of the innocents." Quoting the French historian, Guizot, "From 1561 to 1572 there were about twenty-five massacres, thirty or forty single murders unfortunate enough to be remembered by history. Formal civil war, religious and partisan, broke out in four campaigns signalized by great battles, ending in 1572 with the greatest massacre in French history"--Saint Bartholomew, for slaughtering the innocents. The reign of Charles covered the years 1561-1574, and he was only twenty-four when he died. Not until the Revolution would there be again such "slaughter of the innocents" as filled these blood-drenched years. Trouble began at once with minor slaughters on both the Catholic and Protestant sides. But it was in July, 1562, when the Sun was conjoined with Saturn and both bodies were over the birth Sun of Charles and the birth Mars of Catherine, 14 and 17 degrees of Cancer, that the first religious war was opened.

This quatrain has never been understood by analysts because none has understood the astronomical reference the way Nostradamus used these to date and characterize the thirteen tragic years of this mother-son kingship. We may be sure that there were plenty of people at that time who were quick to grasp the allusions, including Catherine. It may be why the Queen tried so hard in the earlier years of this joint rule to pacify both sides. Catherine didn't want slaughter, she wanted peace, but no woman could have handled and tamed the unbridled, passionate fanaticism which broke all bounds. Later, when it was a question of losing her own power or killing Huguenots, Catherine killed. From her point of view she had no choice.

Some modern students of the Centuries, noting this verse, have wondered if it might not relate to the coming king of France, the prophesied Henry V. In June of 1944 Saturn makes its new ingress into Cancer attended by the Sun, Mercury and Venus in a powerful quadruple conjunction. The present Duke of Guise has his birth Sun and Mars in Cancer. It could be. Interpretations of Nostradamus are tricky, and dualistic, and this is as much due to history as to the prophet. "Destiny is an eternal chain . . . looping upon itself" in repeating patterns, the same and never the same. The author, however, feels that this verse specifically referred to Charles IX and Catherine.

Nostradamus, better than any other in France, understood the terrible threat of the mounting strife. Already it was reaching deeply into Provence and men were dying there for their beliefs. But there were still bright spots to be enjoyed. Chief of this was the promised visit from the Princess Marguerite, who was now the Duchess of Savoy. She came to Salon bringing with her Emmanuel-Philibert. They were on their grand honeymoon swing through the country and probably a little bored with all the public entertainments that were given them everywhere. Nostradamus gave the usual Latin oration on behalf of Salon, as the town always liked him to do for their distinguished visitors. Emmanuel-Philibert seems to have been as charmed by Nostradamus as was his wife. They made quite a stay in the town, longer, that is, than they had planned. They invited Nostradamus to sup with them, and they in turn visited him informally. There were the long and interesting talks that Marguerite had looked forward to. It violated, however, the etiquette of her day, and there was some criticism to mar the pleasure. Nostradamus was a gentleman but not a noble. The sixteenth century made fine distinctions in rank, and Catherine had rigidly tightened all matters of etiquette. She even made such a fuss about the Constable de Montmorency riding his horse into the Louvre courtyard, that he said it was easier for him to win a battle than to get inside the Louvre.

People said that the Savoys were too high in rank to associate with Nostradamus as an equal. It was all right to employ and honor him as a prophet, but not to make a familiar friend of him. The Duchess' new home was now just over the Alps from Provence. The democratic Duchess and her independent husband no doubt valued the intellectual interest of the prophet's friendship above all criticism, and one would like to know if they continued by letter their agreeable acquaintance. So very little is known of the private contacts and friendships of Nostradamus in these late, important years, that we who cannot see through time must regretfully forego the reading of this varied and fascinating chapter of his life. What part he played, what influence he had upon the great who came or sent their messengers to him, as in the days of Delphi, we have no way of knowing.

His friend, the Count de Tende, was increasingly disturbed over heavy Protestant gains through Provence. In 1560 the Governor had occasion to notify the Duke de Guise of an election of entirely Protestant deputies in Languedoc. The Duke de Guise tried accommodatingly to have the deputies killed, but they escaped him. They had been legally elected, and if not murdered could serve, as they did. This heavy conversion to the religion which was going on in Provence was naturally a threat to so prominent a personage and so rigid a Catholic as Nostradamus. The friendship of the Governor was powerful protection, but there must have been times when he and his family went in fear of their lives.

One of the popular and much embroidered stories of the prophet is concerning the personal reading he made for Henry of Navarre, a story of which Tronc de Condoulet is said to have been the author, and he should certainly have known. But Henry was only three years old when Nostradamus went to court, and seems to have made his own court debut not until two years later when his father, King Antoine, took him to Paris. Nostradamus, now ill, living in retirement, would hardly have risked his life in Protestant Béarn, certainly not without the royal protection of that court. Jeanne, Queen of Navarre, mother of Henry, was the inspired and fanatical leader of the Protestants. It is hard to imagine a more unlikely situation than Jeanne allowing her baby to be prophesied for by an old Catholic sorcerer, for as such she would certainly have regarded him. So it is difficult to see how this story could be true. Nostradamus made many prophecies about Henry of Navarre, for which he did not need to see him and probably never did.

The first prophecy made for the house of Navarre by Nostradamus concerned the father of Henry and appeared in the first edition of the Centuries. Since he called by name King Antoine, whom for some reason he seems to have admired, the veiled reference to lead might easily mean the next king of Navarre, Antoine's successor, Henry, whom Nostradamus did not like and never failed to say as much. This verse further gives the lie to the story of the examination of Henry by the prophet. Probably neither of the child's parents would have wanted it. Antoine was a weak man with the turn-coat propensities of his family. He was by turns Protestant and Catholic, but he was Catholic when he died, killed at the siege of Rouen in 1562.

IV-38
The Lice will gnaw great Antoine for his least sordid deed
Even unto the last day of his life.
He who shall covet lead shall, after his election, use his lead as a plumb for depths to which he shall be plunged.

The Lice are of course the Protestants who assailed Antoine and killed him at Rouen. The last lines are a play on words. Lead is the base metal of the alchemists in contrast to gold, the metal of spiritual purity. Henry, the son of

Antoine, shall not value gold, but will covet the baser things, and these will be the measure of the man and his ultimate tragedy of assassination.

In view of the many prophecies in circulation that the heir of Navarre would supplant the Valois, these unflattering comments would have been well understood. It gains in aptness from the fact that both Henry and the prophet, having the same birthday, came under the sign and planet ruling lead. But Nostradamus may have considered that in his own case spiritual alchemy had done its work of transmutation.

The prophet's time was growing short now. The town of Salon, holding many of the religion, had greatly changed, and so had, in consequence, its affection and respect for the prophet. In place of that had come gradually a sullen fear of the strange old man and his secret and sorcerous works. The town avoided him, all but a few close, loyal friends like de Condoulet. He lived in great retirement, receiving distinguished visitors from outside, who were still as numerous as ever, and working on the last group of his Centuries. His strength has greatly failed but he knows to the day how much time he has left.

In 1564-1566, the Queen-mother thought it might be a good and pacific idea if between wars she and Charles made a publicity tour through the whole realm, and let the people see and know their King. Great pomp and ceremony characterized the trip. It was the seventh year since the death of Henry II. Catherine adopted for the trip richer, more elaborate dress, in keeping with the occasion which might be said to mark the end of her official mourning.

When the royal progress brought the King and the Queen-mother to Salon, the town turned out in full array for them. The Mayor and the town fathers were the spearhead of the welcoming, enthusiastic crowd. Among the magistrates stood Nostradamus. It is said that the young King brusquely ignored the demonstration, cutting the Latin oratory short with,

"I have come to see Nostradamus."

The little boy whom the prophet had seen at Blois was growing up into a tall youth whose fierce blue eyes and restless, curt manner were an indication of the changes taking place in him. Catherine, who was stout when Nostradamus had visited the court, was now frankly fat. She might have posed for one of the famous Seine frogs which the old Merovingian kings took for their device. What secret interview took place at this second meeting with royalty was not recounted. Yet surely there was a private meeting, with questions asked and talk of the fulfilled forecasts of the last eight years. The Venetian ambassador, who seems to have wielded an active, if not always accurate pen, was not there to chronicle the rumors, otherwise we might have had a story.

Charles IX confirmed at this time the appointment of Physician-in-Ordinary and Councilor which his father had bestowed on the prophet. Some writers say that it was not Henry, but Charles who first gave it. Others speak of the prophet holding his appointment under three kings, Henry II, Francis II and Charles IX. In view of the facts this seems the more likely assumption.

On his way back to Paris Charles again summoned Nostradamus. On this occasion he gave him a purse of two hundred gold écus. Whether in the past years Nostradamus had carried out secret missions for the crown is not known. There would hardly have been a record of it if it had been so. However, the King, on the occasion of this second meeting, did send the prophet on some kind of embassy which the prophet mentions, together with the King's gift, in his farewell quatrain. It must have been an important, delicate matter which Catherine felt no one else could so well undertake. Otherwise she would scarcely have chosen a man who was crippled with his malady and near death. This was the last time, though it may not have been the first, in which he served the Queen in other than his prophetic capacity.

Nostradamus knew exactly how long he had left to live. After his passing, there was found written in his own hand in his copy of the Ephemeris of Jean Stadius, beside the last date in June, "Hic prope mors est." "Here my death draws near." It was on that day that he sent for the notary and dictated his will.

"June 30th, in the year 1566, Maître Michel Nostradamus, doctor of medicine, astrophile, Physician-in-Ordinary and councilor to the king, bequeaths to his daughter Magdeleine 600 écus of gold, and to his other daughters, Anne and Diane, 500 écus of gold. To his dear wife, Anne Ponsart, 400 écus of gold, together with certain household furniture. I bequeath, moreover, all my books to that one of my sons who improves himself or profits most from study, together with all letters, notes and manuscripts found in the dwelling of the testator, who has not at all desired that an inventory should be taken, but that his effects should be gathered and closed up in one of the rooms of the house until the one who should have them will be of age to receive them."

There follow a few generous bequests to churchly orders, and six hundred écus in gold to be distributed among the poor. Nostradamus was himself a member of the third order of the Cordeliers, a lay rank in which obligations are assumed rather than vows taken.

"The aforesaid testator has furthermore declared that he possesses in currency the sum of 3444 écus in gold and 10 sols, which he declares in the pieces hereinafter specified." Follows a picturesque enumeration of coinage to charm the heart of a numismatist. There were so many of rose nobles, of double ducats and imperials, 1 gold écu of King Louis, 1 gold medal, florins of Germany and pieces called Portuguese.

Nostradamus has without any doubt planted clues to the dates of his undated quatrains. They are all over the place, and if one were versed in the wiles of the rhétoriqueurs and the ancient number cycles, they might perhaps be decoded. The "seven men with seven mops" have been trying, with so far no results. This author has a mop too, but it has not as yet done its perfect work. Nor is there space in this book for speculative findings. No one else has noted, however, that there may be a major clue in the numbers of coins mentioned in the will, but this author believes it is there. Nostradamus, in his letter to his son, prefacing the first edition of the prophecies, mentions the year 3797. This is undoubtedly a cryptic, symbolic date rather than an actual one. If the number of verses in the first edition, 353, is subtracted from the year figure, the difference is 3444, the total number of gold écus in the will. If 353 is added to the date of publication of the first edition, 1555, the sum is 1908, the year of birth of the present Duke de Guise, whose name is Henry, and who, as pretender to the throne of France, may become the Henry V of Nostradamus' prophecy. These number oddities may be only coincidental, but there are a great many curious such correspondencies.

Presage 141
On my return from an embassy, with a gift from the King, my affairs are in order,
Nothing more will happen, I shall have gone to God,
Near to my parents. Friends and brothers of my blood
Will find me dead beside my bed and bench.

On the morning of July 2nd, O. S., they found him at his bench bent in the last study that comes to all. The Ephemeris of Jean Stadius, near at hand, showed for that day the Sun, symbol of man's life, just departed from its conjunction with Saturn, the Grim Reaper, and making an aspect with Neptune, the strange planet of timeless things, still undiscovered in that day. Under the mysterious influence of this star the prophet's gift had been developed, under its guidance this titan of two worlds entered his new home in the farther country of Time, whose boundaries between the seen and unseen lands he had so often crossed.

In the church of the Cordeliers at Salon the prophet was "honorably inhumed" in the tomb which he had long ago prepared for himself, upright in the massive church wall where he still reposes. Above the tomb is the bust which César made of his father from memory. "Quietam posteri ne invidete." "Let those who come after disturb not my peace," was the inscription which Nostradamus caused to be cut in the stone. To these words his wife added her further tribute in a Latin epitaph, inscribed on the tomb, which translated reads:

Here rest the bones of the most illustrious
MICHEL NOSTRADAMUS
alone in the judgment of mortals worthy to record the future events of the entire world under the influence of the stars.
He lived 62 years, 6 months, and 17 days.
He died at Salon in the year 1566. Let not posterity disturb his peace. Anne Ponsart Jumelle wishes her husband true felicity.

So ends all that we know of the Seer of the Centuries. At the close of the third edition of his prophecies, he wrote the word Fin. More fitting words for ending the final chapter of the life story of this timeless traveler and man of tomorrow are
SANS FIN

Part Two: The Cycle of Valois-Navarre

The Seven Children of the King
Presage 40
A succession of fatalities will decimate the house of seven,
Hail, tempests, pestilent misfortune and furies.
A ruler of the Orient will put all the Occident in flight
And subdue those who were once his conquerors.

IV-60
Seven children shall he leave behind him in his house,
The Third Estate will eventually murder one,
Two (people) will be pierced by the sword of one of the children,
Genoa and Florence will contribute to the disorder.

VI-14
The seven branches will be reduced to three,
Death will surprise more than one of the elder born,
The two males will be corrupted to the point of fratricide,
Conspirators will die in their sleep.

ONE OF THE CHILDREN, Francis II, was now gone. The Biblical scourges were unleashing their furies in the religious wars between the Catholics and Protestants, which had begun in 1561, while Nostradamus still lived. Solyman the Great was on the throne of Turkey, his pirates were sweeping the length of the Mediterranean, harrying Venice, preying on the commerce of all Europe. Hatred and rivalry were between Charles IX and his brother, the Duke d'Anjou, Catherine's favorite child.

These three quatrains are like the opening bars of a tragic symphony, giving the leit-motif which the music will interweave with other patterns, amplifying and developing the theme. Covering the reign of Charles IX were the four religious wars which spread death and ruin over the country. The Protestants numbered more than a quarter of the population of France, a large number to do away with or even crush, yet such was the only idea that presented itself to the Catholics.

VIII-85
Between Bayonne and Saint Jean de Luz
The promontory of Mars will rise,
The effort of the Nymph of the North will remove the light,
Then it will be snuffed out at the bedside without help.

In 1565 Catherine and Charles IX met the Duke of Alva at Bayonne to consult about means of quenching the fire of the Protestant menace. The time was set for the massacre which was later postponed until Saint Bartholomew's because the Protestants got wind of it. The Nymph of the North is Queen Elizabeth, whose encouragement and active support were invaluable to the Protestants. The prophet sees the unity of faith lost to France, snuffed out never to return, largely by virtue of this support. Elizabeth also removed the light of the Duke d'Anjou's hope to marry her, which died aborning.

In 1558, two years after the prophet's death, a new and final edition of the Prophecies was published at Lyons by Rigaud. The arrangement of the Centuries was in two parts. The first comprised all of the two previous editions together with the letter to César. The second half consisted of three new Centuries of a hundred verses each, preceded by a letter of dedication to Henry, King of France Second. The edition was brought out under the direction and supervision of Brother Jean Vallier of the monastery of the Mineurs Conventuals, and with the permission of his ecclesiastical superiors. It is evident that this must have been in accordance with a pre-arranged plan made during the prophet's lifetime. It also shows the support and approval which the Church accorded to his prophetic powers.. In this time of high excitement, war and death, the publication of fresh prophecies was an event of prime importance in court circles. So many forecasts had already been fulfilled that, as Nostradamus had predicted, he was even more famous in death than he had been in life.

In this same year occurred another event of importance to the court, and saddening to all France. This was the death of the Princess Elizabeth, then Queen of Spain. Of her marriage to Philip, Nostradamus had this to say:

S-49
Venus, Sun, Jupiter and Mercury
Shall augment events of the class coming under their influence,
A grand alliance will take place in France,
And the blood-sucker of the Midi himself,
The flame of war being extinguished by this extreme remedy,
Will plant the Olive branch in solid ground.

Jupiter and Sun, stars of pomp and royalty, had been in friendly aspect during the splendid, fatal tourney which celebrated the match. Philip, from the time he became King of Sicily, was called by the French the "Blood-Sucker of the Midi." The prophet, remembering the sweet child he had seen at Blois, called the marriage an "extreme remedy," but he saw that the sacrifice was justified for France. The long peace was as foretold. It was only broken after the death of Henry III, when the rise of Navarre, allied with the Nymph of the North, roused Spanish fears.

Crescent and Cross

While the turmoil of civil war was obsessing France, momentous happenings in the Mediterranean were fulfilling more of the prophet's visions, which were a continuation of what Villiers de L'Isle Adam, the soldier of Rhodes, had told him so many years before.

When sword and doctrine are shut up within the fish
There shall go forth one who will wreak worse than war,
His fleet will be well rowed across the sea,
Appearing off the coast of Italy.

IX-61
The pillage made along the seacoast
Will be provoked and induced in the new city, (Geneva)
Certain Christian Knights of Malta, through the act of Messina,
Will be poorly rewarded when they are squeezed in the straits.

In 1565 the Turks boldly attacked Malta, killing eight thousand of the Knights and possessing themselves of half the island. The island had, you will remember, been given to the Knights of Rhodes, under Nostradamus' patient, the Knight Commander de L'Isle Adam, by Spain, as a reward for their valor at Rhodes. Therefore, says Nostradamus, it is poor guerdon for Philip II of Spain and King of Sicily (the deed of Messina, Sicily) to leave them to be squeezed in the straits without sending any help in their dire extremity. John Calvin made Geneva his headquarters. The prophet refers to the "New City," as it was called, in this connection, as contributing to the war.

II-4
From Monaco to Sicily
The whole shore dwells in desolation,
There will not be a town, city or village
Which has not been the prey of Barbarian theft and pillage.

IV-39
The Rhodians will demand help Through the neglect with which their heirs have abandoned them, The Arabian Empire will turn on its course When the Western Nations have redressed the Christian cause.

Lepanto IX-30
From the port of Erzeroum and the country of Saint Nicholas (Turkey) There is Peril to Frenchmen in the Gulf of Fanaticism, From the streets of Constantinople will go up cries and appeals to the house of Capet. Help will go out from Cadiz and the forces of great Philip.

IX-43
The neighboring descendants of the Crusaders
Will be ambushed by the Mussulmans,
But these will be beaten on all sides by the forces of the barque of the Papacy,
They will be promptly assailed by the galleys filled with the picked men of ten nations.
The Holy Father shall heed the cry of Sicily,
All preparations will go forward from the Gulf of Trieste
Extending down to Sicily,
Comprising many galleys. Flee, flee from the horrible scourge.

III-31

From the lands of Media, Arabia, and Armenia
Two great leaders shall thrice assemble expeditions.
Near the shores of Asia Minor the house
Of Sulyman the Great will meet defeat.

III-64
The Shah of Persia will replenish his great commercial navy
When the trireme galleys go against the Mohammedans,
Because of Parthia and Media and the pillage of the Cyclades,
And bring a long peace to the port of Smyrna.

In 1571 the Battle of Lepanto turned back and seriously crippled Turkish sea power. In that year the island of Cyprus, "The neighboring descendants of the Crusaders will be ambushed," was seized by Turkey with a massacre so complete and dreadful that at last Christian Europe was galvanized into action. Individual soldiers went from France to take part in the expedition, as did soldiers from all over Europe and England. But France as a nation remained aloof. Philip of Spain and the Pope were the organizers of the naval expedition which did include ten governments, counting the states of Italy. "The picked men" were the flower of Europe's chivalry. Great princes in person led the boarding parties that took the Moslem ships. Cervantes was among the heroes at the battle. The colorful Don John of Austria was the military commander of the allied fleet.

The losses on both sides were very heavy, but the Christians administered a smashing defeat from which Turkey never recovered. Lepanto is one of the most important naval engagements in history. Its spirit was that of the ancient Crusaders. Its "trireme galleys," little changed from the days when Rome defeated Carthage, saw their last use in a major engagement at Lepanto. These romantic ships of war were shortly discarded for boats of different build adapted to hold the new artillery, and to a complete change in the methods of sea war.

It was some years later, but in direct consequence of Lepanto, that the Shah of Persia seized important Turkish provinces, and also one of the great ports on the Persian Gulf, which enabled him to enrich himself by expansion of his maritime commerce.

The Massacre of Saint Bartholomew

Meanwhile the civil wars of religion went on interminably in France. Leaders on both sides were killed. The ability and faith of Admiral Coligny, after the Prince of Condé died, made him the greatest leader and military commander whom the Protestants had.

VI-75
The master pilot commissioned by the king
Will leave the fleet to assume a higher post,
Seven years later he will be in opposition to his king
At a time when Venice is dreading the coming of Barbarian armies.

V-83
Those whose enterprise is the ruin of France
Of the matchless, powerful and invincible realm of France

Will carry on with deceit. Three nights a watch will be kept
On their leader as he sits at his table reading the Bible.

Presage III
The great bronze bell that rings in the succession of the hours
Will sound full volley at the Tyrant's death,
Tears, groans and cries, but no bread from revolution's icy waters,
Carolus Victor Sanctus abandons peace for the sword.

VIII-85
A hot wind, deliberations going on, tears, hesitations,
Assault by night on one unarmed in bed,
A grand disaster of oppression,
The wedding-song converted into tears and lamentations.

III-30
He who by sword and prowess on the field of battle
Had carried the prize from one of greater rank than he,
In his bed at night will be stabbed to death, by six,
Stripped, without his armor, taken by surprise.

IV-47
When the savage King shall have tried his hand
Bloody with the work of fire, sword and arquebus
The people will be completely terrified
To see the greatest in the land strung up by neck and heels.

Sixain 52
The great City which has but half enough bread to eat (Paris)
Will have the further blow of Saint Bartholomew
Engraved upon the depths of its soul.
Nîmes, Rochelle, Geneva, and Montpellier,
Castres and Lyons, when Mars enters Aries
These cities will have civil war, and all because of a government.

Admiral Coligny resigned his commission as commander-in-chief of the French navy seven years after he had received it, in order to head the Protestant party. He came within an ace of carrying off "the prize" of power by his ascendancy over Charles IX. For a time, he and his party, as well as his enemies, thought that he had. His domination was so great that Catherine dared delay no longer in putting into execution the plans made seven years previously with the Duke of Alva, at Bayonne. And the first death must be Coligny's. An assassin was sent, Maurevert, to kill the Admiral. Guizot says he watched Coligny's house for three days before the Admiral went out, and the killer got his chance. Nostradamus' vivid picture of the old man reading his Bible under the eye of the murderer is a perfect bit. Coligny was only wounded, so that the general mass murder was ordered at once. This occurred on the twenty-fourth of August, 1572. Six days earlier, Marguerite of Valois had married Henry of Navarre, and the court was still celebrating the wedding. The feverish deliberations and last minute conferences which preceded the ringing of the tocsin happened precisely as Nostradamus describes. Coligny was murdered at night, unarmed, by the Duke de Guise, his servant, Besme, and three or four of the Swiss mercenaries. The towns mentioned were those in which Protestants were strong, particularly New La Rochelle.

The prophet had no sympathy for Coligny, the spearhead of the faction he believed undermining France. The anointed King acted within his rights to kill the "Traitor." But he deplored that the savagery of that same King should massacre his people, "the slaughtered innocents" of the quatrain quoted earlier. Charles IX was said to have stood at the palace window, arquebus in hand, and shot down Protestants until exhausted.

Events of importance followed two years later, in 1574.

VII-35
The Important Fish will weep and wail
Because he has been elected. They will be deceived in the times,
Their political guide will not be desirous of making his home with them.
He will be killed by the people of his own language.

The Fish was the Duke d'Anjou. The Pope, in the Centuries, is often called the Fisherman. France, politically and religiously, was always the best-loved fish of the papacy. Henry of Anjou was heir presumptive to the throne. The quarrel between himself and Charles had become so acute that neither was safe from the other. Henry was offered the crown of Poland, which he accepted to get out of France. After sophisticated Paris, he loathed living in Poland. The Poles quite misjudged the character of the times in France when they invited Henry. He was only there three months. Charles IX, racked with remorse and illness, died, soothed at the last only by the old Protestant nurse whom the prophet had seen with the little boy in the gardens of Blois. Henry left Poland at once to become Henry III of France, until such time as one of his own people would murder him.

Duel a Outrance

Henry III was weak, vicious, perverted; but like all the Valois he had charm. The psychopathic jealousy and hatred which he had felt for his brother, Charles IX, now that Charles was dead, he projected upon the strong, brilliant Henry, Duke de Guise, son of the warrior who took Calais. Courtly, eloquent, magnetic, Guise was the idol of Paris. He was twice wounded in action, once in the arm, and again in the leg and head. A bullet clipped his ear and scarred his cheek which gave him his nickname, Le Balafré, in spite of which he was considered very handsome. One of the cardinals at court remarked of the Guises, father and son, that they made other people seem common by comparison.

Guise as the descendant of Charlemagne, and having also the royal blood of the Capet line, was one of the two royal brothers whom Nostradamus describes in the following accurate picture of their deadly duel, which was half personal hatred, half desire for power. Guise, like the Bourbons, wanted the throne. As the leader of the Catholic faction, he was in consequence close to the palace, and had in a fashion the inside track. He was at this time far more powerful than the coming King, Henry of Navarre. Guise had every confidence that he would win the crown. The weak King, Catherine supporting her son with her craft, and the Duke de Guise are the actors in this tragedy.

IV-38
While the Duke, the King and the Queen are in occupation of power
Captives will be taken in Byzantium and Samothrace,
Before the showdown (between the Duke and King) one shall consume the other,
Then the sword will turn against the survivor and its track will be made in blood.

IV-62
Two royal brothers will wage war so powerfully
Against each other that it will be a mortal combat,
Each in turn will occupy the seats of power,
The great quarrel will involve both power and life.

II-54
The insensate ire of furious combat
Will place a gleaming sword between two brothers who were once companions at the same table,
He who is the quarry will be struck to his death,
In the fierce duel that will injure all France.

VIII-45
His hand in a sling and his leg bandaged,
Junior of Calais and a long line of ancestors (Guise),
He will avert his death through a warning of ambush,
His blood will be shed in a palace after Communion.

X-56
King against King and Duke against Prince,
Hatred between them and horrible dissension,
Rage and fury will sweep the whole country,
In France there will be great war and terrible changes.

III-51
Paris conspires to commit a great murder,
Blois will carry it into full effect,
The citizens of Orleans will wish to depose him (the King),
Angers, Troyes, and Langres will commit an offense.

II-57
Before the final conflict and the fall of the wall
A Great Personage (Guise) will be done to death, his end will be sudden and lamented,
The policy of the Church will be imperfect. The greater part of the nation shall welter,
Hard by the river blood will stain the earth.

VII-2
Many will come and will talk about peace
Between the Monarques and their very puissant Lords,
But it will not come about in the near future

Because none of them will swear fealty to any of the others.

VIII-3
Alas what fury! Alas what pity
For what will happen between so many of the nation,
Never will one have seen such good will
Except among diligently coursing wolves.

VIII-4
Much of the nation will wish for negotiation
Between the great Lords who will be responsible for the war,
But no one will be willing to listen to anything,
Alas! If only God would send peace to the earth.

The religious wars were more than a fight between Catholic and Protestant. They were a three-cornered fight for power between Catherine de' Medici, backing successively her sons, and the great competing houses of Guise-Lorraine and Bourbon-Navarre. None of the three would yield to the others; it had to be, as it was, a duel to the death.

Note how the Oriental motif is sustained. Lepanto had defeated Turkey, but not crushed her, and France had not fulfilled her obligation then. No Turkish armies threaten, but the Turk still takes his captives as pirates' prey, while Christian France quarrels internally. The Duke de Guise organized the Catholic League to wrest the power from the King. Spain supported this effort, the King was losing. Assassination was the answer. The King had gone to Blois. The Duke, as Lieutenant-General of France and High Steward of the Royal Household, was also there, both being present for the meeting of the States-General.

So one has the strange picture of these two deadly enemies and rivals under the same roof and dining at the same table. The King summoned the Duke for a private conference. As the Duke raised the tapestry to enter the room, known as the old closet, he was stabbed five times by the King's men. The King and the Duke had taken communion together shortly before the murder.

When the Duke was dead the King exclaimed, "Now I am sole King. The King of Paris is dead!" Catherine said, "You have done the cutting, now we must sew it well." But there was little time for her sewing. Her own death, in bed, occurred thirteen days after the murder of the Duke de Guise. France was outraged at the murder. Orleans turned against the King. The other towns mentioned by the prophet promptly went over to the Protestants, for which Nostradamus blames them. Sixtus V, whom, as we have seen, the prophet did not admire, was subservient to Spain, and in many ways vacillating or afraid to adopt a strong policy. The Cardinal de Guise, brother ("Two shall be killed by one of the children") of Le Balafré, was murdered by Henry a few days after the Duke. The third Guise brother, the Duke de Mayenne, then took over the leadership of the Catholic League.

I-85
The King shall be troubled by the response of the nation,
Ambassadors will scorn their lives in fulfilling their missions,
The Great Personage will act for both his brothers Slain by hatred and malice.

The Great Personage is the Duke de Mayenne.

V-72
For the satisfaction of passing an edict that caters to self-indulgence
Poison will be mingled with holy faith,
Venus in her course will show such power
As will shadow the unalloyed gold of the Sun.

The edict of Poictiers, passed by Henry III in 1577, among other things permitted Protestant ministers to marry. Nostradamus saw this as a threat to Catholicism. It was a temptation away from the ascetic standards of the priesthood, into the freer customs of the Protestant ministry. Venus, here a metaphor for self-indulgence, clouds the Sun of the monarchy.

Henry of Navarre

V-1
Before the onset of the ruin of France
Two shall negotiate within a palace,
A death stroke to the heart, someone mounts a courser,
The Great Personage will be buried without publicity.

II-15
A short while before the King is killed
We shall see Castor and Pollux in the same ship, there will be a comet visible near that time,
The public taxes will have been emptied over land and sea,
Throughout the cities of Italy the land (of France) will be interdict.

The two royal brothers, Henry III and Henry of Navarre, sinking their religious differences and agreeing on a common plan, climb into the same ship of state which is also the barque of religion in a country having a state religion. The condition of the treasury, and the reaction of Italy to the combination of the two rulers were as the prophet indicates.

IV-95
Scant space the two shall hold the reign,
But the war will last three years and seven months.
The two vestals will be in rebellion against France, but from opposite sides.
The victor, from the cadet branch, will plant his foot on Armoric soil (Brittany).
The great King will be taken by a Young Man
Not far from Easter, when there will be confusion and knife thrust,
The perpetration of the deed is at the time when there are captives, and powder in the tower,
This murder follows the death of three brothers who injured themselves.

V-67
While the leader of Perouse (Sixtus V) is afraid to take off his shirt
For fear of being totally despoiled and left bare
The last of the seven will be taken, a shock to court circles,

Father and son both struck in the neck.

Presage 58
When the King--King is no more, destroyed by the Gentle One,
The year will be feverish, stirred with sedition,
Let him who holds hold fast. Not for the nobles (Guise faction) is Lutetia,
He will pass (outlast) the period of his cavillers.

After the furor over the murder of the two Guises, Henry III, twice King, once of Poland, once of France, desperately in need of backing, with the Duke de Mayenne, the third and sole surviving Guise brother, in virtual control of Paris, sought out Henry of Navarre and made an alliance with him. But, "scant space"--only a few months later the King was assassinated by Jacques Clément, believed to be the agent of the Third Estate. "The Third Estate shall murder one." Clément, the name meaning clement or gentle, is exactly indicated by the prophet as the murderer. The alliance with Navarre was at Easter, the murder--"not long after."

Paris, in the hands of the Duke de Mayenne, preparing its defenses and arresting Protestants and royalists, there were "captives and powder." Pope Sixtus, "the leader of Perouse," after the papacy having been despoiled of England by Henry VIII, was terrified lest it happen now with France. Henry II had been struck on his armored neck-piece by Montgomery's lance. Henry III was stabbed in "the little gut," or neck of the colon. "Father and son both struck in the neck." Henry of Navarre, surviving member of the alliance, is advised to hang on, for not to the nobles under the Duke de Mayenne shall fall Lutetia, Paris. Henry will survive his opponents.

The Seven Children of the King are now dead, all but Marguerite, the wife of Henry of Navarre, who had no children. Under the Salic law she cannot rule, and in time Navarre will divorce her.

S-26
There will be two brothers, each the leader of an ecclesiastical faction,
One of them will take France at sword's point.
There will be another coup in six hundred and six
If he is not then afflicted with grave illness.
His armes and power will flourish to six hundred and ten,
His life expectation will hardly go beyond that time.

II-95
Places long peopled will become uninhabitable,
Throughout the country there will be a great division,
Factions of government will be in the hands of men incapable of wisdom,
Between the brothers there will be dissension and death.

X-26
The successor to the kingdom shall avenge his brother-in-law,
He will occupy the realm under the pretense of vengeance,
After the obstacle to his power is cut down, he will show great anger over the death of his own blood,
And Brittany will long be held by France.

VII-24
The buried shall go out from the tomb
To bind with his chains the power of the bridge (of Seine).
Poisoned with the eggs of the great Barbel
   The Leader of Lorraine will be defeated by the Lord Warden of the Marches.

IX-50
Vendôme the deceitful shall soon come into his high power
Putting those of Lorraine somewhat in the background.
The pale Cardinal will be the male of the interregnum,
The young man will be apprehensive, dreading foreign influence.

IX-41
The great Henry will seize Avignon,
From Rome the letters will be bitter-sweet,
   A letter will be dispatched to an accredited agent to go to Chavigny at Chinon,
   Carpentras will be taken by the dark Duke, who wears the Cardinal's panache.

Presage 22
Cut off by sea, trenches are dug around the occupied city,
The Great Personage and the newly chosen King are weakened,
Follow the Fleur de Lis, enter the camp of broken faith.
The white plume will have to put forth a strong effort.

V-18
The unfortunate contender in the duel (the Cardinal) will die,
His victor will celebrate with a hecatomb.
He will draw up an Edict of freedom based on early law,
The wall will fall to the Prince on the seventh day.

I-18
The house of Lorraine will give place to Vendôme,
The high will be put low, and the low exalted to high places,
The son of Amon will be chosen at Rome
And the two great personages will be defeated.

   Cryptic as these verses read, they tell a perfectly straight story. Two brothers in royalty, Navarre and Mayenne, lead the Protestant and Catholic factions. The winner of the war, Navarre, will not live beyond 1610. He was assassinated then. A coup or an illness will mark his year in 1606. He nearly died of illness in 1608, but Guizot speaks of it as if it were of long standing, and it may have begun when the prophet said.
   Henry of Navarre did claim the crown to avenge Henry III, his brother-in-law. He seized Brittany, previously tributary, but autonomous under France. It had belonged to Queen Claude, grandmother of Henry III. Nostradamus said in a verse, previously given, "the cadet branch," the Bourbon, "will plant its foot on Armoric soil." Armorica was the old name of Brittany. Thereafter Brittany remained as a province of the crown.

"The buried" is Coligny who, through his Protestant successor, Henry of Navarre, will enchain the power of Paris. The Barbel is a fish equipped with prongs to spear its prey. The fish, in the Centuries, is always a religious symbol. Here, the Barbel, the vicious fish of the false religion, Protestantism, will poison with the eggs it lays, hopes of the house of the Catholic faction under Guise-Lorraine, so that it is defeated by Navarre. The latter is Lord Warden of the Marches because he comes from the border kingdom of Navarre, a bulwark against Spanish aggression.

But when Henry claimed the throne, the Duke de Mayenne put up a counter-claimant who was none other than Navarre's uncle, the old Cardinal de Bourbon, who had come over to his side. It was in this Cardinal's house that the prophet had lodged while in Paris. But nothing can stop Vendôme (one of the family names of Navarre) although he is worried and doesn't know what Spain is going to do about all this. His first concern was to see that his uncle, whom he had under guard, didn't escape and get himself crowned. The Cardinal was at Chinon in the care of Sieur Chavigny, who was also old, like the Cardinal, and nearly blind. Henry sent a courier with a letter to the governor of Saumur "bidding him at any price" to get the Cardinal away from Chinon and under proper guard, which was done. But the poor old man, "the contender in the duel," died, as the prophet said, not long after.

The battle of Arques, 1589, the first of Navarre's two great victories, was as the prophet indicates it. Mayenne was between Henry and the sea, blocking help. Henry had a complete line of trenches dug surrounding the castle and town of Arques. Nor does Nostradamus forget to mention the white plume of Navarre, so famous in song and story. Victory, he tells us, will crown Navarre in the battle, that is what he means by "follow the Fleur de Lis." It is the beginning of the taking over by the house of Bourbon--to the prophet a faithless line--the royal lily emblem of Capet.

Meanwhile the letters from Sixtus were very bittersweet. He admired Navarre, but he didn't want a Protestant ruling France. Henry of Navarre at once began to put into practice his ideas of toleration which later were shaped into the Edict of Nantes. "The son of Anion," the religious turncoat and heretic, Navarre, of course, was chosen at Rome, after his purely political conversion to Catholicism. Thus were the two great personages, Mayenne and the Cardinal, defeated.

The Cardinal is dead, but we are not yet finished with the Duke de Mayenne. (And, reader, if the history of France seems unduly involved, don't shoot the prophet and the author. Like the pianist, we are doing our best.)

IX-57
A King will replace the line of Dreux (the northern branch)
And will seek a law that will change the situation from Anathema,
While the heaven is thundering with preparations for war
The new brood will destroy themselves and the King too.

X-45
The unfulfillment of the promise made at Cambray,
The shadow over the reign of the faithless Navarre
Will make life very precarious (until)
Accepted as King by Orleans he will find a wall to lean on.

Presage-76
Before the legate of the earth and sea
The head of the Capetian line will accommodate himself to all that is required,
Mayenne will listen in silence
And will, of his own advice, grant as little as he can.

IX-39
In Arbrisselle, Vezame and Crevari,
He shall set out at night in the hope of capturing Savona,
The lively Gascon, with de Givry and La Charry,
Will penetrate the old wall and grab the new palace.

VII-32
Hatred will produce uncommon stratagems,
Rebellion will sow death throughout the country,
When the foreigner returns from his trip
The people will exalt the entry of the Protestant.

Navarre and his rule were under the ban of the Church, they were anathema until his conversion. The prophet in this verse looks forward to Henry's end when fanatical hatred destroys him, and with his passing the new brood, the Protestants, gradually lose their political power, shorn of royal protection. It was, however, hardly true that they were responsible for their own destruction.

Henry had early renounced Protestantism at Chambray, but he hesitated to take the final steps against the feeling of his own party. Only after he was bulwarked by the support of Orleans, which came over to him, did he feel strong enough to take this step, which he did in 1593. He then accommodated himself to the requirements of the Pope, "the legate of the earth and sea."

After his conversion, Henry took Paris the following year. On the 14th of March the civic powers of Paris, having decided to admit him, forbade meetings of the Mayenne faction. Seven days later, as stated by the prophet in a quatrain given earlier, Navarre entered Paris. The reference to the new palace, when Navarre entered the old walls of Paris, is to the Tuileries, which Catherine de' Medici had begun but which was still not entirely finished. De Givry and La Charry are names of two of Navarre's enthusiastic supporters. The three towns mentioned in the same verse were in the Sardinian states with which Henry had a certain amount of fighting and difficulty.

The war continued for a time longer but eventually Mayenne yielded and made the best terms for himself that he could, and became a friend and loyal subject of the King. The Duke of Parma, who led the Spanish forces assisting Mayenne, returned to Spain, and, Spanish influence removed, the people of France, the majority of them, rejoiced in the entry of the Protestant into the monarchy.

VI-70
A world leader shall be Henry the Great,
Respected and feared, he will be more loved long after his passing,
The heavens shall ring with his reputation and praise,
With the sole title of Victorious he will be well content.

IX-45
Never will he be without something more to ask for,
The great personage of Vendôme will obtain his empire (but),
He will spend his time away from court, he will nullify the plans of Piedmont and Picardy, and Paris will
Become like ancient Tyre.

III-88
From Barcelona by sea shall come a great fleet,
All Marseilles will tremble with terror,
Islands will be seized, help blocked by sea,
The traitors will swarm on land.

Philip's plot to seize Marseilles for Spain was in the early years of Henry's rule while he was still fighting for power and had declared war on Spain. When the design was foiled, the traitor killed and dragged in the mud of the streets, Henry exclaimed: "Now I am really King!" Such was the importance, says Guizot, of Marseilles as the queen of the Mediterranean.

The fighting in Picardy was with the Spaniards, mainly, and like that of Piedmont before he came into his full sovereignty.

I-86
The free City (Geneva) which is the slave of liberty
Will give asylum to the defeated and the dreamers.
When France changes her king the application of the law will not be so hard on them

And (in France) for every hundred (formerly) there will now be a thousand.

As true of modern Geneva as in the times of Henry IV. The passing of the Edict of Nantes, the great law of religious toleration, of which the prophet disapproved, permitted the return to France of "the defeated and the dreamers," who had received asylum in Geneva during the religious wars.

Sixain 6
When Biron's traitorous undertaking
Shall put a great Prince and his Lords in a difficult situation.
Lafin will know all about it, his chief will be beheaded.
Plume to the wind and letters sent, for he has a friend in Spain,
The postman will be trapped when he enters France,
The writer throws himself into the water.

Two pieces of treachery marked the reign of Henry IV. One was that of the great soldier, Marshal Biron, whom the King said that he loved like a brother. Biron sold out to Spain. He wanted, he said, to see his head on a coin before he died. If he had lived today it might have gone on a stamp; as it was, it went on the block. His agent was Lafin, who confessed to the King. The other traitor, who also wanted Spanish gold, was an obscure clerk in the diplomatic service. He was trapped through a watch set on the post-office, and when pursued by night, near the Marne, fell in the water and was drowned.

Sixain I
A new cycle begins with a new alliance,

A Lord Warden of the Marches establishes accord with the papal barque,
A galley, uniting a king and a duke, will put out from Florence,
Making port at Marseilles and landing a royal daughter in France
To marry the strong leader who shaved the beard of Catherine.

V-3
The inheritor of the duchy will command advantages
Far beyond the Tuscan sea.
Florence will have a branch in France
And the Frog will be held in the bosom of papal accord.

X-54
Born into this world of a furtive concubine,
Twice raised on high through sad news,
She shall be captured by her enemies
And brought to Malines and Brussels.

Henry IV's second marriage was to Marie de' Medici, who came by galley to Marseilles as Catherine had done so long ago. Her father, the prophet lets us know, did very well for himself when he married his daughter to the King of France. Marie's mother was said to be what Nostradamus called her, but not particularly furtive about it. Marie was twice regent after Henry's death. Richelieu exiled her to the country. She escaped to Brussels and died in Belgium.

III-21
The noise of armes shall long be raised to heaven,
The tree in the midst of the city falls,
There is a vermin-ridden man with a knife opposite Tyson,
Then falls the monarch Henry.

Henry IV was preparing for war when he was stabbed by Ravaillac, while on his way to the Cathedral for his second coronation. Halted by the congestion in the narrow Rue Ferroniere, he was standing, strangely enough, beneath a sign, The Crown Pierced By An Arrow. In this street of the iron-workers there was one little alley which was occupied by the makers of pokers, les tisoniers. The King was standing opposite the entrance to this, "face Tyson," when he was struck down. It is said that before he left the palace to go to the Cathedral, a tree in the courtyard, decorated in gala style according to old custom for such occasions, fell over.

The accession of Henry of Navarre (he had already been ruling for more than a decade) had established the Bourbon dynasty upon "the golden throne." It had brought to fulfillment the long struggle of the Bourbons for the rulership of France which the Constable de Bourbon had begun sixty years before. The prophet could never bring himself to admire the splendid qualities of Henry, though he admits his greatness. To him Navarre was always the faithless scion of a faithless house, whose leader in the days of his youth, the Constable, had brought treachery, plague and slaughter to Rome and to France. He knew, too, that France was not through with the changeable loyalties of the house of Bourbon. Louis de Condé, called The Great, namesake of Bossu, would go against his King, Louis XIII. Philippe Egalité would vote for the beheading of his own brother, Louis XVI. And Louis Philippe would abandon the flag of the Fleur de Lis for the Tricolor. The prophet had spoken bitterly of that; it hurt him. However, with the coming of Henry, the Bourbons were henceforward France, and to those who ruled after Henry, Nostradamus gave spiritual allegiance as he followed them in his prophetic visions.

The author regrets that space forbids the presentation of the great periods intervening between Henry IV and the contemporary scene. It is in our own time, as prophesied by Nostradamus, that the last of the Bourbons is to rule France, the man who is to be her greatest King, who is to arise and guide the nation back to glory. This King will close the cycle of both the Bourbons and the monarchy of France.

It was, however, the reign of Henry of Navarre which closed the cycle of the people Nostradamus knew, born in his lifetime. The world had greatly changed since he came into it. Still, there was always something of its familiar character left while there remained some of those born in his lifetime and acquainted with the old ways. Now that is over. The world which he describes from this time on is a world different from his experience, and known only to his prophet's vision.

It was sometime during the reign of Henry of Navarre that César Nostradamus, nephew of the prophet, and governor of Provence under Henry IV, presented to the King the fifty-eight Sixains and one hundred and forty-one Presages which were among the prophet's effects. In view of Nostradamus' devastating attacks on Henry in so many of his verses, which the King must have seen, it does not seem a too tactful present. One wonders how the King really felt about it, in spite of the records which say that he was interested and pleased. But Henry was a gay, generous, tolerant nature. He probably shrugged it off and, like the vert galant the Gascons still call him, sought out the prettiest woman in the room and told her about it as a jest.

Claude de Savoie

More Mars than Narbonne

CLAUDE DE SAVOIE, Duke de Villars, Marshal-General of France, and the man who was "more like Mars than Narbonne," was the hero of France in the War of the Spanish Succession. That tragic struggle, which involved all Europe from 1701 to 1713, is now chiefly notable for the victories of the Duke of Marlborough, whose reputation has overshadowed that of the scarcely less brilliant Villars.

The story of the war, told by Nostradamus virtually in headlines, is extraordinary for its coverage and detail. His prophecy was superb, if his reporting was somewhat prejudiced in favor of his King.

In these verses, as in a number of others about Louis XIV, the prophet calls Louis the "Æmathion," which means a Macedonian Greek. The term is a good illustration of Nostradamus' power of condensed, laconic expression in which art he could have given lessons to Lacon of Sparta. In this one word, Æmathion, he has made an historical commentary on Le Grand Monarque. The Capetian kings had a real, if shadowy, claim to the blood of Alexander the Great since the days when a Russian princess, descended from Philip of Macedon, Alexander's father, had married an early king of France. Alexander the Great repudiated the paternity of Philip, and called himself the son of the Sun, claiming Apollo for his father. History has repudiated the paternity of the Sun-king, Louis XIV, and his true father is unknown. Both Alexander and Louis were warriors. The conquests of the former were dissipated after he died, while Louis outlived his winnings, which went in this war.

III-92
The world will be approaching its last cycle,
Saturn will be nearing its slow re-entry (into Aries),
The empire (of Spain) will pass to a Germanic nation,
The eye of the man of Narbonne will be torn out by those around him.

IV-2
Because of a death, France will undertake a foreign expedition,
The fleet will put to sea, the army will cross the Pyrenees,
Spain, in a difficult situation, will set her army in motion
Because royal ladies were conducted into France.

I-99
The great Monarch will associate himself with
Two rulers united to him in bonds of friendship,
Oh, how the royal household shall sigh,
What piteous conditions are around the son of Narbonne!

IX-38
The great Æmathion will hold the harbor-mouth at Blaye

Now cleared of English and Rochellese resistance,
The Gauls who wait for help near Agen
Will be fooled in their enterprise, the help will be for the man of Narbonne.

X-69
Savoy approaches, his military array stretches from Lake Geneva,
The great leaders draw up their lines of strength,
Far from the heirs, there will be great fighting around Geneva,
All the people will be involved in flight.

II-34
Livestock savage with hunger will cross rivers,
The greater part of the field will be encamped over against the Danube,
The great general will be taken prisoner (Villefroy)
While German youth are keeping watch on the Rhine.

VIII-73
The Foreign Soldier will smite the great Monarch
Unjustly, when he is already near his end,
The avaricious mother will be the cause of his activity
And plotter and realm will greatly repent of it.

VI-53
The great Celtic prelate suspected by his king
Will lay a course by night and leave the kingdom,
Arranged by the ingenious Duke acting for his British king,
He (the Cardinal) will pass through the towns of Belgium undiscovered.

IV-64
The armies of the Æmathion will cross the Pyrenees,
Mars of Narbonne will not be able to withstand the enemy,
On land and sea so great will be the enemy's advance
That the house of Capet can occupy no terrain in safety.

IV-3
At Arras, Bourges and in Germany the standards of the mighty will be raised,
A large number of Gascons will fight in the infantry,
Soldiers from up and down the Rhone will shed Spanish blood
Close to the mountain where Sagunto sits.

IV-14
The two royal brothers of Spain will be driven out,
The elder will be vanquished beneath the Pyrenees mountains,
The Rhone, Lake Constance and Germany will be red with blood,
Narbonne, eastern Berry and Ath will be regions soiled by the invasions.

VI-56
Fear of the army of Narbonne's enemy
Will terrify the Spaniards very greatly,
Perpignon will be emptied through the blindness of Narbonne,

Barcelona will be taken by naval attack at the point of the pike.

II-59
The French fleet, supporting the country's defense,
Will be in conflict with great Neptune and his trident soldiers,
Provence will be gnawed to the bone to sustain the horde of troops,
The general who is more like Mars than Narbonne will be attacked by the javelins and darts of the enemy.

Presage I
The Ocean and the Tyrrhenian Sea will be under the anchor-watch
Of mighty Neptune and his trident soldiers,
But Provence will be held in safety by the army of the great Tende,
The heroic Villars whose nature will be more like Mars than Narbonne.

The mutation of Saturn and Jupiter in the warlike sign Aries introduced the conflict. Spain was already declining, and Austria was the continental rival of France. Two Spanish princesses married two French Kings, Louis XIII and XIV. The Spanish King, dying without heir, willed his realm to the part-Spanish grandson of Louis XIV. Spain was divided over this arrangement, and the rest of Europe strenuously objected to it. So Louis marched, the others countermarched with a counter claimant, and the fight was on with everybody in it, including England.

Louvet, Louis' war minister, was so jealous of Villars that he would not give him command until a series of disasters had made the French situation desperate. Marshal Villefroy, commanding for the French against Prince Eugene of Savoy and the Duke of Marlborough, was beaten and taken prisoner. Louis started out with two weak allies, and only a German Elector stayed with him. Villars was given command after the damage had been done; he couldn't then stand up against Marlborough, and failed in one battle to foresee his moves. He had his eyes snatched out metaphorically in several ways. The fighting raged from the Danube to the west coast of Spain, and from the lowlands to the Midi. This war saw the first use of the technique so familiar today, the large-scale devastation of areas affecting civilian population, and it was France that used it. Louis was criticized by the rest of the civilized world for doing it. "Livestock maddened by hunger"--but the prophet wouldn't say that it was Louis' fault. Capet could do no wrong.

"The Foreign Soldier" is the Duke of Marlborough. Nostradamus sees him attacking Louis, then an old man, unjustly. The avaricious mother who put him up to it was Queen Anne's England. Marlborough was recalled, and English feeling later turned against him. He was criticized on the home front for the enormous slaughter of Englishmen which marked his victories. Villars said to Louis after Malplaquet, "If our enemies win one more such victory they are ruined."

The Celtic prelate was the Cardinal de Bouillon, who left France and traveled secretly across Belgium under an escort from Marlborough.

Both candidates for the Spanish throne were in turn driven out, but eventually Louis' grandson carried the day, with the rival, descendant of an elder branch, out of the picture, and the era of the Spanish Bourbons began.

England's trident soldiers won her Gibraltar in this war and gave her "the anchor-watch" of the Mediterranean.

In the early part of the war, the Camisards, French Protestants, revolted and expected help would come from the coalition; they awaited it near Agen, but Villars broke their revolt, and the help did not come.

Villars was more than a match for Prince Eugene, and after Marlborough had gone home, won the spectacular victory over him at Denain, which ended the war. Voltaire called Villars "fanfaron plein d'honneur," which is very close to "more Mars than Narbonne." Nostradamus often uses the part to denote the whole. He does this in his mention of "Provence will be safely held--" He means France, but he wanted to imply a tribute too in the recollection which Provence evokes of the earlier Claude de Savoie, his friend, whose valor was more exclusively associated with that part of France.

In the Twentieth Century

As THIS LAST CHAPTER IS BEING assembled with the horrid word "deadline"--Oh, anathema to writers!--ringing in the author's ears, one portion of her attention is on the radio, one on the newspaper, and the rest on the ancient quatrains, written so long ago, and yet so full of meaning for those who live in the present day. Today's news is in the prophecies of the Centuries. Russia and England are now fighting on the same side, while war rages in the Orient, just as Nostradamus predicted. Before this book is off the presses, more striking predictions may have seen fulfillment. And perhaps there will be verses, omitted here because their meaning was not yet clear, which will have become clear through the rapid onrush of events. It is difficult to indicate chronological sequence in events of the future, and any interpreter's confusion on this point in unavoidable. Nostradamus may have juggled order to further mask identification and meaning. Also many of the quatrains had to be omitted for lack of space. Those most pertinent to our time, and to the development of the future, are given first consideration here.

The final chapter of the historic cycle of the Nostradamus predictions is naturally the most exciting to us who live in the midst of its predicted alarms and tragic drama and can foresee, in part, some of the fearsome days of the future. Nostradamus has given in the course of the Centuries many dates, both actual years and astronomically stated times. He has not given, directly, the date for the emergence of France from her yoke of bondage. But in the opinion of this author he has given it in the number of his verses, one of the cryptic methods which he enjoyed using for his half-concealments. The final edition of his work contained ten Centuries which by right should have totaled a thousand quatrains. There were but nine hundred and forty-four. If one takes these two facts as giving the elements of a historic date, and adds them, the date is 1944.

This is not to be taken, however, as the date for the crowning of a new king of France, but rather perhaps of his coming to the fore, or raising the royal standard, together with a new attitude in France. In other words, it is the turning point. Several verses indicate that the stabilization of Europe, and the fullness of a new king's power will not come until 1952-3.

The present Pretender to the French throne is Henri, Duc de Guise. He corresponds in the facts of his life to the description given by the prophet of the coming king. The last king of his line, he would be the first to bear the name Henry since the founder of the Bourbon dynasty, Henry of Navarre, and would complete the cycle of the house of Bourbon-Orleans, whose first ruler was born within the lifetime of Nostradamus.

1914 and its Consequences

A horrible war in the Occident draws near.
The year following its outbreak there will be a scourge
So powerful and terrible that young, old and livestock will be affected.
There will be blood and battle when Mercury, Mars and Jupiter are in

France.

In March, 1915, the second year of World War I, these three planets were in conjunction in Pisces; the Sun, in the chart of the Third Republic, is in the ninth degree of Virgo, the opposing sign to that of the conjunction. The full Moon of that month, occurring March 1st, on the day of the second battle of Ypres, fell on nine of Virgo, exactly on the Sun of the Republic.

The new Moon of the 15th of March fell in Pisces, thus giving emphasis to the other planets in that sign which, since it is opposite Virgo, is the house of enemies of the government, and of war. It is in the precision of such details as this that the vision of Nostradamus seems the most fabulous. For vision it was. No
astrologer on earth, lacking the chart of the Republic (and it was then of course unborn), could have made a forecast based upon it.

VI-81
A bridge made of small boats will be quickly built (pontoons)
To attack the great Prince of the Belgians.
There will be fighting in trenches not far from Brussels,
They (the enemy) will outstrip him, putting seven at a time to the sword.

III-18
After a considerable period of plenty (forty-four years)
The sky will touch the country around Rheims.
Oh, what bloody conflict raging around the people of this locality, draws near.
Nor fathers, nor sons, nor rulers will dare go near it.

Around Rheims, center of the two battles of the Marne, the artillery duel developed such clouds of smoke that the sky seemed to touch the land, and the horror of so many dead deterred even relatives and officials from the agony of the place. The prophet's picture is as accurate as it is harrowing.

VIII-61
Never shall the day dawn to attain the flag of rulership
Until the seats of government are returned to their proper places
And it will be the armed Cock (France)
Who shall bear the gift of Der Tag.

III-7
Fugitives, aerial warfare above the bayonets,
Sportive ravens neighboring the conflict,
The cry goes up from earth for heavenly aid and rescue
When the fighting comes close to the walls (of Paris).

III-6
A cannon shot shall enter within a closed church.
The citizens within shall be killed in their refuge.
Horses, cattle, and men shall suffer. The swelling wave will touch them,
Hunger and thirst will deplete them, even the weakest will be under armes.

In 1917 a shot from a Big Bertha killed people in a church in Paris. The

Seine was very high that year, at times touching the walls.

VIII-48
Saturn in Cancer, Jupiter with Mars,
A university professor, wise as a Chaldean seer, under the aegis of a vigorous young nation, with the fullest round measure will save the country in February.
There will be the fall of Château-fort, and assault on three fronts.
The conflict will take place near Serbia. It is a mortal war.

Saturn was in Cancer throughout the first six months of 1917, leaving the sign at the end of June. On the 3rd of February Woodrow Wilson broke off diplomatic relations with Germany. In June Mars and Jupiter came to conjunction when the first American contingent of troops sailed for France. Nothing could be more precise than this astronomical timing of the period from the first cheering announcement to France of the break which meant this country was coming in, to the sailing of the first troops of the A.E.F. to "save the land."

Nostradamus made use of a triple anagram to characterize President Wilson, which is a triumph of ingenuity and condensation.

III-71
The inhabitants of the isles (Britain) will be blockaded for a long time.
They will summon their vigor and might against the enemies.
Those outside shall die, defeated by hunger.
They will experience a greater hunger than they have ever known.

IX-100
A naval battle will be won in darkness.
The fight will be disastrous to the Occidental navies.
A new ruse will be employed, that of coloring the ships,
There will be wrath toward the vanquished, and the victory won in a drizzle of rain.

X-2
The galleys will screen the ships of the line.
The grand fleet will draw forth the lesser one.
The ships will maneuver to encircle the opponent.
The great navy, which is vanquished, will draw off and reassemble its scattered units.

The battle of Jutland is very well indicated in these two verses and the device of camouflage is duly observed by the prophet.

IV-12
The larger of the countries will be routed and put to flight.
It will hardly be pursued beyond the frontiers (of France).
The country will be reconstructed and a region regained,
Then all of the invaders will have been driven outside of France.

Alsace-Lorraine was regained by this war.

II-82
Through hunger the wolf (Germany) will become the captive of its prey.
The assailant will be driven to great distress.
A man of high birth (the Kaiser) will arrive at his end.
The great leader will not avoid the central pressure.

X-1
The enemy, which is always the same enemy, faithless to its word,
Will not stand fast, nor keep its captives. Its people will be captives.
Taken, overwhelmed, its people dead or stripped to their shirts,
They will give all they have left to be helped.

VII-25
The whole army will be exhausted by long war.
There shall not be found money enough to pay off the troops.
Money will be devalued to the worthlessness of stamped leather.
The ancient Gaulish coinage will shrink (from full moon size) to a crescent.

An illustration in the Jour, for the 26th of February, 1937, showed coins of 1914 as a full moon, those for 1918 as half moon, those for 1936, a quarter crescent, and those for 1937 as a thin crescent. (Extrait du "Jour," Georges Lachapelle, Les Finances de la IIIe République.)

VI-72
By frenzy feigning divine emotion
The wife of a great and powerful man will suffer transgression.
The judges desiring to condemn such teachings
Will sacrifice her as a victim to an ignorant populace.
The Czarina of Russia and the influence of Rasputin.

I-14
The Slavic nation will sing songs and chants, they will present their petitions.
Their Princes will be captured and their Lords imprisoned
At the coming into power of brainless idiots
Who will be accepted as if they were divinely inspired.

This is a clear picture of the Russian Revolution.

X-22
For being unwilling to agree to separation,
He will be recognized thereafter as unfitted and
The King of the Isles will definitely be driven out
And another will occupy the throne when he will no longer sign himself King.

VIII-38
When the kingdom is divided and quarreling over the brothers,
One of them will take the arms and name of Britain.
The English title (of the other) will be tardily considered.
Night overtaking him, he will leave for France.

These are the events around the abdication of Edward VIII.

V-49
Not from Spain but from ancient France
Shall be he who is elected to guide the tossing barque of the Church.
He will have trust in the enemy,
Who during his reign shall become a great scourge.

In the papal elections of 1922 many thought that the papacy would go to the Spanish cardinal, Merry del Val. It was given instead to Monsignor Ratti, Pius XI, who though Italian, came from what was anciently Cisalpine Gaul.

V-92
After the elevation to the papacy, which will last for seventeen years,
Five will change in the revolution of this term,
Then one will be elected from the same time
Who will not be very conformable to the Romans.

Pope Pius XI reigned seventeen years. The five governments which underwent changes in his time were Italy, Germany, Austria, Czechoslovakia and Spain. Pius XII is not too "conformable" to Mussolini's ideas.

The League of Nations
V-13
Near Lake Leman there will be a house of prostitution
Presided over by a foreign woman, who will seek to betray the city.
Before she is murdered by the Germans, there will be a great flight.
Then those from the Rhineland will begin their invasion.

The house is the League of Nations, run by foreign policies. Nostradamus, as we have seen, in earlier quatrains here included, did not trust the League.

X-49
The garden of the world where is the New City (Geneva),
Situated in the corridor between two mountains,
Will be seized and plunged into the vat
And forced to drink the envenomed, sulphurous waters.

I-47
At Lake Leman the preachments will cause irritation.
Days will drag into weeks,
Then months, then years. Then they will fade away completely
And the Judges will condemn their empty laws.

IX-92
The King will desire to enter into the New City
But his enemies will eventually drive him out.
A captive, he will be free. False things will be spoken and perpetrated.
The King, living outside, will keep himself aloof from his enemies.

The captive king is Haile Selassie.

II-64
The gentry of Geneva will be parched with hunger and thirst.
Their closest hope will eventually fade away.
The imposition of the law will have the Genevese trembling on the point of war,
But the fleet will not be able to protect itself in the great port (Toulon)

Yes, that was the time they imposed the Italian sanctions and the British fleet backed down.

I-100
For a long time in the sky a gray bird will be seen Near
Dole and the land of Tuscany
Holding in its beak a green branch.
Soon the great man will die and he will conclude the war.

The reference to the dove and the olive branch of the League of Nations seems to close with a reference to the death of Woodrow Wilson. Perhaps the exigencies of rhyme induced the prophet to mention his concluding war, after the man "will die". The meaning is clear enough, but cart-before-horse.

II-23
The palace birds will be driven off by another bird (German eagle)
Soon after the prince (Hitler) comes into power.
How many times that enemy (Germany) has been driven back across the river (Rhine).
Caught outside its own country the tether of the bird has been seized and held.

I-87
The central fire of the earth which causes temblors
Will make a trembling around the new city.
Two great boulders will for a long time make war (England and Germany)
Then Arethusa's fountain will be red with a new flood.

II-39
A year before Italy is in the conflict
The Germans, French and Spanish will be struggling for power.
The schoolhouse of the republic will fall (League of Nations)
It and its people stifled to death.

IV-59
Two will be besieged with burning anger.
They will quench their thirst in two level cups,
To the strong man who has had the edges of his power filed off, and to the old dreamer.
And to the Genevese, will be exhibited the track of the Aryan country.

The two besieged, or limited, by the League, are Hitler and Mussolini quenching their thirst for power with Czechoslovakia and Ethiopia. The strong man is Daladier; the dreamer, Chamberlain.

1940

II-40
A little later, but no great interval,
By land and sea will come the great tumult.
Naval warfare on a scale greater than ever
With explosions and guns will increase the onslaught.

V-85
The Germans and their neighbors
Will be in a war for the control of the regions of the clouds.
The country will suffer from marine locusts and from gnats (hydroplanes and airplanes),
The faults of Geneva will be laid bare.

III-12
Through the tumult that reigns along the Ebro, the Tagus, the Tiber, and at Rome As well as at Geneva and around the man who is like Aretino, The two great headwaters and the cities of the Garonne will be affected, Captives, dead and injured, the human booty will be divided up.

One can only say that the comparison of Mussolini to Aretino is unflattering to the early journalist and satirist.

The Spanish Revolution
The Greek dame of despicable beauty
With her lucky achievement of innumerable civil processes,
Will be imported into Spain,
Where she will be captured and perish miserably.

Because of the Greek ideas which characterized the French Revolution and Directorate, foreseen by Nostradamus, he usually calls a government la dame, and uses throughout the Centuries the Greek Woman, or Castula to signify it. Here he sees the importation of democratic principles into Spain, crystallized in the Spanish Republic.

I-19
When they shall complete the area of the Coffin
The Spaniards will make trouble for their aristocratic blood.
Their population will be greatly decimated,
Their leader will be in flight, hidden by the troughs of blood.

The author has seen a newspaper reference to the flight of the late ex-King, Alfonso, in a boat carrying a cargo of fresh-killed meat, but cannot cite the reference.

The reference to the Coffin area is fascinating. Bertina Harding, in The Phantom Crown, tells how young Maximilian visited the tombs of his ancestors while in Spain in 1856. "The mystery of Philip II's oracle confronted him. In the octagon-shaped chamber, at the center of the mausoleum, the eccentric monarch had fitted out a permanent abode for his embalmed ancestors. That was not all. After providing accommodation for ten defunct forebears, he had added with dreadful insight, space for as many crowned successors to himself as he deemed probable. Tier on tier the marble coffins stood, thirty in all. And only three were empty ... but the Queen, Isabella II, was fitting up a nursery in her palace at Madrid for this expected heir, Alfonso XII. Would there then be but one more Alfonso? A thirteenth? The Archduke fell into uncomfortable reflections while a phlegmatic guide rattled a bunch of keys.

"'When they are quite full', the man said, pointing at the coffins, 'we will get the Republic.'"

The construction of the tombs (the Coffin) was probably begun by Philip II during the lifetime of Nostradamus.

X-48
In the southernmost part of Spain the standard will be raised
And will go out to the end and the confines of Europe.
The revolution will touch closely the bridgehead of the Aisne.
It will be defeated by the great expedition of a coalition.

It is generally recognized that Franco's revolt was the real beginning of the present world war.

VI-64
No one will keep any treaties of peace.
All who accept them will agitate through deceit.
While peace and truce are protested by land and sea
At Barcelona the fleet will be caught in its activity.

III-75
Pau, Verona, Vicence, Saragossa (throughout Spain and Italy)
There will be the long swords, the lands humid with blood.
The corruption of the great granary will be so great
That though help will be near, the remedies will be very far off.

VI-10
For a time the Church will follow its colors,
Black and white, the two will be intermingled.
The reds and yellows will seem to be like their own.
The land will suffer blood, scourge, hunger, battle and will be maddened by revolution.

The robes of nuns and of the priesthood are black and white. Red and yellow are the Spanish colors. Franco's party will have the confidence of the Church for a while, because ostensibly the Franco revolt is on behalf of royal restoration.

X-14
The Republic of Valencia, without guidance, and by reason of its nature
Will be hardy and timid by turns. Seized by fear, it will be conquered.
Accompanied by its pale prostitutes
It will be convicted in the prisons of Barcelona.
In place of the wife, the daughters will be killed.

Murdered by a criminal fault which will not be allowed to endure.
Little clad, within trenches they will be overwhelmed.
The wife will quench her thirst in the Italian Sea.

The wife is the royal government whose principles will survive, though her children are murdered.

VI-19
The true flame will engulf the government
Which wished to put to death the innocents.
Near the time of assault the at my will become inflamed,
And one will see a prodigious thing in the Bull of Seville.

III-62
Near the Douro, the sea of Cap Cires not having been cut off,
The great mountains of the Pyrenees will be pierced.
The man with the short hand and the pierced tongue (a criminal; meaning the survivors of the Republic)
Will carry his plots into the south of France near Carcassonne.

IV-70
Contiguous to the Pyrenees
A leader will raise a great force against the eagle (Italy),
Exposed and futile forces will be exterminated.
The leader will be pursued as far as Navarre.

III-19
In the south of Spain both blood and prosperity will be spent.
A little before they change their proconsul
There will be great scourge and war; famine and thirst will be seen.
Their prince, their great warden, will die away from his own land.

The recent death of Alfonso XIII confirms his prophecy for Spain's "great warden."

The Second Great War

II-56
When corruption and massacre have not put a stop to the situation
And there is death in the bomb-craters struck from high heaven,
The head of the Church will die when he sees the ruin
And those who are shipwrecked clinging to the rock.
The death of Pius XI in 1939 six months before the outbreak of war.

I-91
The myths acting in human guise
Will be the authors of this great conflict.
Before serene heaven, sword and lance
Will be a less mighty affliction than will be the trend toward the left hand.

The meaning of this is that the old gods and myths revived will dominate human action. Such a revival has been seen in Germany, and Hitler's belief in his relationship to the figures in Wagnerian drama is well known to all readers of magazines and newspapers today. The left hand meant in the prophet's day, not Communism but peace or pacifism. This verse, from a man of peace, is a powerful indictment of the prewar policy of his country.

Interesting is the phraseology of a New York Times editorial (June 22, 1941) on the subject of myths, commenting on a speech by President Conant, of Harvard: "President Conant's new nihilists are the people who believe in the Myth as the great motive force in history. To stir the masses you don't need to tell them the truth. Just tell them anything that gets them excited."

III-26
The kings and the princes will raise up chimeras.
There will be empty prophecies and divination will be exalted.
The golden horn of plenty will be a victim, and from the heaven of the cruel
Will come the interpretations of the oracles.

Everyone has heard that Hitler uses astrology and other occult methods to guide his life and activities as well as the destiny of Germany.

VII-14
Natural topography will come to be falsely abandoned.
The monuments created for posterity will stand as open as pitchers.
Factions will multiply, philosophy will be proclaimed.
Black will be put for white, and green wine drunk for ancient vintage.

Presage 27
Aerial warfare will be over the shores of the Occident,
And of the Midi, rushing even to the Levant.
About half the people will die without being able to take root.
This third age shall belong to Mars the Warrior.

The Firebrands will make their appearance to light the fires, it is the age of the Firebrand, and its end is famine.

X-99
The end of the wolf, the lion, the bull, the ass
And the timid deer will be with the dogs.
No more will sweet manna fall to them.
The watch-dogs will give more vigilance and guardianship.

Italy and Spain
VII-32
Born in a hovel and elevated to a regal height
Is he who, empty and vain, will come to tyrannize over the land.
He will raise a force for the march from Milan,
He will exhaust Fayence and Florence of men and money.

This is Mussolini, even to the "march," by train, from Milan.

VI-36
It is not by earthly battle that good or evil
Will rule the confines of the Perusian plain (Italy).
Pisa and Florence, through revolution, will see the birth of misfortune.
The King wounded by night will be lifted up on his mule and set upon a black saddle-cloth.

The wounding of Victor Emmanuel is metaphorical, as is the black saddle-cloth of Fascism.

II-65
The calamity of a declining economy will afflict
Spain and there will be disaster for Italy.
The Church will be inflamed, there will be corruption and captivity
When Mercury is in the sign of the Archer and Saturn becomes a usurer.

Saturn in Aries is associated with acquisitiveness. The prophet appears here to indicate the period of January 1938, when Saturn entered the sign and Mercury became direct in Sagittarius, to January of 1939 when Saturn turned direct preparatory to leaving the sign, and again Mercury was in the Archer's sign. Nostradamus pays close attention to the times when the planets change from retrograde to direct motion, as did all of the older astrologers who would have noted these details in the prophet's mention of astronomical timing. This time was a period of new and grave economic problems for both Italy, which had not then entered the war, and for the United States whose economic policy, born of the war, was not then fully formulated. The death of a pope during this period would have been felt by Nostradamus as a further deep affliction to Italy.

VII-20
Agents speaking the Italian language
During April and May will cross the Alps and travel overseas.
He of the Calf will explain in a harangue
That he is not coming with the purpose of wiping out the life of France.

This verse seems to describe 1940 in the spring, when Mussolini's agents were active on all fronts before his entrance into the war. He of the Calf is Hitler born under Taurus, sign of the Bull, Ox or Calf. The prophet here implies that he is not only Taurus, but the Golden Calf as well. He, Hitler, was, as one recalls, busily explaining that he had nothing against the French--only their government.

IV-35
When the virgins are faithless to their trust the home-fires will become extinct.
The largest number will join the new league (Hitler's new order).
Rulers alone will have in their keeping the means to make war,
Etruria and Corsica will become a fiery gorge by night.

VI-33
The last army raised by bloody Saul
Will not have power to guarantee the sea.

Between two rivers he shall dread a military power.
The black one of wrath will repent his actions.

Obviously a reference to Mussolini, the dark man with his black-shirt legions. The land between the two rivers, referring to the Po and the Tiber, is Italy. The defeat of the Italians, so recently, is clearly given.

IV-20
The proclaimed union (Axis) will not last a great while. The greater of the two will make changes and reforms.
When the nation is paralyzed in its ships,
Then Rome will have a new Leopard.

It was the Mediterranean defeats of the Italian navy which paralyzed the power of Italy and threw her at the mercy of Britain, causing Hitler to move in and take control.
Leopards were the famous device of the Plantagenets, and Richard I, the Crusader, carried them to the Orient. This provides one analogy to the present crusade of England, and the fact that the Mediterranean battles were fought for control of the Eastern bases.

III-68
The leaderless people of Spain and Italy
Will see death and defeat within Italy.
Their leader (Mussolini) will be betrayed by his irresponsible folly.
Blood will flow everywhere across the latitude (of Spain and Italy).

VII-30
The sack approaches with battle and a fire and a great shedding of blood.
Along the Po and the other great rivers, the initiative will be held by ox-tenders.
After expecting it for a long time, Genoa, Nice, Fossano, Turin, all the way to Savillano will be captured.

Ox-tenders is a play on words referring to Hitler's birth under Taurus, and also is a reference to the low, or ordinary, parentage of Hitler and Mussolini.

IX-76
The Rapacious leader, dark and bloody,
Issued from the hide of inhuman Nero,
Will have his left wing defeated between two waters (Po and Tiber).
He will be destroyed by a young man who will reorganize everything.

Dictatorship organized by Mussolini eventually defeated by the coming Henry V.

VI-98
Ruin to the Italians in terrible plight through the power of fear.
Their great city will be captured, a corrupt deed.
Monarchy, populace and temples will be violated.
The Po and the Tiber will flow reddened with blood.

II-54
By a foreign nation quite different from the Romans
Their great city (Rome) will be affected after they have already gone through a powerful revolution.
The government (Fascist) without forces, because of a different country,
Will see their chief captured for lack of a burnished sword.

It has all been reported in the newspapers. First the Fascist revolution, then the coming of Hitler. Italy helpless, her sword in a beautiful scabbard, but dull and rusty when drawn.

X-20
All the friends who held together the party (Fascism)
Will be pillaged and put to death for their harsh uncivilized propaganda.
Their effects will be declared confiscated,
For never will the people of Rome have been so outraged.

V-21
The death of a Latin monarch
Will involve those whom his rule has assisted.
The fires will be lighted, the booty divided,
There will be public death for his hardy associates (Fascists).

V-14
When Saturn and Mars are (conjoined) in Leo, Spain will be captured,
The African leader will be trapped in the conflict.
Near Malta there will be an engagement. Herod will be taken alive,
The scepter of Rome will be struck down by the Cock.

This warlike conjunction will occur on November 12, 1947. It would seem to indicate General Franco, whose prestige has always been bound up with his African influence; it was from the coast of Africa that he planned and led his invasion of Spain. It also specifies the final overthrow of dictatorial power in Italy. Exit the Fascists and Falangists.

IV-34
The great leader will be led captive in a foreign land.
In chains of gold he will be offered to King Henry.
He who in Italy at Milan will lose the war
With all his host will be put to fire and sword.

Since there was nothing in the rule of Henry of Navarre corresponding with this verse, it must apply to the coming Henry V and the downfall of the Italian dictatorship. Fascism is particularly associated with Milan.

III-54
A man of very high rank will flee into Spain
After the blood-letting of the long wound.
Armed forces will cross the high mountains
Devastating everything, after that he will reign in peace.

The heir to the Spanish throne, Don Juan, or another?

III-21
In Italy, on the Adriatic coast,
There shall appear a horrible fish.
It will have a human face and an aquatic fin,
It will be taken outside on the hook.
Just what this means is uncertain, except that the fish in Nostradamus' writings indicates an heretical religion or ideology.

VII-49
Saturn in Taurus sporting with revolution, Mars in Sagittarius,
The sixth of February will be a day of mortality,
Those of the north of Italy will make a great breach in the walls of Brussels
While at Ponteroso the Barbarian leader dies.

This prediction refers to February 6th, 1971--for readers of another day to check!

The Coming of Hitler
III-76
Germany will give birth to divers creeds
Strongly resembling a happy paganism.
But the heart will be prisoner and there will be little profit.
The people will return to their payment of the true tithe.

II-45
Even the heavens will lament when the Androgyne is born.
Near to those same heavens human blood shall be shed.
Through death too late will a great people be renewed (the French).
Late though early the expected succor will come.

The bi-sexual interests of Hitler have been frequently commented on in the press. Late and early refers to the long interval elapsing between the fall of the monarchy and this modern restoration, which will begin early in the great struggle (1944).

IX-68
From the Aryan height there shall arise one who is both elevated and obscure.
His evil will affect the country at the junction of the Saone and the Rhone (Lyons).
On the Day of Saint Lucia (December 13) his soldiers will be hidden in the woods
Of him who has the most horrible throne ever known.

X-46
In life, destiny and death he will be a base, unworthy man of gold,
But he will not be the new elector of Saxony.
From Brunswick will come the token of affection,

The hypocritical seducer will pose as the restorer of the peoples' rights.

Hitler will not be a second Martin Luther, nor the patron of Luther, the Elector of Saxony. His "reform" movement will not be lasting.

V-5
Under the holy pretense of giving freedom from servitude
He will himself usurp the power of the people and the city.
He will be able to do his worst because of the falsity of the young prostitute (French Republic).
The treacherous, pre-eminent one will read his book to the country.

Probably no one will need to have it pointed out that the dramatis personae of this verse are Hitler, France and Mein Kampf.

X-10
Stained with murder and enormous adulteries,
The great enemy of the entire human race,
Who will be worse than his forefathers, his uncles and his fathers
Will be, in fire, battle and revolution, bloody and inhuman.

This sounds like what a large part of the world thinks of Adolf Hitler today, and recalls to the frivolous, "his sisters and his cousins and his aunts etc."

IV-66
Under the protective coloration of seven revolutionaries
Divers experimenters will sow their seed.
Pits and fountains will run with poison,
These human devourers will be inspired by the power of Italy.

It has been noted that Hitler, who was inspired by Mussolini's success, has consistently surrounded himself with seven leaders who carry out his orders and develop his ideas. Whether this is happenstance or related to some of his ideas on occultism is not known, but the number seven has some association with the occult in the minds of many and its legends are very ancient.

II-9
Nine years the vegetarian will hold his power in peace
Then he will meet downfall in a thirst so bloody
That on account of him a great people without faith or legality
Will be destroyed by one who is more easy-going.

1933 + 9 = 1942 unless the time should be counted from Hitler's rise in 1932.

V-18
The besieged peoples will strain at their agreements
A week after they are faced with the cruel issue.
Blood will flow in their repulse. Seven will get the axe
When the government which wove the fabric of the peace is itself a captive.

This very well describes conditions after the fall of France. The author does not know the exact number of members of the former government now dead or imprisoned at Rion; but it is close on seven. France, through Clemenceau, was responsible for the peace of Versailles.

VIII-13
The crossed brother maddened by lust
Will kill Bellerophon because of Praytus.
The enraged woman whose fleet has sailed for a thou-sound years
Will drink bitter brew, thereafter both shall perish.

This verse is as puzzling as it is intriguing. The Bellerophon was the ship that took Napoleon to Saint Helena. Here it is a symbol of England. Classically, Bellerophon was a hero who retired after involuntarily causing the death of Praytus, his friend and hunting companion, while both were guests in the house of Praytus' father-in-law. The meaning could be that England allied with a government of France, the Republic (which is not the true son of France but an in-law), while both are guests of France, will meet tragedy; that England (at Dunquerque) will be responsible for the death of (Praytus) the French government.

Then the symbolism changes, and seems to indicate Britannia, "for a thousand years" a sea-going power from the days of William the Conqueror, will taste defeat, and thereafter both Britain and her antagonist, Germany, the crossed brother, will perish.

VI-99
The efficient enemy will turn about in confusion.
The great country, sick, will be defeated by ambushes.
Spain and Western Africa will refuse to play along (with Hitler)
There will be defeat near the river where are the remains of antiquity (Tiber).

This appears to be a forecast of the eventual defeat of Italy and Germany, "the efficient enemy."

VIII-90
When among the crossed ones there shall be found a man with a troubled mind,
Then in the Holy Land shall be seen the horned bull.
The home of the Virgin will be filled with swine,
No ruler will be able any more to sustain order there.

Rudolf Hess is said to have fled because his mind was troubled at the thought of occupation and war in the Holy Land which shocked his Catholicism. The horned bull is Hitler, the Taurean, who has brought the war to the Holy Land.

When the Robin Moor was sunk the New York World-Telegram carried a story from the survivors which stated that the submarine hoisted no flag, but was painted with the large device of a red bull. So that it would seem that not only the forces of Hitler, but also his actual astrological insignia are in evidence in the far places.

VI-77
By reason of the fraudulent victory of the leader who shall be cut down,
The two sides will be in battle, when the cycle is closing in Germany.
The leader and his governmental offspring will be destroyed in home territory,
The monarchy and the papacy will be pursued in Rome.

This seems to mean Hitler's destruction by his own people.

VI-18
In the course of events the Great Ruler will be forsaken, and
The Inebriate, drunk not with art but with power, will be no more of this life,
He and his class having been pushed into such high power,
Pardon will be given to the race who hated Christ.

England and Her Allies
IV-50
Libra will see the rise to domination of the Western hemisphere,
From heaven to earth the Monarchy (of France) will hold its power.
The forces of Asia will not have perished.
Only seven more will hold the Hierarchic rank.

Many people interpret the old prophecies concerning the popes to mean that the present pope is the prophesied Pastor Angelicus. Libra is England, so called because of her policy of the balance of power.

II-89
One day the two great masters will become friends, (Hitler and Stalin).
When their grand power will be greatly augmented.
The new world will be at the height of its development,
The bloody one will make an accounting of its resources.

IV-56
The rise of him who will spread fear on a great scale will be sudden
And the principles in the affair will be well concealed;
The red government will no longer be in the public eye,
Little by little the important leaders will become displeased with it.

Joseph Stalin is an ally of England as this goes to press, but here and elsewhere his passing, along with Communism, is predicted.

X-81
The treasures kept within a building by the citizens of the West (Hesperus)
Shall be withdrawn into a secret place.
The building shall open its fastenings to the starving.
Closed up again, it will be ravished, a horrible prey to the populace.

This may refer to the gold hoard of the United States; or it may have reference to Spain, known to the ancients as Hesperus, and often so designated by Nostradamus.

III-3
Mars, Mercury and the Moon in conjunction
Will produce extreme scarcity throughout the south of Europe.
In southernmost Asia the earth will quake (or there will be revolt).
Corinth and Ephesus will then be in a quandary.

This triple conjunction last occurred September 2nd, 1940, just before the invasion of Greece.

Nostradamus lived too near the time of Jeanne d'Arc, and he was too passionately French, to feel other than jealousy and distrust of England, a power which he saw steadily expanding through centuries to greater possessions than his own nation. From early times a prophecy of the downfall of England had been handed down from the Welsh prophet, Merlin. Eustache Deschamps, the French bard of the early fifteenth century, used the Merlin prophecy in one of his satiric poems. Nostradamus has come very near to copying it. Both of these troubadours hoped Merlin was right, and, because of that, one may perhaps discount something of the gloom that hangs about Nostradamus' forecasts for England. The lines of Deschamps are these.

According to the prophet of the Isle of Giants,
Which has since been called Albion,
The people were tardily converted to a belief in God.
The Isle will be completely desolated.
Through their pride will come their day of hardship
Concerning which their prophet Merlin
Predicted their dolorous end
When he wrote: "you will lose life and land."
When that has happened, men will point out to foreigners and those from neighboring countries
Where in former times there was England.

Nostradamus elaborates on the theme in the following verses. No specific dates are indicated in these prophecies for England, some of which may be quite distant.

X-100
England will be a great empire,
The all-powerful land surrounded by water will endure for more than three hundred years.
Her commerce will traverse sea and land,
The Portuguese will not be satisfied with that.

Portugal was the great maritime rival of Britain at the time Nostradamus wrote this. There is something deeply symbolic in the fact that this verse is the closing one of the Centuries. It is as if there were an implication that the end of England would be the end of the world as we know it. It is like the old saying about Rome: "While stands the Colosseum, Rome shall stand, when falls the Colosseum, Rome shall fall, and when Rome, falls the world." The civilized world today has a similar feeling about England and her relationship to all that is held free and precious.

III-70
Great Britain taken together with England
Will become indeed overwhelming on the seas.
The new Ausonian (Italy) league will be active in war
And the two powers will be aligned against each other.

III-57
Seven times you will see the British nation change its dynasty,
Bloodstained, in a period of two hundred and ninety years.
France, by no means because of German backing,
Will mistrust being harnessed to this Arietic ox-pole.

VI-81
Tears, shrieks, wailings, groans and terrors because of
The inhuman heart of a cruel and icy Ruler.
Lake Leman, the British Isles and Italy will be major targets,
There will be bloodshed, famine, and no mercy shown.

The League of Nations and Britain, differently approached, have been Hitler's main objectives.

VI-90
Ignominy stinking and abominable
Will after the event be hailed as felicity.
There will be great excuse for (France) being unfavorable
When Neptune (England) would not be pushed to make peace.

These curious lines, which seem only applicable to 1940, admit that France has played a not quite heroic part--a great admission for the prophet. Yet he manages to blame England for not following in the footsteps of France.

X-32
Everyone will desire to head the great empire,
One shall obtain the power over the others.
But there is little time for his power or life,
Two years his navy will sustain him.

II-100
Within the Isles there will be such a horrible tumult
That nothing will be heard but bellicose factions.
The insults of the brigands (Axis) will become so great
That they will go so far as to range themselves in a strong league.

III-71
Where there is expectation of creating famine
There will be surfeit.
The patrol of the seas, like a dog in the manger,
Will ration oil and wheat to the various nations.

It was all right with Nostradamus when England blockaded the seas in 1914 to the advantage of France. The same situation is all wrong in 1941, and England is then "dog in the manger."

VI-21
When those of the Arctic Pole are united together,
In the Orient there will be a great terror and fear.
The newly elected pope shall sustain the great Church,
Rhodes and Byzantium will be stained with foreign blood.

As this book goes to press, Russia is invaded, and Winston Churchill announces that England will assist her, the two northernmost empires, "those of the Arctic Pole." The fighting and terror in the Orient are at peak.

IV-63
At a time very close to an elongation of Venus
The two great leaders of Asia and Africa will be active.
The arrival of the forces from the Rhine and Danube will be reported.
There will be cries and tears at Malta and the Italian coast.

II-93
The law of More will be seen to decay.
It will be followed by another and much more seductive doctrine.
The premier of Moscow will eventually fall
Defeated by offerings and propaganda of a leader with greater drawing power.

Sir Thomas More, contemporary of the prophet and author of Utopia, was the ancestor of Communism. The prophet seems to blame his ideas beyond those of Rousseau, though he mentions the latter for the tragedies produced by the Communistic ideology. How closely this verse follows the headlines and reports on the Russian-German conflict, as this book goes to press (June, 1941)!

VIII-64
Within the Isles the children will be transported,
Two out of every seven will be in despair.
Those of the soil will be supported by it,
But the name and the skin will be captured by the league, and hope flees.

S-50
A little later after England
Has laid the wolf (Germany) as low as earth,
War will be seen resisting revolution,
Rekindling in such violence
Of human bloodshed that little but the bodily envelope of skin will be left.
Bread will be scarce, but swords abundant.

IX-51
The earthquake occurring at Mortara
Will half engulf the navy of Saint George berthed in near-by waters.
Peace will be asleep, war will awake.

In the Church at Easter the chasms will open.

V-59
The English leader will tarry too long at Nîmes
On the way to Spain to help Ænobarbus.
Many will die through open war that day
When the comet shall fail to strike Artois.

VIII-7
The fortress beside the Thames
Will fall, the government blockaded within.
Thereafter along the coast it will be stripped bare,
Their adversary will behold the corpse, then he will stand inside the barrier.

III-32
The great sepulchre of the people of Aquitaine (England)
Will be off the shores of Tuscany.
Then war will be near the German frontier
And bringing terror to the people of Mantua.

II-78
Great Neptune will lie at the bottom of the sea
In the mingled blood of Arabs and French.
The Isles will go down in blood because they took up their oars too late,
And more, because they concealed their plans so badly.

VIII-97
In the confines of the War the destiny of Britain will change,
Near to the shore where three fine young nations will be born.
Ruin to the people competent through their seniority,
The government of the country will change and never grow again.

IX-6
Across Guienne an enormous number of English
Will come to settle under the name Anglaquitaine (English Aquitanis).
In Toulouse of Languedoc and le Bordelais
They will live and call their settlement Barboxitaine.

France and the Papacy
VI-74
The government which was driven out shall return to power,
Its enemies will be named as conspirators.
More than ever its times will triumph
For three and seventy years until death well assured.

This is a peculiarly interesting verse. In his letter to King Henry the prophet speaks of "the great trembling of the earth together with the increase of the new Babylon, wretched daughter (of the Revolution), augmented by the abomination of the first holocaust (1792). It will hold its power for just seventy-three years and seven months. Then there shall issue from the long barren tree (of the monarchy), born at the 50th Parallel (latitude of the Franco-Belgian border), one who will revitalize the entire Christian Church. And there shall be created a peace, union and concord between the children of opposed and separate races."

If 1944, as previously analyzed from the number of verses and Centuries (this author may possibly be alone in seeing such a connection; certainly the first to say so), it constitutes Nostradamus' date for the beginning of "France Second," over which the new and great Henry V is to rule.

If to the date of the Battle of Sedan, September 1st, 1870, the seventy-three years and seven months of the prophet are added, it brings us to March, 1944. If the seventy-three years are subtracted from the date of the downfall of Napoleon III at Sedan one gets 1797, dating the rise of Napoleon I. Napoleon III died in 1873, which is a kind of echo of the number. Nostradamus mentions, not in a prophetic connection, the Hebrew prophet Joel. This is in the letter to the King. It seemed odd to single out for no reason this one short Biblical book and not to refer to other prophets. But on looking into Joel, one discovers that the book has just three chapters and seventy-three verses. The French Republic has had three chapters too, the First, Second and Third Republics. This number 73 is a peculiar one.

Nostradamus gives the precise date of the French Revolution, also in the letter to the King. "Then will be seen the beginning of events of long duration, and in the first year there will be a great persecution of the Christian Church. This will break out in the year one thousand seven hundred and ninety-two. The people will think that it is a renewing of the age."

If 1792 is taken as a starting point, and two additions of the number of Joel, 73, are made, one has the date of 1938.

Returning to the quatrain, the verse of course refers to the government of Napoleon I, which returned to power under Louis Napoleon. Yet as has been shown, the verse has a much more subtle application, and the seventy-three years does not refer to the tenure of power of either man, but to cycles which included their years. The rise of one and the downfall of the other give points of reference for use of the number.

X-28
The Second and Third Republics will make prime music
And be lifted by a king to the summit of prestige.
But the grass will grow thin to emaciation
And the exposé of false self-indulgence will deprive them of power.

Nostradamus severely blamed Louis Philippe, whose reign was the beginning of the Second Republic, in other verses, for his catering to democratic ideas, and abandoning the flag of the lilies for the tri-color. He is the King referred to here.

IV-30
More than eleven times the populace has refused the monarchy,
All influences have been alternately augmented and lowered,
And so low will they sink that little gold can be sewed up for keeping,

Later there will be famine, corruption and exposés of hidden matters.
There have been twelve elected presidents of France, in addition to the first two who were royalist in sympathy.

VIII-96
The synagogue, sterile and bearing no fruit
Will be received, accepted among the infidels
Of Babylon where its sad, miserable leader will
Have his wings clipped by the daughter of persecution (Paris).

Léon Blum's tenure of office.

IV-32
The times and localities will compel meat to be replaced by fish.
The law of the Commune will work in an opposite fashion.
An old man will hold the power, then he will be removed from office.
The friend of all things pertaining to the mob will be relegated to the background.

The boomerang in both defense and economics which marked the Blum régime is predicted.

VI-50
Within the pits the old bones will be found,
The remains of incest committed by the step-mother.
The state will change, the skeleton will rattle,
And Mars will be ascendant on its star.

Nostradamus never fails to ascribe the faults of democracy in France to its hideous beginnings in the French Revolution, the step-mother of the Third Republic. He hears the rattle of its bones in the revival of Communist ideas in the Blum régime.

I-3
When the blown litter of the whirlwind drives against them,
They will hide their faces with their cloaks,
A new class of people will trouble the Republic
And the Revolutionaries and the Royalists will judge all matters from opposing points of view.

The Cagoulards, or hooded ones, who hid their faces, arose to fight the leftist tendencies of the French Republic, and by so doing played into Hitler's hands.

IX-51
The people will band themselves together against the red factions.
There will be flame, battle and revolution while the heart is avid for peace.
Those who weave their plots will do so at the point of death,
Save one (Hitler), who will bring ruin upon the entire world.

VIII-91
In the country watered by the Rhone,
Where the crossed ones will be almost united
When the two which constrain (Mars and Saturn) are met in Pisces,
A great number will be punished by the deluge.

This probably referred to the conjunction of 1938, when the harmony between the Axis members was at its height. Mention was made in the press of their conspiracies, notably those of burning French ships. They had their headquarters in the valley and mouth of the Rhone. The deluge here is the figurative one of the onset of tragedy.

VIII-1
A number (in the government) will be confused in their expectation.
This will not be forgiven by the population,
Who will be of the opinion that they should persevere in their hope,
But the great leisure to do this will not be given to them.

Sixain 36
Those without power, wishing to acquire power
'Will spread a great rumor all through France.
The honeyed tongue, the veritable chameleons,
The incendiaries, the firebrands, the agitators,
The Toms, Dicks and Harrys, the purveyors of news,
Their bite will be like that of the Scorpion.

VII-33
Through fraudulent government the country will be despoiled of its forces,
The fleet attacked, channels open to espionage.
Two pretended friends will form an alliance
Awakening hatred long lulled to sleep.

The ancient enmity of France and England.

VI-34
The mechanics of flying fire
Will cause the people who are besieged to revolt against their leader.
Within the nation there will be such sedition
That they will be defeated in their despair.

II-77
With projectiles, fire and chemicals they will attack, and be repulsed with fire.
Cries and groans will be heard on the midnight air,
People will be placed within hidden ramparts,
The traitors will escape by an underground route.

VI-43
For a long time the country will be abandoned
Where the Seine and the Marne flow together.
The soldiers from the Thames will be despised,
They will be driven back from those whom they were supposed to guard.

I-41
The City (Paris) will be assailed by night.
Few will escape in the conflict near to the sea (Dunquerque)
The prostitute (Republic), when her son returns to her defeated,

Will perish of poison hidden in the folds of propaganda.

II-8 7
Afterwards there shall come from the neighboring lands
A German prince who shall sit upon the golden throne (France).
In captivity and through experiences with the tides of revolution
The Republic will be reduced to servitude and shall no longer endure.

The golden throne in Nostradamus' writings is always the throne of France, whose ancient emblem was the lilies of gold on the white flag. Nostradamus often uses prince or king when speaking of a foreigner of great power. Here Hitler.

II-5
Near the frontiers, within two cities
There will be two scourges worse than was ever known.
Famine linked with corruption, the people driven at the point of the sword,
They will cry for help to the Great God immortal.

Paris and Vichy. Nostradamus uses such terms as scourge in the Biblical sense of general affliction.

X-85
The tribune so old that he is almost at the point of trembling,
Will be under pressure to deliver up his captive.
The old man, who is not really old, speaking a cautious evil,
Will attempt by legal means to betray his friends.

Pétain, Laval, and the prisoners at Rion.

IV-21
The change will be very difficult,
But the City and province will gain by it.
A prudent man of high courage put in office will be driven out by the clever man,
Land, sea, and population, the status of all will be greatly changed.

This sounds as if it were a reference to Marshal Pétain and Laval or Darlan.

I-61
The Republic, wretched ingrate,
Will be depopulated under its new Magistrate.
There will be a great mass of exiles and witch-doctors,
Who will rob the Germans of their great agreement.

VI-9 7
At the five and fortieth parallel the heavens will flame.
The battle will approach the great new city (Geneva).
On the instant a great scattering blaze will leap up,
Then it will be desirable that the Normans should prove their capacity.

The degree is that of the city of Lyons, which is indicated elsewhere as the route of conquest, up from the south and the path which the coming Henry V will follow. The Normans are the old monarchy of which he is the descendant.

IV-40
The forts of the besieged will be attacked
With fiery explosives that will reduce them to craters.
The bandits will be ground up alive,
At which time there will be never so piteous a schism in the Holy Church.

VIII-6
A lightning splendor appearing at Lyons
Will give illumination; after Malta has been taken will be suddenly smothered.
Don Raz will deceitfully deliver up the Moors
While from Geneva to London the treason of the Cock is proclaimed.

Don Raz is Franco, so called because of his Moorish connections.

III-82
Fréjus, Antibes and the cities around Nice
Will be devastated by land and sea power.
The locusts (airplanes) will be over land and sea when the wind is favorable,

People will be captured, killed, bound and pillaged without regard to the rules of warfare.

S-4
In a round cycle of the lily there shall be born a very great Prince
Come late indeed yet early into his Province.
Saturn will be in Libra, sign of its exaltation.
The standards of self-indulgence will be in decreasing strength.
The Republic after her effort to be masculine will be under her own corpse,
That the happy blood of Bourbon shall be upheld.
Saturn will be in Libra in 1951, when the new King may be expected to reach the fullness of his power.

II-88
When the cycle of the great ruinous activity is accomplished,
There shall arise he who will be the fifth (Henry V) and seventh (of the name of Guise).
At that time Aix will not be able to guarantee Lutetia
Against the foreign Aries warrior and his nation, a third larger than France.

This verse clearly prophesies that the coming King of France will arise at this time when France is under the heel of Germany. Germany, like England, has long been considered by many astrologers to be under the general rulership of the sign Aries. The astrologer Cheiro once told Edward VII that the salvation of both countries lay in peace and agreement because they were both ruled by Aries.

V-53
The law of the monarchy contending against that of self-indulgence
Will confirm the spirit of my prophecy.
Neither the one nor the other of the rival parties (Communism and Fascism) will be successful,
Through the Monarchy the law of the Great Messiah will be upheld.

III-5
Near the long default of two great luminaries
Which will come to pass in April and March,
Oh, what a dearth! But two great and kindly gentlemen
By land and sea will succor all parts.

Nostradamus indicates in verses, not given here, that the coming King of Spain will be a friend and companion-at-arms of Henry V.

I-51
In the watery triplicity there will be born
One who will have Thursday for his gala day.
His reputation, praise, and power will spread
By land and sea, he will be a tempeste to the people of the Orient.

The present Pretender was born July 5, 1908, with the Sun in the watery sign Cancer.

X-71
By the forces of earth and air the very great revolution will be frozen
When in time Thursday shall be venerated.
Never was there one so fair as he shall be,
The four quarters of the earth shall honor him.

Thursday, the day of Jupiter, planet of ecclesiastical hierarchy, is here used in contradistinction to Friday, sacred to the Mohammedans. The meaning is that of the Christian King, Henry V, whose reign will be closely harmonized with the Church.

VI-12
He (Henry V) will assemble forces to carry him to Empire
And in the Vatican the Pope will be of the blood royal (of France).
The Flemish, the English, Spain and Paris
Will fight against Italy and the rest of France.

By Paris, here, one assumes that he must refer to the Free French movement representative of the former government seated in Paris. But the verse is puzzling in advance of the event.

S-15
The newly elected father of the great ship (papacy)
Will for a long time give illumination like a clear flame
Serving as a lamp to this great land,
And at that time the coat-of-arms belonging to his name

Will be linked with that of the happy one of Bourbon.
From the Levant to the Western Ocean and the land
of the Setting Sun his memory will be honored.

X-42
The human rule of Angelic birth
Will base its power on peace and union,
War will be captive and half cloistered,
For a long time peace will be maintained among men.

The Pastor Angelicus, of the prophecy of Malachi, is the pope yet to come, and is the one indicated by the prophet in this verse. Apparently he is to be of royal French blood and hold his office while Henry V is King of France. This prediction does not check with the papal succession given by Malachi.

S-53
Many will die before the Phoenix dies to renew itself.
Until six hundred seventy shall he dwell,
Having passed fifteen years, twenty-one and thirty-nine.
The first is subject to illness,
The second to battle and danger to life,
And to fire and revolution is subject thirty-nine.

If these numbers are added and the sum added to 1870 the resultant date for the rebirth of the Phoenix is 1945.

X-44
When there shall be a ruler who will go contrary to the will of his own people
A scion of Blois (the blood royal of France) will subjugate the Italians,
Memel, Cordova, and the peoples of Dalmatia.
Thereafter the spirit of the seven will be with the King and he will make offerings to the souls of his ancestors.
When Mars and the Scepter shall be conjoined
Under Cancer there will be calamitous war.
Not long thereafter a new king will be anointed
Who for a long period will bring peace to the land.

June, 1951. Both Sun and Mars were in Cancer in 1940 but not close enough for conjunction. This checks the previous verse giving the same year, and indicates that fighting will go on until the turn of the decade.

VIII-52
The king of Blois shall reign in Avignon,
From Amboise he will dispose his forces the length of the Indre.
In the angle of Poictiers he will break the wings of the Holy Empire
In the neighborhood of the Boni.

The angle of Poictiers is what military men still call the strategic position in this terrain which dominates the approach to Paris. The Holy Empire is that of Germany. Boni is thought by Fontbrune to mean the Bohemians--Czechs. This author doubts it, but does not know what the interpretation is. The original line consists of only two words, and there is probably a trick reading. Such verses were an art in the prophet's day.

VIII-1
PAU, NAY, LORON will be a man who is more of fire than of blood.
He will swim in praise. The great man will put down the insurrectionists.
He will refuse entrance to the despoilers.
He will enclose the Name of the Pope in the country where the Durance flows.

In this verse which begins the three Centuries dedicated to Henry, King of France Second, Nostradamus indicates the Bourbon ancestry by addressing the coming King by the name of the birthplace of the Bourbon line, Pau, and two other towns in Béarn. Avignon, the papal city, is near the confluence of the Rhone and Durance.

V-6
The Pope will lay his hand on the King's head
And implore him to establish peace in Italy.
The King will change his scepter to his left hand (token of peace)
And from being a king he will become the pacific Emperor.

VIII-18
The offspring of the Fleur de Lis will cause its death.
A little after its rebirth the old confusion will arise,
The three lilies will come to an end because of it.
The rescued fruit will change and become as crude flesh.

S-34
Princes and Lords, all who are accustomed to make war,
Cousin German, brother with brother,
Ended is The Tree of the happy line of Bourbon.
The very lovable Princes of Jerusalem,
Ended by the commission of an enormous and execrable deed.
The people will feel the effect when the bottom drops out of their economy.

X-75
He who had been so long awaited will never come again
Within Europe. In Asia there will arise
A man of the league, sprung from the Greek tradition (democratic or Communistic)
Who will spread his power over all of the Kings of the Orient.

In the last three verses the tragic end of the house of Bourbon is indicated, and reaction against the monarchy.

VIII-99
By the power of three temporal kings it shall happen.
The Holy See will be changed to another place.
There the bodily substance of the spirit

Will be restored and the new locality will be accepted as the true seat.

V-46
By reason of quarrels and new schisms among the cardinals
When the Pope shall be elected
Great amounts of false doctrine will be produced against him
And Rome will be injured by the Mohammedans.

VIII-98
The blood of the clergy will be shed
Like water in great abundance
And for a long time it will not be stanched.
Woe, woe to the clergy, ruin and sorrow.

There are no dates for these verses.

Discovery of the Tomb of a Saint

The fascinating prophecy given below concerns the finding of a tomb of some early Christian saint, which is to happen in April of whatever year. The prophet does not indicate a closer date except that the "new party" will be founded upon the bones of the saint,

whom he calls the Great Roman. This presumably means the Christian royalist party of the coming King. The saint may possibly be one of the early Christians of the time of Trajan, who journeyed into Gaul and died there. Under Trajan the Roman Empire reached its greatest expansion of territory. It also achieved a very high and wide-spread culture. The persecution of Christians was, however, very severe. The verses seem to point to an analogy between Trajan and the imperialist ambitions of Mussolini, who is perhaps typified in the mention of Prince Ulpian. Trajan's name was Marcus Ulpius Trajan. Nostradamus' reference to the golden lamp of Trajan would seem to mean the spiritual lamp of Christianity which, though buried under persecution, still glows in its secret place in the old Roman province, now Provence. The parallel is made by the prophet between the persecuted Christians of Trajan's day, of whom the old saint may have been one, and the modern Christians, whose lamp must also burn in secret, persecuted by dictators.

VI-66
At the foundation of the new party
Will be found the bones of the Great Roman,
A fissure will reveal the marble of the sepulchre,
Ill covered, after an earthquake in April.

IX-31
Exposure of the government will put an end to the hecatomb.
When the source of the stream is traced
A freshet will lay bare the marble and lead of the tomb
Which will be that of the Great Roman whose motto was Deus In Me.

VIII-59
The weak faction will occupy this locality,

Those in high places will make horrible outcry,
From their vantage point the strong group will stir up trouble,
The tomb will be found near Embrun, where the inscriptions will be uncovered.

VI-15
Beneath the tomb will be found a prince
Worthier than he of Nuremberg.
The Spanish government, its power lessened, will, when the Sun is in Capricorn (January)
Be denounced and betrayed by the Great Leader of Wittemberg.

Nuremberg and Wittemberg refer to Hitler.

V-66
Under the ancient buildings sacred to hearth and home,
Not far from the ruined aqueduct (Pont du Garde at Nîmes)
Are the luminous metals of the Sun and Moon,
There the chased, golden lamp of Trajan is still burning.

VII-66
When the inscription D. M. (Deus In Me) is found
And the ancient tomb with its lamp is discovered,
The law, the King and Prince Ulpian will be put to proof,
The royal standard and the Duke will go into hiding.

III-65
Discovery of the tomb of the Great Roman
Will be followed next day by the election of a new pontiff.
The College of Cardinals, engrossed in quarrels, will not ratify the election.
The sacred chalice (the Church itself) will inhibit the authority of the heir of Saint Peter.

I-25
Lost, refound after concealment for so long a cycle, an age
The shepherd will be venerated as a demigod,
Until the Moon has completed her grand cycle,
When the ancient saint will be dishonored by those of another faith.

The Rise of the Orient

The author, sometime ago, cited some of the predictions in the following verses to a well-known military commentator. He said that they were not news. That men in his particular work who were always scanning future horizons for long-range prophecies of their own had long accepted the rise of the Orient as a fait accompli of the future, and that for this reason the political forecasters gave triple attention to every item that came out of Asia and Africa. Nostradamus in his own day saw the might of the Orient and its menace to Christian Europe, and he knew that cycles return.

VIII-59

Twice lifted to power, twice overthrown,
The Orient like the Occident will weaken.
His adversary after numerous struggles,
Routed by the sea, in a pinch will fall.

IX-60
In the conflict with the Barbarian with the black Head-dress
Bloodshed will make Dalmatia tremble,
The might of Araby will rear its headland,
The frogs will shake with fear, Portugal will give help.

The frogs are the French; that is the ancient name from Merovingian times.

VI-85
The great city of Constaninople will be destroyed by the French;
The forces of the Turban will be taken captive.
Help will come by sea from a great leader of Portugal.
This will happen on the twenty-fifth of May, the day of Saint Urban.

Probably the prophet looks back from this advanced time to what is Portugal today, as this is a small country and may be incorporated in a large one. A modern French commentator, realizing its size, says, naïvely enough, that Portugal will send for the U. S. fleet!

VIII-77
Anti-Christ will be three times annihilated,
Seven and twenty years blood will be shed in war.
Dead heretics, captives and exiles there shall be,
Blood, human corpses, crimson waters and hail upon the earth.

I-18
Through the negligence and discord of France An opening will be given to the followers of Mohammed.
The earth and sea of the north of Italy will be blood-soaked,
The harbor of Marseilles will be filled with ships and sails.

III-44
The ancient monarch driven out of power
Will go to fetch his help among those of the Orient.
For fear of the cross he will fold his standard.
In Greece he will go by land and sea.

V-112
The sea will not be safe for the monarchy,
Those of self-indulgent life will hold all Africa,
No longer will the hypocrites be in occupation,
And a portion of Asia will change.

Life will be frankly hedonistic in Africa without the mask of moral hypocrisy.

V-5
In the country of Arabia Felix
There shall be born a puissant leader of the Mohammedans.
He will trouble Spain and conquer Granada,
And from beyond the sea he shall invade the people of the Italian west coast.

VI-80
From Fez the rule shall attain to the countries of Europe.
Their cities will be fired and their people pierced with a blade,
The chief leader of Asia will bring a great troop by land and sea.
He will pursue the royalists, the priests and the cross to their death.

III-20
Through the lands watered by the great river Bethis
Far within Spain in the kingdom of Granada,
The cross will be driven back by a Mohammedan nation,
A man of Cordova will betray his country.

I-73
France, through her neglect, will be assailed on five fronts,
Tunis and Algiers will be stirred up by the peoples of Asia,
Leon, Seville and Barcelona will fall
And they will not have the fleet of Venice to protect them.

In the coming invasions of Europe, through the rising of the Orient, the prophet makes sarcastic reference to the long years in his own day when the Venetian fleet, unaided, protected Europe against the East while the nations of Europe quarreled amongst themselves. That situation, he says, will come again, and this time there won't be the Venetian fleet.

II-96
A burning torch shall appear in the heaven
Above the Rhone from source to mouth.
Famine, sword will afflict, succor will be tardily brought.
The Persian will turn to the invasion of Macedonia.

IX-73
The Monarch of the blue Turban when he has entered into Foix
Will rule less than an evolution of Saturn (29 years).
The King of the white Turban and the high courage of Byzantium
Will be manifest near the time of holding when Sun, Mars and Mercury are conjoined in Aquarius.

This conjunction takes place February 18, 1981.

Presage 35
France shall be greatly saddened by a death,
The mother and tutrice shall be bereft of the royal blood.
Government and Lords will be made orphans by the Crocodiles,
Strong cities, castles and towns will be taken by surprise,
May Almighty God guard them from these evils.

The Crocodiles are the people of Africa and tropical Asia who will overwhelm France, the mother and tutrice, after the final fall of the Bourbon dynasty.

V-75
The Church of God will be persecuted,
The sacred temples will be despoiled,
The child shall strip the mother of everything,
The Arabs will join the Jews.

V-25
The rule of the Church will succumb by sea
To the Prince of Arabia when Mars, Sun and Venus are conjoined in Leo,
Across Persia will come full near a million troops,
The true serpent will invade Byzantium and Egypt.

The date of this conjunction is August 21, 1987.

The End of the Age

Not only ever since the Christian era, but long before in the songs and lamentations of the Hebrew prophets, the end of the great precessional era of the Fishes, Pisces, has been foretold in a wealth of tragic and saddening detail. It is not the end of the world, as many people of old times thought, but the end of a grand period, and the birth of a new age with a different type of thought and civilization. Nostradamus prophesied that it would be marked by the downfall of old Europe, and be ushered in with earthquakes and eclipses such as the Bible describes in the scene of the Crucifixion.

Science recognizes that from time to time the earth changes the inclination of its axis. They know this from fossil remains (which, for example, show that Alaska had once a warm climate, and other localities show that similar changes have taken place). But science has no knowledge of what causes this change, nor in what cycle of years its return may be expected. Nor does Nostradamus specify the date for this occurrence, but by implication he links it with the phenomenon of the double eclipse which will take place in 1999.

The two eclipses will occur in the sign Leo, a partial one on July 28th, and a total one on August 11. The event is a very rare astronomical phenomenon. Camille Flammarion wrote of it in detail. All astronomers then living will prepare to observe it with every advanced resource of scientific equipment. Nostradamus, in both his letter to the King and in his verses, has given his picture of what he predicts will affect the entire world. Science is just beginning to have an understanding of terrestrial phenomena, such as floods and earthquakes, coming as the result of celestial phenomena, the doctrine held by astrologers for thousands of years. Science has arrived at some limited conclusions forced by the necessity for better long-range weather forecasting. But the study of earthquakes, floods and volcanoes, made in the light of the gravitational and magnetic strains and stresses of the Sun, Moon and planets, is still in its infancy and as yet almost nothing is known about it. The wise men of old knew these things, and Nostradamus knew them. He needed no telescope for the double eclipse, and he not only saw it, but he saw the train of events that came with it, something no giant telescope can show.

In his letter to the King the prophet has this to say of the last years of the twentieth century:

"Then shall begin the great empire of Antichrist in the invasions of Xerxes and Attila ('one who will revive the King of the Angoumois,' and the Oriental invasion) who will come with a countless throng, so that the advent of the Holy Spirit, from the 48th parallel, will make a great change and chase away the abomination of Antichrist that made war on the sovereign Vicar of Christ (the Pope) and against his Church for a time and to the end of time. This will be preceded by an eclipse of the Sun, of denser darkness than has ever been seen since the Creation and up to the passion and crucifixion of Jesus Christ, and from that time until the coming one. There will take place in the month of October a great translation made so that the earth will seem to lose the weight of its natural motion in an abyss of endless darkness. There will be premonitory signs in the spring, and there will be extreme changes, overthrows of kingdoms, and earthquakes."

"In the last period all the Christian kingdoms, and those of the infidels, will be shaken for twenty-five years. The wars and battles will be more injurious. Towns, cities, castles, and other buildings will be burned, laid waste, and destroyed, with great bloodshed of vestals, violation of wives and widows, and children at the breast dashed and broken against the walls of the towns. Satan, the prince infernal, will commit so many evils that nearly the whole world will be afflicted and desolated.

"After this has endured for a certain length of time, Saturn will almost renew his cycle (twenty-nine years), but God the Creator will bring an age of gold. He will heed the affliction of His people, and He will bind Satan and throw him into the abyss. Then shall begin between God and man a universal peace, and Satan will be bound for a thousand years. Then the cycle will return in grand power, Satan will be once more unbound against the Church."

IV-67
The year that Saturn and Mars are conjunct and combust
The air will be very dry and there will be a long trajection (comet),
Through incendiarism a great locality will be consumed by fire,
There will be little rain, with wind, heat, wars and incursions.

This configuration occurs in April, 1998. It is in that year that Nostradamus predicts the great invasion of France. The path of the solar eclipse, which will be total, passes through northern France and Belgium.

V-54
From the Euxine Sea and great Tartary
There will arise a King who will eventually behold Gaul.
He will traverse Turkey and Germany
And in Byzantium will leave his bloody track.

II-29
The Oriental will go out from his home
To cross the Apennines and look on France.
He will traverse the clouds and the snows of heaven,
And everyone will be struck down with his club.

X-72
In the year 1999 and seven months
From the sky will come a great and terrible King
Who will revive the great King of the Angoumois,
Before and after his coming war will rule at full blast.

The Angoumois were an early Gallic people conquered by the invading Goths. The situation will be similar.

III-84
The Great City will be desolate,
Of her inhabitants not one shall remain to dwell there,
Wall, sex, building and virgin will be violated.
By battle, fire, corruption and cannon the people will die.

II-28
The last but one to be called Pope
Will take Diana for his day and his repose,
He will wander afar on account of his distracted head,
Seeking to deliver a great people from economic oppression.

Diana is the Moon, so that Monday will be the Pope's day of rest. The Moon rules changes, travels and voyagings, and it is involved in mental frenzies and distracted mentalities. In the famous prophecy of Malachi, in his descriptions of the popes yet to come he names third before Petrus Romanus (the last one named) De Medietate Lunae. De Medietate Lunae means "relating to the half-Moon, which is the crescent of Diana." Malachi's further description of this pope is: "From the half-moon proceeds this pope sent to Rome by the Divine Doctor, Hail, our well-beloved Pius XII, most holy Mediator, future victim." The present incumbent of the holy See is Pius XII, and more than any previous pope he has "wandered afar." But otherwise the description does not fit, nor does he come in the order given by Malachi. According to the Monk of Padua there will be two popes after the Lunar, and three more before him. Nostradamus names him as the "penultimate" pope. In the times of the Avignon popes and the Great Schism Cardinal Pietro di Luna was one of the false popes. Eustache Deschamps, a famous satiric poet of that time, whose writings were not only familiar to Nostradamus but imitated and quoted by him, wrote a satire called, "Of the Schism in the Church Which is Much Troubled by the Moon" (Luna). Some of Nostradamus' lines are very close to lines in this satire.

III-17
Mount Aventine will be seen flaming in the night.
The sky will be suddenly obscured in Flanders.
When the Monarch drives out his nephew,
The people of the Church will commit scandals.

VIII-15
Toward the north great efforts will be made by mankind,
Almost all of Europe and the whole world will be tormented.
The two eclipses will put men to such pursuit
And will augment life and death among the Hungarians.

These two eclipses, one of the Sun and the other of the Moon, both occur in August of 1999, in the sign Leo, traditionally associated.

VIII-16
In the place where the Almighty has built His ship (Rome)
The deluge will be so great and so sudden
That there will be no spot of earth for a firm foothold.
The wave will cover the Olympus of Fiesole (Apennines).

I-69
The great round mountain of the seven hills (Rome),
After it has gone through peace, war, famine and inundation,
Will tumble far, sending the great country into the abyss,
Even its antiquities will be lost and its great foundation.

I-56
You will see, early and late, great changes take place,
Extremes of horror and prosecutions
As if the Moon were guided by its spirit,
The heavens approach the time of their tilting.

I-84
The Moon obscured in profound darkness,
Her brother (the Sun) will become the color of rust,
The great one hidden for a long time in darkness
Will turn the sword in the bloody wound.

I-47
For forty years the rainbow shall not appear.
For forty years all the days shall behold
A barren earth and increasing scarcity,
And great deluges will be perceived.

X-74
At the revolution of the grand number seven
There will appear the hazards of the hecatomb,
Not far from the great Millennial age
The dead shall go out from their tomb.

X-73
Past and present times together
Will be judged by the great Jehovah,
The world in its late stage will be abandoned by Him
And sentence will be passed on the disloyal clergy.

VII-41
Those whose bones of hands and feet were shut up
In a dwelling long uninhabited by noise
Will be disinherited while they are in the depths of their dream
And translated to a house that is salutary and calm.

Oracles of Nostradamus

Table of Contents

Life of Nostradamus	345
The Preface of Michael Nostradamus to His Prophecies	364
Epistle to Henry II	370
Magic	379
Historical Fragments	386
Henri Quatre	406
Louis XIII	415
Louis XIV	419
Louis XV	426
England	427
French Revolution	456
Louis XVI	464
The National Convention	479
Pius VI	483
Napoleonic Rule	486
Louis XVIII and Louis Philippe	505
Republic, 1848, and Napoleon III	512
Appendix	519

Life of Nostradamus

"In Nature's infinite book of secrecy
A little I can read."
Antony and Cleopatra, i. 2.

"I am Isaiah,—be it spoken with all humility,—to the advancement of God's glory."—Luther's Table Talk, Bohn, p. 12.

Yes, indeed, Luther, with quite Lutheran humility!

"Canys gwn a fydd rhag llaw."
"For I know what has been, and will be hereafter."
TALIESSIN.

"Prophetia est solum futurorum contingentium, quia longe distant ab humana cognitione; sed secundario ad eam pertinent præterita et præsentia."—ST. THO. AQUINATIS, Summa, p. 409.

MICHEL DE NOSTREDAME was born in Provence, in the town of St. Remy, in the year 1503, upon a Thursday, the 14th of December, about noon. Tycho Brahe (1546), D'Herbelot (1625) the great Orientalist, and Bruce (1730) the Abyssinian traveller, were all born on the same day of the month. Coincidences such as these are, perhaps, not worth much; yet, do they interest us less than the rainfall of a month, or the precise pressure of the wind on Cleopatra's needle?—which goes by the name of Cleopatra because Cleopatra had nothing whatever to do with it. Robert Étienne, the great printer, was also born in 1503. What would, however, more have affected the family of Nostradamus is the expulsion of the French from Naples on October 31, 1503, after the famous battles in April, fought on two consecutive Fridays with disaster to the French; the battles namely, of Seminara and Cerignola. Many have said that the evil omen attaching to Friday dates from that period. If we had never heard of Good Friday we also might have been of their opinion.

His father, like Milton's, a notary, was James Nostradamus, a name which is equivalent to de Nôtre Dame. 1 Moreri calls his family "une famille noble;" 1 others say that he was of Jewish descent, but of a family that had been converted to Christianity, and that he claimed to be of the tribe of Issachar, deriving thence his gift of prophecy, for they were "men that had understanding of the times, to know what Israel ought to do" (I Chron. xii. 32); or, as in Esther i. 13, "the seven wise men that knew the times." It is true that but few of the orthodox commentators interpret these passages as signifying astrological or prophetic forecast; but that may be, nevertheless, the real meaning (vid. Poole's "Synopsis").

How could Nostradamus be of Issachar, as that was one of the lost tribes? would be a natural inquiry enough; and one could only answer it, as the wit did, in a case somewhat similar, that He could only resemble Issachar in being a great, "strong ass" (Gen. xlix. 14).

His mother's name was Renee de Saint Remy. Her ancestors by the father's and mother's side were men skilled in mathematics and medicine: one was physician to René, or Renatus, titular King of Jerusalem and Sicily, and Count of Provence; whilst the other was physician to John, Duke of Calabria, who was the son of King René. Our author, in his Commentaries, says that a knowledge of mathematics had traditionally descended (de main en main) to him from his early progenitors; and, in the Preface to his "Centuries," he adds: "Que la parole héréditaire de l'occulte prédiction sera dans son estomac intercluse."

It was his great-grandfather 2 who gave him, almost as in sport, a first taste for the celestial sciences. After the death of this relative he was put to school at Avignon, to study his humanity courses, and thence he went to the university at Montpellier, to acquire philosophy and the theory of medicine.

Montpellier, the Mons Pessulanus of antiquity, contains the most famous school of medicine in all France. It is ancient, and is said to have been founded by Arabian physicians when forced to fly from Spain—Moreri says in the year 1196, by the disciples of Averroes and Avicenna. Its inhabitants are reputed to be witty and most polite. It once had numerous noble churches and many religious establishments, but since the Huguenots became masters of it in 1561, they ruined all this, and made the city the headquarters of their party for a time. Louis XIII. besieged it in 1622, and took it. His first act was to rebuild the Cathedral of St. Peter and the other churches; the desecration of all such edifices being the Puritan and Huguenot fashion there and everywhere. The town seems always to have been a fief of the Crown of France. But a number of kinglets, such as the King of Aragon and the King of Majorca, appear at different times to have had seignorial rights in Montpellier; and many church councils have been held there. All these matters are of some slight interest, as furnishing in a filmy fashion a notion of those influences, mental and physical, that would have been floating around Nostradamus when studying there. The seizure of the town by the Huguenots would have occurred some years before his death. As he was a true Churchman, their successes would have embittered his mind, and may have influenced some of the visions contained in the "Sixains" and "Présages."

It may interest us as Englishmen to know that in the extensive botanical garden at Montpellier lie the remains of Miss Temple, the Narcissa, whose death and funeral are so vividly recounted by Young in the "Night Thoughts." He appears to have considerably misrepresented the transaction; but George Eliot has made up for it by a criticism upon him and his works, conceived, perhaps in the grossest and worst taste that criticism from a woman's pen has ever fallen into. She grows so angry that she can hardly even see that Young is a poet in any sense of the word. She might easily have found out that he was, by comparing some of her own verses with his.

Another point of interest to us in regard to Montpellier is the reversal of public opinion touching the climate of the place. Brompton, sixty or eighty years ago, was, from the mildness and salubrity of its air, coupled with its then semi-rural aspect, called "the Montpellier of London." The analogy could never have been very remarkable, as Brompton is about on a level with the River Thames, whereas Montpellier's splendid promenade of the Place de Peyron is 168 feet above the sea-level, whilst the whole town runs up the hillside, as its name expresses. Still, the phrase testifies to the opinion then prevalent. Owing to the brightness of its atmosphere and the beauty of its suburbs, the town was long recommended by British physicians as a health-resort to patients suffering from pulmonary complaints; but the weather-vane of science has now reversed that opinion entirely. Its climate is found to be changeable, its sunshine is blazing, its atmosphere is charged with dust that is impalpable, all the while that it seems to be clear; and its cold mistral blasts do but portend a spot most singularly hurtful to the lungs. The fashion varies in localities, drugs, theories, and treatment, and as a health resort for English people the reputation of Montpellier has passed away; but the "École de Médecine" still retains its ancient renown as the central seminary of medical instruction in France.

Learned and medical as it was in the days of Nostradamus, it could not escape visitation by a great plague, 1 and Michael Nostradamus had to retreat to Narbonne, Toulouse, and Bordeaux. In these towns he commenced practice, when about twenty-two years of age, and four years later he bethought him of returning to Montpellier for refreshment, and to take his Doctor's degree. This he got through very quickly, and in a manner that won him the admiration and applause of the whole College. In returning to Toulouse he passed through Agen, a town on the Garonne, where he met with no less a person than the learned Jules César Scaliger, 2 with whom he entered at once into the most intimate familiarity. This induced him to take up his permanent residence in the town. But after a while their cordiality grew less, till rivalry and pique sprang up between them, and they thenceforth stood aloof from one another. Here he married a lady "une fort honorable demoiselle," though history has not divulged her name. By her he had two children, who died young; she also died. Finding himself again companionless, he returned to his natal soil of Provence. When he reached Marseilles, he was invited by the Parliament of Provence to come to Aix, where he stayed three years, receiving a salary from the city from the time the plague broke out, in 1546. It seems to have raged fiercely, and it is said that he furnished to the Seigneur de Launay the reports which he has given in his book, "Le Théâtre du Monde."

After the contagion passed away, the town, Moreri records, voted him for several years following a considerable pension. His services must consequently have been recognized as valuable. He has left us the formula of his plague powder in Chapter VIII. of his treatise "Des Fards." As a curious instance of the modesty of the women of Aix, he records that they began to sew themselves up in their winding sheets, as soon as they were attacked by the contagion, that their bodies might not be exposed naked after death ("Penny Cyclopædia"). I suppose we may judge from this that the system of burial during the contagion was as gross and indecent as in the famous plague of London; or is this only a fanciful imitation of the story of the women of Marseilles in classical times?

He went thence to Salon de Craux, which lies midway between Avignon and Marseilles. Here he married for the second time. The lady's name is given by Garencières as Anna Ponce Genelle; Anne Poussart, says Moreri; others say Pons Jumel. (See the epitaph further on.) There is the same incertitude as to his family. Jean Aimes de Chavigny, whom we are following, makes it to consist of six children, three boys and three girls; while Garencières says three sons and one daughter.

It was here, relates our memoir, that, foreseeing great mutations were about to affect all Europe, and that civil wars and troubles were so soon to come upon the kingdom of France, he felt an unaccountable and new enthusiasm springing up uncontrollably in his mind, which at last amounted almost to a maddening fever, till he sat down to write his "Centuries" and other "Presages." The first of these "Presages" is dated 1555, and runs as follows:—

"D'Esprit divin l'ame presage atteinte,
Trouble, famine, peste, guerre courir;
Eaux, siccitez, terre et mer dc sang teinte,
Paix, tresac à naistre, Prelats, Princes mourir!"

He kept them by him for a long time, half afraid to risk the publication; he foresaw there was danger, and that it would lead to infinite detraction, calumny, and backbiting, as indeed it finally fell out. A thing like this is like the fox stolen by the Spartan youth, that eats the heart out, and is sure to get vent sooner or later. His memorialist says, that at last, overcome by a desire to be useful to the public, he produced them. No sooner had he done so than the rumour ran from mouth to mouth, at home and abroad, that some thing marvellous and admirable had appeared. One cannot see of what use they could be to the public, as they could not possibly be understood till they were interpreted after the event and by it. In some of the quatrains he says as much himself. He no doubt published them because he felt an intense longing so to do; and, when the mind of a man reaches this stage of desire, it will not take him long to find some excellent reason for carrying out the impulsion. Public good, the advancement of religion, the sustentation of faith, the psychological inference as to the immorality of the human soul, or any other good phrase, will serve a man as a sufficient reason for doing what he wants to do. That man must be a great searcher into his own consciousness, if he cannot readily assume that the motive assigned in such a case is the causa causativa of the act of putting forth.

Moreri's account is not exactly the same as that of our memoir. Moreri describes him as being invited to Lyons in 1547, but as returning very quickly to Salon, only to find that his popularity at the latter place had greatly abated. The disappointment he experienced from this treatment made him withdraw a good deal from society, and commit himself the more to hard study. He tells us that he had for a long time previously practised divination; now he began to think himself to be directly inspired as to the future. From this time, as the lights occurred to his mind, he began committing them to writing at the moment. He set them down at first in plain prose, if you can call enigmatical sentences plain prose; at any rate, they were not written in verse.

Garencières' version varies again. With him it is, that Nostradamus found by experience that the perfect knowledge of medicine is unattainable without the aid of astrology, to which he now addicted himself. It is an alluring science, and one towards the pursuit of which his natural genius strongly disposed him, so that he made very rapid progress in it. His first publications in this line consisted of almanacs, according to the custom of the time, for profit and recreation's sake; and in these he so happily hit off the conjuncture of events that both he and his publications became greatly sought after. It is somewhat curious that so few of these almanacs appear to be now extant. One would have expected that documents of such interest, once in type, would not perish entirely from all households and libraries. It may, however, be taken as a proof of the maelstrom of time that engulfs everything, so that by the period when posterity grows interested in any event, all its belated questionings are presented with a universal blank. The spirit of literary piracy, too, seems to have been rife in those early days. The success of his work soon became a cause of discredit to him, as it led enterprising printers and booksellers to vend, under his name, almanacs destitute of everything that had constituted the merit of his.

When the work made its appearance, it divided the public. Some called the prophet a simple visionary, or, in coarser phrase, a fool; others accused him of magic, and of being in too close treaty with the Devil to be honest. A few held their judgment in suspense, and would pronounce no opinion on the subject. A vast number of the grandees and of the learned, both at home and abroad, thought that he was endowed with a gift supernatural; and amongst these were Henri II. and Catherine de Medici. It remained to the esprits forts and the ignorant public, who knew nothing of him but his name, to pronounce him a charlatan and impostor. There is one thing certain, he felt much hesitation as to publishing at all; and, when he took that step at last, he addressed the book to his infant son, and not to any public character, in the year 1555. At this period he would be fifty-two. This is not a time of life at which men usually commence a course of imposture. When he is summoned to the Court at Paris, loaded with honours and consulted on high matters (de choses importantes), he displays nothing but moderation and good sense, and returns contentedly to his modest home at Salon. Upon all ordinary lines of human judgment, such conduct seems to indicate genuineness; and this is strengthened, if not established, by his genuine gravity of deportment and serious religious sentiments. Nobody has denied the purity of his life. Still, a certain Lord Pavilion, of his own day, wrote against him, or perhaps against this publishers' figment of a name, rather than his. Further, we find the book led to the bitter epigrammatic distich of the poet Jodele, or as others say, of Beza,—

"Nostradamus cum falsa damus, nam fallere nostrum est,
Et cum falsa damus, nil nisi nostra damus."

This can very easily be turned against the piratical almanac makers, thus:—

"Vera damus cum verba damus quæ Nostradamus dat;
Sed cum nostra damus, nil nisi falsa damus."

In spite of piracy and obloquy, the repute of Nostradamus grew, as we have said, in influential quarters, until it came to the ears of Queen Catherine de Medici and Henri II, on the publication, in March, 1555, of the first seven Centuries of his "Prophecies." The remaining Centuries, the Sixains, and Presages, were not published till long after. In the following year, 1556, they sent for him to attend the Court in Paris: though Garencières says he left Salon on July 14, 1555, and reached Paris on August 15th, a particularity which seems to indicate special knowledge. 1 The Lord Constable Montmorency attended him at his inn, and presented him to the king in person. The king showed him high favour, and ordered him to be lodged at the palace of the Cardinal de Bourbon, Archbishop of Sens, during his stay in the capital.

When there a severe attack of gout seized him, that lasted ten or twelve days. His majesty sent him two hundred crowns in gold (two hundred écus d'or; vid. Moreri) in a velvet purse, and the queen one hundred crowns (Le Pelletier, i. 92). They then despatched him to Blois, to visit their children, the royal princes, and give his astrological opinion. He repaired thither, and seems to have acquitted himself to the satisfaction of the king. It is quite certain that he did not tell them precisely what he thought, 2 for the princes were Francis II., Charles IX., and Henry III., whose tragical fates he has correctly set out, and with unmistakable clearness, as may be seen (at pp. 84, 86, 96) by the forecasts in his strange book. He, however, cast their horoscopes and acquitted himself in this, as in all other transactions, en homme d'esprit. He returned to Salon so much encouraged that he set to work and completed his "Centuries," consisting of three hundred more quatrains. These further quatrains he appears to have printed in 1558, but Garencières says that he dedicated them to the king in 1557. The only thing that is certain is that the Texte-type dates the epistle June 27, 1558. This "Luminary Epistle" to the king, Garencières tells us, discovers future events "from the birth of Louis XIV., now reigning, till the coming of antichrist." 1

Henri II. was killed the following year, 1559, at the tournament of St. Quentin, as we shall see- it fully set forth at Quatrain 35 in Century I.

He had now become quite a court favourite, for Emanuel, the Duke of Savoy, visited him at his house at Salon about this period, in the month of October; and, in the December following, the Princesse Marguerite de France, sister of Henry II., who by the treaty of peace at Cambresis was to marry the duke, came also to Nostradamus, entertaining him very familiarly (Garencières and Moreri).

Charles IX. made a progress through the kingdom in 1564, to quiet the cities that had mutinied; and when he came to Provence, on arriving at Salon, November 17th, he asked first of all for Nostradamus. Nostradamus was in the suite of magistrates around the king, so that he was presented on the instant, upon which the king made him his Physician in Ordinary, and honoured him with the title of Counsellor. He complained rather bitterly of the neglect with which his follow-townsmen treated him. César Nostradamus reports this, saying, "Et de ce, me souviens fort bien, car je fus de la partie" (Moreri). On the return journey he again inquired for Nostradamus, and gave him two hundred ecus. He was at this time over sixty, and with his health fast breaking under severe attacks of gout. He died within about sixteen months of this period, and the salary and profits of Physician in Ordinary must have greatly comforted the old man in his latter days. He enjoyed now the further satisfaction of being flocked to by learned men, grandees, and others, who resorted to him far and near, as to an oracle. "As St. Jerome remarks of Livy, so may we remark of him," says his biographer, Jean Aimes, "that those who came to France sought Nostradamus as the only thing to be seen there."

The closing scene is now drawing very near, and we find him much afflicted with his maladies, notably arthritic gout, as distinguished from podagra, which Dr. Cullen considers as the seat of idiopathic gout. He awaited with firmness his climacteric, as they used to designate a man's sixty-third year. He died on the 2nd of July, 1566, a little before sun. rise, having all his senses yet about him, for the arthrisis turned to dropsy about eight days previously, and early on the second day of the month suffocated him. Jean Aimes says that Nostradamus was well advised of the time, even of the very day and hour, when his death must take place. The prophet reminded him frequently towards the close of the previous June that he had written with his own hand, in the Ephemerides of Jean Stadius, these words in Latin, Hic prope mors est ("Here is death at hand"). "The day," continues this friend, "before he exchanged this life for a better, after I had spent many hours with him, and late at night was taking leave of him until the following morning, he said, 'You will not see me alive at sunrise.'" M. le Pelletier gives (i. 91) Presage 141 as a stanza pointing to his own death; but, as the "Presages" were not printed till 1568, their authenticity may or may not be accepted as the reader feels inclined. The lines run thus, and are remarkable enough, if we admit that they were a genuine forecast; for, although they assign no specific date, yet they sum up the principal facts rather fully:—

"De retour d'Ambassade, don de Roy mis au lieu;
Plus n'en fera; sera allé à Dieu:

Parans plus proches, amis, freres du sang,
Trouvé tout mort près du lict et du banc."

The meaning given to this is, that on his return from Arles, whence he was sent for, in 1564, by Charles IX., to see him a second time, after he had safely put away the three hundred crowns given him by the king and queen, his last transaction would be concluded, and he would then under his soul to God. His nearest relatives, brothers, and friends would find him dead near his bed, seated, as was customary with him, on the bench at its foot, as he could there breathe more freely.

This is the interpretation put upon it by M. le Pelletier. As I understand César Nostradamus, the king did not send for him to Arles, but asked again for him on his majesty's return to Salon; and I should think the word "ambassade" must refer to some private mission the king had sent him upon entirely apart from this, and for which he paid him. Be this as it may, the fact that Nostradamus assigns no date for his death, in this presage, goes to establish its authenticity, one would incline to say. For supposing it to have been foisted in, after his death, surely a fabricator of the marvellous would first of all have made it to show trois vingts et trois bis, and twisted that into some colourable shape. He would have been little likely to add as a prophetical feature that the king's present had been put away in a safe place, as to do so seems anything rather than a supernatural instinct. It is a touch of prose more than of the Python. On the whole, I should incline to take the verse for a genuine emanation from the pen of Nostradamus. Certainly he would recognize, even medically, that, as he found himself to be growing "fort caduc et débile" towards his climacterical year, he would know that his dissolution was at hand. A man's grand climacteric is generally considered to arrive at 63, though some place it at 81, that number being composed of 9 times 9. In either of these periods, if sickness occur, it is considered as especially likely to prove fatal.

There seems to be a diversity of opinion about this, for some say that the annus climactericus is 84, or 12 times 7. Aulus Gellius thinks the opinion to be of immense antiquity, running back to the Chaldeans; and no doubt Pythagoras derived it from the East. Ficinus explains it by saying that the body of man is ruled over by each planet in turn for the space of one year, and, Saturn being the most maleficent, every seventh year falling to his presidency becomes extremely dangerous. This explanation would shut out the nines, except in the sixty-third and eighty-first year, but it would also vitiate the whole scheme of astrology, for the planet under which a man was born (say he were born under Saturn) would dominate his body at birth, and be, one must suppose, the ruling planet that year, and, if it were Saturn, would recur only on his eighth year. Eighty-four would not be in favour generally, as it consists entirely of even numbers, though divisible by seven. Many held that only a number produced by the multiplication of an odd number could be climacterical. Augustus thought it a subject of great rejoicing when he had passed over his sixty-third year. 1 Moreri will have eighty-one to be properly speaking the climacteric, and he notes that at this age died Plato, Diogenes, Eratosthenes the geometer, and many other illustrious personages. Some went so far as to say that political bodies had their climacterical periods; and they certainly, judging from our own country, have periods of fatal folly, whether or no the nines and sevens collide, or the stars fight against Sisera. But amongst other oddities of history may be chronicled the fact that Henri Quatre was the sixty-third King of France, which made Malherbe talk of—

"La vaine étude s'applique,
A trouver la climatérique,
De l'éternelle fleur-de-lis"—
that fleur-de-lis whose terrible withering up in the fatal year of '93 Nostradamus so powerfully forecasts.

Suffice it to say that in this climacterical crisis Nostradamus succumbed in his sixty-third year to gout, which turned to dropsy. 2

Nostradamus was interred at the church of the Franciscan Friars (Les Cordeliers) at Salon, as it is noted, on the left-hand side of the church door (Garencières). His widow erected to him a marble tablet, "representing his figure to the life, and his arms above it." The epitaph is as follows, made, they say, in imitation of that great Livy aforenamed, the Roman historian:—

D. M.
CLARISSIMI OSSA
MICHAELIS NOSTRADAMI,
 UNIUS OMNIUM MORTALIUM JUDICIO DIGNI,
CUJUS PENE DIVINO CALAMO TOTIUS ORBIS,
EX ASTRORUM INFLUXU, FUTURI EVENTUS
CONSCRIBERENTUR.
VIXIT ANNOS LXII. MENSES VI. DIES XVII.
OBIIT SALONE AN. CICICLXVI.
QUIETEM POSTERI NE INVIDETE. ANNA PONTIA GEMELLA
CONJUGI OPT. V. FELICIT.
TRANSLATION.

"Here lie the bones of the illustrious Michael Nostradamus, whose almost divine pen alone, in the judgment of all mortals, was worthy to record, under the influx of the stars, the future events of the whole world. He lived 62 years, 6 months, 17 days. He died at Salon in the year 1566. Posterity, disturb not his sweet rest! Anne Ponce Gemelle hopes for her husband true felicity."

The text of this epitaph is that given by Benoist Rigaud in the edition of Nostradamus published by him in 1568.

In stature he was somewhat undersized, of a robust body, sprightly, and vigorous. He had a broad and open forehead, a straight even nose, grey eyes, of kindly expression, but in anger capable of flashing fire. The general expression was severe, though pleasant, so that a grand humanity shone through the seriousness. Even in age his cheeks were rosy. He had a long thick beard, and excellent health till nearly the close of life; he had his senses, being alert and keen, up to the very last moment. He had a good and lively wit, seizing with quick comprehension everything that he wished to acquire. His judgment was very penetrating, his memory happy and retentive. He was taciturn by nature, thought much and spoke little; but at the right time and occasion he could discourse extremely well. He was quick, and sudden even to irascibility; but very patient where work had to be done. He slept four or five hours only out of the twenty-four. He practised freedom of speech himself and commended it in others. He was cheerful and facetious in conversation, though in jesting a little given to bitterness. He was attached, so says De Chavigny, to the Roman Church, and held fixedly the Catholic faith; out of its pale there was for him no salvation. Though pursuing a line of thought entirely his own, he had no sympathy with the Lutheran heretics of so-called Freethought. He was given to prayer, fasting, and charity. As far as outward observance was concerned, he might be classed with the highly respectable and decent. Le Pelletier says, "Sa fin fut Chrétienne;" but he adds a little further on that his style is very much more like that of the Pagan oracles of Greece and Rome than of the canonical prophets of Hebrew inspiration. He was very generous to the poor, and held it as a sort of maxim that in this sense it was legitimate to make friends with "the mammon of unrighteousness."

Jean Aimes de Chavigny, who seems to have come over from Beaune to play the part of a Boswell to Nostradamus and,—after his friend's death, is said to have devoted twenty-eight years of his life to editing the "Centuries" with notes, 1 says that he collected twelve books of the "Centuries," of which vols. vii., xi., and xii. are imperfect. These are in quatrains, and are classified as Prophéties, and they extend to very remote ages. The Presages, we are told, were written between 1550 and 1567, 1 and. were collected by Aimes and reduced into twelve books in prose, as he thinks them worthy of the attention of posterity. The few Presages thou are in print run to only one hundred and forty-three quatrains in verse; so we must suppose that those written in prose have perished entirely.

Nostradamus left two brothers behind him: one named Bertrand; the other, Jean, who was his junior, and proctor to the Parliament at Aix, composed a History of Provence, and also wrote the lives of the Poets of Provence. 2

Moreri states that by his second wife he had six children, three boys and three girls. Of his sons, César, the eldest, was a person of demonstratively gay and kindly spirit. It was to him, when quite a child, that Nostradamus dedicated the first seven of the "Centuries" published by him. These are the most authentic of all, and Moreri remarks that, if you wish the quatrains to be without interpolation, you should secure early editions. The reader will understand that to be now unnecessary, inasmuch as we have all along been dealing with the Texte-type. César was born at Salon, 1555, and died 1629. He, like his uncle Jean, was an author, and wrote upon the same topics, leaving in manuscript a collection of the most remarkable things happening in Provence from the year 1080 to 1494. In this he included the lives of the poets of Provence. Many years after his death, his nephew and namesake, César Nostradamus, who was Governor of Provence and gentleman in waiting upon the Due de Guise; found them, and himself worked at them, till, in 1603, the Parliament of the province voted him three thousand livres to encourage him to complete the work, which he did; and they were finally printed in Lyons in 1614, under the title of "Chroniques de l'Histoire de Provence." He commences with the Celtic Gauls at the early date of the Deluge. This is worthy of a true scion of the tribe of Issachar. A very strange story is told of César by La Motte le Vayer in his "Instruction pour Monseigneur le Dauphin." He, like his father, Michel, had a taste for forecasting the future, and had ventured to predict that Pouzin, which was besieged, would perish by fire; but it was taken by coup de main. Whilst the pillage was going forward, the foolish prophet was, it is said, seen, match in hand, endeavouring to set it on fire. He was caught; and Saint-Luc, the commander, asked him if he had prophesied anything for himself that day. He replied, "No!" on which the general rode at him with his lance, and killed him on the spot. Moreri relates this story somewhat differently. If either version were true, it would be clear that César did not understand "la parole héréditaire de l'occulte prediction," and that the lancehead instead was "dans son estomac intercluse." From other authorities, however, it would seem that he was busy about his history long after the date thus assigned for his death. Charles, his brother, was very excellent in Provençal poetry,—and several pieces of his arc still extant. Michel's third son, whose name is not given us by

Moreri, became a Capuchin.

An anecdote is related by Garencières, which he throws out as "a merry passage" to recreate his reader. Nostradamus was with Lord Florinville in Lorraine, at the Castle of Faim. He was attending medically his lordship's mother. In the yard where they strolled there were two little pigs, one white and the other black. His lordship inquired of Nostradamus jestingly what would be the fate of those pigs. "We shall eat the black one, and the wolf shall eat the white," said he. Lord Florinville secretly ordered the cook to get ready the white one for supper. When it was spitted ready for roasting, the cook left the kitchen for something, and in his absence a young tame wolf came in and ate a part of it, so that it could not appear at table. The cook immediately killed the black one, and sent it up at the time appointed. His lordship, not knowing what had happened, said to Nostradamus, "Well, Sir, we are now eating the white pig; how shall the wolf get it?" "I do not believe it," rejoined the prophet; "it is the black one that is upon the table." The cook was sent for, and by his confession the truth came out, much to the surprise of everybody present. Another story follows this, that Nostradamus had said that treasure was hidden in a little hill near Faim, that it would not be found if sought for, but that, if the ground was dug for any other reason, it would. Garencières adds that there is great probability about this as it is the site of an ancient temple, and many times since antiquities have been unearthed here. He completes his cock-and-bull story by saying that many such tales are told of Nostradamus all over France but that he passes them by as being "unwilling to write anything without good warrant."

Amongst other nonsensical reports spread was one that he caused himself to be buried alive, and that he continued to write prophecies. This no doubt was set afloat by those honest publishers who in life had done him the honour to pirate his almanacs; at any rate it made for their interest. It has also been pretended that so many in Salon regarded him as an impostor, that for security's sake he was buried in the Franciscan Church.

Those who desire the Bibliography of the editions of Nostradamus up to the year 1840 will consult that which has been admirably drawn up by Eugène Bareste, Paris, 1840, in his work upon "Nostradamus." Or they may find it copied textually, with all due acknowledgment of its excellence, in the first volume of Le Pelletier's edition of the "Oracles."

The works of Nostradamus, besides the "Prophecies," seem. to have been—

Several Almanacs, two of which were translated at once into English, and are given by Watt, "Bib. Brit."

"Almanacke for 1559." London: 1559. 8vo.

"Almanacke et Prognostications." London: 1559. 8vo.

Moreri gives further an—

Almanac for country labourers, to mark the seasons favourable for their work. A true predecessor, this, of Moore's Vox Stellarum.

"Predictions before 1558." London: 1691. 4to. This is named by Watt, and may be a translation of the genuine first edition of the "Seven Centuries," but I have not met with it.

"Prophecies of the Kings and Queens of England." 1715. This is the work by D. D. that we have largely quoted from.

"An excellent Treatise on Contagious Infirmities in 1559-60." Translated into English. London: 1559.

"Traité des Fardements." Lyon: 1552.

"Des Confiteurs," etc. Anvers: 1557.

"Opuscule de plusieurs exquises Receptes, divisé en deux parties." Lyon: 1572. 16mo. This contains both the above.

"La Remède très utile contre la Peste et toutes Fièvres pestilentielles.' Paris: 1651. 8vo.

"Paraphrase de Galien sur 'lexhortation de Menodote aux Études des Beaux Arts." Lyon: 1558. 8vo.

Touching the prophecies of Nostradamus, Théophile de Garencières gives us an interesting fact, that, after the primer, it was the first book at school in which he learnt to read. It was the custom in France then (i.e. 1618) to initiate children by that book. They thought the crabbed and obsolete words, such as long survived in the English law, would give the scholars some idea of the old French language; so that the book got republished from year to year like an almanac. He chronicles that many have run mad from over-studying the prophecies. He dissuades readers from doing this, because interpretation must always be a little uncertain where, like an ancient oracle, the author indulges in a double sense, which he thinks Nostradamus often does. Without a peculiar genius, he does not suppose it possible to get at a right understanding of the quatrain. Even when the prophecy is quite plain, as that the Parliament should put King Charles to death, no reader, until it had happened, could tell when, or how, it would be brought about, Even his astrological signs will not fix things, because the planets go and return again to the same bearings. Some of his reasons are very peculiar, one being that it is not profit able for the vulgar to have knowledge of the future, that God reserves the knowledge of the times to Himself, and that it might trespass upon "business of State" to discover and lay open things which the prudent wish to conceal; and he concludes, oddly enough, that "for these reasons (dear Reader) I would not have thee entangle thyself in the pretentions of knowing future things."

He conceives that there are many concurrent causes tending to diminish the prophetic reputation of Nostradamus. The very ordinary manner in which he conformed to the rules and ritual of the Roman Catholic Church, would lead no one to infer that he enjoyed any extraordinary favour from the Almighty; his proficiency in judicial astrology would furnish matter of prejudice against him in the minds of many learned men; the very devout suspected him of necromancy, and familiarity with the Angel of Darkness; finally the inherent obscurity of his style has been rendered still more difficult by the interminable faults introduced by, the copyists and the carelessness of printers.

Now, it is admitted, he says, and by its ablest defenders, that judicial astrology cannot enable its professor to foretell such particularities as proper names and other circumstances that hang upon the free will of men; and, as our author does foretell such things as these, he must have had recourse to the black art to obtain his results. Accordingly Lord Florimond de Raimond, in his "Birth of Heresies," makes this charge against him; also Lord Spond, in the third volume of his "Annals," in 1566, devised this epitaph for him. "Mortuus est hoc anno nugax ille toto orbe famosus Michel Nostradamus, qui se præscium et presagum eventuum futurorum per astrorum influxum venditavit, sub cujus deinceps nomine quivis homines ingeniosi suas hujus modi cogitationes protendere consueverent, in quem valde apposite lusit qui dixit: Nostra damus cum falsa damus," etc. 1

Provoked thus, Garencières endeavours to prove Nostradamus to have been enlightened by the Holy Spirit. We shall not follow him in this matter any further than to avail ourselves of the facts we may light upon in the course of his arguments, and to record a few of the eulogies upon him that Garencières gathers from eminent authors in times past. To these we may add some authorities who in modern times have named him; but these mostly sum up his forecastings as springing from venality, vanity, and imposture.

Of proper names, that Nostradamus has anticipated, the list is considerable. He names the Lord of Monluc; Captain Charry; Lord de la Mole, Admiral of the Galleys to Henri II.; Entragues, beheaded by Louis XIII.; Clarepegne, the headsman; Sinan, the Pasha who destroyed Hungary; Clément, who murdered Henri III.; the Attorney David and Captain Ampus; Rousseau, the Mayor of Puy; Louis, Prince of Condé; Sixtus V., calling him son of Hamont; Gabrielle d'Estrée; Lord Mutonis; Anthony de Sourdis, Lord Chancellor of France; the Queen Louise; Antony of Portugal. Since Garencières' time other names have been identified: Narbon, the Minister of War; Saulce; Lethuille, for the Tuileries; Lonole, for Old Noll, or Cromwell; Montmorency; Le Grand Chiren, anagram of Henri le Grand; Mendosus, anagram of Vendosme; Norlaris, anagram for Lorrains; Robin, anagram of Biron; Rapis, anagram for Paris; Esleu Cap, for Capet, or Louis XVI.; Varennes, the place where Louis was arrested; the play upon bour and bon, for Bourbon (Cent. vii. 44); Ergaste, anagram of Estrange for Marie Antoinette the Austrian; Mont Gaulfier, for Montgolfier, the æronaut; the island of Elba, mentioned as Æthalia, the ancient name of Elba; Sainct Memire, anagram for Sainct Meri; and the play on "dort leans" for Louis Philippe. This is a goodly list of names to guess at haphazard. Such chance as could so result would rival any prophecy in the miraculous nature of its elements.

Again, as regards the curious things he mentions, one might make out a long list. The date of the Fire of London. The five hundred Marseillais that led the attack upon the Tuileries. The naming of the very year 1792 for the French Revolution; the 22nd of September in that year being the date from which the Republicans began to reckon anew their era. Many more might so easily be gathered as to even weary the reader with their enumeration.

He mentions the birth of persons that were born after his death. Now, judicial astrology could give no help in such cases, since to commence casting a nativity presupposes birth. In his epistle to his son César we shall see what he says of himself and the gifts he possessed; but even there he was obliged to be somewhat obscure, to protect himself from the ridicule of the world on the one side, and from the severities of the Church on the other. He tells his son to eschew the study of the future astrologically, to avoid magic, as prohibited by the Church and Scripture, and that he himself had burnt some books that taught the art of prophesying, although it is pretty evident that he had first read them through very carefully himself. He relates that a mighty flame burst forth from them to the danger of his house, and this he interpreted to be the consequence of their falsity. But yet he seems to have gone through a good many of the magical forms when he was about to devote the night to prophetical studies. He holds that inspired Revelation is "a participation of the Eternal Divinity," though he scarcely lays claim to being a prophet in this sense of the word; in fact, he denies himself to be such a prophet. But, failing to claim inspiration, and denouncing the practice of astrology and the pursuit of magic, one is left somewhat in the dark as to what he really did profess to be the source of fatidical utterance possessed by him. That he had the gift in a marvellous potency this book will show; and that he openly claimed to possess it his whole life proves. It is, in fact, from this I should desire to establish that at least he was no impostor, for he only told others what he began by implicitly believing himself.

As to his obscurity, he himself admits it as a thing to be cultivated both in the times he lived in and in those that were to follow. No one can truthfully deny that obscurity and prophecy seem to be almost interchangeable and convertible terms. The prophecies in Scripture are of such ambiguity that Whitby was commended by many for concluding his Commentary on the Bible with the General Epistle of Jude, without a word bestowed upon the Revelations of St. John. There are those who will hold that prophecies are useless, as they cannot generally be understood until they have been fulfilled. It is obvious that many prophecies are of such a nature as that, if they were clearly understood previous to the event, they would prevent their own fulfilment, and so cease to have been prophecies. What they foretold would never have occurred. The philosophy of history is supposed to show that Providence shapes the course of human events how much soever humanity may seem at every instant to be following out its own collective will. This theory is most in favour amongst erudite modern thinkers, who incline very little towards acquiescence in the old Church doctrine of Predestination. Yet inspired prophecy is a collateral proof of the same principle as that which underlies the philosophy of history. Both of them depend on the finger of God shaping—first shaping chaos into things, and then things into their continuous courses. The shaping is not needed more at the first creation than it is at every successive stage, whether for preservation or for progression. Again, the interest of uninspired prophecy is for mortal man not much less vivid; for, if we have interpreted Nostradamus rightly, we find in him a man living three hundred years ago talking intelligibly, if not clearly, of things that are happening to-day. If there be a power in human nature,—latent in the generality, but in a few alert and quick,—to link far centuries together in anticipatory thought, I take it to be quite clear, that that one fact must revolutionize the whole scheme of human philosophy as accepted now, whether it relates to life, to death, or to futurity. The fatidical capacity implies a spirit of immortality in man. With that once established, we re-enter upon the domain of faith; we recognize that the earth is drossy and the body sin; we re-create the soul, and laugh at the fool (or the philosopher) who doubts, denies, and ridicules it. It gives new ground to teach the immortality of man; it lifts us above the dirt-doctrine of gold; it renders poetry once again possible to lips hallowed with Apollo's fire; it brings back a possibility of worship upon earth, and, with that, prayer, praise, and peace. Bates, the silver-tongued, says well, that for man "it is as natural to pray as to breathe."

Garencières is of opinion that the writings of our prophet were for a century allowed to "be in darkness," but we have seen that in his own day Nostradamus attracted the notice of the learned, of the nobility, and of the king himself. Garencières says that the first book they gave him at school after the primer was "The Centuries," so it was not neglected then; and M. le Pelletier remarks that Nostradamus's fame has now been before the world for three hundred years, with an always growing reception. Of course, as time wanes, and as fresh quatrains become interpreted after accomplishment, the series must shine with an ever augmenting brilliancy and splendour. The kings of France have never been quite indifferent to the Oracles, or at least to such of them as could be shown to refer to them individually. It is reported of Charles Edward Stuart, the

Pretender, that he to the last conned 1 over the volume, anxiously hoping to find in it some stanza promising to his royal line restoration to the throne of England, but in vain (Chambers' "Book of Days," ii. 13).

In modern times prophecy is derided, and our seer, obscurely hinting his strange forecasts, is voted incoherent, rhapsodial, or an impostor. Almost every one has heard his name mentioned, but that is all. Few who come across his work accidentally on a bookshelf can make head or tail of his Provençal and half obsolete terms. Without special study you cannot understand him; and to study a work that lies under a general ban of imposture, in a time when only lucrative study is pursued, is a thing not to be thought of by a littérateur of any intelligence. Consequently in England it is a name, floating far and wide it may be, that nevertheless remains but a name and nothing more. I hope, however, when this book comes to be read by the competent few, it will be seen that there exists far more than a mere name to be dealt with here; that in Nostradamus we have the greatest fatidical seer, not divinely accredited, that the world has ever beheld; that if accepted as being endowed with a rare and curious foresight,—after the severest inquiry into what he has done has been instituted by grammarians, historians, and philosophic critics,—it will next become necessary to try to look into the causes, and so ascertain how he operated. If we cannot succeed in that, and yet cannot deny his work, we must add the faculty, so remarkably developed in him, to the perceptive powers of the human race, as a sixth sense,—generally latent but sometimes developed,—the faculty of anticipating the future. Science, so called, must enlarge its narrow categories, and admit, though never so grudgingly, that a new faculty of vast import must henceforth be accredited to humanity; a faculty which the superstitious and the profoundly religious alike have immemorially admitted, but which philosophers, as such, have as persistently ignored, denied, or even ridiculed. It has often been said by troubled thinkers, with a pretentious flourish of baffled profundity, that "true philosophy begins in doubt." I would whisper it down the wind, but not in Gath, that for the most part there it also ends. Anatomy cuts up a dead man to find life. Analysis reduces final Investigation to a caput mortuum. Philosophy begins in doubt, and travels a wide circle to close in doubt again. Perhaps, after all, the best basis might be faith. Beginning with faith, haply a man might find God accompanying investigation with him step by step through life, even in this world and its miraculous garden, till the hour tome for him to step, through the six-foot wicket, into the Paradise of that glorious world that is adjacent to us but not seen, where sighs are not heaved, and whose glories are incorruptible.

When we come to enumerate some few of the opinions that have been expressed on the writings and character of Nostradamus, it will be seen that a vast number of them condemn him for charlatanry and imposture, especially as we approach our own day. For now what is denominated science accepts nothing for true but what is deducible from the reason; it takes for granted that nothing can be known respecting the future, beyond what cultivated prudence can gather from a politic acquaintance with the past, coupled perhaps with a sagacious estimate of the principles now at work, and the fruit they are likely to engender. In fact, what the knowledge of a wise man can enable him to foresee, covers for such theorists the whole extent and province of all prophecy possible to man,—the sagacity of Mazarin, which detected the revolutionary element in the Cardinal de Retz whilst still a youth; or the prediction of Bishop Butler, in 1741, that the levelling spirit then visible, under the direction of principles that were atheistic, threatened dangers that might menace Europe. But to call this prophecy is to be ignorant of what the word prophecy means. To state it thus, or so to limit it, is to deny the existence of the prophetic faculty altogether. A direct denial of the thing is better than a sceptical definition of it. Scepticism, then, in our day, not believing there can be such a thing as a true presage, concludes that Mother Shipton and Nostradamus stand on precisely the same footing. They read a quatrain of Nostradamus, only understand one line out of four, and say that, although that one may be intelligible, the Sphinx itself could make nothing of the others, and that out of a number of such verses it would be marvellous if something curious were not occasionally let fall. The next inference is that the author set up for a gift that he did not possess, and soon found the imposture was far more lucrative than the dull routine of medical practice, as in those times the superstition of the public was unlimited. The ignorance of the Middle Ages is pointedly contrasted for us now with the wisdom and knowledge of our own day. What, prejudice apart, does this mean, if briefly summed up in an aphorism? Only this: that the wisdom of to-day gives us the Nihilist of no faith, in place of the Astrologer of too much.

We ought to remember in all this that our author had reached the mature age of fifty-two before he printed one word of the work that we are spending time over. He tells us that for generations the family of Nostradamus had inherited and transmitted some share of the prophetic gift (Garencière's Preface, p. 16), that it came to him as a natural genius; in which it seems that his sons partially shared. He had cultivated it long for his private pleasure, and the request in which his almanacs stood seems to have first led him to think he Might more largely utilize the faculty. He never appears to have made any large sum of money through it. He supported himself and brought up his family by steady work in his professional calling. On the very brink of publicity, anticipating malign influences, he still hesitated to take the final plunge; and, when he did take it, he was in his fifty-third year. Men seldom pass through life performing all its duties with credit and decorum, earn a competency, and at fifty-two enter upon a career of contemptible imposture. No; this is not according to human nature. We must acquit him of imposture.

Michel Nostradamus was one of the most learned men of his day, the friend of Jules César Scaliger. He knew many modern languages, and the Hebrew, Greek, and Latin. He had followed medicine from the age of twenty-two, took his Doctor's degree at twenty-six, filled a professional chair at Montpellier, and late in life devoted himself to judicial astrology; in which, and in an intuitive forecast beyond what that can bestow, he has distanced by far all other competitors in the same line. Let a reader thoroughly acquaint himself with all that is here set before him as to Charles I. in England, and its bloody re-enactment in the French Revolution, letting all the rest stand aside; and, if he can rise from the perusal, feeling that there is any kind of imposture discoverable throughout those strange and wonderful revelations then he himself possesses so miraculous a form of judgment, as to leave me without a word further to advance upon the subject.

M. le Pelletier conceives that the Commun Advénement, or l'avénement au règne des gens du commun, which I have rendered "The Vulgar Advent," extending from the death of Louis XVI. to the reign of Antichrist, is the grand object of Nostradamus. It is to paint this lurid epopee that he devotes three-quarters at least of his quatrains, according to le Pelletier. Myself, I think this proportion to be overstated. But our prophet returns to it again and again, elaborates the most minute details, and concentres upon it as in a focus the brightest rays of his mystical genius. Some think that Catharine de Medici was largely influenced in her firm and far-seeing policy by the counsels of Nostradamus, whom she visited expressly at Salon de Craux, in 1564, with her son, Charles IX. This may have been so, but it is a great question whether Nostradamus, for all his visions, curiously as they realize themselves in time, could advise the queen or anybody else at all better than any other wise man of elaborate culture could. His visions would come to him as verses to a great poet, and when written down and the afflatus fled, he would drop back to the ordinary condition of humanity. He would drop back to the level of reason and the discourse of science, with nothing to specially distinguish him from other men well placed to learn such wisdom and knowledge as this world has to bestow upon them. To expect more of him is to expect with the commonalty that if you met Milton in Bread Street he would address you in blank verse, and strain "Good morning" into metre. Great men cut very plain figures in common broadcloth. It is the impostor who is magisterial, and puts on the airs of a Cagliostro.

Nostradamus is sometimes a pillar of fire, but oftener he is a pillar of cloud. He is a past master in words, and depicts events with a terseness that almost baffles parallel; but still his employment of these same words is more practical than artistic, for he never rises to poetry. As an accepted visionary he is perhaps less swayed by the imagination than any man of at all kindred type that one can mention. With him words are as often used to veil as to unfold his meaning. His contempt for simple persons, the ignorant, is very broadly marked. Men of knowledge are to constitute his audience; the heaven of prophecy is in his opinion a region unfit for children. He, clean contrary to the example set forth in St. Mark (x. 14), will suffer none such to approach him. 1 He chiefly predicts the evil to come; what is good only figures in his pages incidentally, and at long intervals. But here it is to be observed that the staple of true prophecy must always run parallel with that of history; whilst, as to the latter, it has grown into an axiom, "Happy is the country that has no history." He fatigues while he fascinates us amid the variety of his combinations; yet a deeper examination will often end in clothing these riddling and vext allusions in a magical and floating investment that lifts them up into a calm sublimity.

Still he is clearly no prophet in the old and Hebrew sense of the word—like Isaiah, Daniel, David, John,—a man who neither respects his own person as regards its safety, nor the person of other men as regards their position. You cannot say of him: "Scimus quia verax es, non enim respicis personam hominum" (St. Matt. xxii. 16), which is the test-touch all the world over of a true prophet. Le Pelletier's summing-up is: c'est un artiste en pronostics. There is a Pythic ring in all he writes and says; a sub-flavour, too, of cabalistic lore far gathered from those ancient compromising books which he saw fit to burn. The outward signs of his procedure and methods are palpably magical, as set forth in the stanzas that open his first Century to the reader. If we know that he professed Christian orthodoxy, equally we know that he practiced judicial astrology, and made unquestionable use of the Pagan ritual of incantation. These rites, uncomprehended by all the erudite in books who wrote about them, were by the divines and fathers of the early Church ignorantly attributed to prestidigitation, Toledan art, and fraudulent compact with the sable fiend. Perhaps they may turn out to have been merely natural excitations, empirically discovered, tending to enable the subject of them more fully to reach a state of semi-conscious ecstasy; to place the cerebral light in the current of latent light that pervades all space (if such an expression be permissible), and so elicit results that are ordinarily unattainable by man. Bouys, who wrote in 1806, plainly considers him to have been a clairvoyant. The animal magnetizers call him a crisiaque. Possibly all these processes only served to place him in a position favourable to clairvoyance; but on all this, respected and gentle reader, construct your own opinion. Let the man be to you prophet, sorcerer, or clairvoyant. Call him what you will, so you free him from the stigma of impostor. M. le Pelletier's judgment as to that ought to be regarded as final: "L'ampleur de son génie, et la sureté inimaginable de son coup d'æil, ne permettent guère de la croire."

It has been well said that the man and his works are an enigma. Everything in our author is ambiguous. the man, the thought, the style. We stumble at every step in the rough paths of his labyrinth. Once we enter, jeering voices seem to deride us from behind each stanza, strophe, word. We try to interrogate, but grow silent before a man of emotionless nerve and of impenetrable mask. What are these "Centuries?" What is Nostradamus? In them and him all may find something; but no man born of woman can find all. The Sphinx of France is here before us; a riddler, riddling of the fate of men: a man at once bold and timid; simple, yet who can plumb his depth? A superficial Christian, a Pagan perhaps at heart; a man rewarded of kings: and yet, so far as we can see, furnishing no one profitable hint to them that could make their life run smoother, or remove a single peril from their path. His leaves a book of things malign, written by one who, albeit, never spoke a word that à tous ne seroit agréable. Behold this Janus of a double face; his very breath is double; the essence of ambiguity lies wrapped incarnate in him, and it moulds the man, the thought, the style. Footnotes

3:1 The facts for this life are taken, where no other reference is given, from a scarce work, entitled, "La première face du Janus François, par Jean Aimes de Chavigny Beaunois, 1594." It is found in the Library at Paris; but not in the British Museum. Fortunately M. le Pelletier gives an almost literal transcript of this "Brief discours sur la vie de M. Michel de Nostredame."

4:1 "Archives du Magnetisme Animal," vol. viii. "Tous deux" (i.e. father and mother) "appartenaient à une famille Juive," converted in the sixteenth century, and of the tribe of Issachar ("Nouvelle Biog. Générale" [Le Pelletier, i. 16 n.]).

4:2 His grandfather, Moreri tells us.

7:1 Moreri assigns this to the year 1525.

7:2 He calls Scaliger in the heyday of friendship "a Virgil in poetry, a Cicero in eloquence, a Galen in medicine," and declares that to him he is indebted for his scientific attainments ("Penny Cyclopædia," s.v. Nostradamus).

12:1 "That the great bulk of French society of his day was impressed by his effusions there can be no doubt" (Chambers' "Book of Days," vol. ii., p. 13).

12:2 Moreri says that nobody knows what his report was.

13:1 Garencières, as we have shown, says Nostradamus dedicated the "Luminary Epistle" to Henri II. in 1557. M. le Pelletier holds (i. 10) that Henri II. never knew of the dedicatory epistle written to him by name, and that, as the events referred to do not concern the House of Valois, they could have had no interest for him had he known of the epistle. M. le Pelletier adds a most singular note to this remark, that the epistle is dedicated "A l'invictissime, très puissant, et très chrestien Henry Roy de France Second." This epigraph he maintains not to be addressed to Henri II., for he remarks that he was no longer alive when it made its appearance. Now, this is not so; for the dedicatory letter was dated in print June 27, 1558, and the king's death only took place in 1559, so that the document was even in print before his death. But, had it not been so, there is no reason whatever why Nostradamus should not have supplied the king with a copy of the letter and quatrains in manuscript long before either of them had been committed to type. Jean de Roux, Curé de Louvicamp, wrongly suggests that it was intended as a prophetical dedication to Louis le Grand or XIV. M. le Pelletier thinks it was not even dedicated to the great Henri Quatre, but to a "Henry, Roy de France Second"—second being the Latin secundus, or prosperous, i.e. some king not less illustrious than Henri Quatre, whose reign is to arise in the future. This it is which furnishes to the reader the secret purpose of Le Pelletier's book, which is to set forth the claims of the Due de Bordeaux, who would have ascended the French throne as Henri Cinq. Accordingly, in the body of the book, he has interpreted five quatrains and one sixain of the prophecies of Nostradamus as referring to this glorious King Henri Second, who has never arrived, and who, being now some years dead, never can. We have seen that the Curé de Louvicamp could even suppose that Louis XIV. could stand for "Henry, Roy de France Second." M. F. Buget, in his "Étude sur Nostradamus," has the same idea, that be does riot address Henri II., because he was not of a character sufficiently great to merit the attribution of such spiritual authority to him by our prophet, as if the flattery of a dedication was to be interpreted au pied de la lettre. It could only be addressed, he thinks to a really great man,—, a saint. M. Buget, in his book of 1862, evidently was another of those who made the fatal error of interpreting Nostradamus out of the future, instead of carefully following the enigmas thrown out p. 14 by him to find their fulfilment in the past. These gentlemen, if they had assiduously read the Epistle itself, instead of consulting their imaginative faculties, would have perceived plainly enough that Nostradamus was writing to the only king he knew, before whom he had personally presented himself, and whom, as he says, he had highly reverenced from "iceluy jour que premierement devant icelle je me presentay." The concluding words of the Dedication are equally plain, and show that he is addressing a king whom he has individually seen with his own eyes: "depuis que mes yeux jurent si proches de vostre splendeur solaire." All the rest is to be set down to the strain of courtly flattery that was customarily addressed to kings, then and down to a period full two hundred years later, especially on occasion of penning royal dedications. The purpose of this long note is to establish, once and for all, I trust, that "Henry, Roy de France Second," stands, without any subtlety at all, simply for King Henry II., and nothing more. It is vain to endeavour to make millstones transparent that we may shoot unexpected rays of light through them. They will answer their purpose by being left in the dark, and will grind grain the better for it. Transparency will in such cases represent frangibility.

58:1 Aulus Gellius, "Noctes Atticæ," xv. 7.
58:2 It was really in the sixth month of his sixty-third year that he died.
20:1 Temple Bar, xli. p. 87, authority for the term of years.
21:1 How any could have been written in 1567, I know not, as Nostradamus died in 1566. But, however this may be, there are twelve Presages, or one for each month throughout the year 1567. The last one is that which we have already given, as relating to his own death.
21:2 The book was entitled, "Les vies des plus célèbres et anciens poëtes

provensaux, qui ont floury du tems des comtes de Provence" (Lyon, 1575); a book still sought for, and rather rare.

26:1 "In 1566 died that trifler, so famous throughout the world, Michael Nostradamus, who boasted while he lived that he knew and could foretell future events by the influence of the stars, in whose name afterwards many ingenious men have put forth their imaginings, justifying him who said so aptly, 'Nostra damus,' etc."

30:1 Bouys does the same for Napoleon I.

36:1 See the ban he utters in Century VI., at the close—"Barbari procul sunto." He shows a quite Horatian and heathen antipathy to the profanam vulgus.

The Preface of Michael Nostradamus to His Prophecies

To César Nostradamus his son, life and felicity. Thy late arrival, 1 César Nostradamus my son, has made me bestow much time, through nightly vigils, to leave you in writing a memorial to refer to, after the corporal extinction of your progenitor, that might serve for the common profit of mankind, out of what the Divine Being has permitted me to learn from the revolution of the stars. And since it has pleased the immortal God that thou shouldst come into the natural light of this terrene abode, and shouldst say that thy years are not yet calculated astronomically, and thy March months are incapable to receive in their weak understanding what I must necessarily record [as to happen] after my time:—seeing also that it is not possible to leave thee in writing what might suffer injury and be obliterated by time; for the inherited gift of occult prediction will remain confined to my own bowels:—considering that events of human proposal are uncertain, whilst all is governed and directed by the incalculable power of Heaven, guiding us, not by Bacchic fury, nor yet by Lymphatic 1 motion, but by astronomical assertion—"Soli numine divino afflati præsagiunt et spirito prophetico particularia." 2

Although for years past I have predicted, a long time in advance, what has afterwards come to pass, and in particular regions attributing the whole accomplishment to divine power and inspiration, also other unfortunate and fortunate occurrences have been pronounced with accelerated promptitude which have since happened in other parts of the world,—for I was willing to maintain silence and to pass over matters that might prove injurious [if published] not only as relates to the present time, but also for the most part of future time, if committed to writing, since kingdoms, sects, and religions will pass through stages so very contrary, and, as regards the present time, diametrically opposed,—that if I were to relate what will happen in the future, governors, sectaries, and ecclesiastics would find it so ill-accordant with [si] their auricular fancy, that they would go near to condemn what future ages will know and perceive to be true. Considering also the sentence of the true Saviour, "Nolite sanctum dare canibus neque mittatis rnargaritas vestras ante porcos, ne forte conculcent eas pedibus suis, et conversi dirumpant vos" [Matt. vii. 6].

This it is which has led me to withhold my tongue from the vulgar, and my pen from paper. But, later on, I thought I would enlarge a little, and declare in dark and abstruse sayings in consideration of [pour] the vulgar advent [vid, Le Pelletier, i. 163] the most urgent of its future causes, as perceived by me, be the revolutionary changes what they may, so only as not to scandalize the auricular frigidity (of my hearers), and write all down under a cloudy figure that shall essentially and above all things be prophetical. Although "Abscondidisti hæc à sapientibus, et prudentibus, id est, potentibus et regibus, et enucleasti ea exiguis et tenuibus." 1 By the grace of God and the good angels, the Prophets have had committed to them the spirit of vaticination, by which they see things at a distance, and are enabled to forecast future events. For there is nothing that can be accomplished without Him, whose power and goodness are so great to all His creatures as long as they put their trust in Him, much as they may be [exposed] or subject to other influences, [yet] on account of their likeness to the nature of their good guardian angel [or genius] that heat and prophetic power draweth nigh to us, as do the rays of the sun which cast their influence alike upon bodies that are elementary and non-elementary. As for ourselves personally who are but human, we can attain to nothing by our own unaided natural knowledge, nor the bent of our intelligence, in the way of deciphering the recondite secrets of God the Creator. "Quia non est nostrum noscere tempora, nec momenta," 1 etc. Although, indeed, now or hereafter some persons may arrive to whom God Almighty may be pleased to reveal by imaginative impression some secrets of the future, as accorded in time past to judicial astrology, when [que for quand] a certain power and volitional faculty came upon them, as a flame of fire appears. 2 They grew inspired, and were able to judge of all inspiration, human and divine, alike. For the divine works, which are absolutely universal, God will complete; those which are contingent, or medial, the good angels direct; and the third sort come under the evil angels. 3

Perhaps, my son, I speak to thee here a little too occultly. But as to the hidden vaticinations which come to one by the subtle spirit of fire, or sometimes by the understanding disturbed, [it may even be, by] contemplating the remotest stars, as being intelligences on the watch, even to giving utterance to declarations [that] being taken down in writing declare, without favour, and without any taint of improper loquacity, that all things whatsoever proceed from the divine power of the great eternal Deity from whom all goodness emanates. Further, my son, although I have inserted the name of prophet, I do not desire to assume a title of so high sublimity at the present moment. For he who "Propheta dicitur hodie, olim vocabatur videns;" 1 for, strictly speaking, my son, a prophet is one who sees things remote from the knowledge of all mankind. Or, to put the case; to the prophet, by means of the perfect light of prophecy, there he opened up very manifestly divine things as well as human; which cannot come about, seeing that the effects of future prediction extend to such remote periods. Now, the secrets of God are incomprehensible, and their efficient virtue belongs to a sphere far remote from natural knowledge; for, deriving their immediate origin from the free will, things set in motion causes that of themselves could never attract such attention as could make them recognized, either by human augury, or by any other knowledge of occult power; it is a thing comprised only within the concavity of heaven itself, from the present fact of all eternity, which comes in itself to embrace all time.

Still, by the means of some eternal power, by an epileptic Herculean agitation, the causes by the celestial movement become known. I do not say, my son, in order that you may fully understand me, that the knowledge of this matter cannot yet impress itself upon thy feeble brain, that very remote future causes may not come within the cognizance of a reasonable being; if they are, notwithstanding, purely the creation of the intellectual soul of things present, future things are not by any means too hidden or concealed. But the perfect knowledge of causes cannot be acquired without divine inspiration; since all prophetic inspiration derives its first motive principle from God the Creator, next from good fortune, and then from nature. Wherefore the independent causes being independently produced, or not produced, the presage partially happens, where it was predicted. For the human understanding, being intellectually create', cannot a penetrate occult causes, otherwise than by the voice of a genius by means of the thin flame (vid. page 68) [showing] to what direction future causes incline to develop themselves. And further, my son, I implore you never to apply your understanding on such reveries and vanities as dry up the body and bring perdition to the soul and disturb all the senses. In like manner, I caution you against the seduction of a more than execrable magic, that has been denounced already by the sacred Scriptures, by the divine canons of the Church—although we have to exempt from this judgment Judicial Astrology. By the aid of this it is, and by divine revelation and inspiration, united with deep calculations, we have reduced our prophecies to writing. And, notwithstanding that this occult philosophy was not reproved by the Church, I have felt no desire to divulge their unbridled promptings. Although many volumes have come before me, which had laid hidden for many ages. But dreading what might happen in the future, after reading them, I presented them to Vulcan, and as the fire kindled them, the flame, licking the air, shot forth an unaccustomed brightness, clearer than the light is of natural flame, resembling more the explosion of powder, casting a subtle illumination over the house as if the whole were wrapped in sudden conflagration.—So that at last you might not in the future be abused by searching for the perfect transformation, lunar or solar, or incorruptible metals hidden under the earth, or the sea, I reduced them to ashes.—But as to the judgment which perfects itself by means of the celestial judgment, that I am desirous to manifest to you: by that method you may have cognizance of things future, avoiding all fantastic imaginations that may arise, and limiting the particularity of the topics by divine and supernatural inspiration; harmonizing with the celestial figures these topics, and that part of time, which the occult property has relation to, by the potential virtue and faculty divine, in whose presence the three aspects of time are clasped in one by eternity—an evolution that connects in one causes past, present, and future—"quia omnia sunt nuda et aperta, etc." 1—

From all which, my son, you can easily comprehend, notwithstanding your tender brain, the things that are to happen can be foretold by nocturnal and celestial lights, which are natural, coupled to a spirit of prophecy,—not that I would assume the name or efficacy of a prophet, but, by revealed inspiration, as a mortal man the senses place me no farther from heaven than the feet are from the earth. "Possum non errare, falli, decipi," 2 (albeit) I am the greatest sinner in this world, and heir to every human affliction. But being surprised sometimes in the ecstatic work, amid prolonged calculation, and engaged in nocturnal studies of sweet odour, I have composed books of prophecies, containing each one hundred astronomic quatrains of forecasts, which I have tried to polish through obscurely, and which are perpetual vaticinations, from now to the year 3797. It is possible that this figure will make some lift up their forehead, at such a vast extent of time, and variety of things to take place under the concave journey of the moon; and this universal treatment of causes, my son, throughout the earth, which, if you reach the natural age, of man, you will see in your climate, under the heaven of your proper nativity, as things that have been foreseen.

Although the everlasting God alone knows the eternity of the light proceeding from Himself, I say frankly to all to whom He has decreed in long and melancholy inspiration to reveal His limitless magnitude, which is beyond both mensuration and comprehension, that by means of this occult cause divinely manifested, principally by two chief causes, comprised in the understanding of the inspired one who prophesies. One is that which comes by infusion, which clarifies the supernatural light, in him who predicts by astral process, or forecasts by inspired revelation, which is practically a participation in the divine eternity, by which means the prophet comes to judge of that which his share of divine spirit has given him, by means of communication with God the Creator, and the natural endowment accorded him. It is to know that what is predicted is true, and has had a heavenly origin; that such light and the thin flame is altogether efficacious; that it descends from above, no less than does natural clearness; and natural light renders philosophers quite sure of their principles, so that by means of the principles of a first cause they have penetrated the profoundest abysses and attained the loftiest doctrines.

But to this end, my son, that I may not wander too profoundly for the future capacity of thy senses, and also because I find that letters shall suffer great and incomparable loss, and that I find the world before the universal conflagration, such deluges and deep submersion, that there will remain scarcely any land not covered with water, and that for so long a period, that everything will perish except Ethnographies and Topographies. Further, after and before these inundations, in many districts the rains will have been so slight, and there will fall from heaven such an abundance of fire and incandescent stones, that scarcely anything will remain unconsumed, and this will occur a short time before the last conflagration. Further, when the planet Mars completes its cycle, at the end of his second period, he will recommence his course. But some will gather in Aquarius through several years, and others in Cancer, which will be of still longer duration. Now that we are conducted by the moon, under the direction of the Creator, and before she has finished her entire circuit the sun will come, and then Saturn. Now, according to the celestial signs, the reign of Saturn shall come back again, so that, all calculated, the world is drawing on towards its anaragonic revolution.

From the time I am writing this, before 177 years 3 months and 11 days, by pestilence, long famine, and wars, and more still by inundations, the world between this day and that, before and after, shall be diminished, and its population so reduced that there will hardly be hands enough to attend to agriculture, and the lands will be left as long without culture as they have been under tillage. This, so far as celestial judgment manifests, that we are now in the seventh millenary, which completes all and introduces us to the eighth, where is the upper firmament of the eighth sphere, which, in a latitudinary dimension, is where the Almighty will come to complete the revolution, where the celestial figures will return to their courses, and the upper motion which renders the earth stable for us and fixed, "non inclinabitur in seculum seculorum," 1 unless His will be accomplished, and no otherwise.

Although by ambiguous opinions exceeding all natural reason by Mahometical dreams, also sometimes God the Creator by the ministry of angels of fire, and missive flame, presents to the external senses, even of our eyes, the causes of future predictions, that indicate the future event which must manifest itself to him who presages anything. For the presage which is made by the exterior light comes infallibly to judge partly with and by means of the exterior flame; although truly the part which seems to come by the eye of the understanding springs only from the lesion of the imaginative sense. The reason is too evident, the whole is predicted by the afflatus of divinity, and by means of the angelic spirit inspired to the man prophesying, rendering him [as it were] anointed with vaticinations, visiting him to illuminate him, and, stirring the forefront of his phantasy by divers nightly apparitions no less than daily certitude, he prophesies by astronomic administration conjoined with the holiest future prediction, taking nothing into his consideration but the hardihood of his free courage.

Come at this hour to understand, my son, that I find by my revelations [astral], and which are in accordance with revealed inspiration, that the sword of death is on its way to us now, in the shape of pestilence, war (more horrible than has been known for three generations of men), and famine, that shall fall upon the earth, and return upon it at frequent intervals. For the stars accord with such a revolution, and with the written word, "Visitabo in virgâ ferrea iniquitates eorum, et in verberibus percutiam eos." 1 For the mercy of God, my son, will not be spread abroad for a time, till the major part of my prophesies shall have been accomplished, and have become by accomplishment resolved. Thus oftentimes in the course of these sinister storms the Lord will say, "Conteram ego, et confringam, et non miserebor." 1 And a thousand other accidents will come by waters and continual rain, as I have more fully and at large set forth in my other Prophecies, which are drawn out at length, in solutâ oratione; 2 (in these I) designate the localities, times, and terms prefixed, that all men who come after may see, recognizing the circumstances that come about by infallible indications. As we have marked by the others where we speak more clearly, for although they are covered with a veil of cloud, they are clear enough to be comprehended by men of good intelligence: "Sed quando submoventa erit ignorantia," 3 the total will stand out with greater clearance still. Making an end here, my son, take now this gift of thy father, Michael Nostradamus, hoping to expound to thee each several prophecy of these quatrains here given, beseeching the immortal Father that He will endue thee with a long life of happy and prospering felicity.

From Salon, this 1st of March, 1555.

Footnotes

39:1 César Nostradamus was born at the beginning of 1555, so he was but a few weeks old when his father dedicated to him the first four "Centuries," published for the first time in 1555, by Macé Bonhonune, the printer at Lyons. In the name of this son the epistle is really a dedication to his spiritual sons; that is, to his interpreters and students in all future ages.

40:1 Lymphatics, Garencières (p. 16) tells, were anciently those who were mad for love; and he absurdly adds that the sign of it was, that such persons threw themselves into the water,—lympha meaning water. Varro says that in Greece those who were mad were believed to have seen the image of nymphs in the water fountains. Others have it that they were afraid of water, as if it were hydrophobia that possessed them. But nympha and lympha approach each other so nearly, that when a man is once caught by a nymph he is, for the time being, mad to all intents and purposes,—"it is not given to a man to love and to be wise." Leaving all this to be settled as it may, there is no question but in the medical technology of Nostradamus a deep melancholy is what was understood by the Lymphatic motion,—melancholy being the temperament most apt for study, poetry, and vaticination. Garencières invents a word for the occasion, or uses one that has since grown obsolete. He employs the verb lymphatize.

40:2 "Such alone as are inspired by the divine power can predict particular events in a spirit of prophecy"

41:1 "Thou hast hidden these things from the wise and prudent, i.e. from the powerful and from kings, and hast revealed them to the small and weak." This is Nostradamus's gloss upon Matt. xi. 25.

42:1 Acts i. 7.

42:2 Nostradamus seems, whenever he alludes to this appearance of flame as preceding vaticination, to have in his mind the descent of tongues of fire at Pentecost (Acts ii. 3),. A flame of fire, be it observed, conveys a double symbol: it resembles a tongue in form. Its luminousness and its purifying tendency express the celestial nature of spirit, as contrasted with matter, and also inspiration. So that intrinsically and extrinsically it represents prophetic utterance. Grotius contributes an unusually good note upon this passage, pointing out that as in Genesis (xi. g), confusion of tongues scattered mankind, so hero (Acts ii. 3) the gift of tongues was to bring men again into one brotherhood.

42:3 This passage is very difficult to bring to a clear sense in translation, Garencières has simply evaded it. It seems to mean that God operates all the great effects in the universe; that, as He is the Maker, so is He the perpetual operator in the world,—its cause and life; but that the guardian angels are good and bad, and are charged with some sort of duty and office, not as affecting the mechanic frame of the world, but in respect of mankind. This is in conformity with the Cabala and Hermetical teaching; but what he precisely means cannot, I think, be quite absolutely stated.

43:1 "He who is called prophet now, once was called seer."

45:1 "For all things are naked and open."

45:2 "I am able not to err, fail, or be deceived."

47:1 "Whence it shall not deviate from age to age."

48:1 "I will visit their iniquities with a rod of iron, and with blows will strike them." This somewhat resembles a passage in the Psalms (ii. 7), but it is not a quotation.

49:1 "I will trample them and break them, and not show pity." This resembles Isai. lxiii. 3.

49:2 In prose, and not in verse, as the quatrains are. These prose forcastings have, I am afraid, been altogether lost.

49:3 "When the time arrives for the removal of ignorance."

Epistle to Henry II

To the most invincible, very puissant, and most Christian Henry King of France the Second: Michael Nostradamus, his most humble, most obedient servant and subject, wishes victory and happiness.

For that sovereign observation that I had, O most Christian and very victorious King, since that my face, long obscured with cloud, presented itself before the deity of your measureless Majesty, since that in that I have been perpetually dazzled, never failing to honour and worthily revere that day, when first before it, as before a singularly humane majesty, I presented myself. I searched for some occasion by which to manifest good heart and frank courage, by the means of which I might grow into greater knowledge of your serene Majesty. I soon found in effect it was impossible for me to declare it, considering the contrast of the solitariness of my long obnubilation and obscurity, and my being suddenly thrust into brilliancy, and transported into the presence of the sovereign eye of the first monarch of the universe. Likewise I have long hung in doubt as to whom I ought to dedicate these three Centuries to, the remainder of my Prophecies amounting now to a thousand. I have long meditated on an act of such audacity. I have at last ventured to address your Majesty, and was not daunted from it as Plutarch, that grave author, relates in the life of Lycurgus, that, seeing the gifts and presents that were made in the way of sacrifice at the temples of the immortal gods so in that age, many were staggered at the expense, and dared not approach the temple to present anything.

Notwithstanding this, I saw your royal splendour to be accompanied with an incomparable humanity, and paid my addresses to it, not as to those Kings of Persia whom it was not permissible to approach. But to a very prudent and very wise Prince I have dedicated my nocturnal and prophetic calculations, composed out of a natural instinct, and accompanied by a poetic fervour, rather than according to the strict rules of poetry. Most part, indeed, has been composed and adjusted by astronomical calculation corresponding to the years, months, and weeks, of the regions, countries, and for the most part towns and cities, throughout Europe, Africa, and a part of Asia, which nearest approach [or resemble] each other in all these climates, and this is composed in a natural manner. Possibly some may answer—who, if so, had better blow his nose [that he may see the clearer by it]—that the rhythm is as easy to be understood, as the sense is hard to get at. Therefore, O most gracious King, the bulk of the prophetic quatrains are so rude, that there is no making way through them, nor is there any interpreter of them. Nevertheless, being always anxious to set down the years, towns, and regions cited, where the events are to occur, even from the year 1585, and the year 1606, dating from the present time, which is the 14th of March, 1557.

Then passing far beyond to things which shall happen at the commencement of the seventh millenary, deeply calculated, so far as my astronomic calculus, and other knowledge, has been able to reach, to the time when the adversaries of Jesus Christ and of His Church shall begin to multiply in great force. The whole has been composed and calculated on days and hours of best election and disposition, and with all the accuracy I could attain to at a moment [blessed] "Minerva libera et non invita," 1 my calculations looking forward to events through a space of time to come that nearly equals that of the past even up to the present, and by this they will know in the lapse of time and in all regions what is to happen, all written down thus particularly, immingled with nothing superfluous.

Notwithstanding that some say, "Quod de futuris non est determinata omnino veritas," 2 I will confess, Sire, that I believed myself capable of presage from the natural instinct I inherit of my ancestors, adjusted and regulated by elaborate calculation, and the endeavour to free the soul, mind, and heart from all care, solicitude, and anxiety, by resting and tranquilizing the spirit, which finally has all to be completed and perfected in one respect tripode æneo [by the brazen tripod]. With all this there will be many to attribute to me as mine, things no more mine than nothing. The Almighty alone, who strictly searches the human heart, pious, just, and pitiful, is the true Judge; to Him I pray to defend me from the calumny of wicked men. Such persons, with equal calumny, will bring into question how all your ancient progenitors the Kings of France have cured the evil; how those of other nations have cured the bite of serpents; others have had a certain instinct in the art of divination, and other faculties that would be too long to recount here. Notwithstanding such as cannot be restrained from the exercise of the malignancy of the evil spirit, [there is hope that] by the lapse of time, and after my extinction here on earth, my writings will be more valued than during my lifetime.

However, if I err in calculation of ages, or find myself unable to please all the world, may it please your Imperial Majesty to forgive me, for I protest before God and His saints, that I purpose to insert nothing whatever in writing this present Epistle that shall militate against the true Catholic Faith, whilst consulting the astronomical calculations to the very best of my knowledge. For the stretch of time of our forefathers [i.e. the age of the world] which has gone before is such, submitting myself to the direction of the soundest chronologists, that the first man, Adam, was about one thousand two hundred and forty years before Noah, not computing time by Gentile records, such as Varro has committed to writing, but taking simply the Sacred Scriptures for the guide in my astronomic reckonings, to the best of my feeble understanding. After Noah, from him and the universal deluge, about one thousand and fourscore years, came Abraham, who was a sovereign astrologer according to some; he first invented the Chaldæan alphabet. Then came Moses, about five hundred and fifteen or sixteen years later. Between the time of David and Moses five hundred and seventy years elapsed. Then after the time of David and the time of our Saviour and Redeemer, Jesus Christ, born of a pure Virgin, there elapsed (according to some chronographers) one thousand three hundred and fifty years.

Some, indeed, may object to this supputation as not true, because it varies from that of Eusebius. Since the time of the human redemption to the hateful apostacy of the Saracens, there have been six hundred and twenty-one years, or thereabouts. Now, from this it is easy to gather what time has elapsed if my supputation be not good and available for all nations, for that all is calculated by the celestial courses, associated in my case with an emotion that steals over me at certain subsecival hours from an emotional tendency handed down to me from a line of ancestors. But the injuriousness of our time, O most serene Sovereign, requires that such secret events should not transpire, except in enigmatic sentences, having but one sense and one only meaning, and quite unmingled with calculation that is of ambiguity or amphibology. Say, rather, under a veiled obscurity from some natural emotional effusion, that resembles the sentential delivery of the thousand and two Prophets, that have been from the Creation of the world, according to the calculation and Punic Chronicle of Joel: "Effundum spiritum meum super omnem carnem, et prophetabunt filii vestri, et filiæ vestræ." 1 But this prophecy proceeded from the mouth of the Holy Spirit, which was the sovereign power eternal, in conjunction with the celestial bodies, has caused some of the number to predict great and marvellous events.

As to myself in this place, I set up no claim to such a title—never, please God. I fully confess that all proceeds from God, and for that I return Him thanks, honour, and immortal praise, and have mingled nothing with it of the divination which proceeds à fato, but à Deo à naturâ, 2 and for the most part accompanied with the movement of the celestial courses. Much as, if looking into a burning mirror [we see], as with darkened vision, the great events, sad or portentous, and calamitous occurrences that are about to fall upon the principal worshippers. First upon the temples of God, secondly upon such as have their support from the earth [i.e. by the kings], this decadence draweth nigh, with a thousand other calamitous incidents that in the course of time will be known to happen.

For God will take notice of the long barrenness of the great Dame, who afterwards will conceive two principal children. But, she being in great danger, the girl she will give birth to with risk at her age of death in the eighteenth year, and not possible to outlive the thirty-sixth, will leave three males and one female, and he will have two who never had any of the same father. The three brothers will be so different, though united and agreed, that the three and four parts of Europe will tremble. By the youngest in years will the Christian monarchy be sustained and augmented; heresies spring up and suddenly cast down, the Arabs driven back, kingdoms united, and new laws promulgated. Of the other children the first shall possess the furious crowned Lions, holding their paws upon the bold escutcheon. The second, accompanied by the Latins, shall penetrate so far that a second trembling and furious descent shall he made, descending Mons Jovis [at Barcelona] to mount the Pyrenees, shall not he translated to the antique monarchy, and a third inundation of human blood shall arise, and March for a long while will not be found in Lent. The daughter shall be given for the preservation of the Christian Church, the dominator falling into the Pagan sect of new infidels, and she will have two children, the one fidelity, the other infidelity, by the confirmation of the Catholic Church. The other, who to his great confusion and tardy repentance wished to ruin her, will have three regions over a wide extent of leagues, that is to say, Roumania, Germany, and Spain, which will entail great intricacy of military handling, stretching from the 50th to the 52nd degree of latitude. And they will have to respect the more distant religions of Europe and the north above the 48th degree of latitude, which at first in a vain timidity will tremble, and then the more western, southern, and eastern will tremble. Their power will become such, that what is brought about by union and concord will prove insuperable by warlike conquest. By nature they will be equal, but exceedingly different in faith.

After this the sterile Dame, of greater power than the second, shall be received by two nations, by the first made obstinate by him who had power over all, by the second, and third, that shall extend his forces towards; the circuit of the east of Europe; [arrived] there his standards will stop and succumb, but by sea he will run on to Trinacria and the Adriatic with his mirmidons. The Germans will succumb wholly and the Barbaric sect will be disquieted and driven back by the whole of the Latin race. Then shall begin the grand Empire of Antichrist in the Atila and Xerxes, [who is] to descend with innumerable multitudes, so that the coming of the Holy Spirit, issuing from the 48th degree, shall make a transmigration, chasing away the abomination of Antichrist, that made war upon the royal person of the great vicar of Jesus Christ, and against His Church, and reign per tempus, et in occasione temporis [for a time, and to the end of time]. This will be preceded by an eclipse of the sun, more obscure and tenebrose than has ever been since the creation of the world, up to the death and passion of Jesus Christ, and from thence till now. There will be in the month of October a grand revolution [translation] made, such that one would think that the librating body of the earth had lost its natural movement in the abyss of perpetual darkness. There will be seen precursive signs in the spring-time, and after extreme changes ensuing, reversal of kingdoms, and great earthquakes [i.e. wars]. All this accompanied with the procreations of the New Babylon [Paris], a miserable prostitute big with the abomination of the first holocaust [death of Louis XVI.]. It will only continue for seventy-three years seven months.

Then there will issue from the stock so long time barren, proceeding from the 50th degree, [one] who will renovate the whole Christian Church. A great peace, union, and concord will then spring up between some of the children of races [long] opposed to each other and separated by diverse kingdoms. Such a peace shall be set up, that the Instigator and promoter of military faction by means of the diversity of religions, shall dwell attached to the bottom of the abyss, and united to the kingdom of the furious, who shall counterfeit the wise. The countries, towns, cities, and provinces that had forsaken their old customs to free themselves, enthralling themselves more deeply, shall become secretly weary of their liberty, and, true religion lost, shall commence by striking off to the left, to return more than ever to the right.

Then replacing holiness, so long desecrated by their former writings [circulating slanders], afterwards the result will be that the great dog will issue as an irresistible mastiff [Napoleon?] who will destroy everything, even to all that may have been prepared in time past, till the churches will be restored as at first, and the clergy reinstated in their pristine condition; till it lapses again into whoredom and luxury, to commit and perpetrate a thousand crimes. And, drawing near to another desolation, then, when she shall be at her highest and sublimest point of dignity, the kings and generals [mains militaires] will come up [against her], and her two swords will be taken from her, and nothing will be left her but the semblance of them. [The following paragraph I can make nothing of, so I give it in the words of Garencières and in inverted commas.] "From which by the means of the crookedness that draweth them, the people causing it to go straight, and not willing to submit unto them by the end opposite to the sharp hand that toucheth the ground they shall provoke." Until there shall be born unto the branch a long time sterile, one who shall deliver the French people from the benign slavery that they voluntarily submitted to, putting himself under the protection of Mars, and stripping Jupiter [Napoleon I.] of all his honours and dignities, for the city constituted free and seated in another narrow Mesopotamia. The chief and governor shall be cast from the midst, and set in a place of the air, ignorant of the conspiracy of the conspirators

[Fouché, Duc d'Otranto, etc.] with the second Thrasibulus, who for a long time had prepared all this. Then shall the impurities and abominations be with great shame set forth and manifested to the darkness of the veiled light, shall cease towards the end of his reign, and the chiefs of the Church shall evince but little of the love of God, whilst many of them shall apostatize from the true faith.

Of the three sects [Lutheran, Catholic, and Mahometan], that which is in the middle, by the action of its own worshippers, will be thrown a little into decadence. The first totally throughout Europe, and the chief part of Africa exterminated by the third, by means of the poor in spirit, who by the madness engendered of libidinous luxury, will commit adultery [i.e. apostatize]. The people will pull down the pillar, and chase away the adherents of the legislators, and it shall seem, from the kingdoms weakened by the Orientals, that God the Creator has loosed Satan from the infernal prisons, to make room for the great Dog and Dohan [Gog and Magog], which will make so great and injurious a breach in the Churches, that neither the reds nor the whites, who are without eyes and without hands [meaning the latter Bourbons, "who learn nothing and forget nothing", cannot judge of the situation, and their power will be taken from them. Then shall commence a persecution of the Church such as never was before. Whilst this is enacting, such a pestilence shall spring up that out of three parts of mankind two shall be removed. To such a length will this proceed that one will neither know nor recognize the fields or houses, and grass will grow in the streets of the cities as high as a man's knees. To the clergy there shall be a total desolation, and the martial men shall usurp what shall come back from the City of the Sun [Rome], and from Malta and the Islands of Hières [off Marseilles], and the great chain of the port shall be opened that takes its name from the marine ox [Bosphorus].

A new incursion shall be made from the maritime shores, eager to give the leap of liberty since the first taking by the Mahometans. Their assaults shall not be at all in vain, and in the place where the habitation of Abraham was, it shall be assailed by those who hold the Jovialists [followers of Jupiter (Napoleon I.?)] in reverence. The city of Achem [in the Island of Sumatra] shall be encompassed and assaulted on all sides by a great force of armed men. Their maritime forces shall be weakened by the Westerns. Upon this kingdom a great desolation shall come, and the great cities shall be depopulated, and such as enter in shall come under the vengeance of the wrath of God. The Holy Sepulchre, for so long a period an object of great veneration, shall remain exposed to the blighting dew of evening under the stars of heaven, and of the sun and moon. The holy place shall be converted into a stable for cattle small and large, and applied to other base purposes. Oh, what a calamitous time will that be for women with child! for then the Sultan of the East will be vanquished, driven for the most part by the Northern and Western men, who will kill him, overthrow him, and put the rest to flight, and his children, the offspring of many women, imprisoned. Then will come to its fulfilment the prophecy of the Royal Prophet, "Ut audiret gemitus compeditorum, et solveret filios interemptorum." 1

What great oppression shall then fall upon the princes and rulers of kingdoms, even on those who are maritime and Oriental, their tongues intermingled from all nations of the earth! Tongues of the Latin nations, mingled with Arabic and North-African communication. All the Eastern kings will be driven away, overthrown, and exterminated, not at all by means of the kings of the North and the drawing near of our age, but by means of the three secretly united who seek out death and snares by ambush sprung upon one another. The renewal of this Triumvirate shall endure for seven years, while its renown shall spread all over the world, and the sacrifice of the holy and immaculate wafer shall be upheld. Then shall two lords of the North conquer the Orientals, and so great report and tumultuary warfare shall issue from these that all the East shall tremble at the noise of these two brothers of the North, who are yet not brothers. And because, Sire, by this discourse I almost introduce confusion into these predictions as to the time when the event of each shall fall out; for the detailed account of the time that follows is very little conformable, if at all, to what I gave above, that indeed could not err, being by astronomic rule and consonant with the Holy Scriptures themselves.

Had I wished to give to every quatrain its detailed date, it could easily have been done, but it would not have been agreeable to all, and still less to interpret them, Sire, until your Majesty should have fully sanctioned me to do this, in order not to furnish calumniators with an opportunity to injure me. Always reckoning the years since the creation of the world to the birth of Noah as being 1506 years, and from that to the completion of the building of the ark at the period of the universal deluge 600 years elapsed (let them be solar years, or lunar, or mixed), I hold that the Scripture takes them to be solar. At the conclusion of this 600 years, Noah entered the ark to escape the deluge. The deluge was universal over the earth, and lasted one year and two months, From the conclusion of the deluge to the birth of Abraham there elapsed 295 years, and 100 years from that to the birth of Isaac. From Isaac to Jacob 60 years. From the time he went into Egypt until his coming out of it was 130 years, and from the entry of Jacob into Egypt to his exit was 436 years; and from that to the building of the Temple by Solomon in the fortieth year of his reign, makes 480 years. From the building of the Temple to Jesus Christ, according to the supputation of the Hierographs, there passed 490 years. Thus by this calculation that I have made, collecting it out of the sacred writings, there are about 4173 years and eight months less or more. Now, from Jesus Christ, in that there is such a diversity of opinion, I pass it by, and having calculated the present prophecies in accordance with the order of the chain which contains the revolution, and the whole by astronomical rule, together with my own hereditary instinct. After some time, and including in it the period Saturn takes to turn between the 7th of April up to the 25th of August; Jupiter from the 14th of June to the 7th of October; Mars from the 17th of April to the 22nd of June; Venus from the 9th of April to the 22nd of May; Mercury from the 3rd of February to the 24th of the same; afterwards from the 1st of June to the 24th of the same; and from the 25th of September to the 16th of October, Saturn in Capricorn, Jupiter in Aquarius, Mars in Scorpio, Venus in Pisces, Mercury within a month in Capricorn, Aquarius, and Pisces; the moon in Aquarius, the Dragon's head in Libra, the tail in her sign opposite. Following the conjunction of Jupiter to Mercury, with a quadrin aspect of Mars to Mercury, and the head of the Dragon shall be with a conjunction of Sol with Jupiter, the year shall be peaceful without eclipse.

Then will be the commencement [of a period] that will comprehend in itself what will long endure [i.e. the vulgar advent of the French Revolution], and in its first year there shall be a great persecution of the Christian Church, fiercer than that in Africa [by the Vandals from 1439 to 15341, and this will burst out [durera] the year one thousand seven hundred and ninety-two; they will think it to be a renovation of time. After this the people of Rome will begin to reconstitute themselves [in 1804, when Napoleon is emperor], and to chase away the obscurity of darkness, recovering some share of their ancient brightness, but not without much division and continual changes. Venice after that, in great force and power, shall raise her wings very high, not much short of the force of ancient Rome. At that time great Bysantine sails, associated with the Piedmontese by the help and power of the North, will so restrain them that the two Cretans will not be able to maintain their faith. The arks built by the ancient warriors will accompany them to the waves of Neptune. In the Adriatic there will be such permutations, that what was united will be separated, and that will be reduced to a house which before was a great city, including the Pampotan and Mesopotamia of Europe, to 45, and others to 41, 42, and 47. And in that time and those countries the infernal power will set the power of the adversaries of its law against the Church of Jesus Christ. This will constitute the second Antichrist, which will persecute that Church and its true vicar, by means of the power of the temporal kings, who in their ignorance will be reduced by tongues that will cut more than any sword in the hands of a madman.

The said reign of Antichrist will only last to the death of him who was born near the [commencement] of the century, and of the other in the city of Plancus [Lyons], accompanied by him the elect of Modena, Fulcy by Ferara, upheld by the Adriatic Piedmontese, and the proximity of the great Trinacria [Sicily]. Afterwards the Gallic Ogmion shall pass the Mount Jovis [Barcelona], accompanied by so great a number that from afar the Empire shall be presented with its grand law, and then and for some time after shall be profusely shed the blood of the innocent by the guilty recently elevated to power. Then by great deluges the memory of things contained in such instruments shall suffer incalculable loss, even to the Alphabet itself. This will happen among the Northerns. By the Divine Will once again Satan will be bound, and universal peace established amongst mankind, and the Church of Jesus Christ delivered from all tribulation, although the Azostains [debauched voluptuaries] would desire to mix with the honey the gall of their pestilent seduction. This will be near the seventh millenary, when the sanctuary of Jesus Christ will no longer be trodden down by the infidels who come from the North; the world [will be then] approaching its great conflagration, although by my supputation in my prophecies, the course of time runs much farther on.

In the epistle that some years since I dedicated to my son César Nostradamus, I have openly enough declared some points without presage. But here, Sire, are comprised many great and marvellous events to come, which those who follow after us shall see. And during the said astrological supputation, harmonized with the sacred Scriptures, the persecution of the Ecclesiastics shall take its rise in the power of the kings of the North, united with the Easterns. And this persecution shall last eleven years, or somewhat less, by which time the chief Northern king shall pass away, which years being run, a united Southern king shall succeed, which shall still more fiercely persecute the clergy of the Church for the space of three years by the Apostolical seduction of one who will take away all the absolute power from the Church Militant, and holy people of God who observe its ritual, and the whole order of religion shall be greatly persecuted and so afflicted that the blood of true ecclesiastics shall float everywhere. To one of those horrible temporal kings such praise shall be given by his adherents that he will have shed more human blood of innocent ecclesiastics, than any could do of wine. This king will commit crimes against the Church that are incredible. Human blood will flow in the public streets and churches, like water after impetuous rain, and will crimson with blood the neighbouring rivers, and by another naval war redden the sea to such a degree that one king shall say to another, "Bellis rubuit navalibus æquor." 1 Then in the same year and those following there will ensue the most horrible pestilence and the most astonishing on account of the famine that will precede, and such tribulation that nothing approaching it ever happened since the first foundation of the Christian Church; this also throughout all the Latin regions, leaving traces in all the countries under the rule of Spain.

Then the third King of the North [Russia?], hearing the complaint of the people from [whom he derives] his principal title, will raise up a mighty army, and pass through the limits [destroits] of his last progenitors and great-grandfathers, to him who will [qui for lui qui] replace almost everything in its old condition. The great Vicar of the Cope shall be put back to his pristine state; but, desolated and abandoned by all, will return to the sanctuary [that was] destroyed by paganism, when the Old and New Testament will be thrust out and burnt. After that Antichrist will be the infernal prince. Then at this last epoch, all the kingdoms of Christianity, as well as of the infidel world, will be shaken during the space of twenty-five years, and the wars and battles will be more grievous, and the towns, cities, castles, and all other edifices will be burnt, desolated, and destroyed with much effusion of vestal blood, married women and widows violated, sucking children dashed and broken against the walls of town; and so many evils will be committed by means of Satan, the prince infernal, that nearly all the world will become undone and desolated. Before the events occur certain strange birds [imperial eagles] will cry in the air, "To-day! to-day!" and after a given time will disappear [June, 1815]. After this has endured for a certain length of time [twenty-five years he has said before, 1790 to 1815], there will be almost renewed another reign of Saturn, the age of gold [this might be the discovery of California, but for what follows]. God the Creator shall say, hearing the affliction of His people, Satan shall be precipitated and bound in the bottomless abyss, and then shall commence between God and men a universal peace. There he shall abide for the space of a thousand years, and shall turn his greatest force against the power of the Church, and shall then be bound again.

How justly are all these figures adapted by the divine letters to visible celestial things, that is to say, by Saturn, Jupiter, and Mars, and others in conjunction with them, as may be seen more at large by some of the quatrains! I would have calculated it more deeply, and adapted the one to the other; but, seeing, O most serene King, that some who are given to censure will raise a difficulty, I shall take the opportunity to retire my pen and seek my nocturnal repose. "Multa etiam, O Rex potentissime præclara, et sane in brevi ventura, sed omnia in hâc tuâ Epistola, innectere non possumus, nec volumus, sed ad intellegenda quædam facta, horrida fata pauca libanda sunt, quamvis tanta sit in omnes tua amplitudo et humanitas homines, deosque pietas, ut solos amplissimo et Christianissimo Regis nomine, et ad quem summa totius religionis auctoritas deferatur dignus esse videare." 1 But I shall only beseech you, O most clement King, by this your singular and most prudent goodness, to understand rather the desire of my heart, and the sovereign wish I have to obey your most excellent Majesty, ever since my eyes approached so nearly to your solar splendour, than the grandeur of my work can attain to or acquire.

Faciebat MICHAEL NOSTRADAMUS.

Solonæ Petræ Provincæ.
From Salon this 27th June, 1558.
Footnotes
52:1 "When Minerva was free and favourable."
52:2 "There can be no truth entirely determined for certain which concerns the future."
54:1 See Joel ii. 28.
54:2 Which proceeds from fate, but from God, and nature.
59:1 "Let the sighing of the prisoner come before thee. to release the children of death" (Ps. lxxviii. 11).
64:1 "The sea blushed red with the blood of naval fights."
66:1 "Many things, O most potent king of all, of the most remarkable kind are shortly to happen, that I neither could nor would interweave them all into this epistle; but in order to comprehend certain facts, a few horrible destinies must be set down in extract, although your amplitude and humanity towards all men is so great, and your piety to the gods, and that you alone seem worthy of the grand title of the most Christian King, and to whom the highest authority in all religion should be deferred."

Magic

BEFORE we enter upon the historical application of the quatrains which admit of interpretation, it will be well to devote a little attention to the views of magic entertained by Nostradamus, to learn from his own mouth what class of readers he proposed to address, and to gather, as far as we may be able, in what manner he proceeded to cultivate the spirit of prophecy and the divine gift with which he thought himself to be endowed. Were he even as certainly an impostor as Cagliostro, this inquiry would have an interest of its own attaching to it; but if we can for a moment suppose that he genuinely believed himself to be endowed with a faculty of divination, the investigation of that assumption on his part would present a considerable psychological interest merely as a human phenomenon. On the other hand, if he were a man truly gifted with forecast, I do not know that, in this age of scepticism as to things spiritual, anything more wholesome could be proposed to our contemplation than a prophetic record fulfilling itself before the eyes of disbelievers and gainsayers; who, wishing to scoff and desiring to suppress such things, find themselves utterly powerless to annul the harmony between the vision recorded three hundred years ago and the event of yesterday. Whether such things are or not, it will be for the reader, when he has gone through the book, to say. At present we will only busy ourselves with what Nostradamus says of himself. He is a notability and worthy of criticism be the final verdict for or against him.

At the end of Century VI. occur four Latin lines headed—

LEGIS CANTIO CONTRA INEPTOS CRITICOS. [I. 51.]
Qui legent hosce versus maturè censunto,
Profanum vulgus et inscium ne attrectato,
Omnesque Astrologi, Blenni, Barbari procul sunto.
Qui aliter facit, is ritè sacer esto.

The sense of these lines is much clearer than the prosody, but that matters little.

Translation.

AN INCANTATION IN ARREST OF INEPT CRITICS.

Let those who read these verses meditate them seriously! Let the profane and ignorant vulgar not handle them! Let astrologers, fools, and savages stand off! Who acts contrary to this, let him he cursed according to the rites of magic.

We now come to the magic formula.

Century I.—Quatrain I. [I. 52.]
Estant assis de nuict secret estude,
Seul, reposé sur la sele 1 d'airain,
Flambe exigue sortant de solitude,
Fait prospèrer 2 qui 3 n'est à croire vain.

Translation.
Gathered at night in study deep I sate,
Alone, upon the tripod stool of brass,
Exiguous flame came out of solitude,

Promise of magic that may be believed.

Being seated at night and wrapt in secret study, entirely alone, I placed myself on the brazen tripod of prophecy. A still small flame came forth of solitude, helping me to realize successfully what it will not prove vain to have believed.

The reader will here refer to the "Preface à mon fils," p. 44.

"L'entendement cree intellectuellement ne peut voir occultement, sinon par la voix faicte au lymbe moyennant la exigue flame, en laquelle partie les causes futures se viendront à incliner."

This passage conveys in prose what the last and the following quatrain conveys in verse.

THE MAGICAL CALL BY WATER. [I. 53.]
Century I.—Quatrain 1.
La verge 1 en main mise au milieu de BRANCHES,
De l'Onde il mouille et le limbe, 2 et le pied:
Un peur et voix fremissent par 3 les manches,
Splendeur divine, Le Divin près s'assied.
Translation.
The rod in hand set in the midst of the Branches,
He moistens with water both the fringe and foot;
Fear and a voice make me quake in my sleeves;
Splendour divine, the God is seated near.

To make this entirely clear is almost impossible. But what we can get at is very curious, showing as it does, if nothing else, that the borderland of the unseen world was actually contiguous with that of the world of Nostradamus. They even overlapped, in his estimation, so as to form an intermediate neutral territory like the marches in the North, where the inhabitants of each district could meet and communicate. We are positive that this is all illusive, superstitious, demoniacal. It may be so. But one effect it undeniably produces. It unites man more to the universe, and less to the world; it makes death less strange and less cold, and furnishes to the soul, and the things of the soul, more nutriment than it can extract from modern life and culture.

The general meaning seems to be that he sat with a wand, branch, or divining-rod of laurel, probably forked like the winchel rod of the water-finders, one fork being held in each hand. This in some way had power to evoke his Genius (or génie familier, as Le Pelletier styles it). When he appeared, he moistened in the brazier that held water, himself, the fringe of his robe (limbe), and his foot. The rod, held as I have suggested, then becoming electrical, caused fear with the sound of a voice and a shuddering up to the elbows. Then shone forth the fatidical splendour of a divine light, and the Deity is present, seated near to him.

M. le Pelletier tells us that there was a pagan rite of the god Branchus that corresponded with this fatidical ceremony practised by Nostradamus. He even suggests that this very Branchus might have been the familiar spirit of our prophet. It must be admitted that in the texte-type, in the words "au milieu de BRANCHES," Branches is printed in capital letters, so that the probable reason for that peculiarity is that the God Branchus, as well as the branches d'un laurier, is shadowed forth. But to suppose that a pagan deity could ever be either the familiar or the guardian angel of a son of the Church of Rome makes such a Renaissance-jumble of the two religions that I think we had better not meddle with it.

As to the assertion that there was a pagan rite of Branchus, I doubt it much; and, if there were, certain it is that Nostradamus speaks here far too covertly for us to assume from his writing that he was discharging any rite special to Branchus. He seems to be following out the usual magical forms employed for establishing vaticinatory connection with the other world, or setting up the counter analogy between mind and spirit, according to that beautiful esoteric verse in Ecclesiasticus (xlvii. 24), "All things are double, one against another; He hath made nothing imperfect." Were such things never to interlink, men might well say, as they do now in the wisdom of science, that spirit and intellect are not doubles, and that no knowledge can be reached save by physical experiment. In this case there will be a particular link missing if science be right. The sage, Estant assis de nuict secret estude, will earnestly desire such assumption may prove to be erroneous. He will readily formulate with St. Paul that the invisible things from creation may be known from the visible; but also that the visible things can never be understood but by the invisible. Recollect that the visible is not visible to the visible, but to the invisible alone. The eye is the machine of sight, but not sight; and who has seen the eye of the eye?

The Greek myth about Branchus, so far as I can see, is this, with sundry forms and variations. He was a youth of Miletus. The reputed son of Smicrus (Lempriere), or Macarcus Varro says, but begotten by Apollo. The mother dreamed that the sun entered her mouth, and, passing through her, the child at birth was named Branchus. Afterwards he kissed Apollo in the woods, and became endowed with the gift of prophecy. He had a temple at Didyma, which Pausanias calls the Temple of Apollo; but Varro goes on to say that after the kiss of the god he prophesied, but quickly after disappeared, when a grand temple was jointly dedicated to him and to Apollo,—Philesius, to kiss. His oracles at Didyma were inferior to none but Delphi. The name Didymean, double or twain, was from the double light of the sun and its reflection in the moonlight. Sun-touched and moon-struck madness and inspiration may in Branchus be said to meet, as out of one throat come things good and evil. The name Didymean was changed to Branchidæ. Strabo (Book xlv.) relates that the priests of this grand temple betrayed its treasures to Xerxes, and accompanied him in his retreat to escape the punishment of their sacrilege. They had settled near to Sogdiana, when Alexander arrived there (Strabo, Book xi.); he destroyed them and their city. This Byronical madman, who could see no iniquity in the slaughter of thousands to gratify the lust of a crack-brained ambition, thought to promote morals by slaughtering the descendants of traitors, they, the descendants, being innocent of everything except being born. The Milesians had long ago rebuilt the temple of Branchus on such a scale that in magnitude it surpassed all others in Greece. It was, in fact, too big to be roofed in, being four or five stadia in compass. Those who wish to see more can consult Suidas, s. v.

The gloss of M. le Pelletier on the quatrain is as follows: that Nostradamus, wand in hand, touches the branches of the tripod, like the priests of Branchus (this I have tried to expunge), and invokes his familiar spirit, which appears to him in the vapour floating above a basin of water, which he had consecrated beforehand according to prescribed magical rites, and in which he dips the fringe of his garment, and his feet. An involuntary shivering (peur) agitates his hand when about to write from the dictation (voix) of the spirit. The fatidical light shines, and the angel is seated at his side. Le Pelletier takes occasion here to remark that mediums at this day write under a spirit of dictation, to which they simply lend their arm as an instrument.

Garencières' interpretation is that of most of the old commentators, even down to the time of M. Bareste, 1840. The rod is a pen, in the middle of the branches means his fingers, the water is the ink, and wetting limb and foot is covering the paper all but the four margins. It is hardly unfair to say that this is both nonsensical and ignorant, although not devoid of ingenuity. I think it will fit the circumstances far better to take it, as I have done, that the wand was a forked laurel branch that dipped forcibly, like the winchel rod, when Nostradamus held it over the water, that it strained, as the hazel-rod does, almost to breaking, and that at this invitation it is to be supposed that the spirit appears. The incantation being completed and successful, the operator must be supposed to set aside the winchel, and assume the pen, quaking with a solemn sense of the spiritual presence. This fear was, Garencières says, to prevent the puffing up of pride, as we read in Daniel, John, and the 4th of Esdras.

Readers who take no interest in this, and are consequently weary by this time of the length we have run into in the investigation, will leap over what follows to get to the next quatrain.

M. le Pelletier refers to Ficinus' translation of Jamblicus' "De Mysteriis Ægyptiorum," 1607. He gives the Latin and French. I will merely introduce here the English translation, as the book is of easy reference to those who wish to examine further for themselves the sources which Nostra, damus had consulted, and from which he drew his summary exposition.

"The sibyl at Delphi received the god in two forms,—either by a subtle and fiery spirit, which burst forth upon any one through the crevice of some cavern, or else sitting on a brazen seat of four or three feet in the inner shrine, dedicated to the god, and where she was exposed on two sides to the divine influx, whence she was irradiate with a divine light" (p. 66).

"Now, the prophetess of Branchus either sits upon a pillar, (r holds in her hand a rod bestowed by some deity, or moistens her feet or the hem of her garment with water, or inhales the vapour of water, and by these means is filled with divine illumination, and. having obtained the deity, she prophesies. By these practices she adapts herself to the god, whom she receives from without" (p. 67).

"Porphyrius says that the art [or magic] is not to be despised which, out of certain vapours due to fire under favourable stellar influences, forms the images of gods spontaneously appearing in the air, in a certain degree like the gods themselves, and possessing a very similar efficacy" (p. 90.

"For amongst the demons there is one who is chief, and who exercises influence at the moment of birth, and apportions to each his demon (or familiar). After this there is present to each one his own guardian, that develops a cultus congruous to his nature, and teaches him both his name and the most suitable form of invocation (to bring him when required), and this method is most congenial to the demons" (p. 171).

These forms of Jamblicus are analogous to those employed by Nostradamus; but there the person prophesying wets the feet and fingers, whilst according to our version Of the quatrains it is the demon or spirit applies them to himself: Le Divin près s'assied. In Jamblicus the one who prophesies becomes possessed by entry of the spirit. Nostradamus describes an external and visible presence which corresponds to Porphyrius' account of deorum idola in aere.

CORPOREAL DEMONS. [I. 59.]
Century I.—Quatrain 42.
La dix Calendes d'Avril de faict gotique
Resuscité encor par gens malins:
Le feu estainct, assemblée diabolique
Cherchant les os du Damant et Pselin. 1
Translation.

The 10th of the Calends of April Gothic computation have been again put in practice by sorcerers (gens malins). The lights put out, the diabolic assembly searching for the Demon [Damant for Démon] treated of by Michael Psellus.

The texte-type is most corrupt in this quatrain; for Damant et Pselin read Démon e (or ex) Pselin, the demon as treated of by Psellus.

The scholium of M. le Pelletier on this is—The magical incantations, which were successful formerly when wrought on the night of Good Friday, were reintroduced into practice by sorcerers of skill on the 10th Calend of April according to the ancient computation (de faict gotique). In a note added he professes that the 10th Calend Old Style would be the last day of March by the Gregorian, and he thinks it probable, that Nostradamus here designates some particular year, when Good Friday fell on the 31st or' March. Garencières upon this notes that it falls on the 23rd of March, called Gothic, because adhered to by the northern nations long after the Gregorian had been adopted at Rome. I do not see how the 10th Calend could ever fall on the 31st, nor indeed what the 31st has to do with the matter. Those who arc more familiar with such calculations may perhaps explain. Like the witches' Sabbath, these diabolic meetings were accompanied by the lewdest rites, as will at once be seen by the following passage from Psellus, which I leave untranslated. It is from the Latin translation of Psellus by Marsilius Ficinus, and will be found in his collected works (ii. 884) in folio ed. 1641.

"Euchetæ et gnosci, ut dæmonia toto concipiant pectore, nefanda sacrificia perpetrant Conveniunt die quo passus est Salvator, 1 vespere, statutur in locum, unà cum puellis sibi notis, et post quædam sacra extinctis luminibus, 2 mistim coëunt, sive cum sorore, sive cum filiâ, sive cum quâlibet" (Psellus as above, p. 894).

"There is a further kind of vaticination by a basin, by means of which rustics frequently predict. just as there is a mode of predicting by means of the air and the leaves of trees, so there is a kind of predictive power in the basin, known and practised by the Assyrians, which has a great similarity to this incarnation or coupling of demons with matter. Thus those about to prophesy take a basin full of water, which attracts the spirits moving stealthily in the depths (dæmonibus congruentem in profunda repentibus.) Le Pelletier translates this, (appropié à l'usage des démons cachés au fond des eaux). The basin then, full of water, seems in sort to breathe (or move) as with sounds (s'il allait émettre des sons); it seems to me that the water was agitated with circular ripples, as from some sound emitted below. Now, this water diffused through the basin differs but little in kind from water out of the basin, but yet it much excels it from a virtue imparted to it by the charms [that have been droned over it], and which have rendered it more apt to receive the spirit of prophecy. For this description of spirit is tetchy and terrene, and much under the influence of composite spells. When the water begins to lend itself as the vehicle of sound, he [the spirit] also presently gives out a thin reedy note [of satisfaction], but devoid of meaning; and close upon that, whilst the water is undulating, certain weak and peeping sounds whisper forth predictions of the future. A spirit of this kind is vagrant everywhere, for he is endowed with the solar pass [so that our terrestrial atmosphere lies everywhere open to him], and that order of spirits, in the work appointed to it, speaks at all times with a subdued voice, that by its indistinct obscurity it may be less easy to seize the falsehoods that it utters" (Psellus as above, p. 885).

From the mode in which Psellus describes the matter in hand, it is very perceptible that he was no great conjuror, and was merely speaking upon hearsay and report. If lies were the business of the spirit, he would be no prophet. Again, if he wished to circulate lies, he must still make things clear enough to his votaries for them to circulate them and work mischief thereby. Are we to suppose that, like an abandoned human being, he had some sense of shame left still, and, like Lord John Russell, would only tell as few lies as possible? Psellus's demon is so foolish that he would soon have been without any one to consult his shrine. He could not have given a reason for his own conduct, in the past or present, and was the last being that any one would resort to to anticipate intelligence of the future. Still the procedure might have been somewhat as Psellus describes it, although the reasons could not.

An historian of the fourth century, and a man of veracity, Marcellinus has given us curious details of how prophetical tripods were considered by the Romans in his day. It comes out quite naturally in the judicial proofs investigating a conspiracy against the life of Valens the Emperor; what we should call a state trial. The conspirators were put to the torture, and as an item in the indictment the figure of j little table becomes prominent, as to which the accused were questioned by the judges. At last one of them, Hillarius, broken by pain, revealed the secret in these words:

"Honoured judges, we constructed this unfortunate little table that you see here after the fashion of the tripod [or, more strictly, the cauldron 1] at Delphi, with dark incantations, out of branches of laurel; and with imprecations of secret song, and numerous ceremonies repeated over daily, we consecrated it by magic rites, till at last we put it in motion. When it reached this capacity of movement, as often as we wished to interrogate it by secret inquiry, we proceeded thus.

It was placed in the middle of a room (in medio domûs) purified throughout by Arabian perfumes; a round dish was simply laid upon it, formed of a composite material of many metals. On the phlange of its outer round were skilfully engraved the scriptile forms of the alphabet separated into as many exactly measured spaces. Over this basin (or dish) a man stood clothed in linen garments and shod with linen socks, his head bound round with a turban-like tuft of hair, and bearing a rod of vervain, the prospering plant. After we had favourably conciliated the deity, who is the giver of all presage, with duly formulated charms and ceremonial knowledge, he communicated a gentle movement to a ring that hung suspended over the basin.... This was tied up by an exceedingly fine Carpathian thread, which had been initiated with mystical observances. This ring, moving by little leaps or jumps, so as to alight upon the distinct intervals with the separate letters inscribed, each in its compartment to itself, gives out in heroic verse answers suitable to the inquiries made, comprehended perfectly in number and measure; such as are called Pythic, or those delivered by the oracles of the Branchidæ.

"To us inquiring who should succeed to the present empire, because it had been already mentioned that it would be one entirely suitable [to our aim and purpose], the leaping ring had glanced upon the two syllables THEO. With the last addition of a letter [that is, D], a man present exclaimed, 'THEODORUM,' the fatal necessity of the portent indicating as much. Nothing further was sought upon this head; for it was agreed amongst us that this was the individual we wanted" (Ammianus Marcellinus, Return Gestarum, xxix. 1).

In this case the ambiguity of the oracle is due to the precipitance of the inquirers. The oracle was true as far as they allowed it to proceed, but had they waited to spell it out they would have learned that the name was not THEODorus, but THEODosius the Great, who was to be the successor to Valens.

This is an authentic passage of high interest. It shows considerable analogy with the table-turning of the moderns; it also gives insight into singular and elaborate processes of divination by magic as being frequently practised at Rome in the fourth century. Clearly the Pagans had no notion in that century that oracles had at all finally ceased on a Good Friday in the first century, or that Pan, the god of rumour, was dead. The sun still shone to them as the Apollo of prophecy, and they still sought presage of a spirit who was made free of the solar order (qui solarem ordinem est sortitus). Footnotes

68:1 Romance tongue, sele for selle, tripod seat, tripode æneo, such as the priestess of Apollo or Pythia sat on to deliver oracles.

68:2 Latin, prosperare, to succeed, or realize an experience.

68:3 Qui for ce qui.

69:1 Latin, virga, branch or wand.

69:2 Latin, limbus, hem, border, fringe.

69:3 Latin, per, in, or through.

74:1 Ex Michaele Psello, de Dæmonibus. Works of Marsilius Ficinus, ii. 884, ed. 1641, folio.

75:1 This refers to some Good Friday evening on the 10th Calend of April Old Style, as set forth in the first line of this quatrain.

75:2 This is exhibited in the third line of the quatrain: Le feu estainct, assemblée diabolique.

77:1 Æneid, iii. 92 and vi. 347.

Historical Fragments

I SHALL now give a few detached historical fragments that relate to France, commencing with the Peace of Cateau-Cambresis, 1559, and running down to the death of Louis XV., 1774, in chronological order, just as M. le Pelletier has found the counterpart to lie embedded in the quatrains of Nostradamus, in a fashion seemingly interpretable to him. This, for any but French readers, will probably be sufficient to indicate the style and value of the presages enveloped in the strange and fatidical diction of the quatrains. I doubt not but that, by original research instituted and by careful re-reading of the text throughout, a good many more of the mysterious stanzas might be unravelled and elucidated; also by collation of all that has been written by commentators on our author, a good deal of light might be thrown upon what they have done, even where their own interpretation has fallen short of clearness. All that my book purposes to accomplish is,—at least for England,—to establish, without doubt, and at once, for all future time, that Nostradamus is no impostor, but, when rightly understood and unlocked, a very wonderful anticipator of events to happen hereafter; and, farther than this, that his works are, to all intents and purposes, the most startling oracles ever put on paper by mortal man not professing divine inspiration. From immemorial time instances of human prescience have occasionally been manifested. The whole human race has an ardent and ingrain desire to search into and anticipate futurity. Very few individuals, however, have from time to time been able to gratify and keep alive their passion in this respect. But no one has done so in a degree that at all sets him on a par with Nostradamus in the felicitous and reiterated coruscations whereby he has anticipated the more prominent points and epochs of time Future; and sometimes in minuteness he even mentions by name some individual who emerges though it be but for an instant from the general obscurity of his life.

THE PEACE OF CATEAU-CAMBRESIS (APRIL 3, 1559). [I. 71.]
Century IX.—Quatrain 52.
La paix s'approche d'un costé, et la guerre
Oncques 1 ne fut la poursuitte si grande:
Plaindre hômes, femmes, sang innocent par terre,
Et ce sera de France a 2 toute bande.
 Translation
Peace approaches on one side, and [as to] war
Never was the pursuit of it so great:
Men and women [have cause] to weep innocent blood on earth;
All through France it shall be from end to end.

The peace was that concluded with Spain at Cateau-Cambresis, whilst the war, carried on with such hot pursuit, was the civil conflict that raged between Romanist and Calvinist. This it was made men and women lament the blood spilt upon the earth in all parts of France, from north to south.

DEATH OF HENRI 11. (JULY 10, 1559). [I. 72.]
 Century I.—Quatrain 35.
 Le lyon jeune le vieux surmontera
 En champ bellique par singulier duelle:p. 81
 Dans cage d'or 1 les yeux lui crevera,
 Deux classes 2 une, 3 puis mourir, mort cruelle.
 Translation.
 The young lion shall overcome the old
 On the field of war in single combat [duelle];
 He will pierce his eyes in a cage of gold.
 This is the first of two loppings, then he dies a cruel death.

Montgomery, who at the moment of the narrative bore the name of Captain Coryes (Garencières, p. 25), afterwards became Earl of Montgomery, overthrew Henri II. (le vieux lion) in the tournay-lists or duel, and pierced him above the eye through the gilt visor of his helmet. This is the first of the two blows that will destroy the dynastic tree of the house of Valois. Henri II., wounded mortally, shall be the first to die a violent death; whilst his son, Henri III., will be the second, who fell by the hand of Jacques Clément.
 August 1. 1589.
 This is a very celebrated quatrain. It is found in the earliest edition of the quatrains published at Lyons in 1555, containing merely 300 quatrains. It lifted Nostradamus into celebrity at once. He had applied it to Henri II. several years before it happened, and had even announced it as a prediction to the King himself. He was well known to Henri II., to whom he dedicated the last three Centuries, in a long and curious epistle, which we have already given in full. The, King seems to have had infinite confidence in Nostradamus, for he let him draw the royal horoscope, as well as that of his two children, in 1556.
 The story of this is curious, as given by Guynaud in his "Concordance des Prophéties de Nostradamus," 1712, 1 pp. 86-91. Henri II., it would seem, proclaimed a tournament in the Rue St. Antoine, the site of the Bastille, then in the country, for July 1, 1559, in honour of the marriage of his daughter Elizabeth of France with Philip II. of Spain. He listed himself as one against all comers. The joust being nearly over and the sun setting, the Duc de Savoie begged him to quit the running, as his side was already victorious; but the King wanted to break another lance over it, and commanded the young Comte de Montgommeri, captain of his Scotch Guard, to run a tilt in conclusion. He excused himself, but the King insisted and grew angry. Of course the young man then obeyed, put spurs to his horse, and struck the King upon the throat, below the vizor. His lance shivered, and the butt raising the vizor, a splinter wounded the King above the right eye, cutting several of the veins of the pia mater. The King swooned. He lived on, however, for ten days in terrible agony, as foretold in the prophecy, Deux classes une, puis mourir, mort cruelle. Nostradamus styles both of them lions, as they both fought under that device. The King wore a gilt helmet, so that the cage d'or was literally fulfilled.
 The strange part is that another astrologer, named Luc Gauric, had once been visited by the King in company with two other gentlemen, to whom he feigned to give precedence; but the astrologer, perhaps knowing him, insisted on addressing him first, and told him he would die in a duel. He also prophesied a violent death to the King's companions, and managed to displease the whole trio. The King said of this, "We are making peace now with the King of Spain,

so it is not very likely that I shall challenge him, and as a king I could in no other way be challenged, whatever may be the fate of the other gentlemen." Guynaud quotes this story from the Princesse de Clèves, who, in the second volume of her writings, represents the Court as discussing the credibility of astrologers, the prevalent opinion apparently being rather strong against them. Still, we know that Henri II. greatly honoured Nostradamus. Prophetic warning is evidently futile, for the King had two separate warnings and heeded neither.

PRINCESSE DE CLÈVES. [II. 145.]

Quelques jours après, le Roy étoit chez la Reine à l'heur du Cercle; l'on parla des Horoscopes et des prédictions. Les opinions étaient partagées sur la croyance que l'on y devoit dormer. La Reine y ajoûtait beaucoup de foi; elle soûtint qu'après tant de choses qui avaient été prédites, et que l'on avait vu arriver, on ne pouvait douter qu'il n'eut quelque certitude dans cette science. D'autres soûtenaient, que parmi ce nombre infini de prédictions, le pea qui se trouvaient veritables, faisait bien voir que se n'etait qu'un effet du hazard.

"J'ai eu autrefois beaucoup de curiosité pour l'avenir," dit le Roy; "mais on m'a dit tant de choses fausses et si peu vraissemblables que je suis demuré convaincu que l'on ne peut rien savoir de véritable. Il y a quelques années qu'il devint ici un homme d'une grande reputation dans l'Astrologie. Tout le monde l'alla voir, j'y allai comme les autres, mais sans lui dire qui j'étais, et je menai Monsieur de Guise et Descars, je les fit passer le premier. L'Astrologue neanmoins s'addressa d'abord à moi, comme s'il m'eut jugé le maitre des autres: Peut-être qu'il me connaissait; cependant il me dit une chose qui ne me convenait pas, s'il m'eut connu. Il me predit que je serai tué en duel. Il dit ensuite à Monsieur de Guise, qu'il serait tué par derrière, et à Descars, qu'il aurait la tête cassée d'un coup de pied de cheval. Monsieur de Guise s'offensa quasi de cette prédiction, comme si l'on eut accusé de devoir fuir. Descars ne fut guerre satisfait de trouver qu'il devait finir par un accident si malheureux. Enfin nous sortimes tous très malcontents de l'astrologue. Je ne scais cc qui arrivera à Monsieur de Guise et à Descars, mais il n'y a guerre d'apparence que je sois tué en duel. Nous venons de faire la paix le Roy d'Espagne et moi; quand nous ne l'aurions pas faite, je doute que nous nous battions, et que je le fisse appeller comme le Roy men père fit rappeller Charles Quint."

The story, as told by the Princesse de Clèves, is fuller than I have given it, but does not correspond at all with the version given to Lord Bacon when in France, as told to him by Dr. Penn, who said (Bacon's "Essay on Prophecies") that the queen-mother, Catherine de Medici, was given to curious arts, and caused the King's nativity to be cast under a false name. The astrologer adjudged that he should be killed in a duel. The queen laughed, supposing her husband to be above challenges to duel; "but he was slain upon a course at tilt, the splinters of the staff of Montgomery going in at his beaver." History, in events large or small, hath so many variants that any man, whose view of things is a little sinister, may well be allowed to say all history is a variant of truth, and all that is sure in it is that it cannot be relied upon at all. In this case the astrologers were right, spite of the odds against them.

ARREST OF MONTGOMERY (May 27, 1574). [I. 73.]
Century III.—Quatrain 30.
Celuy qu'en 1 luitte 2 et fer au faict bellique
Aura porté 3 plus grand qui luy le prix,
De nuict au lict six luy feront la pique,

Nud, sans harnois, subit 4 sera surprins. 5
 Translation.
To him who in strife and armour in the warlike field
Shall have carried away the prize from one greater than himself,
By night in bed six men will stab him;
Unprotected he will be surprised naked and unarmed.

This means that Montgomery, who in joust (au faict bellique,—bellique, we are told, means an engagement on horseback) with lance in hand will have carried away the prize from Henri II. (plus grand que luy) will be suddenly surprised in bed at night, naked and unarmed, by six men, who will deliver him into the vengeful hands of Catherine de Medici.

Some say the dying King gave him free pardon; others report that he fled to England to save himself: but at any rate he came to England, and there embraced Protestantism. When he returned to France, he placed himself at the head of the revolted Huguenots in Normandy, and was besieged in Domfront by the Marshal de Matignon and a large force, to which he was obliged to surrender. The terms of the sur, render guaranteed his life, but by express command of Catherine he was arrested in his own castle of Domfront on the night of May 27, 1574, by six gentlemen of the royal army, and carried to the Château of Caen, thence to the Conciergerie at Paris, and there immured, where the great tower still goes by his name.

THE REGENCY OF CATHERINE DE MEDICI (1559-1574). [I. 74.]
 Century VI.—Quatrain 63.
La Dame seule au regne demeurée,
D'unic esteint premier au lict d'honneur;
Sept ans sera de douleur esplorée,
Puis longue vie au regne par grand heur.
 Translation.
The lady shall remain to rule alone,
Her unique spouse dead, who was first in the field of honour.
She will weep for grief through seven long years,
And gifted with long life will reign long.

Catherine de Medici did not put off her weeds till. August 1, 1566, seven years and a few days from the death of the King in July, 1559. on her return from a progress with her son Charles IX., in the course of which she had visited all the mutinous cities throughout the kingdom, with a view to satisfy them. She survived till the year 1589, and practically retained the whole power during the reigns of her two eldest sons, François II. and Charles IX., but she entirely lost it on the succession of Henri III.

The quatrain applies to no one so well as to Catherine de Medici; and, if it be allowed to be realized as to her person, there is no denying the singular exactitude of the prophecy. We have no evidence that the Queen applied the quatrain to herself, or that her contemporaries bore it in mind; but the second line is remarkable as assuming with reposeful confidence the previous death of the King as predicted. The third line is a startling example of the precision with which our prophet can mark out the duration of a period: seven years the Queen is to wear mourning, and she does so all the time she is travelling. The sceptical will say she did it to fulfil the prophecy; but it looks rather as if that had fallen quite out of remembrance, and as if it was due much more to policy, and for the purpose of creating sympathy, during her state tour, than to motives either of superstition or any singular attachment to her deceased husband. The quatrain is most unobtrusively worded, and yet so confidently assured and searching, that it seems to me, as if perfectly unbiassed and disinterested observers might take it as a kind of moral voucher for the simple integrity of its author. I merely draw attention to it so far, and every reader will form his own judgment upon the point. I hold myself aloof from theory; but this is how the particular fact we are upon impresses my mind, and probably it may affect many others in the same way.

EXTINCTION DES VALOIS (1559-1589). [I. 77]
Presage 40.
De maison Sept par mort mortelle suite;
Gresle, tempeste, pestilent mal, fureurs:
Roi d'Orient, d'Occident tous en fuite,
Subjuguera ses jadis conquereurs.
Translation.
The death of the house of seven by a suite of deaths.
Hail, tempest, pestilence evil, fury.
A king of the East will put all the West to flight,
And will subdue his at-one-time conquerors.

The house of Valois consisted of the seven children of Henri II. By the death of the fourth son, Henri III., in 1589, the whole of the seven were dead except Marguerite, who married Henri IV., so that the family may well be said to have died out by a suite of deaths (mortelle suite). Heresy was rampant (pestilent mal) and civil war. Soliman II., called the Magnificent, threatened all Christendom, and recovered all the Holy Places that the Crusaders had wrested from his predecessors.

CIVIL WAR (1575, 1576). [I. 78.]
Century VI.—Quatrain 11.
Des septs rameaux à trois seront reduicts,
Les plus aisnés seront surprins 1 par mort,
Fratricider les deux seront seduicts
Les conjurés en dormans seront morts.
Translation.
The seven branches when they shall be reduced to three,
And the four eldest shall have been surprised by death,
The two (males) shall entertain fratricidal aims,
And the conspirators sleeping shall be reduced to death.

This means that, when the seven are become but three (i.e. the three youngest), Henri III. and the Duc d'Alençon will enter upon a fratricidal war. In 1575 Alençon escaped from the Court, where he was under surveillance, and put himself at the head of the Malcontents, who were in alliance with the Huguenots. He was successful, and forced the edict of pacification, May 14, 1576, upon his brother the King. Daniel, in his "History of France" under Henri III., shows that they mutually sought each other's death by dagger and poison. The Guise (les conjurés) and the Leaguers will come by their deaths from indulging in a false security.

THE MURDER OF HENRI III. (1589). [I. 79.]
Century V.—Quatrain 67.
Quand chef Perouse n'osera sa tunique,
Sans au couvert tout nud s'expolier. 1
Seront prins 2 sept, faict aristocratique!
Le père et fils morts par poincte au colier.
Translation.
When the chief of Perouse dare not risk casting off his tunic
Without stripping himself entirely naked,
The last of the seven taken, what an event in the upper circles!
Father and son killed by a stab in the throat.

When Sixtus V. (chef de Perouse) will not dare to excommunicate Henri III., having already lost England in 1534, and feeling he must not be entirely stripped by a further Gallican schism, will be rid of the posterity of Henri II. (seront Prins sept) by a tremendous event in aristocratic circles. Father and son will both perish by a thrust in the throat.

DEATH OF THE GUISE (DECEMBER 23, 24, 1588). [I. 80.]
Century IV.—Quatrain 60.
Les sept enfans en hostaine 3 laissés;
Le tiers 4 viendra son enfant trucider 5;
Deux par son fils seront d'estoc percés;
Gennes Florence les viendra enconder. 6
Translation.
Seven children will be left in his house;
The tiers état will come to murder his child;
Two will have been pierced by the sword of his son;
Genoa and Florence will come to disorder them.

This is, Henri II. at his death will leave seven children in his house. The Conseil des Seize (le tiers) will incite Jacques Clément to go to St. Cloud to assassinate Henri III., because he has caused Henri de Guise and the Cardinal to be slain by sword thrusts. Then Charles Emmanuel I., Duke of Savoy (le Génois), and Alexander Farnese, Duke of Parma (le Florentin), General of Philip II., will come to make war on Henri IV., who will be compelled by Farnese to raise the siege of Paris (1590) and Rouen (1592) with precipitation.

Parma was, originally, of Etruscan foundation (Bouillet, "Dictionnaire d'Histoire" s.v. Parme), and in this respect rises above Florence, the capital of Modern Tuscany. This justifies Nostradamus in designating the Duke of Parma as Florence. Genoa, by synecdoche, may stand for Savoy, as being its more commercial emporium.

BURIAL AT ST. DENIS OF THE LAST OF THE VALOIS (1589-1610). [I. 82.]
Century I.—Quatrain 10.
Serpens 1 transmis en la cage de fer
Où les enfans septains du Roy sont pris,
Les vieux et peres sortiront bas 2 de l'enfer, 3
Ains mourir voir de fruict mort et cris.

Translation.
The coffin being lowered behind the grille of iron,
Where the seven children of the King are buried,
The ancestors of the Valois will rise from the depths of the tomb,
And cry out to see their withered fruit thus die.

Henri III. was deposited, provisionally, in 1589, at Compiègne, in the Abbey of St. Corneille; and it was only in 1610 that his body was conveyed to the vaults of St. Denis, at the same time with the bodies of Henry IV. and Catherine de Medici. This quatrain is not very remarkable, but the interpretation hangs pretty well together. It has perhaps this value, that it shows us one incident in a vast procession of historical dissolving views that seem to have passed before the eye of Nostradamus, and one would say in chronological sequence, which he must himself have broken up purposely afterwards, fearing that the chronological clue would often render the prophecy too open to interpretation to be good for either his own safety or the public advantage.

MARRIAGE OF FRANÇOIS II. AND MARY STUART (APRIL 24, 1558). [I. 84.]
Century X.—Quatrain 39.
Premier fils vefve 1 malheureux marriage,
Sans nuts enfants, deux Isles en discord,
Avant dix-huict incompetant age. 2
De l'autre près 3 plus bas sera l'accord.
Translation.
The eldest son leaves, with his wretched marriage,
Widow, no children, and two isles in strife,
And dies before eighteen, incompetent of age.
The younger son will marry earlier still. 4
The matter seems to stand thus. François II., eldest son of Henri II., shall die and leave his wife, Mary Stuart, a widow without children, after an unhappy marriage that extends over less than two years, before he is eighteen, or of competent age. The particularity of this detail is wonderful, and far more like history than prophecy, except as to the brevity with which it is expressed. His enunciations amount to hints only, but they are so pregnant that, when you fill in the indispensably connected particulars, the statement reads like history. So here the instant you recognize that François II. is the subject of the lines, you refer to history for his birth and death, January 19, 1543, December 15, 1560—that is, 17 years, 10 months, and 15 days, or a month and 15 days short of 18 years. Avant dix-huict is Nostradamus's phrase. Again, his death establishes discord between Elizabeth of England and Mary of Scotland (deux Isles en discord). Charles IX., his younger brother, was affianced to Elizabeth of Austria when still younger, at eleven years of age, though he did not marry till twenty. This is how M. le Pelletier harmonizes the line. But, as affiancing is not marriage, this cannot have any affinity at all with marrying at an incompetent age. I should propose to read the line thus. Of the younger one afterwards, and lower down, will the concordance, account, or accord be given; and accordingly we shall have now to enter upon several stanzas that relate to Charles IX.

CHARLES IX. (Le roi farouche). (1560-1574). [I. 86.]
Century III.—Quatrain 66.

Le grand Baillif d'Orleans mis a mort
Sera par un de sang vindicatif:
De mort mérité ne mourra ni par sort;
Des pieds et mains mal le faisoit captif.
Translation.
The great Bailiff of Orleans shall be put to death
By one of vindictive blood:
Not undeserved death shall he die, nor by fate;
For they will insecurely make him captive by feet and hands.

Jérôme Groslot shall be arrested November 9, 1561, and condemned by the Inquisition to beheadal for delivering the city to the Calvinists. But he will not suffer the death merited, nor undergo his fate; his keepers being bribed, he shall escape.

DEFECTION OF ADMIRAL COLIGNY (1559-1567). [I. 87.]
Century VI.—Quatrain 75.
Le grand pillot 1 par Roy sera mandé 2
Laisser la classe 3 pour plus haut lieu atteindre:
Sept ans après sera contrebandé, 4
Barbare armée viendra. Venise craindre. 5
Translation.
He who shall have been appointed admiral by the king,
Shall leave the fleet to take a higher post;
Seven years later, shall take the opposite side to the king;
Venice shall dread an army of barbarians coming.

Gaspard de Coligny, made grand-admiral by Henri II., in 1552, shall quit the fleet in 1559, on the death of the King, and place himself at the head of the Calvinist party. In 1562 he will be general of their forces, and in 1567—that is, seven years after withdrawal from the fleet, he will head the rebellion in the civil war. At the same moment Venice will dread the armies of Selim II., that will wrest Cyprus from her in 1570. The peace between the Catholics and Protestants was signed at St. Germain in this very year. The Venetians, however, in this year gained the naval victory of Lepanto over the Turks in 1570.

MURDER OF LOUIS DE BOURBON, PRINCE OF CONDE (MARCH 13, 1569). [I. 88.]
Century III.—Quatrain 41.
Bossu sera esleu par le conseil:
Plus hideux monstre en terre n'apperceu.
Le coup voulant crevera l'œil 1
Le traistre au Roy pour fidelle receu.
Translation.
Crookback shall be elected by the council:
A more hideous monster never seen on earth.
An intentional shot pierces the eve of the traitor
Who had sworn to be faithful to the king.

Prince Louis of Condé, the Humpback, shall be elected general-in-chief by the council of notables of the Calvinists. Such a monster of wickedness was never seen on earth. Montesquiou killed him with a pistol-shot in the eye, who had twice escaped from his treasonous practices against the King. Here Nostradamus' forecast is miraculously clear, although it has baffled Guynaud to find its concordance with events. He here also exhibits his religious partisanship, A hunchback is always considered to be morally as well as physically deformed; and, as Louis de Bourbon took the side of the Calvinists, he became at once to our prophet le plus hideux monstre en terre. Evidently, however, he was a grand fighting fellow, and spent his life in camps, if we go no further than Moreri for his history. He was condemned for a conspirator in 1560 to lose his head. But the sentence was never carried out, as King François II. died at the moment, and none was bold enough to see to it. When Charles IX. set him at liberty, the Cour des Pairs found out that he was innocent, and declared him so. He perished at the battle of Jarnac. He had his leg broken by the kick of a horse, and was seated at the foot of a bush when Montesquiou, captain of the Duke of Anjou's guards, saw him, and, for some old pique, coolly, but like the veriest coward, shot the wounded Condé in the eye with his pistol. The body was conveyed for burial to St. George of Vendôme, either by chance or insult, on the back of a she ass, at Jarnac; which led to one of those impromptu epitaphial epigrams that the French turn so prettily:

L'an mil cinq cens soixante neuf,
Entre Jarnac et Chateauneuf,
Fut porté mort sur une ânesse
Le grand ennemi de la Messe.   (V. MORERI, s.v. Louis de Bourbon.)

ST. BARTHOLOMEW'S DAY (AUGUST 24, 1572). [I. 89.]
Century IV.—Quatrain 47.
Le Noir 1 farouche, quand aura essayé
Sa main sanguine par feu, fer, arcs tendus, 2
Trestous le peuple sera tant 3 effrayé
Voir les plus grans par col et pieds pendus.
Translation.
The savage king, when he shall have tried
His blood-stained hand with fire, sword, and bows,
All the people shall be terrified
To see the great hung by the neck and feet.

When Charles IX. shall exercise his sanguinary hand with fire, the sword, and the arquebus, the people will be horrified to see the great Calvinist lords strung up by the neck and feet. One of the savage amusements of Charles, in hunting, was to cut off at a single blow the heads of any asses or pigs he came across on the way. During the very massacre he placed himself at a window of the Louvre and took several shots with a long arquebus at the Huguenots who fled from the other side of the Seine in the Faubourg St. Germain. The body of Coligny was dragged by the populace, at the end of a rope, through all the mud of the kennels, and then hung up by one foot to the gibbet at Montfaucon. This 24th of August fell on a Sunday. The King himself died two years after, with some suspicion of poisoning. He is said to have been a man of high courage and of a lively, quick wit, possessing a good share of eloquence; was given much to dissimulation; and full of oaths, unreasonably violent, and without self-control. He turned a verse well, and loved hunting. His poems still remain, but I do not know they can ever command a single reader. In speaking of poets, he used to say they ought to be well fed, like good horses, but not satisfied, or they become lazy. The world in general prefers to starve them if they are first-rate, and enrich them if they are second-rate. We cannot expect people to reward what they cannot understand: though inevitable, we cannot but deplore the arrangement. With good abilities, Charles had so little judgment that his actions would always have been mischievous; the best thing that could have happened was his death at twenty-four. He is said to have remarked, when dying, that he was glad to die young and have no children, for he had sadly learnt, in his own case, how miserable is the conduct of a prince who mounts the throne a child, and so governs through the ministry of others. This only shows a little recovery to sober reason, but none of the remorse that is attributed to him on his death-bed, as being the ostensible author of the blackest act that has ever disfigured Christianity or stained Europe. In perfidy and crime it cannot be surpassed, nor as the outcome of religious perversion. The crimes of an atheistic democracy, perpetrated two hundred years later on the same theatre precisely, have only been able to surpass it, in the carnal lusts exhibited, in the inhuman degradation of the body of man, and in the ubiquity of iniquity, when the whole people are thirsting to satiate their debased passions in sin. Nostradamus has elsewhere called Paris the City of the Sword. It is the wine-press of the earth, fat with the blood of man: Lutetia of mud and blood. Haussmann rebuilt it, but nothing can cleanse it. Their very guillotine is an instrument contrived to publicly gratify the populace in its tiger-taste for the reek of blood in the streets of the City of Blood. If you wish to see the disgrace of religion, read Sully's description of the endeavour of the ferocious priests on that day to have his blood. Look also on the medal of Gregory XIII., 1 struck rejoicingly to commemorate that awful crime. Bonanni shows it; and, as a work of medallic art, the head of the Pope is of the very highest order of beauty and Italian grace. But, then, it commemorates the blood of sixty thousand victims, he says. Ranke (ii. 69) puts it at fifty thousand. Take this number, if you like; it is, enough to satisfy the successor to St. Peter, to whom the special mandate was addressed, "Feed my sheep,"—as other shepherds do for the butcher, is the Gregorian gloss. Trades. men, however, have the decency to shut the shambles on the Sunday morning; but the servus servorum is at home in his ministrations on the Dominical day. That Sunday in August is indeed a Saints' rubric! For that day there is no need of a calendar. Time, till the world ruptures, can never forget it,—nor forgive.

Le noir farouche of this quatrain is, by Guynaud, p. 113, said to stand for Admiral Coligny, who is designated, according to him, very variously in the quatrains. The noir farouche alludes to his rough and forbidding exterior. Le grand Pillot (VI. 75) is another epithet; le tiran (Présage III.) another. The conclusion of the quatrain is admitted, both by Le Pelletier and Guynaud, to stand for Coligny. In the earlier portion, most will, I think, prefer to take noir as the anagram of Roi.

Guynaud gives a surprising account from the historians of Provence and France, of what happened to Coligny when he was at Angoulême in 1568. He set up a gibbet there, and on his own authority hanged upon it Michel Grêlet, Guardian of the Cordéliers, and a most zealous preacher against the heretics. In his dying speech on the scaffold, the latter said, "Admiral, you put me to death very unjustly. I am going to God now to give account to Him of my actions; but remember, you and all the people present here to-day, I predict that in a short time you will yourself be thrown from an upper window, and your body will be cut to pieces." The histories go on to say that an Italian cut off Coligny's head to send it to Cardinal de Lorraine at Rome, whilst other men cut off his hands and other parts of his body; also that at about six in the morning the mob found his body on a dunghill in a stable, dragged it to the Seine, and threw it in. It was again fished out, and hung by the foot to the gibbet of Montfaucon, where it became blackened in the smoke of the fires that were lighted below it. (Guynaud, "Concord. Nostra.," p. 113.)

Sixain 52. [I. 90.]
La grand' Cité qui n'a pain à demy
Encor un coup la Sainct Barthelemy
Engravera au profond de son ame:
Nismes, Rochelle, Geneve et Montpellier,
Castres, Lyon, Mars entrant au Belier,
S'entrebattront; le tout pour une Dame.
Translation.
The great city that has bread at only half rations
Will have the further blow of Saint Bartholomew
Cut deep into its soul:
Nismes, Rochelle, Geneva, and Montpellier,
Castres, Lyons, with Mars entering the Ram,
Will fight one another; and all for the Queen mother.

The great city is, of course, Paris, and une Dame is the Queen, Catherine de Medici. It has to be borne in mind that these sixains were not published till thirty-three years after the massacre of St. Bartholomew's. Naturally, the prediction loses all special authority in this case. It raises, however, a singular question: Why, if it was written after the event, it was not rendered more explicit, if those who published it had an interest in augmenting the fame of the prophet? It looks very much as if the testamentary duties were performed in perfect good faith, mechanically, and without even understanding the purport or meaning of the words.

Another passage relating to St. Bartholomew's massacre occurs in the text of 1605, and its authority is no greater than that of the sixain just quoted, as it was not published till after the event. It goes, however, to strengthen the remark I above made. Those who caused the work to be printed seem to have been perfectly unconscious of the meaning of the stanzas; they regarded the whole procedure as a mere form of respect to the memory of a celebrated relative. Their duty was clear to them, and they performed it; but the writings were to them perfectly unintelligible.

Presage III. (ii. 252) is dated as if written January, 1555 and for anything that I can see there is nothing whatever to make one doubt but that it was so. Having made this point as clear as I can, the reader will take it or reject it as he pleases.

Le gros airain qui les heures ordonne,
Sur le trespas du Tyran cassera: 1
Pleurs, plaintes et cris, eaux, glace pain ne dônc
V. S. C. 2 paix l'arme passera.
Translation.
The brazen bell that rings the daily hours
Will play full volley at the tyrant's death:

Tears, cries, and groans; the waters freeze up bread,
With son of Charles the Fifth a peace is made.

The tyrant here is interpreted by Guynaud (p. 107) a. Coligny, and he appends some interesting remarks from Favin's "Histoire de Navarre," touching St. Bartholomew's Day In Paris. He says they marked the lodgings of the Huguenots that they might know where to find them in the hurry, and it was arranged that at the tocsin of the great bell at the palace, as well as that of the church of St. Germain de l'Auxerrois, they were to lay violent hands (mainbaisse) on all the heretics. Two p.m. was the hour appointed. The Catholics who went into the street were to distinguish themselves by a white cross upon their hats. The bodies of the slain were for the most part thrown into the river. Mezerai records that the queen-mother hastened the signal by a full hour, and that it was, contrary to arrangement, started by the bell of St. Germain de l'Auxerrois, although that was immediately followed up by the big bell of the palace.

Coligny was slain in bed, and flung out of window in his shirt only. His face, being covered with blood, the Duc de Guise coolly wiped it with his handkerchief, to assure himself that it actually was Coligny. We shall shortly see this bloodthirsty villain himself murdered at Blois.

The massacre continued the whole week through, for seven days that is, but the chief fury had spent itself by Tuesday night. The Janus Gallicus professes, though how Aimé could have any certainty of it I cannot tell, that Nostradamus, by tyran, alludes to Coligny, and says that the bell tolled so long that it broke. The quatrain does not necessitate the supposal of any such thing, and I believe the fact is not elsewhere recorded. Of course, if it be, it would be so literal a fulfilment that all the sceptical world would immediately take advantage of what I have pointed out, that this is a prophecy après coup. If so doing should rejoice anybody, I can only say that he has my consent. My business is to put the facts, without a shred of disguise, before the reader; he can weave them into theories for himself. If I at any time manifest what I think, he will be pleased to accept it merely as a contribution towards the same end.

In January, 1572, the river Seine was frozen over for a long time, and the roads became almost impassable. This may perhaps be thought to interpret eaux glace pain ne dône, with such hieroglyphic symbolism of scarcity as oracular utterance delights in. It is pretty certain that provisions did not enter Paris that winter with their usual flow. In allusion to the army mentioned, Guynaud says that the Duc d'Anjou marched with fifty thousand men to the siege of Rochelle, where, after firing thirteen thousand shots, they at last effected a breach. What they battered down, oddly enough, was the Boulevard of the Gospel (Boulevard de l'Évangile), but they could not storm it, and lost twenty thousand men without taking the place.

In that eulogium on Catherine de Medici which de Brantôme ("Panthéon Littéraire," ii. 116) calls her Life, he relates that she died of a broken heart, from grief at having consented to the massacre on this ill-starred day, and that without intending it she (p. 133) had invited the nobles and lords of the land to gather to it. The Cardinal de Bourbon said to her, "Madam, you have brought us all to the butchery without intending it." This touched her to the quick; she took to her bed and never left it again. One can only say this does not quite accord with Mezerai and her sounding the tocsin an hour earlier by anticipation. Further, as the massacre took place in 1572, and the queen-mother did not die at Blois till 1589, seventeen years after, her heart resisted grief much as granite does vinegar. The lady must originally have possessed a very good heart. De Brantôme says poison was talked of; but he considers the broken heart more likely.

CIVIL WAR UNDER HENRI III. (1559-1589). [I. 93.]
Century III.—Quatrain 55.
En l'an qu'un œil en France regnera
La Cour sera en un bien fascheux trouble:
Le Grand de Blois son amy tuera;
Le regne mis en mal et doute double.
Translation.
In the year when a one-eyed man shall reign in France
The Court shall be in very vexatious trouble:
The great one of Blois shall kill his friend;
The Kingdom, plunged into evil and doubt, shall divide in two.

M. le Pelletier's version here seems to be a little forced. The one-eyed man he makes to be Henri II., whose eye was destroyed by Montgomery's lance. The Court is to be in great embarrassment. Henri III. (le Grand de Blois) will convoke at that place the States-General, and will there assassinate the Duc de Guise, first taking with him, in Italian fashion, the Holy Communion, as a sign of entire reconciliation, Then the desolated kingdom will divide into two camps—the Royalists on one side, and the Leaguers On the other.

REGENCY OF CATHERINE DE MEDICI (1537-,574). [I. 94.]
Century VI.—Quatrain 29.
La vefve 1 saincte entendent les nouvelles
De ses rameaux mis en perplex et trouble:
Qui 2 sera duict 3 appaiser 4 les querelles
Par son pourchas 5 des razes 6 fera comble.
Translation.
The holy widow shall receive news
Of the difficulties that perplex and trouble her children;
He whom she calls home to quiet disturbances
Shall bring them to a crisis by his pursuit of shaven heads.

There is a little difficulty in applying the epithet saincte to the queen-mother, and Garencières supposes it to signify Roma la Santa; but, if so, the rest will have no meaning, Nostradamus is so entirely for Henri II., his wife, and the Romish Church, that in spite of his designating her son le roi farouche, he might think the term saincte not inappropriate to her. She sent a private despatch to her son, Henri III., to hurry back from Poland, as we shall see him doing in the next quatrain cited, that he may take the direction of the French Government. He enters into an alliance with Henri IV. and the Huguenots to counterbalance the Catholic League. Thence follows the murder of the Cardinal, brother of the Duc de Guise, who was murdered by the King's order on December 24,1588, one day after his brother. This is the prosecution of the Church (pourchas des razes), coupled with the repression of the League, which culminates the crisis. The only jarring word in this concordance, when once it is comprehended, lies in the word saincte, to which I have already drawn attention, and which may be explained by the devotion felt by Nostradamus to the crown of France and to Rome. It is evident that Brantôme was able to regard her as a most admirable and lovable lady. The tocsin and the blood spoil our appreciation.

HENRI III. RENOUNCES POLAND (JUNE 26, 1574). [I. 96.]
Century VII.—Quatrain 35.
Le grande Pesche 1 viendra plaindre, 2 plorer
D'avoir esleu: trompés seront en l'âge:p. 104
Guiere 1 avec eux ne voudra demourer:
Deceu 2 sera par ceux de son langage.
Translation.
The great gambler 3 shall complain and weep
To have elected him: deceived in his age:
The duke had no desire to stay with them:
He will be slain by men of his own tongue.

Poland, then, will deplore having elected the Duc d'Anjou n 1573, for he stayed only one year with them, and absconded on the 26th of June at night, at his mother's summons, to France. The Comte de Fanchin, the Grand Chamberlain, was sent after him, and overtook him at Piesna, a frontier town in Austria, but the duke was deaf to all intercession (Guynaud, p. 119). He never took the Polish throne because he wished it, but because he was pressed by the Court of France; and now French affairs called him back. Guynaud thinks that the last line means that his friends deceived him into taking it; but this is because he did not discover the Latin meaning in deceu. For certainly Nostradamus meant that he would go home to die by Clement's hand, as he shows in as many words a little later on. Guynaud says that Poland had been deceived as to the prince's age, and that he was represented to be much older than he really was.

EDICT OF POITIERS (OCTOBER 3, 1577). [I. 97.]
Century V.—Quatrain 72.
Pour le plaisir d'edict voluptueux,
On mestera le poison dans la foy:
Venus sera en cours si vertueux, 1
Qu'obfusquera du soleil tout aloy. 2
Translation.
To pass an edict of a sugared sort,
They'll mingle poison with our holy faith:
And Venus darken, in her course robust,
All law and light from out the sacred Sun.

The Sun, in Nostradamus, often stands for the Church or Christianity, by him believed to be within the palisade of Popery. It might also mean France, whose King's name was Rex Christianissimus. Louis XIV. assumed the device of the sun, with the motto nec pluribus impar. Venus stands for sensual pleasure—the world triumphant over the Church. The edict of Poitiers, October 8, 1577, So far favoured the Protestants that they were authorized to hold public services on the reformed footing. Calvinist ministers might marry, and auricular confession was suppressed. Thus did Henri III. mingle the poison of unchastity, etc., with the Catholic faith. The licence of morals (Vénus) became unbridled and tarnished the law of Christendom (Soleil).

Guynaud interprets with Le Pelletier in this, and considers the poison to consist particularly in freeing the Huguenots from the Sacrifice of Penance; in condemning the monastic orders; in encouraging unchastity, by allowing the Calvinist ministers to marry; in abandoning confession. Vénus sera is a line showing that many monks will quit the cloisters to indulge in marriage and other debauchery. The last line may be understood, that the glory of the King will be tarnished, and make him to be ill thought of by the Catholics; or that it will obscure faith in the Church (p. 122).

JOURNÉE DES BARRICADES (MAY 12, 1588). [I. 98.]
 Century III.—Quatrain 50.
La republique de la grande cité
A grand rigueur ne voudra consentir:
Roy sortir hors par trompette cité,
L'eschelle an mur la cité repentir.
 Translation.
The Republic of the great city (Paris)
Would not submit itself to the very rigorous treatment;
The King summoned by trumpet to quit the city,
Which is called to repent by the ladder at the wall.

This quatrain and the event it prefigures are alike wonderful. Garencières is much puzzled over it. What city has a commonwealth? Is it Venice, Genoa, Geneva, Luca? He cannot tell. However, the "great city" in Nostradamus almost always stands for Paris. The League, mistress in Paris, would not submit to the coercive measures of Henri III., and by a call to arms—perhaps the old tocsin of St. Germain de l'Auxerrois sounding the while—told him, as par trompette, he had better quit the city with all speed. Trial and sentence in one word, "Take yourself off,"—for the first time uttered to a king of the race Capetian, in some eight hundred years of history. Later on, the drumming and trumpeting crack-brained citizens, with nothing about them to be called sane but their river, will feel themselves called to repentance when the escalading ladders are laid by Henri III. to the wall.

Let it be noted now that this Day of the Barricades is very remarkable, and, as such, is not to be found at all in Bohn's "Index of Dates." It was, however, repeated in the civil war of the Fronde, August 26, 1648; in the three days' war, July 27, 28, 29, 1830, that set Philippe Citoyen on his rickety perch; and again in June 23, 1848. But close on two hundred years after, in 1789, when the philosophic Republic was at hand and the Bastille was taken; when another Capet was to be handled by the mob; offering cul pour tête to the admiration of a wise world, then was to be best discerned the result of this first reaction from St. Bartholomew's Day; pretty well that tocsin of treason has rung alarum to a world on fire. A further curious analogy demands attention here. The Popes of Rome were the earliest patrons of the principle of regicide, and Clément the monk, whom we shall soon introduce, was the first to practise it; here we see the Catholic League to be the first organized body to repudiate kingship, to set up a republican form, and consecrate a day to revolt and insurrection, which has become memorable in history for ever, though forgotten by Bohn, as la Journée des Barricades. But what shall we say of this forecast by Nostradamus, fifty-three years before the event happened? He is, I think, the first who ever put in type the word Republic as representative of rebellion and revolt, throughout the modern world. But here we have it,—the dough of prophecy made out of the ground wheat-seed of time, and baked by the oven of events into the bread of history; not Walpole's lies, nor the principles, mostly false, that philosopher Hume finds so cleverly for us, but the facts divested of motive.—like a petrified coral. reef of insect humanities concreted into permanence and solidity by the death of myriads. For those who can see, it lies all contained in that linear rune, La république de la grande cité.

MURDER OF THE DUC DE GUISE (DECEMBER 23, 1588). [I. 99.]
Century III.—Quatrain 51.
Paris conjure un grand meutre commetre,
Blois le fera sortir en plein effect:
Ceux d'Orleans voudront leur chef remettre;
Angers, Troye, Langres leur feront un meffait.
Translation.
Paris conspires to commit a great murder;
Blois will carry it into full effect:
The Orléanois will try to place a Leaguer at their head;
Angers, Troye, Langres will try and undo this.

Henri III. at Paris contrived the murder of the Duc de Guise, who had incited and led the Parisians on the day of the Barricades, when Henri was compelled to fly to Chartres. Henri de Lorraine, Duc de Guise, was murdered the day after the Cardinal, his brother, had been, at the Convention of the Estates at Blois. The murder took place at the Chateau de Blois. The Orléanois, on learning this, rose against Balzac d'Entragues, the governor of the town, and set Charles de Lorraine, Chevalier d'Aumale, at their head,—he was one of the chiefs of the League,—whilst Angers, Troyes, and Langres took the side of Henri III. It is not very easy, says Le Pelletier, to distinctly prove the exact position taken up by these three towns, but Nostradamus habitually puts a part to stand for the whole. In the divided interests various cities took differing sides. At the time he wrote there was nothing to show that such internecine separations would take place. He clearly anticipated them, and, so far, is absolutely right. We cannot, it seems, prove him to be right in all the details; but equally, there is nothing to show him wrong.

LE DUC DE MAYENNE (1589-1593). [I. 100.]
Century I.—Quatrain 85.
Par la response dc dame Roy troublé,
Ambassadeurs mespriseront leur vie:
Le Grand ses freres contrefera doublé
Par deux mourront ire, 1 haine, et envie. 2
Translation.
The King shall be troubled by the Queen-mother,
The deputies at risk of life remonstrate:
The Guise will act for both his brothers dead,
The two whom envy, hatred, malice slew.

Henri III. will be troubled by the response of Catherine de Medici, who disapproves of the murder of the Guise; the deputies (ambassadeurs) from both Paris and Blois, make lively remonstrance at the peril of their lives. The Duc de Mayenne (le Grand), when proclaimed chief of the League, will take the title of Lieutenant-General of the Kingdom, and, as if doubled in authority, will represent his two brothers, Henri de Guise and the Cardinal de Lorraine, whom the envy, hatred, and malice of Henri III. and his Court had assassinated. We seem to have here a republic tempered by daggers, in place of what followed, a tyranny tempered with epigrams. This active forging of daggers, knives, and sword-cutlery in France, to carve out an idol of a republic, with its bloodstained heathen Phrygian cap; taken together with its repetition sixty years later, in the Barricades of the Fronde, August, 1648, was clearly generating the poison and concentrating its venom for the most startling act of death known to mankind, but one, in all history,—at Whitehall, on that wintry 30th of January, 1649,—the venom, that by the subtle inoculation of a Raleigh could, for a time, strike silly such a soul as Milton's—"Psalmist of Paradise,"—who, but for this damned virus in the world, might have taught men how to realize a paradise on earth.

CRIME OF JACQUES CLÉMENT (AUGUST 1, 1589). [I. 102.]
Century IX.—Quatrain 36.
Un grand Roy prins 1 entre les mains d'un Joyne 2
Non loin de Pasque, confusion, coup cultre. 3
Perpet, 4 captifs temps que foudre en la husne, 5
Lors que trois freres se blesseront et murtre. 6
Translation.
A great King taken by a young man's hand
Close upon Easter, confusion, and a knife:
There's powder on the tower for captives then,
Three brothers perish; this death takes the last.

Henri III., in his camp at St. Cloud, will be struck by the hand of a young monk,—Joyne might easily be a misprint for Moyne. Jacques Clément was twenty-five. He came straight from receiving the Communion (non loin de Pasque). He thought he did God service (confusion); he struck him in the lower bowel with a knife. The crime will be committed when the Parisians are cut off (captifs) by the King beleaguering, and his vengeance is ready to fall upon their ramparts. This murder completes the violent deaths of the three sons, the issue of Henri II. and Catherine de Medici.

There is no occasion to call attention to the remarkable lucidity of this forecast, when once the linguistic difficulties of its conveyance have been studiously solved. The demilune towers projecting at intervals from the wall, as at the Haute Ville, Boulogne, well enough represent the husne, or tower of vantage, in the quatrain, they need but a shield or belvidere added.

DEATH OF HENRI III. (AUGUST 2, 1589). [I. 103.]
Présage 58.
Le Roy-Roy n'estre, du Doux la pernicie, 1
L'an pestilent, les esmues 2 nubileux.
Tien 3 qui tiendra, les grands non letitie, 4
Et passera terme de cavilleux. 5
Translation.

The twice King dies, by Clement hand is slain;
War and revolt make the year pestilent.
Hold who hold can, the great oppose not well,
Live laughter down and teach the cavillers.

This is a most singular prophecy. Henri III., King, first of Poland then of France is quaintly called Roy-Roy. Le Doux is an excellent synonym for Clément, all must admit. The year was harassed by civil and religious war, and the Leaguers (les esmues) begin to grow anxious about the consequences. Let Henri IV. hold hard his own, the lilied sceptre: "Let Curzon holde what Curzon helde" be his motto. The time is passed for the Catholic grandees (les grands) to woo Lætitia. The King can laugh now at the laughers of the Guise; he laughs best who laughs last.

The murder by Clément of the anti-papal king, Henri III., followed very close upon the setting up of Jesuit Clubs in Paris under papal sanction (Elliot's Horæ Apoc, iii. 321). The pulpits also had been filled by clerical preachers of sedition and bloodshed. Precisely two hundred years later the Bastille was taken, and in the Jacobin Clubs of that day were hung, says Alison, the pictures of Clement and Ravaillac, in the gloomy rooms of the old convent, in which they met like night-birds of ill-omen, and within little wreaths beneath each picture might be seen inscribed the words, "He was fortunate; he killed a king." This is so sentimental, petty, and petulant, that it would move to laughter any large good-natured mind, were it mot for the slaver of malignity that accompanies everything that drops from the tongues of that sack of reptiles gathered out of the Jacobin dunghill, as they crawled forth one by one poisoning and to poison.

Footnotes

80:1 Old word for jamais, never.
80:2 Latin, a. by.
81:1 Bouys [Oracles, p. 103] says that the King alone had the right to a visor of pure gold. I believe this to be pure nonsense. It would be little stronger than lead. It merely means a gilt casque, and I think some of the accounts say so in as many words. If Bouys were right, the King courted death.
81:2 Greek, breaking or lopping.
81:3 Latin, una, the one or first.
82:1 See also Brantôme, Vie des hommes illustres de son temps.
84:1 Qu'en, for qui en.
84:2 Romance, for lutte.
84:3 Porté, pour remporté.
84:4 Latin, subito, suddenly.
84:5 Romance, surprins for surpris.
87:1 Romance, surprins = surpris.
88:1 Latin, exspoliare, totally despoiled.
88:2 Romance, for pris.
88:3 Romance, hostaige, maison, house, palace.
88:4 Romance, tiers, third.
88:5 Latin, trucidare, cut the throat.
88:6 Latin, inconditus, dispersed.
89:1 Greek, wooden case, coffin,
89:2 Sortiront bas, for d'en bas.
89:3 Latin, infernus, subterranean.
90:1 Romance, vefve, veuve. The word is made here to apply to the wife,

Mary Stuart, whom he leaves a widow without children. The grammatical effort is somewhat violent; but vef or veuf is the masculine form, so there is very little choice given.

90:2 In the quatrain this ought to be written eage, as it stands in the texte-type, or the line will not scan.

90:3 Près, for après.

90:4 This is how M. le Pelletier renders the last line.

92:1 Italian, piloto, pilot.

92:2 Latin, mandatus, appointed to a charge.

92:3 Latin, classis, fleet.

92:4 Romance, contrebandé, marching in a contrary band.

92:5 Ordo is, Venise craindra une armie de barbares qui viendra.

93:1 This line is a foot short. Garencières reads:

Le coup volant luy crevera un œil.

94:1 Noir, anagram of roi, cutting off n.

94:2 Arcs tendus, arquebus.

94:3 Latin, tantum, much.

96:1 The family name of Pope Gregory XIII. was Hugo Buon-Compagni. On May 13, 572, he was made Pope. He assumed the name of Gregory out of respect to St. Gregory Nazianzen. He caused the Church to encourage the murder of refractory kings; he promoted the massacre of St. Bartholomew's Day, which Sir Paul Rycaut, the historian of the Popes, does not so much as mention in the life of Gregory. He only says towards the end that "he may be numbered amongst the good Popes." As Buon-Compagni was a good lawyer before he became a good Pope, he was prequalified for a virtuous career in any line of life. He re-confirmed the excommunication of Queen Elizabeth; he rectified the Calendar which goes by his name,—the Gregorian. The Jesuits' College was finished by him at Rome, dedicated so oddly—

Religioni et bonis Artibus.

In his day Japan was, by Jesuit missionary effort, brought within the pale of the Church: on which a wit remarked that Japan varnish was introduced into Europe, and Christian varnish into Japan. He died at eighty-three, and to the last could almost mount on horseback without the help of his servants. His place of retirement, Rycaut says, was Frescati, about ten miles distant from Rome, where the Borghes Palace now is, and was then called Monte Dragone—a most fit name for the residence of the Old Worm of St. Bartholomew's massacre.—V. Paul Rycaut, "Lives of the Popes," ed. 1689, vol. ii. p. 163.

99:1 Will sound in full volley.

99:2 These letters are interpreted by the old commentators and Guynaud (p. 107) as meaning the peace concluded with Philip II. of Spain: V., cinq, S., successeur, C., Charles—i.e., Successor to Charles Quint.

102:1 Romance, vefve = veuve, widow.

102:2 Latin, qui, celui qui.

102:3 Latin, ductus, led.

102:4 Appaiser, for pour apaiser.

102:5 Pourchas, old word, pursuit, active intrigue (proquassatio).

102:6 Razes, tonsured priests and monks (têtes rasées).

103:1 Greek, draught-playing, or gambling. The word was applied to gaming by the Greeks, as we find a story in Plutarch [Liddell and Scott, Lex.], exhibiting Hermes as playing draughts with Selene, and winning five days, which he adds to the year. Guynaud (p. 119) reads poche, which I take to be an abscess, wolf, or devouring ulcer; both he and Le Pelletier interpret it as meaning Poland.

103:2 Plaindre, for se plaindre.

104:1 Guiere. Nobody explains this word, and yet it seems to stand much in need of it. It is given by Roquefort, as from gubernator, a general. Leader, Or we may say dux, for the Duc d'Alençon. It is really guides or guide. Guber, govern, guide, being all three cognate.

104:2 Latin, decisus, cut off, severed.

104:3 This term is applied to Poland by Nostradamus n allusion to its elective throne, which became purely venal—a thing at last coming to be played for as a hazard at dice. But, curiously enough, the less authentic reading poche is almost equally descriptive—a burning ulcer eating into the body politic till it destroys it.

105:1 Latin, virtuosus; according to M. le Pelletier "vigorous." Classical Latin has no such word, and the lower Latin means probus, bonis moribus et virtute præditus. Nostradamus probably meant vertueux, in old French, to be equivalent to robuste.

105:2 Aloi, the quality of the substance of a metal. The battle of French etymologists is very instructive over this word, as may be seen in Littré. Of course, however, it comes from à loi, conformable to law. But I think there is a misprint, and that we ought to read toute loi = toute la loi. Guynaud (p. 122) reads loi in the second line for foy. We might suppose that that variant had been introduced to correct the fourth line, and was only by a "devil" carried to the second instead, by which that imp of mischief contrived to leave two errors in place of one. In confirmation somewhat of this, the texte-type reads tout à loy.

109:1 Latin, ira, anger.

109:2 Ordo, deux mourront par ire, etc.

110:1 Romance, prins, pris.

110:2 Romance, joyne, jeune homme.

110:3 Romance, cultre, couteau.

110:4 Latin, perpetratio.

110:5 Husne, a small tower, or belvidere.

110:6 Romance, murtre, meurtre.

111:1 Latin, pernicies, destruction.

111:2 Romance, esmues, émus, seditious.

111:3 Tien, for tienne.

111:4 Latin, Lætitia, joy, pleasure, and play on Lutetia, Paris.

111:5 Romance, cavilleux, cavillers.

Henri Quatre

THE COMING OF HENRI IV. (AUGUST 2, 1589). [I. 105.]
Century IX.—Quatrain 50.
Mendosus 1 tost viendra à son haut regne,
Mettant arriere un peu les Norlaris: 2
Le rouge blesme, la masle à l'interregne,
Le jeune crainte, et frayeur Barbaris.
Translation.
Mendosus shall soon come to his high dominion,
Setting back those of Lorraine a little.
The old cardinal pale, the male of the interregnum,
The young man timid, and the barbarian alarmed.

HENRI IV. the heretic Vendôme, changed his religion thrice, Jeanne d'Albert, his mother, brought him up a Protestant. To escape St. Bartholomew's Day, he professed Catholicism, in 1572. In 1576, he turned to Protestantism, to head the Calvinist party. He declared himself Catholic to take the throne of France. Through the Salic law he ascended, to the exclusion of the Lorraine princes (Nolaris). In this way, he shut out the old Cardinal de Bourbon, pale (blesme) with age, the Duc de Mayenne, Lieutenant General of the kingdom during the interregnum, the young Duc de Guise, and the barbarously savage Philip II. of Spain, who had pretensions to the crown through Elizabeth his wife, the daughter of Henri II.

The Cardinal is rouge because of the dress of all cardinals. Philip allied himself with the Guises. and supported the Catholic League.

THE DEPRESSION OF THE DE GUISE FAMILY (1589-1593). [I. 107.]
Century X.—Quatrain 18.
Le rang Lorrain fera place à Vendosme,
Le haut mis bas, et le bas mis en haut,
Le fils de Mamon sera esleu 1 en Rome,
Et les deux Grands seront mis en defant.
Translation.
The house of Lorraine yields to the Vendôme,
The high put low, the low put high instead,
The son of Mamon they elect at Rome,
And the Pretenders both are in default.

The house of Lorraine is now eclipsed by that of Vendôme. Mayenne, the chief, is put down, and le petit Béarnais, Henri IV., rises to respect and power. This heretic son of mammon is accepted by choice at Rome for King of France, and neither of the Pretenders will ever be king.

The Cardinal de Bourbon had been actually proclaimed King by the League, as Charles X., but he was dead in 1590. Isabella, the daughter of Philip II., was incapable by the Salic law. So that the only two remaining were the Duc de Mayenne and the young Duc de Guise. They were shut out by Henri IV. and never reached the throne.

HENRI IV. ABJURES PROTESTANTISM (JULY 21, 1593). [I. 108.]
Presage 76.
Par le legat du terrestre et marin,
Le Grande Cape 2 à tout s'accommoder;p. 115
Estre à l'escoute tacite 1 Norlarin, 2
Qu'à 3 son advis ne voudra accorder.
Translation.
Before the legate of the earth and sea,
Henry the Great will yield to all required:
Mayenne to all will listen and not speak a word,
And will grant nothing of his own free will.

Sixtus V. had boldly fulminated an excommunication against Henri Quatre, the great Capet, but the latter subscribes to all required by the legate of him who can bind and loose all on the earth and sea. He abjures Protestantism at St. Denis, on July 25, 1593, the Archbishop of Bourges officiating. The Duc de Mayenne (the Lorraine), Lieutenant-General of France and Master of Paris for the League, will look on in silence, and as far as he can will prevent Paris from receiving the King. The city did not open its gates to him till March 22, 1594, eight months after the abjuration.

MARSEILLES TAKEN BY THE SPANIARDS (FEBRUARY 17, 1596). [I. 109.]
Century III.—Quatrain 88.
De Barselonne par mer si 4 grand' armée,
Toute Marseille de frayeur tremblera:
Isles saisies, de mer ayde fermée,
Ton traditeur 5 en terre nagera. 6
Translation.
From Barcelona a great fleet shall come,
And terror strike into the town Marseilles:
The isles are seized, and help by sea cut off,
But the betrayer is made swim on land.

A Spanish fleet of a dozen galleys, commanded by Charles Doria, was sent by Philip II. to help the Leaguers. He took possession of the islands

Chateau d'If and Ratonneau, and thus cut off all help to seaward. Charles de Casau (le traditeur) was consul, and proposed to place the city in the hands of the Spaniards; Pierre Libertat, however, ran him through with a sword, and the populace dragged the dead body through the muddy channels of the streets.

Guynaud refers to the same event as fulfilling this quatrain in the time of Henri IV., but by a misprint gives 1536 instead of 1596. The islands he mentions are those of St. Honnorat and of St. Marguerite. Black's pretentious Imperial Gazetteer professes to give a plan of the town, and you see a number of nameless vermicelli streets running all about, but not a single island off the coast is visible. One may suppose, however, that the islands are there, and that all the four were occupied by the Spaniards.

BIRON'S PUNISHMENT (DECEMBER 2, 1602). [I. 110.]

Sixain 6.
Quand de Robin 1 la traisteruse enterprise,
Mettra Seigneurs et en peine un grand Prince,
Sceu 2 par la Fin 3 chef on lui tranchera.
La plume au vent, amye clans Espagne, 4
Poste 5 attrappé estant clans la campagne,
Et l'escrivain clans l'eaüe se jettera.
Translation.
When Biron's treason and disastrous act,
Shall put King Henry and his Lords in fear,p. 117
Lafin betrays him, and the King beheads.
Treason dispatched to Spain in amity, 1
The carrier caught when he has entered France, 2
And the scriv'ner will throw himself into the water.

One thing has carefully to be borne in mind in relation to the Sixains, that they were presented to Henri Quatre, and printed for the first time in 1605. That is to say, the) first appeared three years after this had happened. To the sceptically disposed they can furnish no authority, but to ordinary men, who only look for ordinary evidence, it will appear that there is very little as to style that would not appropriately spring from the pen of Nostradamus; and further, that if they are forgeries, the forgers have not taken advantage of their knowledge of the events to make the prophecies any clearer or more striking. These are quite as enigmatical as if our author had written them, and I think that common sense will generally be content to take them for what they are worth, and will regard them as probably genuine "chips of the old block" and as such very curious.

Guynaud in his Concordance, p. 137, gives a full and interesting account of Biron; chiefly extracted from Davila, Montluc, De Thou, Mezeray, Le Père Anselm, and so forth, where the reader can refer for further details, if interested. I may just note that I have copied the date of December 2, 1602, from Le Pelletier, but that Moreri gives the date of Biron's decapitation as July 31, 1602, in the Court of the Bastille. The name of the messenger (poste) was Picoté, a native of Orleans, sold, as they say, to the King of Spain (Guynaud, p. 140).

Garencières has (p. 464) a very elaborate annotation upon this stanza, giving the whole history of Biron and Lafin in twenty-eight folio pages. Biron appears to have been a vain, a violent, and foolish man, though of great courage and audacity in war, which made him highly valued by Henri IV. After Amiens he refused to go to quiet the towns of Picardy, unless his statue were erected in brass before the Louvre. His sudden prosperity had turned his head. The treasonous proposals with Spain were, that he was to have a daughter of the Duke of Savoy in marriage, 500,000 crowns, and sovereign rights in Burgundy. These were negotiated through Lafin; and Lafin told the King. The whole trial is given, with Biron's defence in reply, which is audacious and eloquent, but much of it is highly contradictory. He was condemned and executed in the court of the Bastille, on July 31, 1602, which coincides with Moreri. The superstitious, ignorant, violent, but able soldier comes out most characteristically. He shows in emergency great rapidity of thought, decision, and presence of mind; but a deficient judgment, very little principle, and an overwhelming conceit, that, encouraged by success, almost merged into madness. A man of this sort is always a compound of inconsistencies; accordingly he said to the Chancellor, in speaking of death, "I have not been afraid of it these twenty years." And that was true, when in war, a duel, or hot blood; but in the court of the Bastille he was thought to show great fear of dying. In earlier life he had wondered at himself for fearing nothing from the thrust of a sword, though very nervous over the prick of a lancet, when he had occasion to "be let blood," as they used to phrase it. The fear of death is most in apprehension; but the apprehension is most, perhaps it may be said, of the wicked in cold blood, and of the good in violence, and when the blood is hot, if but the least pause give time for reflection to enter. Garencières notes that the greatest courage and stoutness of a man is nothing in comparison of the weakness of human nature.

Two of Biron's adventures with astrologers are so characteristic of the manners of the time, as recounted by Guynaud [p. 137, etc.], that I think the reader should not be deprived of them. Whatever is strange and rivets the attention must have something of humanity in it, and repay the record, though a few superior people may look down upon such trifling. I shall give them at the risk of running this annotation to too great length.

When at Court with his father, at the age of eighteen or twenty, he had a duel, and killed his man. He had to hide for this, till his father could sue out his pardon, through the, Due d' Espernon, to whom fortunately the father was known. He took the disguise of a letter-carrier, and in this garb consulted an astrologer called La Brosse, who lived in a garret at the top of a house near the Luxembourg. He told the man that it was his master's horoscope he had need of. La Brosse told him that one day he would be a very great man, in fact, might almost be king, but for a caput algol that stood in the way. What this was the man would not explain. Biron, however, continuing to press very hard, got him to say at last that he would be beheaded on a scaffold. Upon this, he burst out with the want of judgment he showed all through his life (forty years in all) and beat the old man mercilessly, leaving him nearly dead. He locked him maliciously into his room, took away the key with him, and kicked down the little ladder that gave access to the loft. But still he believed what had been communicated.

On another occasion he consulted César, who was thought at the time to be the most able astrologer in France. This man also affirmed that he would have good fortune in almost everything. Except for a blow from a Burgundian from behind, he might even be king. But he could not get from him a word more.

When he was confined in the Bastille, a friend called on him, and Biron asked him to ascertain for him from what part of the country the executioner of Paris was; and when he came back and told him that he was a Burgundian, Biron changed colour and said—"There will be no reprieve then; I am as good as dead."

Now as to the fulfilment of the last two lines. It will appear that my rendering is right, and that the scrivener will throw himself into the water. The scrivener turns out to be a man named Nicholas l'Oste, born at Orleans, secretary to Lord Villeroy, Chief Secretary of State, who, finding him a most capable person, confided much in him, and the more so that Oste's father had spent the greater part of his life in his service. When Lord Rochepot was starting as ambassador for Spain, Oste begged to accompany him as secretary. Villeroy immediately recommended him, and he was engaged. In a few months' time he mastered the language to such perfection, and so thoroughly accommodated himself to Spanish manners, that he might well pass for a true-born Spaniard. When Rochepot had got the treaty at Vervins ratified, the King of Spain gave him rich presents—a chain of jewels, and six gold chains valued at a hundred and fifty crowns apiece—to distribute amongst his suite, as he thought fit. Oste was so full of himself that he thought he ought to have one of them, but his master thought otherwise; on which, says Garencières, "the Devil crept into his soul," and, as he wanted money to supply his debaucheries, he determined to betray the State secrets which passed through his hands.

With this in view, he applied to Don Fanchese, a Secretary of State, and made his proposals, but the dignified Spaniard, for some reason or other, received him coolly. "The Catholic King was in good amity with the most Christian one, and required to know no more than the French Ambassador should communicate to him." Nothing discouraged, our traitor hurries off to Don Ydiaques, another secretary, and there meets with excellent reception. He was presented to the Duke of Lerma, to whom he betrayed the Alphabet of Ciphers. He received twelve hundred crowns upon the spot, and was promised the like amount as a yearly pension. By his means the Spanish Council knew the contents of all French instructions as soon as the ambassador himself. When La Rochepot's mission ended, Oste got back into Villeroy's service, and so was able to maintain correspondence with Spain. Tuxis was ambassador from Spain in Paris, and after him Don Baltazar de Caniga. With these men he established a close intimacy, so that finally the Council in Spain got his letters before Des Barreaux at Madrid could receive those from Henri IV.

Des Barreaux told the King that he was always now forestalled. Oste had let a certain reprobate Raffis into his secret, and this fellow, who had been banished, in order to obtain a reprieve of sentence, betrayed Oste to Des Barreaux. When he got his pardon, he gave up the name of Oste. Raffis came to Paris to communicate with Villeroy, and orders were given to detain the two Spanish couriers that had reached the post-office. They then kept a watch upon Oste, who was "doing his devotions at the Charter-house of Paris,"—excellent Catholic, plotter as he was. On reaching the post-office, he soon found he was betrayed; and Descardes, who was to watch him, did not let him out of his sight until he brought him to Villeroy's. When there, he thought his man was safe, and went to announce his capture to Villeroy. Oste instantly ran down to the stable, where his horse stood, still saddled, and galloped away. A hue and cry was soon raised. Oste got a Spanish disguise at De Cuniga's, and made off post-haste for Luxembourg. Postmasters were forbidden to let out horses to any one; but at Meaux the postmaster had received the order too late, for Oste was already on horseback, but no sooner did he begin to gallop than his horse fell under him. His look of dismay impressed the postillion who accompanied him, and he told his master on his return. The postmaster told the sheriff, who came up with him at the second ferry of la Ferte sous Jouare; but he was already on the boat, and threatening the ferryman's life, the man put him ashore, in spite of the sheriff's commands, shouted to him from the bank. He rushed into the bushes and brambles near the Marne, hoping to escape in the darkness of the night, the sheriff scattered his men everywhere, raised the whole country side, and caused bonfires to be lighted in all directions. Oste crept from bush to bush, but, either accidentally or with intention, fell into the river Marne and was drowned. His hat was found next day, stopped between two posts, and his body two days later. So befitting a close to the career of a gifted dastard is a wholesome exemplar of retributive justice, and should not easily be suffered to fall out of men's recollection. Horace thinks that lame-foot justice always trips the sinner. No doubt, if we could see both worlds; but, as we cannot, I wish that here the lame foot were considerably less lame. In England law and the lawyers, her two crutches, seem to reduce Justice to a gouty incapable. With our new Palace of Justice the morals of a Court seem to have dawned upon us.

POPULARITY OF HENRI IV. (AFTER HIS DEATH). [I. 112.]
Century VI.—Quatrain 70.
An chef du monde le grand Chyren 1 sera,
Plus outre après aymé, craint, redouté;
Son bruit et los 2 les cieux surpassera,
Et du seul titre victeur 3 fort contenté.
Translation.
Chief of the world Henri le Grand shall be,
More loved in death than life, more honoured he:
His name and praise shall rise above the skies,
And men will call him victor when he dies.

French self-esteem has always appropriated to France a throne of pre-eminence beyond all other thrones. If it were possible, they would set theirs above that of Jupiter. They pretend a most manly contempt for kings. But the throne, you are to remember, is the work of sans cullottes, French cabinet-makers, and therefore the best thing of its kind in the universe, and so chef du monde. If Nostradamus is no prophet for you, you shall at least admit that he was a Frenchman. The Frenchman whips the old world, and the American whips creation. The rest of us may look forward to an eternity of corporal punishment in spite of the nominal abolition of slavery. Condillac will furnish the logical distinction, that establishes the honour of the throne, when a manly contempt has been duly engendered for the sanctity of the king's majesty. Honest Democrat! Do you read Condillac?

One of Voltaire's rhetorical squibs in the Henriade, which the French are so indulgent as to call not only verse, but poetry, runs—
"Il fut de ses sujets le vainqueur et le père."
"He was the papa and conquestor of his people."
When our Charles II. was addressed as "the father of his people," he said he thought that he might be of a good many of them. But Henri Quatre is too noble a creature for any good and wise man to wish to dwell long upon his foibles. What a contrast between him and the Napoleons!
Footnotes
113:1 Mendosus, anagram of Vendosme (the u standing for v of course), The texte-type reads Mandosus; but as Mendosus is the perfect

anagram of Vendosme, and makes also the Latin word's meaning full of faults, it is best to read Mendosus.

113:2 Norlaris, anagram for Lorrains the patronymic of the Guise family.

114:1 Romance, esleu, élu, chosen.

114:2 Cape, for Capet, a descendant of Hugh Capet.

115:1 Latin, tacite, silently.

115:2 Norlarin, anagram for Lorrain; here it represents the Duc de Mayenne,

115:3 Qu'a for qui à.

115:4 Romance, si for très, very.

115:5 Latin, traditor, traitor.

115:6 His body shall be dragged through the streets in the mud of the gutters.

116:1 Robin, anagram for Biron.

116:2 Romance, sceu for su, known.

116:3 Lafin was the name of the secretary, the accomplice of Biron.

116:4 The ordo here is dans l'Espagne amye which means, then at peace with Henri IV.

116:5 Romance, poste, messenger, postillion.

117:1 La plume au vent is supposed by le Pelletier to stand for currente calamo. I should rather think it means the feather (wing) to the wind. It was written with a quill, and started on its way as a bird flies; but irrevocabile semel emissum. We are to understand this line to relate to l'Oste's treasonable complicity with Spain, of which an account will be given further on. Also, l'escrivain, in the closing line stands for the same individual.

117:2 We shall see that the two Spanish couriers were arrested at the post office in Paris. Le Pelletier confuses all this from not happening to know that l'Oste is the scrivener, so he applies it to the affair of Lafin, whose messenger, when carrying Spanish despatches, had thrown them into the river when he found himself pursued. Unfortunately, when he finds himself in the difficulty which this involves him in, he glazes till he has forced the words to fit his erroneous view. He had far better have stated the difficulty, and said that he could not harmonize the text. But he very rarely trips thus.

123:1 Le Grand Chyren is the anagram of Henri le Grand. Before mounting the throne, he bore the name of Vendosme, from his father Antoine de Bourbon, Duke of Vendôme and King of Navarre. In the first Quatrain of the series, Henri Quatre, Vendosme was anagrammatically given as Mendosus; as to Chiren it is the precise anagram of Henri, as spelt in the old language Henric, from the Latin Henricus. Numerous etymologies have been assigned to Henry. Camden derived it from honore, Verstegan from the Teutonic Han, a haven, and Rice, Saxon for rich. Killian writes it Heynrick, or Heymrick, rich home. This is very nearly right, but now it is generally considered that rick stands for powerful; so chief of a house or district.

123:2 Los, old word for glory. Latin, laus.

"A la sainte divinité,
Soit los, honeur, et potesté."
　　　Le Mystère des Actes des Apôtres.
123:3 Latin, victor, conqueror.

Louis XIII

(1610-1643.)

PUNISHMENT OF THE GREAT MONTMORENCY (OCTOBER 30, 1632.) [I. 113.]

Century IX.—Quatrain 18.
Le lys Dauffois 1 portera 2 dans Nanci
Jusques en Flandres electeur de l'Empire;
Neufve obturée 3 an grand Montmorency,
Hors lieux prouvés 4 delivré 5 á clere peyne. 6

Translation.

The Dauphin shall carry his lily standards into Nancy, just as in Flanders the Elector of Trèves shall be carried prisoner of the Spaniards into Brussels. A new prison will be given to the great Montmorency, who will be delivered for execution into the hands of Clerepeyne. This man will behead him in a spot not devoted to executions.

I HAVE given this in prose, as it could only yield ingenious doggerel in verse.

Louis XIII., of whom it may be remarked that he was the first who bore the title of Dauphin de France since the publication of Century IX., in 1506, entered Nancy on September 25, 1633, a day after his army. In 1635 he enters Flanders on behalf of the Elector, whom the Spaniards had, on t e 26th of March of that year, carried prisoner to Brussels. Nostradamus then reverts to October 30, 1632, when the great Montmorency was executed for rebellion, being first confined in the newly built (neufve obturée) Hotel de Ville at Toulouse. In the courtyard of this building Clerepeyne, a soldier, shall cut off his head, and not, as ought to have been the case, at the place appointed for public executions, such as was La Give at Paris.

It so happens that Clerepeyne's name is fully attested by Étienne Joubert and by the Chevalier de Jant, both contemporary with the event. Further than this, M. Motret has brought to light, after minute historic research, that the family, by solicitation of the King, could obtain only two concessions of mere formality—that the execution should be with closed doors, and by a soldier in lieu of the common headsman. The place publique or marché would be the place mentioned in the official order.

If the reader will carefully give his attention to the full drift of this quatrain, when the mere difficulty of verbal contortion has been resolved, he must feel that the prognostication has to be reckoned as one of the most astounding of oracles ever set forth in history. A French King takes Nancy. The Elector of Trèves is bandied about between France and Spain, like a shuttlecock of State; and then, by name, comes the execution of the great Montmorency, detailed with, it is true, the brevity of Tacitus, but, when understood, with a singular felicity of detail implied in the pregnant words neufve obturée, of the newly built town hall. Not in the market-place is he executed, but in the central courtyard. Let clere peyne (clara pœna) stand merely for celebrated attainder, the thing is still prodigious beyond all precedent. But when you know, in addition, that a part of Nostradamus's prophetic method consists in using every possible play of words, including paronomasia and anagram, and you find that the soldier who acted as headsman—a man called upon by chance to gratify the almost absurd sensibilities of the family—was Clerepeyne, a name that corresponds to a title with the two words employed by the prophet, then, indeed, the marvel mounts into the stupendous. It cannot be paralleled out of the works of the individual we are busy with. It is incredible, and yet you must believe it. It is not to be understood, but it must be accepted. Joubert, de Jant, the Cure de Louvicamp, and Motret, have all contributed to its historical confirmation on independent lines. It was in print, beyond possibility of gainsaying, more than fifty years before any of the events occurred. Clerepeyne could not have been even born at the time his name was being put through the printing press at Lyons. The mind that can realize all these details, and then be content to fall back upon chance to explain them, or upon the verbal fact that visions must be visionary—an axiom quite as philosophic, by-the-bye, as Hume's "Essay on Miracles" is built upon—is a mind not at all to be envied, Such incredulity is more astounding than the prophecy itself. It is easier to believe the prophecy than the philosopher who says he does not believe it. The Tower is below London Bridge. Has anybody ever asked "why?" This 18th quatrain of Century IX. of Nostradamus is just as much a fact as the Tower of London is, and vastly more impregnable. Intelligent people will be amused by an explanation; but the substantive fact can stand without any, till the day of Doom if necessary. It is only some human popinjay, Plato Pry, the philosopher, who would like to gossip to us the How, and so sport another borrowed feather in his feather-brain,—or hum us with another bee from his bonnet; that hive of mad insects.

THE CONSPIRACY OF CINQ MARS (MARCH 13, 1642.) [I. 115.]
   Century VIII—Quatrain 68.
   Vieux Cardinal par la jeusne deccu, 1
   Hors de sa charge sa verra desarmé,
   Arles ne monstres 2 double 3 soit apperceu;
   Et Liqueduct 4 et le Prince embausmé.
   Translation.
   The old cardinal is supplanted by a young man, and will see himself deprived of his charge, and disarmed. [Le Pelletier renders]: If Arles you do not show, in a manner that shall be visible, a counterpart of the treaty, then the man who will cause himself to be conveyed by water will be embalmed, and the Prince also.
   The above is the contortion to which Le Pelletier resorts to force out of it the sense it undoubtedly contains. My proposed reading reduces the difficulty.
   The old Cardinal Richelieu shall find himself supplanted by the young Cinq Mars. He was but twenty-two when he achieved this bit of dexterous Court intrigue against Richelieu, 5 the most rusé fox in Europe, as rumour ran.
   Cinq Mars was his own protégé, and no doubt threw him with a trick learned from his master. A sprightly youngster of the apt breed can learn such things quickly. But when the cardinal was at Arles he learnt that a certain treasonable treaty was negotiated with Spain by his rival in the name of the King's brother, and this made known brought Richelieu back to power straight. Now, if we read the line
   Arles, le monstre double soit apperceu:
   At Arles, let the monster diploma (treacherous treaty) be discovered,—
      or Cinq Mars himself might be the double monster,—it would be but a

gentle emendation in a classic line, and it makes the sense run well. Richelieu returned by water (Liqueduct) from Tarascon to Lyons, by the Rhone, with his bed upon the boat, but sick unto death, carrying Cinq Mars and De Thou prisoners along with him. In the same style he descended the Seine from Fontainebleau to Paris, where he died, two months later, on December 4, 1642. Louis XIII. died on the 14th of the following May. Both were embalmed, which was the practice then customary. The King when dead becomes a Prince again, when the breath was out of the body that 4th of December. Le roi est mort, vive le Roy Louis XIV.

IMPROVEMENT IN FIREARMS (1630-1671.) [I. 116.]
  Century III.—Quatrain 44.
  Quand l'animal à l'homme domestique, 1 p. 130
  Après grands peines et sauts viendra parler,
  Le foudre à vierge 1 sera sit 2 malefique,
  De terre prinse 3 et suspendue en l'air.
  Translation.

When the dog, 4 after many trials, shall begin to leap and speak, the powder loaded by ram-rod shall spread destruction round (sera très malefique.) Powder taken from the earth and exploded in the air.

When the firelock shall have been invented after many trials, and shall speak through the mouth of the gun, with recoil [sauts, or kick], after the powder-charge is well driven home with the ramrod, it will be most murderous by explosion in the air. The invention of the musket dates 1630. Troops, Le Pelletier says, were first armed with it in 1671. Nostradamus, it is to be observed, anticipates by an ingenious amplification and periphrasis the very name chien, by which the French designate this portion of the lock. It would not have served its purpose for the name of the same thing in English. This anticipation of the slang term of manufacture, a hundred years before the thing itself was used or named, seems to show an intimacy with what would be called matters of chance, that is inconceivable and beyond all comprehensibility.

I cannot but append here a translation of Guynaud's remarks upon this quatrain. They are, I think, the funniest that occur in the whole book. He says:

"Nostradamus warns us here that two prodigious things are to occur at last: one, that the industry and care of man will arrive at such a point that a domestic animal, such as dogs are, will be got to speak. For to imagine that this can be intended of birds is out of the question quite, as they are excluded from the list of domestic animals created by God for the service of man, as quadrupeds are. The words of the two first lines of the prophecy are Quand après grande peine l'animal domestique viendra parler a l'homme et qu'il sautera,—just as dogs do in approaching their master. A further thing is to happen that is no less astonishing: a demon is to mingle himself with powder, and suddenly transport a girl into the air, when she will remain suspended for possibly a whole day long, according to these words: 'La foudre â vièrge sera si malefique; de terre prinse et surpendue en l'air.' The critics may suppose that to mean that the girl will be hanged; but this is not so, in my opinion, because the word malefique is derived from the Latin maleficus, which in itself indicates a maleficent spirit delighting to work evil, as the devil always is."—GUYNAUD, "Concordances," p. 271. Footnotes
  125:1 Dauffois, for Dauphinois synonym, for Dauphin.
  125:2 Portera, for supportera, says Le Pelletier. For my part, it seems best

to leave it to its natural rendering, that he will carry his colours into Nancy.

125:3 Latin, obturare, to shut up in.

125:4 Prouvés is for approuvés.

125:5 Delivré, is for livré.

125:6 This is a play upon words, unrecognized by Garencières, as he did not know that Clerepeyne was the name of the man who cut off Montmorency's head, although, of course, Garencières is quite alive to the fact that the quatrain refers to Louis XIII. and the great Montmorency. In Latin clara pœna means celebrated punishment. Here is another instance of the mention of a name of an obscure individual that history for a moment flashes light upon, and then drops him back into the mud of oblivious ooze for ever,—emblem apt of Fame! This was written, if not Printed, a good eighty years before Clerepeyne became the midge-mote of a sunbeam upon that late autumnal day in history, when the night struck chilly on high roofs in Dauphiny.

128:1 Latin, decisus, suppressed cut off.

128:2 Ne monstres. I think there is a printer's error here in the texte-type, and that we should read le monstre.

128:3 Double, diploma, or duplicate of a treaty.

128:4 Latin, ille aquâ ductus, he that is taken by water.

128:5 Richelieu, if you examine him by Philippe de Champagne's splendid triple portrait of him, hanging in our Gallery, may be read as if in life by any physiognomist who pleases to devote the time to it. I have gazed many a time, through long years, with gifted friends and others, and oftener still alone, into those heartless eyes, attracted irresistibly (I only now see why) by the vast discrepancy between the world-wide renown of this French Minister, and his cynically petty face-sly, vulpine, unfeeling, unprincipled, spiteful, a coxcomb of feminine manners, of an p. 129 egotism and paltry vanity inordinate, but of a refinement, showing the highest social culture, a tongue that could gloze with ladies; he might, by lettre de cachet, have shut up a French Walsingham in the Bastille to prevent his own overthrow; but as to coping with him or a Burleigh as a statesman, as an equal in any powerful cabinet in Europe, by force of character, he could not have done it. Artifice, backed by the force of France, then rising into unity of action, or helped by circumstances that tied the hands of his antagonist, he might even throw a giant unawares. Richelieu was an artificial contriver, not a born ruler, if a mature face of fifty be any index to the volume or memoir of a man's life.

129:1 Arrange these words, l'animal domestique à l'homme, i.e. the dog.

130:1 Latinism, fulmen à virgâ, saltpetre; that is, the powder and ram-rod.

130:2 Romance, si, synonym of très, very.

130:3 Romance, prinse, prise, taken, brought.

130:4 The chien is the cock or hammer of the lock.

Louis XIV

(1643-1715.)

COMMENCEMENT OF HIS PERSONAL REIGN (MARCH 10, 1661). [I. 118.]
  Quatrain added to the Xth Century. 1
Quand le fourchu sera soustenu de deux paux, 2
Avec six demy-corps 3 et six sizeaux ouverts,
Le très puissant Seigneur, heritier des crapaux,
Alors subjugera sous soy tout l'univers.
  Translation.
When a fork sustained by two stakes (i.e. V, fourchu, sustained by two stakes upright, II. = M, a thousand,) and six half horns and six scissors open (CCCCCC, XXXXXX). (Half horn is the cor de chasse, or French horn cut in half, like a C, making altogether 1600).
The very mighty King, inheritor of the toads, shall subjugate to his power the whole universe.

THESE TWO first lines are clumsily employed in giving the date, but still were in print fifty-five years before the date named.
Mazarin died on March 9, 1661. The following day Louis XIV. became full inheritor of the lilies, took the reins of government, and subjected everything to his will.
Upon this Le Pelletier remarks that the toads, as emblematic of France, were standards borne under the early kings of the Merovingian race. The fleurs-de-lys were of later introduction, under Clovis, son of Childeric I., the founder of the Christian monarchy of the Franks.

TREATY OF WESTPHALIA, ETC. (1648-1661). [I. 119.]
  Century X.—Quatrain 7.
Le grand conflit qu'on appreste à Nancy;
L'Æmathien 1 dira, tout je soubmets;
L'isle Britanne par 2 vin sel en soucy;
Hem-mi 3 deux Phi 4 longtemps ne tiendra Metz.
  Translation.
A great conflict will approach Nancy;
The Æmathion will say, I submit all to me;
The isle of Britain will be agitated for lack of force and wisdom;
Metz will not hold out long against the two Philips.

Nancy was taken in 1660 by the French, when they razed the fortifications and united it with France. It appears to me that the first two lines of this quatrain should have formed the last two, but how any such error as that could have crept in is quite inexplicable. The reader will discern that a difference of about twelve years exists between the dates involved in the two distichs, that, as they are given, they are contrary to chronology, and that for such disarrangement no reason is assignable. If this is the way in which visions presented themselves to our seer, there is no reason to suppose, as I do, that he shook up the separate quatrains purposely to destroy a sequence that would have rendered them too easy of interpretation. It might have been a printer's error.

We have already seen what is the classical meaning to be attributed to Æmathion—that it relates to the sun and to Alexander the Great. In Nostradamus it refers to Louis XIV. (Louis le Grand). Of him it is to be remembered that he assumed as his emblem and that of France, the sun, with the motto Nec pluribus impar. Now, the sun, in the language of alchemists, stands for gold, and, in the metaphorical language of the Church, for Christianity. Gold is all the Christianity that many Christians possess. Les Solaires, in Nostradamus, is used for Christians. It is especially connected with France, inasmuch as her King is held at Rome, that centre of titles and of prelatical humility, to be Christianissimus. But this stout Capetian glorious King meant it of sovereignty. It was to signify, as Nostradamus has it, tout le soubmets. What is this man's own choice of a posy, to be cut around his signet? Nec pluribus impar. What is the axiom his blind self-pride invents when the death of Mazarin emancipates him from tutelage, and he grips the reins of France in his sole left hand (in 1661)? L'État, c'est Moi. Can insolence rise higher? Wait an odd century or so and see a scaffold spring before your Tuilleries windows, see an Æmathion, but twice removed in blood, roll his head, red, gushing, spurting, and bounding on the sawdust-sprinkled planks there; its motto, could it speak, would be your axiom recast fatally, L'État du Capet! (Caput!)

We have not quite concluded yet. When the treaty of Westphalia shall be agreed to between France and Philip IV. of Spain in 1648, and before the war of Succession to, seat Philip V., grandson of Louis XIV., on the throne, Metz shall be ceded to France, and lose for ever its title of Imperial City, between the two Philips—Philip IV. and, Philip V., protégé of France.

England about the same time, in revolution kindled by that imp of malevolence, Richelieu, shall behead its king, 1649, and be in anxiety because of the want of force and wisdom (vin et sel). This symbol Le Pelletier interprets thus: Wine is the symbol of force, because of its heat; and salt, because of its incorruptibility, is the symbol of wisdom.. I think it clear that this is not to be the interpretation here. He does not allude to want of force and wisdom; but anxiety (soucy) is caused by force and wisdom (à l'envers, as he puts again in reference to England, Century IX. 49; vol. i. 140 applied in the wrong direction.

This, though a highly unsatisfactory quatrain, as I have: shown above, is, nevertheless, one of the most remarkable of the whole series. The time of the Westphalian treaty synchronises with the revolt in England—a revolt which we have seen to be fostered out of mere pique by the vulpine Richelieu; a Churchman plotting royal murder, taught by Rome's consent that regicide was God's service, when a king (Henri III.) stood in her way; and when the Church once corrupted herself, baptizing her St. Bartholomew whose emblem was a knife, in blood, she absolved Paris, [cité au glaive, i. 182] who in midsummer madness stained her kennels red. The example of Whitehall—in re-enactment before the Tuilleries (vin et sel a l'envers), with force and wisdom converted into violence and democratic sensibility,—next turned Paris rouge, and the blood carnation burst into bloom at every street corner.

"When nations are to perish in their sins,
'Tis in the Church the leprosy begins;"

says the wise, mild, thoughtful, but much underrated bard, Cowper, who has done Gilpin inimitably, and Homer better than anybody else, by a long way.

LOSS OF DE LA FERRIÈRE'S SQUADRON (1655). [I. 121.]
Century III.—Quatrain 87.
Classe 1 Gauloise n'approche de Corsegue, 2
Moins de Sardaigne, tu t'en repentiras;
Trestous mourrez frustrès de l'aide grogne;
Sang nagera, captif ne me croiras.
Translation.
Approach not Corsica, thou fleet of France,
Nor yet Sardinia, lest thou rue the chance:
For ye no headland aids, ye all shall die,
The captive drown, for unbelieved am I.

M. le Pelletier tells us of a French squadron, commanded by the Chevalier de la Ferrière in 1655, that foundered in the Gulf of Lyons in coasting Corsica and Sardinia. All hands perished: they did not, he says, pass Cape Pourceau. He points out that Grogne is the synonym of Pourceau, which is a cape with a little port in the Mediterranean. This may have more to support it than appears at first sight, but I think it much simpler to take it for what it says. Grogne is the same as Groin, cape, or headland which runs out into the sea. In other words: nothing will put off to you from the headland where you founder; there will you all be drowned; for what the better will your master pilot be for this advertisement of mine? Jean de Rian was this master pilot, and Le Captif was his nickname, as he had been a slave.

Though perfectly useless for interpretation, Garencières makes annotations on this quatrain, that have an interest of their own. He takes the fulfilment to have been in 1555, just about the time when the quatrains were copied out for presentation to Henri II. But he remarks that Greigne, which is the word in his reading, signifies galley in the Provençal language, which was that of Nostradamus by his mother's side; and this makes very good sense: "they shall all founder without a galley putting out to them from the shore."

Of course Garencières knows nothing about Jean de Rian, or the curious precision with which Nostradamus gives us his nickname Captif; but he appends to his "Poor prisoner, thou shalt not believe me" the following comment that is worth recording, as it may furnish a link to some inquiry in the future:

"We find in this work many examples of those who went to consult with the author concerning the success of their undertakings, as did the Earl of Sommerive, before the besieging of Bagnole; to whom he answered, that he should leave the trees loaded with a new kind of fruit, that is to say, the rebels, whom he caused to be hanged on the trees."

FORTIFICATIONS OF VAUBAN AND THE CANAL OF LANGUENDOC (1659-1666). [I. 122.]
Century IX.—Quatrain 93.
Les ennemies du fort bien esloignés,
Par chariots conduict le bastion,
Par sur les murs de Bourges esgrongnés, 1
Quand Hercules bastira l'Hæmathion. 2

Translation.
When the enemy are driven from French soil,
And earthworks or bastions are brought by carts;
When the walls of Bourges have crumbled by time,
Then will Æmathion undertake a work of Hercules.

When the peace of the Pyrenees, concluded with Spain in 1659, had removed the enemy from the French frontiers, and Vauban had invented earthworks: at least so says Le Pelletier; Nostradamus only says he used them. Moreri tells us that the castle of Grosse Tour at Bourges was not repaired by Louis XIV., and was already partly ruined in 1651. This line seems to be a whimsical, but special announcement of the fact. Then Æmathion, or Louis XIV., will undertake the Herculean labour of constructing the Canal of Languedoc, which opened the Mediterranean to the ocean. It was begun by Paul Riquet in 1666, and terminated in 1681. It cost thirty-four million francs. It is said that when Vauban visited it he gave some useful hints that were acted upon with advantage. Vauban, like Turenne, was a glory, not to France, but to mankind. He was truly great, for he despised riches, and loved truth to indiscretion; yet his life shows that in judgment he much excelled those who loved truth less.

PEACE OF THE PYRENEES (NOVEMBER 7, 1659). [I. 123.]
Century X.—Quatrain 58.
An temps du dueil clue le felin 1 monarque,
Guerroyera le jeune Æmathien:
Gaule bransler, perecliter la barque, 2
Tenter 3 Phossen, 4 an Ponant 5 entretien.
Translation.
When the court of France shall be in mourning, the cat-like monarch shall make war against the young Æmathien. France will stagger; the bark of St. Peter be in danger. Marseilles will be taken. Two great personages will meet in the West of France.

More at large this may be read, that at the death of Louis XIII., when the French Court is in mourning, shrewd Philip IV. of Spain will make war on the boy King. France will be greatly shaken (1648-1653) by the civil war of the Fronde, whilst Rome will be endangered by the growth of Jansenism. This is Le Pelletier's version. Garencières says that Paris is signified, as she carries a ship represented in her arms. The 2nd of March, 1660, Louis XIV. enters Phocea or Marseilles by a breach, after which it submits to him. He then hurries to the west of the Isle of Conference on the Bidassoa, and there concludes the peace of the Pyrenees with Philip IV., and marries his daughter, the infanta Maria Theresa, of Austria.

THE EXPEDITION TO IRELAND IN SUPPORT OF JAMES II. (1689-1691). [I. 125.]
Century II.—Quatrain 68.
De l'Aquilon les efforts seront grands,
Sur l'Ocean sera la porte ouverte,
Le regne en l'Isle sera reintegrand,
Tremblera Londres par 1 voilles 2 descouverte.
Translation.

Ireland, on the north of England, shall make great efforts. The door of the ocean shall be opened to the fleets of France; the kingdom in the island of Ireland shall be set up again; London shall tremble at the discovery of sails.

When William III., in 1688, shall have established himself on the throne, when James II. absconded; Ireland will still be a stronghold, and the French fleets, commanded by Chateau Renaud and Tourville, will convoy the King to Ireland, in spite of the combined fleets of England and Holland, in 1689-1690. They will become masters of the sea, and London will for a moment tremble before the fleets of Louis XIV. This is Le Pelletier's statement. After the fight off Beachy Head on June 30, 1690, it seems to have been pretty much as he relates; for Smollett's account (ed. 1822, i. 93) is that;

"Torrington retreated without further interruption into the mouth of the Thames; and, having taken precautions against any attempts of the enemy in that quarter, returned to London, the inhabitants of which were overwhelmed with consternation."

There is a most remarkable passage in the work of M. Bouys on this quatrain. He professes to apply it to the coming victory that was to confer on Napoleon the coveted command of the seas, saying that you need not always wait until after the event to interpret Nostradamus. His own conduct, however, in this very instance does but enforce the rule. He pretends not to know anything of the fulfilment in 1689-1690. In furtherance of the same view he cites Century VIII., Quatrain 37:

La forteresse auprès de la Thamise
Cherra pour lors le roi dedans serré,
Auprès du pont sera vu en chemise,
Un devant mort, puis dans le fort barré.

The word cherra presents the only difficulty here as to the mere words. It is the future of the verb choir, tomber, to fall. Of the prophecy I know of no interpretation. Garencières significantly quotes Dan. iv. 10: "The dream be to them that hate thee, and the interpretation thereof to thine enemies."

WAR OF THE CAMISARDS (1702-1704). [I. 126.]
Century IX.—Quatrain 38.
L'entrée de Blaye par Rochelle et l'Anglois,
Passera outre le grand Æmathien:
Non loin d'Agen attendra le Gaulois,
Secours Narbonne deceu par entretien.
Translation.

The great Æmathion shall pass out of the Garonne at Blaye, the seaport of Bordeaux, no longer impeded by Rochelle and the English; the Camisards shall look for aid from their co-religionists on the side of Agen and Narbonne, but will be disappointed by an arrangement.

Louis XIV. shall pass out by the Pâté de Blaye, a fort of that name, built by him in 1689 to command the entrance of the Gironde against the English and the Protestants of Rochelle. The Camisards in revolt in the Cévennes (les Gaulois) will wait at Agens and Narbonne for promised help, but quite in vain, after the submission of Jean Cavalier (1704) to Marshal Villars, at a Conference held at Nîmes. Louis XIV. was so beset by the enemies of France that he sent the Marshal into Languedoc to pacify the districts he despaired of subduing by force.

In this quatrain, Garencières shows that there is some analogy between

Æmathien, which we are quite sure is Louis XIV. from the frequency of the application to him. and the country of Macedon, so-called, where Cæsar and Pompey fought their last battle in the field of Pharsalia; and he quotes Lucan's line—

Bella per Æmathios plus quam civilia campos.

It is very probable that line was in the mind of Nostradamus at the moment.

WAR OF THE SPANISH SUCCESSION (1701-1713). [I. 127.]
Century IV.—Quatrain 2.
Par mort la France prendra voyage à faire,
Classe 1 par mer, marcher Incurs Pyrenées,
Espaigne en trouble, marcher gent militaire;
Des plus grands Dames en France emmenées.
Translation.
By reason of a death, France shall, undertake a foreign expedition. The p. 142 fleet will go by sea, the troops will cross the Pyrenees. Spain in trouble will march her military forces, because great ladies have migrated to France.

Philip V., grandson of Louis le Grand, by will of Charles II., will ascend the Spanish throne. But Austria, England, Holland, Prussia, Portugal, and Savoy will coalesce to support the pretensions of the Archduke Charles. The fleets of France will put to sea, her armies will cross the Pyrenees. Spain, in two camps, will be trampled by troops in every direction: all springing out of Bourbon marriages with the two Infantas; one, daughter of Philip III. married to Louis XIII., the other, a daughter of Philip IV., married to Louis XIV. This war lasted twelve years, and was disastrous to France. Philip V. found himself chased from Spain by the Austrians. By the Peace of Utrecht, 1713, the Spanish monarchy was dismembered, and some of his earlier conquests were snatched from Louis XIV.

OVERTHROW OF PHILIP V., grandson of Louis XIV. (1706). [I. 129.]
Century IX.—Quatrain 64.
L'Æmathion passer monts Pyrenées,
En Mars Narbon 1 ne fera resistance,
Par mer terre fera si 2 grand menée,
Cap 3 n'ayant terre seure pour demeurance.
Translation.
The Æmathion is to pass the Pyrenean Mount;
In Narbo Martius no resistance shows;
By sea and land are greatest efforts made;
The Capet holds no foot of land is safe.

Louis XIV. will leap the Pyrenees, and will treat (as we have before seen) with the Camisards of Narbonne. He will make desperate efforts by sea and land. But the Capetian, his grandson, Philip V., will be driven out of Spain by the Imperial forces, and not retain a foot of soil on which to live.

In all these passages of history, quite detached as they seem to be, we find analogies springing up at all points: Æmathion the Macedonian, and Louis le Grand; the Spanish succession which came up again in Louis Philippe's time, even to uniting the very two names of Louis XIV. and his grandson Philip V. in his own baptismal one. Louis wished to expel a Charles, and Louis Philippe actually expelled Charles X. Leibnitz made an express journey to Paris to persuade Louis XIV. to undertake a grand expedition against Egypt. Napoleon, the next Æmathion or Apollon leading France to mischief, was thrust into an Egyptian expedition, and entered into a desperate Spanish war to follow, that crippled France again. History repeats itself, they say. It seems at every turn to be perpetually engaged in a process of replaiting its old lines and once-discarded threads. Footnotes

132:1 Added to the text in the edition of 1605.

132:2 Paux, plural of pal, pieu, a term of blazonry, stake.

132:3 Read cors, horns.

133:1 Æmathien, or Emathion, Le Pelletier says, son of Cephalus and Aurora, who opened the gates of the morning to the sun. I do not find this account of him anywhere. Cephalus is the chaste Joseph of mythology, tempted by Aurora. But Hesiod makes him father of Phaeton by her. Possibly M. le Pelletier has mistaken Emathion for Phaeton. Generally. Emathion is reckoned as son of Titan and Aurora, and a King of Macedonia. His connection in some way however with the sun is certain, and this suffices for the use made of his name by Nostradamus.

133:2 Latin, per, through.

133:3 Romance, emmy, entre, between.

133:4 Phi, for Philip.

136:1 Latin, classis, fleet.

136:2 Carseque, Romance for Corsica.

137:1 Romance, esgrongné, or esgruné, pulverised.

137:2 Turn this; when Æmathion shall build Hercules.

138:1 Latin, felinus, like a cat.

138:2 La barque of St. Peter, the Holy Seat, Rome.

138:3 Latin, tentare, to assail.

138:4 Phocen is another reading. Marseilles, founded by the Phocians, A.C. 660.

138:5 Old word for west, or sundown.

139:1 Latin, per, because of.

139:2 Voiles, for vessels.

141:1 Latin, classis, fleet.

142:1 Latin, Narbo Martius, Narbonne, in the department de l'Aude, said to be so called from its founder Martius. [See p. 140, ix. 38.]

142:2 Romance, si, very.

142:3 Cap, for Capet.

Louis XV

MINORITY OF Louis XV. (SEPTEMBER 1, 1715). [I. 131.]
Century III.—Quatrain 15.
Coeur, vigueur, gloire, le regne changera.
De tous points contre ayant son adversaire:
Lors France enfance par mort subjuguera;
Un grand Regent sera lors plus contraire.
Translation.
Heart, vigour, glory, change with change of reign,—
At every point opposed by something cross:
An infant is set up in France by death;
And a great Regent helps the contrary.

WITH the death of Louis XIV., the splendour of his reign will pass away, and every point show contrary in his successor. By failure of direct inheritors of the throne, Louis XV., a child of five will rule, under Philippe d'Orleans (un grand Regent), whose vices will show him more contrary to Louis XIV. than even to Louis XV.

DECADENCE OF MONARCHY (1715-1774). [I. 132.]
Century V.—Quatrain 38.
Ce grand monarque qu'au mort succedera, 1
Donnera vie illicite lubrique,
Par nonchalance à tous concedera,
Qu'à la parfin faudra 2 la loy Salique.
Translation.
He who succeeds to the great monarch dead, will lead an evil and illicit life. By his neglectful habit he will entrust business to the managementp. 145 of others, so that at last (à la parfin, per finem) the Salic law will fail.

In other words, this is a plain announcement that the reign of Louis XV. will serve as a simple prelude or introduction to the establishment of a Republic; the annihilation of the Salic law; and of the French throne. Footnotes
144:1 Ordo. He who shall succeed to the great monarch dead.
144:2 Faudra, future tense of faillir, fail, or disappear.

England

CHANGES OF GOVERNMENT IN ENGLAND (1501-1791). [I. 135.]
Century VI.—Quatrain 57.
Sept fois changer verrez gent 1 Britannique.
Teints en sang en deux cens nonante an;
Franche 2 non point, par 3 appuy Germanique;
Aries 4 doubte son pole Bastarnan. 5
Translation.
You will see the British nation change seven times, stained with blood, in two hundred and ninety years; but not so France, thanks to the strength of its Germanic Kings [of the Capetian race]. The sign of the Ram will not know (doubte) the northern district (son pole Bastarnan), so changed will it be.

ENGLAND will change its government seven times in a period of 290 years, inundated with blood, says Le Pelletier,—making this long run of years commence at what he calls the Renaissance (1501-1791). Not so in France; thanks to the firmness of the Germanic kings, she will hold out till 1792, I take this to be, in effect, a French endeavour to chalk out a grand epoch in French annals. Poland (la Bastarnie) will be dismembered. The first partition took place in 1772. There will arise in the north of Europe;—Peter the Great ascending the Russian throne, 1682, and Lutheranism triumphing in Germany, 1517,—so that Aries cannot identify the regions adjacent to its northern pole (son pole Bastarnan).

M. le Pelletier gives an elaborate statement of what he conceives to be the seven Revolutions in England (1501-1791). But starting from the Renaissance, at the fancy date 1501, he vitiates the whole of the interpretation as it relates to England; but for the last half of the quatrain he is excellent. His interpretation of the fourth line is masterly. Garencières gives a lengthy annotation, to me in the main unintelligible, but he makes the Period to run out about the year 1845; in which year I can see nothing to chronicle but the Maynooth Grant of £26,000 per annum. He says the two first lines refer to England, and he leaves the English nation to interpret them. We shall shortly try to do so.

(1) The Revolution Le Pelletier dates 1532, when Henry VIII. is proclaimed by Parliament the head of the Church; 1534 this should be. (2) Re-establishment of Popery under Queen Mary. (3) Elizabeth comes back to Protestantism. (4) Commonwealth follows upon death of Charles I. (5) Restoration under Charles II. (6) William III. takes the throne of James II. (7) The House of Hanover succeeds.

This is exceedingly faulty. It omits as one Revolution the most important of all, if consequences are to be regarded,. that is, the lapse of the Tudor race in Elizabeth and the succession of the Stuarts. Another very weak point is the commencing of the 290 years prior to the first issue of the quatrains. According to this, two of the Revolutions were already elapsed. A man does not prophesy of what is past, Nostradamus was writing in the reign of Queen Mary, so that the first Revolution would naturally count from 1558, when Elizabeth re-introduced Protestantism.

Now that we have contrived a firmer basis, let us see what this leads to.

No. 1. Elizabeth comes to the throne, November 17, 1558.

No. 2. James I. (Stuart succession), March 24, 1603. Queen Elizabeth dies exactly one hundred years after her namesake, Queen of Henry VII.

No. 3. Commonwealth on death of Charles I., January 30, 1649; Protectorate, Cromwell, December 16, 1653.

No. 4. Restoration, Charles II., May 29, 1660 (on his 30th birthday).

No. 5. William III. and Mary, November 5, 1668; Revolution (Gunpowder Day).

No. 6. Hanoverian succession, George I., May 21, 1714.

No. 7. Reform Bill, June 17, 1832. (Dulling the lustre of the Crown, as we shall see the French King mitré.)

Those who wish to prophesy pleasant things can do away with the disagreeable date of the Reform Bill, in part, because the No. 3 Revolution can fairly be interpreted as two Revolutions. Cromwell's usurpation belied the pretended principles of his whole life and conduct prior to that assumption, and can be called a new order of things. This arrangement will obviate the necessity of classifying the Reform Bill as the 7th Revolution. But the 290 years must end where they do, though you can regard the matter in what light you please. But I look upon Cromwell's treason, not to the King, but to himself as a man, as being practically part and parcel of the Commonwealth, or a horn growing out of the head of that rhinoceros or unicorn: nothing more. Given a popular revolt, a self-seeking horn always grows out of the forehead of the beast, till, with a ring in its nostril, it is driven whither its sublime liberties shall dictate.

Take it either way, it seems to me quite beyond the reach of the ordinary human mind, simply left to its own resources, to strike out four lines so pregnant as these, and await silently, for three hundred years, an interpretation, so little forced or driven as this is. I may say that to even pack into the space of four lines a mass of assertions so pregnant with hints, is a feat in condensation that no poet has ever equalled. Tacitus, the tersest of historians, has never approached it. No précis writer of the most accomplished skill has ever reduced the facts furnished to him in a well-drawn manuscript to such a compass. He could not, and remain intelligible. To those who will merely look at it in this light it may afford endless matter of reflection and curious study. As a forecast, its appearance to me is purely miraculous. Let any one explain it otherwise who thinks he can; we shall all be ready to learn.

STUART DYNASTY (1603-1649). [I. 138.]
Century X.—Quatrain 40.
La jeunne 1 nay au regne Britannique,
Qu'aura le pere mourant recommandé
Iceluy mort, Lonole 2 donra 3 topique, 4
Et à son fils le regne, demandé.
Translation.
The young Prince of the Kingdom of Britain,
Whose dying father will have recommended him;
This one being dead, Lonole will perorate,
And snatch the kingdom from his very son.

James I. of England and VI. of Scotland was born June 19, 566: the son of Mary Stuart and Henry Lord Darnley; who, before his assassination by Bothwell, had commended the young prince to the fidelity of the Scotch lords.

He ascended the throne of England in 1603, and under him England and Scotland were first denominated Great Britain (au regne Britannique). 1 When King James I. dies (Iceluy mort), Lonole will seduce England with artificial rhetoric, and demand the kingdom and the life of his son Charles I.

Lonole is the right reading, according to the Texte-type; others read Doudlé, and Garencières reads Londre. He also, fancies that the prophecy concerns Charles II., because Charles I. commended him to the people of England.. Cromwell and he have many analogies and points of contact, whether in history, character, or prophecy. But a further anagram, still more wonderful, springs here into view, which, I believe, has hitherto escaped all the commentators. Ole Nol, or Old Noll, has always been the Protector's nickname, and in the first form is letter for letter Lonole. It may stand for Apollyon also, and as such for "Old Nick" too.

I ought not to pass away from this mass and congeries of singular hints and disclosures without pointing out. the remarkable fact or link connecting James I. with Nostradamus, and the particular quatrain we are now dealing with. James I. was born June 19, 1566, and thirteen days after, July 2, 1566, Nostradamus breathed his last. This quatrain, once understood, is one of the clearest and most extraordinary of the forecasts of Nostradamus. The commencing event, the birth of James I., just touches his own death; and the last event, the death of Charles I., 1649, stretches to nearly a hundred years later.

Anagram seems to have been once a passion with the people. We find the white cloth of Lincoln in the thirteenth century alluded to as "Drap blanc de Nicole," that standing for Lincoln. [Le Roux de Lincy "Livre des Prov. Franc." i. 195.]

FALL OF CHARLES I. (MARCH 31, 1646). [I. 139.]
Century III.—Quatrain 80.
Du regne Anglais le digne dechassé, 1
Le conseiller part 2 ire, 3 mis à feu,
Ses adherans iront si has tracer, 4
Que le bastard sera demy receu.
Translation.

He who had the right to reign in England, shall be driven from the throne, his counsellor abandoned (mis à feu) to the fury of the populace (par ire). His adherents will follow so low a track that the usurper (le bastard) will come to be Protector (demy receu, or half King).

Garencières fancies this to relate to Charles II., and, that it is very clear. But evidently le digne dechassé is Charles I. Strafford was surrendered weakly to the unreasoning rage of the people (par ire). The Scotch, his countrymen (ses adherents), will sell him for £40,000 (Hume, vii. 76) to the Independents with unexampled baseness (si bas tracer). After this Cromwell (le bastard) will become Protector, or half king (sera demy receu).

This could scarcely be made more remarkable than it is, had it been written historically after the event, as history, than it is now before it, as prophecy. Look, again, at the overwhelming insight and terseness: the King defeated, Strafford sacrificed, the Covenanters' money bargain, and the Protectorate chalked out in decisive outline nearly a century before the realization: and each event is contained in one metrical phrase.

EXECUTION OF CHARLES I. (JANUARY 30, 1649). [L 141.]
Century IX.—Quatrain 49.
Gand et Bruceles marcheront contre 1 Anvers,
Senat de Londres mettront à mort leur Roy:
Le set et vin luy seront à l'envers,
Pour eux avoir le regne en desarroy.
Translation.
Gand and Brussels will march past Antwerp,
The Senate at London will put their King to death;
Salt and wine will be applied contrariwise,
So that they will set the whole kingdom in disarray.

Philip IV. in the Netherlands, being at war, will move Gand and Brussels towards Antwerp against Holland in revolt. Holland had, in 1579, detached itself from the Low Countries. Thus Antwerp became the border town of the Spanish possessions. Philip claimed rights over her till the treaty of Westphalia, or Munster, of which we have Terburg's curious portraiture in the National Gallery, con, eluded on October 14, 1648; three months only before the death of Charles I., so that the conjunction of the two events is extraordinarily definite and remarkable.

The second line is as definite and marvellous as anything that occurs in Nostradamus. By the treaty of Munster it fixes the date to within three months. Garencières says: "It is the most remarkable of all those [prophecies] that ever Nostradamus was author of." He notifies also, what I think nobody else has, that the number of this quatrain, 49, gives the very year of the occurrence in the seventeenth century For though we in England then called it 1648-49, Nostradamus, by the Gregorian Calendar used in France, would reckon it as 1649. We need lay no stress whatever upon this, for the quatrain wants nothing to strengthen it. Yet, be it the offspring of chance or intention, it is most singular. I have before said how much value lies in mere curiosities, and it is part of my business to point one out whenever I am able.

We have already handled the phrase vin sel at p. 133 and 135 [I. 119], but from a French, and not English point of view; yet even there the line is
L'Isle Britanne par vin set en souci.
—showing the consistency with which the visions must have shaped themselves in the mind of Nostradamus. The one we are treating of now appears in the ninth century of the prophet's quatrains, but the above line occurs in a quatrain of the tenth century. Still, what is said in the one is consistent with what is said in the other. If we call this chance, we shall have to admit an axiom far from self-evident; namely, that method is discernible in chance as well as in madness. Here, as. at disgraceful Old Pancras graveyard, there is clearly a slight derangement of epitaphs,

Bouys and nearly all the commentators treat the figure of le vin et sel, as representing force and wisdom, which were wanting to the King of England. I think we are not at all necessitated to adopt this interpretation. Supposing salt and wine in a good sense to symbolize wisdom and power, before we settle that to be their application here, we shall have to understand what à l'envers means. In the first place, it is not the preposition envers, meaning for, or in regard to. It is a noun substantive, masculine, and stands for the wrong side of a fabric, as contrasted with, or opposed to, the right side, called l'endroit. It means that wisdom and power will present their wrong aspect at this juncture, and become intrigue and violence, and will so stand to him (lui seront à l'envers), as that they will convert into their opposites, intrigue and violence. It has the old sense of inversus, as in the Roman de la Rose. A person is there told that on going to bed no sleep will come, but tossing from one side to the other:

Une heure envers et l'autre adens Come cil qui a mal aus dens.

Here it reads one hour on the back, another on the teeth. Molière says of a character (l'Et. ii. 14):

Vous serez toujours....
Un envers du bon sens, un jugement à gauche.

Nothing can better describe the mockery in Westminster Hall of the trial of the King than un jugement à gauche. The third line of the quatrain is the precise equivalent. Vin so nearly resembles vis that it is sure to mean force, the two extremes of which are power and violence, law and lawlessness. We see this very distinctly in the old French word vimaire, force majeure (vis major) and the word further signified storm, tempest, famine, and pestilence (vide Roquefort, s.v.). That wine does not at all definitely stand for power well directed, is plain enough from "the wine of fornication" (Rev. xvii. 2); and that salt is not to be taken as wisdom personified with fixity may be gathered, if from nothing else, from the sanctification of the sacramental elements in the Church of Rome; where before salt is used, it is first exorcised, to purify it from the stain of original sin, that passed upon all creation at the fall (Auber's "Symbolisme," iii. 394). Whatever wisdom Godwin, Carlyle, and other modern revolutionists may suppose themselves to have discovered in the character of Cromwell, Nostradamus certainly had formed no such notion of him, as we shall immediately feel assured by the next quatrain. Nostradamus's opinion of Cromwell may determine nothing at all as to the final estimate of that man. I adduce it only to help to settle what he meant by the words we are studying, le sel et vin. The next line is plain enough. The Independents set the whole kingdom by the ears.

I think we have reached a point at which every line of this quatrain has become tolerably clear. A wiseacre, writing about it in the Quarterly Review (vol. xxvi. p. 189) says: "Œdipus himself could not give the sense of the whole verse." This is the way in which people treat a difficult, abstruse, and intricate subject. It is so easy to say we have made up our mind about a man; that he is unintelligible, a charlatan, an impostor; that his forecasts are oracular nonsense, meaning nothing, or that if at times they do light on something, chance has more to do with it than seership or vision. You would certainly think that a sane man, finding in a book,—that indubitably was in print,—in 1558 a line prophesying the death of the King of England nearly a hundred years after, "Senat de Londres mettront a Mort leur Roy," would be struck with astonishment at the clearness of that, rather than with the difficulty of making sense of the other three lines. But this is what prejudice can do with us all.

CROMWELL'S PROTECTORATE (1653-1658). [I. 142.]
Century VIII.—Quatrain 76.
Plus Macelin 1 clue Roy en Angleterre,
Lieu obscur nay 2 par force aura l'empire,
Lasche sans foy sans loy saignera terre:
Son temps approche si près que je souspire.
Translation.
A Butcher more than king rules England. A man of no birth will seize the

government by violence. Of loose morals, without faith or law he will bleed the earth. The, hour approaches me so near that I breathe with difficulty.

Here we have a most remarkable forecast. It puts in a clear light what view Nostradamus had formed of Cromwell. There appears to have been visually present to him the butcher-like face of Cromwell, with its fleshly conch and hideous warts. This seems to have struck him with such a sense of vividness and horror, that he is willing to imagine that the time is very near at hand. A full century had, however, to elapse; but he sighs as with a present shudder, and the blood creeps:

Son temps s'approche si près que je souspire.

One of the most remarkable features throughout the work of Nostradamus, is the general absence of any sense of time, apart from the mere enumeration of years as an algebraic or arithmetical formula; further than this, he so regulates and controls his feelings as to appear almost impassable; but this announcement is of such unparalleled and terrific import that he departs from his usual practice and stands horror-stricken as in the presence of a fearful vision.

It was intended to treat here of the portraiture of Cromwell. To complete, however, my observations, I had to go to Chequers Court, the Print Room, and the National Portrait Gallery. These and other necessary steps occupied so much time that the printers had to commence paging; then, as the enlarged matter could not find room here, there was no alternative but an Appendix, which will be found at p. 305. My remarks, which make so little show now that they are done, cost me far more trouble than ten time,, the mere amount of writing would. The final settlement depends on the cast at Florence, if still in existence. I have cleared the road for a decisive conclusion; which, though it is not much, is yet something.

Bouys specially comments (p. 109) upon the word Lasche in this quatrain, and takes it to mean cowardly, the same as lâche does in modern French. Both forms of the word are alike deduced from the Latin, laxare, laxatus, and then if might well mean of loose morals, as I have rendered it. That the Latin may mean this Bailey's "Facciolati" shows, s.v. Laxitas: "Liber membris cum mollibus fingitur, et liquoris feminei dissolutissimus laxitate"; and Cromwell's dissolute life in early youth has been insisted on by many, though, of course, contradicted by others. Frederic Harrison is the last of these, and passes over the charge of vice with a very light hand, saying that "Such testimony as theirs we cannot trust; but we cannot now refute it." Suffice it to say, I do not think cowardice was what Nostradamus meant to impute to Cromwell.

The obscure birth requires a moment's consideration, as none of the French commentators allude in any way to it. The household of Robert Cromwell, Oliver's father, in Huntingdon, was of the industrious, jog-trot, somewhat over-professingly pious, middle-class order, common enough then in the Eastern counties. What is most remarkable, perhaps, is that the homestead, in which he was born, had been built upon the ruins of a convent of Augustine Friars, and that the two estates which came to him, one from his father and the other from his mother's brother, consisted of old church-lands. Oliver's branch of the family had rather fallen away from the county position which such inheritance infers. But it was always the more prominent families that stole, or possessed themselves of, the church-lands at the spoliation, and thus the Cromwells were married in and in with gentry. This scion of the robbers of the Church was soon to develop, on his own account, into a robber of the State; a man of violence and passion quite after the heart of Thomas Carlyle. Carlyle's notion of a hero, is a strong devil in a tantrum, mollifying, now and again, to the drone of a Psalm tune. Cromwell's branch seems to have drifted from the more courtly side to Calvinistic burghers and narrow-souled Independents; whilst Milton, who was born a London citizen, far away from gentry, was floated by his tastes and nature to the Court side of things, to the Bridgewaters, Ludlow Castle (see his deathless Masque of Comus), until a lofty idea of principle,—taken up by an unripe judgment, and dazzled by that false illusion, Liberty,—dashed him headlong into polemics, and irretrievably damaged the greatest poet ever born to England. They were exact opposites—these two. Milton sacrificed himself to his principles, Cromwell his principles to his person. Still, an old brewing concern at Huntingdon may well be designated by Nostradamus lieu obscur, as contrasted with Whitehall, and a burial, if you please, in Westminster Abbey, so wastefully extravagant as that it might well break a nation's treasury to meet it. Such prodigious pageantry belles the professions of the life, and can in no way be harmonized with "Take that bauble hence." Such empty, worthless show has less, for me, of the saint and hero in it, than of the froth of beer, and of the littleness and vanity of man. If this is to be great, prythee, tell us, what is it to be little?

BRITISH ASCENDANCY OF THE SEA (OVER THREE CENTURIES). [I. 143.]
Century X.—Quatrain 100.
Le grand empire sera par Angleterre,
Le pempotam 1 des ans plus de trois cens:
Grandes copies 2 passer par mer et terre,
Les Lusitains 3 n'en seront pas contens.
Translation.
England the Pempotam will rule the great empire (of the waters) for more than three hundred years. Great armies will pass by sea and land; the Portuguese will not be satisfied.

The French render this as meaning the destruction of England by large forces coming to overwhelm her by sea and land, but the reader will see that it does not at all necessarily show this. If we altered the colon, and put it at the end of the third line, it would simply mean that, whilst she was "all powerful" at sea, she moved large bodies of troops by both elements. I do not think it is very clear what the last line intends. But the three hundred years' dominion of the sea is a very palpable and most important object. That it is now drawing to a close is a somewhat melancholy subject for the contemplation of Englishmen, when we consider the searching revolution introduced by steam. If it really forebodes evil to England, it would involve dissatisfaction to the Lusitanians, as, if England fell, Portugal would be overwhelmed simultaneously by Spain.

The Invincible Armada of Philip II. was destroyed in 1588 by storms first, and the residue by Drake in Cadiz Bay. From that epoch we naturally date the maritime supremacy of our country, which, according to Nostradamus, is to last for more than three centuries, but not four. Nelson's death at Trafalgar in 1805 was the culminating event of our naval history. Its salt-sea tale still stirs young hearts in far-off seaboard cottages on stormy nights in winter with a flush of heroism, and that yet more sacred thing, a solemn sense of duty. But the old sobriety and obedient spirit of reverence, that was common in English homes last century is greatly decadent under the rotten knowledge dropping widely from the Upas Board Schools,—with reverence banished and obedience lost. The bare three hundred years ended in 1888. What the plus may count for, with Revolt thus bred at every hearth, a wise Englishman might ask with some emotion now.

It is said, in James's "Naval History," that from 1793 to 1815—I have not referred to verify—two hundred ships of the line, and three to four hundred frigates were taken or destroyed of the fleets opposed to England; and of the sea as at the pouring out of the second vial, it became as the blood of a dead man (Rev. xvi. 3)This completely crushed out all chance of Napoleon's descent upon England; but, with the lying spirit that distinguished his administration at all times, he: managed to disguise the fact from Frenchmen at the time; so that we find Bouys, at p. 92, promising him—out of two misinterpreted quatrains—in 1806, when his fleet was annihilated, the empire of the sea and a conquest of England as complete as that of William the Conqueror. It only proves once more how far from truth is the wish that is father to the thought. Let him stand aloof who would read the future by the light of the lantern of his prejudices.

We are now at the end of the guidance of Le Pelletier. Nevertheless, I will adduce several other quatrains to bring the English sequence down to the succession of the House of Hanover. They will perhaps not be devoid of instruction, though they will not be so remarkable as those already adduced. Several quatrains, more or less intelligibly wrought out, are enumerated in a pamphlet of the year 1715 by D. D. 1 The first relates to Queen Mary.

QUEEN MARY.
Century IV.—Quatrain 96.
La Sœur aisnee de L'Isle Britannique,
Quinze ans devant le frère aura naissance,
Par son promis, moyennant verrifique,
Succedera au Regne dc Balance.
Translation.
The elder sister of the British Isle shall be born fifteen years before her brother; true to her intervening promise, she will succeed to the Kingdom of the Balance.

This means that Mary, elder sister of Edward VI., shall ascend the throne of England. She was not born fifteen years before him. Her birth took place February 18, 1516, whilst Edward VI. was born October 12, 1537, over twenty-one years later. The fulfilment of her truthful promise lay in carrying out her vow to reinstate the Papists, causing even her sister Elizabeth to be imprisoned in the Tower on a charge of conspiracy. Moyennant seems to refer to the temporary nature and duration of her papal restorations; en la moyenne, in the midst or interim, between the Protestantism of her young brother, and that of Elizabeth, who succeeded her. Mary's birth was an event actually contemporary with Nostradamus; a very little inquiry, we may be sure, would have enabled him to have rendered it conformable to the facts of history. As exemplifying his method and procedure, it is very important to find that he took no trouble whatever to do so. It is evident that our prophet acted quite independently of external aids. He seems to have had methods and ways of his own, in which he had the most entire and implicit faith. In whatsoever manner the impressions reached him, he laid himself open to their reception, a reception to all appearance of pure passivity: he took the earliest moment of noting them down, more after the manner of an amanuensis under dictation than as being personally at all responsible for anything he committed to paper. The explanation of D. D. upon this passage is very singular, and implies somewhat of the insight of an adept into magical processes and fatidical language, of which we should be glad to know more. We must, however, content ourselves with it as it is; and even this little glimpse will be valued by those who love to study the human mind in all its byeways, and who are qualified to do so by thrusting aside from their own mind all private prejudice and vain prepossession. He says with regard to the discrepancy:

"But, if he has not known it, then has he either overheard it in raptu whilst his genius dictated unto him one year and three Heptades, or forgot it post raptum, and did write one year and two Heptades. The Lingua Demonum uses Septenarios in numerando, as we do Denarios."

Where he gets this intelligence from I have no idea. What he heard in raptu, could not have been one year and three heptades, for that would have represented twenty-two years, and we have to do with twenty-one years. What he might have heard, supposing we are right as to the lingua demonum, would be "one, plus two heptades," meaning three heptades; and he might have supposed it to mean one year plus two heptades, or fifteen years. If not satisfactory, this at least, has something of plausibility about it.

The phrase Regne de Balance has much of importance attaching to it. Garencières translates the last line, "She shall succeed in the Kingdom of Libra," and he annotates that the princess, whom he does not recognize at all, born so long before her brother, shall be married to a King of France, which is signified by the "Kingdom of Libra." He also says that Louis XIII. was called The Just, because he was born under the sign Libra. I give this for the sake of its being curious, though quite beside the mark, so far as I am able to see.

The phrase Règne de Balance is one of those pithy pregnant sentences, ever and anon dropping instinctively from the pen of Nostradamus, on all topics treated by him or glanced at. The whole bent of England's policy, from Henry VII.'s day to the Treaty of Vienna, has been to maintain a European equipoise, and to provide that no State should grow so strong as to overwhelm the rest. The wise counsels of the statesmen of Elizabeth were all directed in the hope of fortifying it; and it was never seriously infringed until the first partition of Poland in 1772, which was completed by the third in 1795. Napoleon's false profession to restore it in 1806 may count—like all he said, "as false as dicers' oaths"—for nothing. England's permission of that crime,—that satanry of royal crowns, struck her with judicial blindness;—and hired publicists, the venal reptiles that preceded the journalists, soon sprang up in abundance, to confuse and smoke-dry the moral sense of Europe. Poland had established that most unworkable of all governmental schemes, an elective monarchy; an arrangement that insures periodical anarchy at every election, and generally a wrong choice at last. The satanry of Split Eagles gave out, that the Poles could not govern themselves. But the fourth article in Peter the Great's will shows that they were not to be allowed to govern themselves. They were to be kept in continual jealousy, whilst the other powers were to be corrupted by gold, and a share of the plunder; till Russia could retake all. The bribers, the bribed, and the publicists succeeded so well that the very phrase "Balance of power" became, and stilt is, a topic of ridicule in common conversation. By this means its obvious rationality is excluded from any chance of a fair hearing. The Navigation Laws, Corn Laws, and Protection, have all been treated in the same way in our own time, and with the same revolutionary consequences, and loss of English supremacy. The Marquis de Bouillé, in his "Mémoires," ed. 1821, p. 8,—one of the few modern men who is entitled to be called a statesman,—says of England, that it is an empire whose support all other nations stand in need of, and that its happiness is intimately bound up with that of the world at large, but that if its thirst of gold should destroy its patriotism; or that bold demagogues and orators should get power to meddle with its fundamental laws, it would soon become chaotic and fall, leaving nothing behind it but another great ghost of empire perished, to glimmer as an historical beacon through the night of time. Again he says, at p. 24, that for thirty years (speaking about 1783) she has been the happy rival of France, and in some sort the arbitress of Europe. A little later on, when we crushed Napoleon by sea and land, and yet preserved France, we rose to our highest; but at Vienna the Règne de Balance 1 passed, probably for ever, from the sceptre of England; just twenty years after the final partition of Poland. Cursed are those who, with arms in their hands, stand by and allow evil to be done! We repeated the cowardice when France was under the heel of Prussia. If no virtue remained, the common policy of equalization should have weighed, to throw in aid to the weaker side.

QUEEN ELIZABETH (1533-1603).
Century VI.—Quatrain 74.
La dechassee au regne tournera,
Ses ennemies trouvez des conjurez;
Plusque jamais son temps triomphera,
Trois, et Septante, la mort, trop asseurez.
Translation.
The rejected one shall at last reach the throne, her enemies found to have been traitors. More than ever shall her period be triumphant. At seventy she shall go assuredly to death, in the third year of the century.

Elizabeth was long withheld from the throne. When she reached it, of course all enemies were regarded as traitors, and no reign was ever more triumphant. She proved a thorn in the side of popery; overthrew the Armada; and crippled the power of Spain, despoiling it of a large tract of land in America, which has been called after her Virginia; and under Essex, in 1596, inflicted on it a loss of twenty million ducats or pieces of eight, in the Bay of Cadiz. The next quatrain that we shall take seems to refer to the expedition by Essex.

The fourth line is a very singular one. It has no punctuation in the edition of 1558; so I introduce a comma between trois and septante. Septante is "seventy," a good old word that has dropped out of French usage, but which many French scholars think infinitely preferable to the clumsy circumlocution Soixante dix. Trois stands for 1603. Nostradamus often drops the thousands and hundreds from a date. We shall shortly come to a case in point, at the Fire of London, 1666. When Nostradamus describes the doomed city, he writes: "Bruslé par fond, de vingt-trois les six." The nought in 1603 cannot be given, so that, omitting the figures in the tens, hundreds, and thousands, the trois remaining gives the date; so that the line remains "In the third year [of the seventeenth century] and seventy years old, assured death comes." Elizabeth was born September 7, 1533, and she died March 24 (April 3, N.S.), 1603; fulfilling to a nicety the conditions of the line as thus set forth.

ATTACK ON CADIZ BAY (1596).
Century VIII.—Quatrain 94.

Devant le lac ou plus cher fut getté
De sept mois, et son ost desconfit
Seront Hispans par Albanois gastez,
Par delay perte en dormant le conflict.
 Translation.
Before the lake, where much treasure (plus cher) was stranded, after a seven months' voyage, and the host discomforted. Spaniards shall be worsted by the English, by time lost before giving battle.

Garencières here takes Albanois for Albanians, which of course prevents him from reaching any conceivable meaning. It stands for English, as Albanies, or Albions. The quatrain may reasonably enough be interpreted of the attack made by Essex, Howard, and Raleigh, June, 1596, on Cadiz Bay. They destroyed there thirteen ships of war, and forty huge South American galleons, part of the great "silver fleet," or "plate fleet." They had got stranded in their own harbour. Had the Spaniards been alert, they might have unloaded the treasure-ships, and so saved the cargoes. If they had attacked the English at once, instead of awaiting the onset, they might have beaten them off, or at least have kept them out of the harbour. But they were so supine that the Duke de Medina had at last to fire the ships to prevent their capture. The Spartans and Spaniards have been noted as being of small despatch: Mi venga la muerta di Spagna—"Let my death come from Spain, for then it will be sure to be long in coming" (Bacon's Essay on Despatch). Collins does not give this in his Spanish proverbs. But not only did Spaniards and Spartans procrastinate. "Business tomorrow," said the Theban Polymarch, in Plutarch, as he laid under his pillow some despatches relating to a conspiracy, and was killed before he read them. Copyslip wisdom saith "Delays are dangerous."

The bay and harbour of Cadiz may very well be called a lake, being twelve miles one way, and at least six the other, whilst the entrance to it from Rota to the Castle of St. Sebastian is a good six miles. When Essex got possession of the Castle of Puntales, he commanded the whole town and harbour. The idea of lake is actually expressed in the very name of Cadiz, which is derived from the Punic word Gaddir, an enclosed place. The Greeks corrupted this into "neck of land." The Romans contracted either this or the Punic word into Gades, and the Spaniards into Xerez, by the help of their Arabic guttural.

 Century VI.—Quatrain 22.
Dedans la terre du grand temple celique,
Nepueu à Londre par paix feincte meurtry:
La barque alors deviendra scismatique,
Liberté feincte sera an corn' et cry.
 Translation.
In the country of the great heavenly temple the nephew is murdered [by her who comes] to London under a feigned truce. The ship [of Peter] will then become schismatic, and feigned liberty become the hue and cry.

I cannot, I confess. altogether make this out. D. D. interprets it of the murder of Henry Stuart, I 567, and the final establishment of the Reformation. If it mean this, it will be a proof of the uncertainty, and almost caprice with which forecasts are concerned. It is strange that Henry Stuart's murder should find any representation, when, so far as I yet know, nothing is recorded of the fate of Mary Stuart herself. The heavenly temple is, according to D. D., the kingdom of the Angeli, Angels, or Angles, meaning the English. We are by no means forced to accept this interpretation, for Celique may stand for luminous, according to Le Pelletier's Glossary, where he derives the word from Greek though I see no such word. Celique is generally considered to stand for celeste, cælitus, from cælum. We might read it as a misprint for Celtique. Then la terre du grand temple Celtique would be the island in which is placed the great Druid temple of Stonehenge—the island of Apollo, Templum Solis, as Bath is the fountain of the sun, Aqua Solis. I record these hints, not as possessing much value in themselves, but as being possible aids towards future elucidation.

La Barque, in Nostradamus, is no doubt usually to be interpreted of the Popedom, the ship of St. Peter; but if, as I think, the general reference of the quatrain be to England and English affairs, then I should interpret La Barque as the Ship of State, becoming more and more schismatical, and in which the Puritans, Independents, and other Dissenters raise a great hue and cry about liberty, and liberty of conscience (au corn' et cry, or a cor et à cri, which is a variant of the early edition). The Puritans were becoming most troublesome both in England and Scotland all through the reigns of Elizabeth and Mary Stuart. Here D. D. insists upon what it is the business of his book to establish; that the accession of the House of Hanover to the throne of England is one distinct topic of the prophecies of Nostradamus. James I. was the great-grandfather of George I. His daughter Elizabeth married Frederic, the Elector Palatine, and had issue the Princess Sophia, Electress of Brunswick-Lunenberg, the mother of George I.

ENGLAND BECOMES GREAT BRITAIN (1603).
Century III.—Quatrain 70.
La grand Bretaigne comprinse d'Angleterre,
Viendra par eaux si 1 haut à inonder
La Ligue neuve d'Ausonne fera guerre,
Que contre eux ils se viendront bander.
Translation.
Great Britain comprising England, will come to be inundated very forcibly by the waters. The new League in Italy will make war against all such as band together against any one of the cosignatories.

England was politically called Great Britain when Scotland was united to her at the accession of James I. in 1603. Still, in an indefinite way, the term, or kindred terms, had often been employed. To go no further than the "Faerie Queene" of Spenser (Book III. c. ii. § 7), we find:
Far fro my native soyle, that is by name
The Greater Brytayne, here to seeke for praise and fame.

In this passage, Church says, it means Wales, as distinguished from the Lesser Brittany in France. The Greater Brytayne would hardly be Wales, but England and Wales together before the Saxon Heptarchy. This, however, in no way interferes with the propriety of the distinction drawn by Nostradamus. His allusion is clearly to the time of James I., who assumed the title of "King of Great Britain" on October 24, 1604.

The floods spoken of commenced about the end of January, 1607. The principal damage occurred in Somersetshire, where the sea broke down the dykes, and overflowed the country for thirty miles in length and six miles inland, to the destruction of all property and most of the inhabitants. Bristol suffered. The east coast by Norfolk suffered in like manner, though not quite to so great an extent. A long account of it, giving curious details of the calamity, was hunted up by Garencières, and found in an old, almost forgotten Latin book, entitled "Rerum in Galliâ, Belgiâ, Hispaniâ, Angliâ, etc., gestarum anno 1607," à Nicolao Gotardo Artus Dantisco, VII., Book 2.

La Ligue neufve, D. D. says, was a renewal of the Liga Sancta first entered into in 1526 between the King of France, the Pope, and the Venetians. The renewal took place in 1606, and was simply defensive, precisely as the quatrain puts it. Thus the quatrain stretches over a space of three years, from October, 1604, establishing the title of "Great Britain;" the ratification of the Liga Sancta in 1606; and the inundations in Somerset and Norfolk in 1607. The alliance of 1526 goes by the name of the Treaty of Cognac (or Holy League). It was concluded on March 22, 1526, between the Pope, Francis I., Venice, Henry VIII., the Swiss, and Florence. The second or defensive alliance, according to D, D., was between three only of the original signatories; France, the Pope, and the Venetians. I do not find it mentioned, but presume he is right. Garencières evidently writes in entire ignorance of both these treaties; but he says that the League will be of Bordeaux, which is called Ausone, from Ausonius, the famous Latin poet, who was born there. Here it certainly means Italy; but I mention it, as it is quite likely that Nostradamus might so employ the word, though he does not on this occasion. Ausone occurs once again, at least, in Quatrain 22 of Century VII., which I do not know that anybody has yet interpreted.

CHARLES I.
Century V.—Quatrain 93.
Soubs le terroir du rond globe lunaire,
Lors que sera dominateur Mercure:
L'isle d'Escosse fera un luminaire,
Qui les Anglois mettra à deconfiture. 1
Translation.
Under the jurisdiction of the round globe of the moon, when Mercury shall be lord of the ascendant: the island of Scotland will produce a luminary (prince) that shall throw the English into a great discomfiture. 1

Garencières entirely misses the purpose of this, but re, marks that the prophecy must of necessity relate to the past, for since the Union nothing of the kind has happened, Charles I. was born at Dunfermline on November 19, 1600; in astrological language, when Mercury, lord of the horizon, was combust and following Saturn cosmically with the sun: the sun leaning to a conjunction with Mars, and the moon, in her worst location, in quadrature with Mars. He succeeded to the throne in 1625.

D. D. translates the quatrain, oddly enough, as follows:
In regione aëris sublunari,
Mercurius shall govern, p. 173
When a light shall be born in Scotland,
Which will put England into great disorder.

We have here the stars in their courses fighting against King Charles, and, as soon as we had disposed of the historical remarks appended to the quatrain by D. D., our intention was to have thrown together some of the fatalistic signs of the time and the ill omens that attended this unhappy monarch almost throughout life, but unfortunately this intention must be laid aside for the present.

In 1609 James I. tried to induce the Scotch to conform to some sort of uniformity in Church ceremony, but he stopped short of endeavouring to thrust it down their throats. Archbishop Laud was less moderate. With the zealous persistency of a shard-borne beetle flying against a stone wall, he, in 1637, advised Charles to introduce the English Liturgy into the churches of Scotland, auctoritate regis. It was flying in the face of Fate. Quem Deus vult perdere prius dementat.

Next to the folly of establishing it, was the folly of its public withdrawal in less than twelve months' time. It was established by royal mandate, July 23, 1637, and by royal proclamation, June 20, 1638, withdrawn; a further undertaking being given that no English ceremonies should be thrust upon the Church of Scotland. Any tyro in statesmanship would have known that this course was doomed to fall utterly. Having taken the first inconsiderate step, it should have received no other impulse from England; private instructions should have been communicated to the chief clergy that no proceedings would be taken to enforce the law, and it would have died down of itself. As it was, the concession came too late, and gave the Scotch time to enter into a covenant never to permit the establishment of the English ritual; or, as they called it, the English Service Book. The fault was committed that, over and over again, the English commit as to Irish affairs; the yielding to outside pressure. Contentious opposition should be crushed by force first, and then conceded to as of grace. You will never get thanks from any party for having yielded to their threats. This only cemented disaffection; and, in 1643, England, puritanically urged, went further still, and established the Solemn League to like effect. This was a pure piece of political claptrap intended to secure general disaffection.

In 1641 the discontent had spread into Ireland, and, as usual in such cases, English reasoning and Scotch logic developed into bloodshed on the other side of St. George's Channel. The English often content themselves with ink and oratory, but an Irish Celt prefers to record his dissent in a rubric of blood. During the first four months of antagonism, the rebellion under Phelim O'Neil caused the massacre Of 40,000 English Protestants in Ulster: D. D. says 150,000, massacred by Papists, and they could be reckoned up by name. But where he got his list I do not know. His comment on this is: Tantum religio potuit suadere malorum. His quotation is not correct; I hope the same may be said of his statistics.

As we all know, Laud expiated his mistake with his head on Tower Hill, and the King himself was to follow on five years later at Whitehall, after being surrendered for money by the Scotch to the English. As Nostradamus puts it [II. 531, Du juste sang par pris damné sans crime.

King Charles was only twenty-five when he ascended the throne, labouring in that respect under almost the same disadvantage as Louis XVI. Both of these kings could derive but little wisdom from the Council-table. Charles's early acts consequently were rash, and those of the French King speculative rather than practical. Clarendon, in his History (i. 23, ed. 1731), devotes a paragraph or two of great interest to the impeachment of the Earl of Middlesex (Lionel Cranfield). Clarendon admits him to have been "a man of great wit and understanding," and to have held every place with great ability. He had been raised by Buckingham from a city trader to a statesman, and in his success seems to have quite forgotten the patron to whom he owed it. The rash Buckingham, on his return from the Spanish Quixotism, influenced the House of Commons to impeach him; altogether overlooking the consequences of employing such a machinery to revenge a private pique, and he must needs drag in the young Prince Charles to help him. The King foresaw the evil. "The wise King," says

Clarendon, "knew well enough the ill consequence," 1 and he sent for these two,—his son and Buckingham-to lecture them if possible into wisdom. He pointed out that it wounded the Crown and shook his authority, as Ministers would thus have to look to the House, and not to the King alone, as heretofore. At last he burst out in choler: "By God, Steenie, you are a fool, and will shortly repent this folly, and will find that, in this fit of popularity, you are making a rod with which you will be scourged yourself!" He then turned to the prince, and told him: "You will live to have your bellyfull of Parliament impeachments; and, when I shall be dead, you will have too much cause to remember how much you have contributed to the weakening of the Crown by the two precedents you are now so fond of," i.e. engaging the Parliament in the war, and the prosecution of Cranfield. It was, indeed, to teach the many-headed (which is equal to no head) beast to taste blood. Here, indeed, a King turns prophet; foreseeing, from existing facts misdirected, what future evils will arise. This, of course, is quite different from Nostradamus. "Flambe exigue sortant de solitude" [I. 1], and all that can be got out of visions of the night by secret estude or otherwise.

CHARLES II.—CAPITULATION OF EDINBURGH (DECEMBER 12, 1650).
Century VIII.—Quatrain 40.
Le sang du Juste par 1 Taurer la daurade,
Pour se venger contre les Saturnins
Au nouveau lac plongeront la maynade,
Puis marcheront contre les Albanins.

The above is the reading in the texte-type, 1558. D. D.'s version runs as below:
Le sang du juste, par Tore et les Torads,
Pour se venger contre les Saturnins:
Au nouveau lac plongeront la Menade,
Puis marcheront contre les Albanins.

He translates thus—
The blood of the righteous, for Torah and Torees' sakes, cries for vengeance against the Saturnine rebels, who will plunge the priestess of Bacchus, la menade, into the sea of their novelties, and march afterwards against the Scotch.

D. D.'s idea of the interpretation of this is that, for the sake of the law-abiding people (the Torah and Torees), the King's blood cries for vengeance against the Saturnian Roundheads. The intoxicated people shall plunge into a new course of wickedness, and will then march against the Highlanders. He considers that this was fulfilled in 1650, when, after the capitulation, as he calls it, with the Scotch at Breda, Charles II. landed in Scotland on June 23, and joined the royal army, consisting mainly of Highlanders. About the same moment Cromwell reached London from Ireland, and General Fairfax retired from the army. Cromwell, at this critical moment, jumps into his post, and, on June 29, heads the Parliamentary army against the Scots.

Without at all insisting upon the accuracy of this interpretation, I think it furnishes sufficient of curiosity to make it worthy of insertion. What follows, touching the Tories, I give in his own words:

"Some people stick to the Church of England discipline, even to a superstition, and to their last breath. These people had the nickname of Tories, cast on them by the Cromwellites; which is as much as to say some have the law of the Church put upon them, from the Hebrew Torah, which signifies the law, or the law of the Church of God. Perhaps did Cromwell himself, or some of his confident advocates and ministers, designedly invent that cursed name; as it is likely from what happened in the year 1651, when the Parliament ordered the law-books to be translated out of Latin into English, wherein the lawyers took a great deal of freedom by using the verbalia passiva very frequently, and almost on all occasions, according to their own fancy and pleasure. As, for instance, Apellans and Apellatus, they made an Apealer and an Apealee; the Arrestans and Arrestatus, the Challenger and the Challengee; as likewise the Warranter and the Warrantee; the Voucher and the Vouchee; the Leaser and the Leasee; in which manner they used likewise the terms of Torer and Toree; a Torer, in the first place—that is, a promoter of the Common Prayer and Church of England service; and an imposer of human traditions, instead of God's law; and, in the second place, a Toree; that is, one that submits and suffereth such laws to be imposed upon him. Which nomina verbalia passiva, so much in vogue amongst the English lawyers, are not at all English but mere French, and the Participium Passivum itself; and more proper to the neat French than the corrupted Provincial Dialect; which last our Nostradamus very often mixes with his style; wherein they commonly used to say, Les confirmads, les restads, les escilads, instead of les confirmez, les restez, les exilez, etc. And according to this Dialect one must say, LES TORADS, instead of LES TOREZ, and thus does our Poet."

If what he says above has any value, the Toree would be the prelates and clergy; the Torads the laity, who adhere to the Church of England and its discipline and ritual. This in the context would have a greater appropriateness than D. D. himself seems to be aware of, for the word it is contrasted with in the context is les Saturnins. This word in Nostradamus is constantly used for pagans, in contradistinction to Albanins, Christians, robed in white albus. In this quatrain also the men of Albany, if we take them for Scotch, are fighting on the side of Church and State against the Roundheads. Saturne is often put for Antichrist by Nostradamus.

The French of this quatrain, as it stands, does not appear to be correct. The first two lines require a verb understood to connect them: "The blood of the king [cries] few vengeance," etc. The third line has an embarrassed construction: "They will plunge the Menade into a new lake." If Saturnins, again repeated, be understood, it is difficult to see what plunging their mad priestess into the lake can effect. If it could be read as les Menades, then the frantic Bacchantes would plunge into a fresh sea of evil or troubles, and, in their wild intoxication, march northwards. If we could put any interpretation upon Taurer that would be applicable to the rendering, the whole quatrain might then apply to the French Revolution, and not the English. I think that the sang du Juste furnishes thus much of certainty as to the interpretation. It must relate to one of two periods; the death of Charles I. or Louis XVI. Then it would be that the Revolutionists, finding the Royalists to be seeking revenge, declared against the Church, and plunged madly into a new order of things. The Menade would be more appropriate to that period than to the earlier one. Bad as they were in England, there was more of lust, infidelity, and blood, corruption, vice, and madness, in France.

Menade were Bacchantes, the priestesses who celebrated the festivals of Bacchus. Stephanus says that it is to be explained not only as Bacchic, but as frantic; and this is unquestionably the meaning here. The Greek word appears to be connected with the Sanscrit man, to think; and thence the word manyu, anger, is said to be derived. They used to run dishevelled, half-naked, and, brandishing the thyrsus; in their fury they would kill and behead men whom they encountered by the way, and carry off their heads, leaping with rage and joy. According to Nonnus, they were virgins so careful of their chastity that they slept with a cincture of serpents. Juvenal attributes no great severity of virtue to them, but their pretensions to such superlative purism renders them all the fitter emblem of the canting Puritans who won Cromwell's battles for him. In Le Pelletier's Glossary maynade is given as a Romance word for "a child of four or five years;" but this throws no additional light on our difficulty.

THE BATTLE OF DUNBAR (SEPTEMBER 3, 1650).
Century VIII.—Quatrain 56.
La bande foible la terre 1 occupera,
Ceux du haut lieu feront horribles cris: p. 180
Le gros trouppeau d'estre coin troublera,
Tombe pres Dinebro descouvers les escrits.
Translation.

The weak band shall occupy the knoll (or, if preferred, it can be, occupy the ground or field [after the battle]). The Highlanders (Ceux du haut lieu) shall raise horrible shouts (before they engage, and also after their defeat). The large force shall be hampered or cornered (d'estre en coin), and fall close to Edinburgh, their papers even falling into the victor's hands.

This is a very important forecast indeed. The little band on the knoll—for I prefer that reading—is clearly enough Cromwell's small force, very much in the condition he describes it to be in, in his letter to Haslerig at Newcastle, September 2, 1650 (Carlyle's "Cromwell Letters," ii. 201):

"We are upon an engagement very difficult. The enemy hath blocked up our way at the Pass at Copperspath, through which we cannot get without almost a miracle."

Before sunrise Lesley sends down on Monday his horse to cross the small Brocksburn. Whoso wishes to attack must first cross this little brook, in its deep ditch, as they then called it (the picturesque tourist would now say glen), forty feet deep. Lesley's army comes out and places itself in "rather narrow ground," says Carlyle (p. 202) in 1846; d'estre en coin, says Nostradamus in 1558; or 1546, if you like to have it so, for it was probably on paper a clean three hundred years before Carlyle commented; you may even translate him, "takes the trouble to put itself into a corner." "Hampered in narrow, sloping ground," says Carlyle again (p. 206).

The reader who wishes for it can here leave off to peruse Carlyle's very celebrated prose lyric, as they call it, about this "Dunbar Battle," with its "moon" that "gleams out, hard and blue, riding among hailclouds;" whatever "a blue moon" may mean, or not mean. Carlyle makes Nol there, as the level sun shoots up over St. Abb's Head and across the sea, quote the sixty-eighth Psalm, in Rous's doggerel:

"Let God arise, and scattered
  Let all His enemies be;
And let all those that do Him hate
  Before His presence flee!"

Observe here that it is the Saturnins, in a frenzy of antichrist, who do this, according to Nostradamus. But you can take which side you please. "The Lord

General made a halt," says Hodgson, "and sang the hundred-and-seventeenth Psalm" at the foot of Doon Hill; to the tune of Bangor or other, says Carlyle, "strong and great against the sky," this grand strain arises, in which the metre, like the Lord General himself, makes a halt too:

"O give ye praise unto the Lord,
  All nations that be;
Likewise ye people all, accord
  His name to magnify"—

which, to eke out the measure, has to be read, nay-shy-ons, and, for the rhyme's sake, magnifee. This energy is really not dramatic, but it is stagey; on the border-land of sublimity, it curls the lip of humour to a smile.

The poor Highlanders taken prisoners were sold, "not," says Cotton, "to perpetual servitude, but for six, or seven, or eight years, as we do our own" (blessed are they who are of the household of faith); "which is really a mild arrangement," in the estimation of "the Sage of Chelsea" (p. 358).

But now back to our exegesis let us go. Cromwell captured, on this occasion, the whole of the papers of the Scotch, War Office, as well as the Great Seal of Scotland, which he sent forward as a trophy to London. Cromwell's letter to Speaker Lenthall excuses his making "no more frequent address to Parliament," but "it hath now pleased God to bestow a mercy upon you worthy of your knowledge;" and so he goes on, for a space occupying eight closely printed pages 8vo. He says he wishes to treat the Scotch very kindly, for that "God hath a people here fearing his name, though deceived;" and he concludes, in the dirty language of the godly of his century, that he has "offered much love unto such, in the bowels of Christ." His bowels, to the Highlanders made prisoner, awarded slavery, not perpetual, but for eight years only. Here are tender mercies and bowels commiserate for contemplation! sufficient, as we have seen, to make Nostradamus shudder at their approach.

Son temps s'approche si près que je souspire (viii. 76, p. 156).

All that was done here, however, could not prevent Charles from being crowned on January 1, 1654, at Scone, in Scotland. In the next summer he penetrated into England, and was pursued by Cromwell and his Ironsides.

D. D. follows up the Quatrain 56, which we have just treated, with Century VIII., Quatrain 57, which stands next to it:

De Soldat simple parviendra en Empire. [II. 171.]

D. D. interpreting it of Cromwell, as was most natural at that time. Garencières does the same, saying, "I never knew nor heard of anybody to whom this stanza might be better applied than to the late usurper Cromwell;" but unless it be a type of two handles, of the old ecclesiastical sort, I think it will apply still better to Napoleon; and I shall so apply it further on, giving the reasons why it is more appropriate to him than to the Protector. Further than this, as a general rule in regard to the succession of the quatrains in Nostradamus, they have no more affinity to each other than that they lie together, as one bean touches another in a bushel measure. Still, the next we shall treat is in sequence with the two preceding.

CHARLES II. AFTER THE BATTLE OF WORCESTER. (SEPTEMBER 3, 1651).

Century VIII.—Quatrain 58.

Regne en querelle aux frères divisé,
Prendre les armes et le nom Britannique:

Titre Anglican sera tard avisé,
Surprins de nuict mener à l'air Gallique.
Translation.
When a kingdom in quarrel divided between two brothers takes up arms. and the name of Great Britain: The King (Tiltre Anglican) too late advised, surprised at night (is forced) to seek the air of France.

It is rather harsh, but to make sense of this we shall be forced to understand the two brothers to be England and Scotland, or simply civil war. When Charles at last made up his mind to visit Scotland and fight for his crown, it was already too late. The Parliamentary side had developed a strength that he was never equal to cope with. The loss of the battle of Dunbar was a disaster that settled the question. He might as well have quilted the field to Cromwell at once. Instead of that, on the 3rd of September—ominous day! being the anniversary of the Dunbar fight—he engages him again at Worcester. Charles was completely routed and his cause hopelessly broken. He managed, under the cover of night, to escape from the city of Worcester, and, flying from place to place for weeks, as most romantically chronicled in the Boscobel Tracts, he at last, on the 20th of October, got well shipped for Dieppe, and finally rejoined his mother safely at St. Germain.

DEATH OF CROMWELL (SEPTEMBER 3, 1658).

KING CHARLES II.'S FLIGHT AND RESTORATION (SEPTEMBER 3, 1651-1660).
Century X.—Quatrain 4.
Sur la minuict conducteur de l'armée
Se sauvera, subit esvanouy,
Sept ans après la fame non blasmée;
A son retour ne dira one ouy. 1
Translation.
Upon the stroke of midnight, the leader of the army (King Charles II.) shall Save himself (by flight), and suddenly evanish. For seven years longer that is, to a day, till the death of Cromwell, his reputation will survive unchallenged; at his Restoration no one will say anything but yes.

In other words, Nostradamus tells King Charles II. to continue to hope on, for that though he will have to fly by night from Worcester, his memory will be preserved without diminution till the death of his victor, seven years later to a day. Further, that when the day of his Restoration does come round, he will be received back with universal acclaim. Had it been given as neuf ans, it would have been more complete as regards Charles II. personally. But, as it is, the date to a day coinciding with the death of Cromwell, makes one suppose it to have been given to point to that interesting coincidence. It would have been no more wonderful than are many others amongst the quatrains, had this been intended; but whether it shall be so allowed or not rests with the reader,—now that he knows exactly how it stands,—to accept or to reject.

The French used always to engage in a battle willingly on St. Louis's Day, April ii, and the English upon St. George's Day, April 23. But September 3, St. Mansuetus's Day, was ruinous to the Royalists and prosperous to Cromwell. The Battle of Worcester, so decisive in its consequences, was commenced at three o'clock in the afternoon on September 3, 1651; and at three o'clock in the afternoon of September 3, 1658, Cromwell died on what has been called his

Fortunate Day: "Nature herself," says his last chronicler in the ninth edition of the 'Encyclopædia Britannica,' "seeming to prophesy, in the voice of the great tempest that swept over England, that a great power had passed away." 1 It was a tremendous tempest no doubt, and men at the time said the Devil had run away with Old Noll. Some say he died broken-hearted, when the last Parliament convened by him in January, 1658, refused to acknowledge his House of Peers. So great a burden "drank up his spirits," said Maidston.

CROMWELL DECLARED PROTECTOR (DECEMBER 16, 1653).
Century X.—Quatrain 22.
Pour ne vouloir consentir an divorce,
Qui puis après sera cogneu indigne,
Le Roy des isles sera chassé par force:
Mis à son lieu qui de Roy n'aura signe.
Translation.
The King will agree to the divorce of his crown, which would afterwards have been regarded as an unworthy action, and hence will by force be expelled from the island. One who will have no sign of kingship will be put in his place.

Garencières was alive to the true sense of this and its fulfilment. The Republicans murdered the king, gave the government, if not the crown, to Cromwell, and drove Charles II. into France.

CROMWELL THE FOX.
Century VIII.—Quatrain 41.
Esleu sera Renard, ne sonnant mot,
Faisant le saint public, vivant pain d'orge, 1
Tyrannizer après tant 2 à un cop, 3
Mettant à pied des plus grands sur la gorge. 4
Translation.
A Fox shall be elected, uttering not a word, playing saint in public and helping himself to other people's property, in order to tyrannize after a while by a coup d'état, placing his foot on the throat of the greatest.

Garencières thinks this to apply to some Pope, but D. D. refers it much more aptly to Cromwell. If my proposed readings are allowed, the quatrain can fit no one so well, especially as it follows Quatrain 40, which we already have interpreted of the Commonwealth. D. D. reminds us that the Protector was a great Chiliast and Fifth Monarchy man, and certainly Faisant le saint public; even so as to gull, in this our late day, Thomas Carlyle, who allowed the heroism of violence, in this case, to dazzle him into the belief that the hypocrisy of Saintship was Godfearing. As to Cromwell, D. D. says truly, that he was moderate in diet. This he says to strengthen the barley bread, though I feel very strongly that it is differently intended. It might even mean that he got his bread by barley, or John Barleycorn, from the Huntingdon brewery. He was more given to ambition than to pleasure, says D. D., as is the case with men of his saturnine complexion. This may, by such as choose to use it so, connect him with Quatrain 40 and les saturnins. "His fortunate star, Mars," writes D. D., "had brought him the glory of a valiant hero and general."

Here D. D. entertains us, somewhat at large, upon his notion of a "wig, or trimmer, that is, a wavering man or hypocrite, from the original words to wag and to trim about." We, however, know that this etymology is not worth very much.

Our next is a sequence of three quatrains, all of which seem to refer to English affairs.

THE FIRE OF LONDON—DUTCH WAR—PLAGUE (1665-1667).
Century II.—Quatrains 51, 52, 53.
Le sang du juste à Londres fera faute,
Brulez par foudres 1 de vingt trois les six;
La dame 2 antique cherra 3 de place haute,
De mesme secte 4 plusieurs seront occis.
Dans plusieurs nuits la terre tremblera:
Sur le printemps deux effors suite:
Corinthe, Ephèse aux deux mers nagera,
Guerre s'esmeut par deux vaillans de luite. 1
La grand peste de cité maritime
Ne cessera, que mort ne soit vengée
Du juste sang par pris damné sans crime,
De la grand dame 2 par feincte n'outragée.
Translation.

The blood of the just shall be required of London, burnt by fireballs in thrice twenty and six; the old Cathedral shall fall from its high place, and many (edifices) of the same sort shall be destroyed.

Through many nights the earth shall tremble; in the spring two shocks follow each other; Corinth and Ephesus shall swim in the two seas, war arising between two combatants strong in battle.

The great Plague of the maritime city shall not diminish till death is sated for the just blood, basely sold (for £ 2,000,000), and condemned for no fault. The great Cathedral outraged by feigning (saints).

The first quatrain deals most remarkably with the great fire of London; noting the precise year, the burning of St. Paul's, and other injury to the Protestant interest.

The second shows that a bloody sea-war shall rage, the earth quaking under the cannonade from the ships, shaking the cliffs. There was such a war in 1665, 1666, and 1667, between England and the seven united provinces of the Netherlands. Cruising within the narrow seas, he likens to the Ægean waters between Corinth for England, and Ephesus for Antwerp. He describes them as they really occurred, commencing afresh with every ensuing spring,—sur le printemps. D. D. remarks that they were so obstinately contested, all these fights, that they would last for days on a stretch, or, as Nostradamus says, nights: plusieurs nuits la terre tremblera, according to the English custom of reckoning by a fortnight, and not fourteen days. Now the French reckon the fortnight as a quinzaine, that is, up to the fifteenth day, which of course contains only fourteen nights; and you might say la terre tremblera, for the cannon reverberating between the cliffs would move them perceptibly. D. D. thinks that la grande dame in the last quatrain is the great city of London, the metropolis, or mother-city; an Eastern way of speaking. In his learned way, he adds: "The great fire has only metamorphosed the city—ex Ligneâ in Lateritiam," converting it from wood to brick.

The distance at which sounds may be heard seems variable. Captain Parry, in his "Third Voyage," p. 58, relates, it is said, that at Port Bowen a conversation could be carried on distinctly at 6696 feet, which is over a mile. Dr. Clark, in his Travels (ii. 331), whilst sailing from the Gulf of Glaucus to Alexandria, heard the firing of the English upon the fortress of Rachmanie, upon the Nile. All on board heard it, at a distance of 130 miles. The earthquake at Sumbawn, in 1815, was heard 970 miles away (Elliot's "Horæ. Apoc.," iv. 218). In Dereham's "Physico-Theology" (i. p. 185, ed. 1786), a Dr. Hearn is quoted as certifying that guns fired at Stockholm in 1685 were heard at a distance of 180 English miles; and in the above Dutch war, 1672, the guns were heard above two hundred miles (vide Philosophical Transactions, No. 113.) I remember reading, though I have not noted where, that the guns employed at Waterloo were heard, at Hythe in Kent, on the Sunday morning, so that it was known Wellington and Napoleon had engaged in battle somewhere; the fact was confirmed by intelligence shortly after. The buzz of London traffic in 1820 could be heard by putting the ear to the ground on the top of Putney Hill, as Sir Richard Phillips relates in his "Morning's Walk to Kew" (p. 152). But the whole south of Thames was then tricked out rurally in Nature's emerald vest, and herself at case, the earth could transmit vibrations from the troubled town; but now she shudders with a like palsy of her own, and Putney is as rural as Clerkenwell Green. Much of the conveyance of sound depends upon the wind, no doubt. J. p. Malcolm ("Londinium Redivivum," iii. p. 117) has some interesting remarks upon St. Paul's bell. He lived in Somer's Town, and with a strong north-east wind he could hear every hour tolled as clear as if only a quarter of a mile distant, but with the wind east, south-west, or north, not a sound could be heard. Now Somer's Town is north-northwest from St. Paul's, which, in a straight line, is two miles and a half away; so that a north-east wind should convey the vibrations to Lambeth. He found that this wind carried away all the smoke, and so left the air free for the sound to travel through it. A south wind overwhelmed him with noise. He could distinctly hear the guard at St. James's Park beat the tattoo at eight, nine, ten, and eleven, to each distinct roll of the drum. One would judge from this that the wind was blowing nearly due east at Waterloo on that famous Sunday, the 18th of June. It was an east wind at Baalzephon that ruined Pharaoh. I have dwelt thus episodically upon sound to show, if possible, that this tremblement de terre was an effect of sound arising on the waters but vibrating upon land, and not the convulsion of an earthquake.

Quatrain 80 of Century III. we have already treated of by the help of Le Pelletier, and interpreted it of Charles I., and we there made the bastard to stand for Cromwell. D. D. takes the alternative reading of l'indigne, and understands James II. The bastard then is naturally the Duke of Monmouth, natural son of Charles II.; but he was never demy receu; and had it been intended to portray him, he would not have been mentioned after, but before, the abdication. Hence we prefer to leave it as we placed it at first.

WILLIAM III. AND THE REVOLUTION (1688),
Century IV.—Quatrain 89.
Trente do Londres secret conjureront,
Contre leur Roy, sur le pont l'entreprise:
Leuy, satalites là mort de gousteront, 1
Un Roy esleut 2 blonde, natif do Frize.
Translation.
Thirty of London shall conspire secretly against their King; upon the bridge the plot shall be devised. These Satellites shall taste of death. A fair-haired King shall be elected, native of Friesland. D. D. reads for trente, trained. Had the true reading been trained it would have been very wonderful, because the

trained bands of London had not been thought of in Nostradamus's time. Garencières interprets the quatrain to refer to Charles I., and says it is well known that the plotters used to assemble at the Bear at the Bridge foot. This was a celebrated inn on the south side of London Bridge. It was pulled down 1761, when the houses were removed from London Bridge (Public Advertiser, December 26, 1761), "Hist. Sign.," p. 154.

The Quarterly Review (xxvi. 189), in some very disparaging remarks on Nostradamus, says of this particular quatrain that it predicts "the Revolution of 1688 with tolerable clearness," resting upon the last line, which it prints in italics. As, however, William III. was born at the Hague, he was not born in what is called Friesland, but South Holland. I do not know whether it formed a part of Friesland in Nostradamus's time. D. D. is puzzled with the word blonde, and suggests that perhaps William had fair hair in his youth, "or it might be an allusion to his name, Guillaume, because (sic?) of cil, signifying eyebrows." This vermicular wriggle must be permitted to our highly excellent cleric, who is manifestly unable to get the quatrain to say what he wants it to say. We have had numerous quatrains that, when properly understood, have appeared to be clear enough, and which are disparaged as "perplexed verses" by the Quarterly. But this which they find expressed with "tolerable clearness," I do not find clear at all. I find no plot of thirty, no meeting of conspirators at the Bear at the Bridge foot, or at any other bridge, nor satellites who are executed, nor of a blond king, nor of a native of Friesland.

MARLBOROUGH AND THE CARDINAL DE BOUILLON.
Century VI.—Quatrain 53
Le grand Prélat Celtique à Roy suspect,
De nuict par cours sortira hors de regne:
Par Duc fertile à son grand Roy Bretaine,
Bisance à Cypres et Tunes insuspect.
Translation.
The great Celtic Prelate suspected by the King,
Shall post with haste by night out of the realm,
Through Bisance, Ypres, and Bethune, undiscovered,
By aid of the duke fertile (in conquest) to the great King of Britain.

This refers to the Cardinal de Bouillon, Great Almoner of France, who was misrepresented to the French King to such an extent that he could not appear at Court. After some years he threw up his charge and determined to quit France. He was related to Prince Eugène, who was with Marlborough, near Arras. The Cardinal came over to them under cover of night, precisely as described by Nostradamus, under the protection of a strong convoy, sent by Marlborough to protect him from the scouts of Ypres and the other places named. When he reached Antwerp, he simply sent in his ribbon of the Order to the French Court, accompanied with his resignation. He is called "Prelat Celtique" as the Duchy of Bouillon is in Gallia Celtica. D. D. holds that grand Roy is an abbreviation of Royaume. But the sense is better if taken literally as it stands.

I transcribe for the curious reader from D. D. the following passage; it is too singular to be neglected:

"But the allusion on the Duke of Marlborough is still prettier. Had his [Nostradamus's] genius dictated unto him Marnebourg, he might have understood and written down without hesitation, for the English Marl and the French Marne are one and the same. The Dæmons speak all sorts of languages, but Nostradamus did not understand the English, whence it came that at the hearing of the name Marlborough, he startled, and thought, 'Qu'est-ce que Marl?' Thereupon it was inspired to him, 'C'est une terre fertile et graisse,' whereby he is ascribing to him both Nomen and Omen at once; the Duke, by whose indefatigable zeal and incomparable valour the Kingdom of Great Britain should be fertile in conquests."

Century II.—Quatrain 68.

This has already been treated by Le Pelletier (i. 125) under Louis XIV., as fulfilled in the endeavour to re-establish James II. in Ireland. But D. D. refers it to March 23, 1708, when the Pretender cast anchor before Edinburgh, and nobody came out to him. He sailed away, narrowly escaping the English fleet. On this account an Act of Parliament was passed, declaring him a rebel, and setting a reward upon his head. D. D. says that from this time forth Nostradamus always designates him by the title of Rebel. As this quatrain, which we are upon, does not refer to the Pretender, the above remark would only show that Nostradamus always speaks of the Pretender as a rebel. Bouys interprets this, as we have said before, of Napoleon's victories at sea; as also that Bouys was blindly prophesying after the battle of Trafalgar, and in ignorance that such a decisive engagement had been fought. Garencières interprets it as fulfilled in Charles II.'s times: so that with four interpreters we have four interpretations. Sceptics can employ this fact how they like; I am pleased to furnish them with the opportunity. The total of the interpretations seems to me so astounding that we can well afford to submit to deductions such as this. Besides which, I am not endeavouring to establish any point; I wish the facts to establish themselves. What they finally show to be tenable, let us adopt.

GEORGE I.'S SUCCESSION (OCTOBER 20, 1714).
Century VI.—Quatrain 64.
On ne tiendra pache aucune arresté,
Tous recevans iront per tromperie:
De paix et trefue, et terre et mer protesté.
Par Barcelone classe prins d'industrie
Translation.

They will keep no treaty fixedly (arrested). All who have gained by cheating will go (free). Peace and truce are proclaimed by land and sea. Barcelona captured by the perseverance of the fleet.

This quatrain is exceedingly obscure, and very difficult even to translate adequately. D. D., who is writing only a year after the actual events,—the publishing date of his book being 1715,—makes sense of it thus: George I. is proclaimed King, October 20, 1714, and Nostradamus notifies that there shall be a general liberation of all prisoners for debt. But it is hard to extract that sense out of the first two lines, especially as not a word occurs about England, a king, or a throne. The other two lines approach the period well enough. The Peace of Utrecht was concluded in 1713, and the peace between Germany and France at Radstadt followed in March, 1714. The war between France and Spain also was concluded before King George ascended the throne; even Barcelona was taken, before he was crowned (October 20), by the French fleet for the King of Spain, September 12, 1714. At the intercession of Great Britain, honourable terms were conceded to the Catalonians in Barcelona, so that the mention of that city by Nostradamus comes with much felicity and appropriateness, if we decide that he refers to George I. at all here. D. D.'s book must have been written before October 20, 1714, as he says it is hoped that on the Coronation Day the King will empty most of the prisons.

GEORGE 1. (1714).
Century II.—Quatrain 87.
Après viendra des extrèmes contrées,
Prince Germain, dessus le throsne doré;
La servitude et eaux rencontrées,
La dame serve, son temps plus n'adoré.
Translation.
Afterwards shall come, from a distant land, a German prince upon the gilded throne. The slavery and waters shall meet. The lady shall serve, her time no more adored.

D. D. considers this to relate to King George, and he remarks that the King exercised a stronger control than it was possible for Queen Anne to do. The German prince ascending the throne of gold certainly seems to point to George I. But Brunswick is not a very far country. It might be said that modern constitutional government was established first by the Georges, so serfdom and les eaux, or the people and their so-called rights, met together, but then you would have to interpret figuratively the last line: authority (la dame) serves, or is to become subordinate to, the phantom. of Freedom, the time of reverence and good feeling having gone by. This, I say, might be so interpreted, but it does not carry much more conviction with it than does the meaning found by Garencières. He will have it to be a prophecy relating to Gustavus Adolphus of Sweden, called German because of German ancestry. His gilded throne was the gilded ship he sailed in. He made slavery and waters meet, because on landing he began to conquer Germania,—that lady who was no more worshipped afterwards as she had been before.

GEORGE I. AND PEACE (1714-1727).
Century X.—Quatrain 42.
Le regne humain d'Anglique geniture,
Fera son regne paix union tenir:
Captive guerre demy de sa closture,
Longtemps la paix leur fera maintenir.
Translation.
The human throne of English geniture will make its rule to maintain peace and union. War will be captive, or at least confined to half its usual area. (George will contend only with Spain. Peace abroad and an endeavour to maintain union at home, against the Pretender's efforts.) Thus peace will be secured to the country for a long stretch of years.

We have already given our interpretation to D. D.'s next quatrain (III. 57, p. 166). He discovers from it that George shall never want for an heir to the throne up to the Day of Judgment. Myself I see nothing of the kind to be warranted out of Nostradamus. He seems here to be contrasting the numerous changes in Britain with the happy stability of France. I should have made no reference to this, but for the opportunity it affords of introducing some of D. D.'s curious remarks upon the astrological portion of the verses.

At the Creation the Gemini stood in the house or sign Aries, near the equinoctial colure, which has but its own one pole; but they are now in the fourth house called Cancer, near the solstial colure, which has a double pole, viz. Mundi et eclipticæ. Basharion is an Arabic word, and denotes Humanus. Bashar, a substantive Caro, hominis cutis, homo. In the three signs, Aries, Taurus, Gemini, which have successively formed the Caput Zodiaci, none but Gemini is of human figure; that sign must be intended by the word Basharion (especially as the word is not Basharion at all, but Bastarnan); so that, till the age of the world is six or seven thousand years old, i.e., till the Day of Judgment, this will last; and when the great day comes there will be found a direct descendant of that great king sitting on the English throne.

He has taken no notice of the Pempotam and its duration of three hundred years, as a sort of measure of the seven changes, and Nostradamus nowhere says that the seventh change shall endure to the end of time. Like almost all interpreters, D. D. reads his own imagination into the prophecy.

The reader who cares about such explanations as these will find a great deal more of the same sort in Garencières' annotations upon this quatrain. He remarks that the sign of Aries doth govern France, and that by doubling his pole is meant his returning a second time to the same place, so that the stars do promise France a long continuance in exaltation. He adds that if he were a great astrologer himself he should work out exactly the whole calculation, and he thinks Aries should come to that pole in the year 1845. But Garencières seems to have had no inkling whatever of the French Revolution of 1789, as forecast by Nostradamus; nor yet of the second Revolution of 1848, though he translated all the quatrains into English. Footnotes

146:1 Latin, gens, nation.
146:2 Franche, for gent Franche, French nation.
146:3 Latin, per, by reason of.
146:4 Latin; Aries sign of the Ram.
146:5 Bastarnie, corresponding to ancient Poland.
149:1 Romance, nay, né, born.
149:2 Lonole, anagram for destroying, from the verb to destroy. Destroyer.
149:3 Donra, for donnera, will give.
149:4 Topique, flowers of rhetoric, oratory.
150:1
When hempe is sponne,
England's done.

When Elizabeth was in the flower of her age, Bacon remembered well to have heard the above; hempe standing for Henry, Edward, Mary and Philip, and Elizabeth. "Which," says he, "thanks be to God, is verified only in the change of name; for that the King's style is now no more of England but of Britain." Observe the wonderful propriety of the words used by Nostradamus. He noted at the right spot and instant a national change of name; a point of precision that nine out of ten lettered Englishmen would fail to reply to correctly, in answer to the sudden question, When was England first called Great Britain? It would be interesting to know the history of this "trivial prophecy" as his lordship calls it, for it has a good deal of the true spirit of forecast in it. It certainly was genuine, as it evidently was known to the narrator as being in circulation before it was accomplished.

151:1 Romance, dechassé, simply chassé.
151:2 Latin, per, by reason of.
151:3 Latin, ira, anger.

151:4 Romance, tracer, follow a road, track.
152:1 Contre, à côté de, opposite, or near to.
156:1 Italian, macellaio, butcher, from Latin macellum.
156:2 Romance, nay, né, born.
159:1 Pempotam, a shocking word made out of Greek and Latin -potens, all powerful.
159:2 Latin, Copia, military forces.
159:3 Latin, Lusitani, Portuguese.
161:1 The full title runs: "The Prophecies of Nostradamus concerning the fate of all the Kings and Queens of Great Britain since the Reformation, and the succession of his present Majesty King George, and the continuation of the British Crown in his most serene Royal House to the last day of the world. Collected and explained by D. D., 1715." This book is In the British Museum. I do not know whether it is scarce or not. It is not common, for I never meet with it in booksellers catalogues.
164:1 Hume has very ably handled this important question in his Seventh Essay (Hume's "Philosophical Works," iii. 373, Edinburgh, 1826). He there sets out that it is no modern invention as some have maintained, for the Asiatics combined against the Medes and Persians, as Xenophon shows p. 165 in his "Institutions of Cyrus." Likewise Thucydides exhibits the league formed against Athens, which led to the Peloponnesian war, as being grounded on this principle. Afterwards, when Thebes and Lacedæmon disputed the supremacy, Athens always threw her strength into the lighter scale to preserve the balance. She was for Thebes against Sparta till Epaminondas won at Leuctra, and then she immediately changed sides, as of generosity, but really jealous to preserve the balance. If you will read Demosthenes, he says, in the oration for the Megapolitans you may "see the utmost refinements on this principle that ever entered into the head of a Venetian or English speculatist." On the rise of the crafty Macedonian he again bugled the alarm to Greece, which brought the banners together that fell at Chæronea. The principle was right, but the too great delay had knit Fate's smile into a frown. Envy (if you like to call it so, but I call it a jealous prudence) must in a community of States prevent any one from overtopping, as Athenian ostracism expelled the citizen who grew too lush and vigorous for a communion in equality. Flume points out with perspicuous beauty how England went too far. Her emulous antagonism to France made her so alert to defend her allies that they could count upon her as a force of their own. The expenses consequent upon this imprudent course led to funding, i.e. the National Debt; and that has led us into an absurd meekness, a dread of war, and the peace barkings of the Quaker Bright; so that England dares not fire a howitzer when Russia, contrary to her most solemn pledges, annexes Merv, Bokara, and Khiva, and cannot find one word to say when Germany has her foot on the throat of France. Blunders in extravagant advocacy, blunders in parsimonious neglect of a principle, do not diminish its importance; they only emphasize it. With a prophecy out of dry reason Hume says it will become "more prejudical another way, by begetting, as is usual, the opposite extreme, and rendering us totally careless and supine with regard to the fate of Europe." That is how we now stand. In a very recent French cyclopædia, l'équilibre Européan is said to be quite a modern idea, with nothing corresponding to it in antiquity. The writer pretends that it originated with the Church, and that Podichad the King of Bohemia sent Marini to Louis XI. to point out the necessity there was for a Parliament of Kings to adjust matters between the Church and people.

This may be the first form of a Congress. Francis I. carried on the same policy, and Henri IV. extended it to an idea of a Christian republic of federated nations, as against v universal monarchy. This idea enabled Cromwell to meddle as European arbiter, whereas he ought only to have acted as moderator and equalizer of parties. Leibnitz called the House of Hapsburgh a continual conspiracy against the rights of the people, and Richelieu got the equilibrium established and introduced at the Treaty of Westphalia, as a principle of the law of nations, though with the concomitant of Congresses. The princes so assembled plotted against Poland, as might have been anticipated, and p. 166 in the course of seventy years they were enabled entirely to break up the Balance of Power in Europe. Cromwell, Richelieu, Napoleon, and Bismarck, by force, finesse, chicane, and brutal bluntness, have overturned the very groundwork of the principle. The English, having at first stirred up war by means of subventions, have now tumbled, only too laxly, into the stupid doctrine of non-intervention. Congresses should never have been allowed. These "Parliaments of Kings" can only do mischief, as they have no controlling power to refer to. They lack a King above the Parliaments, and as that is impossible, Congresses can only meet for evil. The strongest are irresistible in such congregations. The weaker can get no justice and no sympathy. If they take the field, everybody is against them; if they submit, they are despoiled without hope of a remedy: whereas, formerly, a wrong done might excite a feeling of justice in a neighbour, and so induce him to help; or, where justice was weak, fear of similar treatment might opportunely bring forth the required aid.

170:1 Si, for très.

172:1 Read, Qui mettra les Anglois en déconfiture.

175:1 Observe here how very different is Clarendon's estimate of James I. from the trash that Sir Walter Scott indulges in at the King's expense, in those romances of his from which half the world draw their notions of history.

176:1 Latin, per, during.

179:1 Variant, le tertre, the knoll or rising ground.

184:1 D. D. reads here ne dira t-on qu'ouy, and I think the sense requires it.

185:1 Historical discrepancies ought to be chronicled, for they confuse all investigation, and force every conscientious new comer to commence the whole work over again. A writer in the "Book of Days" pretends to be particularly accurate (ii 309), noting that "the storm in reality happened on Monday, August 30, and must have been pretty well spent before the Friday afternoon, when Oliver breathed his last." Rosse, in his "Index of Dates," says (v. Storms) that there was one on September 3. Carlyle ("Cromwell Letters," iii. 457) chronicles the stormy Monday, but not the stormy Friday. Hume says a violent tempest "immediately succeeded his death." Clarendon, who may be supposed to know better than any of them, writes (v. 648, ed. 1731:) "And this now was a day (i.e. the Friday) very memorable for the greatest storm of wind that had ever been known. for some hours before and after his death."

186:1 This, of course, is "living on barley bread," as everybody translates it. I think, however, it has reference to the phrase faire ses orges, to enrich one's self unscrupulously at the expense of others. If that be so, it becomes excellently applicable in the present context [Noël.] He had sown his wild oats, and now began à faire ses orges.

186:2 Tant, should, I think, be temps.

186:3 Greek, to strike = coup; it may even stand here for a coup d'état. [Borel.]

186:4 Construction is mettant à des plus grands le pied sur la gorge.

187:1 Foudre metaphorically, saltpetre, here fireballs. The belief at the time was that the fire was the work of incendiaries, and it has never been disproved, though it has been ridiculed by those who set up for liberty and enlightenment. The Illuminati will not allow London to have been thus burnt by others; and it is quite certain that they themselves will never set the Thames on fire. What Nostradamus asserts here, history has asserted. That is enough for the present purpose.

187:2 La dame. Garencières takes this for St. Paul's, once dedicated to Diana, who is the ancient dame. We may take it for the mother Church, if we like; and it would not be using much violence if we read le dome, for that might very well mean, as in the Latin, doma, house or church, as St. Jerome uses it—Domus Dei, in fact.

187:3 Cherra, future of the verb choir, tomber, to fall.

187:4 Secte. By this Garencières thinks is meant the eighty-seven churches that were burnt with St. Paul's, belonging to the same Protestant sect. We might read sorte.

188:1 Luite, Romance, for lutte, battle.

188:2 See note on previous page.

191:1 Variant, Luy, satallites la mort degousteront.

191:2 Esteut, or esleu.

French Revolution

THE VULGAR ADVENT. [I. 160.]
Century VI.—Quatrain 74.
La. dechassée 1 an regne tournera,
Ses ennemies trouvés des conjurés:
Plus que jamais son temps triomphera,
Trois et septante à mort trop asseurés.
Translation.
She who was proscribed will return to the kingdom,
Her enemies will be treated as conspirators;
More than ever her time (or empire) will triumph;
Seventy-three years its deathly domination is assured.

THE Revolution (la dechassée), repressed in 1816, shall again obtain the government. Its enemies will be treated as conspirators, and it will be stronger than ever. Seventy-three years are assured to its death-like rule. I give this as M. le Pelletier does, but I see no reason whatever to think that it is correct. Garencières makes it apply to Charles II. of England, and the seventy-three put to death are those who abetted the murder of his father. This is very vague. Garencières reads Le dechassé. Here we may remark that Napoleon himself [p. 280] dates his nobility from the battle of Montenotte, 1797, Seventy-three years added to this yields us the remarkable date of the fall of his dynasty at Sedan, 1870,

Century I.—Quatrain 3. (September 22, 1792.) [I. 162.]
Quand la lictiere du tourbillon versée, 1
Et seront faces de leurs manteaux 2 couvers,
La republique par gens nouveaux vexée, 3
Lors blancs et rouges jugeront à l'envers.
Translation.
When the litter is turned topsy-turvey by the typhoon,
Men will mask their faces with the cloak of hypocrisy.
The republic will be troubled by new-risen men;
The white and red will judge by contraries.

This means that the royalists (les blancs) and the republicans (les rouges) will judge of everything from utterly opposed points of view. What was top will become bottom, when the blast blows the litter over; and, new men rising to power, the rest will cover their faces with hypocrisy, as men do with their cloaks in a storm. Compare the phrase à l'envers with p. 154.

Century II.—Quatrain 30. [I. 163.]
Un qui les dieux d'Annibal infernaux
Fera renaistre, effrayeur des humains.
Oncq' 4 plus d'horreur ne 5 plus pire journaux
Qu'avint viendra par Babel aux Romains. 6

Translation.
There will be one who will revive the infernal gods
Of Hannibal, a terror to mankind.
Never arrived by Babel note horror
Nor worse day's work than will fall upon Roman Catholics.

The meaning is, Napoleon shall arise, who will reawaken the solemn curse on Rome uttered by Hannibal, when he called the infernal gods to witness his hatred to her, to the terror of all mortals. Not Babel at the dispersion brought on the world more horror, nor days of more evil-ploughing for the present or seed-sowing for the future than shall fall upon the Roman world by him. This is much better than to limit it to an ecclesiastical area merely. We shall see that Charles V. is a sort of prototype of Napoleon, and Garencières adduces Charles V. as fulfilling this prophecy. Hannibal is also a prototype of Napoleon in attacking Italy by crossing the Alps.

Century I.—Quatrain 14. (1789-1793.) [I. 164.]
De gent esclave chansons, chants et requestes
Captifs par 1 Princes et Seigneur aux prisons,
A l'advenir par idiots sans testes
Seront receus par 2 divines oraisons.
Translation.
Songs, chants, and refrains of the slavish mob,
Whilst the Princes and King are captive in prison,
Shall be received in the future as oracles divine
By headless idiots deprived of judgment.

Songs—such as the Marseillaise while the King and Princes are imprisoned in the Temple,—songs of the mob (gent esclave) are received by brainless fools for divine utterances, even prayers (divines oraisons). Vox populi, vox Dei, is always the fools' blasphemous formula, when swine chose Barabbas for Pontifex or Generalissimo. A cruelly entreated people; whose burdens are aggravated by wickedness in high places needlessly, above and beyond the grief, which every man is born to by the act of birth into a world of sickness, sorrow, and injustice; sighs heavily at this unduly heaped-up burden, and that sigh, that vox populi, runs upward like a lightning conductor to elicit fire from the clouds, coming back charged with electricity and thunder,—a vox Dei of terrible divinity. But when scum rises to the direction, as with the Revolutionists, and is followed by some brutalized sabreur aggrandizing himself as king of chaos and disorder, with shouts of subservient applause from the smutty mob, saying, "Herod, thou art a god," the vox populi that split the welkin once, is now the vox infernorum demonum, the whole upspring and outcome of which is bestiality and lawlessness enthroned in defiance of the decalogue and heaven. Thenceforth the appeal of all good men and sane is, "Ye who worship God, good and alone from eternity, down with them." The men must work and serve. This fiat is in the air, is in the sea, is on the earth. It is the vox naturæ, in comparison with which the people's voice, vox populi, is nothing, beyond a momentary troubling of the silences.

The following quatrain I give for what it may be thought worth. M. le Pelletier thinks it to relate to the creation of assignats, December 19, 1789. It would be a pity to lose sight of his identification, if even some should presume it to be incorrect.

> Century I.—Quatrain 53. (December 19, 1789.) [I. 165.]
> Las! qu'on verra grand peuple tourmenté,
> Et la loi saincte en totale ruine;
> Par autres loix route la Chrestienté;
> Quand d'or d'argent trouvé nouvelle mine.
> Translation.
> Alas! how great a people shall tormented be,
> And holy law in utter ruin laid:
> By newer laws all Christendom is vexed,
> With a new mine of gold and silver found.

We shall see, alas! the French people (grand peuple) agitated, the Catholic religion (la loy saincte) totally ruined, all Christendom put under new laws, when the National Assembly decrees that four hundred million assignats shall .be issued (nouvelle mine d'or, etc.), secured on the property of the clergy, in the interests of the Revolution.

Older commentators applied this to the paper-money schemes of Law 1716; and Garencières finds the fulfilment in the discovery of the Spanish-American gold and silver mines.

A properly regulated paper-money issue, based on the taxation of a State, having absolutely no intrinsic value whatever in itself, could undoubtedly be converted into a circulating medium that would work more smoothly than any metallic one can, because the market value of the ore, employed as now in coinage, is perpetually introducing a fluctuation of values that conflicts with the nominal standard of the coin, so that the standard is never uniform. The currency required would never amount to a tenth part of the taxation leviable. Paper could therefore be destroyed at the Bank of England, or issued exactly according to the needs of trade and commerce. Fluctuation in the market value of metals would no longer affect the circulating medium in the least. Thus might one cause of recurrent panics be removed for ever. But can bank directors or ministers be trusted with such a responsibility? This hinges on honesty, and there is none to spare.

> Century VII.—Quatrain 14. (1789-1793.) [I. 166.]
> Faux exposer viendra topographie,
> Seront les cruches 1 des monumens ouvertes,
> Pulluler secte, sancte philosophie,
> Pour blanches noires, et pour antiques vertes.
> Translation.
> Topography will soon be falsified,
> The urns and sepulchres stand violate,
> Sects swarm, and babbling sentiment
> Black put for white, and green fruit for the ripe.

The curse be on them for changing old landmarks. The provinces turned into departments (by decree of the Assembly, December 22, 1789). The sepulture of Kings violated at St. Denis. Unholy sects will swarm, and a sentimental philosophy, of Rousseau and other maddened sophists, usurping the office of religion, black will stand for white, and green, crude fruit be substituted for the ripe.

Century IV.—Quatrain 24.
Ouy soubs Terre Sainte Dame 2 voix feinte,
Humaine flamme pour Divine voit luire:
Fera des sœurs de leur sang terre tainte,
Et les saints temples par les impures destruire.
Translation.
Hear from the ground a voice of Halidom,
A human flame pretending light divine.
The blood of sisters stains the earth to red,
And holy temples the impure destroy.

This, I think, refers to the sentimental advocacy of the Rights of man, as substitutionary of religion and faith in the literary movement of the eighteenth century. It would comprise Rousseau's gospel of dirt and sentimentality, Voltaire's substitution of wit for wisdom, and the science of the encyclopædists floating disoriented upon the waters of un,, certainty, in lieu of the deep thought of the solitary thinkers that preceded them. These last were men who, heretofore walking humbly and without association in conspiracy, interrogated the universe, divinely sown with riddles in great abundance by a hand invisible, until they fell asleep into that hand, and awoke to the illuminated answers.

The blood of sisters was the wholesale slaughter of women that distinguished the Revolution, whilst church altars were desecrated by naked women, set there to personate the goddess of impure reason, feigning la sante dame.

The quatrain 25 that follows this in the text of Nostradamus I now give; but this verse 24, so far as I have seen, has never been commented upon nor has the connection been pointed out. Yet this stanza furnishes the reasons why the stars became overclouded to a people that were benighted, par ces raisons, as the reader will perceive by the second line that succeeds this.

Century IV.—Quatrain 25. [I. 167.]
Corps sublimes 1 sans fin à l'œil visibles,
Obnubiler 2 viendront par ces raisons.
Corps front comprins, 3 sens 4 chief 5 et invisibles.
Diminuant les sacrées oraisons.
Translation.
The infinite stars are links that light to doubt,
And drop the pall of night upon the soul:
The eye and front of man,—and soul,—grown cerebral,
God and His host withdraw; and with them prayer!

M. le Pelletier considers that Nostradamus attributes these effects to the reasonings hostile to the faith that improved optical instruments will introduce, as they suggest a plurality of worlds. I quite admit that in many minds this has been the tendency. Almost any discovery, giving a new hint as to infinitude, launches a number of inferior but vigorous brains into new lines of reasoning. We then get great multiplication of secondary volumes, which supply minced Aristotle or chaff to represent any amount of sausage-meat required by the reading public. Of course the further you can see by the telescope the further you put heaven away from the earth-dweller, and he loves it the less; for it is the near things we love, and not the remote. The heart is not universal, and cannot be stretched to it. I look upon the telescope, to an ordinary man, as a drain-pipe, through which he can run off and lose the moisture of his soul and live the worse for it afterwards; to the multitude of men, useless; to the scientific man, a means of inflation and puffing up; and to the really serious and isolated thinker, as the threshold of infinitude that may, though it has hardly yet done so, answer a few out of the ten million astral riddles sown in space. The last-named individual alone may benefit a little by it. But I question if anything at all of this was present to Nostradamus.

He seems to me, in these two closely interlinked quatrains, to enlarge much upon the theme of St. Paul (Rom. i. 28) that, as at the French Revolution, "they did not like to retain God in their knowledge, God gave them over to a reprobate mind;" or one void of judgment, "to do things which are not convenient." So that the earth gave out deceptive voices to them, and false lights for Divine light, to slay women and desecrate the temples; and then that the very stars visible to the eye, which should teach faith to all, will for these reasons veil themselves and leave nothing to mankind but the darkness of night. Pure materialism follows, God and His host withdraw, and prayer is no more heard upon the earth.

Century I.—Quatrain 60. [I. 168.]
Un empereur naistra près d'Italie,
Qui à l'Empire sera vendu bien cher:
Diront avec quels gens il se ralie,
Qu'on trouvera moins prince que boucher.
Translation.
An emperor shall be born near Italy,
Bought by the Empire at a bankrupt rate:
You'd say the herd, he gathers to himself,
Denote him butcher rather than a prince.

An emperor shall be born in Corsica—Napoléon Bonaparte. His advent to the throne of France will prove prodigiously costly to her. It is enough to make one say, from the tribe he surrounds himself with, that he is more like a butcher far, with the steel dangling at his side, and slaughter-man apprentices, than a prince.

It is natural that Bouys, who has hunted Nostradamus for quatrains that will serve for adulation of Napoleon, has passed this over, sub silentio, entirely. Garencières, speaking of this, says it is a prophecy for the future, for that until now (1672) no such emperor has been heard of, born near Italy, that cost so much and proved a butcher.

Century VI.—Quatrain 23. [I. 169.]
D'esprit de regne munismes 1 descriés,
Et seront peuples esmeus contre leur Roy:
Paix, sainct nouveau, sainctes loix empirées,
Rapis 2 onc 3 fut en si trèsdur arroy. 4
Translation.
The rampart of tradition battered down,

The people rise against their King anoint':
Peace, a new Saint, and sacred laws made worse,
Paris was never in such disarray.

The traditions of the French monarchy are thrown to the ground and the people rise against the King, Louis XVI. Peace will succeed the anarchy when Napoleon comes to power. Pius VII., to flatter the Emperor, will interpolate the ritual on the 15th of August with a new saint, the fête of St. Napoleon, 5 who was martyred under Diocletian. The Emperor's interference will hurt the Church greatly, and foreign armies (1814-1815) will reduce Paris to extremities she has never before undergone.

As to the fête of St. Napoleon, the story runs that when it was first instituted its impropriety, if not blasphemy, was much discussed in Catholic circles. An Irish priest from Rome was one day communicating the strange fact at a dinner-table in Dublin, when an Irish gentleman exclaimed with vehemence, "What d——d impudence!" "No, no!" said the priest, "what you mean to call it is the Blessed Assumption," for that day falls on the 15th of August.

Century I.—Quatrain 31. [I. 170.]
Tant 1 d'ans en Gaule les guerres dureront,
Outre 2 la course du Castulon 3 monarque:
Victoire incerte 4 trois grands couronneront,
Aigle, Coq-lune, Lyon-soleil en marque.
Translation.
War draws her length in Gaul for many a day,
Beyond the course of Castula the Queen;
Uncertain victory will crown three thrones,
The Eagle, Cock-moon, Lion-sun, on coin.

Civil war and foreign will last in France long after the ephemeral Republic has perished. Victory, always uncertain, will crown three houses in succession. They will coin money with the Imperial eagle of Napoleon; the revolutionary Gallic cock appearing with the house of Orleans, instituted by revolution, and adding the crescent of Mahomet for successes in Algeria; whilst the Lion represents Louis XVIII. and Charles X. of the Capetian Monarchy, with the sun representing Catholicism. Le Pelletier says the Sun symbolises Christianity, and the moon Mahomet or Antichrist. Myself I think it would be best to consider the sun as the symbol of Christ; the moon as the symbol of atheistic democracy or Antichrist.

This Garencières thought to be interpretable in his time He reads the second line,
"Outre la course du Castulon monarque,"
as, after the death of the King of Spain a Castilian monarch. The eagle as Charles V. [a further analogy with Napoleon]. Henry II., contemporary with Nostradamus, and Soliman, which three crowns met under Leo with uncertain odds in war.

The quatrain that follows this is:

Century I.—Quatrain 32.
Le grand Empire sera tost translaté,

En lieu petit qui bientost viendra croistre,
Lieu bien infime d'exigue comté,
Où au milieu viendra poser son sceptre.
Translation.
The great Empire will soon be translated into a little place that quickly, will expand. An unworthy spot, a mere county, from the midst of which he will come to lay aside his sceptre.

Garencières interprets this of Charles V., who, three years before his death, resigned Spain and the Low Countries to Philip II., his son, and the empire to his brother Ferdinand. He then shut himself up in the Escurial, in Castile, a monastery; which the son afterwards enlarged into a grand palace. accounted by Spaniards as the eighth wonder of the world. But I am not aware that any one has yet pointed out that it fits Napoleon as patly just as it can Charles. His empire was cramped into Elba—Æthalia, the soot island (lieu bien infime); a mere countship was his monarchy there. It soon grew again into an empire, but he only came out of its midst to resign his sceptre a second time and for ever.

After these prelusory flourishes relating to the Vulgar Advent and French Revolution, we are now to enter upon a more special theme; the murder of the King, and the ragged beggars' festival and brawl, called the First Republic of the Sans Culottes. Footnotes

198:1 Romance, dechassé, driven away.

199:1 Versée, for renversée.

199:2 In this high-wind of revolution men will mask their countenances with the cloak of hypocrisy.

199:3 Latin, vexata, troubled.

199:4 Oncques, never, nunquam.

199:5 Romance, ne, ni, nor.

199:6 The order is "Qu'avant oncq' plus d'horreur ni plus pire à Babel qu'il n'adviendra aux Remains par les journaux." This is M. le Pelletier's reading, and he interprets it of Voltaire, the encyclopedists and journalists of the seventeenth century, who assailed the faith and the Church of Rome. But surely the one like Hannibal was Napoléon, and the journaux in this old speech does not stand for journals and newspapers that had no existence, and therefore no name in the time of Nostradamus Journal meant a day's work, such as could, in ploughing, be done by a man with two oxen.

200:1 Latin, per, whilst.

200:2 Latin, pro, for.

203:1 Cruches = urns, Cinerary urns. Garencières read urnes.

203:2 Sainte Dame I take to be equivalent to our English Halidom, consisting of Holy and Dome—a terminative seen in kingdom and Christendom, and signifying rule or lordship. It has also been written as Holidame, as if referring to the Virgin Mary. Of course, if that were the correct etymology, it would furnish the exact rendering of Sainte Dame: but, as it is, it is equivalent. A voice feigning that of the Blessed Virgin may well be represented by a voice feigning that of religion and faith. I take this from Garencières, and not the texte-type.

204:1 Sublimis, high, elevated.

204:2 Latin, obnubilare, to cloud, obscure.

204:3 Romance, comprins, compris, contained in.

204:4 Sens = sans, without.

204:5 Chief = chef, God.

207:1 Latin, munimen, rampart.
207:2 Rapis, anagram, for Paris.
207:3 Latin, nunquam, never.
207:4 Arroi, for desarroi, disorder.
207:5 "On désigne quelquefois sous ce nom un habitant d'Alexandrie dont le véritable nom est Néopol, qui fut martyrisé sous Dioclétien. Outre ce Saint, dont la vie est complètement inconnue, les bollandistes font mention d'un Napoléon, brilliant cavalier, neveu dc Cardinal Fossa-Nuova, qui se tua en tombant de cheval à Rome en 1218. Saint Dominique, temoin de la douleur du pauvre cardinal, ressuscita le jeune homme. Napoléon reconnut ce bienfait en menant une vie fort chretienne et, quand il fut mort pour tout de bon, l'Église le béatifia. Toutefois, il n'avait pas sa place fixe dans le calendrier. Ce fut Pie VII. qui lui assigna pour sa fête la date du 15 août, dans le but sans doute de plaire à Napoléon Bonaparte."—"Grand Dictionnaire Universel du dixneuvième Siècle," par M. Pierre Larousse, tom. xi. p. 804. Paris: 1874.

208:1 Latin, tantum, so much.
208:2 Romance, outre, beyond.
208:3 Latin, castula, tunic. It was a kind of petticoat worn by women next the skin, and fastened under the breasts, which it left exposed. It stands here for the goddess of Republican Liberty, which is generally represented in this dress of the Roman virgins.
208:4 Latin, incerta, uncertain.

Louis XVI

WE enter now upon the lamentable period comprised in the Reign of Louis XVI.—a period whose only parallel in history is the false and Illegal trial of Charles I. of England; the perfectibility of man being evinced only by the increased savagery and augmented moral turpitude exhibited at the later period. The first quatrain that has been adduced as pertaining to this period in the Centuries of Nostradamus is that of:

Century I.—Quatrain 57. [I. 173.]
Par 1 grand discord la terre 2 tremblera,
Accord rompu dressant la teste au ciel,
Bouche sanglante dans le sang nagera,
Au sol la face ointe de laict et miel.
Translation.
By reason of great discord the earth shall quake.
Revolt destroys the old order and lifts its head to heaven.
The [King's] mouth will swim in its own blood,
And his front, anointed with milk and honey, roll upon the sod.

Tremblement de terre is earthquake, and from the time of Virgil, and much earlier than that, has been always taken to forebode convulsions of the State; disturbance of all things rooted and firm, and typifying upheavals of the populace. That it is the King's mouth shall swim in blood is shown unmistakably by the fourth line that follows, where the face is said to be anointed with the milk and honey of the holy ampulla. The Kings of France were crowned at Reims with the oil that was kept there in la sainte ampoule for this purpose. The milk and honey is merely a figurative expression; oil and wine, milk and honey, equally represent the fatness of the land.

Upon this quatrain, about the meaning of which he manifestly could know nothing, Garencières naively says: "The words and sense are plain, and I cannot believe there is any great mystery hidden under these words." Words put a slight upon men's minds to think they understand what they see written; from this it is clear that you may understand the words, and yet comprehend nothing from understanding them. Orators please take note.

Century III.—Quatrain 59. [Bouys, 55.]
Barbare empire par le tiers usurpé.
La plus grand part dc son sang mettra à mort.
Par mort sénile par lui le quart frappé;
De peur que sang par le sang ne soit mort.
Translation.
The rude empire is usurped by the third estate (tiers état).
It will put to death the greatest part of his [the Royal] family.
A quarter [of the kingdom] is struck with senile death;
For fear of retribution of death, from children of those murdered.

This must relate to 1789, as in no country but in France had the third estate usurped exclusive power to itself. Since that period the House of Commons in England has pursued the same lines, in a more covert, gradual, and, as some would say, lawful manner. In the Lyons edition, 1558, the second line reads mettra à mort, which makes better sense, though it spoils the rhythm, unless the a in mettra may suffer elision in old French prosody—a question I lack knowledge to determine. The quarter being destroyed, as old age withers a man, is to be understood analogically of the lives of citizens removed by terror, or emigration, or spoliation of property, or revolutionary taxation, or by imprisonment.

Bouys tells us that sang is to be understood in Nostradamus of children, family, relatives, so that que sang par le sang here would mean, lest the families of the injured should rise against the assassins of their flesh and blood. Such a reaction actually took place in the South, in spite of all the truculent precautions taken. The quatrains exhibit no kind of method or chronological order in their arrangement. So that, out of the thousand and more that exist of them, the commentator must hunt at large until he comes upon something salient that enables him to attach the passage to some event, when often he will be led to the most extraordinary results. The usurpation by the tiers état here, with all but the very phrase supplied, and with the results that would follow from the usurpation so unmistakably set forth, fixes the pertinency of the quatrain almost as perfectly as if it had been headed French Revolution. Yet a reader of less observance and care than is requisite to stay the attention which leads to discovery, might readily pass it over as jargon and mere nonsense. But, once you have deciphered the quaint phrases and their connection, you cannot doubt the meaning, nor the author's vivid gift of expression in conveying ideas, with a terseness more than Tacitean, if less artistic. You discover that Nostradamus can hint in a phrase of three words what would require a long paragraph to make it explicit in an ordinary way. This is truly the language of prophecy. It becomes legible in the light of the event it prefigures, as characters written in milk upon paper become visible at the fire, or when placed in the hot light of the sun.

Century I.—Quatrain 36. [Bouys, 56.]
Tard le monarque se viendra repentir,
De n'avoir mis à mort son adversaire;
Mais viendra bien à plus haut consentir,
(à ce) Que tout son sang par mort fera défaire.
Translation.
The monarch shall too late repent
That he hath not put to death his adversary;
But he will have to permit later on,
That all his family shall suffer for it by death.

Taking this to be the meaning, it is clear that the adversary is the Duke of Orleans,—that centre of all plotting and intrigue against Louis,—who had so forgotten himself as, at a public bed of justice, in 1788, to shake his fist in the King's fact with a most threatening expression of countenance. For this he was only sent into exile when he ought to have suffered death. In the last line sang again stands for family and relatives. This could scarcely be plainer if the names were given; but, had Nostradamus here deviated from the secret idiom of prophetic language, he would have prevented the accomplishment of what he was asserting. Things like this may be happened on by chance, if you choose to say so, but the theory reels under the constant repetition of such chances. Men whose names are prominently before the world can hardly be introduced into prophecy. But we shall see shortly that Nostradamus is able to assign names with precision where the individuals are of a lesser rank, and that their names may so pass unobserved until history has recorded them with her iron pen.

Century IX.—Quatrain 20. (June 20, 1791.) [I. 174.]
De nuict viendra par le forest de Reines,
Deux pars, vaultorte, Herne la pierre blanche,
Le moyne noir en gris dedans Varennes:
Esleu Cap. cause tempeste, feu, sang, tranche.
Translation. [II. P., I. 174.]
By night shall come through the forest of Reines
Two parts, face about, the Queen a white stone,
The black monk in gray within Varennes.
Chosen Cap. causes tempest, fire, blood, slice.

In the translation of this, Garencières leaves the two words vaultorte Herne as in the original French, and does not attempt the translation. He also mistakes Reines for Rennes, the chief town in Little Brittany. He evidently has no conception whatever of the meaning of the quatrain. Bouys and Le Pelletier differ on minor points in rendering these words, Forest, Le Pelletier reads, in Latin, as fores, gate, that is, by the Queen's gate, and he quotes Thiers to show ("Hist. Révol. Fran." i. 309) that the Queen made sure of a secret gate out of the Tuileries, by which they escaped. But Bouys takes it for the forest of Reines, which is on the road to Varennes. Deux pars is husband and wife; voltorte, or vaultorte, is a cross-road, or a divergent road; vaulx, a valley, and torte, tortuous, says Le Pelletier. One does not quite see how to educe cross road from this. Roquefort gives volt for face, and torte would be turned, which seems to me more likely, However, it stands for the road through St. Menehould, on the way to Montmédi. This, it seems, they were forced into by posting arrangements. Prudhomme ("Revol. de Paris," No. 102, p. 542) sets the divergence down to vacillation or change of orders. If that be the correct statement, then my etymology of face about for vaultorte fits it best. Herne is Reine, by metaplasm of h for i. It was permissible in anagrammatic writing to change one letter in a word, but not more than one. The reader can refer for this to the "Dictionnaire de Trévoux," under Anagramme. The white stone stands for this royal or precious stone, the Queen, who was dressed in white. The King was dressed in grey. Prudhomme, in the work mentioned above (p. 554), says he wore a round hat, which hid his face, and had on an iron-grey coat (gris de fer), so he appeared like a Carmelite.

There are nearly fourteen octavo pages of small print (p. 411) of De Bouillé, which it might be well, to print, called "Details du voyage du roi et de la reine à Montmédy et leur arrestation à Varennes dans le Clairmontais, le 22 juin, 1791," full of interesting particulars.

VAULTORTE

"Mais on verra que les circonstances changèrent entièrement jusqu'au moment de l'exécution de son projet; et ce qui était possible au mois de janvier 1791, ne l'était plus au mois de juin."—"Mémoires du Marquis de Bouillé," p.

195, ed. 1821.

"Il [le roi] m'informait qu'il partirait, avec sa famille, dans une seule voiture qu'il ferait faire exprès. Dans la réponse que je fis au roi, je pris la liberté de lui représenter encore une fois que la route par Varennes offrait de grands inconvéniens, à cause des relais qu'il fallait y placer pour suppléer à la poste. . . . J'engageai donc Sa Majesté à prendre la route par Reims, ou celle de Flandre, en passant par Chimay, et en traversant ensuite les Ardennes pour se rendre à Montmédy. Je lui représentais les inconveniens de voyager avec la reine et ses enfants, dans une seule voiture faite exprès, et qui serait remarquée de tout le monde," etc.—"Mémoires du Marquis de Bouillé," p. 217.

This flight occurred on June 20, 1791. On the following day the National Assembly suspended Louis XVI. from his functions. On the 1st of September they passed another decree, that should the King surrender to the will of the people and become a Constitutional King he might do so. This he duly signed and attested on the 14th of the same month; so Capet fut esleu. The title of King of the French instead of the King of France, had been established since October 16, 1789 ("Cyclopædia of Universal History"), which virtually was the same thing. But yet strictly it was not until after the flight that he became Esleu Cap. Madame Campan, in the "Mémoires de Marie-Antoinette," ii. 150, relates that the Queen's hair had become white in a single night and she had had a lock of her white hair mounted in a ring for the Princesse de Lamballe, inscribed Blanchis par le malheur. She had become la pierre plus blanche encore. Her dress was white, and her complexion too. The tranche stands for the slice, or couperet, of the guillotine. Bouys was amongst the first to explain this quatrain in print, and he says he owed the explanation to M. de Vaudeuil, of Nevers, who has written upon Nostradamus.

Century IX.—Quatrain 34. [I. 177.]
Le part 1 solus, 2 Mary 3 sera mitré
Retour: conflict passera sur le thuille,
Par cinq cents: un trahyr 4 sera tittré
Narbon: et Saulce par coutaux 5 avons 6 d'huille.
Translation.

The husband alone afflicted will be mitred on his return. A conflict will take place at the Tuileries by five hundred men. One traitor will be titled—Narbon; and (the other) Saulce, grandfather oilman, will [hand him] over to the soldiery.

The harness broke at Montmirail, and detained them two hours (p. 247). The King showed himself at Chalons, and was recognized by the postmaster, who held his tongue. Everything went wrong owing to the change of date and loss of time on the road. At St. Menehould he was recognized again, and Drouet the postmaster's son, rode on to Varennes to betray him.

On the 15th of June the Marquis de Bouillé received a letter from the King, saying his departure would be delayed till the 20th, at midnight; that he could not take the Marquis d'Agoult, recommended to him by Bouillé (as an "homme d'esprit, ferme et courageux, qui pent se montrer si les circonstances l'exigalent," p. 217), because Madame de Tourzel, the governess of the children, insisted on her right of place never to quit them; and this consideration carried the decision. As if the King could not have let them follow in another vehicle! Anything rather than be forced to show himself on the road as he did (p. 256).

How it all miscarried will be best understood by reading the whole of De Bouillé's account. His arrangements seem to have been masterly, like the noble soldier and statesman that he was; the King's arrangements vacillating, foolish, and even perverse. In this account Monsieur Saulce is not seen at all.

This is to be filled in as follows. Louis XVI. alone, without his wife, will suffer the disgrace of being crowned with the red cap of Liberty, called the Phrygian bonnet or mitre, from its being the headdress of the priests of Mithras. The five hundred Marseillais led the attack upon the Tuileries, a palace begun by Catherine de Medici (1564) on the site of the tile-kilns (le thuille), and not in existence when Nostradamus wrote this (1555). The Count de Narbonne, Minister of War, was of the noblesse, and Saulce, father, son, and grandson, were chandlers and grocers, or oilmen, of Varennes. The father was Procureur-syndic of his commune. These oilmen betrayed him to the populace, and he was arrested per custodes. These sneaks stand as typical of representative traitors of the two classes of noblesse and bourgoisie paying cowardly court to the prolétaire class.

The Madame Campan before alluded to (ii. 158) relates that their Majesties alighted at the grocery shop of the Mayor of Varennes, Saulce; and he could have saved the King. The Queen was seated in the shop between two high-piled stacks of candles, and was talking to Madame Saulce.

The Gazette Nationale, June 25, 1791, reporting what took place in the Assembly the night before, announces that M. Martinet, in addressing the House, described Saulce's conduct as wise and heroic, replying as he did to the promises and caresses of the King and Queen, "J'aime mon roi; mais je resterai fidèle à ma patrie." The result of his heroism was that two months later on the Assembly voted him twenty thousand livres as the reward of his exalted vertue citoyenne. Whether, in the scramble that so soon followed, he ever received the wasteful and ridiculous Judas-gift there is nothing to show; but the bulletin recording the vote of these new-fledged statesmen, liberal of money not their own, still exists. We have here "un Brute Français," apeing the Roman, who loved César well, but blood better.

Thiers' account of the attack upon the Tuileries, June 20, 1792 ("Révol. Fran.," ii. 152), furnishes a pathetic picture of the afflicted King (marri mitré) of the red nightcap, in which he was day-dreaming. The palace was evacuated at about seven in the evening by the populace, which had effected its entry by main force; but, when the crowd had Dow withdrawn peaceably and in good order, the King, Queen, her sister, and the children, all met together, shedding a torrent of tears. The King seemed stunned by what had taken place; the red cap was still upon his head; he now, for the first time for several hours, noticed it, and flung it aside with indignation.

As to the five hundred men named by our oracle, the historian of the French Revolution again comes to our aid (ii. p. 209), saying that Barbaroux had promised the Jacobins the co-operation of his Marseillais, who were on the way to Paris. The project was to assemble at the Tuileries and depose the king (ii. p. 235). They arrived on June 30, 1792, and were five hundred men. Ils étaient cinq cents.

Those who care to see how Narbonne acted against the King, can refer to the "Histoire de la Révolution," by Bertrand de Molleville, for satisfaction.

This stands out certainly as one of the most startling of all the thousand quatrains of our strange seer. It will henceforth and to the end of time speak for itself without comment, if we merely enumerate the historic facts as here anticipated in four lines. The horror of the king at finding himself mitré. The god Mithras is depicted on coins in this very cap, and his priests made it their head-dress; further, it furnishes the lively etymology of the word mitre itself. It was for ages, before the French took it up, the received emblem of that frantic crime that has been called Liberty. I will not say the result of this is, as poetry, artistically beautiful; but, as a phrase of intense expression, it is so terse that at a stroke, beyond that of hydraulic power, it seems able to compress a truss of hay so as it may lie in a husk of beechmast. I do say, nevertheless, that, thus regarded, Dante and Shakespeare can hardly furnish between them three sentences of such compressed force; the matter in it seems to be condensed to adamant. Mari sera mitré, as it has been just explained, will be found, the more profoundly it is thought upon, to be an original miracle in phraseology. It is an actual and an awful prophecy in itself, but to devise a phrase to so convey the idea by human speech to the human mind of another is miraculous. It may sleep for centuries, as this has done, for lack of interpretation; but, when duly interpreted it cannot be resisted; it storms the understanding; and, as a phrase, seems to be a miracle begotten expressly to become the vehicle in which to convey another miracle. This horror of the King mitred is one distinct forecast. The second point is his return to Paris. There is, thirdly, the conflict of the five hundred. Fourthly, the spot, the Tuileries,—at Nostradamus' time, a thing of thin air, where the tiles were still baking, fire-hot to roof houses with, whilst the pen was writing this. Here again, if it is not poetry, it performs the poet's function, which gives to airy nothing a local habitation and a name. Fifthly, comes a titled name-Narbonne. Sixthly, that of Saulce; and finally, the handing over to the custodians. Here are seven distinct prophecies of events historical: two of them, names of men yet to be born at a period two hundred years removed. And, behold, these seven facts are put before you in four lines!

There is a point of particular interest to be noted in. that first line. Bouys (p. 62) remarks that, first line though it be, it should be the last, as the mitre was the closing act of the entire drama; and he supposes that Nostradamus wanted to make the treachery most prominent to the mind of the reader. That is to talk like a chronologer. The first cause and the final are, in spiritual matters, one. The life and death of man are reduced to two points, and epitaphs give enough about most of the lives of mortal men when they chronicle the birth and death dates. "Alone he returned and was mitred." How, step by step, it all came about follows necessarily; and that is how Nostradamus puts it to us. If he had weighted himself with what science calls method, he would have destroyed his own instinct; as science does, just as Saturn ate up the offspring of his proper loins. The soul that does this must grope to its results, but can never jump to them by prophecy.

Before we go to the next quatrain it may be instructive to note Garencières' treatment of the pregnant forecast we have just traversed. He translates thus:

"The separated husband shall wear a mitre,
Returning, battle, he shall go over the tyle,
By five hundred one dignified shall be betrayed,
Narbon and Salces shall have oil by the quintal."

"The verse signifieth, that some certain man who was married shall be parted from his wife, and shall attain to some great ecclesiastical dignity. The second verse is that, coming back from some place or enterprise, he shall be met and fought with, and compelled to escape over the tiles of a house. The third verse is that a man of great account shall be betrayed by five hundred of his men. And the last that, when these things shall come to pass, Narbon and Salces, which are two cities of Languedoc, shall reap and make a great deal of oil."

This shows some skill, but what an unintelligible total we reach. I merely set it down to prove to the sceptical, and those who incline to class Nostradamus authoritatively amongst impostors whose jargon is not worth the pains of interpreting, that they may look at this and learn from it two facts: First, that before the event forecast has happened, all the keys of interpretation are wanting, the prophecy looks like jargon, and is so for all practical purposes; but that, secondly, once it has happened, or as we may say kissed sunlight, the keys appear with it, the light and the understanding awaken together. There is light in potence or in posse now; but even then they will not unlock secrets, if the keys remain in the hands of ignorant or scientific persons [or self-sufficient, which is nearly the same thing as scientific], or in the hands of romance-readers and lazy dullards. You will not unravel "the words of the wise and their dark sayings" by reading a quatrain once through. The interpreter must approach the work in a simple, unprejudiced manner; he must get light from history how he can,—from memoirs, letters, books,—and learn by the success and failure of past commentators. He must be content to work very hard all the while, and with little encouragement from others; and then at last he may so do something, that even his neighbours may allow his work to be,—according to the bent or waterpent of the particular mind of each,—some a discovery, some a revelation. He himself may probably feel that a supreme patience has had more to do with bringing the thing to pass than any other faculty that could easily be named. Things of the spirit must, of course, be spiritually discerned, and all talk about faculties when the individual soul is treated of must sound a little paradoxical. To divide the unique and indivisible unity of the soul into parts and pieces, betrays in the proposer himself perhaps some "want of parts." But from the earliest time until now, this has been the scientific way of treating the human understanding; so let us consider that it is right enough. The soul has almost always been cut into three, and then left to wriggle and wriggle, and at last to join itself together again, as best it can, like a worm in a garden. If this be according to Aristotle, let all Sorbonne profess it for right. What does it matter how we treat one thing, if only our method be perfectly scientific and in accordance with all the rest of the universal phenomena, and with a right interpretation of nature? What can it matter about the invisible, if only our eyes know how to take account of the things that are seen; that is, of the only things truly subject to the cognizance of man?

> Century IX.—Quatrain 92. [Bouys, 64.]
> Le roi voudra en cité neufue entrer.
> Par ennemis expugner l'on viendra.
> Captif libère faux dire et perpétrer,
> Roi dehors estre, loin d'ennemis tiendra.
> Translation.
> The King would enter into the city.
> (By enemies expelled, France will obtain it [or] they will arrive there;)
> It will be false to say and reiterate that the captive is free,
> [And] that the King who is out [of Paris] will keep aloof from enemies

M. le Pelletier does not touch this quatrain. M. Bouys gives his interpretation, which is not very convincing, and I thought of passing it by altogether. But the captif libère so links it with the journey to Varennes of the

Royal family, that it seemed preferable to include it, and leave it to the reader to reject or accept it, as he might think fit. Another determining influence was from my noticing that the cité neuve, or Montmédi, which the King desired to reach, was not French when the quatrain was penned. The VIII., IX., and X. Centuries were not published with the first seven, but were issued at Lyons from the same press, namely that of Pierre Rigaud. Moreri states that Nostradamus felt encouraged by the reception accorded to the seven Centuries to publish three more (i.e. VIII., IX., and X.), in 1558. There is a copy now in the Bibliothèque Royale, to which the authorities give the date of 1558. Pierre Rigaud's name appears on the title, but no date, which is remarkable, as the first volume of 1555 has this imprint: "Ce present livre a été achevé d'imprimer le IIIIe lour de may MDLV," giving a date as if for a nativity. M. le Pelletier demurs to the accuracy of the pretended date, and thinks it must belong to the edition of 1566, by Pierre Rigaud. if so, these three Centuries scarcely appeared in the lifetime of Nostradamus, though they are dedicated to his patron, Henry II.,—who died in 1559,—in an elaborate and interesting epistle dedicatory. In opening this, Nostradamus says he has long been in doubt as to whom he should devote (consacrer) these three Centuries, but at last took courage to lay it at the feet of royalty. Now, the edition of 1566 particularly states that the prophecies n'ont encore jamais esté imprimées. One cannot read the Dedicatory Epistle without feeling sure it was written for the eye of the King, and therefore at least as early as 1558, but probably earlier by a year or two. I therefore assume that he presented them to the King in a fair manuscript, and that having done that he remained content, and that the family at his death, finding the original manuscript, put it in Rigaud's hands to be printed.

My reason for thus inquiring into the dates is this: that the investigation makes it extremely likely the above quatrain was written before 1557, the year in which Montmédi was taken by France, and, if so, it explains the line that I have thrown into a parenthesis in a manner in which it has never been interpreted before. Expugner is not French now; expugnable is all that now remains of it in the language. So that

Par ennemis expugner l'on viendra

may, I think, be regarded as a parenthetic explanation referring to the cité neuve, which was not yet French territory, though on the point of becoming so,—l'on viendra par ennemies expugner, by expulsion of the enemy, in 1557. If this rendering be thought valid, it furnishes one reason the more for explaining this quatrain as one of the series belonging to the Revolutionary epoch, and one more re deemed from the maze of Nostradamus.

It would appear from Bouys, though he does not produce his historical authorities, that immediately the King escaped, France was flooded with announcements that the captive was free, and had their consent to hold himself aloof—loin d'ennemis tiendra. If this be established, it becomes certain that we can in the main determine this quatrain accurately. ("Histoire de la Révolution, par deux amis de la Liberté," in 7 vols., vol. vii. p. 126.)

   Century VIII.—Quatrain 87. [I. 179.]
   Mort conspirée viendra en plein effect,
   Charge donnée et voyage de mort:
   Esleu, créé, receu par siens, deffait.
   Sang d'innocent devant soy par 1 remort.
   Translation.

Death hatched by treason will take its full effect,
A charge imposed, voyage made to death.
Elected, created, received by his own, and undone by them.
The blood of Innocency (rises) before them in remorse (eternal).

Bouys thinks by the last line Nostradamus intended to convey, that the King felt poignant grief at the innocent victims his overthrow would leave without protection to the tender mercies of the States-General. The other is better, connecting it, as it does, with that case analogous, where the mob cursed themselves out of their own mouth, and said "His blood be upon us, and on our children" (Matt. xxvii. 25).

Century X.—Quatrain 43. [I. 180.]
Le trop bon temps, 2 trop de bonté royale,
Fais et deffais, prompt, subit, negligence,
Legier 3 croira faux d'espouse loyalle,
Luy mis à mort par 4 sa benevolence.
Translation.
Too much of good fortune, a too lax Royalty,
That makes and unmakes [appointments] sudden, hasty, negligent,
Lightly believes his loyal Consort false,
And bids good nature lead the way to death.

This is a picture to the life of the fat-making King Louis Seize. The brush of a Velasquez, as it cannot paint the moral, could hardly so well place him before the eye, as in life. He is no picture well-framed, hanging for inspection in a gallery of pictures, but flesh and blood like one's self alive, and moving with us in the gallery a spectator and observer like ourselves. We have here Louis XVI. before us in the flesh.

"He makes and unmakes appointments; yes, indeed." In a little more than eighteen years, sixty-seven ministers take office and relinquish it. Here they are alphabetically, as Bouys enumerates them. Amelot, Barentin, Bertrand de Molleville, Boyne, Breteuil, Brieune, Brogli, Beaulieu, Cahier de Gerville, Calonne, Castries, Champion de Cicé, Clavières, Chambonas, Clugny, Dabancourt, Danton, de Grave, Delessart, de Crosne, de Joly, d'Ormesson, Dabouchage, Dumourier, Duportail, Duport-Dutertre, Duranton, Foulon, Fourgueux, Fleurierès, Joly de Flemy, Lacoste, la Galaisières, Lailliac, la Jarre, la Luzerne, Lamoignon, Lambert, Laporte, Latour-Dupin, Lenoir, Liancourt, Leroux, Malesherbes, Maurepas, Miromeuil, Montmorin, Montbarrey, Mourgues, Narbonne, Necker, Pastoret, Puységur, Roland, Sartines, Ségur, Servan, Saint-Germain, Saint-Priest, Sainte-Croix, Taboureau, Tarbe, Terrier-Monceil, Thevenard, Turgot, Vergennes, Villedeuil. Several of these served twice, and Necker was in three times; so that the number of ministries in the time mentioned is seventy-two —a thing not to be paralleled in history as a course of doing and undoing, of fais and deffais.

His temper was ungovernable and sudden, extending even to rough bathos, but was soon over. Maurepas always said, you must let the King have his first fling of humour out, and then he will soon recover. Secondly, his negligence let everything drift, finance included, till ruin brought collapse. You might think his economists had drawn their singular axiom for statesmenship, Laissez faire, from the example of their royal master. He fell at once into the intrigue of the diamond necklace belonging to Marie Antoinette, which was conveyed by the

Countess of La Motte to the Cardinal de Rohan. Report runs that he even placed his wife under arrest in her own chamber for several days. "Lui mis à mort par sa bénévolence" displays a most wonderful forecast, and it is open to read it now LOUIS mis à mort.

> Century VI.—Quatrain 92. [I. 182.]
> Prince de beauté tant 1 venuste, 2
> An chef menée, le second faict, 3 trahy.
> La cité an glaive de poudre face 4 aduste, 5
> Par trop grand meurtre la chef 6 du Roi hay.
> Translation.
> The prince of very comely beauty (shall be)
> Led to the head, and then betrayed to a second (place).
> The city of the sword, with powder-torch, burns
> The head of the King, hated on account of his illegal murder.

The edition of 1558 gives the reading as above, but the line does not scan; it wants two syllables. Bouys, without comment, reads Prince sera; Le Pelletier understands menée as a synonym for intrigues. But I should read it rather as a misprint for méné. The city of the sword is a graphic name for Paris, where the guillotine was first erected on September 25, 1792, having been perfected by Guillotin, the doctor, whose name was given to it. Roquefort gives the word adusté as brûlé; but Nostradamus uses it as a verb, aduster, in the third person of the present indicative. Paris burnt the king's head with a powder-torch, or burning powder, that is to say with quicklime; and, as having done him wrong, the people hate him, and wish to obliterate the traces of the murder perpetrated.

The body and head of the King were placed in a basket of wicker-work, and carried, according to De Montgaillard ("Histoire de France," iii. p. 415. janvier, 1793 1) to the cemetery of the Madeleine, and thrown into a trench twelve feet deep, which had been spread with quicklime; more was thrown in upon the top of the body, so that decomposition would follow instantly. When the grave was reopened some twenty-four years after, to bestow a more decent burial on the relics, nothing remained but a few fragments of calcined bone.

Garencières reads Princesse de beauté tant venuste, which will not scan any better than the line of the edition of 1558; but he translates au chef menée, I find, as "shall be brought to the general," and the feminine termination is then right. This helps to confirm my rendering above. His annotation says that the only difficulty about the quatrain is as to what city is meant. As, however, he suggests no historical allusion whatever, he leaves every difficulty unsolved.

I think that most readers will be inclined to allow that this is a very extraordinary forecast, and that La cité au glaive as a name for Paris, and what has been perpetrated there, is both poetic and terrific in a very high degree—a sobriquet that, once heard, is likely to cling in the memory for ever. To devise epithets of this simplicity and force constitutes an author at once master of utterance; no matter what may be the shortcomings of the adjacent text. But, when you find these startling felicities perpetually recurring to illustrate facts historical,—facts that will not come into mortal ken for centuries after the death of the writer,—stiff, indeed, must be the reader's neck if he cannot bow it a little, as to a man of God passing by; or, if he would rather have it so, to the occasional divinity shining through man's nature, that will not, cannot wholly die when death has done its worst. From Hecla to the tropics all rational creatures should rejoice at such a fact. What is the new world of Columbus to this? Why, nothing but a new hemisphere of dirt. A spirit, that can read time future, must be a spirit whose habitation is Eternity. It is this hope kindles as we decipher, in the stillness of night, rune upon strange rune of the oracular sage of Salon.

>Century X.—Quatrain 17. [I. 184.]
>La Royne Ergaste 1 voyant sa fille blesme
>Par un regret dans l'estomach enclos:
>Cris lamentables seront lors d'Angolesme,
>Et an germain mariage forclos.
>Translation.
>The stranger Queen, seeing her daughter fading
>By reason of the deep regret she endured inwardly:
>The cries of Angoulême will be lamentable,
>And the marriage with her cousin-germain foreclosed.

The Princess did marry the Duc d'Angoulême in 1799, but there was no issue,—mariage forclos. The Queen wished to marry her daughter to a German Prince: hence all the grief. The Abbé Torné-Chavigny ('L'Histoire prédite et jugée par Nostradamus," ii. 28) had the merit, M. le Pelletier says, of this learned interpretation. I cannot quite see this, as M. Bouys gave the same interpretation as far back as 1806, though with a particularity a little less minute. The prophecy thus unravelled is the more wonderful, as the event seems so little worth recording. There is the same exactitude and precision shown as where a kingdom is at stake.

>Century IX.—Quatrain 77. [I. 185.]
>Le regne prins 1 le Roy convicra,
>La dame prinse à mort jurés à sort,
>La vie a Royne fils on desniera,
>Et la pellix 2 au fort de la consort.

Pierre Rigaud's edition reads conjurera for convicra, and that, at least, makes the line scan, which convicra does not. Bouys says that some ancient editions read conviera, commitari per viam, and then it would mean to arrange the funeral cortège of the King. I think conjurera the best reading, for that might be taken to mean that they condemned the King by jurors, or jury, as the Queen was in the next line.

>Translation.
>The assembly will condemn the King taken,
>[And] the Queen taken to death by jurors sworn by lot;
>They will deny life to the Dauphin (à Royne fils),
>And the prostitute at the fort will partake of the same fate.

Upon the word jurés, in the second line, M. le Pelletier remarks that the Convention, erecting itself into a supreme court of justice, proceeded to condemn the King to death. But the judgment upon Marie-Antoinette was passed by the Tribunal révolutionnaire, newly set up, which proceeded by jurors chosen by lot, jurés à sort. He further says that this jury is an institution borrowed from England, and he erroneously fancies that it had been first introduced into England at the Revolution, and had no existence there, even by name, during the lifetime of Nostradamus. This shows how little a Frenchman, when even well read, cares about English institutions. Pettingal almost proves that the Roman judices, and Greek were jurors. There has been great and profitless dispute, as to whether the Anglo-Saxons had juries, or whether they came in at the Conquest. If they did it would be strange, for they died out in Normandy. If the practice be Roman, it would have prevailed in England as in Normandy, both having been under Roman law forms. Coke, Blackstone, and many others, confidently maintain its existence here prior to the Conquest. If Anglo-Saxon it would still be Roman. Were it Scandinavian in origin, or were it Teutonic, it would equally have prevailed here before the Conquest. So that the whole discussion has an interest merely archæological; and leaves the trial by jury, no matter what its origin, a thing of immemorial usage in these islands. You might as well try, by chemical analysis, to ascertain when oxygen first entered as a component part into the air men breathe. If you could settle the question it would be no use; whilst the time lost in discussing it might otherwise be well employed. But the forensic usage was not so in France itself, as modern Frenchmen think, for in old Glossaries, like Roquefort's, you find jurie, not jurée: "Assise où l'on prononce sur le rapport des jurés."

They delivered the poor Dauphin to the cordonnier Simon, with orders to let him die slowly. The inhuman villains seem to have felt they could not condemn a child to public execution; so they give orders to a murderer to make away with him by ill usage and starvation, a process that would have rendered the guillotine welcome and a boon.

The last line admits of three interpretations. M. le Pelletier takes the pellix to stand for the National Convention itself, saying that it had prostituted justice in condemning an innocent prince over whom it had no jurisdiction. But clearly it had no jurisdiction over the King or Queen. He then takes the fort to be the Conciergerie, to which it consigned its own members, consorts, as an introduction to the scaffold. This is very striking, but the quatrain does not appear to me to threaten members of the Assembly at all. The unity of conception is best maintained by limiting its meaning to the fate of Royalty; and Bouys places an excellent and forcible interpretation upon it without breaking the unity of purpose. He says that it relates to the Dubarri, the King's courtesan, and that the fort is her palace of Luciennes, which had anciently been a strong place or fort. This is good, if the Chateau de Luciennes bears it out; but the fort may so easily be sort with the old s type, which is scarcely distinguishable from an f, that I think we might very well substitute it. We should then construe the last line

"And [consign] the prostitute to the fate of the Queen consort."

This interpretation requires less force to be employed upon the line, and less explanation than any of the others.

The forms of the s and *f* are nearly identical. The reading that brings simplicity with it, and removes stumbling-blocks out of the way, usually proves the safest and the best. Here we remove the complication introduced by the word fort, which otherwise requires explanation, and it runs: The courtesan shares a like fate with the Queen. It is now for the reader to select the best.

Sixaine 55. [I. 186.
Un peu devant ou après très-grand' dame,
Son ame au ciel, et son corps soubs la lame,

De plusieurs gens regrettée sera,
Tous ses parens seront en grand' tristesse,
Pleurs et souspirs d'une dame en jeunesse,
Et à deux Grands la deuil delaissera.
Translation.
A little before or after a very great lady,
The soul [of Madame Elizabeth shall rise] to heaven, her body under the blade,
She will be grieved for by many persons;
All her family connections will be cast into deep sorrow,
One lady very young [Duchesse d'Angoulême will shed] tears and sighs,
And two great ones will be depressed with mourning.

This can be mistaken for no one but Madame Elizabeth, the sister of Louis XVI., her niece, the Duchess d'Angoulême, and the two brothers of Madame Elizabeth, the count of Provence and the Count of Artois. This is not one of the very striking stanzas, but the forecast is still notable, and occupies its position very well as one in a considerable series.

Century I.—Quatrain 58. [I. 187.]
Tranché le ventre naistra avec deux testes
Et quatre bras: quelques ans entiers vivra,
Jour qui 1 Alquiloye 2 celebrera ses festes,
Fossen, Turin, chef Ferrare suivra.
Translation.
The belly cut shall spring again with two heads
And four arms: Aquiloye shall live several years,
In great force (entiers) what (jour qui) time he holds.
Fossen, Turin, Ferrara shall fall under his domination (suivra chef).

This is a very crabbed, but very wonderful quatrain. The elder branch of the Bourbons was cut short in the person of Marie-Antoinette (le ventre tranchée); shall spring up again in two heads, Louis XVIII. and Charles X. The two heads being crowned, the four lesser princes are called arms and uncrowned. They are counted thus: The Duc de Normandy, who died in the Temple, June 8, 1795; the Duc de Berri, assassinated January 13, 1820; the Duc d'Angoulême; and the Duc de Bordeaux, exiled August 16, 1830, who, though he had so many close chances, died without the crown,—an arm only, not a head, a hand tenaciously to the last holding to its white handkerchief as a flag. Zurich and Fossano stand, by synecdoche, for Piedmont, and Ferrara for the Papal States.

This brings us to the end of the Louis Seize series. Let us, before passing on to a fresh series, just give a glance at the ground we have traversed; and endeavour to estimate the value of the historical facts prefigured for us by Nostradamus in his book more than two hundred years before the earliest of them began to take effect upon the stage of actuality.

First, we beheld a section of the nation, the third estate, usurping the sole authority of government, and bringing down upon the whole the desolation that was witnessed in Europe in 1789. Then the intriguing Duc d'Orleans was portrayed, and the poor King was seen repenting that he had not, when insulted by him, publicly punished him by death. The next picture was that of the remarkable flight to Varennes, in which the very travelling habits of the

King and Queen, to their respective colours even, were minutely given, and the precise name hinted of the fallen Capet on the road,—fallen, though elected by the people, esleu cap. At the very last moment we are told their destination was changed by the King, where changing meant his destiny. He was then depicted as betrayed. He had run into the jaws of death, and the very names of the traitors, Narbonne and Saulce, were given; with the further detail, that he was taken back to Paris and mitred with the Phrygian cap, in the desecrated Tuileries, at the dictation of five hundred Marseillais. In another quatrain that journey is called a voyage of death, and in one line is laid before us all that happened to Louis the Unfortunate. He is elected, created king, received by his own people, and undone. To this succeeds that extraordinary picture of the King himself: his best friend could scarcely have portrayed the man so truly to us. Too prosperous at the outset, too good-natured a royalty, sudden in temper, yet dilatory in act, making and unmaking ministries quarterly, and finally done to death by his own benevolence. We then have a stanza devoted to him. We see him as a beautiful youth made chief, then deposed, and his head rolling from the scaffold in the City of the Glave, even to his burial in quicklime at the Madelaine, a procedure so unheard of in the case of kings. Then that curious reference to La Royne Ergaste and the little incident touching her daughter's marriage to D'Angoulême. Then follows the Queen's death, brought about by a jury, a novelty imported from England by the innovators of that period; crowned by cruelty to the Dauphin. There follows a more or less curious sixaine, conveying the fate of Madame Elizabeth, the King's sister; till we close with a brilliant quatrain that exhibits, in a symbolical fashion, the Napoleonic interregnum, when the severed Bourbon race puts out again its last two crowns, above the Eagle-law or Alquiloye,—probably the last appearance it will ever make upon the stage of history. I think we may agree, that it would not be easy to parallel such a series of verified forecasts relating to the most striking historical incidents, that bear upon a single reign, from any one book existing in the world. Footnotes

211:1 Par = per, Latin, by reason of.

211:2 A variant is trombe. We are told that the modern commentators find in this word the anagram of Rome, by syncope of t and b. So you might in rompu, by substitution of e for p and the ellision of u. But as no good comes of doing either, I should suggest to leave them alone.

217:1 Le part is the same word as in the last quatrain, and stands here for the husband.

217:2 Solus, Latin for seul.

217:3 Mary, or marri, is from the old word Marrir, s'affliger, and means afflicted, full of grief.

217:4 Trahyr. Trahitor, trahiter, from Latin traditor = traitre, English traitor.

217:5 Coutaux M. Le Pelletier takes as soldiers. Par coutaux = per custodes. They betrayed him into the hands of guards. I think it may also mean coustiller, a soldier armed with the coustille, a short, straight cutlass.

217:6 Avons = avus, grandfather.

226:1 A variant reads pour.

226:2 Construe Trop de bon temps.

226:3 Legier, for légèrement. Romance language.

226:4 Par, for Latin per, because of.

228:1 Tantum, Latin, very.

228:2 Venustus, Latin, comely.
228:3 Faict, Latin, factus made.
228:4 Face, Latin, fax torch.
228:5 Aduste, Latin, adustus burnt.
228:6 Chef, head.

229:1 Le corps et la tête placés dans un panier d'osier sont à l'instant même portés an cimetière de la Madelaine, jetés aussitôt dans une fosse profonde de douze pieds, ouverte de six, garnie et reconvene de chaux vive, et dissous immédiatement. On l'inhume auprès des personnes qui avaient péri le 20 mai, 1770, jour de la fête donnée par la ville de Paris, à l'occasion de son mariage, et auprès des Suisses morts dans la journée du 10 août."

230:1 Ergaste is estrange in Pierre Rigaud's edition. M. le Pelletier says Ergaster is Latin. It may be, but I do not find it in Facciolati, though ergastulum, a workhouse, is there given. When Marie Antoinette was in the Temple, she was reduced to working with her hands, like a workwoman (ergaste). But ergaste is the anagram of estrange, the one letter n excepted. Probably estrange is the preferable reading, inasmuch as Marie Antoinette was an Austrian, and so étrangère.

231:1 Prins, Latin, prensus, taken, captive.
231:2 Pellix, Latin, pellex, prostitute.
234:1 Qui = Latin cui, to which.
234:2 Alquiloye = Aquilæ lex, law or rule of the Imperial Eagle.

The National Convention

WE now reach a fresh division, and shall treat of the National Convention,—a period of about three years.

    Century VIII.—Quatrain 17. [I. 189.]
Les bien aisés subit 1 seront desmis;
Par les trois freres le monde mis en trouble.
Cité marine saisiront ennemies;
Faim, feu, sang, peste, et de tous maux le double.
 Translation.
The well-to-do [members] shall be suddenly dismissed,
On account of three brothers the world shall suffer trouble.
Enemies shall take possession of the marine city;
Hunger, fire, slaughter, plague, of evils all the double.

Privilege is to be abolished suddenly. The three brothers who trouble the world are the Royal trio, Louis XVI., Louis XVIII., and Charles X. Toulon is the maritime city. We shall come upon it again, further on, in Century VII. 13, where it is treated of more fully. M. le Pelletier interprets feu as being war, and peste as standing for irreligion. As goods were all doubled to Job, so here all evils are to be doubled. On the night of August 4, 1789, feudal privilege was abolished suddenly (subit). The clergy and nobility were dispossessed of property and title. Toulon, taken by the English, is the Cité marine. It was retaken, in the name of Louis XVII., on August 23, 1793, by the French; on the 19th of December, Marie-Antoinette and Égalité, Duc d'Orleans, being both executed during the British tenure.

    Century IX.—Quatrain 17. [I. 191.]
Le tiers 1 premier pis que ne fit Neron,
Vuidez 2 vaillant que 3 sang humain respandre!
Rédifier fera le forneron, 4
Siecle d'or mort, nouveau Roy, grand esclandre!
 Translation.
The third become first does worse than Nero,
See how much valiant human blood it squanders!
It will rebuild the old tile kilns,
The age of gold is dead, a new dynasty, and great scandal.

This interprets itself. M. le Pelletier explains the rebuilding of the kilns as setting up the scaffolds to consume the clergy and nobility. I do not myself see the force or necessity of this. The age of gold yields to that of iron or the sword; the new dynasty (the Napoleonic) is a vast scandal, and reintroduces pomp and ceremonial at the Tuileries.

    Century VIII.—Quatrain 19. [I. 192.]
A 5 soustenir la grand' cappe 6 troublée,

Pour l'esclaircir les rouges marcheront:
De mort famille sera presque accablée,
Les rouges rouges la rouge assommeront.
 Translation.
They will not sustain the great but troubled Capets,
The reds will take steps to purge their number,
They will almost exterminate the family with death,
The red of reds will overwhelm the red.

This very forcibly announces the Reign of Terror to have set in. The reds will do what in them lies to crush the Capets, till they have almost annihilated the family in death; and, then the reddest reds will guillotine the reds,—the Montagnards the Girondists. Bouys does not allude to this, though one would have thought it must strike every reader as far as what is said relating to the conduct of the double-dyed reds against the moderate reds. Garencières' mistakes serve to show how impossible it was to guess at the meaning of a quatrain in the seventeenth century. He fancies this to refer to some conspiracy of red Cardinals against a Pope, to be designated the Red one.

 Century VI.—Quatrain 69. [I. 193.]
La pitié grand' sera sans loing tarder,
Ceux qui dônoyent seront contraints de prendre:
Nuds, affamés, de froid, soif, soy bander,
Les monts passer commettant grand esclandre.
 Translation.
A sight of pity will not long delay,
The almoners will soon be forced to beg:
Hungered, athirst, naked, proscribed, and cold.
In bands they cross the Alps, a scandal to be seen.

This conveys a forcible picture of the calamitous emigration the clergy of France would undergo between 1792 and 1801. Once the clue is supplied, it leads So naturally, that one almost finds insight from it into the manner in which these representations presented themselves to Nostradamus. One feels, that he must have seen the events passing before the field of sight as visions, sometimes accompanied with uttered words; otherwise how could he get intimation of names? But, if it was thus that intuition came to him, the quatrains, that he now scattered up and down throughout the Centuries in utter disorder and disconnection, must have come to him in a sequence, rendering them comprehensible; more or less, indeed, in the very order probably into which the chronology of historical record enables the careful student to replace them now, as soon as they are understood by him. If this be so, a rather curious fact presents itself, in a form approaching to something like a certainty, which is this: disorder must have been the method of the book. We know that generally his practice was to write down the matter in prose, and at leisure convert this into separate quatrains rhymed; these he must afterwards have taken up in a bag or hat, and when inextricably mixed have counted them out into hundreds. I think it quite possible that he found his forecasts became too intelligible when put together in their natural order, and in the sequence of events. No doubt, with regard to those events of his own time and to be soon fulfilled, he first began to perceive the necessity for inverting or displacing the order. Consecutive and interlinking stanzas would form a kind of commentary, and throw mutual light one upon the other; so that the adoption of disorder would follow as a measure of personal security. He thought that his sayings should be dark, as becometh the words of the wise; and that it would be quite time enough, should they grow clear when fulfilled to a reader, who would take sufficient trouble to elucidate them and bring out their meaning.

Century I.—Quatrain 44. [I. 194.]
En bref 1 seront de retour sacrifices,
Contrevenans seront mis à martyre;
Plus ne seront moines, abbés, ne 2 novices,
Le miel sera beaucoup plus cher que cire.

This quatrain exhibits the suppression of the Catholic worship in France, which took place November 10, 1793. What they called the worship of the goddess of Reason was set up; and a return to Paganism is what the first line means.

Translation.
For a short time there will be a return to [Ethnic] sacrifices,
And those who oppose will suffer martyrdom:
There will be no more monks, clergy, nor novices;
Honey will fetch more than wax.

The last line means that wax will be cheapened, as none will be consumed in the churches. The rest explains itself. Garencières can see the meaning of the last two lines; but the first two he considers to have been fulfilled in the time of Henry V. of France and Henry VIII. of England.

Century II.—Quatrain 8. [I. 195.]
Temples sacrés 1 prime 2 façon Romaine,
Rejetterons les gofres 3 fondements,
Prennant leurs loix premieres et humaines,
Chassant non tons des saincts les cultements. 4

Translation.
The temples consecrated in the fashion of early Rome,
They will reject the deep foundations [of Christianity].
Returning to their first and human laws,
They will not entirely abolish all saint-worship.

This A le Pelletier explains to be a forecast of the Fête de l'Être Suprême, which was appointed by decree of the Convention May 7, 1794, and celebrated on the 8th of June of the same year with great pomp.

Century V.—Quatrain 33. [I. 196.]
Des principaux de cité rebellée.
Qui tiendront 1 fort pour liberté r'avoir,
Detranchés 2 masles, infelice 3, meslée,
Cris, hurlements, à Nantes piteux voir!

Translation.
The chief citizens of the revolted city,
Who will struggle hard to recover liberty.
The men beheaded, an unhappy mixture,
Cries, howlings, at Nantes piteous to see.

This was realized at Nantes, in Britany, under the Proconsulate of De Carrier.

The town had, in 1793, become the focus of the Vendean reaction against the National Convention. The men were beheaded generally, but many men and women were stripped naked. They were then tied together, a man to a woman, in couples, or pairs, which their fiendish tormentors styled "republican marriages." In this diabolic connection (infelice meslée) they were precipitated helplessly into the Loire, amidst heartrending cries and howlings. No viler crime was ever committed on this earth, nor can ever be; the infamy of man and the revengeful filth of lust can no further go. From that extraordinary coinage and coupling of words, infelice meslée, you know, or seem to know, that Nostradamus beheld the horrid spectacle in vision—

Estant assis de nuict secret estude (Century I. 1).

Those who believe this to be a recital at haphazard are of a brain-formation singularly constituted.

Century VIII.—Quatrain 88.
Dans la Sardeigne un noble Roy viendra,
Qui ne tiendra que trois ans le royaume.
Plusieurs couleurs avec soy conjoindra, 1
Luy mesme après soin sommeil marrit 2 scome. 3
Translation.
In Sardinia a noble King shall come,
Who will only hold the kingdom during three years.
The tricolour will annex him [the King] to itself;
He after much pains will sleep afflicted and ridiculed.

This is Charles Emmanuel IV. The Republic of the tricolour, "le drapeau tricolor," will despoil him of his continental estate; and he will withdraw to his island, ruling for three years, 1798-1802. He then abdicates to his brother, Victor Emmanuel I., and, après soin much care, will sleep [as regards governing], and, residing at Rome. sad and humiliated, will assume the Jesuit robe, and die in 1819.

Footnotes
238:1 Subit stands for subito, suddenly.
239:1 Tiers = third.
239:2 Vuidez = Latin, videte, see.
239:3 Que = how much.
239:4 Forneron = Latin, fornax, furnace.
239:5 A is the Latin a, privative.
239:6 Cappe, is put for Capet.
241:1 En bref, temps, understood.
241:2 Ne, again used for ni.
242:1 Sacrés, for consacrés.
242:2 Prime, Latin, prima, first.
242:3 Gofres is deep, profound.
242:4 Cultements, Latin, cultus, worship.
243:1 Tiendront fort, will struggle hard.
243:2 Detranchés, Romance for tranchés, tête understood.
243:3 Infelice, Latin, unhappy.
244:1 Le to be understood before conjoindra.
244:2 Marrit, afflicted.
244:3 Scome, Latin, scomme, gibe, taunt.

Pius VI

THE next four quatrains refer to Rome and Pope Pius VI.

Century V.—Quatrain 57. [I. 199.]
Istra 1 de mont Gaulfier 2 et Aventin,
Qui 3 par le trou advertira l'armée.
Entre deux rocs sera prins 4 le butin,
De SEXT 5 mansol 6 faillir la renommée.
Translation.
When a [French] army shall go from Mont Gaulfier to the Aventine,
There will be a man advising them from under the hole.
The booty shall be seized between the two rocks,
And the glory of the sixth celibate shall wither.

This is a very curious stanza. The name of Montgolfier, the aeronaut, is visible enough in the two separate words, mont Gaulfier. M. le Pelletier calls it the grammatical figure of metaplasm; but it is not strictly so. Metaplasm is the forming of cases from a non-existent nominative. This is making two words for things non-existent to represent a proper name. But there is a still greater singularity in the employment of it here. For Nostradamus, as I understand him, makes this fictitious mountain contrast with the real Mount Aventine. He makes it stand, as I think, for one of the two rocks between which the booty is secured. The brothers Montgolfier were paper-makers at Annonay Ardèche, and they gave their own name to their discovery, which dates June 5, 1783. Their balloons opened at the bottom to be filled, so that a man placed in them was under the hole, par le trou. I do not know at what point the Montgolfier was floated to furnish military information to the French, but I suppose on the Italian side of the Alps, so that from that rock or mountain to the Aventine rock would be the points between which the booty was seized. But the former of these Nostradamus seems to me to designate by the man's name, which lends itself to a play upon the word, rather than by a peak of the Alps. M. le Pelletier says that the two rocks refer to Peter, pierre being rock. One is Avignon, in France, and the other Rome, in Italy, and the booty was obtained by the treaty of Tolentino, under date of February 19, 1797. By this the Pope lost Avignon and Venaissin in France, Bolognia, Ferrara, and the Romagnia in Italy, and this he calls the two rocks. The balloon was first used to reconnoitre the position of the Austrians at the battle of Fleurus, June 16, 1794. Almost immediately after the treaty, the Pontiff was dragged from Italy to die at Valence: thus was fulfilled the prophecy of faillir la renommée. Interpret how you may, the mention of the name of Montgolfier so appropriately in this connection, must always stand as proof of the most solid kind that Nostradamus's foresight was miraculous.

Century V.—Quatrain 30. [I. 201.]
Tout à l'entour de la grande cité
Seront soldats logés par champs et villes:
Donner Passaut Paris Rome incité, 1
Sur le pont 2 lors sera faicte grand pille.

Translation.
Compassing all round the great city
There shall be soldiers camping in the fields and towns:
A Frenchman [Paris will take] Rome excited;
There will then be perpetrated on the Pope a great pillage.

The Executive Directory, in defiance of the Constitution which formally forbade it, encamped troops around Paris, la grande cité, on September 4, 1797. This was to quell, or keep in awe, the counter revolution. A Frenchman [Paris], General Berthier, took Rome by assault, February 10, 1798. the pretext being that General Duphot had lost his life in an émeute [dans Rome incité]. Pope Pius VI. was dispossessed of his states, arrested in his palace, and subjected to general pillage.

Century VIII.—Quatrain 46. [I. 202.]
Pol 1 mensole 2 mourra trois lieües du Rosne;
Fuis 3 les deux prochains 4 tarasc 5 destrois: 6
Car Mars 7 fera le plus horrible trosne
De Coq, et d'Aigle, de France Freres trois.
Translation.
The grand Celibate shall die three leagues from the Rhone;
The two dejected brothers shall fly tumult:
For war shall make a most horrible throne
For the three brothers of France by the Cock and Eagle.

The Pope, that is, shall die at Valence, a few leagues from the Rhone. The two brothers [afterwards Louis XVIII. and Charles X.], alarmed at the movement of the populace, take flight. War inflicts sad havoc on the throne of the three brothers [Louis XVI., Louis XVIII., Charles X.] by the Orleans Cock, and Napoleonic Eagle.

Century II.—Quatrain 99. [I. 203.]
Terroir Romain qu'interpretoit Augure 1
Par gent 2 Gauloise par trop sera vexée:
Mais nation Celtique craindra l'heure,
Boreas 3 classe 4 trop loing l'avoir poussée. 5
Translation.
The Roman territory that the Pope governed
The French will cruelly vex:
But that Celtic nation should fear the hour
When it has advanced its army too far to the north.

I render this in the main in accordance with M. le Pelletier; but perhaps some may think that the Pope cannot be called an augur without great violence. Interprétoit can hardly stand for spiritual government. It is also difficult to make classis into army. Classis represented the orders of the people of Rome; that divided them into bands and companies for governmental and electoral purposes, not for war. The only classis of war was the fleet, and Garencières renders it by navy, although he is entirely abroad in every other respect ill his interpretation of the quatrain. Though he forces a fulfilment upon it in the time of Henry II. of France, still, evidently Rome is meant, whatever the Augur may interpret. The Roman territory was twice trampled on by the French: first by General Berthier against Plus VI, and again by General Miollis, who in 1809 removed Pope Pius VII. The closing couplet is clearly a forecast of Napoleon's defeat in Russia. That will not be affected by the manner in which we interpret classe; but I cannot imagine for a moment that Nostradamus would employ the Latin classis so erroneously for an army, which no Roman would ever use it for. Certamen classicum is a sea-fight, but never employed for engagements on land. The result of this minute verbal inquiry will, I think, end by establishing the more remarkably the prescience and forecast of this consummate seer. He uses the word classe in one of its late eighteenth, or early nineteenth century acceptions, for that body of young men, which is called out every year in France by, lot to serve in the army; or all those called to the colours, who are drawn for service in the same year. It is an administrative word, that sprang into use out of the conscription, and which will die out again when that fraud, passed upon the nations of Europe, has been detected and abolished; that institution which fosters war and makes its otherwise intermittent evils permanent and perpetual upon humanity. To enlarge the area of this view is to doom conscription to death and sure oblivion. Conscription is an invention of Beelzebub, when seeking his bath of blood, under the euphonic guise of a patriotic defence of the mother soil. Mourir pour la patrie is the glozing lie of Roget de l'Isle, that supplements, or drowns, the true cry of "Blood for Moloch." So we will read, for the first time now, the passage thus: But let the Celtic nation beware the hour when her conscript columns are pushed too far to the Boreal northeast. In brief, beware of Moscow. If this sixteenth century anticipation of a nineteenth century idiom be nothing, then let the Alps be called a molehill, and the hollow sea a cup. Here we close the prefiguration of the Papal torment appropriately enough; it closes with a terrible hint to its tormentor. Footnotes

245:1 Istra = ira, will go, or will go forth.
245:2 Montgolfier, the inventor of ærostatics.
245:3 Qui, Latin for who, a man who.
245:4 Prins, taken.
245:5 Sext, for sextus.
245:6 Mansol, man, sol. Manens solus means celibate, or priest under vows.
246:1 Latin, incitatus, agitated.
246:2 Pont. pour Pontificat, or Pontifex.
247:1 grand, considerable.
247:2 Man. sol., manens solus, as before.
247:3 The ordo is, les deux prochains destrois fuiront le tarasc.
247:4 Prochain = proche parent, who partakes in a heritage.
247:5 tumult.
247:6 Romance, destrois, afflicted, dejected.
247:7 Mars, god of war.
248:1 Augur, for Roman priest.
248:2 Gens is Latin for nation.
248:3 Boreas is north wind, or north.
248:4 Classis, Latin, is a body of men, used here as army.
248:5 The ordo is, [où elle] aura poussé son armée trop loin vers le nord.

Napoleonic Rule

    Century III.—Quatrain 35. [I. 205.]
    Du plus profond de l'Occident d'Europe,
    De pauvres gens un jeune enfant naistra,
    Qui par sa langue seduira grande troupe,
    Son bruit au regne d'Orient plus croitra.
    Translation.
    In the Southern extremity of Western Europe
    A child shall be born of poor parents,
    Who by his tongue shall seduce the French army;
    His bruit shall extend to the kingdom of the East.

    IN the island of Corsica was born, of an ancient but impoverished family, a child, Napoleon Bonaparte, whose proclamations electrified the French troops. His expedition, by order of the Directory, to Egypt, which was meant to ruin his career, conferred upon him a world-wide renown. This man was not eloquent as orators are eloquent; verbosity is their gift. Even the endowment of Cicero lay much in words; and in their multitude, which wanteth not folly: Solomon says sin. A plethora of words becomes the apoplexy of reason. But this man's phrases are all portable, made for the knapsack: they fly to the lip as lightning does to metal; poetry, passion, and energy are in them, but fused to an aerolite, till they fall like a luminous bolt, only to burn in man's memory for ever after. They are not winged, but lightning-shod. Fulminants are matter etherealized to an interlinking with spirit. But this man's words are spirit itself, and burn their niche in Time, to last as long as that will. Take two of them: "Soldiers, forty centuries look down upon you!" and again, "Behold the sun of Austerlitz!" When you speak, speak thus to men; such words are deeds; and come not as from one who beateth the air to the pitchpipe of the tibicen Ciceronical, but as the bullet to its butt; speak swordpoints, that press between the joints and marrow. But I will stop here, to escape oratory. That may still fetch its price, and seduce the zebra troup in the courts of legal falsity, or in the Babel-room down by the river-Minster.

    Century I.—Quatrain 76. [I. 206.]
    D'un nom farouche tel proferé sera,
    Que les trois seurs 1 auront fato 2 le nom;
    Puis grand peuple par langue et faict dira, 3
    Plus que nul autre aura bruit et renom.
    Translation.
    Of a savage name there shall be such publishing
    That the three sisters shall have by Fate the same name:
    Then he will lead a great nation by tongue and deed,
    And have more glory and fame than any other.

    Here M. le Pelletier takes le proferé for a thing placed before, and understands it as being the prenomen of Bonaparte, viz. Napoleon. But I cannot see how that is shown to be the meaning of proferé. That word, if from the Latin proferre, never was used for cognomen or prænomen. One of the meanings of proferre is palam facere, to make public or publish, and I think it would be safer to render it as I have done. It will still equally draw attention to the name Napoleon, in contradistinction to the name of Bonaparte; because, when he mounted the throne as Emperor, he adopted the new name and abandoned the previous one. This selection of a new name seems to be a natural instinct of humanity on entering upon a new phase of life. The popes take a new name on assuming the pontifical rank; monks and nuns do so on entering the religious life; commoners leave their name behind when created peers; women do so when they marry; and here Napoleon does it. But I do not think it desirable to consider this to be indicated by the word proferé. Nostradamus says that it is such a fatal name that the Parcæ themselves will adopt it. He then repeats that he will lead,—I think it should be seduce (séduira),—the grande nation by speech and deeds, and raise a name unrivalled in the universe. This was certainly true, and the prefiguration of it is, beyond the denial of prejudice, marvellous.

We have now to deal with the word itself, which will furnish to investigation a few interesting hints. Of course some may think them intricate and far-fetched. There is no great importance to be attached to them perhaps, but they must interest the curious; and curiosity that is innocent has a value of its own. Who could see in Sloane's strange Chelsea gallery the shape, dimension, and value of the museum of Bloomsbury and its affiliations?

Century IX.—Quatrain 33. [I. 208.]
Hercules Roy de Rome et D'annemarc, 1
De Gaule trois Guion 2 surnommé,
Trembler l'Italie et l'unde 3 de Sainct Marc,
Premier sur tons monarque renommé.
Translation.
Hercules, King of Rome and Denmark,
Surnamed the triple Giant of France,
Shall make Italy tremble and the wave of St. Mark,
First in renown of all monarchs.

There was a Celtic Hercules fabled to draw men by their ears: Par langue et faict il conduira, as we have just seen, so that this Hercules means the Napoleonic dynasty. As to King of Rome, Napoleon actually assumed that title, and later on he conferred it upon his son by Marie Louise. In the "Memorial de Sainte-Helene," 1840 [i. 79], by Las Cases, it is said that during his consulate somebody published a genealogy connecting his family with the ancient kings of the north. This Napoleon ridiculed in the public journals, stating that his nobility dated only from Montenotte or the 18th Brumaire. Things were not yet ripe for royal pretensions. The Bonaparte family in Italy can trace to the thirteenth century. One branch was settled at Treviso, the other at Florence, and both held an honourable position; a third was at Sarzana, in Genoa. A Charles Bonaparte settled in Corsica in 1612, and lived in obscurity, says Le Pelletier, till this family of kings was born. Taine has discovered that the family was of condottiere stock, and De Staël and Stendal had, before that, both of them found Napoleon's character more analogous to that, than to any other type known to them. Taine finds him to be a Sforza or a Malatesta born belated by three centuries. He is as unscrupulous, searching, and ambitious as Macchiavelli; and, curiously enough, the only book 1 he is known to have ever annotated profusely is Macchiavelli's "Prince," which was found in his baggage at Waterloo, and has since been published; and an intensely interesting book it is; enormously wicked and shrewd, but diabolically wise in the Devil's gay antics. It is a scientific treatise on government without God in the world. Its moral axiom would seem to be that even murder should be directed by good sense in the hands of a craft-master. In this respect I think it is even superior to the clemency of César. The "Prince" evidently fascinated him deeply. He treats his author quite imperially, as Bentley or any other great critic might do, and points out condescendingly where the priest is but a theorist and errs for want of knowledge, such as can only be gained from the practical handling of affairs by a man of the Napoleon calibre. I don't know that you can read so deep into the very spirit (for I will not mention heart in the same breath with Napoleon) of the man of blood and brain, as you may by the pencil interlineations by him jotted down in this his Italian vade mecum; from time to time as he recurs to the book, enlarging in view from general to first consul, and from first consul to emperor. You seem to sit with him, as in a magical cave, with terrible writings that come and go upon the wall before you, writings which are the words of this book, and are lit up with a lurid phosphoresence, the light of which emanates from his own putrescent brain.

It is not historically true to say, as M. le Pelletier does, that the family lived in obscurity in Corsica. The house at Ajaccio was the largest in the place, a palace even as compared with the other residences. The title of King of Rome was precious to Napoleon, as it enabled him to claim succession to the Empire of Charlemagne. Although Garencières, in his interpretation, fails of attaching any individual fulfilment to the words, he is able, from this title, to say that whoever it belongs to will attain to the Roman Empire.

Guion is equivalent to Terræfilius or Earthborn, and means giant; in fact, it almost seems a variant of géants; but why three giants of France? I do not know that this has ever been explained. Hercules mythologically was distinguished by three symbols (Martinii, "Etymologicon," s.v. Hercules),—a lion's skin, key, and three apples. The three apples were, not to get angry, not to love money, not to love pleasure. This need only be mentioned for the sake of the double triplication and as marking so far the propriety of the term Hercules. Master of Rome, i.e. Italy; of Venice, i.e. Austria; of Paris, i.e. France; as ruled over by Napoleon as General, Consul, Emperor. That he was "the first of monarchs over all renowned" needs no elucidation.

> Century VIII.—Quatrain 61. [I. 209.]
> Jamais par le descouvrement du jour
> Ne parviendra an signe 1 sceptrifere 2
> Que tout ses sieges 3 ne soyent en sejour, 4
> Portant au coq don du TAG 5 armifere. 6
> Translation.
> Never shall he in broad daylight
> Reach to the symbol of sceptre-bearing rule.
> Of all his positions none will be of a settled permanency,
> Conferring on the Gallic cock a gift of the armed Legion.

In other words, the Emperor will never enjoy a settled seat of firmly established government, and he will confer upon France, either the ruinous legacy or bequest or gift of the legionary conscription, which converts Europe into an armed camp,—an evil gift, indeed; or those who prefer it, may render it as the gift to France of a huge burial-place in Spain and Portugal, where so many thousands of men, her best blood, fell. But conscription is of the wider issue, and the more permanent evil, as it affects Europe to this hour. It makes peace an interlude to war, and very little less costly than war.

Our next quatrain is a great rarity, for it seems to be in pure Provençal, and extremely pleasing it is, a great deal more honied, to the ear in sound than the present French language; which is excellent for conversation and the salon, where society grimaces, but where true souls are struck dumb and poetry has ceased to be possible; or only possible to rebellion, such as that of Victor Hugo.

> Century IV.—Quatrain 26. [I. 211.]
> Lou grand eyssame se lèvera d'abelhos,
> Que non sauran don te siegen venguddos.
> De nuech l'embousq. Lou gach dessous les treilhos,
> Ciutad trahido per cinq langos non nudos.
> Translation.
> The great swarm of bees shall rise,
> That none can tell from whence they came.p. 257
> Night's ambush. The jay 1 beneath the tiles.
> City betrayed by five tongues not naked.
> "A peacock moulted, and a jay
>   Assumed the feathers fine,
> And, strutting in a peacock-way,
>   Thought 'now I look divine.'
> "The first who met him laughed outright;
>   Others he found to sneer;
> The peacocks voted him a fright,
> His brother jays all quizzed 'the sight,'
>   But none would have him near.
> "Of biped jays like this, there are
> Thousands from here to Zanzibar;
>   We call them 'plagiarist!'
> But hush! For setting souls ajar
>   Is not my line, I wist."

The bees stand for the Bonapartist army and the Empire. The second line is understood, by M. le Pelletier, to refer to the origin of the family, and it may be so; but I think it refers to the surprising suddenness with which the rouges, sans-culottes, and republicans,—in pretended love with equality and freedom,—were found to welcome tyranny and Rule of One, that used to be spoken of as Monarchy. Guillotined in that form, Frenchmen hailed it as a sword-saviour in the new dictator. It seems to me to be the sudden conversion of such opposed principles to Bonapartism on the night of the 18th Brumaire [November 9, 1799],—De neuch l'embousq, an ambuscade of night,—that startles Nostradamus. Certainly there was no doubt whatever whence the Napoleon family sprang; a family with a history more or less traceable for five hundred years can scarcely be described with propriety as one "whose origin is lost in the night of time." Yet this is the meaning M. le Pelletier would have us put upon it.

Next, like the jay in the fable, tricked out in pea-cock feathers and spoils of the Capetian kings, Napoleon makes their palace of the Tuileries [Treilhos] his head-quarters. The city is given over to him by cinq langos, five prodigious talkers of the long robe. Far from naked as to words or clothing were they, but as to principles very nude and bare, quite unable to cope face to face with the audacity of this unscrupulous cut-throat, this gunner of Ajaccio.

The men of no principles and no practice were simply ciphers before this man of practice, par langue et faict; this ethnic Hercules of tongue and sword; this servant, as Daniel has it, of "the God of Forces;" this fly-pest Beelzebub, man of Vespres et mouches, grown to a dynamic King. Where men have lost their virtue, the poor sceptics are given over to believe a lie of their own making; tongues have they to lie withal, but never a hand amongst them to furnish help at need.

> Century VII.—Quatrain 13. [I. 213.]
> De la cité marine et tributaire
> La teste rase 1 prendra la satrapie:
> Chasser sordide 2 qui puis 3 sera contraire;
> Par 4 quatorze ans tiendra la tyrannie.
> Translation.
> The short-haired man shall assume authority
> In maritime Toulon tributary to the enemy:
> He will afterwards dismiss as sordid all who oppose him;
> And for fourteen years direct a tyranny.

The English had seized Toulon in the name of Louis XVII., and held it a few months till Bonaparte retook it. He overturned the Directory (sordide), and suppressed its partisans with the Republic, and enjoyed the tyranny for fourteen years, from 18th Brumaire, November 9, 1799, to April 13, 1814. We have already seen (p. 238) that the cité marine is Toulon. Garencières fancies this to have been fulfilled when Richelieu made himself governor of Havre de Grace, where he kept his treasure and tyrannized for about fourteen years.

> Century VIII.—Quatrain 57. [I. 214.]
> De soldat simple parviendra en empire,
> De robbe courte parviendra à la longue:
> Vaillant aux armes, en Eglise, où plus pire,
> Vexer 1 les prestres comme l'eau fait l'esponge.
> Translation.
> From a simple soldier he will rise to the empire,
> From the short robe he will attain the long:
> Able in arms, in Church government he shows less skill;
> He raises or depresses the priests as water a sponge.

This is a very remarkable quatrain, that Bouys and Le Pelletier, and I suppose all French commentators, pronounce to belong to Napoleon; and it certainly fits him very well. But, with almost as little injury to historical fact, it may be applied to Cromwell, and accordingly Garencières does so apply it. He writes: "I never knew nor heard of anybody to whom this stanza might be applied, than to the late usurper Cromwell; for from a simple soldier he became to be Lord Protector, and from a student in the University he became a graduate in Oxford, he was valiant in arms, and the worst Churchman that could be found; as for vexing the priests, I mean the prelatical clergy, I believe none went beyond him."

The circumstances of the French Revolution and the English Commonwealth times are so much alike in many respects that it is not surprising that such a description as this of a soldier who seized power and afflicted the clergy should fit both the usurpers, Napoleon and Cromwell, almost equally well.

Napoleon was a plain lieutenant in 1785, Consul for life in 1799, and Emperor from 1804 to 1814. He changed the short robe for the long, is understood by M. le Pelletier as being the consular robe for the imperial. There is no need to interpret thus. The military dress or that of the civilian is the short robe. Nostradamus takes but little heed, so far as we have yet seen, of the consular dignity. In the last quatrain he designates the duration of the tyranny, not as one of ten years, which would represent the Empire, but of fourteen, which regards the consulship and empire as one period. If we take Cromwell's protectorate, however, from the death of Charles I. to the death of Cromwell, the term will correspond with Napoleon's imperial career. But the interregnum in England was a period of twelve years, and that in France under Napoleon was of fourteen (quatorze ans); hence this quatrain must not be applied to Cromwell, though it in other respects is as true of him as of Napoleon.

Valiant in arms, but in ecclesiastical matters less successful, still he thoroughly vexes them, penetrating into every place and corner, as water does into a sponge. We cannot accept M. le Pelletier's rendering of vexare as meaning to raise and cast down. It was used in the sense of to trouble, cruciare,—to anger, commovere; or to harass with care, curarum œstu fluctuare; but never to alternately swell and depress, as in filling or squeezing out a sponge.

Century II.—Quatrain 69. [I. 215.]
Le Roy Gaulois par la Celtique dextre, 1
Voyant discorde 2 de la grand Monarchie,
Sur les trois parts fera florir son sceptre,
Centre la Cappe 3 de la grand Hierarchie.
Translation.
The Gallic King by means of the Celtic sword-hand,
Seeing the discord of the great monarchy,
Shall make his sceptre flourish by restoring the three parts,
As against the Capets, and the Popedom.

Garencières understands as "the Cap of the great Hierarchy," Spain in the Netherlands, which was the great upholder of the Popedom. His application of this to history is of no value. But if we understand Cap as Capet, and the ancient connection of the French crown with the Papal Hierarchy, I think we elicit a better sense than that of M. le Pelletier, which makes the Capet and the Hierarchy one. The three parts restored, M. le Pelletier makes to consist of clergy, nobility, and tiers état. I feel that the three parts under Napoleon were Emperor, Senate, and Chamber of Deputies, which would be head (or Caput instead of Capet), Senate representing the higher classes, and the Chambers the people. That would constitute les trois parts of the quatrain.

Century I.—Quatrain 88. [I. 216.]
Le divin mal surprendra le grand Prince,
Un pen devant aura femme espousée: 1
Son appuy et credit à un coup 2 viendra mince, 3
Conseil mourra pour la teste rasée.
Translation.
He shall have married a woman just before
The divine wrath falleth on the great Prince;
And his support shall dwindle in a sudden atrophy;

Counsel shall perish from this shaven head.

This divine evil that surprises the Prince a little after his marriage with Marie-Louise of Austria and his mean-spirited repudiation of Josephine, is most excellently rendered by Garencières as "the falling sickness, called by the Greeks Epilepsia, and by the Latins Morbus sacer." Garencières was a Fellow of the London College of Physicians, and a man versed in the medical nomenclature of his day; so that le mal divin should here be rendered epilepsy. It has never yet been so rendered, except by Garencières, and he has no application to make of it whatever, though, as a mere matter of translation, he says, "the construction of the whole is easie." It strikes me that this forecast, thus interpreted, will throw light from Nostradamus on what history has heretofore overlooked, and will necessitate the re-writing of Napoleon's life from the date of his wicked prostitution of the marriage rite. Napoleon, Cromwell, Mahomet, César, were all epileptic, and probably Alexander. But this particular scoundrel first committed, from the purely sordid motive of self-aggrandisement, a moral crime, and that brought on the convulsion of the brain, that practically discharged for ever the mighty Leyden jar or electric battery, with which this potent brain-fiend had dealt out merciless torpedo-shocks to Europe, and death as from the hot wind Samyel. Inflated vanity, the epileptic stroke, the reaction of external forces on the weakened centre, made the cerebral pap, still of gigantic power, entertain new Phantasms huger than ever, with a terribly diminished power of reason, to bring them to birth by the practical handling of circumjacent facts and time-tendencies. Now, said the fool of this western parable, now am I master of events, and may swim against the sea,—not with it, as I and common mortals heretofore have done, but against it, and to win. Well, he did carry the big dream into Russia, and as far as the nightmare of Borodino. He also still found a mighty utterance of lurid glory, with which to pin that evil minute in letters of fire and phosphorus upon the curtain of eternity, "Behold the sun of Austerlitz!" The looming mot d'ordre, the old work, the old guards, and the old drillings, guided once again to a Pyrrhic victory; two such will damn a kingdom. Reader, read Ségur [Comte de Ségur, "Napoléon et la Grande Armée," liv. vii. ch. viii. p. 179], and there perceive the giant unbrained and drivelling about his bastard boy called "King of Rome," and what else belongs to mon étoile effacée. "All the supports dwindle," says Nostradamus, "and counsel will perish from the shaven head." Garencières is right, and the diagnosis true. It is the falling sickness. It is not Jove fulminant that strikes the reeling Pagod from without, as with César 'twas, but an epiletic withdrawal of electricity from within, backwards. Emperor and empire will soon roll together in the dust; man's posthumous analysis, and that of all the evil works wrought by him, though the good live after.

Century I.—Quatrain 4. [I. 127.]
Par 1 l'univers sera faict un monarque
Qu'en 2 paix et vie ne sera longuement:
Lors se perdra la piscature barque,
Sera regie en plus grand detriment.
 Translation.
Throughout the universe a monarch shall arise,
Who will not be long in peace nor life;
The bark of St. Peter will then lose itself,
Being directed to its greatest detriment.

The Emperor Napoleon, reviving pretensions to the old Roman empire or universe, will neither enjoy peace nor life for very long. In his time the Holy Seat, la piscature barque, shall so guide itself to greatest detriment as to be cast away and lost (under Pius VII.).

Pope Pius was made a prisoner by General Miollis, July 6, 1809, and carried to Savone, then to Fontainebleau, and kept under strict guard by Napoleon till March 10, 1814, when he was set at liberty. Garencières interprets this as being fulfilled in the time of Henri II. of France, who was slain by Montgomery in the tilt yard. Through all his reign he was at war with the Emperor Charles V. This Emperor sacked Rome, and Pope Clement VII. was made a prisoner (vide Garencières, "Tiber," p. 77).

Century V.—Quatrain 60. [I. 218.]
Par teste rase viendra bien mal eslire,
Plus clue sa charge ne porte 1 passera;
Si grande 2 fureur et rage fera dire
Qu'à feu et sang tout sexe tranchera. 3
Translation.
In the shorn head France will have made so bad a choice;
It will be heavier than its force will enable it to endure.
So great fury and rage will make men say
That he will exterminate the male sex by fire and sword.

The period of the fulfilment of this event M. le Pelletier gives as extending from 1813 to 1815. It asks no further interpretation than that afforded by the translation.

Century IV.—Quatrain 82. [I. 219.]
Amas s'approche venant d'Esclavonie, 4
L'Olestant 5 vieux cité ruynera,
Fort desolée verra sa Romanie,
Puis grande flamme esteindre ne scaura.
Translation.
A troop approaches, coming through Sclavonia;
The destroyer will ruin an old city;
He will see all Romania desolated,
Nor will he know how to extinguish such a blaze.

A mass of troops is wending from Sclavonia. The destroyer, Napoleon, will ruin old Moscow altogether, and see Roumania desolated; such a conflagration he will not know how to extinguish. It was Rostopchin, in 1812, fired Moscow to prevent the French from wintering there, and it settled the fate of the campaign.

Century II.—Quatrain 44. [I. 220.]
L'aigle poussée 1 entour 2 de pavillions,
Par autres oyseaux d'entour 3 sera chassée,
Quand bruit des cymbres 4 tube, 5 et sonnaillons 6
Rendront le sens de la dame insensée.
Translation.
The eagle, drifting in her cloud of flags,
By other circling birds is beaten home.
Till war's hoarse trumpet and the clarion shrill,
Recall her senses to th' insenate dame.

This is one of the few quatrains that lend themselves freely to a poetic rendering. The Napoleonic eagle driven back to France with all its retreating flags about it, or chased by a surrounding of other eagles, Austrian, Russian, Prussian. The din of cymbals, trumpets, and clarions restore France to reason, the insensate dame.

Garencières's annotation here is extremely funny, and should not be unrecorded. He says: "It is an eagle driven from the tents by other birds, when a mad lady shall recover her senses by the noise of cymbals, trumpets, and bells."

Century X.—Quatrain 86. [I. 221.]
Comme un gryphon viendra le Roy d'Europe,
Accompagné de ceux d'Aquilon, 7 p. 267
De rouges et blancs conduira grand 1 troupe,
Et iront contre 2 le Roy de Babylon.
Translation.
Like a griffin the King of Europe will come, Accompanied with those of the north. Of red and white there will be a great number, And they will go against the King of Babylon.

The King of Europe is Louis XVIII.; shall come like a griffin , a fabulous animal, with hooked beak: v. Liddell and Scott; v. Griffe, Noel; Griffeau, Roquefort, Littré, Gwillim, Brunet, etc.), accompanied with those of the north. He will conduct grand battalions of red and white uniforms, i.e. English and Austrian, and they will march as one against the King of Babylon, which is Paris. Louis, as the descendant of Hugh Capet, may be styled the first of European Kings. The King of Paris is Napoleon, who ruled the Revolution there, and brought order to confusion or Babel. But we can bring it home to Paris even more intimately than this, for the old name of Paris was Lutetia, or mud-place, where the toads, crapauds, or Frankish frogs dwelt, and out of whose mud, or bourbe, came the Bourbon family. So that Paris, their chief city, en calembour, yields Bourbe ville, Babyl, Babel.

Garencières thinks to see Gustavus Adolphus here as the most eminent King of Europe in his day, and he came from Aquilon, the north, and warred upon the Emperor, who was King of Babylon, from propping the popedom, or from the Babel of confusion. He had regiments red, white, blue, and yellow and green, in the hope of creating emulation amongst them. If he had only had regiments red and white we might have hesitated, and gone further to examine where the clue would lead to. But what begins by proving too much is like other overshooting, and misses the mark entirely.

Century VI.—Quatrain 89. [I. 222.]
Entre deux cymbes 1 pieds et mains attachés
De miel face oingt et de laict substanté,
Guespes et mouches, fitine, 2 amour, fachés,
Poccilateur 3 faucet 4 Cyphe 5 tenté.
We have now rather laboriously cleared the way for a
Translation.
Between two prisons, bound hand and foot,
With his face anointed with honey, and fed with milk,
Exposed to wasps and flies, and tormented with the love of his child,
His cupbearer will false the cup that aims at suicide.

M. le Pelletier renders this: Napoleon, after being consecrated by Pius VII., and anointed from the sacred ampulla with honey and milk, underwent a double imprisonment in Elba and St. Helena. The imperial bees—for so he translates the wasps and flies—are desolated as to their love for the child, and his surgeon, Yvan (pocillator), has falsified the death by poison, on the night of April 12 to 13, 1814. Now, as it was not his own soldiers that tormented him, I think we ought to read it faché: he was desolated by wasps, flies, his child, and love. His soldiers are called abeilles before, never guêpes; these are the enemy tormenting, who will not let him abdicate in favour of his son . We shall do better here to follow Garencières's example, drawn from the life of Artaxerxes, King of Persia. The Persians used to punish poisoners by laying them between two troughs, here called boats, with their face uncovered, bedaubed with honey to attract the wasps and flies, and fed them with milk to prolong the torment, which if they refused, they ran needles into their eyes most persuasively, and then left them till vermin ate them up. So that it means: he was tormented between two prisons bodily and mentally, with the ruin of his family, insomuch that he would have been glad to have escaped it all by poison. Whenever Napoleon was thoroughly frustrated in his plans, he evidently tried to fall back upon, what he had never deserved, human sympathy; which in prosperity he had never thought of nor desired. He first showed this softening, rather of the brain than heart, at Borodino, as we have said before.

We will now take the substance of what happened at the abdication, as given by M. le Pelletier from the Manuscrit de 1814, by the Baron Faim. He abdicated [here may we say, "Woe unto him that buildeth a town with blood" (Habakkuk, ii. 12)] at Fontainebleau April 4, 1814, reserving the Regency for the Empress Marie Louise, and his son. He was thrown into despair when he found the allies to be masters of Paris, and to reject any such conditions. Baron Faim was his private secretary, and describes what occurred on the night of the 12th and 13th of April, before the day of his unconditional abdication. Fontainebleau really became a prison under the surveillance of strangers. There were no terms left to him to save even his life. Still he let the day close without yielding.

For some days previously he had seemed altogether preoccupied in revolving some design. His conversation turned always upon the voluntary death that the great men of antiquity courted when in situations such as his. The Empress had reached Orleans on her way to rejoin him, but he had given orders not to allow her to do so. He dreaded such an interview as likely to unman him for the resolution he meditated.

It was a terrible night of suspense; the long corridors of the palace resounded with the footsteps of servants going and coming, the candles were burning in the private apartments. Doctor Yvan is suddenly called upon to attend, the Duc de Vincence is sent for, and they hurry to fetch the Duc de Bassano from the Chancellory; they are all taken to the bedroom as they drop in one after another. Sobs and sighs escape, but not a word is yet dropped to satisfy curiosity. On a sudden the doctor leaves the apartment, descends to the courtyard, finds a horse ready saddled, and quits the place at a hand-gallop.

All that transpires on the occasion is that, at the retreat from Moscow, Napoleon had provided himself with a means of escape, should he fall alive into the hands of the enemy. Yvan, his surgeon, had given him a packet of opium, which he had ever since carried round his neck. The valet heard him rise in the night, and saw through the half-opened door that he mixed something in a glass of water, drank it off, and returned to bed. He quickly felt that his end was approaching, and had his most trusted followers called to his bedside, Yvan amongst the rest; but, when he heard Napoleon complain that the action of the poison was too slow, he precipitately quitted Fontainebleau, as we have seen.

A very heavy slumber supervened, accompanied with profuse perspiration, and when he awoke the symptoms had disappeared, the dose having proved of insufficient quantity, or time had deprived it of its efficacy. Napoleon, astonished at the failure, simply exclaimed, "Dieu ne le veut pas!" and professing, perhaps for the first time in his life, to yield to Providence, resigned himself quietly to his new destiny, On board the Northumberland he strongly reprobated suicide. It would have been instructive to have heard the arguments employed by this intellectual giant, merely as a mental acrobat exhibiting, and as showing how far the intellect may be effective in illustrating the path of duty. But on nothing could Napoleon's opinion be worth so little as on a question of morals, where the soul's instinct is chief guide. The rats ate his heart, it is said, in an interim of the medical dissection. I doubt it; he had eaten it himself long before he left Brienne.

On the morning of the 13th, Napoleon rose and dressed as usual. His objections had vanished, and his next act was to ratify the treaty—a solemn act, which he took the earliest opportunity that offered to betray and break.

>Century X.—Quatrain 24. [I. 227.]
>Le captif prince aux Itales 1 vaincu
>Passera Gennes par mer 2 jusqu'a Marseille,
>Par grand effort des forains 3 survaincu,
>Sauf 4 coup de feu, 5 barril liqueur d'abeille.
> Translation.
>The captive prince, conquered, is sent to Elba;
>He will sail across the Gulf of Genoa to Marseilles.
>By a great effort of the foreign forces he is overcome,
>Though he escapes the fire, his bees yield blood by the barrel.

He ran the blockade, March 1, 1815, and landed at Cannes, close to Marseilles, crossing the Gulf of Genoa, till defeated at Waterloo on the 18th of June, "seeking death," says Le Pelletier, "without being able to find it," (où il sera sauf de coups de feu). When the smoke rises from the bottomless pit, "shall men seek death and not find it; and shall desire to die, and death shall flee from them" (Rev. ix. 6). Napoleon comes out of the island Æthalia, or metallic smoke, and escapes the murderous artillery that kills his men, though it were far fitter he should die. His beehive is not burned with fire, but other liquor than honey flows freely,—the life-blood of his bees.

>Century II.—Quatrain 70.
>Le dard du ciel 6 fera 7 son estandue, 8
>Morts en parlant, grande execution.p. 273
>La pierre en l'arbre, la fiere gent 1 rendue,
>Bruit humain monstre 2 purge expiation.

The third and fourth lines will neither of them scan. La fiere genit should be written la fier' gent, fier being read as one syllable.

Bruit, in the fourth line, is to be read as one syllable. Garencières has Brait, which, though it have no meaning, shows perhaps that it was one syllable.

>Translation.
>The thunderbolt shall strike his standard;
>He shall die speaking proud words, great is the execution.
>The stone is in the tree, the proud nation yields,
>The monster purges his human fame by expiation.

The thunderbolt from heaven shall strike down his standard, and he fails or dies 3 uttering haughty words. There is terrible execution done. The stone 4 is in the tree. The proud nation yields. The hero purges by expiation his human renown.

In spite of all these doubts interposed, this yields us a quatrain of a sufficiently clear sense, in conveying two leading ideas; a providential and mighty overthrow of a giant leader and braggart of swelling words; and of a proud nation split in battle, as a tree is by thunder-stroke. The forcible picture is not unworthy of Waterloo or the Battle of Mont Saint-Jean, as the French call it; even though it may not be impossible to find some other battle since the death. of Nostradamus that it might represent almost as well, if not quite so fully, as the tremendous day of Waterloo, June: 18, 1815. Englishmen seem half afraid now to mention the day with pride, for fear of hurting French susceptibilities. To mention it insultingly, or in a hostile spirit, is unpardonable; but to speak of it modestly and thankfully, and of Wellington as a great soldier and benefactor to us, is only manly and proper. The man who has not the courage to do this firmly and inoffensively in the company of Frenchmen is only one of the many cowards amongst us, who lead the French to think that, however great things our fathers may have done in the past, the spirit has fled from us that would repeat them in the future.

Century IX.—Quatrain 86. [I. 230.]
Du Bourg la reyne parviêdront droit à Chartres,
Et feront près du pont Anthoni pause:
Sept pour la paix cauteleux comme martres,
Feront entrée 1 d'armée à Paris clause. 2
 Translation.
From Bourg la Reine they shall march on Chartres,
They shall camp close to Pont Anthony:
Seven chiefs for peace, cautious as martens,
Shall enter Paris cut off from its army.

The generals of the seven nations coalesced shall, under pretext of peace, but really out of jealousy of France, says M. le Pelletier, and in virtue of the capitulation of the 3rd of July, enter Paris; now cut off from her army (clos d'armee), which retreats upon Chartres, passing by Bourg la Reine and Pont d'Anthony, where it camps. The quatrain does not at all obviously read so, but we must suppose that it is the French army which goes to Chartres. We are not, however, bound to believe that the marten-like and cunning seven only pretended to establish peace out of jealousy to France. All Europe and France herself sighed for peace; and if, when victorious, the enemies were inclined to take back what France had robbed them of severally, that would not be very wonderful. The seven nations signatory to the treaties of 1815 were England, Austria, Prussia, Russia, Spain, Sweden, and Portugal.

This is a very remarkable forecast, and shows that although Nostradamus is a national prophet of France, and nearly all his one thousand quatrains turn upon her and her interests, he seldom exhibits a particle of partisanship, and you would not know he was a Frenchman from any word that he lets fall. He strictly limits himself to the utterance of his vision in the tersest phrase, and the most forcible words that he can bring to bear for that purpose. I think there is no other instance known of such inviolable temperance. A man sits down in his study and prophecies; commits his visions to paper in prose; turns them deliberately afterwards, and in cold blood, into the pithiest poetry he knows how; shakes up in a hat, as we have previously remarked, all the quatrains together, and, when he has effectually destroyed all sequence and order, counts them out into even hundreds; then, without a word of note or comment, he sends them forth in type into the world to sink or swim; be ridiculed or admired, be understood or mistaken, perish or endure; until such period as their fulfilment in the centuries of time is realized, and the sleeping world awakens to the miracle, that has slept also, beside the sleeping world, till light arose to make both clear qt once.

Century II.—Quatrain 67. [I. 232.]
Le blonde au nez forche 1 viendra commettre 2
Par 3 la duelle 4 et chassera dehors:p. 276
Les exilés dedans fera remettre,
Aux lieux marins commettant 1 les plus fors. 2
Translation.
The light-haired one will come to blows with the hooked nose
For the second time, and chase him out:
The exiled will replace him within,
Consigning the strongest of the party to a fortress in the sea.

Louis XVIII. is designated Le blond au nez fourchu according to Le Pelletier. Le blond is, no doubt, the sign of the Capets, as shown by several other stanzas in Nostradamus, but not the aquiline nose, I think; that, I believe, is intended for Napoleon. So that Louis XVIII. comes to blows with the hooked nose, or Napoleon, for the second time and drives him out; he who was exiled before now replacing him within. The strongest, that is Napoleon and his officers, are committed aux lieux marins; which either means to the English, who go down to the sea in ships, or else to St. Helena, a prison in the sea.

Century X.—Quatrain 90. [I. 233.]
Cent fois mourra le tyran inhumain;
Mis à son lieu sçavant et debonnaire:
Tout le senat sera dessous sa main,
Fasché sera par malin 3 temeraire.
Translation.
The inhuman tyrant shall die a hundred times;
A learned and debonnaire King shall take his place:
All the senate shall be under his control,
And he shall be grieved by a bold criminal.

Napoleon is the inhuman tyrant to die a hundred deaths: one his suicidal attempt; another Elba, with its cinerary and fuliginous ashes; another Waterloo; and lastly St. Helena, with its ten times ten remorseful hours, regrets, and studious falsifications of the history of his life. Debonnaire is, with Nostradamus, an epithet of the Capet family, and stands doubtless for Louis XVIII. put into his place. The King finds the Senate quite submissive to his will, but he is cut to the heart by the daring attempt of the criminal Louvel upon the Duc de Berri, February 13, 1820.

This is the excellent interpretation of M. le Pelletier. Bouys (p. 80), writing in 1806 under the full influence of the demon of Napoleon, gives it a very different reading. The inhuman tyrant with him can be nobody but Robes pierre, who, with a pistol shot, endeavoured to put an end to himself ineffectually, but blew away half his face, suffering thirty hours of fearful torment, and finally was dragged to the place of execution amidst the maledictions of the populace. The sçavant et debonnaire to Bouys is, of course, Napoleon. The malin teméraire is a forgotten Georges, whose conspiracy gave a little momentary anxiety to Napoleon. Here terminate the oracles assigned to Napoleon by A le Pelletier. But Bouys adduces several others, which sufficiently relate to the Emperor to be enumerated here. It is painful to see how men manipulate these things to suit their theories. We will give now a quatrain that Bouys cites, as he thinks it favourable to Napoleon; but he carefully omits the one next to it in the same Century, purely, as it seems, because it is unfavourable to Napoleon,

> Century II.—Quatrain 29. [Bouys, 82.]
> L'oriental sortira de son siège,
> Passer les monts Apennons voir la Gaule:
> Transpercera le ciel, les eaux et neige,
> Et un chacun frappera de sa gaule.
> Translation.
> The oriental will quit his post,
> To cross the Apennines and see after Gaul: p. 278
> He will transfix the heaven, the mountain ice and snows,
> Striking each of them with his magic wand.

The Oriental, i.e. Napoleon in Egypt, will leave his army behind there, after almost turning Mahometan; return and cross the Apennines and Alps to look after the Directory and their doings in France. He will soon even subdue the elements and Nature by his marvellous roads over the mountains of ice and snow, and will strike each as with the rod of Moses, or the wand of a magician; for the archaic and unusual word gaule may mean that, as well as a riding switch. Bouys misses the plainer meaning of the first line, but is determined it shall represent Napoleon, so he takes Oriental to be Corsica, as being east of Toulon. The passage of Mont St. Bernard with cavalry and artillery he gives rightly enough; the Alps have to be introduced for the Apennines. The quatrain following next to this he passes sub silentio, for the reason above assigned, though it is pregnant with meaning; and how this should have been over. looked by M. le Pelletier, I cannot quite understand; but so it is.

> Century II.—Quatrain 30. [II. 45.]
> On qui les dieux d'Annibal infernaux,
> Fera 1 renaistre, effrayeur des humains.
> Oncq' plus d'horreur ne plus pire journaux,
> Qu'avint 2 viendra 3 par Babel aux Romains.
> Translation.
> One whom the gods of Hannibal from the lower regions
> Shall cause to be born again [shall be], a terror to mankind.
> Never will more horror, nor more evil days,
> Come upon the Romans. The confusion will be like that before from Babel.

Hannibal and Napoleon are the only great generals who ever forced their military way over the Alps successfully; Hannibal, with his acetum, vinegar, or hatchet, as some have interpreted Livy; and Napoleon for cavalry and heavy pieces of artillery. He seemed to be the marvellous Carthaginian born again out of the shades of Hades, a scourge and flail of men: Babel itself not worse in the confusion that fell upon Rome, and the Church of Rome through him. We have given this before, at p. 199, but repeat it here with further enlargement, as it belongs more to Napoleon than to the Revolution. Garencières thinks it was fulfilled when Charles V. sacked Rome. If we consider, as I do, that the two stanzas are inseparable, they will fit only Napoleon.

We come now to a quatrain that M. le Pelletier has overlooked, but which Bouys (p. 83) with some reason attributes to Napoleon.

> Century IV.—Quatrain 54.
> Du nom qui onque 1 ne fut un Roi Gaulois
> Jamais ne fut un foudre si crantif.
> Tremblant l'Italie, 2 l'Espagne et les Anglois,
> De femme estrangiers 3 grandement attentif.
> Translation.
> Of a name that never belonged to Gallic king,
> Never was there so terrible a thunderbolt.
> He made Italy tremble, Spain and the English.
> He wooed a foreign lady with assiduity.

Bouys introduces into his interpretation of this a good deal of foolish adulation of Napoleon; pretending that he was not only crantif towards his enemies, which we must render a cause of terror, but also that he was himself crantif, very tender of the lives of his troops. To prove this monstrous proposition, he quotes the claptrap uttered by him before the battle of Austerlitz: "I regret to think how many of these brave fellows I shall lose. I feel for them as if veritably they were my own children. Indeed I sometimes reproach myself for this sentiment of tenderness; I sometimes fear it may end in rendering me unfit to carry on war." This was, indeed, an heroic fear, says Bouys. We are content to let its heroism wrestle with its hypocrisy; we foresee which will come by the first fall.

Garencières translates that the warrior, whoever he may be, will follow after strange women; and that would fit Napoleon, though not specially. But we think it better to render it with Bouys as indicating the Empress Josephine, who was of Creole blood, and therefore foreign; or Marie Louise, equally foreign. If the latter, Estrange would stand for Austrian (v. Century I., Quatrain 83).

> Century VIII.—Quatrain 53. [I. 269.]
> Dedans Bolongne voudra laver ses fautes, 1
> Il ne pourra au temple du soleil
> Il volera faisant choses si 2 hautes,
> En hierarchie n'en fut oncq un pareil.
> Translation.
> In Boulogne he would make up for his shortcomings,
> But cannot penetrate the temple of the sun.
> He hastens away to perform the very highest things.
> In the hierarchy he never had an equal.

This is a singularly interesting quatrain. It has received three different interpretations; all three somewhat curious, Garencières opens the ball. He says there are two towns called Bolloin, one in Italy, one in France; that is, Bologna in Italy, and Boulogne in France. He thinks Boulogne is intended, and that Richelieu, a man of high things, and beyond the hierarchy, vowed, a little before his death, that if he recovered he would make a pilgrimage to Boulogne; to the Temple of Miracles there, dedicated to the Virgin, here described as the Sun, from that passage in the Revelation, "And there appeared a woman clothed with the sun;" but the cardinal took the road of death, which led, not through Boulogne, to the shades below, and certainly not to the Temple of the Sun. This has an interest of its own, but, as an interpretation, is utterly wide of the mark. Richelieu on a repentant pilgrimage to the Temple of the Sun would have been admirable as a caricature in Rabelais; but, would be no fitter subject for Nostradamus's pen, than if a lady of title went to Aix-les-Bains to take the waters there. And observe, he had to invent a Temple of the Sun to send him to, for never was there such a temple at Boulogne.

We have also Le Pelletier trying his hand, and he realizes it in Louis Napoleon, in his escapade of 1840. When he was made Emperor, his Italian exploit is represented as a flight to the Temple of the Sun. But how he could suppose that inferior mortal, to be referred to in n'en fut oncq un pareil, I cannot divine.

Bouys and others attribute it to Napoleon, and his intention to descend upon England from Boulogne in the flotilla. Is there not a column there, ridiculously built to commemorate the failure? Is there not also a Boulogne medal struck (Ford's "Spain," i. 272) with one of the Napoleonic falsehoods (an endless series) imprinted on its face, which runs, "Descente en Angleterre frappé à Londres"? These are the ridiculous touches; but now let us enter on the serious interpretation and see what that will yield us.

At Boulogne the Emperor will endeavour to blot England from the map of Europe, and so redeem all his previous shortcomings in that direction. He promises himself the satisfaction of dictating his terms in London, and possibly entertained, in that strange brain of his, some dream that he would be crowned on that royalty-confirming stone of Scone in Westminster Abbey; where, tradition tells, the Temple of Apollo was shaken down by earthquake, A.D. 154, the Temple of the Sun. But Il ne pourra au temple du soleil, says Nostradamus: and history has thought fit in this as on so many other occasions to endorse the forecast of the prophet. Bouys adds, "Napoléon finira par faire la conquête de l'Angleterre;" but Bouys is not Nostradamus; and Napoleon, like Richelieu, went to the shades below from St. Helena, and did not go to the Temple of the Sun nor to the Stone of Scone. He went away, however, from Boulogne to very great things, as men count greatness; and was quite without an equal in the hierarchy of kings. Footnotes

251:1 Seur = sœur.

251:2 Fatum, Latin, fate, destiny.

251:3 Duira, for conduira.

252:1 Princedom of Dan. The old Kings of Denmark pretended to derive from Dan, seventh son of Jacob, it is said.

252:2 son of earth. Terræfilius, giant.

252:3 Unda, wave, onde.

253:1 The title of this book is "Machiavel Commenté par Non Buonaparte," 1816, published by H. Nicolle, 12, Rue de Seine. I have a copy, but there is none in the British Museum. The Preface and the Introductory Discourse on Macchiavelli are full of ability. The translation of the "Prince" in French occupies the left-hand column of each page, and seems well done; on the right-hand column are given the emperor's annotations, p. 254 where they occur, otherwise it stands blank. They are severally initialled G., R. C., or E—General, Republican Consul, Emperor,—according to the period at which Napoleon may be supposed to have written them. Some of the remarks are clever, but perhaps scarcely show the grip of Napoleon; which, whether right or wrong, was always that of an iron vice. I now imagine it to be an ingenious forgery, but it is quite curious enough to merit further inquiry. This footnote, it will be seen, does not correspond with what I have said in the text. I wrote that under the impression that the document was genuine, and it would be just, if the book were true. But I leave it as it is, though it tells slightly against myself, as the contrast, between the first and second thoughts seems to me instructive. It shows that, let a man walk by right faith or by wrong, he must steer by the belief that is present with him.

255:1 Signum, ensign, standard, or perhaps symbol of rule or domination.

255:2 Sceptrum ferre, sceptre-bearing, reigning.

255:3 Siége, position, situation.

255:4 En séjour, permanent, durable.

255:5 Coq, the Gallic cock.

255:6 Tago, or tango, to touch or take, le Pelletier says; but it does not yield very good sense. Perhaps a regular body of soldiers, in Dion Cassius it stands for the Roman legion. Garencières reads here TAG à misère, "The tag to misery," and says it is wretchedness to come from p. 256 Portugal to France, Tag being the Tagus, on which Lisbon is situated. This might be interpreted well to mean the mischief arising to the empire from the successes of Wellington in the Peninsular war.

257:1 The jay, of course, is Esop's Fable of that bird, tricked out in finer feathers than its own. The elegant rendering by La Fontaine [iv. 9, Ed., 1838] of Le Geai paré des plumes du Paon had, when Nostradamus wrote, not then taken shape. The original is so accessible, that it may suffice to give here the English version.

258:1 This curious phrase manifestly points to Napoleon wearing short hair, in military fashion, as distinguished from the flowing locks of the line of Capet,—shaven as contrasted with bewigged. This is one of the many coincidences that connect the Commonwealth of England with the French repetition of it at the Revolution. Croppies, or Roundheads, distinguished the sanctimonious insurgents of the Commonwealth from the cavaliers with their flowing locks. The Tory cavaliers wore wigs; the Whigs undermined the bewigged.

258:2 Sordide should be written sordid', and teste, test', if we wish the line to scan.

258:3 Puis, for depuis.

258:4 Latin, per, pendant.

259:1 Latin, vexare, raise, inflate, according to Le Pelletier; but Facciolati gives no such meaning. "Vexed Bermoothes" gives it.

261:1 Dextera, Latin, right hand, or sword hand.

261:2 Discorde should be discord', or the line will not scan. These may be minor matters, but those who think them unimportant are not wise. It is an excellent rule in literature to let nothing remain wrong that can be set right by a little scholarship and industry. In the world it is very different; there you should never put anything right, for everything wrong has a host of latent friends, that will fight very savagely in its defence.

261:3 Cappe, for Capet, says M. le Pelletier. The texte-type gives a variation here as la Chappe. This yields no help at all, except as showing by the variant that there is something wants altering. The line will not scan as it s. I think it should be altered to le Cap. If it stands for Capet it is Masculine, and when it occurred before, in Quatrain 20 of Century IX, it was given as Esleu Cap.

262:1 These two lines furnish an hyperbaton and will be best transposed, that the great Prince will have married a woman before the divine wrath falls upon him.

262:2 This is equivalent to tout d'un coup, suddenly.

262:3 This line is too long by a foot; appuy et credit mean the same thing, and one should be omitted. The line should be corrected thus:

Et son appuy à un coup viendra mince.
264:1 Par is Latin, per, throughout.
264:2 Equals qui en.
265:1 The texte-type furnishes porter, with porte as a variant. M. le Pelletier embodies this in his text. I should replace the word that he excludes. Further, I should regard passera as being a form of the Latin patior, and the French pâtir, and therefore read pâtira. Porter pâtira will then mean suffer it to bear. Charge, for the scansion, should be charg'.
265:2 Grande should be grand', for the scansion.
265:3 Tranchera should read il tranchena.
265:4 Esclavonie is put for modern Hungary
265:5 Olestant is another variation of the nom fatidique de Napoleon.
266:1 Poussée, for repoussé.
266:2 Entour should be entour', for entouré.
266:3 Entour here is for entourage.
266:4 Cymbres, cymbals.
266:5 Tube, tuba, trumpet.
266:6 Sonnaillons, literally, bell-ringing, but perhaps clarion may serve.
266:7 This line cannot be scanned; we must read de l'Aquillon.
267:1 This requires, for both grammar and scansion, grande.
267:2 The E in contre must suffer elision, thus: contr'. It is right in Garencières's.
268:1 is a cup, usually, in Greek. M. le Pelletier gives it as a cavity or precipice. I find no such meaning as precipice. There is a great difficulty to settle the meaning here. It could means a cup, a boat, a wallet. We should perhaps simplify the issue by confining ourselves strictly to the Latin word, Cymba, which is boat or skiff. Always a light boat, as in the Georgics, i. 136, where the little boats were made of alnos cavatas, the riverside alders hollowed out. It is rather a craft for a small lake than for the sea; as Ovid charmingly puts it:

"Non ideo debet pelago se credere, signa
Audet in exiguo ludere cymba lacu."

But, then, what sense would it yield, "a man being between two boats, tied hand and foot?" Between two abysses, M. le Pelletier interprets; but, then, we do not find that, either in Greek or Latin, the word yields that meaning. He interprets it of Elba and St. Helena. But was an island ever called an abyss; I think as seldom as ever . In Martinius's "Lexicon Etymol.," there is a very curious quotation from Isidore, Bk. 19., which makes the cymba to be the space occupied by a ship in the displacement of the water beneath it. I think out of all this we may extract a meaning for the deux cymbes. As two places, or recessed prisons, hollowed out of the sea, he shall be put, bound hand and foot. The line, to scan correctly, should have the word et left out.
268:2 Fitine, plant, scion, child.
268:3 Pocillator is cupbearer.
268:4 Faucer is fauser, to trick.
268:5 Scyphus, cup. There is a singular appropriateness in this word, whether intended or not by Nostradamus, for Athenaeus describes the Bœotians as first using huge silver drinking-cups, or scyphi, which were denominated Herculean, because Hercules, who was very fond of feasting, used such, and first invented the cry of "no heel taps!" ut libantes nihil in calice vini relinquerent. The reader will bear in mind the Hercules de Gaule of a former quatrain.
272:1 Itales, Ætalia, Elba.
272:2 Par mer, Gulf of Genoa.

272:3 Forains, Latin, foris, strangers.
272:4 Sauf, Latin, sabous, English, safe.
272:5 Sauf de coup de feu.
272:6 Le dard du ceil is the thunderbolt.
272:7 Latin, ferire, to strike.
272:8 Estandue is standard.
273:1 Latin, gens, nation.
273:2 Latin, monstrum, prodigy.

273:3 Morts should be read Meurt, perhaps, as referring to Napoleon, who, showed great delight, it is said, when he found that Wellington intended. to fight him. It cannot refer, as Le Pelletier would have it to do, to, the celebrated mot of Cambronne or General Michel, as it has been proved that it was never uttered at all, but manufactured by a wit après coup.

273:4 The stone is in the tree. Le Pelletier would here understand silex, the flint axe of primitive ages. This seems to me to be very far fetched., and I would rather read, with Garencières, the stone into thunderstone or aerolite, which seems to be far less forced.

274:1 Hyperbaton. the construction is feront entrée a Paris clos d'armée.
274:2 Latin, clausus, shut, cut off from the French army.
275:1 Forche, fourchu, or forked. Latin, furca, hooked.
275:2 Commettre, ellipsis for se commettre, to come to blows with any one.
275:3 Latin, per, through, or by means of.
275:4 Latin, duo, a second repetition.
276:1 Consigning.
276:2 Plus fors, read plus forts.
276:3 Malignus, Latin, a criminal.
278:1 Fera should be feront, I think.
278:2 Avint I take to mean avant.
278:3 Viendra for viendront.
279:1 Onque should be oncq', to scan.

279:2 Italie is the reading of the texte-type. Bouys reads Itale, and then this line will scan.

279:3 Estrangiers was probably pronounced as of two syllables only, but it is difficult to make this line scan.

280:1 Fautes, to be taken as shortcomings.
280:2 Si—very.

Louis XVIII and Louis Philippe

WE now come to the Restoration of Louis XVIII.

 Presage 38. [I. 235.]
Roy salué Victeur, 1 Impereateur, 2
La foy faussée. Le Royal fait 3 congnu: 4
Sang 5 Mathien 6 Roy fait 7 supereateur, 8
De gent 9 superbe humble 10 par 11 pleurs venu. 12
 This is a very crabbed quatrain.
Translation.
The King is saluted victor and dominator,
The oath falsified: The King makes himself known again:
Grandson of Louis XIV. becomes King,
Is called back by the proud people humiliated to tears.

 Louis XVIII. is proclaimed King, May 3, 1814, but the people take up Napoleon from Elba, March 1, 1815, thus breaking faith. Louis XVIII. (Le Royal) is again recognized, July 8, 1815; the grandson of Louis XIV. (sang Æmathien), a name conferred by Nostradamus on Louis XIV., who assumed the emblem of the Sun, Æmathien being son of Aurora, who opens the gates of the morning sun. This grandson becomes now undisputed King, the humiliated French nation recalling him with tears.

 Century X.—Quatrain 16. [I. 236.]
Heureux au regne de France, heureux de vie,
Ignorant sang, mort fureur et rapine,
Par nom flateur 1 sera mis en envie:
Roy desrobé, 2 trop de foye en cuisine.
 Translation.
Happy in the kingdom of France, happy in life,
Free from blood, violent death and angry rapine,
He will have a flattering name, and be an object of desire:
A King retired, with too much faith in the kitchen.

 Here we are to take Louis XVIII. as restored to the throne of France: his life passes happily, without violent experiences of blood, death, rage, or rapine. The flattering name was given to him of Desiré that is prophetically hinted in the words "il sera mis en envie." He will not devote sufficient attention to his public duties, so that he may be described as desrobé, retired or retained at home; and he will be too much addicted to enjoyments of the table,—trop defoye en cuisine. The gastronomy was proverbial; the obesity consequent upon it made him grow inert, so that he gradually let the affairs of State drift without giving them due attention.

 Century III.—Quatrain 96. [I. 238.]
Chef de Fossan 3 aura gorge couppée
Par le ducteur 4 du limier et levrier;p. 285

Le faict patré 1 par ceux du mont Tarpée, 2
Saturne en Leo 3 13 de Fevrier.
Translation.
A prince of Fossano shall have his throat cut
By the keeper of his hounds and greyhounds:
The attempt will be made by those of the Tarpeian rock,
Saturn being in Leo on 13th February.

Fossana is put, by synecdoche, for Sardinia. A prince, therefore, of Sardinia shall be stabbed by the Keeper of the Kennel, instigated by Republicans, when Saturn is in opposition to the sign of the Lion, on February 13, 1820. M. le Pelletier, who seems somewhat learned in the houses of the stars, says that Saturn was in opposition to, and not in conjunction with, Leo on this occasion. But Nostradamus leaves it open. The Tarpeian rock is figuratively employed to signify the Mountain, or the demagogues and the Republicans generally. The Mons Tarpeius was first named from murder, and was for ages a scene of murder. Tarpeia, who betrayed the Capitol to the Sabines, was crushed by their shields at the gate, and her father, Spurius Tarpeius, was thrown over the battlements by order of Romulus. Children ill-formed at birth were flung from its heights. It was better known as Capitolinus, so called (caput Toli) from the head of Tolus, found there when digging foundations for the Temple of Jupiter: thus the place of the skull, a Golgotha from the beginning of Rome. Later on criminals were sentenced to be thrown from it. Many of these deadly associations were, no doubt, present to the mind of Nostradamus, and made this mountain of death seem to him fit to foreshadow the death that should emanate from the French mountain. To dwell upon this is of physiological interest, as showing how very closely the natures of the poet and the prophet overlap each other; so that, as in the rainbow colours, there is no line to be drawn as to where one begins or another ends:—they may be seen, but not severed.

The Duc de Berri was the son of Marie Therèse of Savoy, married to the Comte d'Artois, she being the daughter of Victor-Amédée III., King of Sardinia. This Sardinian was to have ruled France, and, with but one intervening, to have followed the Corsican in the occupation of the throne. Louvel, the murderer, stabbed him coming from the opera, and wore the King's livery at the moment of the attempt. The forecast is again wonderful in prefiguring every particular short of the names of the two individuals. The nationalities are given, the calling of Louvel, and the day of the month. If all this be Chance, some hare-brained few would prefer it to what they know of Certainty.

Century V.—Quatrain 4. [I. 240.]
Le gros mastin de cité dechassé, 1
Sera fasché de l'estrange 2 alliance:
Après aux champs avoir le cerf chassé, 3
Le loup et l'ours se donront 4 defiance.
Translation.
The great mastiff chased from the city
Will be afflicted by the strange alliance:
When the stag is driven to the fields,
The wolf and bear will commence to mistrust each other.

The Duc de Bordeaux is the great mastiff, dethroned August 9, 1830, by Louis Philippe, in the dog-days, when the star Sirius is in opposition. Le Grand Chien burning in the horizon is a synonym for the gros mastin; the city, of course, is Paris. Charles X., who was fond of the chase, is turned from the great huntsman to the stag. The wolf is Louis Philippe, a name which lends itself to Lou. P. The bear represents, according to M. le Pelletier, la Montagne, in the assembly, because bears make their lair in the highest situations. We need not insist on this resemblance or characteristic pointed out by Le Pelletier.

There are six quatrains devoted by Le Pelletier to the Duc de Bordeaux,—the Henri Cinq that was never to be,—that Royal Prince whom all the Princes should see to be heaven-descended. But as we, who are not royal, have seen that nothing came of him; and that, being now dead, nothing can come of him, we shall pass over the six quatrains in silence. The quatrains of Nostradamus lend themselves most kindly to elucidation once you find the clue, but they most persistently refuse to have a meaning read into them from without.

M. le Pelletier has elaborated the meaning of the six quatrains, about Louis Philippe with so much ingenious learning that we must give the whole of them, and let the reader take them at his own valuation.

Century VI.—Quatrain 84.
Celuy qu'en 1 Sparte Claude 2 ne peut regner,
Il fera tant par voye seductive,
Que du court, long le fera araigner, 3
Que contre Roy fera sa perspective. 4
Translation.
He who will cause that the lame cannot reign in Paris, 1
He will effect so much in his seductive way
That from the short to long he will attain,
Who has brought to bear his deception against the King.

The meaning of this is that Louis Philippe d'Orléans will cause the Duc de Bordeaux to be unable to hold the reins of government in Paris. The anagrammatic substitution of Sparte for Paris is doubly ingenious, inasmuch as Lycurgus at Sparta established a double kingship so-called. Of course the office could not be that of king at all, but there was the name if not the fact, and that suffices for this prince of dexterous analogists, Nostradamus. Louis Philippe will achieve this by the byeways of seduction, and will usurp successfully his nephew's throne (araigner), putting himself in opposition, says Le Pelletier, to his lawful King. Faire sa perspective he renders opposition. I do not think this is the meaning of the phrase. There is an extract from Fontenelle (I cannot refer to it in his works at present), in which he speaks of a perspective that will make an emperor or a beggar out of the same figure, according to the point of view from which you regard it. That is an optical illusion. Descartes, in his "L'Homme," mentions the pictures placed at the end of corridors to cheat the eye agreeably, and adds, "L'exemple des tableaux de perspective montre combien il est facile de s'y tromper." And then there were those perspectives that Holbein and his contemporaries used to introduce into their pictures, of a skull, or death's head, so painted that you could not quite tell what it was till you reached the right point of view, when it would suddenly contract and draw its elongated self together to a true skull by a process the reverse of foreshortening. By the words sa perspective, I conceive that Nostradamus meant that Louis Philippe brought his deception to bear against the King.

Century V.—Quatrain 69. [I. 250.]

Plus ne sera le Grand en faux sommeil,
L'inquietude viendra prendre repos:
Dresser phalange 1 d'or, azur, et vermeil,
Subjuger Afrique, la ronger jusques os.
Translation.
Le Grand will pretend no longer a false sleep;
His disquietude will now lull itself in security,
Arrange his army under gold, blue, and red,
Subjugate Africa, gnawing it to the very bone.

Louis Philippe, now King, and so become le Grand, says M. le Pelletier (though, as applied to the individual, it looks quite like a misnomer), will now unmask his designs, and take his repose in security. He will adopt the tricolour of the Revolution and complete the conquest of Algeria; Pelissier roasting the refugees in caves, to the very bone. Everything but the word Grand justifies the interpretation to a nicety.

Century I.—Quatrain 39. [I. 251.]
De nuict dans lict le supresme 1 estranglé,
Pour avoir trop sejourné blond esleu,
Par trois 2 l'Empire subrogé 3 exanclé 4
A mort mettra carte 5 et pacquet ne leu. 6
Translation.
When France shall be dominated by three parties,
The last of the family shall be strangled at night in bed,
For having lent too much to the fair Capet.
Put to death because a paper and packet were not read.

When France is dominated by three alternately (Orleanists, Republicans, Bonapartists), the Prince de Bourbon, Condé, last of his race, shall be strangled, at night in his bed, for desiring to follow in the suite of the Duc de Bordeaux. A new will, duly sealed up, in favor of the Bourbon, but not read, is the cause of his death. The "not read" means, not read by the Duc de Bordeaux, in whose favour it was drawn. The Baronne de Feuchères, whose interests were allied to those of Louis Philippe, defeated this by the murder. M. le Pelletier acquits Louis Philippe of complicity in the crime, but he remarks that the interest of the baronne was incidentally that of the King. Her crime was incited by the desire to do away with the new will, by which she would be a heavy loser. It is curious that Garencières considers this quatrain to have been fulfilled in Philip II. of Spain, who had his own son, Don Carlos, strangled in bed. The coincidence of the name Philip is singular, but the remaining two lines he does not attempt to interpret.

Century VIII.—Quatrain 42. [I. 253.]
Par avarice, par force et violence
Viendra vexer les siens chef d'Orleans;
Près Sainct Memire 1 assaut et resistance,
Mort dans sa tante, 2 diront qu'il dort leans. 3
Translation.
By cupidity and abuse of power, force, and violence,
The chief of Orleans will come to vex his own;
Near St. Memire resistance will be made;
Dead in his palace he will ever after sleep.

Avarice was always the fault of Louis Philippe. By extortion and abuse he raised resistance at Saint Meri; in and near the church he forced the republicans to submission, dort leans a play upon the name, never again showed energy, but slept a sleep as of death in his palace (dans sa tente). The insurrection that was quelled took place on June 5 and 6, 1832.

Century IX.—Quatrain 89. [I. 254.]
Sept ans sera Philipp; fortune prospere:
Rabaissera des Arabes effort;
Puis son midy perplex 4 rebors 5 affaire,
Jeune Ognion 6 abismera son fort.
Translation.
Seven years will Philip's fortune prosper well;
He will defeat every effort of the Arabs;
In his embarrassed middle period all goes against the grain,
Young Ogmion will overwhelm his fort.

Fortune will favour Louis Philippe for the first seven years. He will repress the Arabs. But in the middle of his reign the Eastern question will spring up, and cover him with disgrace (this culminated July 15, 1840). For the next seven years all will go against the grain, and the new Republic (jeune Ogmion) will overturn his throne and his Bastille; the Paris he thought he had so strongly fortified.

Garencières again introduces Philip II. of Spain, and there seems to exist some analogy between these two kings. The Spaniard also was prosperous for some seven years, and in the person of his brother, Don Juan of Austria, beat the Turks in the Battle of Lepanto. Garencières reads Barbares for Arabs. Later on he had to put his son to death, and was opposed by young Ogmion; the King, Henri Quatre, of France and Navarre.

Century V.—Quatrain 92. [I. 255.]
Après le siege tenu dix-sept ans,
Cinq changeront en tel revolu terme:
Puis sera l'un esleu de mesme temps,
Qui les Romains ne sera trop conforme.
Translation.
After the throne has been held for seventeen years,
Five shall change when that term has run out:
Then, at the same time, one shall be elected,
Who will not be very conformable to the wishes of the Romanists.

After the reign of Louis Philippe, during seventeen years, five of his sons lost the throne with himself; and with much manœuvring have never been able to reapproach it. They were the Comte de Paris, representative of Chartres, Duc de Nemours, Joinville, Montpensier, and Due d'Aumale. The election that followed was that of Louis Napoleon, whose mixed, or no policy, suited neither the Revolutionary party nor the Roman Catholics. There is nothing here but the seventeen years to connect this with Louis Philippe. For the five who changed with the revolt would be six if Louis Philippe himself were counted, and he certainly ought to be. The concluding two lines are very vague, and may or may not belong to Louis Napoleon. I merely cite it, as one of the ingenuities of M. le Pelletier.

There are three prophecies cited relating to the Due de Chartres, which seem fairly well interpreted; and very wonderful they would be if they stood alone or related to any one whose fate was of any importance in the opening scroll of history. All the little interest of Louis Philippe is centred in himself, and therefore I omit the three quatrains relating to his son, not because they are not curious, if rightly interpreted of the son, but that, even supposing them to be so, the Due de Chartres is a person and a character not deserving of serious mention in history. The gossip of a barber's shop in Nostradamus's own day would be even more interesting to any rational investigator of human affairs. Footnotes

283:1 Latin, victor, conqueror.
283:2 Latin, Imperator.
283:3 Latin, factum, action, act.
283:4 Congnu = connu, known.
283:5 Sang, son or grandson.
283:6 Mathien, Æmathien.
283:7 Latinism, factus, made, become.
283:8 Latin, superator, rule, dominator.
283:9 Latin, gens, nation.
283:10 Humble = humiliated, perhaps humblée.
283:11 Latin, per, by reason of.
283:12 The order is, "venu à cause des pleurs de la superbe nation humiliée."
284:1 The original text is corrupt here, but this yields the best sense.
284:2 Desrobé, withdrawn, or shut up.
284:3 Fossano is the alternative reading, a town in the Sardinian States.
284:4 Keeper of the hounds and greyhounds.
285:1 Latin, patratus, done, committed.
285:2 The Tarpeian rock at Rome.
285:3 Latin, Leo, the astronomical sign of the Lion.
286:1 Dechassé = chassé, chased away.
286:2 Estrange has again the meaning of foreign, or out of the family.
286:3 The order is après avoir chassé le cerf aux champs.
286:4 Donront = donneront.
287:1 Celuy qu'en = Celuy qui fera qu'en.
287:2 Latin, Claudus, lame. This Le Pelletier has before endeavoured, with surprising dexterity, to show to be the Due de Bordeaux.
287:3 This whole line is difficult. Araigner, in the Romance language, is said to mean to plead and gain a cause against another. The court and long we had before, in Century VIII., 57, applied to Napoleon, as rising from a soldier to the long-robed Emperor; here he had to refer to Talma to teach him how to carry it. Now, again, it means the rise from a mere dignitary to Kingship.
287:4 Latin, qui.
288:1 Sparte = Paris. The letters te may be considered as one letter, the v being mute. It will then convert, according to the rule of the anagram.
289:1 Phalange, flag, standard, writes M. le Pelletier. As far as I can discover anything, this statement appears to be entirely erroneous. The word "phalanx," as connected with matters military, always signifies a body of men in military order. It may in the plural even stand indefinitely for armies. In the singular it is very confusing. It may stand for a party of twenty-eight men or eight thousand (Potter's "Antiquities," ii. 56). Danet says six thousand men. Gibbon introduces one of his constantly recurring slovenly phrases about it,—absurd in fact, but philosophic in form. He is comparing the legion with the phalanx (i. 22), and tells us, "It was soon discovered by reflection, as well as by the event," that it could not contend with the

legion. It is obvious here, that if it had been discovered by reflection it would never have been tried by the event. This somewhat justifies the sarcasm of Porson, that schoolboys ought to be set to translate Gibbon into English. As a pleasing variety, Smith sets the number when complete at about sixteen thousand men. One feels inclined to say that these classical guides are conveying us to that ditch, which is never far to seek, when the blind are leading the blind. Martinius, in his curious "Lex. Phil.," cites Pliny to show that the Africans first fought the Egyptians fustibus, with staves, which they called phalanges in the plural, or phalanx in the singular, so that it is an African word, in Hebrew phalag, is a staff. Also there is a spider called phalangion; and as the pikes of the first five ranks in a phalanx were interlaced, they were somewhat like a web of staves. Many may regard all this as extremely useless; perhaps they will concede that it is curious; if so, I shall consider it to be useful. I have long found that whatever is very curious is useful. It sets the mind agreeably in movement, and often throws a new light on things that previously had no interest and seemed obscure. At any rate, we have now established that phalange is not to be rendered standard, but troops, army.

290:1 Latin, supremus, the last.
290:2 The order is, "Quand l'Empire sera exanclé par trois subrogés."
290:3 Latin, subrogatus, substituted; read subrogés.
290:4 Exancillatus, subdued to, under the yoke of.
290:5 Latin, charta, paper
290:6 Romance, ne leu, not read.
291:1 Sainct Memire is the anagram of S'Meri. To make this pass, M. le Pelletier drops one m and one e.
291:2 Tante is to be read tente.
291:3 Leans is an old word for là dedans.
291:4 Latin, perplexus, troubled.
291:5 Rebors = rebours; à rebours is against the grain.
291:6 Ognion is Ogmius, the Celtic Mercury or Gallic Hercules. It has p. 292 figured in 1792, 1848, and again after the German war, 872. At the two first periods they put the figure of this Hercules on their five franc pieces, with that idle exergue, Liberté, Égalité, Fraternité. This vocable, Ogmion, is equivalent to Oignon, onion, or bulbous root of the lily. If there could be any doubt at all about this, Nostradamus has taken care to remove it, calling it le grand mercure d'Hercule fleur de lys, in Century X. 79.

Republic, 1848, and Napoleon III

Century IX.—Quatrain 5. [I. 261.]
Tiers 1 doigt du pied au premier semblera,
A un nouveau monarque de bas haut: 2
Qui 3 Pyse et Luques tyran occupera,
Du precedent coriger le deffaut.
Translation.
The third 4 shall be a stepping-stone to the throne,
To a new monarch from low position to the top;
He will as tyrant have taken a military post in Tuscany, 5
And will seek to correct the defects of his predecessor.

THE National Assembly of 1848 shall serve as a foot to Louis Napoleon to step from private life into a conspicuous position. He had in his youth been concerned in the Revolution of Tuscany, and purposed correcting the defect of his predecessor.

This might mean that he purposed to guide France better than Louis Philippe had done, or than in four years the Republic had done, or, which is most probable from his Idées Napoléoniennes, to carry to completion the policy of his uncle Napoleon I. I cannot think it refers to Napoleon II., Duc de Reichstadt. The entire application of the quatrain is neither very clear nor very important.

The quatrain on Cavaignac, I think, is hardly made out satisfactorily, so I omit it.

Century VIII.—Quatrain 43. [I. 265.]
Par le decide 1 de deux choses bastards,
Nepveu du sang 2 occupera le regne: 3
Dedans Lectoyre 4 seront les coups de dards,
Nepveu par peur pliera l'enseigne.
Translation.
By the fall or ruin of two bastard things
The nephew by blood will occupy the empire;
In Lectoyre there will be deaths by arrow,
The nephew will fold up his standard for very fear.

By the overthrow of Louis Philippe and the Republic two bastard governments, Louis Napoleon will now succeed to the throne, a nephew by blood of Napoleon Bonaparte; and, what is not generally known, he was the only one of the Bonaparte family born in the Palace of the Tuileries. In battle afterwards at Lectoyre (coups de dards must be taken simply as battle) the nephew will furl his standard through fear.

Writing in 1866, M. le Pelletier particularly remarks that the epoch is left undetermined, and, as to the enigma of Lectoyre, nothing can be known till the event has transpired. It may then be interpreted, he thinks, in some of the idioms known to Nostradamus—Greek, Hebrew, Latin, Celtic, Languedoc, etc. He considers the standard to present a further enigma, and asks "What standard?" This difficulty I do not quite recognize. The imperial standard that is adopted by him, whatever it may be. To furl a standard is to close and shut it up, so that no one will rally to it any more. It symbolizes that the cause it represents is brought to the ground finally, and that it is no longer flying.

As to the word Lectoyre, we now know that, if it is to be interpreted at all, it will have to be found in connection with Sedan,—the noblest reminiscence connected with which is that it was the birthplace of that great soldier and greater man, Marshal Turenne. He may well be called La gloire de Sedan, whilst as appropriately may Napoleon the Little be designated as Cédant de la gloire, with that furled ensign, qu'il par peur pliera. 1

After much difficulty and searching I have at last come upon two old maps, printed at Amsterdam by Blaeuw; the one dated 1620 and the other 1650, styled "Les Soverainetez de Sedan." In both of these the embattled town of Sedan is given, as seated on the right bank of the river Meuse, whilst on the left bank is shown an extensive territory named Grand Torcy and Petit Torcy. In another map it is given as Torsy. These maps give no indication of the points of the compass. But from another map, indicating them, the river-bend on which the town is seated appears to run from east to west; and, if so, Torcy lies south or south-west of Sedan. In a more modern map it appears as Le Grand Torcy and is described as lying "sur la route impériale de Mezieres a Sedan." Evidently therefore we are entitled to place Le Torcy at Sedan. The French must determine for themselves, by their military bureau, whether the French camp was pitched in the meadows of Le Torcy; but nothing can alter the great fact, as now for the first time made plain, that the Nepveu du sang furled his standard for ever at Sedan or Lectoyre, as the oracle gives it. Now Lectoyre is the precise anagram, letter for letter, of Le Torcey, though the commoner spelling is without the second e, Le Torcy. If we are to reckon this as being a chance coincidence, my only further comment will be, that such chance as this is quite as miraculous as any miracle in the world could be.

As regards the words "nepveu du sang," there was a caricature very popular in France at the time of the candidature for the French presidency, consisting of two pictures. In one the Prince de Joinville was commending himself to the French people for election, having the young Comte de Paris by the hand, and saying, "I am the uncle of my nephew." On the other side Louis Napoleon presses his suit by pointing to a statuette of Napoleon Bonaparte and uttering the words, "I am the nephew of my uncle;" showing how characteristically nepveu du sang designates Prince Louis Napoleon. He may almost be said to have chosen it himself as a cognomen.

Century VIII.—Quatrain 44. [I. 267.]
Le procrée naturel d'Ogmion 1
De sept à neuf du chemin destorner:
A roy de longue amy et 2 au my hom 3
Doit à Navarre fort de Pau prosterner.

I propose here to make the meaning as clear as I can without a translation.

Napoleon III. (le procrée), the natural offspring of the French Republic (Ogmion), will turn from the right road for seven or nine years before his fall. Le Pelletier interprets otherwise. He says that the war in Italy began in the seventh year of the Empire, 1869, and from that date throughout the nine following years he changed his policy. I think the line means that from seven to nine years before the end of his reign he changed his policy. That is to say, from seven years previous to the close of his reign, when Charles August Louis, Duc de Morny, died, i.e. in 1865; and even for two years previously to that, things took a different turn. De Morny no longer exercised active control, and his was the head that had guided I all along. When he died, all ran to destruction. The roi de longue and his friend my hom, Le Pelletier states to be Victor Emmanuel and Garibaldi; one of long race and one of low birth, the tallow-smelter. I think it is Frederic William, de longue vie, and Bismarck, the bi-valve man, which it becomes, if we read it as my-homme. I have a great idea that à Navarre is a misprint for le nepveu. Whether fort de Pau may mean with his health re-established by staying at Pau or not, I cannot say. But, anyhow, I think that the two last lines are to be read together, and that he is to prostrate himself to the King and his friend. Louis Napoleon's whole reign must be represented as a failure, if you read it with Le Pelletier; mine makes it a failure during the last seven to nine years. My King and friend bring about the catastrophe far below the date that his will do. My emendation to le nepveu certainly clarifies the meaning. The explanation of Pau is not quite so comprehensible as I could wish; had Ham been a variant it would have spoken for itself.

The Quatrain 53 of Century VIII., which I have already explained as the flotilla of Napoleon Bonaparte, M. le Pelletier fixes as the ludicrous Boulogne expedition of Louis Napoleon, and the Italian campaign after he became Emperor; but I think he entirely fails in reading the symbols.

Century V.—Quatrain 8. [I. 270.]
Sera laissé feu vif, mort caché,
Dedans les globes, horrible espouvantable,
De nuict a classe 1 cité en poudre lasché,
La cité à feu, l'ennemy favourable.
Translation.
Live fire, hidden death, shall be left
In bombs, a horrible and frightful thing:
By a band at night the city shall be fired with powder;
The city seems on fire, it helps though intended to destroy.

Fulminating mercury (feu vif) in bombs in terrible explosion contains death hidden. The city, Paris, will be startled with powder liberated (lasché, loosed) by assassins by night. The city will seem on fire. But the enemy (in spite of himself) will prove favourable to Napoleon. This, of course, is Orsini's attempt of January 14, 1858.

The next verse follows up the thread.

Century V.—Quatrain 9. [I. 271.]
Jusques au fond la grand arq 2 demolue 3
Par chef captif l'amy anticipé, 4
Naistra de dame front, face chevelue,
Lors par astuce duc 5 mort atrapé.
Translation.
When the peristyle is thoroughly demolished
By the chief prisoner, the friend being taken before,
A plot born of the woman, long beard and hairy face;
Then by cunning the leader caught will be executed.

The peristyle (la grand arq') of the opera shall be completely shattered. Pieri, the friend of Orsini, the chief captive, is seized beforehand by Hébert, head of the detective service, who recognized him in the crowd. The plot was conceived in the secret lodges of the Demagoguy [de Dame], whose members wear the beard and hair long. Orsini, the leader of the whole, will be surprised astutely by the confessions of Gomez at the restaurant Broggi, whither he had fled, and, being taken, will be sentenced to death.

I do not feel very confident as to this interpretation, but give it much as I find it in M. le Pelletier.

    Century V.—Quatrain 10. [I. 272.]
    Un 1 chef Celtique dans le conflict blessé,
    Auprès de cave 2 voyant siens mort abbatre,
    De sang et playes et d'ennemis pressé,
    Et secours par incogneus 3 de quatre.
    Translation.
    The Celtic chief is wounded in the strife,
    Seeing death strike down his friends near the theatre,
    Surrounded with blood and wounds and pressed by enemies,
    He escapes the four 4 assassins, by unknown aid.

The Emperor, slightly struck in the eye by a fragment of glass, shall see his people strewn in death about the entrance of the Grand Opera. Pressed by the conspirators, four in number, he will receive unknown help; whether of angels or pure spirits, M. le Pelletier cannot quite say. We now know that he had still to see Sedan; but it would be curious if pure spirits had interested themselves greatly to protect the cold-blooded murderer of the Champs de Mars. and Coup d'État.

    Century VI.—Quatrain 4. [I. 273.]
    Le second chef du regne D'annemarc, 1
    Par ceux de Frize 2 et l'Isle Britannique,
    Fera despendre 3 plus de cent mille marc, 4
    Vain exploicter voyage en Italique.

The second of the Napoleonic race in power will cause England and Hanover to expend 100,000 marks in fortifications and war material. Fearing invasion after the Orsini effort, he will then exploit the Italian campaign, though vainly, as he will not reap the results he looks for.

This corresponds so clearly with what happened that probably most will agree that it is a very remarkable forecast.

    Century III.—Quatrain 37. [I. 274.]
    Avant l'assaut l'oraison 5 prononcée,
    Milan prins 6 d'Aigle par embusches deceus, 7
    Muraille antique par canons enfoncée,
    Par feu et sang à mercy pen receus.
    Translation.
    Before assault a harangue is pronounced;
    Lombardy is taken by the eagle, being cut off by ambuscade.
    An ancient wall driven in by cannon,
    Fire and blood, but little mercy shown.

Before the declaration of war, the Emperor will pronounce (January 1, 1859), in the presence of the diplomatic corps, a threatening discourse against Austria.

Lombardy (Milan, part for the whole) will be ceded by Austria at the Treaty of Zurich (October 17, 1859); Austria, an old wall, will yield to cannon, fire, and blood.

> Century V.—Quatrain 20. [I. 275.]
> De là 1 les Alpes grande armée passera
> Un peu devant naistra monstre vapin, 2
> Prodigieux et subit 3 tournera 4
> Le grand Tosquan à son lieu plus propin. 5
> Translation.
> A great army will pass beyond the Alps,
> A little before a prodigious scamp will come to power;
> He will drive the grand Duke of Tuscany
> To his nearer home with astounding suddenness.

In 1859 Napoleon III.'s army will pass the Alps. A little before a prominent scamp will have come to the front, who will suddenly and in a most startling fashion drive the Grand Duke of Tuscany to seek refuge in Austria (son lieu le plus propin).

We have to note here that Nostradamus, whenever he emerges from the impassability of the secret estude, it is to exhibit a profound hostility to the genius of Democracy and Revolution. There is therefore little doubt but that the powerful epithet here employed of the monstre vapin relates to the red-shirted Garibaldi.

We have now reached the point which covers the last of the Oracles of Nostradamus that commentary has yet been able to lay before the world with its meaning rendered transparent by the correspondence of interpretation with an event in history. The number of such correlations of occurrence with forecast falls immensely short of the number of the quatrains themselves. In fact, only about one hundred and fifty-one, out of a thousand. The rest give no scintillation as yet, but lie without sign of existence traceable, dead as a flint, till the iron stroke of Time's heel shall develop the spark. Lateat scintillula forsan. One or two Presages and two or three Sixains have been also resolved, Enough, we trust, has been opened up to show what a treasure-house it is that we have entered into, how rich in curiosity, if in nothing more. What may still lie perdu in the bulky remainder of eight hundred and fifty it is impossible to say; whether, though unidentified, they have been realized already, or are yet to bud in the future. If nothing more be ever done with Nostradamus than this book gives, still the work must for one reason or other hereafter stand out as the most wonderful book of its kind that was ever written or printed in this world. It has now to go forth and take its chance, good or evil, of notice or of neglect amongst the mass of printed matter, largely rubbish, that deluges our life. It is certainly calculated, so far as it can secure any attention whatever, to severely shock the prejudices now prevalent amongst mankind. The half-educated will find it troublesome to read, and disturbing, perhaps, to think about; whilst the scientific may even denounce it as a locust-cloud of darkness mediæval in its tendency. Undoubtedly it must have the effect that Nostradamus in his preface to his son (see p. 45) says very graphically it will have, "que possible fera retirer le front à quelques uns." Although, as he says again, the forecasts may be clouded, they will be understood by men of sense, and they will grow clearer as ignorance dies out (see p. 49); which should be our care now.

To all objectors I rejoin, gentlemen, investigate, please, all the points in question as searchingly as you can; find every fault in my work, and in that of the other Nostradamic commentators, that you can; expose all that is weak or illusive,

wherever you find it to be so. Let us see, then, how far all the learning and acuteness you can bring to bear, coupled with whatever established prejudice, and its rancour at being disturbed in comfortable somnolency, can suggest, to overthrow what other men heretofore, and I now, have taken so much pains to bring together and give shape to. Consciously I have not set down a single word with any other desire than that the truth should prevail; and if your criticism can establish the opposite, I shall still repeat, "Let truth prevail." But I do not think you can do this: and if not, there is only one other thing, open to the learned and the wise that can be done,—that is, to rewrite their philosophies, so as to make room for the reception of this rather awkward piece of truth that has here got in the way of our old theories, and cannot be got out of the way again. To the really competent and candid reader I have nothing whatever to add beyond begging him to refer back to the closing words of my preface, as to him they will he found to contain my whole and entire message.
Footnotes

294:1 Tiers, pour le tiers État. The third order now claiming to govern itself.

294:2 De bas haut, for de bas en haut elevated from a low to a higher and conspicuous position.

294:3 Latin, qui, he, who.

294:4 The third estate will serve, as a toe of the foot to the first rank, a stepping-stone to place.

294:5 Lucca and Pisa stand for all Tuscany, where, in 1831, Louis Napoleon and Charles Bonaparte, his elder brother, had, with one cannon served by himself and a few Italian partisans, possessed himself of Civita-Castellana, in the Pontifical States.

295:1 Latin, decidium, a word not of classical usage, signifying ruin, or a fall.

295:2 Romance sang, family.

295:3 Latin, regnum, empire.

295:4 Lectoyre, a town in France, in the department of Gers. Garencières adopts the variant Lectoure, which he says is a town in Gascony. The word occurs again, Century VII. 12, and there he says it is a city of Guyenne. Lectora was the Latin name. It was a place of great strength, and picturesque; but, unless we can find it to be an anagram, there is nothing to connect the town in any way with the fortunes of Louis Napoleon.

296:1 The word pliera, is of course, only an archaic transposition of pleira. The line here can in no way be made to scan, being two syllables or one whole foot short. I would suggest it be read Nepveu (du sang) par peur pleira l'enseigne.

297:1 Ogmion has been explained already to be the symbol of the French Republic.

297:2 The texte-type reads et amy au.

297:3 My-hom, Le Pelletier says, is demy-homme, a man of low birth, and Roy de longue = de vieille race. I prefer to read de longue vie, and understand the King of Prussia; and my-hom I take to be the bivalve-man, or Bismarck.

299:1 Latin, classis, band; à classe, by a band [sic?]. It might be better here to render classe as "crash," ??????, brisure. De nuict la classe, a crash by night.

299:2 Latin, arca, chest, or dam.

299:3 Latin, demolitus, demolished.

299:4 Latin, antecaptus, seized beforehand.

299:5 Latin, dux, leader.

300:1 Latin, unus, the first.

300:2 Latin, cavea, theatre.

300:3 Romance, incogneus, unknown.

300:4 The four were Orsini, Pieri, de Rudio, and Gomez.
301:1 Greek, as we had it before (v. p. 252).
301:2 Frise, Hanover.
301:3 Latin, dependere, to weigh out, spend.
301:4 M. le Pelletier calculates that the golden mark was equal to 250 grammes, or 100,000 marks = 10,000,000 francs.
301:5 Latin, oratio, harangue.
301:6 Romance, prins, pris, taken.
301:7 Latin, decisus, cut off.
302:1 Delà, for au delà.
302:2 Italian, vappa, scamp.
302:3 Latin, subito, suddenly.
302:4 Il tournera, for il fera tourner.
302:5 Latin, propinque, at hand, near.

Appendix

THE genuine and spurious portraits of Cromwell are numerous to such a degree, that they may almost be called innumerable; for they can never be counted, as no one man can get at them all to reckon them up. Their main authority is said to depend upon the works of four artists, Lely, Cooper, Walker, Faithorne. Samuel Butler, the author of the ever-marvelous "Hudibras," is thought to have painted a likeness, but it counts for nothing, as it is not now to be identified as existing in any collection. The first-named three are painters, the fourth is a great engraver.

In all these, Mr. Frederic Harrison professes to discover "singular resemblance" ["Cromwell," p. 32,] but considers that Cooper's is the most successful of them all. I find the first to be a most misleading statement. and one that may be disproved by anybody who will compare Cooper's likeness, as given in Carlyle's "Cromwell Letters" with the picture by Walker in the National Portrait Gallery. They differ in every particular,—in character, feature, temperament, and conformation. Scarcely do they agree even in the wart. There is nothing to identify them as representing the same individual. Either Lely copied Cooper, or Cooper copied Lely, and they accordingly, of course, correspond with each other; but truth is too much sacrificed to flattery by both these courtly painters, for us to suppose that their work corresponds very accurately with the sitter. Such examples of Faithorne as are readily accessible in the Print Room at the Museum convey no adequate idea of the man. Neither do they resemble Cooper, Lely, nor Walker's work. There is a profile print by Houbraken, an excellent performance, which is interesting as showing that both the chin and forehead receded greatly. There is also a very peculiar engraving of Thomas Simon's medal, which is very beautiful as a work of art. But here again the facial angle is simply villainous, with very mean diminutive eyes, and the dress almost clerical. The engraving from the Cooper at Sidney College gives the wart on the left brow instead of the right.

From such discrepant things it seems to me next to impossible to derive any correct notion regarding the face of Cromwell, except that the facial angle of the side face must have been unusually bad. Yet Mr. Harrison is able to express himself as follows:– "No human countenance recorded is more familiar to us than that broad, solid face with the thick and prominent red nose; the heavy gnarled brow, with its historic wart; eyes firm, penetrating, sad; square jaw, and close-set mouth; scanty tufts of hair on lip and chin; long loose brown locks flowing down in waves on to the shoulder. His whole air breathing energy, firmness, passion, pity, and sorrow." Carlyle's fancy version is given below. 1

This being derived from a falsity, must itself be false. But is it not somewhat curious that friends and foes of Cromwell should alike sit down contentedly before this admirably executed miniature of Cooper's without devoting a second thought to its representative value as a portrait of the man in question? Its artistic felicity should be as nothing to the historical inquirer. Taken as a mere portrait, this Cooper is as valueless as Veronese's presentment of Alexander the Great; or as any fancy portrait of Oliver would be, if sent in by some skilled modern hand to the next May show at Burlington House.

Our sense of surprise increases, when we come to remember that we possess an authentic original to go by, in the shape of a mask still extant that was taken at death. Historians draw up rigmarole pen-and-ink portraits of their own, but are all silent about this, or make only casual mention of it as "the mask at the Statuaries," just as though it corresponded in every particular with Samuel Cooper's exquisite pigment-figment. Romancists delight in coloured detail gathered from history; and historians revel in romance when it saves them from searching into dry detail. In this case historical gossip slips in to illustrate the stringent veracity of Cromwell. When Lely was to take his portrait, he is said to have ordered him to be faithful in representing every blemish and defect, to paint warts and all, or he would not be paid. Lely knew what this meant, and acted accordingly. All portrait-painters flatter, they must to secure a practice; but, they ought to select the best aspect possible, for so far it is what it professes to be, a likeness. Now the strong point with your court painter is, to throw in skillfully what is not there. In this Lely and Cooper have succeeded to admiration.

Walker, in his several portraits, gives us another set of varieties. His picture in the Portrait Gallery [Granger, "Biog. Hist.," iii. p. 290.] with Cromwell's son Richard as page tying on the father's scarf, has been finely engraved by Pierre Lombart. In this picture, which is a little wooden, we get an average-looking gentleman going to battle. A man we should have to look at three or four times before we should individualize him at all in the memory. Mr. Nobody riding to nowhere particular is the impression derived. Of the engraving, however, Evelyn says, and he knew Cromwell perfectly well, "that it gives the strongest resemblance of him." He therein physiognomically discovers "characters of the greatest dissimulation, boldness, cruelty, and ambition, in every stroke and touch." I can say nothing of this, for I have not seen the Lombart engraving. The picture does not convey the idea.

How pliantly subservient art was in those days, is well illustrated in another Cromwell engraving by the same Lombart. This artist had done, after Vandyke, a "Charles on horseback," from which he erased the face, and substituted that of Cromwell. The slender figure of the king had to do duty for the heavy-built brewer of Huntingdon. But times change, and we with them. So Peter reinstated the king. There must be impressions of this turn-face print in its three states; for no doubt copies were sold at every stage. The King is dead. God save the Protector! The Protector is dead. God save the King! The dead lion is never so good for the crowd as the live ass; irrespective of the latter creature being far more representative. A quality much sought after in modern governors.

There is a portrait of Cromwell affixed to Isaac Kimber's "Life of Oliver Cromwell," which he published anonymously [Granger, iii. 297]. This is pronounced in the "Letters of Mr. Hughes" to be most like the authentic family pictures of Cromwell. Vertue engraved it in 1724 for Rapin's "History of England," and when Granger wrote the picture was in the possession of Sir Thomas Frankland of Old Bond Street. I suppose this to be still in the hands of the Frankland-Russells of Chequers Court, who also possess a plaster cast of Cromwell's face. By the courtesy of the family I have been permitted to examine this; but it seems to me of ne value, and it has no history.

We come now to the terra-cotta bust by Edward Pierce, which is in the National Portrait Gallery, said to be taken from life. Pierce was an artist in the second generation. His father, of the same Christian name, was a painter, and assistant of Vandyke. Our Edward was trained for a statuary, and because the pupil of Edward Bird: he also acted as assistant to Sir Christopher Wren, and is said to have built St. Clement Danes under him. He did a bust of Wren, for the theatre at Oxford, and also one of Newton, He died at Surrey street in the Strand, and was buried at the old Savoy. This bust of Cromwell was, to all appearance, modelled by him from a cast taken from life, and must therefore, as to measurement and bulk, be of life size.

I was kindly permitted by Mr. George Scharf, of the National Portrait Gallery, to take the dimensions of this bust by measurement, but practically they are not very useful, inasmuch as the head has a great abundance of short curly hair which of course in terra-cotta becomes perfectly solid, and thereby increases the circumference of the head by many inches.

The circumference, hair and all, at his brow is 28 2/8 inches.

Nape of neck to frontal bone, where it unites with nose 15 4/8 "

Breadth from car to ear at level of the central hole of each ear as near as can be approximated 6 2/8 "

This last measurement is, I believe, correct, but it is a dimension that only a large forceps could take with perfect certainty. It is so small, however, that I feel sure that the other two dimensions must be very far from giving the true osseous formation, so that several inches will have to be allowed off them for the hair. Again, the measurement between the tip of nose and back of head (9 5/8 inches) would also require that deductions be made for a wad of hair at the back. This measurement when reduced, and coupled with the third measurement given, indicates an undersized skull for a broad-built man of five feet eleven in stature.

As for the physiognomy, the nose, though far from fine, is somewhat aquiline, and the best of all the features of the face. The forehead is low, ill-formed, and mean. The mouth firm, cruel, deceitful. The jowl and chin sensual and gross almost to brutality. It is the face of a man of low passions, possibly ambitious, but of great duplicity, of a low-bred type, the type as of one sprung from a lower stratum of society than his history indicates him to have sprung from; and you may readily suppose that in exchanges of coarse buffoonery with the roughest trooper of his corps, he would have been quite within his own province and at home. His mother's portrait shows her also to have been a very masculine coarse-featured woman.

It is well perhaps to mention here a bust that Grose in a letter to Granger in 1774, calls "a masterly and spirited bust of Oliver Cromwell by one Bannier." It was then in Mr. Gostling's collection. He says it is like that engraving given in Rapin's "History." I imagine it therefore to be a fancy rendering, and of very small historic value.

The expert historians, and of course the general public together with them, are perfectly satisfied with the Cromwell presented to them by Samuel Cooper. I confess that I think it a most laughable presentment, and of quite impossible credence. I do not think Pierce's bust to be satisfactory, but I most certainly consider that it is the only likeness I have had the opportunity of examining that conveys even a hint of what can be supposed to be the real appearance of the man. There is but one way now remaining to settle this question. It is very much to be regretted that, with so much pretence of a desire for historical accuracy, we should have allowed two hundred and fifty years to elapse without making the least attempt to settle this question.

We learn from Breval's "Travels" that at the Old Palace at Florence there is a cast preserved of Oliver Cromwell. The mould was obtained from Cromwell's face a few minutes after his decease, "through the dexterous management of the Tuscan resident in London." This, or a cast from it, ought immediately to be secured for our National Portrait Gallery. A copy of it would cost very little in either time, money, or trouble to secure; and when secured three or four should be cast in bronze, and placed in different museums so that one fire could not destroy all of them at once.

I feel almost sure that it will be found to confirm the bust of Pierce,, as being more like Cromwell than anything else that we possess. And further, as Pierce's work is by no means a grand achievement in the sculptor's art, I should hope to find in the Florence cast characteristic indications that are absent from Pierce's work. Grandeur of soul is incompatible with such a face as Pierce gives us. But I confess that I see no grandeur whatever that could be expressed by a man whose history it that of Oliver. His base success the world may worship if it will. I despise success if it must be obtained by Cromwell's methods. I observe that the great in history are always mean in fact; and I well know that you must say to all the men who have been triumphant, let no probing moralist come near you. Pitiable and contemptible is the man who can envy the great in the greatness of their crimes. I do not expect that the cast, if procured, will make the reading any better for Cromwell; but, if it should, I am quite ready to give him all the advantage of it. At present I hold that the face is villainous, like the man.

". . . ducitur unco,
Spectandus: gaudent omnes. Quæ labra? Quis illi
Vultus erat? Nunquam, si quid mihi credis, amavi
Hunc hominem."

JUVENAL, x. 66.

Still, love or no love, we have reached the end; and if we should confirm Pierce, the flesh and bones of the man thus revived will also confirm the epithets of Nostradamus, which first induced me to enter upon this investigation.

"Sir, I perceive that thou art a prophet."—John iv. 19.
"Quod est ante pedes, nemo spectat: cœli scrutantur plagas."—Cic., Divin., ii. 13.
This granted, a pig is nearest wisdom.
—WITSIUS, Miscel., p. 14.
The best analogist is the best prophet.
"L'observation des analogies universelles a été negligée, et c'est pour cela qu'on ne croit plus a la divination."—LEVI, Clef des Mystères, p. 216.
—Prov. xvi. 10, LXX.
There is divination on a king's lips, and judgment fails not in his mouth.
ENVOY
"He that knows anything worth communicating and does not communicate it, let him be hanged by the neck."—Talmud, Sucah, p. 58. Footnotes
306:1 "Stands some five feet ten or more; a man of strong solid stature, and dignified, now partly military carriage: the expression of him valour and devout intelligence,—-energy and delicacy on a basis of simplicity. Fifty-four years old, gone April last; ruddy-fair complexion, bronzed by toil and age; light brown hair and moustache are getting streaked with grey. A figure of sufficient impressiveness;—not lovely to the man—milliner species, nor pretending to be so. Massive stature; big massive head, of somewhat leonine aspect, 'evident workshop and storehouse of a vast treasury of natural parts.' Wart above the right eyebrow; nose of considerable blunt aquiline proportions; strict yet copious lips, full of all tremulous sensibilities, and also, if need were, of all fierceness and rigours; deep loving eyes, call them grave, call them stern, looking from under those craggy brows, as if in life-long sorrow, and yet not thinking it sorrow, thinking it only labour, and endeavour:—on the whole. a right noble lion-face, and hero-face." (Carlyle, "Cromwell Letters," ii. p. 435).

www.ingramcontent.com/pod-product-compliance
Lightning Source LLC
Chambersburg PA
CBHW020344170426
43200CB00005B/45